Encyclopedia of
Asian American Issues Today

Encyclopedia of
Asian American Issues Today

VOLUME 2

Edith Wen-Chu Chen and
Grace J. Yoo,
Editors

GREENWOOD PRESS

An Imprint of ABC-CLIO, LLC

A B C 🌐 C L I O

Santa Barbara, California • Denver, Colorado • Oxford, England

Library of Congress Cataloging-in-Publication Data

Encyclopedia of Asian American issues today / Edith Wen-Chu Chen, Grace J. Yoo,
editors.
      v. cm.
  Includes bibliographical references and index.
   ISBN 978-0-313-34749-8 (set : alk. paper) — ISBN 978-0-313-34751-1 (v. 1 : alk.
paper) — ISBN 978-0-313-34753-5 (v. 2 : alk. paper) — ISBN 978-0-313-34750-4
(set ebook) — ISBN 978-0-313-34752-8 (v. 1 ebook) — ISBN 978-0-313-34754-2
(v. 2 ebook)
  1. Asian Americans—Encyclopedias. 2. Asian Americans—Social conditions—
Encyclopedias. I. Chen, Edith Wen-Chu, 1966- II. Yoo, Grace J.
  E184.A75E53 2009
  305.895'073—dc22   2009046475

14 13 12 11 10   1 2 3 4 5

This book is also available on the World Wide Web as an eBook.
Visit www.abc-clio.com for details.

ABC-CLIO, LLC
130 Cremona Drive, P.O. Box 1911
Santa Barbara, California 93116-1911

This book is printed on acid-free paper ∞
Manufactured in the United States of America

In honor of our parents,
Flora Huang Chung-Hsia and Mo-Shing Chen
and
Wendy Wangsook and Frank Sungkung Yoo

Contents

Section 6:

IMMIGRATION, REFUGEES, AND CITIZENSHIP

Section Editor: Bill Ong Hing

OVERVIEW: EXAMINING KEY ISSUES

Bill Ong Hing

Immigration and refugee policies have shaped Asian American communities since the 1800s. Asian immigrants were always welcomed in some quarters, but they were vilified by many detractors. Long before the Page Law of 1875, when Chinese women were excluded under the pretext that they were prostitutes, or the Chinese Exclusion Act of 1882, local ordinances and state laws sought to regulate immigration outright or discourage Asian immigrants from settling for long, even as they were recruited by some employers. The tension between welcome and exclusion has left its imprint on every Asian American community in the United States.

Key aspects of the Asian American profile are attributable to immigration and refugee policies. How the Asian American population is distributed across the country, gender ratios, educational achievement, income, and political views can all be linked to these policies. Chinese American and Filipino American populations are the largest subgroups because of family immigration policies. The existence of Hmong, Cambodian, and Vietnamese communities, who relied on public assistance upon arrival, is attributable to refugee policies. Within Asian American communities, except for Japanese Americans, most people are foreign-born. That means that immigration and refugee selection criteria affect the continuing development of Asian America.

Asian America today is not simply a West Coast story or even a West Coast–East Coast bifurcated phenomenon. The story of Asian America, which is very much a story about immigration policy, includes the story of Vietnamese American victims of Hurricane Katrina; Hmong vendors at farmers markets in

Minnesota and Wisconsin, Indian entrepreneurs in Louisville, KY, Korean store owners in Denver, CO, and youth violence and gangs in many locations. Compared with the pre-1965 era, the relative generosity of U.S. immigration policies makes the Asian America story more diverse and more complex.

Today, the range of immigration-related issues faced by Asian Americans is vast. A sampling provides a taste for the many ways that immigrant and immigration policies affect Asian America. Immigration and refugee policies explain much about Asian America. This section features essays on some of the most important aspects of Asian America that are related to these policies that have affected Asian Americans in the last decade. They include descriptions and commentary on family immigration, naturalization, integration, Asian American women, the effects of 9/11, deportation, undocumented immigration, public benefits, human trafficking, and Southeast Asian refugees.

THE POST-9/11 ERA

September 11, 2001, marked a major turning point in U.S. immigration policies. Like 1882, 1917, 1924, and 1965, "9/11" represents the beginning of an era that has affected Asian Americans in important ways. Not long after the tragic terrorist attacks, immigration and deportation enforcement strategies were stepped up, the USA PATRIOT Act was enacted, and discussions of progressive immigration reforms were placed on the back burner. Harsh immigration laws were enacted in 1996, but it took the tragedy of 9/11 to fuel the enforcement of these laws and policies in a manner that began to include Asian Americans in the target—often in the name of combating terrorism.

Profiling and Hate Crimes

Perhaps the failure of the use of immigration policies to catch terrorists is best illustrated by the results of the special registration program. The call-in program required male noncitizens from twenty-five mostly Arab and Muslim countries to register with immigration authorities between November 2002 and April 2003. In addition to nationals of North Korea and the Middle East, the domestic call-in registration program included those from Pakistan, Indonesia, and Bangladesh. About eighty-three thousand men came forward, and nearly thirteen thousand were placed in deportation proceedings. Many (the actual number is unknown) were, in fact, deported for minor immigration violations, but no one was charged with crimes related to terrorism.

These officially sanctioned efforts have provided the impetus for many private citizens to commit hate crimes against those who they think do not meet the racial profile of a true American. Within hours of the terrorist attacks, Americans of Muslim, Middle Eastern, and South Asian descent found themselves targets for acts of hate and racial profiling. In Huntington, NY, a seventy-five-year-old man tried to run over a Pakistani woman in the parking lot of a shopping mall. He then followed the woman into the store and threatened to kill her for "destroying my country." Near San Diego, a Sikh woman was attacked by a knife-wielding man, shouting, "This is what you get for what you've done to us." Another Sikh, a truck driver in the Phoenix area, was shot by two young men who were driving by, yelling, "Go back to where you belong." These are the acts of vigilante racists who are emboldened by the government's own marginalization of these victims through profiling.

After 9/11, hate crimes against Muslims soared, rising more than 1,500 percent. Discrimination in the workplace climbed as well. So overwhelming was the number of complaints that the Equal Employment Opportunity Commission, which monitors job discrimination, created a new category to track acts of discrimination against Middle Eastern, Muslim, and South Asian workers after 9/11.

Deportation

Kim Ho Ma was a happy man on July 9, 1999. After more than two years in state prison and several more months in the custody of immigration authorities, Kim Ho was released by court order. In his own words, "I can work. I pay the taxes. I just want to live the American life."[1] Within three years, however, the United States would deport Kim Ho to a country he had left at the age of two, where he would be unable to speak the language and be ill-equipped for a completely foreign environment.

Kim Ho was born in Cambodia in 1977, in the midst of the Khmer Rouge regime's sinister oppression and genocide. Kim Ho's mother, eight months pregnant, was sentenced to dig holes in one of Pol Pot's work camps. The idea was to teach her humility, and when she collapsed from exhaustion, she expected to be killed. Instead, the guards walked away. When Kim Ho was two, his mother carried him through minefields, fleeing the oppression of the Khmer Rouge, first to refugee camps in Thailand and the Philippines, and eventually to the United States at the age of seven.

Kim Ho's first home in America was a housing project in Seattle, where he and other Cambodian refugees had the misfortune of being resettled in the middle of a new war—one between black and Latino gangs. Both sides taunted Kim Ho and his friends, beating them up for fun. His mother, still affected by the trauma she experienced in Cambodia and preoccupied with two minimum wage jobs, did not understand what was happening to her son. Determined that they would not be pushed around, Kim Ho and his friends formed their own gang.

In 1995, at age seventeen, Kim Ho and two friends ambushed a member of a rival gang; Kim Ho was convicted of first-degree manslaughter. With no previous criminal record, Kim Ho was sentenced to thirty-eight months imprisonment. Earning time off for good behavior, Kim Ho served twenty-six months and was released into the custody of immigration officials.

His conviction for an "aggravated felony" led to a removal (or deportation) order. Upon entry of a final order of deportation, the Immigration and Nationality Act directs the Attorney General to deport the individual from the United States within ninety days. The Immigration and Naturalization Service ("INS") could not effectuate Kim Ho's deportation to Cambodia within the ninety-day removal period, however, because the United States and Cambodia did not have a repatriation agreement. The ninety-day removal period expired in early 1999, but the INS continued to keep Kim Ho in custody. The INS's rationale was that, in light of his former gang membership, the nature of his crime, and his planned participation in a prison hunger strike, it was unable to conclude that Kim Ho would remain nonviolent.

Kim Ho challenged the custody order in federal court, and eventually he was released. The lower courts and the Supreme Court ruled that there was no realistic chance that Cambodia, which had no repatriation treaty with the United States at the time, would accept Kim Ho. The law did not permit indefinite detention. The Supreme Court stated that preventive detention should be limited to especially dangerous individuals, and Kim Ho was not such a person.

That all changed when the Cambodian government signed a repatriation memorandum of understanding in March 2002 to facilitate the return of removable Cambodian refugees. Kim Ho was among the first deported on October 2, 2002. The deportation of other Cambodians have followed—most of whom entered the United States as infants and toddlers—and approximately 1,500 other Cambodians await deportation. In 2008, a similar repatriation agreement was signed between Vietnam and the United States, opening the door to the deportation of Vietnamese Americans who have been convicted of aggravated felonies, even though they, too, may have grown up in the United States after entering at a young age.

CRIMINALITY

The deportation of Cambodians and other Asian noncitizens who are products of U.S. society demonstrates the challenges that young immigrants and their newcomer parents have in their new environment. While most appear to do fine, many others are caught in the middle of the tensions between their own culture and tradition and that of their new home. For many, their environment is overwhelming and can lead to violence and crime. Consider the path of Duc Ta, a young man whose parents entered as refugees from Vietnam and settled in Los Angeles.

As Duc grew up, he often got into fights at school or at the park. Other children would taunt him for wearing the same clothes nearly every day and for his breath smelling like onions. At first, he did not fight back. He would just run or curl up on the ground as he was getting pummeled. When he arrived home with bruises, his father would punish Duc for fighting at school, and the father would beat him. Eventually, Duc got tired of the daily beatings from the other kids and from his own father. He thought to myself, "I'm gonna get beat by my father anyways, might as well fight these kids." He fought nearly every day after that until he was expelled in the fourth grade.

After that, Duc's parents would not let him attend any neighborhood schools. The streets were always full of drug dealers, gangsters, and hookers. So his parents signed him up for elementary school in San Fernando Valley. Duc rode the school bus every day more than an hour each way. The school was predominantly white and middle class. The first day there he was quickly labeled the "poor kid."

He was teased and called names. Kids would stretch their eyes and mock the way he talked. It did not take long for his first fight at the new school. Duc had no sense of belonging at that school; his grades were low and he was suspended several times.

Duc's father would beat him endlessly for getting into fights. His mother would stand on the side cheering on. All the while, Duc would try and run away from his father, screaming and pleading for him to stop. Duc would try to explain that the fights were not his fault, that others would initiate the conflicts. That never worked, and the beatings continued. Duc would close the bedroom door, lock it, and look at himself in the mirror. Teary-eyed with a body covered with bruises, he would ask God why he was in such a family. His father would tell him to open the door to let him in. The father would tell Duc that he beat him because he loved him.

The years went by and things got worse. Duc got kicked out of school after school after school. He flunked eighth grade and ended up in an alternative school. There was racial tension between the Asians and the Latinos; the Asians hung out together watching each others' backs. They hung out in school and eventually gave each other rides home to avoid getting shot or stabbed.

One day, just like any other day, Duc drove to his friend's home; Duc was not in a gang, but his friends were. While driving, they saw two guys from another gang, and they decided to pull up to fight them. But, when they pulled up, Duc heard four or five shots coming from his car. Everything happened quickly, in a blink of an eye, they were all in handcuffs sitting on the sidewalk. No one was injured.

Even though they were only 16 years old, Duc and his friends were charged as adults with first-degree attempted murder and personal use of a firearm with a gang enhancement. Even though Duc did not fire the shots and was not a gang member, they all received the same sentence: 35 years to life.

TRAFFICKING

One of the ugly sides of immigration law relates to the human trafficking of immigrants to the United States through smuggling and other methods of circumventing immigration restrictions. Attracted by promises of high-paying jobs, the victims often pay exorbitant down payments and agree to additional fees, only to find themselves trapped in slave-like conditions in low-wage jobs from which they are unable to extract themselves. Trafficking situations are about coercion, force, fraud and exploitation for money. These forced situations can involve labor or sexual exploitation and may include debt bondage, forced labor or slavery. Victims have been found in low-wage industries but also in the commercial sex industry and even in private homes.

Seventy-one Thai garment workers at a sweatshop in a suburb of Los Angeles, CA. They were discovered in August 1995. They had been held in a two-story apartment complex with seven units, where they were forced to work, live, eat, and sleep for seven years. A ring of razor wire and iron inward-pointing spikes surrounded the complex to ensure that workers would not escape. The workers, sixty-seven of whom were women, lived under the constant threat of harm to themselves and their families. They were told that if they tried to resist or escape, their homes in Thailand would be burned, their families murdered, and they would be beaten. As proof, the captors caught a worker trying to escape, beat him, and took of picture of his bruised and battered body to show the other workers. They also were told that if they reported what was happening to anyone, they would be sent to immigration authorities for deportation. The workers were not permitted to make unmonitored phone calls or write or receive uncensored letters. Armed guards imposed discipline.

Although eighteen-hour days were the norm, sometimes the workday was longer depending on how quickly the manufacturers and retailers wanted their orders. Sleep arrangements were on the floor, with up to ten people in a room, and often infested with rats and cockroaches. Because of the poor housing and work conditions, workers became ill with respiratory illnesses and eye problems, and the lack of proper medical attention often resulted in untreated dental conditions and even cancerous growths.

After the situation was exposed to police and immigration authorities, the workers were taken into immigration custody. With the aid of community lawyers, eventually the workers were released, and most were allowed to remain in the country as they pursued legal remedies against their captors. In the process, their plight helped to transform California law to enable recovery for past wages and to amend immigration laws to allow certain victims of trafficking to be issued special visas.

Incidents of human trafficking are on the increase. Estimates on the scope and magnitude of modern-day slavery cover a wide range. Worldwide, there are more than 12 million people in forced labor, bonded labor, forced child labor, and sexual servitude. The majority of these trafficked victims are women, girls, and minors. Trafficked women are often promised a better life, including work opportunities, marital prospects, and even educational opportunities. Women are promised work as babysitters, housekeepers, waitresses or models—but most often they end up sent into commercial sexual exploitation.[2] Fraudulent recruiters, employers, and corrupt officials seek to reap unlawful profits through those trafficked.

WELFARE REFORM

In its final incarnation, the "welfare reform" bill enacted in the summer of 1996 was as much or more about immigrant policy reform and budget savings as it was about improving the welfare system. Almost half of the money saved as a result of the 1996 Personal Responsibility Act came out of the pockets of immigrants. Congress' stated purpose in barring immigrants from receipt of federal and state benefits was to encourage self-sufficiency and to remove incentives for legal and undocumented migration to the United States. The structure of the bill and the resulting political fallout revealed, however, that a fundamental reason for the legislative choice was economic: eliminating coverage for immigrants saved an estimated $23.7 billion over the first six years, and constituted 44 percent of the total $53.4 billion savings package.

Policy reform involving immigrants and welfare was in large measure a battle waged through popular images. The image advanced by anti-immigrant forces, particularly with regard to the Asian American community, was of the wealthy immigrant professional who rips off the welfare system on behalf of his or her foreign-born parents. Advocacy groups countered with an image of a despondent, elderly legal immigrant contemplating suicide at the prospect of losing his or her benefits.

Accounts of purported immigrant welfare abuse carried the day in the summer of 1996. Such images gave Congress, frustrated by delays in the reform of immigration, a politically convenient way to target immigrants in welfare policy. Even while signing the welfare reform bill, however, President Bill Clinton acknowledged its disproportionate impact on immigrants. Within a year, Congress partially relented, agreeing to restore most benefits to needy refugees and immigrants. By that time, Congress had been heavily lobbied with a different set of images: suicides, sympathetic refugees, and elderly immigrants who had not abused the system. But for future immigrants, the message remained clear: the familiar, poetic inscription upon the Statue of Liberty— "Give us your poor, your tired, your huddled masses"—cannot be taken as the invitation it appears to be.

By eliminating a federal commitment to provide even a minimal level of assistance to America's poorest, the 1996 legislation carried harsh consequences for a range of economically vulnerable individuals and families. Since the act specifically targeted immigrants for major cuts, its effects were felt quickly and severely by noncitizen immigrants in economic need. In the wake of the 1996 Act, many legal immigrants began the process of naturalization because citizens would still be eligible for benefits. Some who failed or who were not eligible for naturalization had access to local cash assistance programs, such as General Assistance. Others who were frightened by the prospect of losing benefits committed or contemplated committing suicide.

The Personal Responsibility Act makes legal immigrants ineligible to receive a number of federally funded public benefits. It similarly authorizes state and local governments to deny locally funded benefits to legal immigrants, transgressing the long-held constitutional requirement that states treat citizens and legal immigrants alike in terms of public benefits eligibility.

By August 5, 1997, a year after the passage of the welfare reform legislation, the Clinton administration and congressional leaders compromised and restored most disability benefits to immigrants who were in the country and covered before the initial legislation. Restrictions on most programs, however, were retained. Even after the second wave of reform, counties and states were still confronted by major cost increases.

Public discourse ignores the fact that a significant portion of welfare dispensed to immigrants actually benefits refugees. In fact, if the class of "immigrants" is defined so as to exclude people from certain refugee-originating countries, the evidence indicates that, nationwide, use of all public programs (e.g., low-income assistance, social insurance, education, and health services) or services (e.g., fire and police protection) by immigrants does not impose any unusual fiscal burden.

Refugees have strong equitable claims to welfare receipt, which justifies excluding them from calculations of immigrant welfare use. The higher rate of welfare use among refugees is understandable because they are fleeing persecution and have fewer economic or family ties in the United States than other immigrants. As a matter of refugee policy, under the Immigration and Nationality Act, the United States admits migrant refugees only after they have established that they have a "well-founded fear of persecution on account of race, religion, nationality, membership in a particular social group, or political opinion." In the last two decades, most refugees who were granted admission have fled persecution from Southeast Asia, Eastern Europe and the former Soviet Union, and the Middle East. The injustices that they and their families have suffered have left them tormented by the scars of war, violence, torture, and economic oppression. They generally have been able to flee their homes with little more than the clothes on their backs. Given a national policy of admitting individuals so in need of shelter, it is irrational to assume that they will never need welfare, even for transitional purposes.

In fact, statistics for the second generation of refugees specifically demonstrate that refugee welfare use is transitional rather than permanent. A telling sign of what use refugees who seek welfare make of their assistance is the minuscule welfare rate among their offspring who have reached adulthood. Thus, although refugee parents and families may have used welfare at some point, that use was transitional and a cycle of dependency was not established. More specifically, second-generation Asian Pacific Americans, including refugees, are one-third as likely to use welfare as first-generation immigrants. The rate of welfare use for second-generation Asian families is less than half that for all white American families. All second-generation Asian Pacific Americans have a low Supplemental Security Income participation rate of 1.5 percent compared with 10.5 percent for all Asian Pacific Americans and 3.3 percent for all white Americans.[3]

INTEGRATION AND REFUGEE IDENTITY

Asian newcomers to the United States face the challenge that most immigrants face: how to become integrated into a society that is vastly different from where they came. The response to this challenge varies from group to group. The responses by Asian newcomers, such as young members of the Hmong and Iu Mien communities, are unique.

Shortly after the U.S. military withdrawal from the Vietnam War in April 1975, Iu Mien and Hmong refugees began arriving in the United States. For those individuals and families, the challenge to their traditions of cultural retention appears impossible to withstand. Many of the children of these refugee groups—some born in Laos or in Thai refugee camps, others born in the United States—are now young adults facing questions of cultural identity that have challenged the children of immigrants and refugees before them.

The Americanization experience for the children of Iu Mien and Hmong refugees is unique. Certainly their experience bears some resemblance to the experience of other immigrants and refugees. After all, other refugees and immigrants have resettled in a variety of settings and enclaves that can be hostile or friendly; however, the Iu Mien and Hmong were part of a Southeast Asian refugee program that presented the largest numerical challenge that the U.S. government ever faced, and officials responded with special resettlement policies. The Iu Mien and Hmong refugee communities are relatively small in size, and they do not have a geo-political "homeland" nation the way that other immigrants, and even Vietnamese, Cambodian, and Laotians, might claim. Other refugees may find it logistically difficult to travel to homelands to renew cultural awareness, but Iu Mien and Hmong refugees face an even bigger hurdle without a country that was ever their own. And unlike other Asian immigrant groups such as Chinese, Filipinos, Indians, and Koreans, who have significant numbers of new immigrant members each year fueling those communities culturally, relatively few Iu Mien and Hmong refugees enter the United States each year. Thus, the cultural identity formation process for Iu Mien and Hmong children is likely quite different from the process the children of the larger Asian American groups go through.

Much can be learned from the process of listening to the voices of those affected by refugee policies. Because few new Hmong and Iu Mien refugees enter each year, questions of intergenerational tension, identity, and cultural and language retention that arise in every group of new Americans are particularly acute in these two communities. Government policies have laid the foundation for environmental effects on their Americanization, but their voices show that Iu Mien and Hmong young adults are active participants in the development of their cultural identities. They are exercising choices affected by the policies that brought them to this country, the cultural identities of their parents, pop culture, interaction with other Asian Americans, the attitudes of other Americans, and a range of other factors.

These two ethnic groups from the mountains of Laos—the Hmong and the Iu Mien—originated from China. The Hmong are better known in the United States. Unlike most new Americans, Hmong refugees are involuntary migrants. The Hmong left China in the nineteenth century to "resist assimilation," and they fled to the United States for the same reason. They came not only to save their lives but also to save their Hmong ethnicity. They wanted to be "left alone to be Hmong," to be self-sufficient, and to grow their own crops. Some carried farming tools with them upon arrival.

Everywhere the Iu Mien have migrated, they have been a minority. This has been true in China, Vietnam, Laos, Thailand, and Burma. They are a small group that has preserved its ethnicity relative to the dominant Chinese, Vietnamese, Lao, Shan (in Burma), Thai, and French. In some respects, this position relative to larger and more organized groups seems to be, by definition, part of Mien ethnicity. Throughout the Iu Mien cultural history, revolt has been common. Despite the inclination to revolution, there are few reported attempts of political organization by the Iu Mien. These attempts were primarily reliant on the coercive powers of a Mien patron and not founded on any incipient form of Mien state structure. In essence, the Mien have been a colonized people for some 2,000 years. While this status has certainly not been without bloodshed, the Iu Mien mostly have dealt with their subordinate position through a combined process of selective assimilation and political manipulation within the context of patron-client relationships.

Like refugees who have entered before, Iu Mien and Hmong refugees who entered the United States as adults face some very serious cultural and social adjustment challenges. Uprooted by war and devastation, they have resettled in societies that are completely foreign. The languages and customs they encountered on arrival could not have been more different. They were unfamiliar with modern conveniences like refrigerators, stoves, and even toilets. The assimilation process for many of the adults has been very slow. And given the history of how the Hmong and Iu Mien were recruited to fight for the United States during the Vietnam War, how they fought heroically for the cause, and how promises of protection were made to them, a case can be made that they should be allowed to live in the United States in peace, free from overbearing pressure to assimilate.

The assimilation story for the Iu Mien and Hmong children is different. The 1.5 generation (born abroad, but entering as children) and second generation are caught between their parents' generation and the world outside their homes. This results in a tension-filled dynamic over identity and culture. In college, they react in a variety of ways to this tension; the formation of their cultural identity does not necessarily fit within standard visions of assimilation.

The cultural identity being developed by Iu Mien and Hmong young adults is based on their experience as the children of refugees, most of whom were on public assistance. They may identify with other Asian Americans with whom they interact, but without that interaction race alone may not be a sufficient marker to bridge a common identity with Chinese, Japanese, and Koreans. Real and perceived class differences with Chinese, Japanese, and Koreans may compel Iu Mien and Hmong children to see commonalities with African Americans and perhaps other low-income groups. Of course they are aware of the subordination that their own communities face racially and classwise in the United States, but they may not see themselves in the same boat as other Asians, especially those driving the model minority image.

In the process of cultural identity formation, some Iu Mien and Hmong are choosing to incorporate aspects of their culture out of respect for and in tribute to their elders and centuries of tradition, but on their own terms. For them, the development of cultural identity is a statement of individualism. Theirs is a statement of dissent and independence from mainstream culture, Asian American culture dominated by Chinese American and Japanese American life, and their own parents' cultures. Yet their unique identities may be influenced by each other. They adamantly refuse to be essentialized as Southeast Asian refugees, much less as simply Asian Americans.

FAMILY IMMIGRATION

Promoting family reunification has been a major feature of immigration policy for decades. Prior to 1965, allowing spouses of U.S. citizens, relatives of lawful permanent residents, and even siblings of U.S. citizens to immigrate were important aspects of the immigration selection system. And after the 1965 reforms, family reunification is the major cornerstone of the immigration admission system.

Over time, Asian and Latin immigration came to dominate most of the immigration to the Untied States. By 1976, a worldwide preference system (which included the Western Hemisphere) quota of 270,000 was in place that continued to reserve 80 percent for kinship provisions, and the category of immediate relatives of the United States citizens remained numerically unlimited. The effects of this priority were demonstrated vividly in the subsequent flow of Asian immigration, even though nations such as those in Africa and Asia, with low rates of immigration prior to 1965, were handicapped. In other words, the nations with large numbers of descendants in the United States were expected to benefit from a kinship-based system, and in 1965, fewer than a million Asian Americans resided in the country. Although the kinship priority meant that Asians were beginning on an unequal footing, at least Asians were on par numerically, in terms of the per-country quotas. Gradually, by using the family categories to the extent they could be used and the labor employment route, Asians built a family base from which to use the kinship categories more and more. By the late 1980s, virtually 90 percent of all immigration to the United States—including Asian immigration—was through the kinship categories. And by the 1990s, the vast majority of these immigrants were from Asia and Latin America.

Once Asian and Latin immigrants began to dominate the family immigration categories, the kinship system was attacked. Arguing that the system was nepotistic or that the country would be better off with a skills-based system became a popular claim. Without an empirical foundation for attacking the entry of some family immigrants with low job skills, critics of the current system simply argue that there is a better way of doing things. These critics are not satisfied that immigration fills needed job shortages and aids economic growth as a result of the entry of ambitious, hard-working family immigrants and their children, many of whom are professionals as well as unskilled workers with a propensity for saving and investment.

The economic data on today's kinship immigrants are favorable for the country. The entry of even low-skilled immigrants leads to faster economic growth by increasing the size of the market, thereby boosting productivity, investment, and technological practice. Technological advances are made by immigrants who are neither well-educated nor well-paid in addition to those by white-collar immigrants. Moreover, many kinship-based immigrants open new businesses that employ natives as well as other immigrants; this is important because small businesses are now the most important source of new jobs in the country. The current system results in designers, business leaders, investors, and Silicon Valley-type engineers. And much of the flexibility available to American entrepreneurs in experimenting with risky labor-intensive business ventures is afforded by the presence of low-wage immigrant workers. In short, kinship immigrants contribute greatly to this country's vitality and growth.

Beyond the obvious economic benefits of the current system, advocates have suggested that a thorough consideration of the benefits of the family-based immigration system includes the psychic values of such a system. The psychic value of family reunification is generally overlooked by empiricists, perhaps because of the difficulty in making exact calculations.

Immigration and refugee policies explain much about Asian America. This section features entries on some of the most important aspects of Asian America related to these policies. They include descriptions and commentary on family immigration, naturalization, integration, the effects of 9/11, women, deportation, undocumented immigration, public benefits, human trafficking, and Southeast Asian refugees. Many believe that Asian America needs to pay close attention to immigration policy and enforcement debates. The outcomes of those debates will continue to shape who Asian Americans are, how they define themselves, and how others define Asian Americans.

NOTES

1. Morning Edition, NPR radio broadcast, June 29, 2001.

2. Briefing on the Eighth Annual Trafficking in Persons, Ambassador Mark P. Lagon, Director of the Office to Monitor and Combat Trafficking in Persons, http://www .america.gov/st/texttrans-english/2008/June/20080604195900eaifas0.7583429.html& distid=ucs.

3. Thomas MaCurdy and Margaret O'Brien-Strain, *Who Will Be Affected by Welfare Reform in California*. San Francisco: Public Policy Institute of California, Feb. 1997, http://www.ppic.org/content/pubs/report/R_297TMR.pdf.

CITIZENSHIP AND NATURALIZATION RATES

Kyung Jin Lee

Immigrants who have become naturalized have involved themselves in civic participation through voting and running for office. With the historic elections of 2008, Asian Americans, including a high number of naturalized citizens, came out in record numbers to participate in elections, as 62 percent voted for President Barack Obama, and 35 percent voted for Republican candidate John McCain, which constituted 2 percent of the total vote.[1] For immigrants, the benefits of obtaining U.S. citizenship through naturalization are significant. A citizen has greater access to civic participation through voting and even running for political office. Federal civil service jobs and many state and local government jobs are limited to citizens. Citizenship also enables broader family reunification through immigration laws, permits greater and longer access to public benefits, and protects against the threat of deportation.

In 2007, a total of 660,447 people naturalized as U.S. citizens. Among those from Asia, Filipinos had the highest rate for citizenship and naturalization followed by immigrants from China and Vietnam.[2] Women naturalized at a higher rate than men, and married people naturalized at higher rates than those who were single.[3] California led all states in naturalization rates for all immigrants. Asian immigrants from states such as Illinois, Hawaii, New York, Texas, and Massachusetts came in second and third for Vietnamese immigrants.[4] Filipino and Chinese immigrants who have naturalized were more often employed in the management and professional sections. For Vietnamese immigrants, those who naturalized were more often employed in the production, transportation, and service industries.[5]

Historically, the passage of the nation's immigration laws in 1965 resulted in exponential growth of Asian immigration from the 1970s to the 1990s. In 1970, 64 percent of all legal permanent residents naturalized. That figure declined to 51 percent in 1980, then further dipped to 38 percent by 1990.[6] Among those who naturalized, 33.5 percent were of Asian descent between 1971 and 1980, but then the figure rose to 48.8 percent between 1981 and 1990.[7]

The percentage has continued to grow in recent years. Individuals have their own reasons for seeking citizenship, but there are several major factors that drove individuals, families, and communities to seek permanent allegiance to the United States. This entry examines the rates of naturalization for different Asian American groups and discusses various trends. Case studies and statistics are used to examine those trends. While individuals may have their own unique reasons for seeking citizenship, a dramatic increase in naturalization among Asian immigrant and refugee communities correlates with factors such as welfare and immigration legislation reform, as well as fee hikes implemented by the United States Citizenship and Immigration Services (USCIS), the federal government agency within the Department of Homeland Security that oversees lawful immigration to the United States.

NATURALIZATION PRE-1996

Between 1952 and 1965, there was a strict quota system that allotted one hundred immigrant visas to the countries of South and East Asia, through the passage of the Immigration and Nationality Act of 1952 (The McCarran-Walter Act). In 1943 and 1946, racial restrictions against nationals of China, India, and the Philippines had been repealed, and the 1952 law repealed the legal bars for those from other Asian countries, but added that any "individual with one or more Asian parent, born anywhere in the world and possessing the citizenship of any nation, would be counted under the national quota of the Asian nation of his or her ethnicity or against a generic quota for the 'Asian Pacific Triangle.'"[8]

The 1965 amendments repealed the quota system, and each country was given the same immigration numerical limitation of 20,000 immigrant visas, in addition to special quota free visas for immediate relatives of U.S. citizens. So after 1965, many Asian immigrants were motivated to naturalize in order to petition for family members in their homeland. Family petitions for legal permanent residents are restricted to spouses and unmarried children, while U.S. citizens are allowed to petition parents, spouses, married and unmarried children, and siblings.[9] In order to become eligible to become a citizen, one must be at least 18 years old and have lived in the United States continuously for five years. They must be able to read, write, and speak English and answer questions that demonstrate knowledge of U.S. government and history. They must also take an oath of citizenship.

1996 ACTS

In August and September of 1996, President Bill Clinton signed the Personal Responsibility and Work Opportunity Reconciliation Act (PRWOR) and the Illegal Immigration and Immigrant Responsibility Act (IIRAIRA), which drastically changed the rights and protections for immigrants. Under PRWOR, only U.S. citizens would be eligible for certain public benefits, including Supplemental Security Income (SSI), and other restrictions were placed on recent legal permanent residents seeking other public benefits including Medicaid. IIRAIRA expanded the likelihood of deportation for legal permanent residents who commit criminal offenses. The consequences of these new laws changed the landscape for immigrants. Since 1996, the rates of legal permanent residents seeking naturalization have surged. Fee hikes implemented by the USCIS in 2007 resulted in another spike in naturalization applications prior to the increase.

These welfare changes threatened loss of a safety net and protections provided by the public welfare system. While proponents described the PRWOR as "a comprehensive bipartisan welfare reform plan that will dramatically change the nation's welfare system into one that requires work in exchange for time-limited assistance," there was also much public outcry and criticism from immigrant rights, labor, women's rights, and religious organizations throughout the country.[10] The legislation replaced the Aid to Families with Dependent Children (AFDC) program to the Temporary Assistance for Needy Families (TANF), which is administered through individual states via block grants from the federal government. This radical change to the welfare system eventually removed from aid millions of families in need and required those who were eligible to remain on the rolls to find work within two years of receiving the temporary aid.

IIRAIRA made immigrants convicted of an "aggravated felony" ineligible for relief from deportation. Furthermore, the classification of aggravated felonies was expanded. Between 1988 and 1996, aggravated felony offenses included only murder, drug trafficking, and firearms trafficking; however, after 1997, the definition grew to include relatively minor offenses that could result in a year in prison.[11]

Within the Asian American population, the Southeast Asian community was most adversely affected by the 1996 legislation. Many refugees from Vietnam, Cambodia, and Laos who had fled to the United States after 1975 did not naturalize and remained legal permanent residents after IIRAIRA passed. Those immigrants who were convicted of aggravated felonies were ordered removed (deported), but because of the lack of diplomatic relations, they could not be deported, although many were kept in immigration detention for lengthy periods. The U.S. State Department now has signed repatriation agreements with the governments of Cambodia and Vietnam, and the deportation of former Cambodian refugees has gone on for many years.

The passage of IIRAIRA in 1996 was the culmination of anti-immigration sentiment during that time. Even prior to 1996, states passed restrictive laws, such as California's Proposition 187, which would have denied undocumented immigrants access to social services, public health, and education. These new punitive measures drove millions of permanent residents to apply for naturalization, which created a huge backlog in naturalization applications.

In 1995, Asian immigrants (as well as Middle Easterners) accounted for 190,205 of those naturalized; however, in 1996, that figure jumped to 307,451. Within the Asian population, Filipino immigrants ranked first in naturalization numbers, followed by Vietnamese immigrants. Third were Chinese immigrants, followed by Indian immigrants and Korean immigrants. The overall naturalization numbers for all immigrants were 488,088 in 1995 and 1,044,689 in 1996.[12] Other factors for the dramatic increase in naturalization numbers were the streamlined naturalization exam process called the Citizenship USA initiative in 1995, as well as increased interest in participating in the 1996 presidential election.[13]

CHALLENGES TO CITIZENSHIP

On January 31, 2007, the USCIS announced a proposal for increased fees for those seeking immigration benefits, beginning July 30, 2007. Naturalization fees rose 80 percent, from $330 to $595, plus $80 for biometrics (fingerprints); all other immigration application fees also rose significantly. This dramatic increase in service fees motivated 1,383,275 residents to file for naturalization that year, marking the second largest spike in USCIS/INS history, just behind the 1996 surge.[14] In July 2007 alone, more than 460,000 residents filed for naturalization, an increase of more than seven times the number from the previous year.[15] The USCIS claimed it needed to increase fees so it could improve customer service, delivery, and processing time and meet national security.[16]

Just after the fee increase, however, the overwhelming numbers of applications drove the processing time back for all applications, including naturalization. At the end of 2007, almost one million naturalization cases were still awaiting adjudication by the USCIS.[17]

In 2000, the USCIS announced plans to launch a new naturalization test re-design because of the inconsistencies of the test's contents, administration, and scoring throughout the local CIS offices in the country.[18] These new changes include a complete overhaul of the reading and writing portion of the exam, as well as a newly designed list of one hundred U.S. history and government questions. The new exam was officially introduced on September 27, 2007, and was fully implemented by October 1, 2008. Many immigrants, especially limited English speakers such as the elderly, have expressed hesitancy and anxiety over the redesigned exam.

There are many barriers that prevent Asian immigrants and refuges from applying for citizenship. Several of the requirements for attaining citizenship—specifically, the need to be able to speak, write, read and understand basic English, and to answer questions that demonstrate knowledge of U.S. government and history—are especially challenging for recent, elderly or disabled immigrants. The most recent cost of $675 for the application fee is also prohibitive for low-income immigrants with very little disposable income.

While there are specific English waivers provided by U.S. Citizenship and Immigration Services with regard to long-time elderly residents (these waivers are given to those who are older than fifty-five years and have been a legal permanent resident for more than fifteen years; or more than fifty years old and have retained their resident status for at least twenty years), others who apply have felt intimidated by the process of attaining citizenship as well as by the individual officers who conduct interviews. Once someone files for citizenship benefits, this gives consent to the United States government to go through his or her immigration history and files, and allows the officers to ask historical and personal questions about the applicant when deemed necessary. For those with limited English skills and/or those with minor criminal convictions, this can be very intimidating, especially when the officer is curt or unfriendly.

In addition to the fear and intimidation of the process of obtaining citizenship, there are many who consciously refuse to become a U.S. citizen, even after twenty, thirty or even forty years of residing in the United States. Again, the reasons are as varied as the individuals themselves, but anecdotal evidence suggests that national pride for their home countries is a big factor not to naturalize. Other factors include material reasons, such as specific laws in their countries of birth that prohibit foreigner nationals from owning property or that levy heavy taxes on foreign ownership of land, lasting thoughts of returning to their homelands in the future, or for political reasons. This is especially true for the Southeast Asian refugee communities, where a small but significant number remain stateless after migrating to the United States in the early 1980s.

Hind Makki, left, with the Council of Islamic Organizations of Greater Chicago, and Soo Ji Min, executive director of the Korean American Community Services, listen during a news conference February 21, 2005, in Chicago as Alfonso Aguilar, chief of the U.S. Office of Citizenship in Washington, outlined Illinois' New Americans Initiative. The $3 million program was to help legal immigrants attain U.S. citizenship, with money going for ads and a network of agencies to help those negotiating the complex process. (AP Photo/Nam Y. Huh)

Throughout the past fifteen years, many Asian immigrants chose to naturalize because of external forces, such as dramatic changes in immigration laws and fee hikes imposed by the USCIS. There are also thousands of immigrants who chose to naturalize to reunite family members and to fully participate in the civic life in the United States and/or a combination of both internal and external factors. Within the Asian subgroups, Filipino, Vietnamese, Chinese, Indian and Korean immigrants were naturalized at the highest numbers, respectively. The reasons why are as varied as the communities they represent; however, one common theme why Asian immigrants choose to naturalize is to further integrate into their adopted homeland. National and local immigration organizations continue to struggle over reducing the growing backlog of pending family immigration cases, bringing the nearly 2 million Asian immigrants who remain without proper documents out of the shadows, and providing children of undocumented immigrants in-state tuition for public universities.

FURTHER READING

Asian American Legal Defense and Education Fund Voting Rights Project. http://www.aaldef.org/voting.php.

Banks, Jeremy and Bergeron, Claire. *Behind the Naturalization Backlog: Causes, Context, and Concerns* [Online, February 2008]. Migration Policy Institute. http://www.migrationpolicy.org.

Department of Homeland Security Immigration Data & Statistics. http://www.dhs.gov/ximgtn/statistics/data/.

Passel, Jeffrey S. "Growing Share of Immigrants Choosing Naturalization" [Online, March 2007]. Pew Hispanic http://www.pewhispanic.org.

NOTES

1. CNN Politics.com, "Local Exit Polls—Election Center 2008," http://www.cnn.com/ELECTION/2008/results/polls/#val=USP00p1.

2. Annual Flow Report 2007, "Naturalizations in the United States: 2007," http://www.dhs.gov/xlibrary/assets/statistics/publications/natz_fr_07.pdf.

3. Homeland Security Web site, "Profiles on Naturalized Citizens: 2007," http://www.dhs.gov/ximgtn/statistics/data/DSNat07c.shtm.

4. Homeland Security Web site, "Profiles on Naturalized Citizens: 2007," http://www.dhs.gov/ximgtn/statistics/data/DSNat07c.shtm.

5. Homeland Security Web site, "Profiles on Naturalized Citizens: 2007," http://www.dhs.gov/ximgtn/statistics/data/DSNat07c.shtm.

6. Homeland Security Web site, "Profiles on Naturalized Citizens: 2007," http://www.dhs.gov/ximgtn/statistics/data/DSNat07c.shtm.

7. Naturalizations Fiscal Year 1999: http://www.dhs.gov/xlibrary/assets/statistics/yearbook/1999/Natz99text.pdf.

8. USCIC; Service & Benefits; Permanent Residence (Green Card); Immigration Through a Family Member: http://www.uscis.gov/portal/site/uscis/menuitem.5af9bb95919f35e66f614176543f6d1a/?vgnextoid=0775667706f7d010VgnVCM10000048f3d6a1RCRD.

9. Department of State Visa Bulletin Web site: http://travel.state.gov/visa/frvi/bulletin/bulletin_4252.html.

10. *Source Watch Encyclopedia*, "1996 Personal Responsibility and Work Opportunity Reconciliation Act," http://www.sourcewatch.org/index.php?title=1996_Welfare_Reform_Act.

11. American Immigration Lawyer's Association IIRIRA Fact Sheet: http://www.aila.org/content/default.aspx?bc=6714%7C6729%7C11769%7C3545.

12. *Department of Homeland Security: 2004 Yearbook of Immigration Statistics:* Table 32. Persons naturalized by region and country of birth: fiscal years 1986–2004.

13. Naturalization Fiscal Year 1999: http://www.dhs.gov/xlibrary/assets/statistics/yearbook/1999/Natz99text.pdf.

14. *Department of Homeland Security: 2004 Yearbook of Immigration Statistics Table 31*: Petitions for Naturalizations Filed, Persons Naturalized , and Petitions for Naturalization Denied: Fiscal Years 1907-2004; http://www.dhs.gov/ximgtn/statistics/publications/YrBk04Na.shtm.

15. Migration Policy Institute Immigration Facts series, Feb. 2008.

16. *Federal Register* 72, no. 21, (Feb. 1, 2007), http://edocket.access.gpo.gov/2007/pdf/E7-1631.pdf.

17. Migration Policy Institute Immigration Facts series Feb. 2008, http://www.migrationpolicy.org/pubs/FS21_NaturalizationBacklog_022608.pdf (accessed on July 21, 2009).

18. "The Redesigned Naturalization Test," Office of Citizenship, USCIC, M-685, Sept. 2007.

DETENTION AND DEPORTATION

Bo Han Yang, Angie Junck, and Sin Yen Ling

The Asian immigrant community is often overlooked when issues of deportation and detention are raised. The common misperception is that only Latinos—and mostly Mexicans—are in the United States unlawfully and therefore they are the only ones in danger of deportation. In fact, among Asian immigrant communities, Chinese, Filipinos, Cambodians, Laotian, and Vietnamese immigrants experience high rates of deportation. Exact figures on how many Asian immigrants are subject to detention and deportation every year are unavailable; however, in 2006, it was estimated that 9,967 Asian noncitizens were deportable, compared with 3,507 African noncitizens and 3,255 European noncitizens.[1]

Detention and deportation are the two primary means through which the U.S. government enforces its immigration law. If a person is found to have violated the immigration laws of the United States, he or she may be held in detention until deportation (physical removal) from the United States, or until a U.S. immigration judge decides to grants permission to stay in the country.

In 1996, a series of anti-immigrant bills were signed into law, including the Illegal Immigration Reform and Immigrant Responsibility Act (IIRIRA), which drastically changed United States immigration law ("the 1996 laws"). This legislation increased the reasons for which noncitizens could be detained and deported from the United States, and in many instances made deportations mandatory. The legislation severely restricted the ability of noncitizens to seek asylum and to immigrate to the United States to reunify with their families. The 1996 laws also eliminated important legal rights to challenge deportation and due process protections that helped ensure that the government was treating immigrants fairly and justly under the law.

Since 1996, the federal government has been aggressively enforcing immigration laws resulting in the deportation of more than 1.5 million people. Many people believe that noncitizens are being deported as a result of laws passed after the events of September 11, 2001. However, no new laws regarding deportation and detention were passed in the wake of 9/11. Instead, 9/11 had the effect of increasing enforcement of the 1996 laws. Now, with the collapse of comprehensive immigration reform to legalize the 12 million undocumented people in the country, coupled with emphasis on enforcing our existing immigration laws, the government aims to detain and deport all deportable noncitizens in the United States.

The United States government, through the Department of Homeland Security (DHS), arrests, detains, and deports immigrants, including Asian noncitizens, for violations of immigration law. The DHS operates through two sub-agencies: Immigration and Customs Enforcement (ICE), which enforces immigration laws within the interior of the United States, and Customs and Border Protection (CBP), which enforces immigration laws at the border and all ports of entry, such as airports.

DEPORTATION

Deportation is the forced return and exile of an individual to one's country of origin at the government's expense. Anyone who is not a U.S. citizen can be subject to deportation. This includes refugees who were invited by the U.S. to participate in refugee resettlement programs from Vietnam, Laos, and Cambodia. Student visa and business visa holders can also be deported. Regardless of their individual circumstances, even longtime legal residents with green cards can be deported if they are convicted of a first-time, minor criminal offense that does not result in any jail time. The fact that deportees have a spouse and children who are U.S. citizens, have been in the United States since they themselves were children, or can demonstrate rehabilitation is not relevant in deportation proceedings. Asian noncitizens are found deportable from the United States for any immigration violation ranging from overstaying a visa to be being convicted of a criminal offense.

The deportation process typically begins when an ICE or Border Patrol agent discovers and arrests a person who has violated an immigration law. Either agency generally will place the noncitizen in detention and give him or her the opportunity to have the case heard before an immigration judge. The immigration judge will render a decision as to whether the noncitizen will be deported. In some circumstances, such as where a person who is found at a port of entry with no documentation, the person will not get a hearing before an immigration judge prior to being deported.

IMMIGRATION ENFORCEMENT

Many noncitizens are arrested and subject to deportation as a result of ICE immigration raids. These raids can occur at homes, on the street, or in the workplace. While the majority of noncitizens targeted by these raids are Latinos, in some instances, Asian noncitizens are targeted as well.

Raids are planned operations by the DHS to find and arrest certain deportable individuals within the United States. DHS investigates and gathers information about those who have violated immigration laws and then prioritizes who it believes to be the most serious offenders. Current high ICE priorities target those who have evaded deportation orders or orders to appear, those with criminal records, and those who previously or currently are alleged to be affiliated with street gangs. Because many Asian noncitizens fall within the latter two categories, they are significantly affected. For instance, ICE has arrested and deported large numbers of Vietnamese, Cambodian, Hmong, and Filipino immigrants, including youths, who are thought to be affiliated in some way with street gangs. In the San Francisco Bay Area, ICE also targeted the homecare industry, arresting a number of homecare givers who are predominantly undocumented Filipino workers. Many of these Filipina workers were live-in caregivers providing care for senior citizens, the disabled and displaced young people. Arresting these Filipino workers had broad ramifications on this area of the health industry. Each worker was responsible for several patients at a time for a 24-hour period. When ICE arrested the workers, patients faced a shortage of care while the workers sat in detention centers or were too afraid to return to work. ICE also targeted many Asian noncitizens, who have been ordered deported without even knowing they had deportation orders against them. Asian noncitizens who have committed criminal offenses have also been arrested.

While communities are aware of these raids because they are so visible, ICE often enforces immigration law through lesser-known tactics. One of these tactics is to simply wait for noncitizens to appear before them. In fact, this is the primary way that ICE and the Citizenship and Immigration Services agencies identify the majority of Asian noncitizens for detention and deportation. Noncitizens can come into contact with either agency voluntarily or mandatorily—and when they do, the agency will use the opportunity to initiate detention and deportation. This happens when unsuspecting noncitizens apply for a status change (such as citizenship, permanent residency, or a green card), when they go to an immigration office to renew a green card, when they appear before CBP at borders or airports as they return from travel abroad, or when they come into contact with ICE agents who patrol the criminal justice system (including for those arrested or stopped for a traffic violation).

If noncitizen have any immigration violation on their record, they are probably susceptible to arrest and deportation. This is true regardless of how minor the violation seems to be or how long ago it occurred. For example, if a person is a legal permanent resident and committed a minor crime years ago, he could still be in jeopardy today. Arrests and deportations can happen at any time. Some individuals have gone through the entire citizenship process only to be arrested during their citizenship interview. Others have repeatedly traveled abroad to visit family and re-enter every year and then are suddenly

From Fleeing Persecution to Life on the Streets

At the age of seven, Many Uch, his mother, and two older brothers came to the United States under horrific conditions. Under the brutal Pol Pot–led Khmer Rouge regime, Many's family was captured by the Khmer Rouge army. Separated from their father and forced from their home into the jungle, Many's family was found by Red Cross workers among the sick and the dead and placed them in a refugee camp. Many's family eventually came to the United States as refugees and settled in Seattle, WA.

Many was placed in a school that had a high crime rate. Riding the bus home from school, students would make fun of Many for getting off in the "projects." They would also tell him to "go back to his country." In his elementary school English as a Second Language (ESL) class, Many befriended a group of guys from similar backgrounds who had similar problems. If other kids picked on one, the rest would stand up for that person. To him, they were a much–needed support group, but to police, they were a gang.

As Many grew older, life in the street got more intense; he found himself committing crimes to get by. Fighting and stealing became a way of life. When Many was 18, he was convicted of robbery and sent to prison.

Ironically, it was in prison where he would have the opportunity to improve himself in a manner that he was unable to in his neighborhood. In prison he read books, went to school, and learned the law. He used this knowledge to petition for his release. After a tough battle, Many eventually won his freedom.

Since 2002, when Cambodia signed a repatriation agreement, the U.S. government has deported many refugee youth such as Many; however, Many has not let this threat stop him from working to improve the lives of others and moving on with his life, including getting married and raising a family. Yet because of his conviction, he may still be deported, even though he already served time for the crime.

—Bill Ong Hing

arrested at the airport on one particular trip home. Still others were at the immigration office to renew a green card or apply for some other immigration benefit. Chinese senior citizens who immigrated to the United States to reunite with their citizen adult children may face deportation problems. These senior citizens often return to their home country to seek health care subsidized by the Chinese government. Because they are unable to find suitable health care in the United States, many Chinese seniors are placed in removal proceedings after being absent from the United States for more than a year. ICE alleges that they have abandoned their U.S. residence.

The result of these enforcement efforts is an increase in the detention and deportation Asian immigrants.

REASONS FOR DEPORTATION

Asian noncitizens are deportable from the United States for many different reasons. They overstay their student or tourist visas; they may misrepresent an important fact to immigration officials or engage in marriage fraud to get legal immigration status; they use false documents to enter the United States; they commit and/or are convicted of certain criminal offenses, even minor nonviolent offenses for which they have already served a criminal sentence many years ago.

Overstaying a Visa

Many people believe that all undocumented noncitizens in the United States have crossed the border illegally. Many undocumented noncitizens from Mexico, Canada, and Central America do cross the border without inspection; however, most Asian noncitizens do not cross the border in that manner. Instead, the vast majority of Asian noncitizens enter the United States with immigrant visas or with temporary visas, such as tourist or student visas. Those with temporary or nonimmigrant visas often overstay the time permitted on their visas. Once their visas expire, they become undocumented like those who crossed the border without inspection.

Many Asians arrive in the United States from the Philippines, China, India, and Korea as student visa holders. After 9/11, pursuant to the new program called SEVIS (Student Exchange Visitor and Information System), students' failure to comply with their student visa restrictions requires their university to report them to ICE. Noncompliance can include many things, from failure to pay tuition to failure to carry the required credits for the semester. If a university fails to report noncompliant student visa holders to ICE, it risks accreditation problems. Students reported to ICE often face a home raid and are subsequently taken into ICE custody.

Asians are the second largest subgroup of undocumented immigrants in the United States because of these visa overstays. These overstays amount to approximately 13 percent (about 1.5 million) of the estimated 12 million undocumented individuals in the United States.[2] In the San Francisco Bay Area alone, for example, it is estimated that there are approximately 80,000 to 180,000 undocumented Asian immigrants, with Chinese individuals accounting for 23 percent, followed by Filipinos at 17 percent, Asian Indians at 14 percent, and Koreans at 11 percent.[3]

Document and Marriage Fraud

People may be deported if they defraud the government. Specifically, individuals who are found to have committed document or marriage fraud to enter or stay in the United States may be deportable.

Tongans, Fijians, Southeast Asians, Filipinos, and Chinese have often been denied entry to the United States at airports because of their use of falsified visas and passports. Some Filipinos, for instance, have attempted to enter the country with another person's U.S. passport. If detected by the DHS, the person is immediately sent back to the home country or detained, pending a legal proceeding.

Some prospective immigrants are parties to "fake marriages" between citizens and noncitizens so that the noncitizen can become a legal permanent resident and then ultimately, a U.S. citizen. A "fake" or "sham" marriage constitutes fraud and can result in the noncitizen's deportation.

Criminal Convictions

A noncitizen may be deported for the conviction of a variety of crimes. These can range from minor offenses such as shoplifting to more serious ones such as assault and drug trafficking. Asian noncitizens are quite affected by the criminal grounds of deportation. In 2006 alone, the DHS deported 272,389 people based on criminal grounds. Of those individuals, 4,614 were deported to Asian countries. In comparison, 3,101 were deported to European countries and 1,921 to countries in Africa.[4] The majority of Asian noncitizens affected by the criminal grounds of deportation are refugees from Vietnam, Laos, Cambodia, or the Philippines.

The 1996 laws significantly changed the deportation and detention provisions relating to criminal convictions, and this has had a devastating impact on Asian noncitizens. Specifically, the laws dramatically increased the number and kinds of offenses for which noncitizens could be mandatorily detained and deported. In addition, many of the changes are retroactive; they apply to crimes that were committed long ago and can now trigger deportation. Many offenses that were misdemeanors or nonviolent offenses were designated "aggravated felonies" under immigration law, resulting in mandatory detention and deportation from the United States without any hope of a pardon. These provisions restricted a judge's power to hear cases of longtime legal residents and to consider whether the immigrants deserve to remain in the United States with their families.

These radical legal changes have sharply increased the number of longtime Asian permanent residents being deported and separated from their families. Many were their family's breadwinners and were refugees who fled persecution from Cambodia, who came to the United States as children and know no other home. These individuals often have spouses and children who are U.S. citizens and have no ties to the countries to which they are being deported. Many have no family, no knowledge of the language and culture, and no financial means to fend for themselves in the countries to where they are deported. Although they may have committed crimes, they have completed their criminal sentences and have rehabilitated themselves, but they find themselves facing permanent banishment from the United States.

Consider the story of Loeun Lun, a Cambodian refugee who fled the Khmer Rouge regime in Cambodia while an infant and went from labor camp to labor camp until he ultimately arrived in the United States at age six. Loeun, like many other impoverished Cambodian refugees, did not receive adequate services from the U.S. refugee resettlement program that brought him to the United States; he grew up in a crime-ridden housing project in Tacoma, WA. Eventually, Loeun dropped out of high school so that he could work full time to support his mother, who suffered from depression and trauma.

In 1995, at age nineteen, Loeun was convicted of two counts of assault for shooting his gun into the air after being harassed by other kids. No one was hurt, but Loeun served 11 months in jail. After he served his sentence, Loeun married a U.S. citizen and had two daughters. From 1996 to 1999, he changed his life around and held a factory job to provide for his family. He paid off his debts and rebuilt his credit, became the primary caretaker for his mother, and had no other trouble with the law. In 1999, thinking his past was behind him, Loeun applied for U.S. citizenship.

In 2002, seven years after his conviction, Loeun inquired about the status of his citizenship application but was arrested by ICE. DHS had discovered Loeun's 1995 conviction for an "aggravated felony," triggering mandatory deportation with no possibility of a relief from deportation. The immigration judge was forced to order Loeun deported because the 1996 laws do not allow judges to consider the individual's extenuating circumstances when it comes to deportation based on an aggravated felony. The judge could do nothing, even though Loeun had lived lawfully in the United States for most of his life, had a wife and two daughters who are U.S. citizens, and had rehabilitated himself. Loeun was deported to Cambodia in 2003, leaving his wife and infant daughters behind.

In recent years the United States established repatriation agreements with Cambodia and Vietnam as a means of immigration enforcement to effectuate deportation of Asian noncitizen refugees for criminal convictions. These agreements resulted from considerable pressure by the U.S. government on the governments of those countries to accept deportees from the United States. Many of these refugees who are subject to deportation came to the United States at an early age, have been legal residents of the United States for the majority of their lives, have U.S. citizen families, and have long since been rehabilitated.

While the Vietnamese repatriation agreement is in the early stages of implementation, the Cambodian agreement has resulted in the deportation of at least 150 individuals, while another 1,500 are still waiting to be deported. Many of these individuals have been waiting since 2002 and do not know when they will be scheduled for deportation. Currently, the only Asian country that lacks a repatriation agreement with the United States is Laos. Laotians who are ordered deported are allowed back into the community on supervised release. They have no official legal status in the United States and must check in regularly with DHS.

Terrorism

People may be deported if they are deemed to be a threat to the security to the United States. Since the 9/11 terrorist attacks, the DHS has focused on the monitoring and removal of individuals with possible Muslim terrorist connections or perceived connections.

A post-9/11 program called the National Security Exit-Entry Registration System (NSEERS) requires that certain nationals report to the former Immigration and Naturalization Service (INS) for interrogation, fingerprinting, and deportation. Of the twenty-four Muslim countries involved, several are Asian countries, including North Korea, Bangladesh, Indonesia, and Pakistan. According to a report by the Asian American Legal Defense and Education Fund, 77 percent of those who have registered reported spending longer than 5 hours at ICE and 59 percent spent more than 10 hours at ICE. Those who spent more than 10 hours at ICE were denied access to counsel. Nationwide, of the 83,000 individuals who reported for the program, approximately 13,000 were placed in deportation proceedings. In New York City, the disproportionate impact of the program meant that entire communities were eliminated, such as Pakistanis in Brooklyn and Indonesians in Queens.

Years after 9/11, these policies continue to be selectively enforced against certain nationals, many from India, Pakistan, and the Philippines. In 2007, male Filipinos over the age of 18 were increasingly being targeted for deportation because of their possible ties to Muslim militias in the southern Philippines. Many people from a Muslim minority in western China face a similar predicament. The DHS justification for this is that men older than 18 who are originally from these regions are more likely to be involved with the Muslim militias and therefore pose a greater threat to the security of the United States. For example, in 2007, a Pakistani national was detained for approximately five months at California's Santa Clara County Jail, because of claims that he had provided material support to an International Muslim organization. He was a Silicon Valley worker, married to a U.S. citizen, and had two U.S. citizen children. Five years after filing his adjustment application, he was taken into ICE custody when his application was denied. His application was denied on the basis that he was a board member of a U.S. domestic Muslim nonprofit organization that provides services to inner city Muslim youth.

DETENTION

Immigration detention is the lock-up of noncitizens in facilities equivalent to jails or prisons while they await a final determination on their deportation cases. Many Asian noncitizens who are deportable because of document fraud or criminal convictions are detained. These individuals include asylum-seekers and long-term legal U.S. residents. The time spent in detention can last a few years, many years, or, for some, indefinitely.

The 1996 laws vastly increased the number of noncitizens eligible to be detained pending deportation from the United States. When combined with recent aggressive immigration enforcement, this has resulted in a sharp increase in the number of immigrants being housed in detention centers across the country. These detention centers often are located in remote places, far from the detainees' home states where their families and communities are located. These increased mandatory detention requirements have resulted in an explosion of the U.S. immigration detention system. According to current statistics, ICE holds about 32,000 people in detention each day and about 300,000 each year. This is more than a 300 percent increase since 2001, while the former INS detained about 9,500 people each year. To accommodate this sudden surge of ICE detentions, DHS has converted medium security prisons into immigration detention centers, created "family detention centers," and contracted with private prisons. Currently, the government allocates ICE more than $1.2 billion per year to operate more than 440 detention centers and to contract with private prison corporations such as the Corrections Corporation of America (CCA) to manage these facilities. Detainees are now generally held in one of three places: local county jails, CCA-managed private prisons, or federal immigration detention centers.

As a result of this burgeoning system, which is often run for profit, immigrants' rights are frequently violated during detention. While detainees have the right to be represented by counsel, immigrants are often sent to remote locations far from their counsel—and frequently far from any counsel at all. While detainees should have the right to visit with family members, the detention center rules and locations often make it difficult. Detention centers often have unhealthy food, and inadequate medical care. In fact, the conditions in many of the detention facilities are so poor that there have been many reports of detainee deaths as a result of inadequate medical care. Detainees also consistently face problems such as overcrowding, lack of recreational or educational programs, and little access to phones, legal materials, and fresh air.[5]

According to the 2006 Yearbook of Immigration Statistics, approximately 10,000 immigrants deported are from Asian countries. An unknown percentage of these are detained in immigration facilities or local county jails. Individuals are detained while they are facing deportation or going through their deportation hearings. Chinese nationals are detained for a variety of reasons: minors who are smuggled in by Chinese gangs to work as indentured servants, for example, are detained, and others are detained for white-collar crimes. Southeast Asians, including Cambodians, Vietnamese, and Laotians, are detained for criminal convictions related to socioeconomic challenges facing refugees in the United States. Filipinos are detained for perceived terrorist activities, prior criminal convictions, entering the United States with fake documentation, and as individuals with final orders of removal. Pacific Islanders such as Tongans and Fijians are detained for overstaying their visa and face

Sarath Suong shouts chants through a bullhorn as Cambodian children surround him before a rally in Providence, Rhode Island, in August 2002. Members of the Cambodian Society of Rhode Island and Providence Youth Student Movement held the rally to protest the deportation of convicted Cambodians. (AP Photo/Victoria Arocho)

indefinite detention because they, more often than other Asian ethnic groups, are unable to post bail or bond out of detention.

Long-term legal residents with criminal convictions (mostly Cambodians, Laotians, Vietnamese, and Filipinos) are often subject to mandatory detention until their cases are completed. Previously, Cambodians and Vietnamese only stayed in detention long enough to sign their deportation order because they could not be physically returned to their countries of origin. Now they must stay in detention as long as necessary to fight their case. Laotians, on the other hand, still cannot be removed to their country and, as a result, are likely to stay in detention for shorter periods of time. Prolonged detention, which can last up to several years, is a common problem for these Asian noncitizens. Many give up hope and simply accept the deportation order even though they have a right to fight or appeal their case. Many choose deportation over the prospect of being locked up because the process could mean several years in immigration detention.

FURTHER READING

Asian American Legal Defense and Education Fund. http://www.aaldef.org.
Detention Watch Network. http://www.detentionwatchnetwork.org.
Hing, Bill Ong. *Deporting Our Souls: Values, Morality, and Immigration Policy* (Cambridge, UK: Cambridge Press, 2006).

Hing, Bill Ong. "Detention to Deportation—Rethinking the Removal of Cambodian Refugees." *University of Davis Law Review* (2005), 38 University of California–Davis Law Review, 891.

Human Rights Watch. "Forced Apart: Families Separated and Immigrants Harmed by United States Deportation Policy" [online, July 2007]. Human Rights Watch Web site. http://www.hrw.org/reports/2007/us0707/.

Immigrant Justice Network. www.ilrc.org/immigrantjusticenetwork/.

Southeast Asia Resource Action Center: http://www.searac.org.

NOTES

1. DHS Yearbook of Immigration Statistics, 2006, http://www.dhs.gov/ximgtn/statistics/publications/YrBk06En.shtm.

2. Vanessa Hua, "Amnesty Touches Home for Bay Area Asians," *San Francisco Chronicle*, April 18, 2006, citing the Pew Hispanic Report, April 2006, http://www.sfgate.com/cgi-bin/article.cgi?f=/c/a/2006/05/18/MNG7JITSJA1. DTL&hw=Filipinos%2BFor%2BAffirmative%2BAction&sn=001&sc=1000.

3. Hua, "Amnesty Touches Home for Bay Area Asians."

4. DHS 2006 Yearbook of Immigration Statistics, http://www.dhs.gov/ximgtn/statistics/publications/YrBk06En.shtm.

5. Amnesty USA International. "Jailed without Justice: Immigration Detention in the USA," http://www.amnestyusa.org/uploads/JailedWithoutJustice.pdf.

FAMILY IMMIGRATION

Joren Lyons

From 1924 to 1965, immigration to the United States was regulated by a complex national origins quota system, in which each country had a different annual immigration quota based on the proportion of individuals in the 1890 census with ancestors from that country.[1] As a result, Asian immigration via this system was almost impossible, even when not blocked by other specific bans or agreements (although in 1952 a token yearly quota of 2,000 was set for immigrants from the former Asiatic Barred Zone, renamed the Asia-Pacific Triangle).[2] By 1965, the growing domestic civil rights movement and the need to present a more positive international image planted the seeds of change.[3] The foundation of the United States' current family immigration system was laid that year with the passage of the Hart-Celler Act.[4] This bill abolished the national origins quota system, and in its place created a system in which a U.S. citizen or permanent resident (green card holder) can file a petition requesting permission for close family members to immigrate to the United States and be granted permanent resident status here. The same bill established employment-based immigration categories under which an American employer can sponsor a worker for permanent resident status, as long as the company can show the Department of Labor that a fair wage is being offered and that no qualified American worker is available to do the job.

DRAMATIC INCREASE IN IMMIGRATION

While supporters of the Hart-Celler Act recognized that it would place immigrants from non-Western countries on a more equal footing, even key backers such as Senator Ted Kennedy (D-MA) failed to appreciate the magnitude of the shift in the ethnic composition of immigration that would take place once the new law took effect in 1968. Senator Kennedy remarked during the debate over the bill that "the ethnic mix of this country will not be upset. . . . Contrary to the charges in some quarters, [the new system] will not inundate America with immigrants from any one country or area, or the most populated and deprived nations of Africa and Asia."[5]

Such predictions proved completely wrong as far as Asians were concerned. In fiscal year 2007, 383,508 people born in Asia were granted permanent resident status in the United States, making up 36.4 percent of the 1,052,415 total new permanent residents for the year.[6] Of these Asian-born immigrants, 240,447, or 62.7 percent were family-based immigrants, roughly in line with the 65.5 percent of all 2006 immigrants who were family-based. Asians are also major beneficiaries of the employment-based categories; 24 percent of Asian immigrants in 2006 received their permanent resident status via an employer, as compared to 15.4 percent of all immigrants that year. Asians made up 56.8 percent of all employment-based immigrants for the year. Despite this heavy usage of employment-based immigration, Asian family immigrants continue to outnumber employment-based immigrants by more than 2.5 to 1.

Major contributions to the number of Asian-born immigrants came from mainland China (76,655), the Philippines (72,596), India (65,353), Vietnam (28,691), and South Korea (22,405), all of them among the top ten countries of birth among new permanent residents in 2007. While in the 1970s and 1980s, most arrivals from Southeast Asian countries came as refugees, in recent years family immigration from the region has far surpassed new refugee admissions. In fiscal year 2006, there were 3,039 new Vietnamese refugee arrivals, by far the largest number from any Asian country, but still dwarfed by the 27,910 Vietnamese immigrants that received their green cards via the family immigration system that year.[7]

"IMMEDIATE RELATIVES" AND FAMILY PREFERENCE CATEGORIES

Under the family immigration system enacted in 1965 and still in effect, U.S. citizens can petition for "immediate relatives" (spouses, unmarried children under age 21, and parents) without being subject to an annual cap or quota, meaning that an immigrant visa can be obtained fairly quickly, often in less than a year.[8] All other family petitions fall into various "preference" categories subject to annual limits that have resulted in substantial waiting lists. Citizens can use these categories to petition for their adult unmarried or married children and their siblings, while permanent residents are limited to sponsoring spouses and unmarried children of any age.[9] While immediate relatives can receive their immigrant visas fairly quickly, they cannot bring their spouses or children with them; each immediate relative must have a direct relationship with a petitioning U.S. citizen.[10] Those in the preference categories must wait much longer to immigrate, but they are entitled to issuance of "derivative beneficiary" immigrant visas to allow their spouses and unmarried, minor children to obtain permanent resident status together with the principal beneficiary.[11]

Through the years, a number of legislators have sought to eliminate various family preference categories. Senator Alan Simpson (R-WY) teamed up with Rep. Romano Mazzoli (D-KY) in multiple efforts to eliminate the sibling category in the early 1980s, galvanizing the Asian American community in opposition and leading to a successful campaign to defend the category.[12] More recently, in 2007 a proposal to scrap most of the family immigration system (in favor of a skills-based point system similar to that used in Canada and Australia) emerged from the Senate's negotiations with the Bush administration as part of a larger immigration reform effort, but the larger reform effort was attacked by both the left and the right and failed to win enough votes to move forward.[13] Thus the family immigration categories today essentially remain the same as those established in 1965.

ANNUAL QUOTAS AND THE GROWTH OF BACKLOGS

Within each preference category, the length of the waiting list is governed by the Visa Bulletin, a monthly report issued by the State Department's Visa Office in which officials determine, to the best of their ability, how many immigrant visas can be issued each month while staying within the annual quota set by law.[14] These limits are of two types: the annual number of visas that can be issued for each family category, and the number that can be issued to natives of any single country (20,000 per year, with no more than 7 percent of total combined employment and family preference visas going to immigrants born in any one country).[15]

Congress can set the annual limits wherever it chooses, but the current numbers have remained unchanged since 1990, despite several attempts to slash them over the years. Notably, Senator Alan Simpson (R-WY) tried to greatly reduce family immigration quotas in the 104th Congress of 1995–96, but failed when his proposal was split into two bills, one dealing with legal immigration levels and the other with undocumented immigrants and noncitizens convicted of crimes.[16] This latter bill eventually became the Illegal Immigration Reform and Immigrant Responsibility Act of 1996 and was signed into law by President Clinton; Simpson's effort to cut legal immigration found little traction once separated from the larger bill. As a result, present levels of legal immigration remain as fixed in 1990, with no limit for a citizen's spouse, parent, or unmarried child under 21 and at least 226,000 immigrant visas available yearly for the family preference categories, divided as follows:[17]

Family Visa Petition Filed by a U.S. Citizen	Family Visa Petition Filed by a Legal Permanent Resident
First preference (adult unmarried son or daughter): 23,400 per year	Preference 2A (spouses and unmarried children under 21): 87,934 per year
Third preference (married son or daughter): 23,400 per year	Preference 2B (unmarried son or daughter over age 21): 26,266 per year
Fourth preference (brother or sister, married or single): 65,000 per year	

Victims of the Backlogs

Many immigration categories for prospective immigrants from Asia are seriously backlogged. Siblings of U.S. citizens must wait more than twenty years in the case of the Philippines, and relatives of lawful permanent residents (often called "green card holders") from other Asian countries must wait from four to twelve years. The delay in family reunification can result in severe emotional impact on the family. Consider Annie Soo Hoo. She was able to emigrate from China in the 1930s as the wife of a U.S. citizen. She left behind a sister, with whom she was very close. Within ten years of immigrating, Soo Hoo was able to become a U.S. citizen because the prohibition against Chinese immigrants becoming naturalized citizens was repealed in 1943. When Soo Hoo first began the process attempting to help her sister immigrate, she ran into paperwork problems. In rural parts of China, standard documents such as birth certificates and marriage certificates were not issued. So Soo Hoo had to go through a long time-consuming process of gathering supporting statements from people who knew they were sisters, finding old family photographs that pictured her with her sister, and translating letters they had written to each other to prove that they were indeed sisters. After the 1965 immigration law amendments, the processing time for the sibling category gradually grew longer and longer. The People's Republic of China also made it difficult for residents of China to obtain travel documents out of China in the 1970s. When Soo Hoo received word that her sister had passed away in the late 1970s still on the waitlist, she cried for weeks; she had endured pain for decades being separated from her sister.

—Bill Ong Hing

Where there are more applicants than available visas, the cases are handled in the order in which they were filed by the petitioning relatives in the United States. The date that the petition (Form I-130) was filed with U.S. Citizenship and Immigration Services or its predecessor, the Immigration and Naturalization Service, is known as the priority date. The State Department's monthly Visa Bulletin lists the priority date that is current for each category; potential immigrants with visa petitions filed before that date are eligible for an interview and visa issuance. Because U.S. citizens and permanent residents from particular countries have filed more petitions than others, backlogs for natives of those countries are longer. (The "country of chargeability" is determined by country of birth of the prospective immigrant, rather than country of current nationality or citizenship.)

In the most extreme case, Philippines-born siblings of U.S. citizens must wait twenty-two years to immigrate. Over the past decade, the most dramatic growth in the backlog has been in the first preference (unmarried adult sons and daughters of U.S. citizens) and third preference (married sons and daughters of U.S. citizens) categories, which respectively grew from fifteen months to six and a half years, and from three and a half years to more than eight years.[18] In fact, the first preference category of unmarried adult sons and daughters of U.S. citizens could immigrate without any delay at all as late as September 1996.

In 2000, Congress took special note of the lengthy backlog for spouses and minor children of permanent residents, which had already reached four and half years, and authorized a temporary "V-visa" program that allowed these family members to travel to the United States once their petition had been pending for

---

Victims of the Backlog

To understand the sometimes harsh effects of the growth in family immigration backlogs, it may help to look at a particular family. Minh Tran emigrated from Saigon, Vietnam, to San Francisco in 1998, under a fourth preference petition filed in 1988 by his sister Thao, a former refugee who had passed the naturalization test and become a U.S. citizen. Minh was accompanied by his wife, Hanh, and their nineteen-year-old daughter, Vi. Their son, Giang, was forced to remain in Vietnam because he had just turned twenty-one and was no longer considered a part of Minh's immediate family under the law at the time. As soon as the family settled in San Francisco, Hanh filed a petition for Minh under the 2B preference. But after nine years of waiting, just before the priority date was ready for Giang to immigrate, Hanh died suddenly, and her petition for her son was canceled. Now, twenty years after the original petition was filed for his family's immigration, Giang has been forced to begin waiting all over again, this time with Minh (now a U.S. citizen) petitioning for him under the first preference.

three years.[19] While the program did not speed up the actual granting of permanent resident status, it did reunite families during the latter part of their waiting period. The V-visa program is rarely useful today, however, because of its built-in closing date: it was available only to beneficiaries of 2A-preference family visa petitions filed before December 21, 2000.

In 2002, Congress addressed a long-standing problem with the preference categories: because of the mechanics of the annual quotas and the relative number of people waiting to immigrate in each category, Philippines-born unmarried sons and daughters of U.S. citizens must wait longer than those of permanent residents. For many years, this "naturalization penalty" made Filipinos reluctant to apply for U.S. citizenship because their children's immigration would be delayed. As part of the Child Status Protection Act of 2002, Congress remedied this situation by allowing the unmarried son or daughter of a permanent resident to opt out of the conversion from the 2B preference to the first preference that would normally result from the naturalization of the petitioning parent.[20]

FINANCIAL SPONSOR FOR FAMILY IMMIGRANTS

Until the passage of welfare reform legislation in 1996, family immigrants needed a financial sponsor, but the required paperwork was limited in scope. The 1996 amendments created a legally binding contract that the petitioning relative signs, promising to provide adequate support to the new immigrant.[21] This "affidavit of support" allows the immigrant to sue the sponsor for support if necessary, and also provides that the federal, state, or local government can sue the sponsor for reimbursement if the immigrant receives any "means-tested public benefits" (primarily monthly cash assistance programs available only to low-income individuals). The necessary level of support is set at 125 percent of the federal poverty guidelines, and the petitioning relative must show enough income or assets to support both existing household members and the new arrivals. When the petitioner's income and assets fall short, a co-sponsor may be used. The support obligation lasts until the sponsored immigrant becomes a U.S. citizen, is credited with 40 quarters of work under Social Security rules, dies, or permanently leaves the United States and gives up permanent resident status. While this law created a requirement that some families struggle to meet, it has not noticeably slowed immigration from Asia or other regions during the past decade.[22]

OUTLOOK

During the past forty years, family immigration has been and continues to be the primary growth engine of the Asian American community. Such notable Asian Americans as Jerry Yang, former CEO of Yahoo, arrived via the family preference system.[23] Even for those immigrants who originally arrived here via an employer's sponsorship or as refugees, the family petitioning process has enabled them to gradually reunite their families here in the United States, an opportunity that is very limited under other countries' immigration systems, such as those in Australia and Canada. As a result, the inevitable future efforts to alter the U.S. family immigration system will merit close attention from all segments of the Asian American immigrant community.

FURTHER READING

Hing, Bill Ong. *Making and Remaking Asian America through Immigration Policy, 1850–1990*. Stanford: Stanford University Press, 1993.

Office of Immigration Statistics, U.S. Department of Homeland Security. *2007 Yearbook of Immigration Statistics*. Washington, DC: National Technical Information Service, U.S. Department of Commerce, 2008. http://www.dhs.gov/ximgtn/statistics/publications/yearbook.shtm.

Tamayo, William R. "Asian Americans and Present U.S. Immigration Policies: A Legacy of Asian Exclusion." In *Asian Americans and the Supreme Court*, Hyung-Chan Kim, ed., 1105–1130. Westport, CT: Greenwood Press, 1992.

NOTES

1. David Weissbrodt, *Immigration Law and Procedure,* 4th ed. (St. Paul, MN: West Publishing Group, 1998), 10–17.

2. Hing, Bill Ong, *Making and Remaking Asian America through Immigration Policy, 1850–1990* (Stanford: Stanford University Press, 1993) 37–38.

3. Weissbrodt, *Immigration Law and Procedure,* 17; Hing, *Making and Remaking Asian America through Immigration Policy,* 79.

4. Pub. L. No. 89-236.

5. U.S. Senate, Subcommittee on Immigration and Naturalization of the Committee on the Judiciary, Washington, DC, Hearing Transcript of Feb. 10, 1965, pp. 1–3.

6. Office of Immigration Statistics, U.S. Department of Homeland Security, *2007 Yearbook of Immigration Statistics* (Washington, D.C: National Technical Information Service, U.S. Department of Commerce, 2008), http://www.dhs.gov/ximgtn/statistics/publications/yearbook.shtm. Figures cited in this paragraph and the following one are from this source.

7. Office of Immigration Statistics, U.S. Department of Homeland Security, *2006 Yearbook of Immigration Statistics* (Washington, D.C: National Technical Information Service, U.S. Department of Commerce 2007), http://www.dhs.gov/ximgtn/statistics/publications/yearbook.shtm.

8. 8 USC § 1151(b)(2)(A)(i).

9. 8 USC § 1153(a).

10. 8 CFR § 204.2(a)(4).

11. 8 USC § 1153(d).

12. Tamayo, William R., "Asian Americans and Present U.S. Immigration Policies: A Legacy of Asian Exclusion," in *Asian Americans and the Supreme Court,* ed. Hyung-Chan Kim (Westport, CT: Greenwood, 1992), 1115–1118.

13. Dana Bash and Andrea Koppel, "Senate Immigration Bill Suffers Crushing Defeat" (June 28, 2007), http://www.cnn.com/2007/POLITICS/06/28/immigration.congress/index.html.

14. The Visa Bulletin http://travel.state.gov/visa/frvi/bulletin/bulletin_1360.html.

15. 8 USC § 1152(a)(2).

16. Schmitt, Eric, "Bill to Limit Immigration Faces a Setback in Senate," *New York Times*, March 14, 1996, http://www.nytimes.com/1996/03/14/us/bill-to-limit-immigration-faces-a-setback-in-senate.html?n=Top%2FReference%2FTimes%20Topics%2FSubjects%2FI%2FIllegal%20Aliens.

17. 8 USC § 1153(a).

18. The Visa Bulletin Archive, http://travel.state.gov/visa/frvi/bulletin/bulletin_1360.html.

19. 8 USC § 1101(a)(15)(V).

20. Section 6, Pub. L. No. 107-208.

21. 8 USC § 1183a.

22. Office of Immigration Statistics, U.S. Department of Homeland Security, *2007 Yearbook of Immigration Statistics* (Washington, DC: National Technical Information Service, U.S. Department of Commerce, 2008), http://www.dhs.gov/ximgtn/statistics/publications/yearbook.shtm.

23. "Benefits to the American Economy of a More Educated Workforce," Hearing before the House Immigration Subcommittee, 106th Congress, 1st Session (March 25, 1999), Serial No. 35, p. 137 (remarks of Rep. Zoe Lofgren).

HUMAN TRAFFICKING

Pahole Yotin Sookkasikon

Human trafficking occurs when people are attained, drafted, or brought in by coercion, force, and/or fraud for the ultimate purposes of subjection to commercial sex, forced labor, and/or indentured servitude. Worldwide, human trafficking brings in an estimated $32 billion to $44.3 billion per year. Sex trafficking—seen more often among victimized Asian immigrants—alone generates $7 billion to $8 billion per year.[1] Internationally, it is estimated that 4 million to 27 million people have been forced into this universally illegal and underground trade.[2] Of this annual number, the majority of victims are women and girls, and many are young children. In the United States, 45,000 to 50,000 individuals per year are brought into the country under various guises and for different purposes. Approximately 30,000 of those people smuggled into the United States are from Asia—primarily from Thailand, Vietnam, China, and other Asian nations where poverty levels are high.[3]

General consensus defines human trafficking as the illegal movement of people(s) across national borders. U.S. law defines human trafficking as the following: "a) sex trafficking in which a commercial sex act is induced by force, fraud, or coercion, or in which the person persuaded to perform such an act has not attained 18 years of age; or b) the recruitment, harboring, transportation, provision, or obtaining of a person for labor or services, through the use of force, fraud, or coercion for the purpose of subjection to involuntary servitude, peonage, debt bondage, or slavery."[4]

Human traffickers prey on individuals who are quite vulnerable, recruiting victims through coercion and manipulation. These victims tend to come from impoverished nations—at times called "source countries"—and typically travel to states with greater economic opportunities and higher levels of income—"destination countries."[5] Those trafficked from Asian countries are usually forced and manipulated into services such as involuntary sex work; domestic servitude; labor and child exploitation; as well as the more recent, servile marriages—a marriage that a woman was promised or given into without her consent, specifically seen in mail-order brides. Often these migrant sufferers face unwilling servitude because of various abuses, which include the misuse of a working contract; inadequate local laws that govern the recruitment and employment of migrant laborers; and the intentional imposition of debts that continuously incur while remaining in their captors' possession.

HUMAN TRAFFICKING CASES

On August 2, 1995, it was discovered that seventy-two Thai workers were held captive as slave labor in an apartment-based sweatshop in the southern Californian suburb of El Monte. The Manasurangkun family, fellow Thai immigrants, was held responsible for holding migrants captive while enforcing and abusing laborers with constant deadlines, inhumane treatment, little time off, and corrupt work ethics. Like many stories that involve illegal trafficking, most of the individuals—predominantly ethnic Thai women, and some men— were introduced to the prospect of a better economic opportunity by word-of-mouth or an acquaintance in their native homeland. These men and women typically came from a rural socioeconomic background and were in need of an economic alternative. They then migrated to the United States under fabricated documents and fake identities, assuming an entirely new life concocted and controlled by their traffickers. Many of them did not second-guess or run from their captors during the process of migration because they did not suspect or know they were being trafficked until it was too late. Those who have testified against the Manasurangkun family said that, upon arrival, their rights and freedoms were restricted; conversation to and with other workers was closely monitored; work was thoroughly enforced; and they were held captive from the outside world—locked inside the seven-unit complex, with barbed-wired fences.

From its earlier stages in 1988 to the final raid in August 1995, the operators of the El Monte sweatshop intimidated their victims by making them work sixteen-hours a day seven days a week, increased their debts, made threats of physical harm to them and to their families in Thailand, and kept them under tight surveillance to prevent them from escaping. Workers were forced to sew garments for large, brand-name clothing lines—such as High Sierra, B.U.M., and Anchor Blue, which were sold at Miller's Outpost, Nordstrom's, Target, and Sears—for less than $2 an hour.[6] Although they sewed for many well-known clothing lines, the men and women of El Monte rarely saw any profit. Malinan Radomphon, an El Monte interviewee, recalled that on a monthly basis, laborers would receive $400 to $500 per month.[7] For the most part, a high percentage of their earnings were stripped away and used to pay off the increasing debt that each individual owed. With the little money left over, laborers had no choice but to use those earnings to purchase food or personal products through the Manasurangkun family at extorted prices.

When law enforcement finally raided the sweatshop, acting on a tip from the boyfriend of an escaped worker, they arrested eight of the garment shop operators and the Immigration and Naturalization Service detained the seventy-two workers in their custody. Nine days after being detained, the INS released the workers and granted them temporary residency in the United States as material witnesses to testify against the operators of El Monte. By 1999, eleven companies—Mervyn's, Montgomery Ward, Tomato, Bum International, L. F. Sportswear, Miller's Outpost, Balmara, Beniko, F-40 California, Ms. Tops, and Topson Downs—agreed to pay more than $3.7 million to the 150 workers who labored in the El Monte sweatshop and its storefront operation. As in most cases involving the exploitation of undocumented laborers and large-clothing companies, these large corporations argued that they had no knowledge of the type of labor used to sew their apparel and were just fooled by the contractors. After this ordeal many of the workers were granted legal residency. Most are expected to apply for legal citizenship in the United States.

SEX TRAFFICKING

The most prominently known form of human trafficking is illegal sex work, which is generally defined as an exchange of capital and goods for sexual services. Out of the 30,000 Asian individuals—commonly women—who are trafficked into the United States annually, a large percentage of them consequently end up taking this route of human barter. These victims are chiefly exported from developing nations such as the Philippines, Sri Lanka, Thailand, and are emerging in Vietnam and Cambodia. Similar to the case of El Monte, individuals involved in sex trafficking were and are lured by the promises of better economic options for the possibility of a more thriving and successful livelihood.

It is estimated that 10,000 Asian women are trafficked into the Los Angeles underground sex trade yearly.[8] About twenty to thirty Thai women are illegally imported into Canadian and U.S. brothels (typically disguised as a massage parlor) a month.[9] Along with these women, approximately 25,000 Filipinas have been brought into the United States to work in numerous states, in different forms of the sex trade, as well as near U.S. military bases and camps.[10] Furthermore, the women typically are locked inside the place of business and forced to have sex with as many as a dozen men a day. Sometimes victims are forced to live in the brothel where five or six "co-workers" are crammed into one room.[11]

Generally, most of the victims are promised work as hostesses, waitresses, models, and other small jobs to pay debts.[12] Upon arrival to the U.S., many awake to the reality of enforced sexual servitude with little hope of escape until expenses—travel costs, housing, visas and passports, food, and personal hygiene products—are paid off. In one case, a Korean woman who was trafficked was told that she owed her employers $11,000 for her journey—$4,000 more than she had originally agreed to. This woman was sold into an escort service where women were sold into brothels, massage parlors, and strip clubs.[13] Being forced to navigate herself throughout the underground sex industry of California, she ended up in the Tenderloin district of San Francisco, where she eventually saved enough money to pay off expenses and buy her freedom; she gave $30,000 plus a $1,200 fee to her employer.[14]

Individuals who free themselves from their traffickers are able to use many resources that are available to them and usually qualify for the government-issued T-1 visa, allowing them to stay in the country for three years and eventually apply for a green card if it is proved that they were a victim of enforced sexual servitude. Although the U.S. government allots 5,000 visas annually for victims, typically only 1,000 are issued because those who apply must first testify against their trafficker, which many are not prepared to do, fearing physical harm to their family and themselves. This becomes problematic, and both the authorities and traffickers know it. Because of the lack of evidence to convict traffickers, the penalty that they face is minimal compared with the amount of distress and trauma they have caused victims. For example, in San Francisco, only a handful of problem massage parlors have been fined $2,500 for health code violations and threatened with 60- and 90-day permit suspensions if more violations are discovered.[15]

ADVOCACY FOR VICTIMS

Although at times reparation sometimes seems like a fleeting dream to victims, many organizations have begun to advocate and provide substantial services for victimized individuals during and after their ordeal. For example, the U.S. government—in most cases—is able to adjust the immigration and citizenship status of most trafficked laborers, obtain local and federal assistance for individuals, and begin to rebuild fractured lives through rehabilitation. Additionally, the government—through the U.S. Department of Health and Human Services (HHS)—facilitates federally funded relief to victims who are of non-U.S. residency and status. Victims are also able to access services through HHS such as federal and government-mandated health care, food provisions, and assistance in finding occupations and employment. Most importantly, with more to offer than the basic necessities given to victims, the HHS connects reluctant parties who are fearful of deportation and incarceration with nonprofit organizations that exclusively handle situations such as these.

Asian American nonprofit and grassroots organizations such as the GABRIELA Network, Asian Pacific Islander Legal Outreach (APILO), the Coalition to Abolish Slavery and Trafficking (CAST), Asian Pacific American

Legal Center, Asian Law Caucus, and others are organized to campaign and raise awareness so others can fully understand the scope of this international problem. Some of their main goals are to provide cohesion—through networking, recognition, and similar aspirations—among groups and individuals, which help empower and give voice to those victimized. Groups also advocate civil rights, produce educational tools and awareness, and in some cases, provide legal services that assist victims ascertain some sense of security.

The services they offer are sometimes seen as legal routes that help educate community-based organizations, government offices, social and legal providers, and shelters to give more resources to victims in the United States. Through this awareness and action as a middleman, grassroots Asian American organizations and policy groups play an important role by providing culturally appropriate direct services, community education, policy research and legislative advocacy that are sensitive to the particular needs of trafficked persons.[16]

Many organizations and people refuse to ignore the problem and answer the call of victims because this is not just an international issue, but a domestic one

Garment industry worker Nantha Jaknang, right, embraces Rini Chakraborty of the Asian Pacific American Legal Center (APALC). Jaknang, who was involved in the 1995 El Monte raid where Thai workers were taken as prisoners, spoke about the difficulty she had trying to exercise her rights under California's anti-sweatshop law at a news conference at the APALC in Los Angeles, 2005. (AP Photo/Reed Saxon)

as well. As the number of Asian and Asian American people trafficked continues to increase, so do the organizations that help advocate on their behalf and bring attention to this undercover and unlawful occurrence. For many, it is the desire to bring attention that allows individuals to understand and follow the signs that aid and heal the trauma for those who struggle silently. It is the desire for an end to this modern-day slavery that makes people take action.

FURTHER READING

American Civil Liberties Union (ACLU), http://www.aclu.org/ and http://www.aclu.org/womensrights/index.html.
Asian Anti Trafficking Collaborative (AATC), http://endtrafficking.wordpress.com/.
Foo, Lora Jo. *Asian American Women: Issues, Concerns, and Responsive Human and Civil Rights Advocacy*. New York: iUniverse, Inc., 2003.
Gabriela Network (GABNet), http://www.gabnet.org/.
Office to Monitor and Combat Trafficking in Persons, http://www.state.gov/g/tip/.
Rebugio, Liezl Tomas. *Rights to Survival & Mobility: An Anti-Trafficking Activist's Agenda*. [Online, 2008]. National Asian Pacific American Woman's Forum Web site. http://www.napawf.org/file/events/AT_Agenda.pdf.
Sweatshop Watch, http://www.sweatshopwatch.org/.

NOTES

1. U.S. Department of State, *Trafficking in Persons* Report (*TIP Report*), available at http://www.state.gov/g/tip/rls/tiprpt/2008/index.htm (June 4, 2008); American Civil Liberties Union, *Human Trafficking: Modern Enslavement of Immigrant Women in the United States*, http://www.aclu.org/womensrights/humanrights/34683res20070531.html (May 31, 2007).

2. U.S. Department of State, *Trafficking in Persons Report*.

3. Lora Jo Foo, *Asian American Women: Issues, Concerns, and Responsive Human and Civil Rights Advocacy* (New York: iUniverse, Inc., 2003).

4. *Trafficking Victims Protection Act* ("*TVPA*") of 2000, 22 U.S.C. § 7102(8).

5. Ivy O Suriyopas, "Toll on Human Trafficking," *Filipino Reporter* 36, no. 13 (2008): 55.

6. Liezl Tomas Rebugio, "Rights to Survival & Mobility: An Anti-Trafficking Activist's Agenda," *National Asian Pacific American Woman's Forum,* 2008, http://www.napawf.org/file/events/AT_Agenda.pdf.

7. Peter Leibhold and Harry R. Rubenstein, *Between a Rock and a Hard Place: A History of American Sweatshops, 1820–Present* (Los Angeles: UCLA Asian American Studies Center and Simon Wiesenthal Center Museum of Tolerance, 1999), 78.

8. Foo, *Asian American Women*. 2003.

9. Foo, *Asian American Women*, 2003.

10. Gabriela Network, "Trafficking in the United States," *The Purple Rose Campaign: Against Trafficking Filipino Women and Children*, 2005–2009, http://www.gabnet.org/campaigns.php?page=2.2.

11. Meredith May, "Diary of a Sex Slave," *SFGate.com*, Oct. 6–10, 2006, http://www.sfgate.com/sextrafficking/.

12. May, "Diary of a Sex Slave."

13. May, "Diary of a Sex Slave."

14. May, "Diary of a Sex Slave."

15. May, "Diary of a Sex Slave."

16. Liezl Tomas Rebugio, "Rights to Survival & Mobility: An Anti-Trafficking Activist's Agenda," *National Asian Pacific American Woman's Forum,* 2008, http://www.napawf.org/file/events/AT_Agenda.pdf.

PUBLIC BENEFITS

Jonathan Blazer and Tanya Broder

The availability of public benefits is an important matter for many Asian Americans. The vast majority of Asian Americans are foreign-born, and a substantial number—particularly among those who entered the country as refugees—rely on public assistance as they adjust to life in the United States. Many Asian Americans are denied access to critical services, however, because of immigrant restrictions imposed in many benefits programs. Since the inception of federal programs providing food, cash assistance, and health insurance to low-income persons, undocumented immigrants and immigrants with temporary visas generally have been ineligible for assistance. However, enactment of 1996 welfare and immigration laws marked an unprecedented new era of restrictionism.[1] Prior to the 1996 laws, lawfully residing immigrants generally were eligible for assistance in a similar manner as citizens. Thereafter, most lawfully residing immigrants were barred from receiving assistance under the major federal benefits programs for five years or longer. Even where eligibility for immigrants was preserved by the 1996 laws or restored by subsequent legislation, many immigrant families hesitate to enroll in critical health care, job-training, nutrition, and cash assistance programs because of fear and confusion about these laws. As a result, the participation of legal immigrants in public benefit programs decreased sharply since passage of the 1996 law, leaving many poor and low-income families in severe hardship, lacking even the minimal support available to other low-income families.[2]

Many states have worked to fill in the significant gaps in noncitizen coverage created by the 1996 laws. In fact, more than half of the states spend their own money to cover at least some of the immigrants who are ineligible for federally funded services. A growing number of states or counties provide health coverage to children and/or pregnant women, regardless of their immigration status. State-funded programs are often temporary or subject to state budget battles. In determining an immigrant's eligibility for benefits, it is important to understand both the federal rules and the rules of the individual state in which an immigrant resides.

POVERTY AND IMMIGRANTS

Although only one in eight persons living in the U.S. is foreign-born, immigrants comprise one-fifth of the nation's low-wage workforce. Although many immigrants do well economically, many others work long hours at low-wage jobs with no health insurance or other benefits. In fact, nearly half of immigrant workers earn less than twice the minimum wage, and only 26 percent of immigrants have job-based health insurance.[3]

In recent decades, the population of immigrants from Asian countries living in the United States has grown dramatically, increasing by 65 percent between 1990 and 2000 alone. In 2000, these immigrants comprised more than a quarter of the foreign-born, second only to Latin American immigrants in foreign-born population by world region. Among the top five countries sending refugees to the United States from 1983–2004, three are Southeast Asian countries.[4]

Although, as a broad category, Asian immigrants have higher earnings and lower rates of unemployment and poverty than the overall foreign-born population, there is a great deal of variation among immigrants based on their country of birth. Approximately one in every seven Asian immigrants lives in poverty, which indicates that many are financially eligible for federal public benefit programs that assist low-income persons. There is wide variation in poverty rates among foreign-born Asian populations, ranging from 6 percent (Philippines) to 43.2 percent (Mongolia), and of course there is also enormous variation among individual persons within country populations.[5]

Overall, approximately 18 percent of all Asian Americans lack health insurance, compared to 11 percent of non-Hispanic whites. Two factors help explain the discrepancy. First, despite their high rates of employment, Asian Americans are less likely to work in jobs providing employer-sponsored coverage. For example, Korean Americans and Southeast Asians, nearly half of whom are uninsured, are also the least likely to have employment-based coverage. Second, Asian immigrants are often excluded from the public health programs intended to assist low-income persons who lack job-based insurance because of the various eligibility restrictions and other barriers described in this article. Indeed, Asian Americans use Medicaid and Medicare relatively infrequently (18.3% vs. 26.1% for whites) despite their higher poverty rates and lower rate of employer-sponsored coverage. That said, public programs play a critical role in providing health care access for many Asian American groups. For example, Asian American children are somewhat more likely than white children to have government health insurance, such as Medicaid, SCHIP, or military health care (22.4% vs. 18.4%).[6]

IMMIGRANT ELIGIBILITY RESTRICTIONS

The 1996 welfare law created two categories of immigrants for benefits eligibility purposes: "qualified" and "not qualified." The qualified immigrant category includes lawful permanent residents, refugees, asylees, and other more specialized categories.[7] All other immigrants, ranging from undocumented immigrants to many people who are lawfully present in the United States, are considered "not qualified." The federal law prohibits "not qualified" immigrants from enrolling in most federal public benefit programs.[8] Federal public benefits include a variety of safety net services paid for by federal funds.[9]

Congress restricted eligibility even for many qualified immigrants by arbitrarily distinguishing between those who entered the United States before or "on or after" the date the law was enacted, August 22, 1996. The law bars most immigrants who entered the United States on or after that date from "federal means-tested public benefits" during the five years after they secure qualified immigrant status.[10] Federal agencies clarified that "federal means-tested public benefits" are Medicaid (except for emergency care), SCHIP, TANF, Food Stamps, and Supplemental Security Income.[11] "Humanitarian immigrants"—refugees, people granted asylum or withholding of deportation/removal, Cuban/Haitian entrants, certain Amerasian immigrants, and victims of trafficking—are exempt from the five-year bar, as are "qualified" immigrant veterans, active duty military, and their spouses and children.

States can receive federal funding for TANF, Medicaid, and SCHIP to serve "qualified" immigrants who have completed the federal five-year bar.[12] Approximately half of the states use state funds to provide TANF, Medicaid, and/or SCHIP to some or all of the immigrants who are subject to the five-year bar on federally funded services, or to a broader group of immigrants.[13] Although the 1996 law severely restricted immigrant eligibility for food stamps, subsequent legislation restored access for many of these immigrants. Other "qualified" immigrant adults, however, must wait until they have been in qualified status for five years before their eligibility for food stamps can be considered.

Congress imposed its most severe restrictions on immigrant seniors and immigrants with disabilities, who seek assistance under the SSI program.[14] Although advocacy efforts in the years following the welfare law's passage achieved a partial restoration of these benefits, significant gaps in eligibility remain. SSI, for example, continues to exclude "not qualified" immigrants who were not already receiving the benefits, as well as most "qualified" immigrants who entered the country after the welfare law passed and seniors without disabilities who were in the United States before that date.[15]

"Not qualified" immigrants remain eligible for emergency Medicaid, if they are otherwise eligible for their state's Medicaid program.[16] The 1996 law does not restrict access to public health programs providing immunizations and/or treatment of communicable disease symptoms (whether or not those symptoms are caused by such a disease). School breakfast and lunch programs remain open to all children regardless of immigration status, and every state has opted to provide access to the Special Supplemental Nutrition Program for Women, Infants and Children (WIC).[17] Also exempted from the restrictions are in-kind services necessary to protect life or safety, as long as the program is not conditioned on a person's income or resources.[18]

OTHER BARRIERS IMPEDING ACCESS TO BENEFITS

Asian American immigrants confront numerous barriers when attempting to secure public benefits. Confusion about eligibility rules pervades not only benefit agencies but also Asian American and immigrant health and service providers.[19] The confusion stems from the complex interaction of the immigration and welfare laws, differences in eligibility criteria for various state and federal programs, and a lack of adequate training on the rules as clarified by federal agencies. Consequently, many eligible immigrants have assumed that they should not seek services, and eligibility workers mistakenly have turned away eligible immigrants. Asian immigrants and their families are often confused by these federal laws and wary of applying for public benefits because they do not want to jeopardize their immigration status. The failure of benefits and other agencies to provide linguistically appropriate information has compounded the problem.

Many Asian immigrants fear that use of public benefits could jeopardize their immigration status.[20] Current immigration laws allow officials to deny applications for permanent residence if the authorities determine that the immigrant seeking permanent residence is "likely to become a public charge." In deciding whether an immigrant is likely to become a public charge, immigration or consular officials look at the "totality of the circumstances," including an immigrant's health, age, income, education and skills, and affidavits of support. In May 1999, the Immigration and Naturalization Service issued helpful guidance and a proposed regulation on the public charge doctrine.[21] The guidance clarifies that receipt of health care and other noncash benefits will not jeopardize the immigration status of recipients or their family members by putting them at risk of being considered a public charge.[22] Nevertheless, after the issuance of this guidance, confusion and concern about the public charge rules remain, deterring many eligible immigrants from seeking benefits for which they are eligible.

In the Asian American community, immigrants and their families also have been deterred from using public benefits because they fear that their use of benefits will have negative repercussions for their "sponsors."[23] Under the 1996 welfare and immigration laws, family members who file a petition to help a person immigrate must become financial sponsors of the immigrant by signing a contract with the government (an affidavit of support). Under this affidavit, the sponsor promises to support the immigrant and to repay certain benefits that the immigrant may use. The particular federal benefits for which sponsors may be liable have been defined to be TANF, SSI, food stamps, nonemergency Medicaid, and SCHIP. Recently issued regulations on the affidavits of support make clear that states are not obligated to pursue sponsors and that states cannot collect reimbursement for services used prior to public notification that they are considered means-tested public benefits for which sponsors will be liable. Most states have not designated the programs that would give rise to sponsor liability. The specter of sponsor liability, however, has deterred some eligible immigrants from applying for benefits, based on concerns about exposing their sponsors to government collection efforts.

Many Asian immigrants face significant linguistic and cultural barriers to obtaining benefits. As a group, Asian immigrants are somewhat more likely to be proficient in English than the overall foreign-born population; however, more than one-third of Asians Americans do not speak English "very well." These limited English proficient (LEP) residents cannot effectively apply for benefits or meaningfully communicate with a health care provider without language assistance. Title VI of the Civil Rights Act of 1964 prohibits recipients of federal funding from discriminating on the basis of national origin, and such discrimination can include failure to address language barriers that prevent LEP individuals from securing assistance. Compliance with this nondiscrimination requirement has been limited. In August 2000, the White House issued an executive order directing federal agencies, by December 11, 2000, to submit to the U.S. Department of Justice (DOJ) plans to improve language access and to publish guidance for programs receiving federal financial assistance regarding compliance with the Title VI requirement to take "reasonable steps" to assure "meaningful access" to federally funded services.[24] The DOJ published final guidance to its recipients on June 18, 2002.[25] Several agencies, including HHS, developed and published guidance for public comment, but many remain delinquent.[26]

As a result of federal welfare law changes and the confusion that ensued, many local, statewide and national Asian American organizations such as the Asian Pacific Islander American Health Forum, the Asian American Justice Center, the National Korean American Service and Education Consortium, the Southeast Asian Resource Center, and National Asian Pacific Women's Forum have made it a priority to engage in education and continued advocacy in many Asian immigrant communities to address the various barriers preventing immigrants from securing public benefits.

OUTLOOK

The 1996 welfare law produced sharp decreases in public benefits participation, particularly among immigrants. Proponents of welfare reform see that fact as evidence of the bill's success, noting that a reduction of welfare "dependency," particularly among immigrants, was precisely what the legislation intended. Critics question, among other things, the fairness of excluding immigrants from programs that are supported by the taxes that the immigrants themselves pay. In Asian American communities, the 1996 welfare law marked a time to challenge policy makers on their decisions to curtail immigrants access to benefit programs. Working in coalitions with other local and national organizations, they worked to advocate that immigrants—regardless of their citizenship or immigration status—deserved essential services such as preventive health care.[27] Later, after the passage of the federal welfare law, many of these groups worked together to challenge and to restore many of the lost benefits. Today, national Asian American organizations continue to collaborate with other organizations to engage with local and statewide groups and policy makers in addressing the inequalities and barriers that prevent immigrants from participating in benefit programs.

FURTHER READING

Asian Pacific Islander American Health Forum. http//:www.apiahf.org.

National Immigration Law Center, *Guide to Immigrant Eligibility for Federal Programs*, 4th ed. Washington, DC: National Immigration Law Center, 2002.

National Immigration Law Center, *Federal Guidance on Public Charge: When is it safe to use public benefits?* http://www.nilc.org/ce/nilc/Public_Charge_Nat-06-01-05.pdf.

National Immigration Law Center, *Sponsored Immigrants and Benefits* http://www.nilc.org/ce/nilc/sponsoredimms&bens_na_2006-07.pdf.

Southeast Asia Resource Action Center, http://www.searac.org.

NOTES

1. Personal Responsibility and Work Opportunity Reconciliation Act of 1996 (hereinafter "welfare law"), Pub. L. No. 104–193, 110 Stat. 2105 (Aug. 22, 1996); and Illegal Immigration Reform and Immigrant Responsibility Act of 1996 (hereinafter "IIRIRA"), enacted as Division C of the Defense Department Appropriations Act, 1997, Pub. L. No. 104–208, 110 Stat. 3008 (Sept. 30, 1996).

2. Michael Fix and Jeffrey Passel, "The Scope and Impact of Welfare Reform's Immigrant Provisions." *Assessing the New Federalism* Discussion Paper No. 02-03. Washington, DC: The Urban Institute, 2002.

3. Leighton Ku and Shannon Blaney, "Health Coverage for Legal Immigrant Children: New Census Data Highlight Importance of Restoring Medicaid and SCHIP Coverage," (Washington, DC: Center on Budget and Policy Priorities, October 2000).

4. Audrey Singer and Jill H Wilson, "Refugee Resettlement in Metropolitan America," Migration Policy Institute, March 2007.

5. David Dixon, "Characteristics of the Asian Born in the United States," Migration Policy Institute, March 2006 (compiling data from the 2000 Census).

6. Asian & Pacific Islander American Health Forum, "Health Coverage: Asian American and Pacific Islanders" (December 2006) (summarizing primary source data), http://www.apiahf.org/resources/pdf/AAPI_Insurance_coverage_Fact_Sheet.pdf.

7. The following groups are defined as "qualified" immigrants: lawful permanent residents; refugees, persons granted asylum or withholding of deportation/removal, Cuban and Haitian entrants and conditional entrants; people granted parole by the Department of Homeland Security (DHS) for a period of at least one year; and certain abused immigrants, their children, and/or their parents. Victims of trafficking and their derivative beneficiaries, while not technically "qualified" immigrants, are eligible for benefits to the same extent as refugees. Some states continue to provide services to a broader range of immigrants using state or local funds.

8. Welfare law § 401 (8 U.S.C. § 1611).

9. "Federal public benefit" is defined in the 1996 welfare law as any grant, contract, loan, professional license, or commercial license provided by an agency of the United States or by appropriated funds of the United States, and any retirement, welfare, health, disability, public or assisted housing, postsecondary education, food assistance, unemployment, benefit, or any other similar benefit for which payments or assistance are provided to an individual, household, or family eligibility unit by an agency of the United States or appropriated funds of the United States; see http://www.acf.hhs.gov/programs/ocs/liheap/guidance/special_topics/im98-25.html.

10. Welfare law § 403 (8 U.S.C. § 1613).

11. HHS, Personal Responsibility and Work Opportunity Reconciliation Act of 1996 (PRWORA), "Interpretation of 'Federal Means-Tested Public Benefit,'" 62 FR 45256 (August 26, 1997); U.S. Department of Agriculture (USDA), "Federal Means-Tested Public Benefits," 63 FR 36653 (July 7, 1998); Health Care Financing Administration, "The Administration's Response to Questions about the State Child Health Insurance Program," Question 19(a) (Sept. 11, 1997).

12. The Children's Health Insurance Program Reauthorization Act of 2009 granted states the option to provide federally funded Medicaid and CHIP to "lawfully residing" children and pregnant women, regardless of their date of entry into the United States. Public Law 111-113.

13. See *Guide to Immigrant Eligibility for Federal Programs*, 4th ed. (Los Angeles: National Immigrant Law Center, 2002), and updated tables at http://www.nilc.org/pubs/Guide_update.htm.

14. Welfare law § 402(a) (8 U.S.C. § 1612(a)).

15. Most new entrants cannot receive SSI until they become citizens or secure credit for 40 quarters of work history (including work performed by a spouse during marriage, persons "holding out to the community" as spouses, and by parents before the immigrant was 18 years old).

16. Emergency Medicaid covers the treatment of an emergency medical conditions, which is defined as: " a medical condition (including emergency labor and delivery) manifesting itself by acute symptoms of sufficient severity (including severe pain) such that the absence of immediate medical attention could reasonably be expected to result in: (A) placing the patient's health in serious jeopardy, (B) serious impairment to bodily functions: or (C) serious dysfunction of any bodily organ or part." 42 U.S.C. §1396b(v); Welfare law § 401(b)(1)(A) (8 U.S.C. § 1611(b)(1)(A)).

17. Welfare law § 742 (8 U.S.C. § 1615).

18. U.S. Department of Justice (DOJ), "Final Specification of Community Programs Necessary for Protection of Life or Safety under Welfare Reform Legislation," A.G. Order No. 2353–2001, published in 66 FR 3613–16 (Jan. 16, 2001).

19. L. S. Park and G. J. Yoo, "Impact of 'Public Charge' Policy on Immigrant Women's Access to Medi-Cal," *Policy Report to the California Policy Research Center's California Program on Access to Care* (2002).

20. Park and Yoo, "Impact of 'Public Charge' Policy."

21. DOJ, "Field Guidance on Deportability and Inadmissibility on Public Charge Grounds," 64 FR 28689–93 (May 26, 1999); see also DOJ, "Inadmissibility and Deportability on Public Charge Grounds," 64 FR 28676–88 (May 26, 1999); U.S. Department of State, INA 212(A)(4) Public Charge: Policy Guidance, 9 FAM 40.41.

22. The use of all health care programs, except for long-term institutionalization (e.g. Medicaid payment for nursing home care), was declared to be irrelevant to public charge determinations. Programs providing cash assistance for income maintenance purposes

Encyclopedia of Asian American Issues Today

are the only other programs that are relevant in the public charge determination. The determination is based on the "totality of a person's circumstances" and therefore the past use of cash assistance can be weighed against other favorable factors, such as a person's current income or skills or the contract signed by a sponsor promising to support the intending immigrant.

23. Park and Yoo, "Impact of "Public Charge" Policy".

24. Personal Responsibility and Work Opportunity Reconciliation Act of 1996.

25. Fix and Passel, "The Scope and Impact of Welfare Reform's Immigrant Provisions."

26. Ku and Blaney, *Health Coverage for Legal Immigrant Children.*

27. Yoo, "The Fight to Save Welfare for Low-Income Older Asian Immigrants: The Role of National Asian American Organizations," *Asian Americans & Pacific Islanders Policy, Practice and Community* 1, No. 1: 85–103.

SOUTH ASIANS IN A POST–SEPTEMBER 11TH ENVIRONMENT

Deepa Iyer

The post-September 11th environment has been framed as a watershed moment for South Asian community members and organizations in the United States. During the months and years that followed the September 11th attacks, South Asians experienced unprecedented levels of harassment, targeting, profiling, and discrimination from members of the general public, entities such as employers or businesses, and governmental entities.

More than 2.7 million South Asians reside in the United States. South Asians trace their backgrounds to Bangladesh, Bhutan, India, the Maldives, Nepal, Pakistan, Sri Lanka, and the diaspora that includes the Caribbean, Africa, and Europe. South Asians are diverse in terms of national origin, languages spoken, economic status, and religious affiliation. The majority of South Asians who live in the United States are foreign-born, with more than 75 percent of the population born outside of the United States. The metropolitan areas with the largest South Asian populations include New York/New Jersey, the San Francisco Bay Area, Chicago, Los Angeles, and the Washington, DC, metropolitan area.[1]

For South Asian communities, the post–September 11th backlash was a wakeup call in many ways. While South Asians had experienced discrimination, violence, and profiling prior to September 11th, the general feeling of comfort and security that many community members enjoyed was shaken like never before.

The post September 11th backlash occurred as a result of either action by private actors and entities, or of policies implemented by legislative or executive branches of government. While the post–September 11th backlash manifested in different ways, it stems from the scapegoating of South Asian, Muslim, and Arab American communities and suspicions of disloyalty about them. It results from the belief that South Asians, Muslims, and Arab Americans—and anyone who is perceived as being part of those communities—could be potential terrorists or have links to terrorist activities simply because they either resemble or come from the same countries as those who masterminded the September 11th attacks.

PUBLIC BACKLASH

In the wake of September 11th, South Asians, Arab Americans, Sikhs, Muslims, and anyone perceived to be connected to those communities were targeted by members of the general public and private entities. The backlash ranged from hate crimes and streetside assaults to refusals of service at places of accommodation (such as restaurants and hotels), workplace harassment and discrimination to bullying or teasing at schools and on university campuses. In 2001, the Federal Bureau of Investigation reported a 1600 percent-plus increase in anti-Muslim hate crimes (from 28 in 2000 to 481 in 2001).[2] The Civil Rights Division of the Department of Justice, the Federal Bureau of Investigation, and the U.S. Attorney's Office have investigated more than 750 incidents involving violence, threats, vandalism, and arson against Arabs, Muslims, South Asians, and Sikhs between September 11th and March 2007.[3]

At least three individuals—and potentially four more —were murdered as a result of anti-Arab or anti-Muslim backlash.[4] These individuals include Balbir Singh Sodhi, a forty-nine-year-old turbaned Sikh and father of three, who was shot and killed while planting flowers at his gas station on September 15, 2002. His killer, Frank Roque, earlier said that he intended to "kill the ragheads responsible for September 11th."[5] After shooting Sodhi, Roque also allegedly fired shots into the home of an Afghani American and at two Lebanese gas station clerks. Other victims of the post-9/11 backlash included Waquar Hassan, a forty-six-year-old Pakistani man, who was killed while he worked at his grocery store near Dallas, TX, on September 15, 2001.[6]

In addition to hate crimes, South Asians experienced verbal harassment, ethnic and religious slurs, and assaults in cars and on streets. The violence also extended to places of worship, including the Islamic Center of El Paso Mosque, where an individual threw a "Molotov Cocktail," and the Islamic Center Mosque in Tallahassee, FL, where an individual crashed his truck into the building.[7] In Bedford, OH, an individual threw three Molotov cocktails into the Guru Gobind Singh Sikh Gurdwara.[8]

South Asians also confronted discrimination in the workplace and at public places of accommodation. The Equal Employment Opportunity Commission (EEOC), a federal agency that investigates complaints of workplace discrimination on the basis of race, color, religion, sex, or national origin, reported receiving in 2003 more than 800 complaints of backlash discrimination since

September 11th.[9] In most cases, these complaints involved discharge or workplace hostility from coworkers or supervisors. An example of a lawsuit filed by the EEOC was that against the Plaza Hotel and Fairmont Hotel and Resorts in New York City, where a class of employees claimed that they were subjected to hostile conditions and harassment at the workplace. South Asian, Muslim, and Arab employees claimed that they were called "Dumb Muslim," and "Taliban" and were accused of perpetrating the 9/11 attacks.[10]

As the backlash began to spread across the country, South Asians joined with friends, families and allies at vigils and rallies to remember the victims of the September 11th attacks and to remind Americans of the country's commitment to racial, religious, and ethnic diversity. Even though bias attacks lessened in frequency, they would continue over subsequent years, and they would be further compounded as federal agencies began to target certain communities through enforcement policies and initiatives.

GOVERNMENT ENFORCEMENT ACTIONS

Through legislation such as the USA PATRIOT Act and a number of far-reaching executive orders and internal policies, federal government agencies obtained expanded surveillance and enforcement powers in the months and years after September 11th. As a result, South Asians, Arab Americans, Sikhs, and Muslims have reported increased incidents of profiling, detentions and deportations, and denials of basic constitutional due process rights.

Since September 11th, South Asians have reported high incidents of profiling, which is a law enforcement tactic that connects individuals to crimes based on certain characteristics that are unrelated to the criminal conduct under investigation. After September 11th, airport security personnel, immigration enforcement agencies, and state and local law enforcement have singled out South Asians for additional scrutiny and investigation based on characteristics related to national origin, ethnicity, religious affiliation, and perceived immigration status—with no relation to terrorist activities or links with terrorism. For example, many South Asians have been prevented from flying because their names are identical or similar to those on "no-fly" lists maintained by the Transportation Security Administration. South Asians have also reported experiencing excessive screenings and questioning by U.S. Customs and Border Protection (CBP) agents when returning from trips abroad.[11] In addition, Sikh travelers who wear turbans and Muslim women who wear headscarves are frequently subjected to additional secondary screenings simply based upon their attire.[12]

Other government-sponsored actions after September 11th were related to the use of immigration laws to investigate and detain individuals suspected of having connections to terrorist activities. Shortly after September 11th, more than 1,200 individuals were secretly arrested and detained after nationwide sweeps in connection with terrorism investigations.[13] More than 750 of these detainees were designed as "special interest" detainees.[14] For the most part, the detainees were men from South Asian or Middle Eastern nations with the largest number of detainees (33%) coming from Pakistan.[15] In many circumstances, FBI agents and local police identified and detained individuals based not on evidence of potential ties to terrorism but on tips from the public and chance encounters. For example, on November 25, 2001, a resident in Torrington, CT, informed police that he had heard two "Arabs" talking about anthrax. Police followed the two suspects and arrested them, along with an Indian businessman who had been working at the gas station, as well as another man from Pakistan who happened to be at the station at the same time. Police did not offer explanations for the detention of the Indian businessman and detained him for 18 days before releasing him on bond.[16]

Detainees discovered that once detained, government officials could use administrative rules to hold them for longer periods of time without charging them with any crimes. In fact, on September 20, 2001, the U,S. Department of Justice issued an interim rule that allowed the detention of noncitizens for 48 hours or longer if necessary—without pressing any charges against them.[17] In fact, of the 752 special interest detainees, 317 were held without charge for more than 48 hours, 36 were held for 28 days or more without charges, 13 were held for more than 40 days without charges, and 9 were held for more than 50 days without charges.[18] In addition to being held for long periods of time with no charges, many special interest detainees reported that they were subjected to verbal and physical abuse inside detention centers. Many did not receive adequate medical attention and could not comply with religious customs related to diet and prayer.

In addition, the detainees were often unable to exercise basic fundamental rights that are guaranteed to all people (regardless of citizenship status) under the U.S. Constitution. These due process rights include the ability to challenge one's detention, receive information about the charges being brought, and present oneself before a neutral judge in a timely fashion. Many of these rights effectively disappeared for detainees in the post–September 11th environment.[19] In addition, hundreds were subjected to secret immigration hearings where the public, media, and even family and friends were excluded. More than half of the special interest detainees were charged with immigration violations, but no special interest detainees were charged in relation to the 9/11 attacks, and almost no special interest detainees were charged with terrorism-related offenses.[20]

In addition to the nationwide sweeps and arbitrary detentions, the U.S. government implemented several policies that officials claimed were related to protecting national security. One of the most disturbing policies was called Special Registration in 2002. The Department of Justice required under this policy that nonimmigrant males sixteen years and older from twenty-five designated countries would need to report to the immigration agency upon arrival; 30 days after arrival; every 12 months after arrival; upon events such as a change of address, employment or school; and upon departure from the country.[21] The government justified Special Registration through a national security argument (related to needing knowledge about the movement of nonimmigrants in and out of the United States), although only individuals from countries with significant Muslim populations were required to comply. The twenty-five countries included: Afghanistan, Algeria, Bahrain, Bangladesh, Egypt, Eritrea, Indonesia, Iran, Iraq, Jordan, Kuwait, Lebanon, Libya, Morocco, North Korea, Oman, Pakistan, Qatar, Saudi Arabia, Somalia, Sudan, Syria, Tunisia, United Arab Emirates, and Yemen.[22]

Between December 2002 and early 2003, 83,000 individuals from these countries complied with the program.[23] When Special Registration was completed, 13,000 men of the 83,000 who complied were set to be deported.[24] Thirty-five percent of those who have been or will be deported are of Pakistani descent.[25]

IMPACT

Governmental policies and actions after September 11th compounded the public backlash against South Asians. At its core, the post–September 11th backlash stems from the assumption that individuals from countries in the Middle East or South Asia are prone to disloyalty and anti-American sentiment, and places the burden on these individuals to prove their loyalty—a concept that is in stark contrast to the United States' legal safeguard of "presumed innocent until proven guilty."

The type of profiling that occurred after September 11th is also a reminder of the U.S. government's internment of more than 100,000 individuals of Japanese descent based on presumed disloyalty. Policies implemented since September 11th bear an eerie similarity to those that led to the Japanese American internment.[26]

Even with the passage of time, South Asians continue to experience the impact of the post–September 11th backlash, and the post–September 11th backlash is far-reaching. For example, community members are less inclined now to turn to law enforcement to report crimes for fear of being investigated for unrelated issues, such as immigration status or links to terrorism. In addition, many South Asian families have left their neighborhoods and jobs to find other lands of opportunity. For example, in Brooklyn, NY, where more than 120,000 Pakistanis used to live, approximately 15,000 have left for Canada, Europe, or Pakistan.[27]

In the wake of September 11th, many South Asian communities that had previously been separated along religious, ethnic, or linguistic lines came together to address the impact of the post–September 11th backlash. South Asian organizations around the United States have been working with community members to address immediate needs stemming from the backlash through social service provision, referrals, advocacy, organizing, and community education. In fact, some South Asian organizations were formed as a direct response to the post–September 11th backlash. South Asians have also developed partnerships with Arab American organizations since September 11th to address common issues and concerns.

Bangladeshi immigrant Abdul Mosobbir, now of Brooklyn, prays on a bridge over-looking the World Trade Center site in New York, Sept. 11, 2003, before the start of ceremonies on the second anniversary of the attacks. Mosobbir lost his brother Shabbir Ahmed, who worked at the restaurant Windows on the World in the World Trade Center attacks. (AP Photo/Kathy Willens, Pool)

FURTHER READING

Asian American Legal Defense and Education Fund. "Special Registration: Discrimination and Xenophobia as Government Policy." 2004. http://www.aaldef.org.

Council on American-Islamic Relations. http://www.cair.com/.

Desis Rising Up and Moving. http://www.drumnation.org.

Gohil, N., and Sidhu, D., "The Sikh Turban: Post 9/11 Challenges to this Article of Faith." *Rutgers Journal of Law and Religion* 9 (2008), 10.

Hing, Bill Ong. "Vigilante Racism: The De-Americanization of Immigrant America." *Michigan Journal of Race and Law* 441 (2002).

Muslim Advocates. http://www.muslimadvocates.org.

Muslim Public Affairs Council. http://www.mpac.org.

National Asian Pacific American Legal Consortium. "Backlash: 2001 Audit of Violence Against Asian Pacific Americans." 2002. http://www.advancingequality.org.

Sikh American Legal Defense and Education Fund. http://www.saldef.org.

Sikh Coalition. http://www.sikhcoalition.org.

South Asian Americans Leading Together. http://www.saalt.org.

South Asian Network. http://www.southasiannetwork.org.

UNITED SIKHS. http://www.unitedsikhs.org.

NOTES

1. All statistics and content in this paragraph derived from *A National Action Agenda*, The National Coalition of South Asian Organizations (online, June 2008), http://saalt.org/national_coalition.html.

2. Tanya Schevitz, "FBI Sees Leap in Anti-Muslim Hate Crimes," *San Francisco Chronicle* (online, Nov. 26, 2002), http://www.sfgate.com/cgi-bin/article.cgi?f=/c/a/2002/11/26/MN224441.DTL.

3. All statistics and content in this paragraph derived from *A National Action Agenda*.

4. Human Rights Watch, "We are Not the Enemy: Hate Crimes Against Arabs, Muslims, and Those Perceived to be Arab or Muslim after September 11th," *Human Rights Watch* 14, no. 6 (online, November 2002), http://www.hrw.org/reports/2002/usahate/.

5. Human Rights Watch, "We Are Not the Enemy."

6. Human Rights Watch, "We Are Not the Enemy."

7. U.S. Department of Justice, Civil Rights Division, *Enforcement and Outreach Following the September 11 Terrorist Attacks* (online, May 2008), http://www.usdoj.gov/crt/legalinfo/discrimupdate.htm.

8. Human Rights Watch, "We Are Not the Enemy."

9. Equal Employment Opportunity Commission, *EEOC Sues Plaza Hotel and Fairmont Hotels and Resorts for Post–9/11 Backlash Discrimination* (online, September 2003), http://www.eeoc.gov/press/9-30-03b.html.

10. Equal Employment Opportunity Commission, *EEOC Sues Plaza Hotel.*

11. Complaint for Injunctive Relief for *Violation of the Freedom of Information Act*, Asian Law Caucus and Electronic Frontier Foundation v. U.S. Department of Homeland Security (N.D. Cal. 2008).

12. The Sikh Coalition, *The TSA Report Card: A Quarterly Review of Security Screenings of Sikh Travelers in the U.S. Airports* (April 2008); Council on American-Islamic Relations, *The Status of Muslim Civil Rights in the United States* (2007).

13. Rights Working Group, *Equal Treatment Denied: United States Immigration Enforcement Policies*, A Shadow Report to the U.N. Committee on Elimination of Racial Discrimination (March 2008).

14. Rights Working Group, *Equal Treatment Denied.*

15. Office of the Inspector General, *The September 11 Detainees: A Review of the Treatment of Aliens, Held on Immigration Charges in Connection with the Investigation of the September 11 Attacks* (June 2003).

16. Human Rights Watch, "Presumption of Guilt: Human Rights Abuses of Post–September 11 Detainees," *Human Rights Watch* 14, no. 4(G) (Aug. 2002).

17. 66 Fed. Reg. 48, 334 (Sept. 20, 2001).

18. Rights Working Group, *Equal Treatment Denied.*

19. Nancy Chang, "How Democracy Dies: The War on Civil Liberties," in *Lost Liberties: Ashcroft and the Assault on Personal Freedom*, ed. Cynthia Brown (New York: The New Press, 2003), 34–35, 48.

20. Rights Working Group, *Equal Treatment Denied.*

21. 67 Fed. Reg. 52584 (Aug. 12, 2002).

22. 67 Fed. Reg. 52584.

23. Nurith C. Aizenmann and Edward Walsh, "Immigrants Fear Deportation After Registration," *Washington Post* (July 28, 2003), http://www.alakhbar-usa.com/AAguide/immgration.html.

24. Executive Order No. 13166, "Improving Access to Services for Persons with Limited English Proficiency," 65 FR 50121 (Aug. 16, 2000).

25. "Guidance to Federal Financial Assistance Recipients Regarding Title VI Prohibition against National Origin Discrimination Affecting Limited English Proficient Persons," 67 FR 41455 (June 18, 2002).

26. See the federal interagency language access Web site, http://www.lep.gov.

27. Michael Powell, "An Exodus Grows in Brooklyn," *Washington Post* (May 29, 2003), http://www.google.com/url?sa=t&source=web&ct=res&cd=1&url=http%3A%2F%2Fciapnyc.org%2Fuploads%2FExodusGrowsinBrooklyn.pdf&ei=XtpUSubpDIfgswOnmLSODw&rct=j&q=An+Exodus+Grows+in+Brooklyn&usg=AFQjCNHIijGFW1gpZrmwJ8C6zjrrsHTckg

SOUTHEAST ASIAN REFUGEES

Helly Lee, Catherina Nou, Naomi Steinberg, and Doua Thor

In the aftermath of the Vietnam War, Southeast Asians from Cambodia, Laos, and Vietnam became the largest group of refugees to resettle in the United States.[1] Between 1975 and 2002, more than 145,000 refugees from Cambodia, 241,000 from Laos, and 759,000 from Vietnam arrived in the United States. Today, with a national population of nearly 2 million according to the 2000 census, Southeast Asian Americans are a significant thread in the diverse fabric of America. They have established themselves and created homes in every state across the nation, most notably in California and Texas, where Southeast Asian Americans number more than 700,000 and 160,000, respectively.[2]

Despite many community successes since their first arrival in the United States, many Southeast Asian refugees still face numerous challenges as new Americans. Having fled oppressive government regimes, they were unfamiliar with the participatory governmental style of the United States. They are now beginning to realize the importance of becoming civically engaged and empowered, in order to build relationships and exchange ideas with government officials and agencies. They understand that creating systemic changes through the engagement of communities and the enactment of public policy is necessary to ensure that the needs of Southeast Asian American communities are not overlooked.

INTEGRATION AND CITIZENSHIP

As new Americans, issues of integration and full civic participation through citizenship are priorities for Southeast Asian Americans; however, increasing naturalization fees remains a barrier for many who have low incomes. In July

2007, naturalization fees increased from $400 to $675. In addition, the U.S. Citizenship and Immigration Services (USCIS) implemented a new citizenship test on October 2008. The new test includes revised, open-ended and multiple-choice questions that many community members and advocates contend make it more difficult, especially for the elderly and English language learners.[3]

IMMIGRATION

Immigration issues and policies have a great impact on Southeast Asian American communities. For many who were separated from their family members as they were fleeing their country in times of war and conflict, a robust family-based immigration system is one of the very few ways refugees in America can be reunited with long-lost family members. Family-based immigration allows former refugees who have obtained lawful permanent residence (LPR) status to petition for their spouse or unmarried son or daughter to be reunited with them in the United States. Those who become naturalized citizens may petition to be reunited with their spouse, child (unmarried or married), sibling, or parents. Given the backlog in many family immigration categories, however, this method of reunification results in lengthy waiting periods.

The issue of deportation is also a concern within Southeast Asian American communities. Immigration laws demand the deportation of individuals who are not citizens who have committed certain crimes, especially "aggravated felonies." This means that refugees who arrived in the United States who do not yet possess their citizenship, even if they have LPR status, can be deported.

In 1996, Congress passed the Antiterrorism and Effective Death Penalty Act (AEDPA) and the Illegal Immigration Reform and Immigrant Responsibility Act (IIRIRA). These laws dramatically increased the numbers of the kinds of offenses for which noncitizens can be detained and deported. The laws were made retroactive, which means that an LPR who was convicted of an "aggravated felony" prior to the passage of the law can still be removed. In addition, the laws severely restrict the ability of immigration judges to consider the individual circumstances of a person before ordering deportation.

Since May 3, 2002, when the United States and Cambodia signed a repatriation agreement to send Cambodians who have been convicted of crimes back to Cambodia, approximately 187 have been deported out of an estimated 1,400 who have received notice of potential deportation.[4] On January 22, 2008, the Vietnam government followed suit and signed a Memorandum of Understanding (MOU) with the United States to accept deportable Vietnamese nationals who arrived in the United States on or after July 12, 1995. Until 2008, the Vietnamese government did not have a formal agreement with the United States to accept deportees from this country.[5] According to a statement released by Immigration and Customs Enforcement (ICE), approximately 1,500 Vietnamese nationals will potentially be affected.[6] Laos remains one of the few countries in the world that does not have a repatriation agreement with the United States.

As refugee communities, deportation is an issue of particular concern because individuals are being returned to the very countries they fled. Many arrived in the United States as infants and young children, grew up as Americans, and have little to no knowledge of the countries in which they were born.[7] There are no safeguards for how these former refugees will be treated once they are deported, and there are very limited resources, if any, to assist with integration in their countries of origin.[8]

Southeast Asian Americans recognize how their communities are affected by deportation and have been instrumental in further educating their communities, the general public, and lawmakers about these issues. For example, after the signing of the repatriation agreement between Vietnam and the United States in early 2008, college students in California organized statewide teach-ins and rallies to educate others about the impact of deportation in their communities. Local youth-led groups such as Khmer In Action (KIA) in Seattle, WA, and the Providence Youth Student Movement (PrYSM) in Providence, RI, have been successful in engaging young Southeast Asian American community members in education and organizing around the issue of deportation, as well as providing a supportive space for individuals affected by the deportation of a family member.

EDUCATION

Education is key to ending the cycle of poverty for all communities, including Southeast Asian American communities. The educational needs of many Southeast Asian American students, however, are often overlooked because of the "model minority" myth that all Asian Americans excel academically. Although available data shows that Asian Americans overall do well academically, when Southeast Asian Americans are viewed separately, the disparities are apparent. For example, while more than 80 percent of the overall U.S. population age 25 and over hold at least a high school degree, individual data reveals that only 47 percent of Cambodian, 41 percent of Hmong, 51 percent of Laotian and 62 percent of Vietnamese Americans hold a high school degree or higher.[9]

In the realm of higher education, Asian Americans are touted as the exemplary minority group with outstanding achievements. According to the 2000 U.S. Census, however, while more than 40 percent of Asian Americans collectively possess an undergraduate degree, only 9.1 percent of Cambodian Americans, 7.4 percent of Hmong Americans, 7.6 percent of Lao Americans and 19.5 percent of Vietnamese Americans have attained a bachelor's degree. To address this and other disparities, in 2007 Congress enacted the College Cost Reduction Act, which established Asian American and Native American Pacific Islander Serving Institutions (AANAPISI) (for two years from the date of enactment). Like the Historically Black Colleges and Universities and Hispanic Serving Institutions, the law designates discretionary grants to eligible institutions of higher education serving large populations of low-income Asian Americans and Pacific Islanders.[10] Subsequently, in August 2008, the Higher

Education Opportunity Act was enacted, helping to expand provisions and funding opportunities for AANAPISI. These laws represent a positive movement toward alleviating higher education disparities for Southeast Asian Americans through funding allocated to outreach, retention, and research of underrepresented Asian American groups. They also increased opportunities for partnering with community-based organizations to be a part of these activities.[11]

ECONOMIC WELL-BEING

As new Americans, Southeast Asian Americans are some of the most economically disadvantaged populations in the United States. The 2000 Census reveals that 29 percent of Cambodians, 37 percent of Hmong, 19 percent of Laotians and 16 percent of Vietnamese Americans live below the poverty level, compared with 12 percent of the total U.S. population.

In addition, elderly and disabled Southeast Asian individuals have a higher risk of poverty, which is especially significant given the high rates of disability within these communities. For example, in California the disability rates for those age 65 and over range from 63 percent for Laotians, to 68 percent for Cambodians, and 71 percent for Hmong compared to approximately 42 percent for all Californians.

For many elderly and disabled refugees, Supplemental Security Income provides the bare means for survival—no more than $623 per month for an individual or $934 for a couple.[12] As part of the 1996 Federal Welfare Reform law, SSI was restricted to a seven-year limit for elderly and disabled refugees and humanitarian immigrants who are not able to obtain their citizenship within that time frame. This change has been particularly harmful because new refugees must wait one year before obtaining their LPR status. Once having done so, individuals must wait five years before applying for citizenship, which constitutes six of the seven years during which elderly and disabled refugees are expected to obtain citizenship in order to maintain their SSI benefits. Many refugees are unable to obtain citizenship within that short time frame for a variety of reasons, including limited availability of English language courses, increasing citizenship fees, lengthy backlogs in processing citizenship applications, advanced age, and physical or mental health issues. The challenge to obtain citizenship within seven years is also great for many Southeast Asian American elders, many who have arrived in the United States with little to no formal schooling.[13] Moreover, overcoming this barrier with advancing age becomes extremely difficult as the ability to learn and retain new information becomes less likely and often impossible.[14] As a result, many Southeast Asian Americans were among the 20,000 refugees projected to lose their SSI by 2008.[15]

For many years, advocates and Congress have tried to provide a temporary fix to the seven-year SSI cutoff through legislation that would extend the number of years refugees and humanitarian immigrants may receive SSI to nine years. In July 2007, the U.S. House of Representatives passed legislation that would provide a temporary two-year extension to the seven-year cutoff. In July 2008, the Senate also passed the temporary two-year extension to SSI for elderly and disabled refugees. There continues to be a need, however, for a long-term solution because the current legislation only provides the two-year extension until 2010 (those with pending citizenship applications may extend their SSI eligibility until 2011).[16]

OUTLOOK

Southeast Asian Americans face many challenges, including the rising costs associated with becoming naturalized citizens, stalled immigration reform efforts, deportation, limited access to sustainable benefits, and limited access to high-quality educational opportunities. As daunting as these challenges may seem, Southeast Asian American communities are poised and ready to address these issues through civic engagement and developing strong community organizations and leaders. The vast majority of Southeast Asian American community-based organizations, also known as mutual assistance associations (MAAs), identified by the Southeast Asia Resource Action Center (SEARAC) offer citizenship or civic engagement class.[17] Through the combined efforts of community-based organizations, policy makers, university researchers and broad-based advocacy coalitions, Southeast Asian Americans will continue to break barriers and contribute to American society.

FURTHER READING

Igasaki, Paul, and Max Niedzwiecki. *Aging among Southeast Asian Americans in California: Assessing Strengths and Challenges, Strategizing for the Future*, 2004. http://www.searac.org/aging-seaamer-fin.pdf.

Niedzwiecki, Max, and T. C. Duong. *Southeast Asian American Statistical Profile*. Washington, DC: Southeast Asia Resource Action Center (SEARAC), 2004. http://www.searac.org/seastatprofilemay04.pdf.

Southeast Asia Resource Action Center (SEARAC). http://www.searac.org.

Um, Khatharya. *A Dream Denied: Educational Experiences of Southeast Asian American Youth*. Washington, DC: Southeast Asia Resource Action Center (SEARAC), 2003. http://www.searac.org/ydfinal-2_03.pdf.

NOTES

1. Here, Southeast Asians refer to those with history from Cambodia, Laos, and Vietnam. The Office of Refugee Resettlement also includes Burmese in this calculation of the largest group of refugees admitted to the U.S. Office of Refugee Resettlement, *2005 Annual Report to Congress*, http://www.acf.hhs.gov/programs/orr/data/05arc7.htm.

2. T. Duong and M. Niedzwiecki, "Southeast Asian American Statistical Profile," (Washington, DC: Southeast Asia Resource Action Center, 2004): 1–30.

3. Refugee Women's Alliance, Naturalization Services for Refugees and Immigrants on Public Assistance, http://www.rewa.org/files/position-paper-citizenship-2008-legislative-day.pdf.

4. This number includes the additional thirteen deported on August 12, 2008. Immigration and Customs Enforcement. 2006, http://www.ice.gov/pi/nr/0808/080814 seattle.htm; Southeast Asia Resource Action Center, "Deportation of Cambodians from the United States," http://searac.org/cambdeptactalt6_02.html.

5. U.S. Embassy, Vietnam, "United States Signs Historical Agreement with Vietnam," http://vietnam.usembassy.gov/pr012208.html.

6. U.S. Immigration and Customs Enforcement, "ICE Assistant Secretary Myers signs historical MOU with Vietnam," http://www.ice.gov/pi/news/newsreleases/articles/080122washington.htm.

7. PBS Documentary, "Sentenced Home," http://www.pbs.org/independentlens/sentencedhome/immigration.html.

8. PBS Documentary, "Sentenced Home."

9. Duong, *Southeast Asian American Statistical Profile*.

10. Committee on Education and Labor, "College Cost Reduction and Access Act," http://edlabor.house.gov/micro/ccraa.shtml.

11. Committee on Education and Labor, "Chairman Miller Statement on signing of the Higher Education Opportunity Act," http://www.house.gov/apps/list/speech/edlabor_dem/BushHEOA081408.html.

12. U.S. Social Security Administration, "SSI Monthly Statistics, January 2007," http://www.ssa.gov/policy/docs/statcomps/ssi_monthly/2007-01/table07.html.

13. K. Mathavongsy, "Southeast Asian American Elders in California: Barriers to Accessing Social Services," Southeast Asia Resource Action Center, http://www.searac.org/tst-helpkham6-15-06.pdf.

14. S. Earm, M. Niedzwiecki, and K. Yang, *Southeast Asian American Elders in California: Demographics and Service Priorities Revealed by the 2000 Census and a Survey of Mutual Assistance Associations (MAAs) and Faith-Based Organizations (FBOs)* (Washington, DC: Southeast Asia Resource Action Center, 2003).

15. Zoe Neuberger, "Loss of SSI Aid is Impoverishing Thousands of Refugees: Congress Could Prevent Further Hardship," Center on Budget and Policy Priorities http://www.cbpp.org/2-8-07ssi.htm, 2007.

16. At the time of the writing of this document, the House and Senate have yet to reconvene to finalize changes that were made to the SSI extension bill, (HR 2608), and the bill has not been signed into law.

17. B. King et al., *Directory of Southeast Asian American Community-Based Organizations 2004: Mutual Assistance Associations (MAAs) and Religious Organizations Providing Social Services* (Washington, DC: Southeast Asia Resource Action Center, 2004).

UNDOCUMENTED IMMIGRANTS

Rodolfo-Jose Blanco Quiambao

An undocumented immigrant is any person whose presence in the United States is deemed unlawful, and the term is commonly used to describe someone who has entered the country without authorization. Undocumented immigrants enter the country in two ways: by physically crossing over U.S. borders without an immigrant visa, or by remaining in the U.S. after their nonimmigrant visa has expired, also known as "overstaying." Nonimmigrants such as students and tourists obtain visas through an application process that determines their eligibility based on several admissible categories. Nonimmigrant visas are only issued for a certain period and must be renewed. If nonimmigrants allow their visa to expire without renewal, they are "overstaying" their visa, and are thus considered undocumented.

Discussion on undocumented immigrants focuses primarily on people of Mexican or other Hispanic origin. While the majority of undocumented immigrants originate from Latin America and South America, 12 percent of undocumented immigrants are Asian.[1] Most of the undocumented Asian population is Filipino, with a 2006 estimation of 280,000, making up roughly 2 percent of the total undocumented immigrant population. Asian Indians, Koreans, Chinese, and Vietnamese also have large numbers of undocumented individuals.[2] Undocumented Asian immigrants usually enter the country through overstaying.[3] This method of entry is common because of the distance and geographical barriers that separate the United States and Asia, leaving travel by air or sea—which is heavily monitored—as the most plausible routes. Asian immigrants must first obtain a visa permitting their stay in the United States, meaning they initially qualify for entry based on family or employment-based preferences for admission. Contemporary immigration laws are designed to exclude aliens who are "likely to become a public charge," or dependent on public assistance. Because of these regulations, Asian immigrants tend to be educated or skilled, have family who will support them, or possess the financial resources to convince immigration officials they will not become reliant on public assistance.

Undocumented Asian immigrants may also be physically smuggled into the United States. Human smuggling can be a lucrative, albeit illegal, enterprise. Smugglers typically transported their human cargo by boat. In 1993, a ship carrying 286 undocumented Chinese ran aground off the coast of New York. This event is commonly referred to as the "Golden Venture incident." It brought attention to seaborne human trafficking, and as a result, land-based smuggling operations through Mexico or the United States are more common. In 2008, the U.S. Border Patrol detained 837 Chinese immigrants attempting to cross the Mexico border, and 500 were caught between January and August.[4] Within Chinese and Chinese American communities, smugglers are referred to as "snakeheads." More than half of all snakeheads are also undocumented, and almost 30 percent are employed as small business owners.[5] Other strategies for circumventing immigration laws, including the forgery or procurement of visas and passports, bribery of immigration officials, and false marriages to U.S. citizens, are mediated by smugglers as well.

ACCESS TO SOCIAL SERVICES, HEALTH CARE, AND EDUCATION

All undocumented immigrants, including those of Asian descent, are severely limited from accessing social services, health care, and education. The Personal Responsibility and Work Opportunity Act (PRWORA) of 1996 was passed by President Bill Clinton as part of an initiative to wean the U.S. population off welfare. Research revealed the number of immigrants relying on public assistance had doubled between 1986 and 1994, totaling approximately $4 billion. Furthermore, about half of all immigrants became reliant on welfare within four years of entry.[6] After studies showed immigrants were indeed becoming a public charge, PRWORA made welfare temporary for noncitizens, setting their eligibility for only five years. PRWORA also denied public assistance, Social Security, and Medicaid for undocumented immigrants, as a means of discouraging their entry.

Denying undocumented immigrants social services as a preventative measure was a trend set at the state level. California, the state with the highest population of both documented and undocumented immigrants, passed Proposition 187 in 1994, two years before PRWORA. Proposition 187, which was declared unconstitutional, made undocumented immigrants ineligible for public services, containing nativist language stating that society "suffers economic hardship caused by illegal aliens" and "citizens have a right to the protection of their government from any person or person entering the country."[7]

Undocumented immigrants, already an underprivileged, undereducated class, are essentially denied social mobility because they are not eligible for most public assistance programs.

Many U.S. cities, however, have passed ordinances that do not require a declaration of legal status in exchange for services and are referred to as "sanctuary cities." Sanctuary cities offer services without reviewing legal status, and when legal status must be disclosed, immigrants are not reported to Immigration and Customs Enforcement (ICE). Aside from its economic advantages, sanctuary cities assist local law enforcement in apprehending criminals within immigrant communities, because undocumented noncitizens may come forward with information leading to an arrest without fear of leaving themselves vulnerable. Sanctuary cities increase opportunities for undocumented immigrants. The University of California system has reported that approximately 40 to 44 percent of their undocumented student population is Asian.[8] Berkeley, Los Angeles, Santa Cruz, and San Diego are designated sanctuary cities with a University of California campus. Stigma and shame are associated with undocumented status, causing many undocumented Asians to be silent. Combined with the possible limited English skills of first-generation immigrants, undocumented Asians may not be aware of available privileges and be reluctant to ask for help.

ENFORCEMENT

For the undocumented immigrant, the consequence of being caught is deportation. Deportation proceedings are expedited under current immigration laws, essentially denying immigrants many basic rights such as right to counsel at government expense or the right to bail in many cases. Any immigrant suspected of being undocumented can be arrested and detained without a warrant. Furthermore, although deportation proceedings are expedited, the actual hearing could take place months after the arrest, meaning that immigrants could be imprisoned without a trial for many weeks or months. Undocumented Asians may not understand the intricacies of U.S. immigration law, or they may avoid seeking counsel because of the associated stigma or in fear of being discovered. Regardless, deportation can be a devastating punishment. The following deportation cases have put undocumented Asian immigrants in the spotlight.

Hui Lui Ng immigrated to the United States in 1992 from Hong Kong on a tourist visa. When his visa expired, he applied for asylum. In the meantime, Ng went to school, obtained a degree, found work, and married, although his plea for asylum was later rejected. After getting married, he and his spouse filed requisite papers for his green card. In 2001, a subpoena for Ng to appear at an immigration hearing was delivered to a nonexistent address, and when he failed to show, the judge ordered his deportation. On July 19, 2007, Ng and his wife went to his green card interview, where ICE officials were waiting for him, and he was immediately arrested and detained. Over the next year, his family hired lawyers seeking his release. In April 2008, Ng's health began to fail, and he began complaining of extreme lower back pain. His condition steadily worsened, and he eventually became too weak to stand. On July 30, 2008, guards forcefully dragged the shackled, ailing Ng from a detention center in Rhode Island and drove him two hours to a lockup in Hartford, CT, where he was pressured by an immigration official to withdraw his appeals. They then took him back to Rhode Island, on the same day, to prove he was faking his illness. A judge heard his petition for habeas corpus on August 1st and insisted that Ng receive medical treatment. Ng was diagnosed with terminal cancer and a fractured spine. He died five days later.[9]

In June 2004, the Cuevas Family was deported to the Philippines after living in the United States for nearly twenty years.[10] Delfin Cuevas immigrated to the United States in December 1984 on a tourist visa, escaping the economic and political turmoil of the Philippines under Ferdinand Marcos. Within a year, he was joined by his wife, Lily, and their three children, Donna, Dale, and Dominique. The Cuevas family overstayed their visas and lived in undocumented status, residing in California's Bay Area. Incorrectly believing their chances of gaining discretionary relief would increase the longer they stayed in the United States, they waited to resolve their status until the Illegal Immigration Reform and Immigrant Responsibility (IIRIRA) Act of 1996 was passed, which changed the qualifications for eligibility. The Cuevas Family was unable to meet these new standards and sought help from an immigration lawyer to secure a hearing before IIRIRA came into effect. Because of the heavy backlog of applications from others who hoped to do the same, a judge did not rule on their case until 2000. The judge ruled the Cuevas Family should be deported, and his decision was upheld in appeal hearings in 2002 and December 2004. Their children were not aware of their undocumented status until they received their deportation orders in the mail. The Cuevases were forced to sell their home and other possessions and move to the Philippines. Although their case is not uncommon, they were one of only a few to publicly speak on their situation.

Recently, ICE raids have become an increasing problem within the Asian American community. ICE has quadrupled the numbers of their Fugitive Operation Teams, who conduct the raids. In 2007, ICE reported more than 100,000 arrests of fugitive aliens.[11] In September 2008, ICE led a high-profile raid within California's Bay Area, targeting Chinese restaurants and resulting in the arrest of twenty-one undocumented immigrants, including nine from China, two from Indonesia, and one from Singapore.[12] ICE is also known for aggressively pursuing the undocumented in their homes and detaining occupants regardless of status, with nothing more than a deportation order. Such tactics intimidate undocumented immigrants, further adding to their apprehension in seeking assistance.

REFORM

The Development, Relief, and Education for Alien Minors (DREAM) Act first appeared unsuccessfully as an amendment to IIRIRA, seeking to grant undocumented immigrant children a path toward legal citizenship. In order to qualify for citizenship under the stipulations of the DREAM Act, children had to have lived in the United States before the age of fifteen and be under the age of twenty-one, with no criminal history, and either enlist in military service or enroll into college.[13] Introduced again in 2003, the DREAM Act languished in Congress for years. If it had passed, Hui Lui Ng, the children of the Cuevas family, and other undocumented Asian students would have had the opportunity to remain in the United States, rather than being deported. The Comprehensive Immigration Reform Act of 2007 sought to form a compromise between undocumented immigrant supporters and opponents, including a provision that resurrected the original DREAM Act in its entirety. The bipartisan bill would have granted amnesty to undocumented immigrants currently living in the United States by adjusting the definition of "legal permanent resident" to any alien who can prove a continuous physical presence in the country, ongoing employment, tax payment, and proficiency of basic citizenship skills.[14] The tradeoff for amnesty involved a profound increase in border security and the elimination of visa backlogs. Clearing visa backlogs would bring an end to the current system of family-reunification immigration. Asian Americans, who rely on family-reunification preferences for emotional and economic support, would be heavily affected if visa backlogs were eliminated; however, the Comprehensive Immigration Reform Act was not enacted.

Various Asian American advocacy groups work with undocumented immigrants because immigration is a constant within the Asian American community. Most support comes at the local level because of the sensitivity around legal status. The San Francisco-based Asian Law Caucus is a primary resource for legal immigration assistance, representing a number of immigrants in removal proceedings and providing free immigration clinics, as well as working toward reforming current policies. Asian Pacific Islander Legal Outreach (formerly Nihonmachi Legal Outreach) provides similar services of representation and community education. The Asian Pacific American Legal Center (APALC) provides assistance to the undocumented in Los Angeles and Southern California. In New York, Asian American Legal Defense (AALDef) is also a major advocate for immigrant rights. Nationally, groups such as the Organization of Chinese Americans, the Asian American Justice Center (AAJC), and the Southeast Asian Refugee Action Center (SEARAC) work toward reform through community education and fostering civic engagement.

FURTHER READING

Asian American Justice Center. http://www.advancingequality.org/.

Asian Law Causus. http://www.asianlawcaucus.org/.

Critical Filipina and Filipino Studies Collective. "Resisting Homeland Security: Organizing Against Unjust Removals of U.S. Filipinos," San Jose, CA: Critical Filipina and Filipino Studies Collective, December 2004.

Park, Edward J. W., and John S. W. Park. *Probationary Americans: Contemporary Immigration Policies and the Shaping of Asian American Communities.* New York: Routledge, 2005.

NOTES

1. Jeffrey F. Passel and D'Vera Cohn, "Trends in Unauthorized Immigration: Unauthorized Inflow Now Trails Legal Inflow," Pew Hispanic Center, Oct. 2, 2008.

2. David Seminara, "No Coyote Needed: U.S. Visas Still an Easy Ticket in Developing Countries," Center for Immigration Studies. (March 2008): 4.

3. Pew Hispanic Center, "Modes of Entry for the Unauthorized Migrant Population," Fact Sheet. May 22, 2006. A 2003 report from the U.S. Government Accountability Office states, "There is no accurate list of visa overstays" because of the lack of departure and arrival forms being collected, and the difficulty of matching the forms together. Robert Warren, formerly of the INS, developed a method of estimating the number of visa overstays. As of 1996, an estimated 91 percent of undocumented migrants outside of Mexico and Latin America entered the country through overstaying.

4. Jeff McShan, "Illegal Chinese immigrants slip into Texas," khou.com, Dec. 24, 2008. http://www.khou.com/news/local/stories/khou081223_mp_asian-aliens.39f0f80 .html.

5. National Institute of Justice, "Characteristics of Chinese Human Smugglers," U.S. Department of Justice, August 2004.

6. Edward J. W. Park and John S. W. Park, *Probationary Americans: Contemporary Immigration Policies and the Shaping of Asian American Communities* (New York: Routledge, 2005), 66.

7. *Statutes of California*, 1993–1994. A-317.

8. Beleza Chan, "Undocumented Asian Students Face Stigma," *AsianWeek*. Oct. 13, 2008, http://news.newamericamedia.org/news/view_article.html?article_id=dadc 30476b263a037ac68c65f32704c6.

9. Nina Bernstein, "Ill and in Pain, Detainee Dies in U.S. Hands," *The New York Times*, Aug. 12, 2008, http://www.nytimes.com/2008/08/13/nyregion/13detain.html.

10. Cicero Estrella, "Exiles of the American Dream: 'All-American' Exiles," *San Francisco Chronicle*. July 1, 2004, http://www.sfgate.com/cgi-bin/article.cgi?f=/c/a/ 2004/07/01/MNGV47EUPF1.DTL&type=printable.

11. U.S. Immigration and Customs Enforcement, *ICE Fiscal Year 2007 Annual Report*.

12. Henry K. Lee, "21 Illegal Immigrants Arrested in North Bay," *San Francisco Chronicle*. Sept. 20, 2008, http://www.sfgate.com/cgi-bin/article.cgi?f=/c/a/2008/ 09/20/BACP131843.DTL.

13. Development, Relief, and Education for Alien Minors Act of 2003 (DREAM Act) Sponsored by Senator Orrin G. Hatch, S. 1545 108–224.

14. Comprehensive Immigration Reform Bill of 2007.

WOMEN IMMIGRANTS

Eun Sook Lee

The primary means of entry to the United States for Asian American women has been overwhelmingly through dependent relationships, such as family sponsorship visas, including international marriages as war brides, mail-order brides, fiancés, or simply brides. Additionally, a significant number of women have arrived as refugees and asylees fleeing wars or persecution. With the exception of those women who work in traditionally female professions such as nursing, few women have had the resources or educational training to legally enter the United States independent of men.

MIGRATION OF WOMEN

At 90 million, women now make up close to half of the world's migrants, from 46 percent in 1960 to 49 percent in 2000.[1] The population of women who migrate out of Asia has grown significantly, from 13.5 million in 1960 to close to 19 million in 2000.[2] Comparatively, the United States is home to the largest number of international migrants, 35 million in 2000.[3] The forms of migration vary, from legal immigration as dependent family members or as principal wage earners to forced migration as asylees or victims of human trafficking.

Not surprisingly, economics is a primary impetus for women to migrate. The desire and need to provide economic stability and sustainability for self and family are common themes for all immigrants, but women are affected in significantly different ways than men. With today's globalized economy, more men and women seek jobs abroad. Additionally, the countries of origin benefit from remittances to the families who remain there. For example, the total amount of remittances to countries in Asia ballooned from $8.6 billion in 1990 to $35.8 billion in 2003.[4] Although migrant women generally earn less than migrant men, women are believed to remit a greater share of their income to their families abroad.[5]

Another impetus for women to migrate is the desire to leave behind traditional patriarchal expectations in the home country in search of greater independence and equality. Yet, these women often find that the destination country, because of similarly entrenched notions of patriarchy, perpetuates gender stereotypes and limits their employment opportunities to stereotypical and undervalued female roles, such as childcare, cleaning, or sewing. Women are disproportionately underrepresented in high-skilled, degreed professions, with the exception of the health care industry (for example, nursing).

RACE AND GENDER PROFILE OF U.S. IMMIGRATION LAWS

Historically, U.S. immigration laws have intentionally discriminated against and restricted access of women and people of color, including Asian Americans. The first naturalization laws of the United States, the 1790 Naturalization Act, granted citizenship to only "free white persons," and excluded Africans, indentured servants, and women. Women could only be granted citizenship as dependents of their husbands. A female U.S. citizen also could lose her citizenship if she married an immigrant man. Female U.S. citizens could not file an immigration petition for their foreign-born husbands, but the same was not true for male U.S. citizens.[6]

In 1875, Congress enacted the Alien Prostitution Importation Act or "Page Law," the first immigration law that excluded the entry of a specific group of people: women from China, Japan or any "Oriental" country for the alleged purpose of prostitution.[7] Although the Page Law and many other discriminatory laws were repealed or eliminated with the Immigration and Nationality Act (INA) of 1952 and the 1965 immigration amendments, gender discrimination in immigration policies did not end.[8] For example, the 1986 Immigration Marriage Fraud Amendment Act (IMFA) required immigrant spouses, who are disproportionately women, to reside as conditional residents for two years before being granted legal permanent resident status. Domestic violence advocates opposed the IMFA because it granted petitioners the "license to abuse" their spouses.[9]

IMMIGRATION OF WOMEN TO THE UNITED STATES

Consistent with the recent "feminization" of global migration, immigrant women now make up a greater percentage of the legal immigrants admitted to the U.S. from 49.8 percent in 1985 to 54.6 percent in 2004.[10] Women in the U.S. comprise slightly more than 50 percent of the foreign-born population since 1970. This figure dropped slightly from a high of 53.9 percent in 1980 to 51.9 percent in 1990, and 50.4 percent in 2000, largely attributable to the surge in the undocumented, predominantly male population.[11] Immigrant women mostly are from the same countries as immigrant men, but with some differences. The top Asian countries of origin for immigrant women are China, Philippines, India, Vietnam, South Korea, Japan, Laos, Pakistan, Thailand, and Cambodia.[12] The first five also are part of the top countries of origin for all immigrants.

FAMILY SPONSORSHIP AND INTERNATIONAL MARRIAGES

The primary channel for entry into the United States for women has been through family sponsorships beginning with the 1945 War Brides Act, which enabled foreign spouses of U.S. servicemen to immigrate into the United States. Enacted following World War II, the law shifted the dominance of men as the legal immigrant population. From 1945 to 1948 for example, 25 percent of all legal immigrants were women married to U.S. soldiers. In total, 200,000 women from throughout Asia have entered the U.S. as war brides since the end of World War II.[13] Following the Korean War (1950–1953), women from Korea began to arrive in large numbers. From 1950 to 1989, 40,278 women from Korea arrived, representing the second immigration wave for Korean Americans. In fact, Korean war brides are seen as a primary engine of growth for the Korean American community, with 40 percent of all Korean immigrants as either descendants of or sponsored by Korean war brides.[14]

The family-oriented immigration amendments of 1965, which now account for two-thirds of permanent immigration to the United States, led to the dominance of immigrant women in family-based immigration, particularly as spouses or parents of U.S. citizens or legal permanent residents.[15] In 2005, women made up 54.6 percent of all legal immigrants to the U.S. and dominated entry through the immediate relative category.[16] Six million or 76 percent of the immigrants from Asia entered the U.S. within the last twenty-five years and 4.3 million or 43 percent entered within the last fifteen years.[17]

Another form of family sponsorship that has grown rapidly is immigration through fiancé visas. From 1998 to 2002, the number has doubled, and this has been largely attributed to the rising number of marriages between American men and foreign women, brokered by third party, for-profit matchmaking businesses.[18] International marriages are part of the global phenomenon of women who are trafficked from developing countries in Asia and the former USSR to industrialized Western countries. In response to high-profile cases of abuse and violence by U.S. citizen men against foreign spouses, Congress enacted the International Marriage Brokers Regulation Act of 2005 (IMBRA). Although IMBRA is written in gender-neutral language, the undeniable reality is that international marriages are by and large between male U.S. citizens and female foreign spouses. The inherent power imbalance results in abuse and exploitation of the female spouses.

In summary, immigration through family sponsorship is generally the male sponsorship of female spouses into the United States. This real or perceived dependency of immigrant women to their male sponsor/spouse can aggravate the relationships of power between men and women. Such an imbalance is more apparent and expected in the case of war brides who marry U.S. soldiers or with international marriages involving the "purchase" of an Asian wife by a U.S. citizen husband through an International Marriage Broker because of the clear race distinctions.

In all cases, immigrant women, as war brides, mail-order brides, or simply brides have faced multiple barriers of race, language, culture, and even class in adjusting to life in the United States. Moreover, the circumstances leading to their immigration into the United States as dependents of male sponsors can prohibit their ability to speak freely or exercise their full rights. A clear example is in the case of domestic violence, which cuts across race, class, and culture and is considered the single greatest health risk for women.[19] Immigrant women are often trapped in abusive relationships because exiting would mean imperiling their lawful immigration status.

In the context of today's substantial immigration backlogs, family reunification is a primary concern for both Asian Americans and women. An estimated 1.5 million Asian American family members of U.S. citizens and lawful permanent residents are forced to wait years, even decades, to be reunited with their family members. Historically, three of the top four countries with the longest backlogs are from Asia—China, India, Korea, and the Philippines. For example, a Korean legal permanent resident must wait at least 5 years to be reunited with a spouse or minor child. The longest estimated wait time is faced by Filipino American U.S. citizens, who may have to wait more than 20 years to be reunited with a sibling.[20] The wait time is painful, particularly for women left in the country of origin, often with the economic and emotional burdens of raising children alone and maintaining the family household.

EMPLOYMENT-BASED IMMIGRATION

Family-based immigration typically consists of women who reunite with the men who typically migrate for labor and employment. Conventional gender roles in the United States and Asian countries make it less likely that women would immigrate as independent immigrant workers. In time, this trend is expected to change with shifting attitudes that no longer restrict the immigration of women to the United States. Today, however, compared with men, women make up a smaller percentage of the recipients of employment-based visas. In 2004, 26.8 percent of women and 65.3 percent of men received employment-based visas as principal visa holders (compared with 73.2 percent of women and 34.7 percent of men who were dependents of a principal visa holder).[21] In contrast, in 1979, women represented 3 percent of primary beneficiaries of employment-based immigrant visas.[22]

With the exception of traditionally female professions, men dominate employment-based immigration visas. The 1948 Exchange Visitors Program (EVP), created after World War II to fill labor shortages in certain professions, allowed an increased number of female nurses from the Philippines, who made up 80 percent of the participants by the 1960s. Many of these EVP participants remained in the United States after they had stayed their maximum two years. The 1965 immigration law subsequently allowed an additional increase in female nurses from the Philippines and South Korea. For this reason, immigrant women from the Philippines (59%) and South Korea (56%) outnumber immigrant men from the two countries today.[23] The global disparity in the educational opportunities for women compared to men, coupled with prevailing perceptions of social and economic roles for women, has confined the majority of immigrant women to low-wage and domestic employment.

ADOPTEES

Immigration through overseas adoption is noteworthy because of the predominance of adopted female Asian babies. Today, China is now the leading "exporter" of children sent abroad for overseas adoption.[24] Girls far outnumber boys in overseas adoption. The 2005 figures from the U.S. Department of Homeland Security report 14,982 or 66 percent of the 22,710 children adopted were girls. Of that total, 10,558 children were from Asia and 8,753 (83%) were girls. Thus, 7,545 (95%) of the 7,939 children adopted from China were girls.

UNDOCUMENTED WOMEN

Of the 10 percent to 15 percent of the undocumented population in the United States that is estimated to be from Asia, there is limited data on the number of undocumented immigrant women from Asia. Perhaps 44 percent are women and one out of five are single women.[25]

Undocumented immigrant women have the lowest employment rate at 56 percent compared with 64 percent for legal immigrant women and 73 percent for U.S. citizen women. As a point of reference, undocumented immigrant men have the highest rate of employment at 92 percent, compared with 86 percent for legal immigrant men and 83 percent for native-born men. In the case of women, the low figure is attributed to two realities: the likelihood that most are the caregivers in the home and the difficulty of finding employment without documentation.[26]

In general, undocumented immigrants are concentrated in low-wage occupations and earn a family income that is 40 percent less than that of legal immigrants or native-born citizens. They are overrepresented in domestic work, and the leisure and hospitality, and construction and manufacturing industries. Twenty-seven percent live in poverty, and 59 percent of the adults do not have health insurance.[27]

REFUGEES AND ASYLEES

Women and children make up 80 percent of the world's refugees, and in 2003, refugees and asylees who adjusted their status comprised 6.4 percent of all legal permanent residents.[28] The U.S. recognizes refugees and asylees as individuals fearing persecution on the basis of race, religion, membership in a social group, political opinion, or national origin.

The largest group of refugees from Asia are those from Southeast Asia, primarily Cambodia, Laos, and Vietnam. From 1975 to 2002, close to 1,146,650 Southeast Asians arrived as refugees. In 2005, 53,813 people were admitted into the United States as refugees, and the leading countries of origin were Somalia, Laos, and Cuba. In 2005, of the total refugee admittance population, 15,048 were from the countries of East Asia and Near East/South Asia. Another 25,257 were granted asylum, and the leading countries of origin were China, Colombia, and Haiti. After September 11, 2001, the U.S. refugee program was tremendously affected, and the admittance of refugees decreased from 69,304 in 2001 to 27,110 in 2002. In 2006, the program increased to admitting an estimated 50,000 refugees a year. Additionally, the rate of asylum cases granted has fallen significantly. In 2001, 43 percent of asylum cases were granted, whereas, in 2003, 29 percent were granted.[29]

In the past twenty years, immigration laws have made it more difficult for asylum seekers by placing a one-year time limit for application, denying work authorization and implementation of expedited removal procedures. For example, a woman seeking asylum as a rape or domestic violence survivor may be deported because of the summary expedited removal process. Asylum seekers are granted only a cursory review by an immigration officer at the port of entry rather than a full legal hearing. For those who pass the initial screening, they are still subject to indefinite and mandatory detention.

DETENTION AND DEPORTATION

Since the 1980s, the INS and later the DHS reversed policy on detentions by making it a central enforcement tool. Aggravating this situation was the 1996 Illegal Immigration Reform and Immigrant Responsibility Act, which introduced sweeping changes to the immigration laws and led to the increasing number of people subject to deportation and mandatory detention. In 1995, the daily capacity of the detention program was 7,000 beds, and this has tripled to 20,000 today.[30] The estimated total is now close to 24,000 detained throughout the year. Given this tremendous expansion, the industrial prison complex has greatly profited from the incarceration of 60 percent of all immigration detainees.[31]

In addition to those who committed violent crimes, asylum seekers and legal permanent residents are detained and placed into deportation proceedings because they committed minor and nonviolent crimes, some several years earlier. The U.S. Citizenship and Immigration Services has been unwilling to release information on the detainee population by country of origin or by gender. However, the Southeast Asia Resource Action Center has compiled and published data regarding the number of Southeast Asians who have orders of removal (those detained, detained and released, or deported): 1,400 from Cambodia, 1,900 from Laos and 4,000 from Vietnam. It is also estimated that 5 percent of those held are asylum seekers, 7 percent are women and 3 percent are children.[32] Because women make up a smaller portion of the total detainee population, they are more likely to be kept with the general criminal population.[33]

Given the very reason why many refugee and asylum seekers came to the United States, there is tremendous concern about returning to a country that had persecuted them. While there are unjust and unfair practices occurring because of deportation, what is overlooked is the direct impact on refugee women as wives and mothers. Often those who are deported had been the sole financial provider for their families. Women are left without a financial network to support and raise their children. More gravely, refugee women had risked their lives to bring their children to the United States only to face more loss and suffering.

With respect to detentions, in 2002, the Women's Commission for Refugee Women and Children released its report on the conditions at the Krome Detention Center in Florida that reveal "widespread sexual, physical, verbal and emotional abuse of detainees, especially women." Sexual abuse from rape to molestation was particularly prevalent, as were cases of prolonged detention and failure to provide legal access or address language needs of detainees who were Limited English Proficient, particularly non-English or non-Spanish speakers.

POST–SEPTEMBER 11

Immigrant women faced a myriad of consequences in the wake of September 11. South Asian women were the indirect victims of the policies that primarily targeted men of Middle Eastern and South Asian descent. As their fathers, brothers, and sons were being detained, questioned, and even deported, women had to assume the roles of sole breadwinners in their families, as well as raise children and maintain the family unit. Another consequence of the post-9/11 targeting is more complicated. For women suffering in abusive situations, the government's targeting of the abusers in their lives may have led to some amount of relief.

One of the most pressing issues affecting women and all refugees in the aftermath of September 11 is the "Material Support" admission bar. Because of broad interpretation of anti-terrorism provisions in the PATRIOT Act and other laws, refugee status is now denied to anyone who has provided "material support" to a terrorist organization. Unfortunately, refugees who are deemed to have provided material support—any financial, physical, or material assistance, no matter if the amount was insignificant or given inadvertently without direct intent to help an armed resistance group against a country's government—are barred from entering the United States. For example, there are large numbers of prodemocracy Burmese living in refugee camps in Thailand, waiting for resettlement in a third country. Given this broad definition of "material support," a Burmese woman found to provide "material support," even under duress, to an individual or group defined in the PATRIOT Act as a "terrorist" and/or "terrorist organization" or committed a "terrorist activity" would not be eligible to be resettled as a refugee in the United States, even if her resettlement has been cleared by the United Nations High Commission for

Refugees. The denial rate on the basis of the Material Support bar means that almost one-quarter of the refugee population would not be eligible for resettlement in the United States.[34]

OUTLOOK

According to national advocates, Asian American women's data, voices, and perspectives have been underacknowledged in the description of the immigrant experience, public research, and political discourse. Immigration policies and prevailing global patriarchal norms, long have had a discriminatory impact on Asian American women. The primary means of entry to the United States for Asian American women have been overwhelmingly through dependent relationships, such as family sponsorship visas, including adoptions, and international marriages as war brides, mail-order brides, fiancés or simply brides. Significant numbers arrive as refugees and asylees as well. Scholars and advocates agree that understanding the role that Asian American women have played in the community's immigrant experience is critical if we are to understand the effects of public policy on Asian American communities in the past and in the future.

FURTHER READING

Department of Economic and Social Affairs Division for the Advancement of Women. "2004 World Survey on the Role of Women in Development: Women and International Migration." New York: United Nations, 2006.

Fitzpatrick, Joan. "The Gender Dimension of U.S. Immigration Policy." *Yale Journal of Law and Feminism* 9, no. 1 (1997).

Pearce, Susan. "Immigrant Women in the United States: A Demographic Portrait Special Report, Summer 2006." Washington, DC: Immigration Policy Center, 2006.

Strum, Philippa, Danielle Tarantolo, and Woodrow Wilson, eds. "Women Immigrants in the United States." Washington, DC: International Center for Scholars and Migration Policy Institute, 2002.

NOTES

1. Department of Economic and Social Affairs Division for the Advancement of Women (DAW), "2004 World Survey on the Role of Women in Development: Women and International Migration," United Nations, New York (2006): 9.

2. DAW, "2004 World Survey on the Role of Women in Development," 10.

3. DAW, "2004 World Survey on the Role of Women in Development," 8.

4. DAW, "2004 World Survey on the Role of Women in Development," 20.

5. DAW, "2004 World Survey on the Role of Women in Development," 21.

6. Susan Pearce, "Immigrant Women in the United States: A Demographic Portrait Special Report, Summer 2006," Immigration Policy Center, Washington, DC (2006): 3.

7. Jennifer M. Chacon, "Misery and Myopia: Understanding the Failures of U.S. Efforts to Stop Human Trafficking," *Fordham Law Review* (2006).

8. Pearce, "Immigrant Women in the United States," 3; Sucheng Chan, *Asian Americans: An Interpretive History* (New York: Twyane Publishers, 1991), 145.

9. Joan Fitzpatrick, "The Gender Dimension of U.S. Immigration Policy," *Yale Journal of Law and Feminism* 9, no.1 (1997): 31.

10. Pearce, "Immigrant Women in the United States," 1.

11. Pearce, "Immigrant Women in the United States," 4–6.

12. Pearce, "Immigrant Women in the United States," 8.

13. State of Washington Commission on APA Affairs, http://www.capaa.wa.gov.

14. Bonnie Demrose Stone and Betty Sowers Alt, *Uncle Sam's Brides: The World of Military Wives* (New York: Walter and Company, 1990), 128–129.

15. Ramah McKay, "Family Reunification," *Migration Policy Institute,* Washington, DC (2003): 1.

16. Pearce, "Immigrant Women in the United States," 7; 47.3 percent of women entered through the immediate family category compared to 37.6 percent of men. At the same time, family-sponsored preference categories of third and fourth preference (adult children or siblings of U.S. citizens) showed minor differences between women at 22.4 percent and men at 23.0 percent.

17. Department of Homeland Security, *Annual Flow Report: April 2006*, page 5 http://www.uscis.gov/graphics/shared/statistics/publications/USLegalPermEst_5.pdf; Department of Homeland Security, *2005 Yearbook of Immigration Statistics*, Table 9, page 26. http://www.dhs.gov/xlibrary/assets/statistics/yearbook/2005/OIS_2005_Yearbook.pdf18. H.R. 3657, International Marriage Broker Act, 109th 1st session, Section 1.

19. Aardvarc.org, "Commonly Used Domestic Violence Citations," http://www.aardvarc.org/dv/statistics.shtml#cites.

20. Mary A. Nies and Melanie McEwan, *Community Health Nursing: Promoting the Health of Populations,* 3rd ed., Elsevier Saunders, 2001.

21. Pearce, "Immigrant Women in the United States," 7.

22. Fitzpatrick, "The Gender Dimension of U.S. Immigration Policy," 25.

23. Pearce, "Immigrant Women in the United States," 9–10.

24. Koreans and Amerasians also comprise a significant portion of the U.S. adoptee population. Of the more than 150,000 children adopted overseas, 100,000 were adopted into U.S. homes. Adoptees from Korea make up 10 percent of today's Korean American population and are part of the second immigration wave of Korean Americans. (U.S. Census) The other significant entry of children from Asia was "Amerasian" children (children born in Vietnam to Vietnamese women and U.S. servicemen). Since the Vietnam War (1957–1975) close to 100,000 Amerasians entered the United States. (http://www.searac.org).

25. Jeffrey S. Passel, "Unauthorized Migrants: Numbers and Characteristics," Pew Hispanic Center, June 2005, p. 18, http://pewhispanic.org/files/reports/46.pdf.

26. Passel, "Unauthorized Migrants," 25.

27. Passel, "Unauthorized Migrants," 26–30,

28. Jeanne Batalova, "Spotlight on Legal Immigration to the United States," Migration Policy Institute, Washington, DC (June 2005): 4.

29. The number of asylum cases that have been filed has dropped dramatically from 123,884 in 1994 to 27,704 in 2004. Kelly Jefferys, "Annual Flow Report—Refugees and Asylees: 2005, Office of Immigration Statistics, Department of Homeland Security, pages 1–5.

30. Wendy Young, "Behind Locked Doors: Abuse of Refugee Women at Krome," *Women's Commission for Refugee Women and Children*, New York (October 2000): 2.

31. "Immigration Detention—An Overview," Detention Watch Network, 2006. Washington, DC (2006): 2.

32. Young, "Behind Locked Doors" 2.

33. Immigration Detention, 2.

34. Refugee Council USA, "The Stories: Refugees Hurt by the Material Support Bar on Admission," April 5, 2006, http://www.rcusa.org/uploads/pdfs/ms-caseexamples-2006.pdf.

RESOURCE GUIDE

Suggested Reading

California Alliance to Combat Trafficking and Slavery Task Force, Human Trafficking in California (2007).

Hing, Bill Ong. *Defining America through Immigration Policy*. Philadelphia: Temple University Press, 2004.

Hing, Bill Ong. *Deporting Our Souls: Values, Morality, and Immigration Policy*. Cambridge, UK: Cambridge University Press, 2006.

Hing, Bill Ong. "Detention to Deportation—Rethinking the Removal of Cambodian Refugees." *U. C.–Davis Law Review* 38 (2005): 891.

Hing, Bill Ong. "Don't Give Me Your Tired, Your Poor: Conflicted Immigrant Stories and Welfare Reform." *Harvard Civil Rights-Civil Liberties Law Review* 33 (1998): 159.

Hing, Bill Ong. *Making and Remaking Asian America through Immigration Policy*. Palo Alto, CA: Stanford Press, 1993.

Hing, Bill Ong. "Refugee Policy and Cultural Identity: In the Voice of Hmong and Iu Mien Young Adults." *Hastings Race & Poverty Law Journal* 1 (2003): 111.

Hing, Bill Ong. *To Be an American: Cultural Pluralism and the Rhetoric of Assimilation*. New York: NYU Press 1997.

Su, Julie. "Making the Invisible Visible: The Garment Industry's Dirty Laundry." *Journal of Gender, Race and Justice* 1 (1998): 405.

Films

Becoming American: The Chinese American Experience. 2003. Bill Moyers. PBS. (360 minutes). This documentary focuses on the history of Chinese Americans from the California Gold Rush to the present. It also explores generation and the personal journeys around history, racism and identity of Chinese Americans.

Juvies. 2004. Dir. Leslie Neale. Chance Films. DVD (66 minutes). A documentary focusing on the lives of twelve juveniles, tried as adults and facing long-term sentences. The juveniles were taught basic video production and interviewing skills that are featured in the film. Duc Ta is one of the twelve juvenile participants.

Sentenced Home. 2005. Dir. Nicole Newnham and David Grabias. IndiePix. DVD (76 minutes). This documentary focuses on three Cambodian-American immigrants living in Seattle. In the early 1980s, these children were among multitudes of Cambodian refugees given shelter from the genocidal Khmer Rouge in Seattle's housing projects. Now, their teenage rebellions have caught up with them in a horrific way, and the confluence of their noncitizenship (they are "permanent residents") and post 9/11 anti-terrorism laws lead to their immediate deportation. The film follows the men back to their native Cambodia, a country that is unfamiliar and fearsome to them.

Organizations

Asian American Justice Center. http://www.advancingequality.org/. An organization working to advance Asian American human and civil rights through advocacy, public policy initiatives, public education and litigation.

Asian American Legal Defense and Education Fund. https://www.aaldef.org/. National organization focused on key issues impacting Asian American civil rights and provides litigation, legal resources, education and training.

Asian Law Caucus. http://www.asianlawcaucus.org/site/alc_dev/. Serves low-income Asian Pacific American communities in promoting, advancing and representing their legal and civil rights.

Immigrant Legal Resource Center. http://www.ilrc.org/. Provides information on immigration law and current publications that educate and inform immigrants and their advocates.

Southeast Asian Refugee Action Center. http://www.searac.org/. National organization features information about Cambodian, Laotian, and Vietnamese Americans and relevant issues impacting these communities.

Web Sites

ACLU Immigrant Rights Project. http://www.aclu.org/immigrants/index.html. Discussion of the most pressing constitutional challenges faced by immigrants and other noncitizens in the United States.

American Immigration Lawyers Association. http://www.aila.org/. Immigration on the rights of immigrants and available legal services across the nation.

Detention Watch Network. http://www.detentionwatchnetwork.org/. advocates on behalf of immigrants who are held in custody under unreasonable conditions and procedures.

DHS Immigration Statistics. http://www.dhs.gov/ximgtn/statistics/. Regular reports from the Department of Homeland Security on immigration, refugee, and deportation data in the United States.

Immigration Policy Center. http://www.immigrationpolicy.org/. Policy and advocacy position papers on a variety of current immigration issues.

ImmigrationProf Blog. http://lawprofessors.typepad.com/immigration/. Daily coverage of immigration and refugee issues from a legal and community-based perspective.

Law Offices of Carl Shusterman. http://www.shusterman.com/. Comprehensive Web site on immigration procedures, requirements, visa backlogs, and current immigration legal issues.

National Immigration Forum. http://www.immigrationforum.org/. Up-to-date information on legislative and policy proposals affecting immigrants in the United States.

National Immigration Law Center. http://www.nilc.org/. Devoted to policy relevant information impacting immigrants and refugees, including education, public assistance, and labor rights.

National Network for Immigrant & Refugee Rights. http://www.nnirr.org/. Advocacy information on immigrant and refugee rights from a grassroots and community-based perspective.

Section 7:

LAW

Section Editor: Angelo Ancheta

LEGAL ISSUES, PAST AND PRESENT

Angelo Ancheta

Law and the legal system have had strong and lasting effects on the lives of Asian Americans since the founding of the nation. During most of American history, Asian Americans have faced various racially discriminatory laws, and guarantees of civil rights have been elusive. Social movements and revisions in federal and state policies have brought important changes in the law in recent decades, but discrimination in the law and insufficient civil rights protections remain leading issues. Both historical discrimination against Asian Americans and contemporary legal issues reflect recurring problems rooted in race, ethnicity, immigration and citizenship status, and language access. In many instances, the discrimination reflects racism that is intertwined with nativism and anti-American sentiment—where Asian Americans, even those whose families have been in the U.S. for generations, are treated as if they are foreigners.

HISTORICAL IMMIGRATION AND DISCRIMINATION

The history of Asians in the United States dates back to the founding of the country, and the waves of immigrant laborers who entered the country in the nineteenth and early twentieth centuries produced significant Asian populations in Hawai'i and several western states. Chinese immigrants first arrived in the mid-1800s to work on plantations in Hawai'i , as well as in the mining and railroad industries on the West Coast; Japanese, Filipino, Korean, and Asian Indian workers entered in later decades as demands for low-wage labor increased. In time, however, economic downturns and overt racism led to serious discrimination against immigrant populations. Anti-Asian laws came in three major forms: federal citizenship laws that created racial barriers for Asians seeking naturalized citizenship, federal immigration laws that severely limited the number of immigrants from Asian countries, and state and local laws that discriminated against Asians, often based on their ineligibility for American citizenship.

RACE AND NATURALIZED CITIZENSHIP

In 1790, Congress passed the Nationality Act of 1790, which stated that "any alien, being a *free white person* who shall have resided within the limits and under the jurisdiction of the United States for a term of two years, may be admitted to become a citizen thereof."[1] The act was originally intended to exclude blacks and Native Americans from citizenship, but as immigrant populations grew in the 1800s, the law was used to deny citizenship to Asians as well. Even after the addition of the Fourteenth Amendment to the federal Constitution, which guaranteed that any person born in the United States would be an American citizen, the naturalization laws excluded Asians from eligibility. Federal legislation amended the naturalization laws in 1870 to grant "aliens of African nativity and persons of African descent" the right to become naturalized citizens, but Congress rejected legislation to make Chinese immigrants eligible for citizenship.

Restrictions on naturalized citizenship also cast doubt on the birthright citizenship of American-born children of Asian immigrants, and the basic issue was not resolved until 1898 in the case of *United States v. Wong Kim Ark.*[2] Wong Kim Ark had been born in San Francisco to Chinese immigrant parents, but after returning to the United States from a trip to China, he was prevented from entering the country based on the government's allegation that he was not an American citizen. The Supreme Court ruled in favor of Wong and held that all people born in the United States, even those born to parents ineligible for citizenship, become citizens under the Fourteenth Amendment. At the same time, however, the Court reaffirmed Congress' power to deny naturalized citizenship to Wong's parents.

During the 1920s the Supreme Court confirmed that various Asian immigrant groups were ineligible for naturalization. In *Ozawa v. United States,* the Court ruled that Japanese immigrants were ineligible for naturalized citizenship. Ozawa, who had spent almost his entire life in the U.S, argued that Japanese were included within the category of "free white persons" because of their skin color.[3] The Court rejected his argument, proposing that the words "white person" were not based on skin color; instead, the term was meant to include only members of the Caucasian race. In *United States v. Thind,* the Supreme Court ruled that Asian Indians were ineligible for citizenship, even though anthropological science at the time classified Indians as Caucasian.[4] Popular conceptions of Caucasian, the Court concluded, did not include Indians because their physical characteristics made them "readily distinguishable from the various persons in this country commonly recognized as white."[5]

Federal citizenship laws even went so far as to take away American citizenship from women who married Asian immigrants. The Cable Act, passed in 1922, stated that any woman citizen who married an alien ineligible to citizenship would cease to be a citizen of the United States. At the time, the citizenship of a husband and a wife was considered identical, and the husband's citizenship took precedence over the wife's citizenship; thus the government could strip away American citizenship from a woman who married an immigrant subject to the racial bar.

The federal courts never overturned the racial bar on naturalization as unconstitutional, and it was not until the 1940s and 1950s that Congress removed the prohibition, largely in response to World War II alliances between the United States and Asian countries. Chinese immigrants became eligible to naturalize in 1943, and Asian Indians and Filipinos became eligible in 1946. It was not until 1952 that the racial limitation on naturalized citizenship was finally removed altogether from the law.

EXCLUSIONARY IMMIGRATION LAWS

While racial barriers to naturalization prevented Asian immigrants from gaining citizenship, race-based immigration restrictions prevented Asians from entering the country in the first place. Congress passed a series of laws limiting Asian immigration during the late nineteenth and early twentieth centuries in response to calls to curtail the flow of Asian labor during economic recessions. The laws first sought to end Chinese migration, but they were extended in time to include all Asian groups in the United States.

Among the earliest laws was the Page Law of 1875, a law designed to prevent the entry of prostitutes but was applied almost entirely against Chinese women, who were routinely classified as prostitutes. In 1882, Congress passed the Chinese Exclusion Act, which excluded Chinese laborers from entering the United States for a full decade; as a result, the number of Chinese who entered the country declined from over 39,000 in 1882 to just ten in 1888. The Scott Act of 1888 extended Chinese exclusion by prohibiting the entry of Chinese laborers who left the United States temporarily and failed to return by a set date.

The Supreme Court upheld the constitutionality of the Scott Act in *Chae Chan Ping v. United States (The Chinese Exclusion Case),* ruling that Congress had broad powers to regulate immigration and that if the government considered "the presence of foreigners of a different race in this country, who will not assimilate with us, to be dangerous to its peace and security, their exclusion [would] not to be stayed."[6] The Geary Act of 1892 extended Chinese exclusion for an additional ten years and added the requirement that any Chinese immigrant who failed to register with the government within a year would become subject to deportation. In *Fong Yue Ting v. United States,* the Supreme Court upheld the constitutionality of the Geary Act as consistent with Congress' powers.[7] Congress renewed the exclusion laws in 1902 and in 1904 passed legislation that extended exclusion indefinitely.

With the decline of Chinese migration, renewed calls for low-wage labor led to increased migration from Japan. The Japanese government tightly regulated early migration and focused on sending laborers to Hawai'i and California for agricultural work. In time, however, calls for immigration restrictions abounded on the West Coast. Diplomatic solutions to address anti-Japanese sentiment led to a "Gentleman's Agreement," which was first negotiated in 1907 to voluntarily limit Japanese migration. Under the agreement, the Japanese government ceased issuing travel documents to U.S.-bound workers; in exchange, the spouses and children of Japanese laborers were allowed to enter the United States.

Racist sentiment against Korean and Indian immigrants grew in the early twentieth century as well. Congress passed the Immigration Act of 1917, which created an "Asiatic barred zone," which covered South Asia from Arabia to Indochina, and included India, Burma, Siam, the Malay states, the East Indian islands, Asiatic Russia, the Polynesian islands, and parts of Arabia and Afghanistan. Congress later passed the Immigration Act of 1924, an immigration law that established national origin quotas that were heavily biased in favor of migrants from Northern and Western Europe. The 1924 act also excluded any "alien ineligible to citizenship," which targeted Asian migration through the racial bar on naturalization.

Filipinos, who were U.S. nationals for many years because of the Philippines' status as an American colony in the early twentieth century, were not directly affected by the first restrictive immigration laws. Although initially welcomed as laborers, Filipinos were eventually targeted for immigration restrictions, resulting in Congress' passage of the Tydings-McDuffie Act of 1934. The law granted commonwealth status to the Philippines, which eventually became independent in 1946, but it stripped Filipinos in the United States of their status as nationals and made them deportable. Filipinos became subject to the immigration laws, and annual quotas limited the entry of Filipinos to the United States to approximately fifty per year.

Because of the immigration laws, Asian migration was drastically reduced and some immigrant populations in the United States even declined over time. The McCarran-Walter Act of 1952 revised much of the federal immigration system, but it kept the basic quota system that limited Asian immigration. The 1952 act also created an "Asia-Pacific triangle" that allowed only two thousand immigrants to enter the country each year; moreover, annual quotas for each Asian country typically allowed only one hundred migrants per year. It was not until 1965 that the laws were amended to remove overtly race-based exclusions from the federal immigration laws.

STATE AND LOCAL LAWS

Racially discriminatory laws at the state and local level had the most powerful effects on Asian Americans. Many of the laws discriminated through explicit language based on race or ethnicity, but other laws relied on the racial bar on naturalized citizenship to target Asian immigrants. Laws designed to deny legal rights to "aliens ineligible to citizenship" had the unmistakable effect of discriminating against Asian immigrants and their family members. In 1852, for example, California enacted a foreign miners' license tax, which imposed a three-dollar monthly tax on every foreign miner who could not become an American citizen. Until it was overridden by federal statute, the tax generated from one-fourth to one-half of California's total state revenue. In 1855, the California legislature passed a law entitled "An Act to Discourage the Immigration to this State of Persons Who Cannot Become Citizens Thereof," which imposed a landing tax of fifty dollars per person on ship owners transporting Asian immigrants.

State courts also actively engaged in discrimination against Chinese immigrants. In 1854, for example, the California Supreme Court in *People v. Hall* overturned the criminal conviction of a white man whose conviction for murdering a Chinese man was based in part on the testimony of Chinese witnesses.[8] The court ruled that a Chinese witness could not testify based on a state law which stated that "[n]o Black or Mulatto person, or Indian, shall be allowed to give evidence in favor of, or against any white person." The court ruled that the law included Chinese because Indians and Chinese were from the same racial stock, because the word "black" included all individuals other than whites, and because accepting the testimony of unassimilated Chinese immigrants would be unwise public policy.

Local laws also imposed discriminatory burdens on Chinese immigrants and immigrant-owned businesses. A San Francisco ordinance, for example, imposed a tax schedule of $1.25 on laundries with one horse-drawn vehicle, $4 on laundries with two horse-drawn vehicles, $15 on laundries with more than two horse-drawn vehicles, and $15 on laundries with no horse-drawn vehicles at all. The law targeted Chinese laundries because practically no Chinese laundry operated a horse-drawn vehicle. San Francisco also enacted a "Cubic Air Ordinance," which mandated that living areas have a minimum of five hundred cubic feet of space per person; the law was enforced only in Chinatown.

One of the rare instances in which an ordinance was struck down as unconstitutional was in the landmark 1886 case of *Yick Wo v. Hopkins,* in which the Supreme Court struck down a San Francisco ordinance that prohibited wood-constructed laundries.[9] The government denied renewal licenses to Yick Wo and hundreds of Chinese laundry owners under the ordinance, even though they had been operating their laundries for more than two decades. Almost all non-Chinese laundries, including ones with wooden buildings, were granted renewals. The Court held in favor of Yick Wo, ruling that noncitizens were protected by the Equal Protection Clause of the Fourteenth Amendment, and that even a law that was not racially discriminatory on its face could violate the Equal Protection Clause if it was administered in a discriminatory manner.

The property rights of Asian immigrants were also limited through state "alien land laws." For example, the Alien Land Law of 1913 targeted Japanese farmers in California by prohibiting aliens ineligible for citizenship from purchasing land and by limiting lease terms to no more than three years. The

California law was expanded in the 1920s to prevent American-born Asian children from gaining title to land and having their parents act as guardians. The U.S. Supreme Court upheld alien land laws against constitutional challenge in the 1920s, ruling in *Terrace v. Thompson* that Asian immigrants did not enjoy the same rights as citizens.[10] The Court concluded that because a noncitizen lacked sufficient interest in the welfare of the state, the state could properly deny him the right to own and lease real property.

Another common form of discrimination came in the form of school segregation laws. In 1860, California barred Asians, blacks, and Native Americans from attending public schools altogether. In the 1880s, after the law banning minority students was declared unconstitutional, the laws established racially segregated schools. For example, Chinese and other Asian students in cities such as San Francisco were often sent to "Oriental schools" and other minority-only schools. In 1927, the U.S. Supreme Court ruled in *Gong Lum v. Rice* that requiring a Chinese American student to enroll in a Mississippi school designed for the "colored races" was constitutional.[11] *Gong Lum* remained in place until it was overruled by the Supreme Court in 1954 in *Brown v. Board of Education.*

Antimiscegenation laws that banned many interracial marriages were also widely used to discriminate against Asian Americans. In the 1880s, for example, California enacted an antimiscegenation law that prohibited marriages between whites and "Negroes, mulattoes, or Mongolians"; the law was extended in the 1930s to include Filipinos, who had been ruled by the courts to be members of the "Malay race." As reflections of white supremacy—intermarriage between nonwhites was allowed but intermarriage between whites and nonwhites was banned—antimiscegenation laws against blacks and Asians were common in western states, and many laws remained on the books until the U.S. Supreme Court declared them unconstitutional in 1967.

WORLD WAR II INTERNMENT OF JAPANESE AMERICANS

Among the most serious acts of discrimination against an Asian American population was the relocation and internment of Japanese Americans during World War II. After the attack on Pearl Harbor, longstanding sentiment against Japanese immigrants led to calls for the removal of Japanese Americans from the West Coast. On February 19, 1942, President Franklin D. Roosevelt issued Executive Order 9066, which authorized the creation of military areas from which all persons could be excluded in the interest of national defense. Although also applicable to individuals of German and Italian origin, the executive order was targeted almost entirely against Japanese Americans, and military plans to evacuate all people of Japanese descent from the West Coast soon followed. More than 110,000 Japanese Americans, most of whom were American-born citizens, were placed into internment camps in the interior of the United States for the duration of the war.

Four Japanese Americans challenged the military orders and appealed their cases in the courts. Gordon Hirabayashi, Minoru Yasui, and Fred Korematsu were each arrested and imprisoned for violating military orders, and challenged their convictions as violations of due process and equal protection under the law; Mitsuye Endo, who had been interned in both California and Utah, filed a writ of habeas corpus arguing that her detention was illegal. In 1943, in *Hirabayashi v. United States*, the Supreme Court ruled that a curfew order restricting the movement and presence of Japanese Americans was constitutional.[12] The Court noted that Hirabayashi's conviction was based on a racial classification, but concluded that military necessity justified the conviction. In *Yasui v. United States,* the Supreme Court employed similar reasoning and overturned a lower court ruling that the curfew order was unconstitutional as applied to American citizens.[13]

In 1944, in *Korematsu v. United States*, the Supreme Court upheld the constitutionality of the military's exclusion order.[14] The Court wrote that while "all legal restrictions which curtail the civil rights of a single racial group are immediately suspect," some restrictions could be constitutional because "[p]ressing public necessity must sometimes justify the existence of such restrictions." In *Ex Parte Endo,* the Court provided Endo with a personal victory but did not confront the constitutionality of the internment itself.[15] The Supreme Court limited its decision to whether Endo's detention was valid, and after finding Endo's loyalty to be unquestioned, the Court ordered her release. The exclusion orders were eventually rescinded by the military near the end of World War II, allowing Japanese Americans to return to the West Coast.

Nearly forty years after the internment, documents showing that the government had altered key reports and had suppressed evidence of Japanese American loyalty were used to vacate the original convictions of Hirabayashi and Korematsu. In both instances, the courts concluded that the federal government had committed prosecutorial misconduct. Yasui's conviction was also vacated, but without a court finding of misconduct; Yasui passed away during the course of his appeal. The Civil Liberties Act of 1988, which issued a governmental apology for the internment and granted redress payments to former internees, was later enacted to provide compensation and a measure of closure on the internment.

POST–WORLD WAR II REFORMS

Notwithstanding the government's discriminatory treatment of Japanese Americans during the war, the fight for democracy abroad during the 1940s helped usher in a period of legal reform and increased civil rights protections for Asian Americans. For example, in *Oyama v. California,* the U.S. Supreme Court ruled in 1948 that California's alien land law was unconstitutional because it violated the equal protection rights of an American citizen who was a child of Japanese immigrants.[16]

The Supreme Court also held in 1948 that racially restrictive housing covenants, provisions within deeds and other real estate contracts that had been used to prevent Asian Americans from owning homes, were unconstitutional and could not be enforced by the courts. And the Supreme Court's landmark decision in *Brown v. Board of Education* in 1954 prohibited public school segregation and led to the dismantling of "separate but equal" schools for Asian Americans.[17] During the late 1940s and 1950s, state legislatures and state courts also began reversing earlier laws that discriminated against Asian Americans. The Oregon Supreme Court declared the state's alien land law unconstitutional in 1949, followed by the California Supreme Court in 1952. In 1948, in *Perez v. Sharp*, the California Supreme Court declared California's antimiscegenation law to be unconstitutional.[18]

The federal government's reversal of discriminatory immigration and naturalization laws began in the 1940s and culminated with the passage of the Immigration Act of 1965. The Chinese exclusion laws were repealed in 1943, and Chinese immigrants were also allowed to become naturalized citizens. Asian Indian and Filipino immigrants gained the right to naturalize in 1946, and the 1952 McCarran-Walter Act fully removed the racial bar to naturalization. The Immigration Act of 1965 abolished the Asia-Pacific triangle put into place by the McCarran-Walter Act and removed the discriminatory national origin quotas dating back to the 1924 act, which limited visas for most Asian countries to one hundred per year. The 1965 act established a much higher allocation of visas per country and turned to a preference system based on reuniting families and meeting the needs of the American economy through the entry of professional and skilled workers.

CONTEMPORARY LEGAL ISSUES

Along with major civil rights legislation of the 1960s—including the Civil Rights Act of 1964 and the Voting Rights Act of 1965—the Immigration Act of 1965 marked a significant shift in the federal government's commitment to antidiscrimination law and racial equality. As a result, Asian Americans began benefiting directly from governmental prohibitions on discrimination in employment, education, housing, public accommodations, and voting. Moreover, Asian Americans began being included in a range of affirmative action programs designed to remedy past discrimination in areas such as public contracting and public employment, as well as in many programs designed to promote diversity in employment and higher education. Nonetheless, there are still ongoing problems tied to overt racial discrimination, immigration, immigrant rights, language access, national security and racial profiling, and full inclusion in civil rights programs. The legal system provides rights and remedies for many victims of discrimination, but in many cases the law itself plays a central role in the discriminatory treatment of Asian Americans.

Racial Violence

One area of racial discrimination that continues to pose problems for Asian American communities as a whole—one that is tied both to lingering problems of nativism and to inadequate civil rights enforcement—revolves around racial violence. Anti-Asian violence is deeply rooted in the history of Asian immigrant communities that endured acts of violence, ranging from assaults and killings to property damage and harassment to race rioting. In more recent decades, prominent incidents of racial violence, such as the killings of Vincent Chin in Detroit in 1982, Jim (Ming Hai) Loo in North Carolina in 1989, Joseph Ileto in Southern California in 1999, and Cha Vang in Wisconsin in 2007, have reflected nativist racism motivated by antagonisms rooted in economic competition with Asian countries, lingering hostilities related to the Vietnam War and other military conflicts, and overt racism. In the post–September 11th environment, violence against individuals of South Asian and Muslim origin, as well as individuals perceived to be members of those groups, has been a particularly serious problem.[19] Anti-Asian violence is especially threatening to entire communities because many incidents of violence cut across ethnic boundaries and reflect discrimination based on the victims' perceived status as a foreigner.

Civil rights organizations monitoring anti-Asian violence nationwide have tracked a wide variety of crimes in recent years, including graffiti, vandalism, cross burnings, property damage, arson, hate mail, intimidation, physical assaults, homicides, and police misconduct.[20] Data collection is incomplete, however, and problems of underreporting, particularly among limited-English-speaking immigrants, makes accurate monitoring and enforcement difficult. And even with national reports and prominent incidents of anti-Asian violence, there are ongoing problems related to the recognition of anti-Asian violence as a serious issue, the weak enforcement of civil rights laws, and inadequate punishment for many hate crimes.

Racial Profiling and National Security

Since the 1990s and after the terrorist attacks of September 11th, national security policies and antiterrorism efforts have had important effects on Asian American populations. For example, the attempted prosecution of nuclear scientist Wen Ho Lee in 1999 highlighted racial profiling by the federal government against Asian Americans whose basic loyalties to the United States were questioned. The government's case against Lee, a Taiwanese American who had resided in the United States since the 1960s, fell apart as evidence demonstrated that he had not stolen classified information and passed it on to the Chinese government. But the adverse effects of racial profiling on Asian Americans, particularly those seeking work in technology and defense industries, became clear as individuals were often discouraged from applying for jobs or asked to comply with higher standards for security clearances. (For more on racial profiling, see the sidebar on page 627.)

The war on terrorism has further generated problems of anti-Asian sentiment— by the government and by private sector actors who have engaged in discrimination ranging from limitations in airline travel and airport security to harassment on the job and in public life. South Asians, along with Arab Americans and Muslims, have borne the brunt of many of these acts. Government rhetoric has not been as overtly discriminatory as during the time of the Japanese American internment, but the federal government has also implemented significant immigration and criminal justice policies with powerful effects on Asian Americans. For example, policies such as the Absconder Apprehension Initiative, a deportation policy begun in 2002 that targeted individuals from countries with significant Al Qaeda activities, led to the removal of hundreds of individuals with unsubstantiated links to terrorism, including dozens of individuals from Asian countries such as the Philippines and Indonesia.

Immigration Restrictions and Anti-Immigrant Legislation

Anti-immigrant legislation enacted since the 1980s in response to the large number of immigrants from Asia and Latin America has created programs that have caused discrimination against Asian Americans or produced changes in the law affecting significant numbers of Asian immigrants. In 1986, for example, Congress passed the Immigration Reform and Control Act (IRCA) to address undocumented migration to the United States. The law created programs to legalize qualified undocumented immigrants, but it also established a system of employment verification and employer sanctions for hiring unauthorized workers. Because of employer sanctions, discrimination against Asian Americans and Latinos increased significantly after IRCA went into effect.

State and local laws affecting immigrants have also been enacted. In 1994, for example, the voters of California passed Proposition 187, a ballot initiative designed to address immigration by denying basic rights and government services to undocumented immigrants. Under Proposition 187, undocumented immigrants would have been denied access to public school education, non-emergency health care, and social services. Although the courts declared most of its provisions unconstitutional, Proposition 187 had immediate effects on immigrants, who removed their children from schools and avoided seeking health and social services. Similar ballot initiatives were unable to qualify for the ballots of other states, but efforts in Congress led to the passage of measures further limiting the rights of immigrants.

In 1996, Congress passed the Personal Responsibility and Work Opportunity Reconciliation Act, a law intended to overhaul the nation's welfare system. The legislation contained provisions that discriminated against lawful permanent residents living in the United States by removing their eligibility for public entitlements, including Food Stamps and Supplemental Security Income for the elderly, blind, and disabled. Like earlier law that discriminated against "aliens ineligible to citizenship," the welfare reform law was race-neutral on its face, but its impact fell most heavily on the Asian American and Latino immigrant communities. Recent immigration laws such as the Illegal Immigration Reform and Immigrant Responsibility Act of 1996 that limited the rights of undocumented immigrants to receive federal entitlements, that cut back on the due process rights of applicants for political asylum, and that increased immigration enforcement by local officials have also had significant effects on Asian immigrant populations.

Language Access and Language Discrimination

Because two-thirds of the Asian American population is foreign-born, many of whom have limited English-speaking abilities, language access and language discrimination issues have long been core civil rights issues for Asian Americans, and Asian Americans have been at the forefront of advancing language rights. In 1974, for example, the U.S. Supreme Court ruled in *Lau v. Nichols*[21] that the San Francisco Unified School District violated Title VI of the Civil Rights Act of 1964 when the district discriminated against limited–English-speaking Chinese students by failing to provide equal educational opportunities through bilingual or supplemental instruction in English. The *Lau* case, in turn, led to expansions in bilingual education throughout the country and to increased guarantees for language assistance in a wide range of government services.

Nevertheless, with the growth of Asian immigrant populations and dozens of individual language groups, issues of language access still pose significant problems for limited–English-speaking Asian Americans, including some of the largest immigrant communities such as the Chinese, Vietnamese, and Korean communities, in key areas such as education, voting, criminal justice, and social and health care services. Bilingual education and bilingual ballots, for example, are not always available to smaller Asian language populations, and the result is unequal educational opportunities and even the denial of basic rights such as the right to vote. In critical areas such as health care, the lack of access to language assistance can often have dire consequences.

English-only policies, both by government and private-sector employers, have presented another source of language discrimination. During the 1980s and 1990s, a number of state and local governmental bodies enacted laws that made English the official language of government, which often curtailed key services for limited–English-speaking Asian immigrants. Although a number of English-only laws have been ruled unconstitutional or in violation of civil rights laws by the courts, many laws and policies continue to send symbolic signals to limited–English-speaking populations that they are not entirely welcome within political communities or within particular workplaces.

RECURRING THEMES OF LAW AND HISTORY

Patterns of discrimination involving nativism and anti-immigrant scapegoating have been recurring themes in the statutes and court cases of the twentieth and twenty-first centuries, just as they were in the nineteenth century. Even during economic upturns, Asian Americans have been treated as perpetual foreigners, and even today, many of the anti-Asian court decisions from earlier eras—including *The Chinese Exclusion Case* and the *Korematsu* case—continue to be cited as valid legal precedents. The legal history of Asian Americans shows that Asian Americans must continue to be vigilant about protecting their civil and human rights.

NOTES

1. *Statutes at Large* 1 (1790): 103 (emphasis added).
2. 169 U.S. 649 (1898).
3. 260 U.S. 178 (1922).
4. 261 U.S. 204 (1923).
5. *United States v. Thind* at 215.
6. 130 U.S. 581, 606 (1889).
7. 149 U.S. 698 (1893).
8. 4 Cal. 399 (1854).
9. 118 U.S. 356 (1886).
10. 263 U.S. 197 (1923).
11. 275 U.S. 78 (1927).
12. 320 U.S. 81 (1943).
13. 320 U.S. 115 (1943).
14. 323 U.S. 214 (1944).
15. 323 U.S. 283 (1944).
16. 332 U.S. 633 (1948).
17. 347 U.S. 483 (1954).
18. 32 Cal.2d 711 (1948).

19. National Asian Pacific American Legal Consortium, *2002 Audit of Violence Against Asian Pacific Americans: Tenth Annual Report* (Washington, DC: National Asian Pacific American Legal Consortium, 2004).

20. National Asian Pacific American Legal Consortium, *2002 Audit of Violence Against Asian Pacific Americans.*

21. 414 U.S. 563 (1974).

AFFIRMATIVE ACTION

Angelo Ancheta

Affirmative action policies that consider an individual's race or ethnicity in employment, government contracting, or higher education admissions are commonly used to remedy past racial discrimination or to promote diversity within institutions. Affirmative action programs remain controversial, however, and have been subject to legal and constitutional challenges. In recent years, some race-conscious programs have been upheld as constitutional, but a number have been struck down by the U.S. Supreme Court and other federal courts. In addition, a number of states have chosen to eliminate racial preferences in various areas of government decision-making, including public employment, public contracting, and admissions at public universities.

Asian Americans have been at the center of many of these controversies because they are not treated as underrepresented minorities in some affirmative action programs, particularly in higher education, and they are frequently perceived to be victims of discrimination because of affirmative action. Because programs designed to assist members of other racial minority groups might lead to the denial of positions to members of other racial groups, Asian Americans are sometimes seen as beneficiaries of policies or court rulings that eliminate affirmative action. Indeed, there are significant differences of opinion among Asian American advocates regarding the constitutionality and soundness of affirmative action policies, and in many leading court cases and policy debates, Asian American advocates can often be found on both sides of the issue. Nevertheless, Asian Americans have achieved progress in a wide range of fields because of affirmative action and can be expected to be included in many race-conscious programs in the future.

LEGAL LIMITS

Because of numerous court challenges to race-conscious programs, the scope of affirmative action has been limited in recent years. In the area of private-sector employment, the Supreme Court has recognized that carefully crafted affirmative action programs can, consistent with Title VII of the Civil Rights Act of 1964, attempt to address longstanding racial imbalances in traditionally segregated jobs. In areas involving governmental action, such as public-sector employment, government contracting, and higher education admissions at state universities, the Supreme Court has been more restrictive and has recognized only two compelling interests that can justify race-conscious affirmative action: remedying the effects of an institution's past discrimination and promoting educational diversity in higher education. Moreover, even if one of these interests is used to justify a particular program, the policy must be "narrowly tailored" to the government's interest; this means that the use of race must be limited and flexible, that nonminorities must not be unduly burdened by the policy, that policies must be subject to time limits or regular review, and that race-neutral alternatives must be considered before adopting race-conscious policies.

In the area of higher education admissions, for example, the U.S. Supreme Court's 2003 decisions in *Grutter v. Bollinger*[1] and *Gratz v. Bollinger*[2] make clear that race-conscious admissions policies designed to promote student body diversity can employ race as a "plus" factor among many factors considered in a competitive admissions process. Thus, race can be considered in an applicant's file, along with factors such as grade-point average, standardized test scores, work and life experiences, geography, special skills or talents, athletic contributions, and past social or economic disadvantage. A lawful admissions policy, however, must not employ race mechanically or weigh race so heavily that the policy guarantees admission to minorities. Quotas or special admissions tracks for minority applicants are prohibited in diversity-based admissions, and the use of race cannot be inflexible and cannot be overly burdensome for non-minority students.

Although the courts have defined the constitutional limits of affirmative action policies in recent years, there is no constitutional requirement that government must employ affirmative action policies. A number of states, including California, Washington, Florida, and Michigan, have recently enacted laws and policies that prohibit racial preferences in areas such as public employment, public contracting, and public education. These policies have eliminated many governmental affirmative action programs, and participation by racial minorities, including Asian Americans, has declined in a variety of sectors within those states. At the same time, however, in some sectors such as higher education, Asian American representation has been expected to increase because of the elimination of some affirmative action policies. These changes have led to increased enrollments of Asian American students at a number of universities, but they continue to generate controversy because of the perception that Asian Americans are gaining seats in colleges and universities at the expense of other racial and ethnic minorities.

UNDERREPRESENTATION

The "model minority" stereotype that suggests that Asian Americans do not suffer from discrimination and have achieved success comparable to whites has often led to proposals to exclude Asian Americans from affirmative action programs. Yet, the underrepresentation of Asian Americans in a range of areas supports their inclusion in affirmative action policies that address both past and ongoing discrimination. In the employment arena, for example, Asian Americans often face a "glass ceiling" that prevents their advancing to upper-level management positions, even though Asian Americans, on average, may have higher education levels and may fill the professional ranks of businesses in proportionately greater numbers than whites.[3] For example, wage disparities between whites and Asian Americans are also persistent, with Asian Americans possessing the same levels of education and comparable jobs often receiving lower salaries than whites. The failure to command equal wages or to obtain promotions to management and other high-level positions can often be attributed to negative stereotypes about Asian Americans—such as being passive or unassertive, lacking effective communication skills, or possessing inadequate preparation for leadership roles. In some sectors of public employment, such as police and firefighting, Asian Americans have often been underrepresented, and the statistical disparities can be striking. In Southern California during the 1990s, for example, Asian Americans constituted more than 10 percent of the population in both Los Angeles County and Orange County, but just more than 2 percent of the Los Angeles County firefighters and Orange County firefighters were Asian American. Percentages were even lower among county sheriffs—just more than 1 percent of the Orange County sheriff's officers were Asian American—and several departments in the Southern California area had no Asian American officers or firefighters at all.[4]

In other areas of government activity, such as public contracting, Asian American business owners have often been unable to gain access to competitive processes because of discrimination. In many instances, local government agencies have employed inconsistent bidding and contract procedures and have withheld information from minority contractors; in addition, there is often little or no outreach to minority-owned and women-owned businesses. Asian American businesses may already carry serious disadvantages in accessing capital and credit resulting from discrimination, and as a result of unequal access, these businesses may be unable to bid on government contracts at all. In San Francisco during the 1980s, for example, Asian American construction firms received less than 1 percent of the city's construction contracts, even though Asian American firms constituted 20 percent of the available pool.[5]

Affirmative action programs designed to remedy past discrimination have employed various forms of race-conscious outreach and recruitment, and have set specific goals and timetables that have enabled Asian Americans and other racial minority groups to gain significant ground. For example, under a 1988 court-enforced settlement agreement, the San Francisco Fire Department initiated a race-conscious and gender-conscious hiring and promotion policy, with goals designed to remedy past discrimination against racial minorities and women.[6] Because of affirmative action, the number of Asian American firefighters increased fivefold during a ten-year period.

HIGHER EDUCATION AND DIVERSITY

In the area of higher education admissions, race-conscious policies are frequently employed to promote diversity within college and university student bodies. Historically, Asian Americans were included with other racial and ethnic minority groups in many higher education affirmative action programs, whether those programs were designed to remedy past discrimination or to promote diversity. In more recent years, however, Asian Americans have not been treated as underrepresented minorities in many affirmative action programs because they have become numerically well represented within student bodies. Indeed, many believe that race-conscious affirmative action programs in higher education are detrimental to Asian Americans because they prevent many Asian American students with strong grades and standardized test scores from being admitted to elite universities.

The assertion that Asian Americans are adequately represented or even overrepresented within college student bodies has generated a number of difficult questions. During the late 1980s and 1990s, for example, the federal government investigated a number of admissions programs, including a number of Ivy League schools and major research universities such as UCLA and the University of California–Berkeley, that were alleged to be discriminating against Asian American applicants because of the perception that there were too many Asians within undergraduate and graduate student bodies.[7] Although most of these programs were found not to be discriminating against Asian American students, a handful of practices were problematic. The graduate mathematics program at UCLA, for example, was found by the Department of Education's Office for Civil Rights to be illegally favoring white applicants over Asian American applicants, and the admissions policy was subsequently revised.

The exclusion of Asian Americans from affirmative action programs is even more complicated because some Asian ethnic groups continue to suffer economic and social disadvantage and are not well represented within college student bodies. For example, Southeast Asian groups, including Vietnamese, Cambodian, Laotian, and Hmong, have lower levels of grade completion and fall below the national average for high school graduation and college completion. Yet because Asian Americans are typically treated as a single racial group for affirmative action purposes, members of underrepresented Asian American subgroups are often omitted from university affirmative action programs.

Debates within the Asian American community itself have also complicated the picture. Many civil rights groups continue to be strong advocates for the inclusion of Asian Americans in higher education affirmative action programs, but some organizations have taken the position that Asian Americans have been harmed by affirmative action because they have been denied seats in selective colleges and universities that have gone to other racial minority applicants. For example, during the litigation of the University of Michigan affirmative action cases in the Supreme Court in 2003, the Asian American Legal Foundation, based in northern California, submitted a friend-of-the-court brief in support of the plaintiffs who were challenging the university's affirmative action policies; leading civil rights organizations such as the Asian American Justice Center, however, took the position in support of the university's affirmative action programs.[8]

The questions generated by Asian American admissions in higher education have led to calls for adopting other types of admissions policies, including class-based affirmative action policies that focus on family income and socioeconomic status rather than on race. Yet, class-based affirmative action policies have been shown to be less effective than race-conscious policies in promoting racial diversity, and the benefits of diversity achieved through race-conscious admissions have been fully recognized by the Supreme Court. Race-conscious policies are thus likely to be used for many years at selective universities. Whether Asian Americans as a whole will continue to be excluded from programs, or whether specific Asian subgroups, based on socioeconomic disadvantage as well as racial and ethnic considerations, will be included in affirmative action programs remains an open question.

OUTLOOK

Affirmative action programs can be expected to generate controversy as the nation continues to struggle with racial inequality and denials of equal opportunity. Opponents of affirmative action can be expected to challenge policies that push the legal limits set by the Supreme Court in recent years, and attempts to eliminate affirmative action at the state and local level—whether through legislation or ballot initiatives—are expected to continue in many parts of the country. Controversies within the Asian American community concerning affirmative action, especially in the arena of higher education, will no doubt remain prominent as well. Yet, affirmative action has led to genuine progress for Asian Americans in a host of arenas, and its supporters can be expected to continue to fight for its retention.

FURTHER READING

Asian American Justice Center. http://www.advancingequality.org.

Kidder, William C. "Situating Asian Pacific Americans in the Law School Affirmative Action Debate: Empirical Facts About Thernstrom's Rhetorical Acts," *Asian Law Journal* 7 (2000): 29–68.

Takagi, Dana Y. *The Retreat from Race: Asian-American Admissions and Racial Politics.* New Brunswick, N.J.: Rutgers University Press, 1992.

United States Commission on Civil Rights. *Civil Rights Issues Facing Asian Americans in the 1990s.* Washington, DC, February 1992.

Wu, Frank H. *Yellow: Race in America Beyond Black and White.* New York: Basic Books, 2002.

Yamamoto, Eric, Margaret Chon, Carol L. Izumi, Jerry Kang and Frank Wu. *Race, Rights and Reparation: Law and the Japanese American Internment*. Gaithersburg: Aspen Law & Business, 2001.

NOTES

1. 539 U.S. 306 (2003).

2. 539 U.S. 244 (2003).

3. United States Commission on Civil Rights. *Civil Rights Issues Facing Asian Americans in the 1990s.* (Washington, DC, February 1992).

4. American Civil Liberties Union of Southern California, *Of the Community and For the Community: Racial and Gender Integration in Southern California Police and Fire Departments* (Los Angeles: American Civil Liberties Union of Southern California, 1994).

5. City and County of San Francisco, *Progress Report: Minority/Women/Local Business Enterprise Ordinance II* (San Francisco: City and County of San Francisco, 1990), 14.

6. *United States v. City and County of San Francisco,* 696 F. Supp. 1287 (N.D. Cal. 1988).

7. Dana Y. Takagi, *The Retreat from Race: Asian-American Admissions and Racial Politics* (New Brunswick, N.J.: Rutgers University Press, 1992), 102–139.

8. David G. Savage, "Affirmative Action Case Splits Asian Americans; University's Policy, Set for Debate in High Court, Is Seen as Limited and Needed, Lawyers Say," *Los Angeles Times,* March 30, 2003, A13.

CIVIL RIGHTS AND COMMUNITY LEGAL ADVOCACY

Angelo Ancheta

Civil rights advocacy has a long history within Asian American communities, and lawyers and legal organizations have played key roles in advocacy efforts, beginning with the earliest challenges to racial segregation and anti-Asian immigration laws in the nineteenth century and moving forward into this century. Contemporary legal advocates continue to address an array of civil rights issues, such as racial violence, immigrants' rights, language access, citizenship and political empowerment, and affirmative action. National organizations such as the Asian American Justice Center, as well as local, state, and regional organizations throughout the United States, employ an array of strategies, including litigation, community education, community organizing, legislative advocacy, media advocacy, and community-based research and training to address ongoing civil rights issues.

LEADING ISSUES

During multiple decades, Asian Americans have challenged racially discriminatory laws and policies through litigation in the federal and state courts, including the U.S. Supreme Court. Lawsuits contesting exclusionary immigration laws, the internment of Japanese Americans during World War II, and segregation laws involving education, housing, marriage, and other key areas of American life were all actively litigated. Although many early cases challenging anti-Asian laws were unsuccessful, the litigation of key issues helped pave the way for groundbreaking changes in the laws. For example, landmark cases such as *Yick Wo v. Hopkins,* the 1886 case which established basic constitutional protections for noncitizens under the Equal Protection Clause of the Fourteenth Amendment, grew out of legal challenges to racial segregation and violations of Asian Americans' rights.[1]

With the shift in constitutional norms following the Supreme Court's *Brown v. Board of Education* decision in 1954, the emergence of civil rights movements in the 1950s and 1960s, and the development of antidiscrimination laws protecting racial minorities—coupled with the growth of Asian American immigrant populations in more recent years—civil rights advocacy has confronted not only problems involving explicit racial discrimination but expanded to include a broad range of problems affecting Asian Americans:

- Immigration Status and Citizenship: Addressing the rights of Asian American immigrants, both lawful and undocumented, who are more vulnerable to discrimination and abridgments of their rights because of their noncitizen status.
- National Security Discrimination: Challenging overinclusive or unconstitutional policies that abridge the rights of individuals who are members of groups that have been targeted for antiterrorism and other national security efforts.
- Language Access: Seeking increased accommodations and language access for immigrants who are limited English proficient through the provision of interpreters, translated materials, and other forms of assistance.
- Glass Ceiling Issues: Promoting private- and public-sector employment policies that address the underrepresentation of Asian Americans in positions of leadership and management.
- Political Empowerment: Enforcing election and redistricting policies that promote voting rights and greater access to the political process.
- Accurate Census Counts and Data Collection: Advocating for thorough and accurate data collection related to Asian American communities to address problems of undercounting and to ensure proper political representation and allocation of government resources.
- Interracial and Interminority Relations: Pursuing policies that promote interracial harmony and improved relations between racial and ethnic minority groups.
- Defense of Race-Conscious Policies: Promoting policies that provide greater opportunities for Asian Americans and other minorities, such as affirmative action and voluntary school desegregation.

Nonetheless, problems of overt racial discrimination, such as hate violence and discrimination in housing and employment, continue to afflict Asian American communities, and advocacy to strengthen government enforcement and the prosecution of civil rights violations remains a high priority for many organizations and advocates.

MODELS OF ADVOCACY

Litigation and court-centered strategies have dominated the agendas of many civil rights organizations, and law reform efforts pioneered by leading groups such as the NAACP Legal Defense and Educational Fund, whose work culminated in *Brown v. Board of Education,* have served as a basic model for advocacy on behalf of Asian Americans and other minority groups. For example, in *Lau v. Nichols,* the 1974 case establishing educational rights for limited–English-proficient students under Title VI of the Civil Rights Act of 1964, community-based advocates and parents worked closely with legal aid lawyers to challenge school policies that had ignored the learning needs of Chinese American students with limited English proficiency; the school district had denied the students additional instruction to learn English and to develop competency for learning other subjects.[2] The *Lau* case, in turn, established broader frameworks for the civil rights of English-language learners that eventually led to federal legislation, as well as state and local policies, promoting bilingual education and other forms of supplemental language instruction.

Litigation has been only one element, however, that legal advocates have employed in contemporary civil rights work. Because the U.S. Supreme Court and other federal courts have become increasingly conservative in recent years, strategies that focus on public education, community organizing, lobbying, and other forms of policy advocacy have become important supplements to litigation. During the 1970s, for example, legislative advocacy to expand the federal Voting Rights Act to include explicit coverage for language minority groups and to establish new requirements for multilingual assistance for limited–English-proficient voters came on the heels of the *Lau* case, but it was cemented by the lobbying and educational work of civil rights organizations in the Asian American, Latino, and Native American communities.

Multipronged strategies that combine litigation, education and organizing, media relations, and lobbying are typically employed in tandem to advance civil rights issues. During the 1980s, for example, efforts to gain redress and reparations for Japanese Americans who were interned during World War II took on multiple dimensions over the course of the decade. Public education and organizing efforts were developed within Asian American communities and through coalitions with various civil rights, labor, and social justice groups. A government-sponsored commission engaged in fact-finding and developed public education strategies and policy recommendations for redress. Litigation seeking internment-related monetary damages through the courts was initiated, as was litigation challenging the wartime convictions of key individuals who violated curfew and exclusion orders during the war. These multiple efforts combined with strong legislative advocacy to culminate in the enactment of the Civil Liberties Act of 1988, the federal legislation that granted redress payments to each surviving internee and created an educational fund to inform the public about the internment and to prevent future occurrences.

Lawyers, Judges, and Law Students

The number of Asian Americans in law schools and in the legal profession has increased steadily since the 1960s, when opportunities to obtain a legal education and to move into the profession were expanded through equal opportunity programs and affirmative action.

Law school enrollments, for example, rose from 1.2 percent of the nation's students in the 1977–78 academic year to 2.2 percent in the 1987–88 year, and to 6.0 percent in the 1997–98 year.[1] In the 2003–04 year, Asian Americans constituted 7.3 percent of the law students nationwide. Much of this growth has occurred even though Asian Americans are now excluded from many affirmative action programs designed to increase the representation of racial minority groups.

Asian Americans have entered the legal profession in increasing numbers as well. In 2000, Asian Americans comprised 2.3 percent of the lawyers nationwide, up from 1.4 percent in 1990. In 2002, Asian Americans made up 7.9 percent of the federal government lawyers, and in 2003, Asian American law firm associates comprised more than 48 percent of the minority associates at the nation's 250 largest law firms.

Still, Asian American representation in the legal profession falls below Asian American representation in other professions. In 2000, for example, while 2.3 percent of the nation's lawyers were Asian American, 3.6 percent of the civilian workforce was Asian American, and 14.9 percent of physicians/surgeons, 10.3 percent of computer scientists, 7.4 percent of accountants, and 8.8 percent of dentists were Asian Americans.

Progress has been even slower in some key sectors of the law, where Asian Americans constitute a minute percentage of the membership. For example, among federal judgeships, which include some of the most prestigious judicial positions, such as the U.S. Supreme Court and the U.S. Courts of Appeals, Asian Americans are seriously underrepresented. There has never been an Asian American on the U.S. Supreme Court, and Asian Americans fill less than 1 percent of the more than 800 active federal judgeships in the country. Similarly, only 1.8 percent of the full professors at the nation's law schools were Asian American in 2001–02, and less than 1 percent of the law school deans were Asian American.

Yet, as the population of Asian Americans increases nationwide and the number of Asian American law school graduates grows as well, one can expect that the disparities and gaps in some of these important positions will be bridged, and Asian Americans will fill the ranks of judgeships, professorships, and other key positions in increasing numbers.

1. Statistics are from Elizabeth Chambliss, *Miles to Go: Progress of Minorities in the Legal Profession* (Chicago: American Bar Association, 2004).

—Angelo Ancheta

LEGAL ORGANIZATIONS

Legal organizations play a central role in civil rights advocacy on behalf of Asian Americans. While they are not the sole source of civil rights activity, legal organizations focusing on Asian American communities often play key positions in developing civil rights initiatives, coordinating strategies, and implementing legal reforms when those strategies require use of the courts and litigation.

A number of community-based legal organizations founded in the 1970s, such as the San Francisco–based Asian Law Caucus, the New York City–based Asian American Legal Defense and Educational Fund, and the San Jose–based Asian Law Alliance, have long histories of civil rights advocacy focusing on racial discrimination, immigrant rights, labor rights, hate violence, and political empowerment. The Los Angeles–based Asian Pacific American Legal Center of Southern California, founded in the 1980s, has developed similar programs and has expanded its activities to include areas such as community-based research initiatives and leadership training in interethnic relations. Coalitions of organizations are also key elements in implementing civil rights strategies: in California, for example, Asian Americans for Civil Rights and Equality has been a joint project of Chinese for Affirmative Action, the Asian Law Caucus, and the Asian Pacific American Legal Center that focuses on legislative advocacy in the state capital of Sacramento.

On the national level, civil rights legal organizations play an important role in coordinating national strategies and working with coalitions focusing on major litigation or federal legislation. Founded in the mid-1990s, the Washington, DC–based Asian American Justice Center (formerly the National Asian Pacific American Legal Consortium) has become a leading national organization for both policy advocacy, strategy development and research, and cooperative activities with regional affiliates such as the Asian Law Caucus, the Asian Pacific American Legal Center, and the Chicago-based Asian American Institute, as well as an array of community partner organizations throughout the country. Working in conjunction with social justice groups involved in the DC-based Leadership Conference on Civil Rights, the Asian American Justice Center is also a leading advocate for federal civil rights legislation addressing Asian American interests and the interests of other groups suffering discrimination.

FURTHER READING

Ancheta, Angelo N. *Race, Rights, and the Asian American Experience.* 2nd ed. New Brunswick, N.J.: Rutgers University Press, 2006.
Asian American Institute. http://www.aaichicago.org.
Asian American Justice Center. http:// www.advancingequality.org.
Asian American Legal Defense and Educational Fund. http://www.aaldef.org.
Asian Law Alliance. http://www.asianlawalliance.org.
Asian Law Caucus. http:// www.asianlawcaucus.org.

Yamamoto, Eric, Margaret Chon, Carol L. Izumi, Jerry Kang and Frank Wu. *Race, Rights and Reparation: Law and the Japanese American Internment.* Gaithersburg, MD: Aspen Law & Business, 2001.

NOTES

1. 118 U.S. 356 (1886).
2. 414 U.S. 563 (1974).

CULTURAL DEFENSE

Angelo Ancheta

A "cultural defense" refers to the use of evidence related to a criminal defendant's culture that attempts to excuse or to lessen a criminal charge against the defendant. A cultural defense can also be used to attempt to reduce the defendant's sentence after pleading guilty to a crime or after being convicted. While no American jurisdictions formally recognize a cultural defense, cultural evidence has been introduced in a number of prominent criminal cases involving Asian immigrant defendants, with mixed success.

Assertions of a cultural defense have been controversial. Proponents suggest that accepting a cultural defense in appropriate cases recognizes legitimate cultural differences among immigrant groups and demonstrates a commitment within the legal system to a pluralistic society. Opponents of cultural defenses, however, have proposed that they promote stereotypes of immigrants and that they violate antidiscrimination principles and constitutional requirements of equal protection under the law by favoring immigrants and ethnic minorities over other Americans.

Opponents have also argued against admitting evidence of cultural difference because it can further harm a victim of violence, who is often a woman or a child; in cases involving male defendants who have injured or killed female victims, accepting a cultural defense may appear to condone the violence. Despite their controversial nature, cultural defenses can be expected to appear in future criminal cases involving immigrants whose home-country cultural norms differ in significant ways from American cultural norms.

CONTEXT

Because most criminal offenses require proof of both an illegal act and a particular mental state, defendants may offer evidence of cultural differences to show that they lacked the necessary mental state required to be convicted of a particular crime. A cultural defense can also be used to strengthen a traditional legal defense, such as self-defense or insanity. A defendant may also offer cultural evidence in support of obtaining a more lenient sentence.

In *People v. Chen,* for example, a Chinese immigrant killed his wife by striking her multiple times with a claw hammer after discovering her marital infidelity. Chen was charged with second-degree murder for the killing.[1] At trial, Chen's attorney called on the testimony of a cultural anthropologist who argued that the defendant's violent reaction to his wife's confession of infidelity was not unusual, given his Chinese cultural background. The anthropologist proposed that in traditional Chinese culture, a man might threaten to kill his wife upon learning of her infidelity, but community safeguards would stop him from carrying out his threat; because Chen was in the United States, the community safeguards were not in place to prevent the killing.

The judge in the case accepted the expert testimony and acquitted Chen of murder; instead, the judge found Chen guilty of the lesser charge of manslaughter and sentenced him to five years of probation. The judge explained that if the defendant had been born and raised in America, or if he had been born elsewhere and raised in America, even in the Chinese American community, then the manslaughter conviction would have been inappropriate. According to the judge, the cultural evidence did not excuse the defendant's actions, but it did justify reducing the charge and the sentence.

Although cultural defenses have become most prominent in homicide and assault cases involving Asian immigrants, they can also be asserted in a wide range of cases. Another area where cultural conflicts and criminal defenses have prominence is in the area of animal cruelty law enforcement. Conflicting interests have developed around food preparation and eating customs among Asian immigrants, where preparation of certain dishes that feature fish or amphibians or the consumption of certain animal meats, such as dog meat, has led to charges of animal cruelty. In San Francisco, for example, for a number of years animal rights activists called for the passage of specific animal cruelty laws that would have targeted vendors in the Chinatown area in order to prevent businesses from selling live animals or engaging in particular practices.[2]

PROMINENT CASES

There is little empirical research on the cultural defense because of the lack of systematic data on its use in criminal cases; however, cultural defenses have appeared in a number of well-known cases involving Asian immigrants. For example, in cases involving Asian immigrant women who have attempted to kill themselves and their children in response to a husband's infidelity, cultural evidence has been employed to show that the defendants lacked the necessary mental state to be convicted of murder.

In *People v. Kimura,* a Japanese immigrant woman who had discovered that her husband had been having an extramarital affair attempted to kill herself and her two young children by walking into the Pacific Ocean.[3] Kimura was rescued, but her children drowned. In Japan, the act of parent-child suicide, known as *oyako shinju,* is justified as a practice that can rid a parent of shame and spare children from being left behind without a parent. Kimura was originally charged with first-degree murder and felony child endangerment, but after Japanese American community pressure to acknowledge the cultural basis for *oyako shinju,* she was later allowed to plead guilty to manslaughter and received a sentence of one year in prison and five years probation.

Similarly, in *People v. Wu,* a Chinese immigrant woman killed her nine-year-old child and then tried to kill herself.[4] Wu initially received a murder conviction and was sentenced to a prison term of fifteen years to life. On appeal, she argued that the trial judge had erred by failing to instruct the jury on how her cultural background as a Chinese immigrant might have affected her state of mind when she killed her child. The appeals court agreed and ordered a new trial requiring that the jurors be instructed to consider Wu's cultural background in assessing whether she had the mental state necessary for a murder conviction. Wu was eventually convicted of the lesser charge of voluntary manslaughter and sentenced to eleven years in prison.

Another set of cultural defense cases has involved Hmong American men who have been charged with rape, but who have argued that the acts of sexual intercourse were consensual because of the Hmong custom of "marriage by capture." In *People v. Moua,* a Hmong man was charged with both kidnapping and rape after he took a Hmong woman from her college dormitory room to a family member's house and then engaged in sexual intercourse with her.[5] Moua defended his actions as consistent with the custom of *zij paj niam,* in which a Hmong man takes his future bride from her home, brings her to his home, and then consummates the marriage by engaging in sexual intercourse over her protests.

Moua argued that his cultural background led him to believe honestly and reasonably that the woman had consented to the sexual acts. Because such a belief could serve as an affirmative defense to a rape charge, Moua was eventually allowed to plead guilty to a lesser charge of false imprisonment, for which he received three months in jail and was ordered to pay $1,000 in restitution. "Marriage by capture" cultural defenses have been rejected in other cases involving Hmong men, however, resulting in rape convictions against the defendants; moreover, the practice is no longer widely accepted in the Hmong American community and has been condemned by many Hmong community and religious organizations.

Another well-known case of cultural conflict occurred in Long Beach, CA, when two Cambodian Americans were charged with animal cruelty for bludgeoning a puppy that they eventually ate as part of a meal.[6] The case raised a number of cultural questions about the practice of dog eating, anti-Asian stereotypes, and tensions between traditional cultural belief systems and American legal standards and practices. The defendants asserted that their actions were rooted in culturally specific norms, because dog eating was an acceptable, albeit atypical, practice in Cambodia. Ultimately, the charges of animal cruelty were dismissed, but California law was changed to prohibit the practice.[7] Asian American groups also played a role in ensuring that the law did not reinforce stereotypes about Asian Americans by advocating for the inclusion of a wide range of pet animals, and not only dogs, in the ban.

PROBLEMS

Recent cases provide examples of successful cultural defenses, but they also show how cultural defenses can raise serious problems in obtaining justice for victims of crime and in reinforcing negative racial and sexual stereotypes about Asian Americans. As the leading cases involving cultural defenses show, innocent victims of crime (including spouses, children, and unconsenting partners) are harmed by acts of violence, regardless of the cultural norms and customs that may be driving the defendants to act.

In addition, cultural defenses can undergird incorrect and negative stereotypes about Asian Americans, whether those stereotypes involve the perception that all Asian Americans are foreigners, that Asian cultures are vastly and irreconcilably different from American culture, that Asian women are submissive and subservient, and that extreme and brutal forms of violence are tolerated—and perhaps even encouraged—in some Asian cultures. At the very least, the use of cultural defenses in criminal cases suggests that defendants and their lawyers, while seeking the best outcomes for their clients, must be mindful of the implications of cultural evidence both for the case at hand and for Asian American communities more generally.

FURTHER READING

Ly, Choua. "The Conflict Between Law and Culture: The Case of the Hmong in America," *Wisconsin Law Review* 2001 (2001): 471–499.

Renteln, Alison Dundes. *The Cultural Defense.* New York: Oxford University Press, 2004.

Volpp, Leti. "Cultural Defenses in the Criminal Legal System." http://www.apiahf.org/adidvinstitute/CriticalIssues/volpp.htm.

Volpp, Leti. "(Mis)Identifying Culture: Asian Women and the 'Cultural Defense,'" *Harvard Women's Law Journal* 17 (1994): 57–101.

NOTES

1. No. 87-7774 (Supreme Court, N.Y. County, Dec. 2, 1988).
2. "Assembly Bill Threatens Traditional Markets," May 25, 2000, at http://www.asianweek.com/2000/05/25/assembly-bill-threatens-traditional-markets/.

3. No. A-091133, Superior Court, Los Angeles County, April 24, 1985.

4. 286 Cal. Rptr. 868 (Ct. App. 1991).

5. No. 315972-0, Superior Court, Fresno County, CA, Feb. 7, 1985.

6. Frank H. Wu, *Yellow: Race in American Beyond Black and White* (New York: Basic Books, 2001), 218–226.

7. California Penal Code section 598a.

DOMESTIC VIOLENCE AND IMMIGRANT WOMEN

Angelo Ancheta

Domestic violence is a serious problem cutting across all sectors of American society, but issues affecting Asian immigrant women can be especially challenging because of barriers rooted in culture, language ability, socioeconomic status, and immigration status. Domestic violence is often portrayed within Asian American communities as a nonexistent or marginal problem, and can be treated as if part of a "traditional" element of a community's patriarchal culture. Cultural pressures can also prevent victims of domestic violence from seeking assistance, and the legal system and service providers that help victims of domestic violence are often inadequately equipped to address some of the special problems of language access and cultural difference facing Asian immigrants. Nevertheless, agencies that focus specifically on Asian immigrant women have provided support in many parts of the country, and, increasingly, federal, state, and local government have paid greater attention to problems such as gaining lawful immigration status for women who are victims of domestic violence and related crimes such as human trafficking.

NATURE AND EXTENT OF THE PROBLEM

Statistics on domestic violence among Asian Americans are difficult to obtain and incomplete, but compilations of studies suggest a significant prevalence of domestic violence in many communities. One survey conducted in the late-1990s, for example, found that nearly 13 percent of Asian and Pacific Islander women reported experiencing physical assault by an intimate partner at least once during their lifetime, and that rate was considerably lower than might be expected, likely because of underreporting.[1] Community surveys of individual Asian ethnic groups suggest even higher rates of between 40 and 60 percent of respondents reporting some form physical or emotional abuse during their lifetimes.[2] For example, a 2002 study of South Asian women who were married or in a heterosexual relationship living in the greater Boston area found that more than 40 percent of the women sampled had been physically or sexually abused by the male partners in their lifetime, and more than 36 percent reported having been victimized in the previous year; a study by the Asian Task Force Against Domestic Violence in Boston found that 47 percent of Cambodians, 44 percent of South Asians, and 39 percent of Vietnamese surveyed knew a woman who had been physically abused or injured by her partner.

Although domestic violence transcends lines of race, economic class, religion, education, and immigration status, research suggests that the dynamics of domestic violence in Asian American communities carry added dimensions.[3] Cultural and community pressures may lead both victims and abusers to see abandonment of a relationship and divorce as options that cannot be pursued. Additionally, although spousal abuse is typically seen as the primary source of domestic violence, in many Asian American households there may be multiple abusers within a home, including various in-law relatives, adult siblings, and ex- or new wives; multiple perpetrators can cause increased blame and shame for a victim of domestic violence and can further compound the devaluation of a victim.

Gender roles are often defined much more restrictively within many Asian American households, making it difficult for many women to exercise full control over their own lives. Added problems such as forced marriages, threats to immigration status because a women is dependent on her spouse for lawful status, and problems of sexual violence associated with young women who are victims of human trafficking (including mail-order brides, sex workers, or indentured workers) further complicate the picture.

Domestic violence–related homicides pose another difficult and troubling problem. Homicides include a broader range of deaths carried out through honor killings (killings by family members of a woman or girl who has shamed the family), contract killings, and suicides resulting from longstanding abuse by spouses or in-laws. For example, in July 2008, a Pakistani American living in the Atlanta, GA, area was accused of strangling and killing his twenty-five-year-old daughter because she sought to get out of an arranged marriage that had been initiated in Pakistan but to which she had not fully agreed.

BARRIERS TO SEEKING ASSISTANCE

Community norms can often exacerbate problems of gender violence and domestic abuse.[4] For example, in many Asian American communities, gender discrimination can be directed against girls beginning in early childhood by withholding proper nutrition and nourishment, education, and health care.

Support for batterers, whether implicit or explicit, and the lack of community-based sanctions for domestic violence, can embolden abusive spouses or other members of a victims' household. And community norms can further lock in patterns of domestic violence through blaming and shaming of a victim, through silencing or ignoring calls for help, and through rejecting and even ostracizing victims from a particular community.

Asian immigrants who do seek assistance from the legal system can face additional barriers because of cultural conflicts and access limitations based on their limited English proficiency. Distrust of the police can deter women from seeking official intervention, and difficulties in navigating the family law system to obtain restraining orders, divorces, and child and spousal support payments can further deter victims from continuing with procedures within the legal system. Although jurisdictions with significant Asian and Pacific Islander populations have been providing interpreter services, written translations of materials, and other forms of language assistance to victims of domestic violence, problems often arise when immigrant populations are relatively small and there are limited language resources among law enforcement, the courts, and service providers.

For several years, organizations such as the San Francisco-based Asian Women's Shelter have focused on providing culturally competent and linguistically appropriate services involving safety, food, shelter, advocacy, and other resources for Asian immigrant women.[5] Comprehensive services can be essential because many immigrant women can fall between the cracks in navigating the multiple governmental agencies that address elements of domestic violence, and many agencies may lack the cultural competence and language assistance that immigrants require. Nonprofit legal organizations focusing on Asian American populations also play a key role in providing help in obtaining restraining orders against batterers, processing divorces, and obtaining financial support through child support payments. Yet, resources such as shelter space and long-term transitional services are very limited, and the demand for services can greatly exceed the supply of services among these organizations.

IMMIGRATION STATUS

Asian immigrants who are victims of domestic violence may also face a variety of problems because they lack lawful immigration status or because their continuing lawful status is dependent upon an abusive spouse. For example, a spouse may threaten to withdraw a petition for lawful immigration status in order to maintain control over a domestic violence victim, leaving the victim the difficult choice of either remaining in an unsafe situation in the home or losing lawful immigration status if she decides to seek shelter elsewhere. In other situations, an abuser may threaten to report an undocumented immigrant to the federal authorities and use the threat of removal from the United States as a bargaining tool in an abusive relationship. Options for obtaining lawful immigration status are even more limited when neither the abuser nor the victim possesses lawful status and potential removal from the country becomes a real danger.

With the passage of the federal Violence Against Women Act (VAWA) in 1994, immigration laws have contained more options for victims of domestic violence. For example, under VAWA the spouses and children of U.S. citizens or lawful permanent residents may "self-petition" to obtain lawful permanent residency. The self-petitioning process allows certain battered immigrants to file for immigration relief without a spouse's assistance or knowledge, thus making it possible to seek safety and independence from an abusive spouse. Newer immigration laws have also provided possibilities for obtaining temporary lawful status for immigrants who have suffered abuse because of criminal activities and who can provide assistance to law enforcement. The "U-visa" was created by the Victims of Trafficking and Violence Prevention Act of 2000, and it is available to immigrants who have suffered substantial physical or mental abuse resulting from a wide range of criminal activity and who have been helpful or are likely to be helpful with the investigation or prosecution of a crime. The U-visa provides eligible immigrants with an authorized stay in the United States and employment authorization allowing them to work in the United States.

ADDRESSING PROBLEMS

Reforms within the legal system will continue to focus on strengthening criminal justice enforcement of crimes of domestic violence, improving language and cultural accessibility for Asian immigrants seeking restraining orders and divorces, and addressing issues of lawful immigration status for victims of domestic violence. For example, the U-visa, which is available to some noncitizen victims of domestic violence who assist with criminal investigations and prosecutions, has an extensive list of requirements that can pose challenges for limited–English-speaking immigrants unfamiliar with the legal system and does not guarantee long-term immigration status. Making the process more accessible and clearing paths to lawful permanent residency are important improvements that can aid victims of crimes of domestic violence.

Comprehensive reforms that expand immigrants' ability to access the criminal justice system, the civil justice system to obtain court orders and divorces, and the immigration law system will no doubt provide longer-term solutions for Asian immigrant women who struggle against domestic violence. Yet the root causes and contributing factors of culture and family roles that often complicate domestic violence within Asian immigrant communities will continue to pose challenges both within and outside the legal system. The problems of domestic violence in Asian American communities are longstanding ones that do not have easy or ready solutions. Organizations focusing on domestic violence issues remain committed to advancing agendas that can address the multiple dimensions of domestic violence in immigrant communities.

For example, the Asian & Pacific Islander Institute on Domestic Violence has offered an extensive set of goals and strategies, all of which may be necessary to address the many problems of domestic violence in immigrant communities: raising awareness in Asian and Pacific Islander communities about the damaging effects of domestic violence on individuals, families, and communities; addressing the root causes of violence, the various forms of violence employed, and community complicity in violence; promoting cultural transformation and new social norms; expanding leadership and expertise within communities about prevention, intervention, advocacy, and research; promoting culturally relevant programming, research, and advocacy by identifying promising practices; formulating national policies that foster state and local initiatives to address violence; and strengthening an anti-violence movement by forging links with other communities and organizations.[6]

FURTHER READING

Asian & Pacific Islander Institute on Domestic Violence. http://www.apiahf.org/apidvinstitute/.

Asian & Pacific Islander Institute on Domestic Violence. *National Directory, Asian American, Native Hawaiian and Pacific Islander Domestic Violence Agencies and Programs* (San Francisco: Asian & Pacific Islander American Health Forum, 2008), http://www.apiahf.org/apidvinstitute/PDF/Directory_API_Programs.pdf.

Foo, Lora Jo. *Asian American Women: Issues, Concerns, and Responsive Human and Civil Rights Advocacy* (New York: Ford Foundation, 2003).

NOTES

1. Tjaden, Patricia, and Nancy Thoennes, *Extent, Nature, and Consequences of Intimate Partner Violence,* (Washington, DC: National Institute of Justice and the Centers for Disease Control, July 2000), available at http://www.ncjrs.gov/txtfiles1/nij/181867.txt.

2. Dabby, Firoza Chic, *Gender Violence in Asian & Pacific Islander Communities* (San Francisco, CA: Asian & Pacific Islander American Health Forum, Asian & Pacific Islander Institute on Domestic Violence, 2007), 10–12, available at http://www.apiahf.org/images/stories/Documents/publications_database/Gender_Violence_2-2007.pdf.

3. Dabby, 7–9.

4. Dabby, 9.

5. http://www.sfaws.org/ (Web site of San Francisco–based Asian Women's Shelter, a comprehensive domestic violence shelter and community building program that provides shelter, food, advocacy, and other resources to women and children affected by domestic violence).

6. http://www.apiahf.org/index.php/programs/domestic-violence.html (Web site of Asian & Pacific Islander Institute on Domestic Violence, a national resource center and clearinghouse based at the Asian & Pacific Islander American Health Forum focusing on gender violence in Asian American, Native Hawaiian, and Pacific Islander communities).

HOMELAND SECURITY AND RACISM

Peter Chua

In 2002, the U.S. government reorganized its Immigration and Naturalization Services agency to be part of the new Department of Homeland Security (DHS) to manage and coordinate more effectively antiterrorism, national security, and immigration activities. This reorganization formally ushered in racism in homeland security. This novel form of institutional racism has negatively and disproportionably targeted particular racial and ethnic heritage groups for social exclusion, harassment, and violence, thereby maintaining white racial supremacy. These groups include U.S. Asians such as Pakistanis, Filipinos, Cambodians, and Chinese, in addition to Middle Easterners, Latinos, and Africans who have been typically known to be targets of government monitoring and civil liberties curtailment.

BACKGROUND AND CONTEXTS

The September 11, 2001, events in New York City and other U.S. areas brought destruction, social misery, and the national crystallization of homeland security racist policies. Months after these events, mass media depicted images of government agents searching, interrogating, and detaining individuals as possible so-called foreign terrorists and undesired residents. Those affected ranged from Pakistanis and other Asian individuals with Muslim or Middle Eastern–sounding surnames, and Filipinos working as checkpoint agents and baggage handlers at airports to Chinese immigrant scientists working at national defense laboratories.

The logic and apparatus of homeland security racism draws from earlier anti-nativist practices that consider certain racial and ethnic groups as national outsiders.[1] For example, the U.S. government enacted the Chinese Exclusion Act, criminalized particular "Asian" cultural practices, interned people of Japanese background, and deported U.S. Filipino labor organizers as suspected communists. These antinativist and Eurocentric practices asserted the inadmissibility of cultural group traits common to certain Asian and other groups and the impossibility of assimilation based on these cultural traits.

While earlier legal gains in the Asian American immigrant movement gave the pretense of national openness and societal inclusion of Asians in the United States, restrictive and racist state policies have reemerged since the 1990s. In particular, the 1996 Illegal Immigration Reform and Immigrant Responsibility Act (IIRAIRA), implemented by President Clinton, dramatically derailed immigrant rights by seeking to curtail unauthorized residence in the United States and removing undesirables, including those with legal permanent U.S. residence status.[2]

With the September 11, 2001, events and the 2002 enactment of the Uniting and Strengthening America by Providing Appropriate Tools Required to Intercept and Obstruct Terrorism (USA PATRIOT) Act, the Homeland Security Act, and other similar legislation, President George W. Bush sought to subsume immigration into national security under the pretext of capturing suspected al-Qaeda–linked terrorists. This newer legislation provided the mechanisms and procedures to implement IIRAIRA on a broad national scale under the new DHS. The policy underlying these legislations assumes undesired "foreigners," such as those from Asian Muslim communities, are terrorist suspects and that a broad entrapment net is the optimal approach to safeguard the nation.

PROLIFERATION

Institutional racism results from DHS policies, procedures, and programs that systemically and selectively target particular racial-ethnic communities for harassment, detention, and mass removal.[3] These policies, procedures, and programs have not been enforced uniformly, without regard to racial-ethnicity, cultural heritage, and national origins. Instead, DHS and other government agencies monitor personal cues drawn from physical bodily appearances (such as clothing), markers of group identification (such as birth place, first name, and last name), and racial-ethnic and national-cultural practices (such as food preferences on air travel) to profile and determine the possible conduct of political activities to destabilize governmental institutions. Based on such personal cues, the U.S. government targets individuals and communities for harassment, mass detention, and mass removal.

U.S. Asian communities have been severely affected. The full scope of homeland security racism on these communities has not been fully determined because of the secretive aspects of homeland security activities. Mass media accounts and the release of limited government records demonstrate the extensive network of selected surveillance with the intent to harass, detain, and remove particular racial-ethnic groups.

For example, the government has contracted private air carriers to transport possible terrorists, criminals, and undesirables from national security "immigration" detention centers to their countries of origin or ancestry. These contracts were arranged prior to the capturing of the "criminals." Furthermore, formal agreements with receiving countries have allowed these private carriers to transport the individuals and their families, to land, and to grant those removed some form of legal status of residence in the receiving countries. Cambodian young men who entered the United States as refugees and who had legal resident status provide a notable example of this. These men—many of whom spent their lives in the United States, are not fluent in the Cambodian language, and have no relatives in Cambodia—were deported for suspected gang activities. They were transported to Cambodia via private air carriers, and placed indefinitely in Cambodian prisons for suspected criminal activities in the United States. In this way, the Cambodian government becomes a strong ally of the United States in its war against global terror and, as a result, garners favorable economic and humanitarian benefits from the United States.

Removal is one of the severe examples of racism in homeland security. Formally, DHS considered inadmissibility and deportation as two forms of removal. Inadmissibility usually occurs at the port of entry when DHS officers do not allow tourists, U.S. legal residents, or U.S. citizens to enter or return to the U.S. because of violation of federal laws, certain "inadmissible" convictions, or suspected security, criminal and health reasons. These officers rely on government electronic databases—which bring together demographic characteristics, corporate information (involving credit cards, banks, air travel, and so on), and governmental details (from DHS, the Internal Revenue Service, Social Security, public schools, employment records, public library, and so on)—to flag people who would be inadmissible. Once inadmissible, an individual has to initiate the challenge of database errors from outside the United States.

Regardless of legal resident status, individuals can be deported because of certain criminal convictions, procedural violations, or deemed security risks. The USA PATRIOT Act expands grounds for deportation and detention to include U.S. citizens. Detention during the processes of inadmissibility and deportation can be short-term, extended, or indefinite.

The post–September 11, 2001, effect of homeland security racism can be seen in the analysis of DHS removal data from 2001 to 2003. Filipinos and Pakistanis residing in the United States were systematically targeted for deportation. Filipinos were ranked seventh for "noncriminals" removed, with one hundred people removed in 2001 and increases of more than fifty each year in the following two years; Pakistanis were ranked ninth. The others at the top of the list include those with Lebanese, Egyptian, Jordanian, and Moroccan heritage. In the case of U.S. Filipinos, there was a 65 percent increase of removal. In contrast, for all groups combined, there was only a 5 percent increase. This is significant because it shows that the U.S. Filipinos are removed at a greater rate than the overall removal rate. A significant number of U.S. Filipinos who were removed were permanent residents. More than 42 percent had legal documents, and they were removed because of felony convictions. DHS stopped making public these figures after 2003. In total in 2003, DHS expected to remove 85,000 Filipinos.

The experiential impacts of racism in homeland security have been far-reaching. Many who have been targeted for mass removal face greater uncertainty. They have been caught by surprise with immediate deportation, inadmissibility, and detention, without a sense of their human rights and without economic resources to respond adequately. Since the implementation of these, they have lacked adequate understanding, capable legal counsel, and adequate due process.

Individuals and families have faced greater economic and social hardships. Some, if not all, family members have lost jobs, homes, and economic security. Their careers and schooling are interrupted. They have lacked support from friends and neighbors because of racial, religious, and political stigmas. While isolated, they have lacked family and community networks, forcing spouses and children to rebuild their lives alone. Some have sought greater support and services from public assistance and underfunded local agencies.

As a result, racism in homeland security has made it difficult for Asians living in the United States, regardless of citizenship status. They have been

Amardeep Singh, left, legal director of the Sikh Coalition, discusses a new policy by the Metropolitan Transit Authority (MTA) that requires Sikh employees to wear MTA logos on their turbans, during a news conference in 2005 in New York. Five Sikh station agents announced their intention to file discrimination charges against the MTA. The Sikh workers charge that a post-9/11 policy requiring them to brand their turbans with an MTA logo amounts to religious discrimination, and to put an MTA logo on their turban would be equivalent to asking a Christian to put the logo on the cross. (AP Photo/Julie Jacobson)

unduly targeted for unjust mass detention and removals and placed under detrimental legal uncertainties. They have faced greater family hardships and have been living through legislatively generated fear and harassment.

While racism in homeland security remains invisible to many, some grassroots community organizations have been transforming themselves from simply focusing on immigrant rights and citizenship advocacy to more broadly addressing homeland security criminalization, incarceration, and racism. Instead of simply demanding comprehensive immigration reform, the organizations have been considering the need to demand for the dismantling of DHS and termination of racist practices. They have been forging a broader struggle against the increasing suspension of civil liberties by the U.S. government and organizing for social justice and their human rights and security.

FURTHER READING

Bâli, Ash Ü. "Scapegoating the Vulnerable: Preventive Detention of Immigrants in America's 'War or Terror.' " In Austin Sarat, ed, *Studies in Law, Politics, and Society*, 38, Greenwich, CT: JAI Press, 2006: 25–69.

Criminal and Deportation Defense. The National Immigration Project. http://www .nationalimmigrationproject.org/CrimPage/CrimPage.html.

Hing, Bill Ong. *Defining America through Immigration Policy*. Philadelphia: Temple University Press, 2004.

Puar, Jasbir K. and Amit Rai. "Monster, Terrorist, Fag: The War on Terrorism and the Production of Docile Patriots." *Social Text* 72 (2002): 117–148.

NOTES

1. See Mae M. Ngai, *Impossible Subjects: Illegal Aliens and the Making of Modern America.* (Princeton, NJ: Princeton University Press, 2004), 1–14.

2. See Edward W. Park and John W. Park. *Probationary Americans: Contemporary Immigration Policies and the Shaping of Asian American Communities.* (New York: Routledge. 2005), 45–62.

3. See Critical Filipina and Filipino Studies Collective, *Resisting Homeland Security: Organizing Against Unjust Removal of U.S. Filipinos* (San Jose, CA: Critical Filipina and Filipino Studies Collective and the National Alliance for Filipino Concerns, 2004).

LANGUAGE RIGHTS AND LANGUAGE DISCRIMINATION

Angelo Ancheta

For many Asian Americans, lacking proficiency in the English language poses a serious barrier to full participation in American life. The inability to communicate well in English implies having difficulty in school, lacking access to many jobs and areas of business, facing serious barriers in accessing the range of public services, including emergency services and health care, and limitations in exercising basic political rights, such as the right to vote. Providing equal language access to Asian immigrants poses an especially significant challenge for government and other institutions because of the multiplicity of Asian languages; there is no single Asian language, and members of some Asian ethnic groups often speak entirely different dialects and languages.

Consequently, the protections of the law and the legal system for limited–English-speaking individuals are often incomplete, and various forms of discrimination have emerged because of the growth of immigrant communities. Federal civil rights laws guaranteeing degrees of language assistance can be found in areas such as public education, criminal justice, and voting, but there are also gaps in many key areas such as health care and social services. In addition, resentment and hostility to immigrants has generated various types of language discrimination, including "Official English" laws making English the official language of government, English-only policies at workplaces, and accent-based discrimination.

LANGUAGE ACCESS AND LANGUAGE RIGHTS

The U.S. Supreme Court's landmark case of *Lau v. Nichols,* decided in 1974, signaled a major shift in the interpretation of civil rights laws and the recognition of language difference as a basis for violations of federal rights.[1] In *Lau,* the Supreme Court addressed the question of whether the failure of the San Francisco Unified School district to offer significant language assistance to nearly 3,000 limited–English-speaking Chinese American students violated Title VI of the Civil Rights Act of 1964, which prohibits discrimination based on race or national origin by programs receiving federal funding. The Court ruled that the school district's refusal to take appropriate action to help the students overcome language barriers was a form of national origin discrimination that deprived them of equal educational opportunity.

The *Lau* decision did not require specific types of instruction, such as bilingual education, but it helped usher in language assistance programs in the nation's public school systems and led to reforms in a number of areas of law, including the criminal justice system and in voting. For example, because of legislation first added to the federal Voting Rights Act during the mid-1970s, many U.S. counties with sizable language minority populations are required to provide language assistance in Asian languages based on satisfying a triggering formula and census data requirements. After the 2000 Census, the County of Los Angeles, for example, was required to provide translated ballots and election materials, as well as oral assistance, to five large Asian language minority groups (Chinese, Filipino, Japanese, Korean, and Vietnamese).

Similarly, Executive Order 13166, issued by President Clinton in 2000, requires federal agencies to assess services provided to limited–English-proficient individuals and to develop adequate plans and guidelines to ensure meaningful access to agency services. Executive Order 13166 also requires that federal agencies ensure that recipients of federal funding, including many state and local government agencies, provide meaningful access to limited–English-proficient applicants and beneficiaries. Consequently, service providers in areas such as health care, social services, and criminal justice must provide language assistance through translated materials and interpreter services.

Yet, many guarantees of language rights are incomplete because of limitations in the law and because of the difficulty of covering the wide array of languages spoken in Asian American communities. The guarantees of *Lau* have not been extended to all areas of law, and national policies such as Executive 13166 can still have gaps in individual agency guidelines and services. And even with the requirements of *Lau* and federal law, supplemental language instruction in public education is not applied consistently across the country. Some states have even enacted laws that mandate pedagogically questionable "immersion" methods as the required form of instruction for limited–English-proficient students. For example, Proposition 227 was passed in 1998 by the voters of California, and similar ballot measures were passed in Arizona in 2001 and in Massachusetts in 2002; these initiatives adopt a one-size-fits-all model of instruction that requires English-language acquisition within the course of a year, even though acquiring the necessary English language skills to perform on the same level as native speakers can take a much longer amount of time and many Asian American students can be left behind their classmates.

The problem of multiple Asian languages also results in the underaddressing of language needs. For example, many Asian American students who belong to smaller language groups are not able to gain access to full bilingual education services that are available to larger language groups. Language assistance in voting is only mandated for language groups that meet certain thresholds; groups below the thresholds are not required to receive language assistance, and the right to vote can be compromised. For example, in Los Angeles County, groups such as Cambodians and Laotians have sizable populations in some areas of the county, but in the aggregate may not have sufficient numbers to trigger the language assistance requirements of the Voting Rights Act. And assistance for key government services such as medical care can be abridged because institutions lack the capacity to address the needs of smaller language groups, particularly among populations such as the Hmong, who lack a written language tradition.

LANGUAGE DISCRIMINATION

Language-based discrimination is also a common problem associated with limited English proficiency. For example, the differential treatment of individuals who are non–English-speaking or limited–English-speaking can lead to unlawful discrimination in situations where a certain degree of English proficiency is not necessary—such as when a high level of proficiency is required for a job in which English communication skills are not truly essential. In recent years, language discrimination has also come in the form of English-only laws and policies that limit the use of languages other than English in particular settings, as well as policies that discriminate on the basis of language-related characteristics such as accent.

Beginning in the 1980s, a number of states and localities began enacting "Official English" laws in response to concerns that the increasing use of foreign languages in immigrant communities had diminished both the stature of the English language and the acquisition of English by immigrants. Although the laws varied in content—ranging from the merely symbolic to establishing significant limits on the use of non-English languages by government employees and curtailing the development of government materials in other languages—they were designed largely to assert the primacy of English over other languages. For example, in 1986, the voters of California enacted Proposition 63, which made English the official language of the state but did not prohibit the use of languages other than English in the provision of government services or in government workplaces. On the other hand, in 1988 the voters of Arizona enacted Proposition 106, which required all levels of state and local government to "act in English and no other language." Because of the severe restrictions on the use of languages other than English by the government, the Arizona law was challenged in federal and state court and ultimately struck down as unconstitutional by the Arizona Supreme Court.[2]

Some jurisdictions with large numbers of Asian American businesses also developed laws that limited the uses of Asian languages on business signs;

although motivated in part to ensure access for emergency police and fire services, English-mandated signage laws represented attempts to suppress Asian languages in those business areas dominated by Asian immigrants. For example, in the late 1980s, the Southern California city of Monterey Park, a largely suburban community with a sizable Asian American population, passed an ordinance requiring that business signs be posted in English, along with a moratorium on new construction that effectively blocked the building of many Asian American businesses. The law was enacted largely in response to the influx of Chinese American businesses and the use of signs written in Chinese. A change in the membership of the city council that included Chinese Americans who opposed the ordinance led to the law's eventual repeal.

Legal challenges based on the First Amendment and other constitutional grounds have also tempered some of the harsher laws. In *Asian American Business Group v. City of Pomona,* for example, a federal court struck down a city ordinance that required local businesses displaying "foreign alphabetical characters" to also devote one-half of the area of a sign to advertising in English.[3] The court ruled that the Pomona law violated both the First Amendment and the Equal Protection Clause of the Fourteenth Amendment because the choice of language is an expression of national origin and culture, the ordinance discriminated on the basis of national origin, and the city's interest in providing emergency services could just as easily have been accomplished through a requirement that a street number be posted rather than requiring that half the sign contain English. Nonetheless, many Official English laws remain on the books, and proposals to adopt new laws continue to be circulated.

English-only policies also commonly appear in employment settings, where employers limit the uses of other languages to serve a core business need such as preventing accidents, as well as to maintain employer interests in workplace harmony and positive employee relations. Federal regulations have linked English-only policies to national origin discrimination under Title VII of the Civil Rights Act of 1964; English-only rules are considered illegal in most instances, unless they serve a business necessity designed to promote workplace safety, efficiency, or effective communications with customers. English-only rules that impose a complete ban on the use of other languages, even during break hours, are likely to be illegal. Still, some employment policies limiting the use of languages other than English have been upheld; for example, in *Dimaranan v. Pomona Valley Hospital Medical Center,* a "no-Tagalog" rule that targeted Filipino nurses was ruled not to be national origin discrimination because the court concluded that limits on Tagalog were necessary to maintain communication and conformity within the workplace.[4]

Accent discrimination has also been a common form of discrimination against Asian Americans, even those who are fully fluent in English but still possess a non-American accent because English is their second or third language. In *Carino v. University of Oklahoma Board of Regents,* for example, a federal court concluded that a Filipino American who was unlawfully demoted from his position as a supervisor and was not considered for a position in a new facility suffered discrimination based on his Filipino accent.[5] Nevertheless, accent discrimination has been upheld as a legitimate employer decision when oral communication skills are necessary to perform job duties and the person's accent materially interferes with the ability to perform job duties.

Language rights and language discrimination issues are expected to be ongoing civil rights issues for Asian Americans as immigrant populations continue to grow. Community organizations, as well as national advocacy groups such as the Asian American Justice Center and the Asian and Pacific Islander American Health Forum, have made language access a high priority and continue to advocate for the expansion of language rights and the elimination of English-only laws and policies. As immigrant language groups increase in size and number, their inclusion in programs that guarantee language access and assistance should also expand, but racial and ethnic tensions may also make language discrimination more problematic as governmental bodies and private-sector institutions impose policies that limit the use of languages other than English.

FURTHER READING

Asian American Justice Center. http://www.advancingequality.org.

Asian and Pacific Islander American Health Forum. http://www.apiahf.org.

Crawford, James. *Hold Your Tongue: Bilingualism and the Politics of "English Only."* Reading, Mass.: Addison-Wesley Publishing Co., 1992.

Crawford, James, ed. *Language Loyalties: A Source Book on the Official English Controversy.* Chicago: University of Chicago Press, 1992.

Magpantay, Glenn D. "Asian American Access to the Vote: The Language Assistance Provisions (Section 203) of the Voting Rights Act and Beyond," *Asian Law Journal* 11 (2004): 31–56.

NOTES

1. 414 U.S. 563 (1974).
2. Ruiz v. Hull, 191 Ariz. 441, 957 P.2d 984 (1998).
3. 716 F. Supp. 1328 (C.D. Cal. 1989).
4. 775 F. Supp. 338 (C.D. Cal. 1991).
5. 750 F.2d 815 (10th Cir. 1984).

PRISONERS

Angela E. Oh and Karen Umemoto

Asian Americans and Pacific Islanders (API) have been among the growing prison population in the United States. From 1980 to 1999, the national prison population increased fourfold, from 330,000 to nearly 1.4 million, and the incarceration rate during that same time increased from about 140 to 476 per 100,000 residents.[1] By the early 2000s, 600,000 to 700,000 individuals were being released annually from state and federal prisons.[2] Many prisoners who return home often have difficulties reconnecting with jobs, housing, and their families or have substance abuse and health problems. Many are returned to prison for new crimes or parole violations. Within three years of release, nearly two-thirds of released prisoners are rearrested for a felony or serious misdemeanor. Such high recidivism rates translate into new victimizations each year. While incarcerated, few gain the skills and rehabilitative treatment needed to successfully reintegrate upon their release. Public health data also show that reentering prisoners are disproportionately afflicted with chronic health problems and communicable diseases.

INMATE ESTIMATES

There are different estimates of the number of API prisoners due to varied methods of documentation and data collection. According to the "1997 Survey of Inmates in State and Federal Correctional Facilities" conducted for the U.S. Department of Justice, API male inmates comprised 3.4 percent of the California state prison population and 1.3 percent of the total U.S. state prison population.[3] According to the 2000 U.S. Census, APIs comprise approximately

13 percent of the California population and 4.5 percent of the U.S. population.[4] The proportion of APIs among the imprisoned population in the U.S. as a whole is lower than their representation in the overall population, when grouped as one single racial category of "Asian American and Pacific Islander." In Hawai'i, however, the proportion of API prisoners is close to their share of the overall population, comprising two-thirds of the inmate population. According to the 2000 Census, Asian Americans and Pacific Islanders (both full and part) comprise approximately 70.8 percent of the Hawai'i state population.[5]

In Hawai'i, there is a disproportionate number of Native Hawaiians in prison (Table 1). This number is somewhat inflated because of the fact that, unlike other ethnic groups, anyone who has any Native Hawaiian ancestry is counted fully as Native Hawaiian despite the fact that almost all are of mixed ancestry. Disproportionate confinement cannot be separated from the effects of colonialism and the displacement of Hawaiians from their native lands. Native Hawaiians, like other indigenous peoples, score lowest on the major indicators of economic and physical well-being among the various ethnic groups in the state. In a study of criminal justice and Hawaiians in the 1990s, Hawaiians comprised nearly 40 percent of prison admissions while at that time comprising only 18.6 percent of the state's males aged 19 to 35. During the 1980s, the prison population in Hawai'i had been rising approximately 18 percent per year. The study also found that the odds in favor of incarceration, longer sentences, and rearrests were greater for Hawaiians for most felony offense types.[6]

Table 1. Number and Percentage of Prisoners in Hawai'i by Race or Ethnicity, 2004

Ethnic or Racial Group	Number	Percentage
Hawaiian (full or part)	1,708	41.2
Caucasian	884	21.3
Filipino	513	12.4
Samoan	216	5.2
Japanese	202	4.9
African American	180	4.3
Hispanic	107	2.6
Chinese	42	1.0
Other Pacific Islander	23	0.6
Native American	22	0.5
Korean	21	0.5
Unknown/Other	228	5.5
Total	4,146	100

Source: State of Hawai'i, Department of Public Safety, 2004.

REENTRY IMPACT ON COMMUNITIES

In the continental United States, immigrant and refugee communities often bear the biggest impact of API prisoner reentry. In California, for example, 64.6 percent of API prisoners are immigrants and refugees. Among API prisoners in California, the largest percentages of inmates are Vietnamese (21.9%) and Filipino (19.8%), followed by Pacific Islander (9.9%) and Laotian (8.5%).[7] The concentrated nature of the prison population in California magnifies the impact that the release of prisoners has on already-distressed ethnic enclaves and counties. Almost two-thirds of all API prisoners come from six counties (Table 2).[8]

This distribution concurs with state parole figures. According to the California Department of Corrections, parole units with the highest number of API parolees include San Jose, Sacramento, Los Angeles, Chula Vista, El Monte, Fresno, Long Beach, Orange County, San Diego, and San Francisco.[9]

In contrast to the continental U.S., the API prisoner population in Hawai'i is largely U.S.-born. The vast majority of those with Asian, Native Hawaiian and other Pacific Islander ancestry were born in the United States or the U.S. territories. Those born in the Philippines are the largest immigrant group, comprising less than 4 percent of the API inmate population.[10] Following Native Hawaiians and Caucasians in numbers, inmates of Philippine ancestry, including both U.S.- and Philippine-born, comprise 12.4 percent of the total prison population.

Table 2. Top 10 California Counties with API Prisoners

	TOTAL		MALE		FEMALE	
	Number	**%**	**Number**	**%**	**Number**	**%**
Santa Clara	403	24	382	22	21	1
Los Angeles	269	16	233	14	36	2
San Diego	131	8	111	6	20	1
San Mateo	111	6	106	6	5	0
Orange	110	6	94	5	16	1
Sacramento	101	6	97	6	4	0
Alameda	79	5	77	5	2	0
San Francisco	64	4	62	4	2	0
San Joaquin	59	3	55	3	4	0
Solano	52	3	49	3	3	0
Total and Percentage of All Counties*	1711	81	1266	74	113	7

*All percentages are based on the number of inmates out of the total API inmate population of 1,711.
Source: State of California, Department of Corrections, Offender Information Service Branch, May 2004.

AGE AT INCARCERATION

In California, Asian and Pacific Islander prisoners are incarcerated at a younger age than prisoners of other racial backgrounds. Half of all API prisoners were age twenty-seven and younger (Figure 1), while that age group accounted for 37.8 percent of African American prisoners and 28.3 percent of Caucasians prisoners. Similar to API prisoners in their age distribution, nearly half of Latinos were twenty-seven and younger.[11] In contrast, the API prisoners in Hawai'i are generally older. The largest commitment age group in California was age eighteen to twenty-two (30.9 percent of API prisoners) while the largest age group in Hawai'i was age thirty to thirty-five (24.8 percent of API prisoners).

The young age of many of the API prisoners in California is indicative of the growing number of API youth also incarcerated in youth correctional facilities. According to a 2004 study of API wards under the supervision of the California

Figure 1. Age at Incarceration of API Male and Female Prisoners in California, 2004

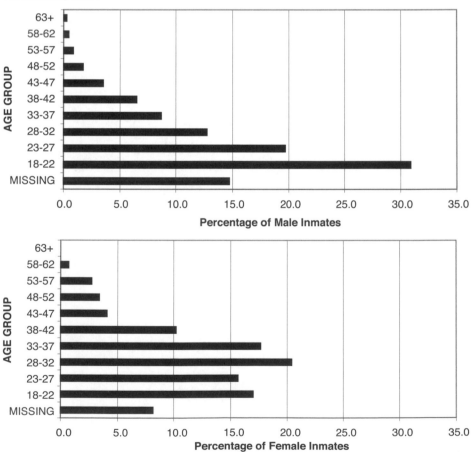

Source: State of California, Department of Corrections, Offender Information Service Branch, May 2004.

Youth Authority (CYA), API youth comprised 5 percent of the wards under the CYA in 2002.[12] The API youth group shows the following breakdown: Laotian (26%), Vietnamese (20%), and Cambodian (15%), with Filipino, Thai and Pacific Islander at 10 percent each. If these youth remain in the criminal justice system into adulthood, Southeast Asian inmate numbers in California prisons will likely continue to increase.

TYPES OF OFFENSES

API inmates in the United States had the highest proportion of violent crime offenses compared to other racial groups. Violent offenses include murder, manslaughter, assault, robbery and other crimes against people. According to the "1997 Survey of Inmates in State and Federal Correctional Facilities," 56 percent of API inmates were incarcerated for violent offenses compared with 48 percent for all state prisoners. Conversely, API inmates had among the lowest proportions of offenses for property and drug offenses (Table 3). This difference is more pronounced in California than in the United States as a whole: 64 percent of Californian API inmates were incarcerated for violent offenses compared with 39 percent for all Californian prisoners.[13] More recent data from the California Department of Corrections show that in 2004 more than two-thirds of API inmates were charged with violent offenses compared to two-fifths for all other groups.

The severity of offenses between API male inmates in Hawai'i and California varies considerably (see Table 3). Among API prisoners in Hawai'i, a much smaller proportion of Asian Americans (48.9%) and Native Hawaiians and Pacific Islanders (49.3%) were incarcerated for violent offenses compared to API inmates in California (67.7%) and the rest of the nation (55.8%). Also, a greater proportion of API prisoners in California were charged with violent offenses compared to other racial groups. While more than two-thirds of API prisoners had violent offenses, only half of those identified with other racial groups fell in the same summary offense category. This relatively high proportion of violent offenses among API prisoners can be seen in other states, according to a 1997 survey. This marked variation in California may reflect a more serious pattern of offending among API males, or it may reflect a higher rate of arrest for property and drug-related crimes for other groups. Disproportionate sentencing of African Americans under California's Three Strikes law may also account for some of this variation.[14]

Regardless of the offense, prisoners are released into society with the same amount of preparation, which is very little, across all racial groups. Those who have committed more serious violent crimes, however, may have to overcome greater social and psychological challenges to successfully reintegrate. In tighter knit communities, relations with victims and their families may still remain a salient factor in the reintegration process. Also, those charged with more serious crimes tend to serve longer sentences. More than one-fifth of API inmates in California serve sentences of twenty-five or more years and serve the longest sentences compared with all other racial groups.[15] Those who spend

Table 3. Offense Type by Race

	U.S.[a]		California[b]			Hawai'i[c]	
	APIs	All Other Groups	APIs	All Other Groups	Asian American	Native Hawaiian and Pacific Islander	All Other Groups
Violent	55.8	47.8	67.7	50.2	48.9	49.3	50.7
Property	15.2	21.5	16.9	21.2	20.6	24.2	24.0
Drug	17.8	19.5	10.0	21.4	25.9	19.9	18.8
Other or missing	11.1	11.1	5.3	7.2	4.6	6.5	6.5
Total	100	100	100	100	100	100	100

[a]Survey of Inmates in State and Federal Facilities, 1997.
[b]California Department of Corrections, Data Analysis Unit, Offender Information Branch, May 2004.
[c]Hawai'i Department of Public Safety, June 2004.

more time in prison are at greater risk of becoming more deeply steeped in criminal lifestyles, as criminologists suggest.[16]

RECIDIVISM

Among API inmates, the recidivism rate appears to be lower than other racial groups, according to a study of state prisoners released in 1994 and tracked over a three-year period. In California, slightly more than two-fifths of API inmates were rearrested within three years of release compared with almost three-quarters of all those released. Less than one fifth of API inmates were reconvicted and less than one in ten were sent to prison for a new offense within three years of release. For the overall population, the percentage rates of reconviction and resentencing were 49.9 and 27.9, respectively (Table 4). There is no conclusive evidence that spending more time in prison leads to higher rates of recidivism.[17] Recidivism studies have shown that those who committed more serious violent crimes had somewhat lower rates of recidivism than those sentenced for robbery, various property, or drug offenses.[18]

PARTICIPATION IN PROGRAMS

The demand for comprehensive prisoner reentry programs has increased. As the prison and parole population has grown during the past twenty years, the demand for comprehensive prisoner reentry programs has also increased. Yet, most prisoner reentry programs do not have specific components to address the linguistic or cultural needs of API ex-offenders. Current information about the participation of the general prison population shows the need for mental health services, education, and job training.

Table 4. Survey of California Male Inmates Rearrested, Reconvicted, and Resentenced to Prison within Three Years of 1994 Release from Prison by Race

	Released[a]	Re-Arrested	Re-Convicted	Re-Sentenced[b]	Returned to Prison[d]
White	62,261	42,324 (68)[c]	29,790 (47.8)[c]	16,585 (26.6)[c]	39,762 (63.9)[a]
Black	31,223	24,989 (80.0)	17,280 (55.3)	9,752 (31.2)	23,088 (73.9)
American Indian/ Aleutian	567	345 (60.8)	254 (44.8)	94 (16.6)	417 (73.5)
Asian/ Pacific Islander	904	386 (42.7)	161 (17.8)	73 (8.1)	424 (46.9)
Unknown	182	24 (13.3)	21 (11.6)	20 (11.0)	51 (28.2)
Total	95,137	68,068 (71.5)	47,506 (49.9)	26,524 (27.9)	63,742 (67.0)

[a]Weighted sample size for California male inmates released in 1994 was 95,136.
[b]Prisoners only returned to prison for technical violations of his/her parole are not included.
[c]Numbers in parentheses represent the percentage of those released within each racial category.
[d]Percentage returned to prison also includes those returned for technical violation of their release, such as failing a drug test or failing to report to their parole officer.
Source: U.S. Department of Justice, Bureau of Justice Statistics, Recidivism of Prisoners Released in 1994.

FUTURE TRENDS

A growing concern is the fate of API juveniles who are entering the juvenile justice system. The youth prison population presents a separate set of problems and potential reentry issues. According to the report by the National Council on Crime and Delinquency, API youth were one of the smaller racial groups, accounting for 5 percent of the total juvenile justice system population in 2002.[19] They are increasing in number, however, and if these trends continue, a continued increase in the API adult prison population will likely be seen. Better data collection on each of the specific API ethnic groups will be important in tracking these trends.

The API community has a long and proud tradition of advocating for and working to meet the needs of its most vulnerable members. Ex-offenders and their families, seeking to reestablish their lives after a prison term, are among those in most need. An early assessment of the process of prisoner reentry will likely maintain and strengthen the Asian and Pacific Islander community. In addition, foundations and other social institutions have an opportunity to invest in programs to address some of the root causes of criminality and give those caught in the system a second chance. This support can help break the cycle of poverty and violence that erode the social capital and well-being of communities, especially those in greatest distress.

FURTHER READING

Braithwaite, J. *Restorative Justice and Responsive Regulation.* New York: Oxford University Press, 2002.
Le, Thao. "Delinquency among Asian/Pacific Islanders: Review of the literature." *The Justice Professional* 15 (2002): 57–70.
National Council on Crime and Delinquency. "Promising approaches: A nationwide resource guide to Asian/Pacific Islander youth organizations and programs." Oakland, CA: National Council on Crime and Delinquency, 2007.
Petersilia, Joan. *When Prisoners Come Home: Parole and Prisoner Reentry.* Oxford and New York: Oxford University Press, 2003.
U.S. Dept. of Justice, Bureau of Justice Statistics. Survey of Inmates in State and Federal Correctional Facilities, 2004 [Computer file]. ICPSR04572-v1. Ann Arbor, MI: Inter-University Consortium for Political and Social Research [producer and distributor], 2007-02-28. doi:10.3886/ICPSR04572. [Online, Jan. 2009]. http://www.icpsr.umich.edu/NACJD/sisfcf/.

NOTES

1. James P. Lynch and William. J. Sabol. "Prisoner Reentry in Perspective," *Crime Policy Report.* 3 (Washington, DC: Urban Institute, 2001).

2. The Bureau of Justice Statistics estimates that 585,400 prisoners were released in 2000. Allen J. Beck, "State and Federal Prisoners Returning to the Community: Findings from the Bureau of Justice Statistics." (Washington, DC: U.S. Department of Justice, Bureau of Justice Statistics, 2000).

3. The "1997 Survey of Inmates in State and Federal Correctional Facilities" conducted for the U.S. Department of Justice used a weighted sample of the prison population. For California, the weighted sample represented 4,824 of 141,667 inmates while the U.S. sample represented 12,445 of 992,968 inmates.

4. U.S. Department of Justice, Bureau of Justice Statistics, "1997 Survey of Inmates in State and Federal Correctional Facilities." U.S. Bureau of the Census, The Asian Population: 2000. Census 2000 Brief, 2002. This estimate appears to corroborate with data from the Offender-Based Transaction Statistics (OBTS) administered by the California Department of Corrections that APIs comprised 2 percent of those sentenced in California to prison in 2002. Since API inmates tend to serve longer prison terms due to more serious offenses, their proportion of the prison population would likely be higher than 2 percent. There seems to be some discrepancy in the California data. Routine reports from the California Department of Corrections categorize APIs along with Native Americans as "other," which in February 2004 comprised 5.7 percent of the inmate population. See California Department of Corrections, Data Analysis Unit, Offender Information Services Branch, "Characteristics of Inmate Population," February 2004, http://www.corr.ca.gov/OffenderInfoServices/Reports/Quarterly/Strike1/STRIKE1d0406.pdf, accessed November 22, 2004. In a data set by the California

Department of Corrections, Data Analysis Unit, Offender Information Services Branch, generated in May 2004, which included API and American Indian categories, the proportion of API and Native American inmates were counted as 1.1 percent and 1.0 percent respectively. This adds up to less than the 5.7 percent categorized as "other" in the February report.

5. U.S. Department of Justice, Bureau of Justice Statistics, "1997 Survey of Inmates in State and Federal Correctional Facilities." U.S. Bureau of the Census, The Asian Population: 2000. Census 2000 Brief, 2002. See also Brian Niiya and Karen Umemoto, "A Demographic Profile of Asian Pacific Americans in Hawai'i," in Eric Lai and Dennis Arguelles, eds. *The New Face of Asian Pacific America: Numbers, Diversity and Change in the 21st Century* (San Francisco: *Asian Week*, 2003).

6. Gene Kassebaum, "Criminal Justice and Hawaiians in the 1990s: Ethnic Differences in Imprisonment Rates in the State of Hawai'i," October 1993, unpublished report.

7. California Department of Corrections, Data Analysis Unit, Offender Information Services Branch, May 2004. These data were similar to the "1997 Survey of Inmates in State and Federal Facilities," which reported the place of birth of California inmates. According to this survey, 58 percent of API inmates were born outside of the U.S. Among these, 40 percent were born in Vietnam, 13.7 percent in the Philippines, 16.7 percent in the Pacific Islands, and 9.7 percent in Laos.

8. State of California, Department of Corrections, Offender Information Services Branch (May 2004).

9. State of California Department of Corrections, Statewide Parolee Database, June 2004.

10. State of Hawai'i, Department of Public Safety, July 2004.

11. Data from California Department of Corrections, Data Analysis Unit, Offender Information Branch, May 2004 (see Appendix I).

12. National Council on Crime and Delinquency, *Asian American and Pacific Islander Youth in the California Youth Authority (CYA)*, 2004, unpublished report.

13. Data from "Survey of Inmates in State and Federal Correctional Facilities, 1997" (see Appendix I).

14. In 2002, about 25 percent of the prison population in California was subject to sentencing enhancements under the Three Strikes law. African Americans, who comprise 30 percent of the California prison population, have received a greater number of second and third strikes relative to their population in California. See *Second and Third Strikers in the Institution Population: December 2002.* (Sacramento: California Department of Corrections: Data Analysis Unit, 2003).

15. In contrast, most API females (51.7 percent) serve sentences of 2 years or less, with only 11 percent serving sentences of 15 years or more. California Department of Corrections, Data Analysis Unit, Offender Information Services Branch, May 2004.

16. See Joan Petersilia, *When Prisoners Come Home: Parole and Prisoner Reentry.* (Oxford and New York: Oxford University Press, 2003), 21–53.

17. Patrick A. Langan, and David. J. Levin, "Recidivism of Prisoners Released in 1994." Special report. (Washington, DC: U.S. Department of Justice, Office of Justice Programs, 2002).

18. Langan and Levin, "Recidivism of Prisoners Released in 1994."

19. National Council on Crime and Delinquency, *Asian American and Pacific Islander Youth in the California Youth Authority (CYA)*, 2004.

RACIAL VIOLENCE AND HATE CRIMES

Angelo Ancheta

Racial violence has been a longstanding problem facing Asian American communities. Discriminatory acts of violence, including vandalism, property damage, assaults, and killings, have been unfortunate hallmarks of Asian American history, and laws and the legal system have often been unresponsive to problems of hate violence. Incidents of contemporary anti-Asian violence typically reveal not only overt racism but close connections between race and the perception of Asian Americans as foreigners. Epithets such as "Go home!" or "Why don't you go back to your own country?" often accompany anti-Asian violence, and many acts of violence have been tied to anti-immigrant sentiment, economic competition, past military conflicts with Asian countries, and national security and anti-terrorism efforts by the U.S. government.

MAJOR EXAMPLES OF ANTI-ASIAN VIOLENCE

Anti-Asian violence has a history dating back to the earliest Asian immigrant communities in the United States and has even been sanctioned by law. During the nineteenth century, for example, the California Supreme Court ruled that Chinese Americans could not testify against white defendants in criminal cases, which had the practical effect of licensing racial violence against Chinese immigrants. Individual crimes of violence, as well as race riots, were frequent occurrences, ranging from multiple attacks on Chinese laborers during the nineteenth century to race riots against Filipino immigrants in agricultural areas of northern California in the 1930s. More recent incidents of anti-Asian violence continue to reflect anti-immigrant sentiment, but problems of economic competition with countries such as Japan and past military conflicts with countries such as Vietnam have generated especially violent crimes against Asian Americans.

The Murder of Cha Vang: A Hate Crime?

Cha Vang, 30, a Hmong factory worker from Green Bay, WI, was found dead from stabbing and shotgun wounds and partially hidden under brush in the Peshtigo Harbor Wildlife Area on January 6, 2007. He had been reported missing on January 5, after failing to return from his weekend hunting trip to the 5,000-acre reserve.

James A. Nichols, 28, of Peshtigo was subsequently targeted as a person of interest after he sought medical care for two gunshot wounds, one to each hand. He was also in custody as an ex-felon (a convicted burglar) in possession of a firearm. Marinette County Sheriff James Kanikula told reporters that Vang and his killer met accidentally in the woods, where they were involved in an altercation that obviously turned violent. Nichols claimed that Vang was the aggressor and that Nichols acted in self-defense. There were no witnesses to the confrontation.

The death of Cha Vang followed the 2004 slayings of six white men by a Hmong hunter in Rice Lake, WI. Chai Soua Vang of St. Paul, MN, shot eight hunters who had accused him of trespassing on private land and who had tried to force him away from the area. During his trial, Vang said that the white hunters had shouted racial slurs and then began to shoot at him. The surviving wounded denied that they shouted racial slurs and said that Chai Soua Vang was the aggressor who fired first. Chai Soua Vang was convicted and sentenced to life in prison.

The effect of all the slayings fed more fuel to continuing racial tensions in the area. Since the late 1970s, the region has been immersed in an often-fierce political and judicial argument over treaties that reserve Native Americans' rights to spearfish to the exclusion of others. In the late 1980s, there were several violent attacks on Native Americans during a time of open conflict with whites over hunting rights. Many residents of the area believe that the conflicts will certainly worsen as more Hmong immigrants from Southeast Asia arrive.

Hmong men are traditional hunters. Their skills were an important asset in the harsh and remote refugee camps of Thailand and Laos after the retreat of the United States and its allies from Vietnam. Thousands of Hmong evacuated from the last of the refugee centers in Asia that had been set up after the evacuation of Westerners and a significant number of the social and economic elite of South Vietnam, the departure of U.S. and allied military forces, and the rapid fall of South Vietnam that followed.

On their arrival in the United States, government-run refugee resettlement programs distributed Hmong to areas with low Asian populations, such as northern Minnesota and Wisconsin, as a method of hastening their adjustment to and acceptance into American society. According to local newspaper accounts, the approximately six thousand Hmong in Wisconsin's northwoods have had very limited interaction with the white majority, who are predominantly farmers and long-term and often multigenerational residents. Negative stereotypes of the Hmong—who are viewed as invaders—run rampant. Academics at the University of Wisconsin with expertise in both media and racial issues believe that lack of interaction nurtures stereotypes. In 2007, a high school in Minocqua, about 140 miles northwest of Peshtigo, was locked down after racial threats were found written in graffiti on school property and violence broke out between white and Native American students. Some white residents have begun to address what they have been forced to recognize as open, generational racism in their communities by offering cultural diversity programs.

Prosecution of James Nichols

Despite pressure from the Hmong community, Wisconsin Attorney General J. B. Van Hollen and Marinette County District Attorney Brent DeBord did not add hate crime charges to the prosecution of Nichols in January 2007 for the killing of Cha Vang. Their decision to exclude hate crime provisions brought immediate and forceful criticism from the Hmong community, which was joined by a broad range of supporters, including Asian American legal service and legal rights advocacy groups, community service agencies, and local and national organizations and associations with interests in civil and human rights issues.

Controversy

The argument about how this crime should have been prosecuted sheds light on how state laws define hate crimes, and what evidence is needed to secure a conviction for a hate crime. Those who argue that the case should have been tried as a hate crime point to the degree of violence shown in the physical evidence of the killing, the number and nature of the victim's wounds, the condition of Vang's body when it was found, and the defendant's own statements before and after the homicide as indicators of racial hatred. The autopsy of the victim revealed that Nichols had shot Vang at close range with a shotgun, wounding him in the right arm, neck and torso while he was turned away. Nichols also stabbed Vang six times, five wounds to the front of his neck and one to his left cheek. Vang also suffered a laceration behind his right ear, and his body was found with a 4-inch wooden stick protruding from his mouth. According to the official police report, Nichols made disparaging racial comments throughout their initial interview about Hmong people and about the victim.

Wisconsin hate crime statutes (Wisconsin Statute 939645) provide for increased fines and sentences when the crimes charged were committed because the defendant "intentionally selects the person against whom the crime is committed" and because of his or her "belief or perception" about "the race, religion, color, disability, sexual orientation, national origin or ancestry" of the person or property harmed by the crime.

Given the specific language of the applicable state code regarding the requirement of an "intentional selection" of the victim of a crime, two reasonable prosecutorial concerns arise: is there sufficient evidence that would convince a jury to convict with the hate crime enhancement attached, and should the jury conclude that enhancement of the criminal punishment does *not* apply, is there a risk that they might convict for a lesser offense— manslaughter rather than murder, for example—and then assess much less than a maximum penalty? Defense counsel could easily argue that the initial encounter between the victim and his killer—both hunters in a reserve— was by chance rather than design and thus rebut the "intentional selection" of Cha Vang because of his race or ethnicity.

Epilogue and Lessons Learned

Nichols was convicted for second-degree intentional homicide (known as second-degree murder in some states) on October 7, 2007, for the killing of Cha Vang. He received the maximum sentence of sixty-nine years on November 28, 2007. According to Wisconsin news media, the Hmong community was heartened by the maximum sentence despite the lack of hate crime enhancement.

The Asian Law Caucus (ALC) of San Francisco has been providing legal services and law-related political advocacy on a local and national basis for nearly four decades. In a 2004 report, the ALC cited frequent resistance from law enforcement, including district attorneys, to giving serious consideration to victims' descriptions of actions consistent with racist motivations on the part of their attackers. Resistance or reluctance on the part of the police to investigate whether racial or other forms of hate crime may have been committed might be the result of weak institutional policy, procedures or protocols. It may also be attributable to law enforcement culture or a combination of these factors.

The ALC report also cites underreporting of hate crimes as a continuing problem. An annual audit of violence against Asian Americans conducted jointly by the National Asian Pacific American Legal Consortium, the Asian Pacific American Legal Center and the ALC showed 35 percent more incidents of racial hatred perpetrated against Asians and Pacific Islanders per year than stated in the official report constructed and published by the California Attorney General's office (2004).

Legislatures and courts will continue to further define standards for intent and underlying motivation. As is often the case, the specific language of the laws is key to ready and effective enforcement of penalties against any crimes, including those motivated by racial hatred. What is clear from the overall history of hate crime is that, throughout the nation, prosecutions and positive policy reform usually come only after close monitoring, firm advocacy politics, and continuous pressure, including media coverage, from the victims' communities and their allies.

—Daniel Phil Gonzales

Perhaps the best-known incident of anti-Asian violence was the killing of Vincent Chin in 1982, a case that generated national attention and helped galvanize social and political movements against anti-Asian violence. Chin, a twenty-seven-year-old Chinese American, was celebrating at his bachelor's party at a Detroit bar when he was initially confronted by Ronald Ebens and Michael Nitz, two white autoworkers. Ebens and Nitz believed that Chin was Japanese and blamed him for the loss of jobs in the Detroit-area automobile industry. After another confrontation involving racial epithets, Ebens and Nitz caught Chin in a parking lot and beat him repeatedly with a baseball bat. Chin died from severe head injuries a few days later.

The Vincent Chin case led to widespread community organizing among Asian Americans in both the Detroit area and across the country, especially after Ebens and Nitz pleaded guilty to manslaughter but received only probation and a fine. Ebens was later convicted of federal civil rights violations, but his conviction was overturned on appeal and he was acquitted on retrial. Thus, despite the severity of their crime and the notoriety of the case, neither Ebens nor Nitz spent any time in prison for the killing. The case did, however, bring national attention to the problem of anti-Asian violence, particularly its linkages to economic competition and nativist sentiment.

Another prominent killing occurred in Raleigh, NC, with the murder of Ming Hai "Jim" Loo in 1989. Loo had been playing pool with several friends when he was approached by Robert Piche and his brother Lloyd. They began calling Loo and his friends "chinks" and "gooks" and blaming them for the death of Americans in the Vietnam War. Robert Piche pistol-whipped Loo on the back of the head, which eventually led to Loo's death a few days later. Piche was convicted and sentenced to more than thirty years in prison, while his brother was sentenced to both a state prison term and federal prison term for civil rights violations.

Another major incident in 1989 involved multiple killings of Asian American children at the Cleveland Elementary School in Stockton, CA. The assailant, Patrick Purdy, used an AK-47 assault rifle to shoot bullets into a schoolyard, killing five children and wounding several others before turning the gun on himself. A state government report concluded that the shooter had focused on the school because it was heavily populated by Southeast Asian children.

Perpetrators who are known to be white supremacists or are affiliated with organized hate groups have also been responsible for serious anti-Asian crimes. During the early 1980s, for example, tensions erupted between Vietnamese immigrant fishermen and native-born fishermen along the Gulf Coast of Texas, and the Ku Klux Klan engaged in extensive harassment and violence against the Vietnamese fishermen. In 1999, Joseph Ileto, a Filipino American postal worker, was gunned down in Southern California by a white supremacist who had also riddled a Jewish community center with bullets from a semi-automatic weapon and wounded several individuals. The killer shot Ileto nine times and admitted that he had targeted Ileto because he thought Ileto was "a chink or a spic"; the killer was eventually sentenced to multiple life sentences without the possibility of parole.

Other instances of racial violence have occurred where there have been ongoing racial tensions among groups. For example, the 2007 killing of Cha Vang, a Hmong American who was shot and stabbed multiple times by a white individual while hunting in northern Wisconsin, came in the aftermath of the fatal shootings of six white hunters by a Hmong American in 2004. Tensions among whites and the Hmong community had been strained for an extended period of time, and the Cha Vang killing was especially brutal because a wooden stick had been placed in his clenched teeth, and his body was hidden in a ditch covered by wood and other debris. Hmong American and other community leaders, who feared that the Cha Vang killing was retaliation for the earlier shootings, called for racial violence prosecutions in the case, but the government declined to prosecute a hate crime; ultimately, Cha Vang's killer was convicted of second-degree homicide and sentenced to sixty-nine years in prison.

Serious incidents of anti-Asian violence have also arisen from conflicts among racial minorities. For example, the rioting that occurred in Southern California after the verdicts in the Rodney King police brutality cases revealed deep interracial and interethnic tensions. It led to the destruction of many businesses owned by Korean Americans and other Asian Americans in the region. Another example from the early 1990s occurred in San Francisco's public housing projects, where many Southeast Asian families were subjected to harassment and violence by African American tenants. Poorly developed institutional policies, including flawed security and integration strategies, exacerbated conflicts among the tenants and led to numerous assaults.

DOCUMENTING AND ADDRESSING HATE CRIMES

Reports by both the government and civil rights organizations have attempted to document the extensiveness of anti-Asian violence in recent decades. For example, a 1986 report by the U.S. Commission on Civil Rights concluded that anti-Asian activity in the form of violence, harassment, intimidation, and vandalism was a problem across the nation.[1] The Asian American Justice Center (formerly known as the National Asian Pacific American Legal Consortium) has monitored anti-Asian violence during the 1990s and 2000s and has tracked a wide variety of crimes, including vandalism, graffiti, property damage, arson, intimidation, hate mail, cross burnings, assaults, homicides, and even police misconduct.[2]

Calculating accurate figures can be difficult because of victims' underreporting of crime; the problem can be especially serious for crimes involving recent immigrants who face English language barriers or are afraid to report crimes to law enforcement. The figures that are available are troubling. During the eight-year period from 1995 to 2002, audits of anti-Asian violence by the Asian American Justice Center compiled a nationwide total of 3,581 incidents against Asian Americans, with more than 400 incidents logged for almost every year during the period.[3] A sample of incidents drawn from a 2002 audit illustrates a wide range of problems that highlight the treatment of Asian Americans as immigrants, foreigners, and even as terrorists:

- A Japanese American man in Rancho Santa Margarita, CA, was attacked in his front yard by a perpetrator who threw eggs at him and shouted, "You dirty Jap!" while leaving the scene.
- In a supermarket parking lot in Fort Lee, NJ, a Korean American woman was verbally assaulted by a couple, one of whom yelled: "Where did you learn to drive? You chink!" After confronting the couple, the woman was threatened by another customer who yelled, "Yeah, go back to your own country!"
- While leaving a casino in Lake Tahoe, NV, three Chinese American families were verbally and physically assaulted by an individual who, after already having confronted a security guard, shouted out: "This is America, you fucking Chinks. Do you want some of me?" During the perpetrator's detention by security guards, he told one of the guards: "Hey man, I can respect you. Not like these fucking spics and slant-eyes who are just there to take our money."
- At a business in Los Angeles, a perpetrator brandished a knife and told a South Asian American victim, "I don't like Indians or Pakistanis and if you don't go back to your country, I'll kill you."
- In Beverly Hills, CA, a South Asian American man working as a restaurant valet was accosted by an individual who called the man an "Indian motherfucker" and asked "Are you a terrorist?" before attempting to assault the victim.[4]

Hate crimes laws on the national level, such as the Hate Crimes Statistics Act of 1990 and federal civil rights laws addressing violence and criminal conspiracies, as well as various state laws that track hate crimes and increase punishment for bias-motivated acts, provide the legal foundation for addressing anti-Asian violence. In addition, state civil rights laws often allow civil lawsuits to be filed so that victims of racial violence can obtain monetary damages. The U.S. Supreme Court in *Wisconsin v. Mitchell* has also upheld the constitutionality of criminal penalty enhancement laws designed both to deter and to punish hate violence.[5]

Nevertheless, several problems remain unaddressed by government and the law. These include: insufficient monitoring by law enforcement; incomplete or weakly written hate crimes laws; inadequate training of law enforcement; and major barriers to reporting, including the absence of language-appropriate services for limited–English-speaking immigrants. For example, immigrants who are unable to speak or understand English may be subjected to racial violence, but language and cultural barriers may occur at several points: in understanding the nature of a crime (not comprehending the racial insults or epithets accompanying an attack), in contacting and explaining the crime to law enforcement, and in properly characterizing the crime as a hate crime. Thus, law enforcement may not receive a crime report at all, or, even if a report is filed, may not consider the act of violence a true hate crime. The lack of culturally relevant training for law enforcement in assessing hate crimes against immigrants only compounds the barriers.

Even where reporting mechanisms and laws are in place, prosecuting hate crimes can be problematic: inadequately trained officers may not collect sufficient evidence, and government attorneys may be reluctant to prosecute hate crimes cases because of the difficulty of proving discriminatory intent by the perpetrator. Hate crimes laws have often been on the books for years in many states, but the number of prosecutions remains relatively small; evidence of a defendant's intention to commit an act of violence because of the victim's race or ethnicity may only come through racial epithets or obvious racial hostility accompanying the act of violence, and this type of evidence may be missing or ambiguous in a particular case, despite the actual intent of the perpetrator. This can be a serious problem because even though a perpetrator may be convicted under a non–hate-crime law for a crime such as homicide or assault and receive a significant punishment, the preventive role of the prosecution will be more limited. Unless a hate crime is prosecuted and the public is made aware of the serious nature of an offense, hate crimes laws will have little deterrent effect on future hate crimes.

Because racial violence remains an issue for organizing communities, Asian American civil rights groups and community-based organizations no doubt will continue to advocate for stronger laws and better tracking of bias-motivated incidents, and to push local law enforcement and prosecutors to address racial violence through appropriate prosecutions and just sentences. The Asian American Justice Center, for example, works with a nationwide network of local community organization to track hate crimes against Asian Americans and advocates for stronger laws at the national, state, and local levels; the organization also employs rapid-response strategies to call attention to incidents of racial violence and works with attorneys in many parts of the country to assist victims in asserting their legal rights. As a result of longstanding advocacy efforts, many police departments and local district attorney offices now have designated officers or special units that focus on hate crimes.

Chou Vang, sister of Chai Soua Vang, reacts as she talks outside the Sawyer County Courthouse in September 2005, in Hayward, Wisconsin. A jury found Chai Soua Vang guilty of murdering six deer hunters and wounding two others during a confrontation over trespassing, rejecting his claims he shot in self-defense after one hunter used racial slurs and another fired at him. At right is Chai Soua Vang's mother Sao Hang. (AP Photo/Morry Gash)

RACIAL PROFILING

Racial profiling is basing racial or ethnic traits as a source of reasoning when suspecting individuals involved in crime. Historically, occurrences such as the internment of Japanese Americans during World War II, the unlawful persecution of Chinese Americans during the McCarthy/Cold War era, and the recent treatment of South Asian Americans post-9/11 all are examples of unjust racial profiling. These issues occur because of mainstream society's and policy makers' inadequate comprehension of the Asian American experience. There are still everyday occurrences of such practices, especially for urban Asian Pacific Islander youth. Many in Southeast Asian communities, as well as other concentrated community enclaves such as "Chinatowns" and "Koreatowns," encounter harassment for being "prospective" gang members.

For the Asian American community, racial profiling has meant harassment as well as unlawful arrests and even fatalities committed by law enforcement officers. As the Asian populations in the United States have grown in the past few decades, there have been many instances of police brutality, wrongful incarceration and wrongful death in the Asian American community. For many Asian immigrants who have been convicted wrongfully or otherwise of criminal charges, they also have to face the issue of deportation from U.S. soil.

Police Brutality

March 2008, Milwaukee, WI: Thirty-nine-year-old Hmong immigrant Koua Moua was beaten after officers claimed that Moua was being non-compliant after being pulled over for drunk driving. Supporters of Moua argue that he does not speak English and that what happened to him was excessive force by the officers. Moua is about 4 foot, 10 inches in height.

Wrongful Incarceration

December 2004, Clinton, NY: David Wong, a Chinese immigrant, having served 17 years for a crime he did not commit, had the murder charges against him dropped after years of struggle from his lawyers and others. In 1987, David Wong was tasked with a 25 year jail sentence when he was charged with second-degree murder. He had been serving an 8-to-25-year sentence at Clinton Correctional Facility in New York when this occurred.

March 2006, Queens, NY: Shih-Wei Su, a Taiwanese-born immigrant who had served 12 years for a murder charge that he did not commit, intends to sue the Queens prosecutors for withholding evidence and providing false testimony for his wrongful conviction. His case was overturned in 2003 after his lawyer successfully uncovered documents that proved prosecutorial misconduct. Su was 18 when he started his sentence. He stated that his lack of English prevented him from understanding his initial court trials.

Wrongful Death

July 2004, Minneapolis, MN: Nineteen-year-old Fong Lee (Hmong) was gunned and killed by police officers at a local elementary school yard. Although the police reported that Lee had attacked first with a loaded weapon, evidence from eyewitnesses and video surveillance make those claims highly unlikely. Members of the community respond with anger and called out for the erroneous evidence filed by the police department. Lee's fingerprints were not found on the weapon that was claimed to be the one that was in his possession.

July 2003, San Jose, CA: Twenty-five-year-old mother of two, Cau Tran (Vietnamese) was fatally shot in the chest inside her own home. A neighbor had called the police concerned that Tran's toddler was playing unsupervised outside their apartment. By the time the police arrived, Tran was standing in the kitchen with a utensil in her hand. The officer later testified that he thought she was waving a cleaver at him and that he instructed her twice to drop it. He estimated that he shot Tran within five to seven seconds of entering her apartment. The utensil that was in her hand turned out to be a "dao bao," a vegetable peeler commonly used in Asia. Her children were in the next room, as her husband witnessed the murder in a state of disbelief. The officer was later cleared of all charges.

August 2005, Dublin, CA: After a call to the police because of a domestic disturbance, officers arrived at the home of Richard Kim (Korean). His brother-in-law Kwang Tae Lee was visiting from Korea. When police arrived, Lee had a knife in hand and was threatening to get into the room where Kim had been hiding. When Lee did not comply with the officers' demands to drop his weapon, he was shot five times and killed. During the shootout, a bullet penetrated the bedroom door and injured Kim; he died three days later. The district attorney's report was released 9 months later, claiming that the officers reacted in self defense and no liability charges were to be filed. Many Korean American organizations in the Bay Area voiced their call for justice in these deaths and attested that the shootings were unjustified.

Controversy of Deportation

Under the Antiterrorism and Effective Death Penalty Act (AEDPA) and the Illegal Immigration Reform and Immigrant Responsibility Act (IIRAIRA) passed in 1996, many convicted and incarcerated Asians face the issue of deportation. The law is retroactive and affects permanent legal residents regardless of the amount of time they have resided in the United States. A felony, misdemeanor, or first-time offense can lead to removal from the United States.

—Mitchel Wu

FURTHER READING

Asian American Justice Center. http://www.advancingequality.org.

Kang, Jerry. "Racial Violence Against Asian Americans," *Harvard Law Review* 106 (1993) 1926–1943.

National Asian Pacific American Legal Consortium. *2002 Audit of Violence against Asian Pacific Americans: Tenth Annual Report*. Washington, DC: National Asian Pacific American Legal Consortium, 2004.

United States Commission on Civil Rights. *Civil Rights Issues Facing Asian Americans in the 1990s*. Washington, DC, February 1992.

Yamamoto, Eric, Margaret Chon, Carol L. Izumi, Jerry Kang and Frank Wu. *Race, Rights and Reparation: Law and the Japanese American Internment*. Gaithersburg, MD: Aspen Law & Business, 2001.

NOTES

1. United States Commission on Civil Rights, *Recent Activities against Citizens and Residents of Asian Descent*, Clearinghouse Publication No. 88 (Washington, DC, 1986), 5.

2. National Asian Pacific American Legal Consortium, *1995 Audit of Violence against Asian Pacific Americans* (Washington, DC: National Asian Pacific American Legal Consortium, 1996).

3. National Asian Pacific American Legal Consortium, *2002 Audit of Violence Against Asian Pacific Americans: Tenth Annual Report* (Washington, DC: National Asian Pacific American Legal Consortium, 2004), 11.

4. National Asian Pacific American Legal Consortium, *2002 Audit of Violence Against Asian Pacific Americans: Tenth Annual Report* (Washington, DC: National Asian Pacific American Legal Consortium, 2004), 14–23.

5. 508 U.S. 476 (1993).

RESOURCE GUIDE

Suggested Reading

Ancheta, Angelo N. *Race, Rights, and the Asian American Experience.* 2nd ed. New Brunswick, NJ: Rutgers University Press, 2006.

Foo, Lora Jo. *Asian American Women: Issues, Concerns, and Responsive Human and Civil Rights Advocacy* (New York: Ford Foundation, 2003).

Kim, Hyung-chan, ed. *Asian Americans and the Supreme Court: A Documentary History.* Westport, CT: Greenwood Press, 1992.

Okihiro, Gary Y. *Margins & Mainstreams: Asians in American History and Culture.* Seattle: University of Washington Press, 1994.

Takagi, Dana Y. *The Retreat from Race: Asian-American Admissions and Racial Politics.* New Brunswick, N.J.: Rutgers University Press, 1992.

Takaki, Ronald. *Strangers from a Different Shore: A History of Asian Americans.* Boston: Little, Brown & Company, 1989.

United States Commission on Civil Rights. *Civil Rights Issues Facing Asian Americans in the 1990s.* Washington, DC, February 1992.

Wu, Frank H. *Yellow: Race in America Beyond Black and White.* New York: Basic Books, 2002.

Yamamoto, Eric, Margaret Chon, Carol L. Izumi, Jerry Kang and Frank Wu. *Race, Rights and Reparation: Law and the Japanese American Internment.* Gaithersburg, MD: Aspen Law & Business, 2001.

Films

Of Civil Wrongs and Rights: The Fred Korematsu Story, DVD, directed by Eric Paul Fournier. (San Francisco: National Asian American Telecommunications Association, 2000) (60 min.). Examines the life Fred Korematsu, one of a number of Japanese Americans who challenged the orders requiring the evacuation and internment of Japanese Americans on the West Coast during World War II. The film covers his U.S. Supreme Court case, as well as his legal victory nearly forty years later in having his original conviction overturned.

Unfinished Business: The Japanese American Internment Cases, DVD, directed by Steven Okazaki. (San Francisco: Mouchette Films, 1986). (58 min.). Focuses on three

Japanese Americans—Fred Korematsu, Gordon Hirabayashi, and Min Yasui—who resisted military orders targeting Japanese Americans on the West Coast during World War II and took their cases to the U.S. Supreme Court.

Who Killed Vincent Chin? VHS, directed by Christine Choy. (New York: Filmakers Library, 1988). (82 min.). Documentary examining the killing of Vincent Chin in Detroit in 1982, as well as community responses to the crime. The film examines themes of racism in working-class America, Asian American activism, and social justice.

Organizations

Asian American Justice Center. http://www.advancingequality.org. The Asian American Justice Center (formerly the National Asian Pacific American Legal Consortium) is a Washington, DC–based organization that advances the civil rights of Asian Americans through advocacy, public policy, publication, education, and litigation. Its affiliates include the Asian Law Caucus (San Francisco), the Asian Pacific American Legal Center (Los Angeles), and the Asian American Institute (Chicago).

Asian Law Caucus. http://www.asianlawcaucus.org. Nation's oldest legal and civil rights organization serving the low-income Asian Pacific American communities, with a mission to promote, advance and represent the legal and civil rights of the Asian and Pacific Islander communities.

National Asian Pacific American Bar Association. http://www.napaba.org. National association of Asian Pacific American attorneys, judges, law professors, and law students, providing a national network for its members and affiliates. NAPABA advocates for the legal needs and interests of the Asian Pacific American community and represents the interests of more than 40,000 attorneys and approximately fifty-seven local bar associations, with practice settings ranging from solo practices to large firms, corporations, legal services organizations, nonprofit organizations, law schools, and governmental agencies.

Web Sites

Asian American Justice Center. http://www.advancingequality.org. Washington, DC–based organization that advances the civil rights of Asian Americans through advocacy, public policy, publication, education, and litigation. The Web site offers readings, resources, and policy briefings on key civil rights issues.

Asian American Institute. http://www.aaichicago.org. Established in 1992 as a pan-Asian not-for-profit 501(c)(3) organization. Its mission is to empower the Asian American community through advocacy, using research, education, and coalition building. Specifically, the institute works to improve cooperation and mutual understanding by bringing ethnic Asian American communities together; raises the visibility of the Asian American community and spotlights its concerns so that elected officials, policy makers and the general public will understand; and gathers and disseminates data about Asian American communities.

Asian American Legal Defense and Education Fund. http://www.aaldef.org. Founded in 1974, the Asian American Legal Defense and Education Fund (AALDEF) is a national organization that protects and promotes the civil rights of Asian Americans. By combining litigation, advocacy, education, and organizing, AALDEF works with Asian American communities across the country to secure human rights for all. AALDEF focuses on critical issues affecting Asian Americans, including immigrant rights, civic participation and voting rights, economic justice for workers, language access to services, Census policy, affirmative action, youth rights and educational equity, and the elimination of anti-Asian violence, police misconduct, and human trafficking.

Asian Americans for Civil Rights and Equality. http://www.aacre.org. Progressive voice advocating for justice in California. As the first and only project based in California's capital with a focus on state legislative and budget advocacy for Asian and Pacific Islander Americans, AACRE fights for critical legislation and funding on behalf of our diverse communities, and empowers APIAs to be an active and effective force in advancing civil rights and social justice.

Asian & Pacific Islander Institute on Domestic Violence. http://www.apiahf.org/apidvin-stitute. National network of advocates; community members; professionals from health, mental health, law, education, and social services; survivors; scholars; researchers; and activists from public policy, community organizations, youth programs, immigrants' rights networks, communities of color, women's groups, lesbian/gay/bisexual/transgender communities, and other social justice organizations. It serves as a forum for, and clearinghouse on, information, research, resources and critical issues about violence against women in Asian and Pacific Islander communities.

Asian Law Alliance. http://www.asianlawalliance.org. Founded in 1977, the San Jose–based Asian Law Alliance is a nonprofit law office addressing the needs of Asian Americans and Pacific Islanders in Santa Clara County through multilingual legal services, preventative community legal education, and community organizing and impact work.

Asian Pacific American Legal Center. http://www.apalc.org. The Asian Pacific American Legal Center of Southern California (APALC) is the nation's largest legal organiza-tion serving the Asian and Pacific Islander (API) communities. Founded in 1983, APALC provides traditional legal services as well as civil rights advocacy through lit-igation. These include landmark and key civil rights cases involving English-only workplace policies, education inequity at public high schools and universities, sweat-shop abuse, redress for Japanese American internees, and racially discriminatory employment practices.

Asian Pacific American Legal Resource Center. http://www.apalrc.org. The Asian Pacific American Legal Resource Center (APALRC) is a nonprofit organization dedicated to advancing the legal and civil rights of Asian Americans in the Washington, DC, met-ropolitan community through direct services, education, and advocacy. Through its innovative programs and strategic partnerships, the APALRC's main goals are two-fold: to address the individual legal needs of low-income and limited-English profi-cient Asian Americans, particularly in the areas of workers' rights, domestic violence, and immigration, and to advocate for broad-based systemic change on civil rights issues impacting Asian Americans.

CivilRights.org. http://www.civilrights.org. A collaboration of the Leadership Confer-ence on Civil Rights and the Leadership Conference on Civil Rights Education Fund. Its mission is to serve as the site of record for relevant and up-to-the minute civil rights news and information.

National Asian Pacific American Law Student Association. http://www.napalsa.org. A national law student organization whose goals include educating, representing, and advocating on a national level in the interests of APA law students and Asian Pacific Americans in America; educating and promoting a deeper understanding of the polit-ical, financial, social and historical role, contributions, and status of Asian Pacific Americans in America; and serving as a national network of communication among the APA law student community for fostering the exchange of ideas and information.

Section 8:

MEDIA

*Section Editors: Valerie Soe, Allan Aquino,
and Edith Wen-Chu Chen*

PORTRAYALS IN FILM AND TELEVISION

Timothy P. Fong, Valerie Soe, and Allan Aquino

Today's images of Asian Americans in popular culture have improved and provide more breadth than in the past. In earlier days popular images of Asians and Asian Americans were predominantly mediated by non-Asian studio executives and writers—as a consequence, Hollywood's earlier characterizations of Asians and Asian Americans were often quite negative and demeaning. Some of these images are still perpetuated today, and Asian American media watchers and critics continue to complain about racist stereotypes that emerge in popular culture. Many film scholars argue that Hollywood films and television programs are not merely harmless entertainment, but are reflective of race, class, and gender ideologies and pressing social and political concerns.[1]

HISTORICAL IMAGES

Images of Asians in mainstream Hollywood motion pictures can be traced back to the mid-to-late 1800s when Asian migrants first arrived in large numbers to the United States.

Popular comic strips such as "The Yellow Kid" and "The Ting-Ling Kids" emerged in the 1890s and depicted racial caricatures of Chinese Americans for mass audiences. Throughout the ensuing decades, Asians were commonly portrayed in the press as the "Yellow Peril," an invasion of faceless and destructive Asiatics who would eventually overtake the nation and wreak social and economic havoc. The dominant ideology of Western superiority versus Eastern inferiority eventually led to the passage of the 1882 Chinese Exclusion Law, as well as a multitude of other anti-Asian legislation.

Silent films included early moving images of Asian Americans such as *Tsing Fu, the Yellow Devil* (1910), where the sinister Chinese wizard plots revenge against a white woman who rejects his lecherous intentions. The rise of Japan as a military and industrial power following the 1905 Russo-Japanese War was the inspiration for *The Japanese Investigation* (1909), which prominently featured the threat of U.S. involvement in an Asiatic war. For decades Hollywood films have consistently played on the theme of "Orientals" as the "other."

YELLOWFACE

Popular Asian characters such as Charlie Chan and Fu Manchu were created by white writers and producers and usually portrayed by white actors grotesquely made up to look Asian. All of the Asian characters in Fu Manchu movies were played by non-Asian actors. The first two Charlie Chan movies hired Japanese American actors for the lead role, but as the films gained popularity, they were quickly replaced by white actors who colored their hair jet black and used scotch tape to alter the shape of their eyes.

This practice, commonly known as yellowface, entails non-Asian performers playing Asian characters. Yellowface is a variation on the term "blackface," the practice popular in the late nineteenth and early twentieth centuries of white performers darkening their faces in order to impersonate African Americans. As with blackface performers, actors in yellowface take on the most exaggerated and stereotypical attributes of the race they are imitating. In the case of Asians, this includes buck teeth, slanted eyes and accented English. Yellowface has a long tradition in Hollywood films. Its popularity is partly because of several factors, including overt racism and discrimination against Asian American performers. One of the main institutionalized causes of the use of yellowface was the United States Motion Picture Production Code of 1930, or the "Hays Code," Hollywood's self-censoring doctrine that forbade, among many other things, portrayals of miscegenation, or intimate relationships between performers of different races. Because of this, non-Asian actors could not be depicted in romantic relationships with Asian actors—when the plot of the film called for this aspect, non-Asian performers were cast as Asian characters in yellowface, with their eyes cosmetically masked, their skin darkened and their teeth made prominent with prosthetics.

In classic yellowface performances, Paul Muni and Louise Rainer, both Austrian Jews, played the lead roles in the epic *The Good Earth* (1937), the film adaptation of Pearl Buck's classic novel about heroic Chinese peasants. Other well-known actors played roles in yellowface that were simply not available to Asian Americans. For example, Katharine Hepburn played a feisty Chinese peasant woman in *Dragon Seed* (1941), and Marlon Brando played a Japanese interpreter in *Teahouse of the August Moon* (1956). Another famous yellowface character was Charlie Chan, depicted by non-Asians including Warner Oland, Sidney Toler, and Roland Winter in the *Charlie Chan* film series (1931–44). In *Breakfast at Tiffany's* (1961), Mickey Rooney plays perhaps the most infamous example of a yellowface role, as a Japanese photographer with thick glasses, squinty eyes, and buck teeth. *The Year of Living Dangerously* (1983), starring Mel Gibson and Sigourney Weaver also holds another notable yellowface performance, in which actress Linda Hunt plays Billy Kwan, a male Chinese-Australian photographer. Other well-respected actors who have performed in yellowface include Shirley MacLaine, Peter Sellers, Nicolas Cage, and Eddie Murphy, among others.

Television also has a famous example of yellowface in the series, *Kung Fu* (1972–1975). The program was originally conceived by Bruce Lee, who desperately wanted to play the lead role of a Shaolin priest who escapes China in the late nineteenth century after avenging the death of his mentor, and finds adventure wandering around the American West. It would have been the perfect vehicle for Lee to fully demonstrate his potent martial arts prowess in front of a national audience that wanted more after his debut in *The Green Hornet*. When *Kung Fu* eventually premiered on television, the starring role was given to actor David Carradine. In addition, the character was changed from Chinese to half-Chinese, half-white. Lee was terribly embittered by this rejection, and it was at this point he left the United States to make his mark in Hong Kong martial arts films.

Yellowface fell out of general practice by the 1990s, although recent films including *Grindhouse* (2007), *Balls of Fury* (2007), and *I Now Pronounce You Chuck And Larry*, (2007) continue this unfortunate tradition. However, a more subtle form of yellowface, known as whitewashing, in which characters that are originally Asian are changed to white characters, took place with the casting of the film *21* (2008). Based on the best-selling book *Bringing Down the House*, the story focused on the MIT Blackjack Team that used sophisticated card-counting techniques to win thousands of dollars at casinos across the country. Most of the team members featured in the book were Asian American, but producers of *21* changed the ethnicity of these characters, including main character Jeff Ma, to white. Asian Americans protested the whitewashing of the characters but the producers were unapologetic, stating, "most of the film's actors would be white, with perhaps an Asian female." Similarly, the live-action version of the popular animated series *Avatar: The Last Airbender* (2010), which is set in Asia, was cast entirely with white leading actors, further prompting protest from the Asian American community. In response to the complaints, actor Jackson Rathbone stated, "I think it's one of those things where I pull my hair up, shave the sides, and I definitely need a tan. It's one of those things where, hopefully, the audience will suspend disbelief a little bit."[2] Though not as flagrantly offensive as classic yellowface performances, whitewashing continues decades-old practices of excluding and erasing Asian American roles from Hollywood screens.

PORTRAYALS OF ASIAN MEN

Evil Villains

Asian American men have often been portrayed as evil villains, bad guys and enemy combatants. Typical representations include despotic, cruel villains such as Ming the Merciless, from the popular *Buck Rogers* film series (1939); Fu Manchu (*The Mask of Fu Manchu*, 1932), first popularized in Sax Rohmer's pulp fictions of the early 20th century; and the buck-toothed, fanatical Japanese kamikazes and enemy soldiers found in World War II films propaganda films from the United States. Popular media images of Asian males have historically been depicted as either uncontrollably lustful or completely asexual. Fu Manchu's lasciviousness toward white women was, of course, never directly acted upon on screen, but the threat was always there, which only served to enhance the most negative images of Asians and the Yellow Peril. On one hand, Fu Manchu possessed superhuman intellect and ambition, and on the other, he was subhuman in his immorality and ruthlessness.

These portrayals have continued in the last couple of decades. Chow Yun-Fat appeared in *Pirates of the Caribbean 3: At World's End* (2007) as Sao Feng, a Singaporean pirate described as "an unscrupulous and honour-less coward who will do anything to join with the winning, even if it means betraying his best friends." He wears a queue, a Fu-Manchu style mustache, and long, "mandarin" fingernails and meets his violent demise while attempting to rape the film's heroine, Elizabeth. When the film was released in China, ten minutes of footage of Sao Feng were cut from the film, presumably because its stereotypical nature was offensive to the Chinese people.[3]

Jet Li also portrayed an evil villain character, in *The Mummy: Tomb of the Dragon Emperor* (2008), in which the martial arts superstar played Emperor Han, a malevolent resurrected mummy who "threatens to plunge the world into his merciless, unending service."

These characterizations perpetuate the stereotype of Asian men as inhuman killers bent on fanatical destruction, with an unnatural lust for white women and, in many cases, desiring world domination and the destruction of Western civilization. Such portrayals depict Asians as subhuman, perhaps as a justification for World War II atrocities such as Hiroshima and Nagasaki, and later conflicts such as the Korean and Vietnam wars.

Emasculated Males

In another recurring Hollywood stereotype, Asian American men are emasculated, sexless males who are clumsy rather than threatening in their attraction to white women. Charlie Chan, the cherubic and inscrutable Chinese

American detective from Honolulu, originated in a series of novels by Earl Derr Biggers and quickly made it into the movie houses, with almost fifty Charlie Chan movies released between 1926 and 1949. Chan exemplified the completely asexual Asian male character. Although he was married and had a large family, the films only introduced two of his sons. Audiences never saw his wife and Chan was never enticed by other women nor were any women enticed by him.

This stereotype came to full fruition in the character of Long Duk Dong in John Hughes's teen comedy *Sixteen Candles* (1984). In this popular film, Gedde Watanabe portrayed a nerdy, socially inept, and decidedly unsexy Japanese exchange student nicknamed "The Donger," who uttered comical phrases such as "What's happenin', hot stuff?" and "No more yanky my wanky!" As Eric Nakamura, editor of *Giant Robot*, notes, "It's like every bad stereotype possible, loaded into one character."[4] Even virile Bruce Lee in his megahit *Enter the Dragon* (1972) was precluded from having any interest in women, unlike his white and black costars. Lee may have been one of the very few sexually chaste action heroes in Hollywood. A similar example can be found in Chow Yun-Fat's first Hollywood feature film, *The Replacement Killers* (1998), where at the end he says goodbye to his female costar, Mira Sorvino. In the theater version of the film, Chow touches Sorvino's face, and they both walk away in opposite directions, assuring no sexual tension or contact. In the alternative ending that is included in the DVD release of the film, Chow passionately kisses Sorvino before the two separate. As they walk away in opposite directions they both turn around and look longingly at each other, creating at least an image of sexual attraction, albeit unrequited.

Further enforcing this stereotype, *Fargo* (1996) included a scene where a nerdy Japanese American male made inappropriate romantic overtures to the main female character. Other iterations of the emasculated, sexless Asian American male appeared in *Anna and the King* (2000), in which the romance between the lead characters played by Jodie Foster and Chow Yun-Fat culminated in a chaste dance, and in *Romeo Must Die*, (2000), which concluded with leads Jet Li and Aaliyah, as the modern-day Romeo and Juliet, sharing not a kiss but a platonic embrace. In *Deuce Bigalow: European Gigolo* (2005), an Asian male prostitute further perpetuates the stereotype of the emasculated, poorly endowed Asian male, stating, "I take my three inches elsewhere!"

Even the most famous Asian American male on television, Lt. Sulu (George Takei), in the original *Star Trek* series (1966–1969), was an obvious sexless character. While all the primary male members on the starship *Enterprise* had intergalactic encounters with women—human and alien—Lt. Sulu was almost always left alone.

However, the Jackie Chan film, *The Medallion* (2003), does end with Chan and his female costar, Claire Forlani, running off together as a couple ready for the next fight. This was a genuine rarity for an Asian man in Hollywood.

Who is Harlemm Lee?

In the summer of 2003, Harlemm Lee (born Gerry Woo) won the national television talent show *FAME*. Aired on the NBC-TV network, *FAME's* contestants gave live vocal performances on a weekly basis. Audience viewers telephoned their votes for who among the featured singers performed best; singers with the most votes would return to compete in the following week's broadcast. Lee, 35 at the time, had struggled for years in the recording industry, yet bested a number of his younger fellow competitors. Week after week, primetimes viewers voted for Lee and, as a result, he won a management deal from a top music manager, a year of training at the Debbie Allen Dance Academy, and free accommodations at the W Hotel in Los Angeles to help him launch his career. Soon after this victory, Lee would fall into obscurity.

By November 2003, Lee released his album, *Introducing Harlemm Lee*, which, despite positive reviews, moved only five hundred copies and was pulled from shelves because of low sales. In June 2004, Lee posted a message on his Web site thanking fans for his support, admitting his disappointment at the state of his post-*FAME* career. "I have been completely invisible since winning *FAME* and unable to capitalize from all my hard work and national exposure," he wrote. "If it weren't for my unemployment checks and my year-long stay at the W Hotel, I would be completely penniless and homeless." Lee stated that he was denied the most basic promotion and marketing resources, with justification given to him by industry executives was that his story was not "compelling enough." In his Web site message, Lee added "without [the industry's] machinery behind you, you will definitely not be seen or heard."

By contrast, Lee's story could not be more different (or as well known) as singer William Hung's. In January of 2004, Hung, then a 21-year-old engineering student from University of California–Berkeley, gained instant notoriety with his performance of the Ricky Martin song "She Bangs" for the enormously popular *American Idol* talent show. Accompanying his off-key vocals with an odd jig, Hung completed only the first chorus when judge Simon Cowell stopped him. After Hung questioned Cowell's intensely adamant disapproval, Cowell replied, "You can't sing, you can't dance, so what do you want me to say?"

With complete sincerity, Hung declared that he had no professional vocal training and had "no regrets at all." Perhaps it was in his grace in the face of his rejection that captured attention, but Hung became an instant comic pop star. He was featured in numerous television talk shows, news programs, commercials, music videos, and print articles; he has his own fan Web site, has given concerts across the U.S. and Asia, and has released three CDs.

Unlike Harlemm Lee, William Hung's first CD, *Inspiration*, sold more than 3,000 units on the day of its release. He has since sold tens of thousands more. According to Chi-hui Yang, director of the San Francisco International Asian American Film Festival, Hung's popularity was based upon his image: "What informs that kind of humor is something that is deeply rooted in the American depiction of Asian men as ineffective, effeminate, or wimpy, and I think William Hung fits right into it." Hung's popularity has persisted, much to the chagrin of many who view him as a racial caricature reflecting previous decades of stereotypes. Primary among these is the image of the asexual and buffoonish foreigner often exploited as a comic device—in Hung's case, a clumsy "oriental" with a discordant accent. "On the other hand," Yang continues, "someone like Harlemm Lee, who is enormously talented, has not gone very far. [Hung] feeds back into the people with the marketing dollars and knowing what the American public wants to see or what is familiar."

—Timothy P. Fong and Allan Aquino

Servants and Sidekicks

One of the most common roles for Asian American males in Hollywood was as domestic servants to whites. Easily the most famous Chinese domestic servant was Victor Sen Yung, who was the character Hop Sing in the *Bonanza* series that ran for fourteen years (1959–1973). Even Bruce Lee got his start on television as the faithful houseboy Kato in the show *The Green Hornet* (1966–1967).

Drawing from the Charlie Chan stereotype, police detectives are another common role for Asian American males on television. A recent example is seen in the San Francisco–based show, *Nash Bridges* (1996–2001) starring Don Johnson, where Cary-Hiroyuki Tagawa had a reoccurring role as Lt. A. J. Shimamura. Except for Sammo Hung in *Martial Law* (1998–2000) and Pat Morita starring in his own short-lived series, *Ohara* (1987–1988), all Asian American detectives have played sidekick roles to white males. For example, Jack Soo as Sergeant Nick Yemana had a secondary role in the program *Barney Miller* (1975–1982). In the popular television show *Hawaii Five-0* (1968–1980), actors Jack Lord and James MacArthur led a group of Asian American detectives to solve crimes in the aloha state. Asian American actors Kam Fong and Zulu, among others, played silent background roles, rushing off when orders were given. In the series *Midnight Caller* (1988–1991), actor Dennis Dun played Billy Po, the assistant to the show's lead star, Jack Killian (Gary Cole), a radio talk show host who worked to solve crimes in his spare time. Although Dun's character was much more developed than the standard Asian detective sidekick, his role was clearly the helper to the hero.

Asian Actors in Hollywood

The best-known Asian actors in Hollywood all came to the United States following phenomenal success in Asia and nearly all are limited to martial arts/action hero roles. Of these, the most well-known are Jackie Chan, Chow Yun-Fat, and Jet Li. Chan was born in Hong Kong and was formally trained at the China Drama Academy, where he learned martial arts, acrobatics, singing, and acting. His breakthrough Hong Kong martial arts movie was *The New Fist of Fury* (1976), which was a remake of the original Bruce Lee classic of the same name. For the next two decades Chan made numerous action/comedy films in Asia, where he became widely popular; however, it wasn't until the Hong Kong–made *Rumble in the Bronx* (1996) that Chan caught the eye of Hollywood producers. Chan's first major U.S.-made movie was *Rush Hour* (1998), which was unique in the sense that it combined Chan's martial arts/comedy skills together with a culture clash with his partner, an African American cop (Chris Tucker). The film was a smash hit, and Chan went on to star in a string of other comedies of the same general formula that feature his marital arts prowess, including *Shanghai Noon* (2000), *Rush Hour 2* (2001), *The Tuxedo* (2002), *Shanghai Knights* (2003), *The Medallion* (2003), and *Around the World in 80 Days* (2004). Although his movies are popular and make lots of money, Chan yearns to move on beyond his typecast roles. "It's all the same, cop from Hong Kong, cop from China," Chan admits. "Jet Li, Chow Yun-Fat and I all face the same problem. Our roles are limited."[5]

Chow Yun-Fat made more than seventy films and was Asia's biggest star before making his film debut in the United States. His first two Hollywood films, *The Replacement Killers* (1998) and the *Corruptor* (1999), were both full of action but empty in plot. His third film, *Anna and the King* (2000), was a big-budget extravaganza that also starred Jodie Foster. This film provided him the opportunity to temporarily break out of the action film mold, but he returned to the action-film genre in *Crouching Tiger, Hidden Dragon* (2000) and again in *Bulletproof Monk* (2003). His recent roles have been more varied, and he has appeared in both action-adventure films, such as *Curse of the Golden Flower* (2006), *Pirates of the Caribbean: At World's End* (2007), and *Dragonball Evolution* (2010), and dramatic films, including *The Children of Huang-Chi* (2007) and *Shanghai* (2009). Chow, however, has still not replicated his enormous popularity in Asia in the many years since his move to Hollywood.

As a child, Jet Li was a national martial arts champion in China before beginning his film career. After becoming one of the most popular movies stars in Asia in films such as *Once Upon A Time In China* (1991) and *Fist Of Legend* (1994), Li made his Hollywood debut in the first villainous role of his career, in *Lethal Weapon 4* (1999). He has since had martial arts–related starring roles in several Hollywood films, such as *Romeo Must Die* (2000), *Kiss of the Dragon* (2001), *Unleashed* (2005), and *War* (2007). In 2007 Li returned to Asia to star in the historical epic *The Warlords* (2008) and teamed up for the first time with his main martial-arts movie star rival, Jackie Chan, for a Hollywood version of the legend of the Monkey King, *The Forbidden Kingdom* (2008).

Because of the visibility of these three Hong Kong imports who work primarily in action films, as well as the success of Bruce Lee in the 1970s, martial art roles still predominate for Asian men in Hollywood. Recent examples include *Batman Begins* (2005), which includes martial arts training sessions by a mysterious Asian master and the animated film *Kung Fu Panda* (2008). Asian martial artists also frequently appear as antagonists in films by white action stars such as Jean Claude Van Damme (*Kickboxer*, 1989), Chuck Norris, (*Missing In Action*, 1984) and Stephen Seagal (*Out For A Kill*, 2003; *Into The Sun*, 2005). These roles also update the evil villain stereotype, portraying Asians as inhuman killing machines who are therefore expendable.

Asian American Actors in Hollywood

Asian American men with talent but without accents have had a much more difficult time in Hollywood than their compatriots from Hong Kong. In *La Bamba* (1987), Lou Diamond Phillips portrayed rock star Ritchie Valens, a romantic lead, and soon after gained fame playing Mexican American or Native American characters in popular films like *Stand and Deliver* (1988) and the *Young Guns* series (1988–1990). Though Phillips is Filipino American, his film career has been largely based upon non-Asian roles. Phillips notably wrote and starred in the 1991 thriller *Ambition*, which cast Dr. Haing S. Ngor as a character called "Tatay" (Tagalog for father). In 2008 he played Bolivian Socialist Mario Monje in *Che: Part Two—Guerilla*, whose character dialogue was entirely in Spanish. Likewise, Enrique Iglesias, known primarily as an international "Latin Pop" recording artist, has played non-Asian characters in films like *Once Upon a Time in Mexico* (2003) and television shows such as *Two and a Half Men* (2007). Unbeknownst to the public at large, Enrique and his brother, Julio Iglesias Jr., are of Filipino *mestizo* descent.

In the early 1990s Jason Scott Lee emerged as another Asian American actor cast as a romantic lead with broad major market appeal, paralleling the career of Japanese American actor Sessue Hayakawa in the early silent screen era. Hayakawa was a short-lived and extremely rare exception to the more typical evil Asian male stereotype in films made in the past. Lee starred in *Map of the Human Heart* (1992), *Dragon: The Bruce Lee Story* (1993), and *Jungle Book* (1994). He also provided his voice to animated cartoons *Lilo & Stich* (2002) and *Lilo & Stich 2* (2005). Paolo Montelban, the handsome Filipino American singer and actor best known for his role as Prince Charming in the Disney movie, *Cinderella* (1997), has also learned the limits of casting for Asian American men. Following his critically acclaimed film debut in *Cinderella*, he was immediately cast as the lead in the short-lived television martial arts show *Mortal Kombat* (1998–1999).

He was not seen on the big screen again until he appeared in the Filipino American independent film, *American Adobo* (2001) and in a small role in *The Great Raid* (2005).

Dwayne "The Rock" Johnson, a multiracial Samoan American, emerged as a popular World Wrestling Federation personality in the late 1990s. He soon built a significant film resumé, starring in big-budget action vehicles, such as *The Scorpion King* (2001), and comedies, such as *Get Smart* (2008). His characters are typically of nondescript racial or ethnic backgrounds, and his roles depend upon his large, muscular phenotype for physical spectacle.

Korean American actor John Cho made his film debut in the independent Asian American film *Shopping for Fangs* (1997). Cho later appeared in other Asian American films, including *Yellow* (1998) and *Better Luck Tomorrow* (2002), while also taking small roles in Hollywood productions including *American Pie* (1999) and *American Beauty* (1999). His breakout Hollywood role was in the stoner comedy *Harold and Kumar Go to White Castle* (2004). He was then cast as Mr. Sulu, one of the lead characters in the 2009 big-screen installment of *Star Trek* (2009), and was also named one of People Magazine's 2006 Sexiest Men Alive, which belies the stereotype of the emasculated Asian male. It remains to be seen whether Cho will continue on to dramatic or romantic leading-man roles in Hollywood.

PORTRAYALS OF ASIAN AMERICAN WOMEN

Asian American women have two dominant stereotypes in mainstream American film and television. The dragon lady stereotype originated in the early twentieth century and was codified in several roles by Chinese American actress Anna May Wong (*Thief of Bagdad*, 1924; *Shanghai Express*, 1932; *Daughter of the Dragon*, 1931). The dragon lady stereotype typically portrays an Asian woman who is sneaky, untrustworthy, and devious, and who uses her sexuality as a weapon to deceive and ensnare unfortunate men. More recent variations on the dragon lady stereotype include several portrayed by Lucy Liu in films such as *Payback* (1999), *Kill Bill: Vol. 1* (2003), and the television series *Ally McBeal*, in which Liu plays the scheming lawyer Ling Woo, whose theme music was from the Wizard of Oz's Wicked Witch of the West. Liu's role in the animated film *Afro Samurai: Resurrection* (2009) has the actress voicing Sio, "a seductive and sadistic mastermind out to destroy (the) samurai."

The other prevalent stereotype of Asian American women is known variously as the lotus blossom, geisha girl, china doll, or Suzie Wong (for the seminal title character in the 1957 Richard Quine film *The World of Suzie Wong*). This characterization presents Asian women as passive, sexually compliant and easy to seduce, often as willing partners to European American men. A continuation of long-held stereotypes of Asian women as prostitutes (see the Page Act, 1875), the popularity of these roles grew exponentially after World War II, during which many U.S. servicemen in the Pacific Theater first encountered Asian populations. Films such as *Love Is a Many Splendored Thing*

(1955), *Teahouse of the August Moon* (1956), *Sayonara* (1957), *The World of Suzie Wong, A Girl Named Tamiko* (1962), and *You Only Live Twice* (1967) engraved the image of sexy, submissive Asian woman into the American consciousness. Later films such *as Full Metal Jacket* (1987), *Braddock: Missing in Action 3* (1988), and *Balls of Fury* (2007) continued to perpetuate this stereotype. In *I Now Pronounce You Chuck and Larry* (2007), several Asian women (including Tila Tequila) are seen as scantily clad "Hooters" girls, who sexually perform for the white male protagonists.

The Asian Girlfriend

Another common representation of Asian American women portrays characters who are romantically involved with white men. Asian American film scholars suggest that this practice reflects white male privilege, in which white men enjoy the license to sexually, politically, and socially dominate women of color.[6] The last year of the hit program *M*A*S*H* (1972–1983) featured a female Asian character, Soon-Lee (Rosalind Chao), who eventually married the cross-dressing corporal Max Klinger (Jamie Farr). Their marriage continued into a post-*M*A*S*H* spinoff, *AfterMASH* (1983–1984). Chao also regularly appeared in the show *Star Trek: The Next Generation* (1987–1994) and its spinoff *Star Trek: Deep Space Nine* (1993–1999) as botanist Keiko Ishikawa, wife of Transporter Chief Miles O'Brian (Colm Meaney). In the hit comedy series, *Friends* (1994–2004) Lauren Tom had a recurring role from 1995 through 1996 as Julie, the girlfriend of one of the show's main characters, while Ming-Na played a sharp-talking gallery owner, social butterfly, and love interest in the show *The Single Guy* (1995–1997).

OTHER STEREOTYPES

Perpetual Foreigner

Asian Americans have often been portrayed as "perpetual foreigners," nonnative interlopers into American culture. Characteristics of this stereotype include camera-wielding Japanese tourists (*Armageddon*, 1998), hostile Korean merchants and shopkeepers speaking strongly accented English (*Falling Down*, 1993; *Menace II Society*, 1993; *Do The Right Thing*, 1989), unethical bad drivers (*Crash*, 2006), and other depictions that emphasize the "foreign-ness" of Asians in the United States. The hit independent film *Juno* (2007) further reinforced the perpetual foreigner stereotype—its only Asian character is a girl found protesting outside of a family-planning clinic. The character proclaims that "babies want to be borned," in broken yet unaccented English, suggesting that even American-born Asians are unable to speak English correctly. By inference, Asians can never fully belong in this country, are not fully American, and are undermining American culture with their barbaric, backward customs and manners. The perceived inability of Asians to acculturate in the United States thus prevents their full acceptance into mainstream American life.

Model Minority

Asian Americans are perceived as the model minority: successful, well-behaved, assimilated members of mainstream American society who have overcome prejudice and racism. In mainstream media this manifests itself in guises such as Asian Americans in high-paying professions—doctors, lawyers, and accountants. These roles are often supporting characters with little depth or development. These portrayals also contradict the reality that many Asian Americans, notably Southeast Asians and Pacific Islanders, live near or below the poverty line and often struggle to survive in the United States.

Another version of the model minority is the Asian geek, often a computer nerd, who is a straight-A student who brings up the bell curve. A recent characterization of this type is Hiro Nakamura of the television series *Heroes* (2006-present, NBC-TV), a nerdy, bespectacled Japanese office worker who loves science fiction and "manga," or Japanese comic books. However, because Hiro is a featured character on the show, his character has been much more layered and developed than previous, more one-dimensional representations such as those mentioned above. Another film that both exploits and deconstructs the model minority stereotype is *Harold and Kumar Go to White Castle* (2004). The title characters at first appear to be typical model minorities—Harold, a Korean American, is an investment banker, and Kumar, of Indian descent, is applying for medical school. Most of the film, however, centers on their getting stoned, pursuing women, and searching for White Castle hamburgers, activities that counter the model minority myth.

PROGRESS IN REPRESENTATIONS

Canadian born Sandra Oh began her career acting in independent Asian Canadian and Asian American films, winning two Best Actress Genies (the Canadian equivalent of the Academy Awards) for her roles in those films. Her breakout role in the award-winning film *Sideways* (2004) led to a recurring role in the television drama *Grey's Anatomy*, for which she has won a Golden Globe award as well as several Emmy nominations. Oh's character, Cristina Yang, is multilayered and complex and evades the simplistic characterizations and stereotyping too often found in roles for Asian women in Hollywood.

In the fall of 1994, Korean American comedian Margaret Cho was the first Asian American woman to star in her own situation comedy, *All-American Girl*. The show floundered creatively, however, and was canceled after one season. It was also somewhat controversial in the Asian American community, as some Asian Americans thought that the program perpetuated stereotypes, notably of Asian American men.

Following the cancellation of the series, Cho concentrated on her stand-up comedy career and her one-woman stage shows, including *I'm The One That I Want* (in which she chronicled her misadventures with *All-American Girl*), *Notorious C.H.O.* (2002), and *Assassin* (2005), which became popular and

Margaret Cho poses for a portrait at the Gay Pride Parade in San Francisco, June 2008. (AP Images for VH1/Kevin Sam)

critical successes. In 2008 Cho launched a new television series, a reality show on cable channel VH1 titled *The Cho Show,* over which, as writer and producer, she maintained creative control. A combination of unscripted elements and set-up situations, the series followed Cho in her daily life as a comedian in Los Angeles. The show was a success and presented a much more realistic and interesting view of Cho than her earlier sitcom, in part because of the program's focus on her strong, unconventional personality.

In 2008, Clint Eastwood directed and co-starred in *Gran Torino*, the first mainstream film to feature a Hmong American cast. In the film, Eastwood portrays Walt Kowalski, a Korean War veteran and former Detroit autoworker who is compelled to resolve his guilt and racial prejudice after being welcomed into his Hmong neighbors' social circle. The film pushes beyond the typical stereotypes of other Hollywood portrayals of Southeast Asians as "chinks" or "commie gooks" and provides cursory insights about this otherwise invisible Asian American group. Casualties of the CIA's secret, illegal war in Laos, the Hmong characters are depicted with complexity and humanity as they struggle with their new lives in the United States.[7]

LACK OF PRESENCE IN TELEVISION

Despite these gains, Asian Americans still lack a solid presence in the television mainstream. A 2007 analysis of Asian Americans on television from the National Asian Pacific American Legal Consortium (NAPALC) shows 2.5 percent Asian Pacific Islander American (APIA) representation on television, which is only slightly more than the representation a decade ago. In total, there were eighteen APIA actors on prime-time television. Out of 113 prime time programs, only thirteen featured at least one reoccurring Asian American, Pacific Islander, or multiracial Asian American/Pacific Islander character. Only three programs on television in fall 2004 had more than one APIA character (*ER*, *Hawaii*, and *Lost*).

Other findings were as follows:

- Of the thirteen television programs, APIA actors were featured far less than non-APIA actors. White actors took up 83.3 percent of the screen time on these thirteen specific programs, while APIA characters consistently had the lowest screen time. The multiracial APIA actors, some of whom played white characters, received significantly more screen time than nonmultiracial APIA actors. In this study, male APIA actors (11) outnumbered female APIA actors (7).

- A number of television programs were located in cities such as Honolulu, San Francisco, Queens (New York), Seattle, and New York City that have large APIA populations, but had no regular APIA cast member. For example, the programs *Half and Half* on UPN and *Charmed* on WB were set in San Francisco but neither had an APIA cast member. There were seven television programs set in Los Angeles that had no regular APIA cast member. Two shows set in Honolulu, *Hawaii* on NBC and *North Shore* on FOX, had relatively high APIA representation on the cast (27 percent), although APIAs represent 63 percent of the city's population.

The characterizations of APIAs on television are not as stereotypical and limited as in the past. Of the eighteen APIA characters on television, five were in the medical field (two doctors, one medical examiner, one forensic psychologist, and one paramedic), three were in law enforcement (one captain and two officers). There was one linguistic specialist, one bartender/nightclub owner, one "brainy student," and two whose occupation is unknown because they are survivors of a plane crash forced to live on a remote island (*Lost*).

ORGANIZING FOR CHANGE

Because their representation in Hollywood has often been negligible or distorted, Asian Americans have organized in various ways to speak out against and take action in support of more realistic images. Founded in 1992, the Media Action Network for Asian Americans (MANAA) monitors television, motion pictures, print, advertising, and radio, advocating for balanced, sensitive, and positive portrayals of Asian Americans.

Since 1999 NAPALC has led the Asian Pacific American Media Coalition, a group of nineteen organizations, in a campaign against the lack of diversity in television programming. More recently, Web sites such as AngryAsianMan.com have been effective loci for Asian Americans organizing to protest inaccuracies and stereotypes in representations of Asians in Hollywood. These include campaigns against the whitewashing of the film versions of *Avatar: The Last Airbender* and *21*.

OUTLOOK

In recent years, the medium of cyberspace has played an influential role, especially in terms of mass audience access for Asian American artists. Internet-only performers Happy Slip (Filipina American Christine Gambito), KevJumba, and David Choi have thousands of subscribers on their YouTube channels, bypassing traditional means of distribution to directly reach their target audiences. Because they maintain complete creative control over their output, these performers are not subject to the stereotyping that is prevalent in conventional mainstream media.

Asian Americans have also found success in television's reality and talent shows, where unscripted programming allows them to represent themselves on their own terms. In 2003, Dat Phan was the winner of *Last Comic Standing*, the popular NBC stand-up comedy competition reality show. Much of his material is based upon his experience growing up as a Vietnamese American and pokes fun at Asian stereotypes. Filipino American comedian Jo Koy (Joseph Glenn Herbert) also has gained notoriety with his edgy observational humor and original insights. Recent appearances include *BET's Comic View, Showtime at the Apollo,* and *The Tonight Show with Jay Leno.*

In 2006, Korean American Yul Kwon became the first Asian American to win *Survivor*, the popular CBS-TV reality show. On the show Kwon was a strong, intelligent, and empathetic leader, whose negotiating skills led to his victory. Because of his famously toned physique and good looks, he also became an object of desire and was named one of *People* Magazine's Sexiest Men in 2006, countering the stereotype of the emasculated Asian male. In 2009, Filipino American Lou Diamond Phillips was the winner on ABC-TV's *Survivor*-like series *I'm a Celebrity . . . Get Me Out of Here!*

In 2007, the dance crew JabbaWockeeZ, with several Asian American members, won MTV's *America's Best Dance Crew* competition. (Kaba Modern, another Asian American crew, also competed on the show). Jabbawokeez has achieved mainstream success and recognition, and its widespread appeal offers hope for the further dissolution of barriers for Asian Americans in mass media. Crew members notably danced with Shaquille O'Neal in an exhibition performance during the 2009 NBA All-Star Game. As one admirer notes, "I'm an African American woman who has always had an eye on hip-hop internationally, so when my friends act shocked about Asians in hip-hop, I just tell them the Asian community has been bringin' it for years." [8]

Outside of the Hollywood mainstream, Asian American independent filmmakers are also making their mark on the screen, as discussed further in the Independent Film entry.

NOTES

1. Darrell Y. Hamamoto, *Monitored Peril: Asian Americans and the Politics of TV Representation* (Minneapolis: University of Minnesota Press, 1994), 3.

2. Larry Carroll, "'Twilight' Star Jackson Rathbone Hopes To 'Show His Range' In 'Last Airbender'," *MTV*, Jan. 15, 2009.

3. "China Gives Bald Pirate the Chop," Associated Press. June 15, 2007, http://www .cnn.com/2007/SHOWBIZ/Movies/06/15/china.pirates.ap/index.html.

4. Alison MacAdam, "Long Duk Dong: Last of the Hollywood Stereotypes?" *All Things Considered,* National Public Radio, March 24, 2008.

5. "Chan Complains of Limited Roles," *AsianWeek*, Oct. 7, 2004, http://www .committee100.org/publications/outsourcing/jackychan.htm (accessed on August 3, 2009).

6. Darryl Hamamoto, *Monitored Peril* (Minneapolis: University of Minnesota Press, 1994), 46.

7. Kurashige, Scott. "Living for Change: An American Icon Looks in the Mirror". *Michigan Citizen*. January 11–17, 2009, http://www.boggscenter.org/fi-scott _kurashige-01-17-09_grand_torino.html.

8. "Letters to the Editor: Chol Soo Lee, AZN TV, R.I.P., JabbaWockeeZ Love" *AsianWeek*. April 9, 2008.

DIRECTORS IN HOLLYWOOD

Valerie Soe

Prior to the 1990s very few Asian American filmmakers had directed mainstream Hollywood films. Since then, several Asian Americans have become successful studio film directors. This is significant because Asian Americans have been historically mis- or underrepresented in Hollywood, both on-screen and behind the camera. Asian American scholars note that until recently Asian Americans have been systematically excluded from positions of influence in mainstream film production in the United States.[1] Overt institutional racism, such as the Chinese Exclusion Act (in effect until its repeal in 1943) and the internment of Japanese Americans during World War II, as well as more subtle forms of discrimination, barred most Asian Americans from succeeding in the film industry.[2] By the 1990s, conditions for Asian Americans in Hollywood had improved somewhat.

One of the earliest Asian American directors to break through in Hollywood was Wayne Wang. Born and raised in Hong Kong, Wang went to film school in the United States. His earliest feature films were independent productions, often dealing with Asian American stories and with primarily Asian American casts, including *Chan Is Missing* (1981), *Dim Sum: A Little Bit Of Heart* (1985), and *Eat A Bowl Of Tea* (1989). In 1993 Wang directed the film version of Amy Tan's bestselling novel *The Joy Luck Club*, which was a surprise hit despite focusing on an Asian American story and having no movie stars in the cast. He followed this with a pair of successful independent films, *Smoke* (1995) and *Blue In The Face* (1995), which did not deal with Asian American themes, with actors including Harvey Keitel, William Hurt, and Forest Whitaker. Since then Wang has gone on to direct several Hollywood studio pictures with bankable stars, including *Anywhere But Here* (1999), with Susan Sarandon and Natalie Portman; *Maid In Manhattan* (2002), with Jennifer Lopez; and *Last Holiday* (2006), with Queen Latifah. However, Wang has also retained his interest in independent films, often with Asian and Asian American-themed stories, such as *Chinese Box* (1997), a psychological drama set during the handover of Hong Kong in 1997. In 2007 he directed a pair of low-budget independent feature films on digital video, *The Princess Of Nebraska* and *A Thousand Years Of Good Prayers*, which were based on the short stories of Chinese American writer Yiyun Li.

Another Asian American director who has succeeded in Hollywood is the Taiwanese American Ang Lee. Like Wang, Lee was born in Asia but went to film school in the United States, at New York University. His films often deal with issues of self and the search for identity in the face of discrimination or societal disapproval. His first feature film, *Pushing Hands* (1992), about a Chinese immigrant to New York City, was an independent production, as was his second, *The Wedding Banquet* (1993), which dealt with a gay New Yorker's struggle to hide his sexuality from his Taiwanese parents. This film, however, was a critical and commercial success and was the highest-grossing film of the year in relation to its production costs. Lee followed *The Wedding Banquet* with *Eat Drink Man Woman* (1994), which followed the story of a Taiwanese family's various interpersonal struggles and which was the third of what he calls his "father knows best" trilogy, so named for its focus on family conflicts and challenges to traditional Chinese patriarchal values. He then directed a very popular and well-received adaptation of Jane Austen's *Sense and Sensibility* (1995), set in England and starring Emma Thompson and Hugh Grant.

Following this, Lee has directed both Asian-themed and non-Asian themed films to great success. In 2000 he directed the martial-arts fantasy film *Crouching Tiger, Hidden Dragon*, which was a critical and commercial success. It was the highest-grossing foreign-language film in the United States and was nominated for four Academy Awards, including Best Foreign Language Film, for which it won the Oscar. Lee then directed *The Hulk* (2003), based on the Marvel Comic book, which flopped critically and at the box office.

Following the disappointment of *The Hulk*, Lee directed *Brokeback Mountain* (2005), which became his most acclaimed film to date. The story of two male Wyoming ranch hands who fall in love, *Brokeback Mountain* won more than seventy awards, including three Academy Awards. One Oscar was for best director for Lee, the first Asian to receive this honor. The film was heavily favored to also win the Oscar for Best Picture but was upset by Paul Haggis's *Crash*.

Lee returned to an Asian-themed story with *Lust, Caution* (2005), which outlined the relationship between an actress and an official in 1950s China. The film's explicit sex scenes earned it an NC-17 rating in the United States, which prevented its screening in some theaters, yet it grossed more than $4 million in limited release. It was also a great success in Asia, as one of the top-grossing films of the year in China, Hong Kong, and Taiwan. It won the Golden Lion award at the Venice Film Festival, as well as several Golden Horse awards in Taiwan.

Although India has longstanding, thriving film industry, it is dominated by "Bollywood," the Hindi-language film production center based in Mumbai, as well as smaller commercial film centers in the South and other regions. Some independent Indian directors such as Deepa Mehta have gained prominence as well. Mehta and British-born Gurinder Chadha, as well as Mira Nair, are among some of the well-known diasporic Indian filmmakers. Mira Nair has had success in directing both independent and Hollywood films. Her work is discussed further in the sidebar.

Born in India and raised in a suburb of Philadelphia, M. Night Shyamalan graduated from New York University's Tisch School of the Arts, where he directed and starred in his first feature, *Praying with Anger* (1992), which looked at an Indian American's struggle to reconcile with his family and his culture. He came to prominence after his third feature, *The Sixth Sense* (1999), became a box office hit. Starring Bruce Willis and Haley Joel Osment, with a supernatural story and ending plot twist, the film was one of the top grossing pictures of the year in the United States and was nominated for six Academy Awards. Shyamalan has since directed several thrillers in Hollywood, including *Unbreakable* (2000), *Signs* (2002), *The Village* (2004), and *Lady in the Water* (2006), all of which are known for their surprise endings.

Chinese American director Justin Lin was born in Taiwan and raised in Orange County, CA. After attending film school at UCLA, Lin co-directed *Shopping for Fangs* (1997) with fellow UCLA alumnus, Quentin Lee. The film, which linked several characters, including a man who thinks he is turning into a werewolf, an amnesiac housewife and a mysterious Chinese American lesbian waitress in a blonde wig and sunglasses, was well-received on the festival circuit and went on to limited theatrical release. His next feature, *Better Luck Tomorrow* (2002), which looked at the shadow lives of several Asian American teenagers in Orange County, caused a sensation at the Sundance Film Festival and was subsequently picked up for distribution by MTV films and went on to commercial and critical success. Lin's next film *Annapolis* (2006), set in the Naval Academy with a multiracial cast including James Franco, Tyrese Gibson, and Roger Fan, was less popular in its theatrical release but has since had a successful DVD release. Lin was then hired to direct *The Fast and the Furious: Tokyo Drift* (2006), the third installment of the action car racing franchise, which has grossed more than $158 million to date. Lin followed this with another independent release, *Finishing the Game* (2007), which traced the fictional account of the search

Mira Nair

South Asian filmmaker Mira Nair has directed several mainstream commercial films in the United States. Born and raised in India, Nair attended Harvard University and lives in New York City. One of the few women of color who has succeeded as a director in Hollywood, she is known primarily for films that examine the connections and conflicts between Indian and Western culture.

Nair started out as a documentary producer, then directed several well-received independent films including *Salaam, Bombay!* (1988), which was nominated for an Academy Award for Best Foreign Film; *Mississippi Masala* (1991), about an interracial relationship between an Indian woman and an African American man in the South; *The Perez Family* (1995), which looked at a group of Cuban refugees in the U.S., and *Kama Sutra: A Tale of Love* (1996), based in part on the famous Indian text. She then directed *Monsoon Wedding* (2001), a love story set in India that was a commercial success in the United States and abroad. She followed this with *Vanity Fair* (2004), based on the novel by English author William Thackeray, which starred Reese Witherspoon, and *The Namesake* (2006), which was set in India and Boston and featured Indian actors Tabu and Irfan Khan as well as Indian American actor Kal Penn (*Harold and Kumar Go To White Castle*). Her latest production is *Shantaram*, starring Johnny Depp, which will shoot in India and the United Kingdom.

Nair has also directed films for television, including *My Own Country*, from the true story and the book of the same name about Dr. Abraham Verghese, a South Asian physician who moves to rural Tennessee and becomes a specialist in AIDS and other infectious diseases. Like *Mississippi Masala*, film deals with relationships between South Asians and African Americans. Additionally, she directed the TV film *Hysterical Blindness*, starring Uma Thurman, Gena Rowlands, and Juliette Lewis, which examines the romantic lives of three women in New Jersey. Nair also returned to documentary production with short film *The Laughing Club of India* (2002). She also produced short segments of the omnibus films *New York, I Love You* and *11'09"01—September 11*.

Nair also mentors emerging international filmmakers, most significantly through the Maisha Film Lab, which she founded in 2004. Based in Uganda, Maisha selects South Asian (India, Pakistan, Sri Lanka, and Bangladesh) and East African (Uganda, Kenya, Tanzania, and Rwanda) filmmakers for extensive training in screenwriting, storytelling, and film production. According to Maisha's mission statement, "Maisha is motivated by the belief that a film which explores the truths and idiosyncrasies of the specifically local often has the power to cross over and become significantly universal."[1]

Nair is well regarded in her home country of India and in 2007 was given the "Pride of India" award at the ninth Bollywood Film Awards. Upon receiving the award Nair noted the influence of Indian arts and culture on her work, saying, "To those who worry about filmmakers becoming more international than Indian, I say this—it is because my roots are so strong that I can fly."[2]

FURTHER READING

Muir, John Kenneth, *Mercy in Her Eyes: The Films of Mira Nair,* Applause Theatre and Cinema Books (2006)

Notes

1. Maisha Film Lab, http://www.maishafilmlab.com/.
2. Press Trust of India, "Bollywood to Honour Mira Nair with 'Pride of India' Award," Hindustan Times, Feb. 4, 2007.

—Valerie Soe

for a successor to Bruce Lee. Lin is also the director for *Fast and Furious 4,* released in 2009.

Other Asian Americans who have recently directed films in Hollywood include Joan Chen (*Autumn in New York*, 2000), Joseph Kahn (*Torque*, 2003), Gregg Araki (*Mysterious Skin*, 2004), and James Wong (*Dragonball Evolution*, 2009; *The One*, 2001).

Justin Lin arrives at the premiere of *Fast and Furious 4* in Los Angeles on March 2009. (AP Photo/Matt Sayles)

FURTHER READING

Dilley, Whitney Crothers. *The Cinema of Ang Lee: The Other Side of the Screen, Directors' Cuts.* London: Wallflower Press, 2007.
Muir, John Kenneth. *Mercy in Her Eyes: The Films of Mira Nair.* Applause Theatre and Cinema Books (2006).

NOTES

1. Darrell Hamamoto, *Countervisions: Asian American Film Criticism* (Philadelphia: Temple University Press, 2000), 1.

2. Yoshio Kishi, "Final Mix: Unscheduled," *Moving The Image: Independent Asian Pacific American Media Arts* (Los Angeles: UCLA Asian American Studies Center and Visual Communications, 1991), 157.

INDEPENDENT FILM

Valerie Soe

Asian American independent film has thrived since the early 1970s, when Asian Americans began making work in large numbers. Work by Asian American producers intersects with and reflects issues of the Asian American community, such as self-definition, self-determination, and empowerment, and Asian American independent films are often tools for social change and political activism. These films reflect the diversity of the Asian American community, with its many different nationalities and languages, from new immigrants to American-born Asians, living in many different parts of the United States. The films bring to light stories not found in mainstream film and television, from an Asian American perspective, by Asian American people.

The Asian American independent film movement was part of the broader social and political activism of the 1960s, which included the civil rights and antiwar movements of the 1950s and 1960s and the 1968 Third World Strike at San Francisco State University. As young people and people of color began to rise up and take their struggle to the streets, Asian American filmmakers began to voice the concerns of the Asian American community. Culture, identity, racism, activism, and equal rights all became subjects for the nascent Asian American film movement.

Early Asian American films from the 1970s and 1980s often reflected this activism through community-based, grassroots production. As film historian Russell Leong notes: "We did not see ourselves as making art for others to consume. We did not separate ourselves from everyday activities of eating, drinking, working or making love in our neighborhoods. Rather, community collaboration was integral to planning, producing and presenting our works."[1] Films such as *Hito Hata: Raise The Banner* (1970), which chronicled the struggles of first-generation Japanese Americans, *The Fall of the I-Hotel* (1984), which looked at community efforts to save a landmark Manilatown institution, and *Who Killed Vincent Chin?* (1988), which outlined the circumstances of the infamous 1982 murder of a Chinese American man in Detroit, all reflected issues significant to the Asian American community at the time.[2] Although several Asian American documentaries screened on public television, many other of these earlier productions were primarily exhibited within the Asian American community, at film festivals and other community gatherings.

The first Asian American Film Festival took place in New York City in 1976. Since then, more than a dozen Asian American film festivals have been established across the country, in cities including San Francisco (where the ten-day festival presents more than 120 films), Los Angeles, Seattle, Austin, Chicago, Washington, DC, and Vancouver and Toronto in Canada. These festivals provide important support and visibility for Asian American independent films and aid producers and directors in finding theatrical, broadcast, and educational distribution for their films.

Many early Asian American independent films sought to clarify and illuminate Asian American history and identity. Eddie Wong's short documentary *Wong Sinsaang* (1971) paid tribute to the simple, iconic life of his laundryman father. Loni Ding's two-part series *Ancestors In America* traced the story of the Chinese in America—Ding also produced *The Color of Honor: The Japanese American Soldier in WWII* (1987). Steven Okazaki's documentaries *Survivors* (1982) and *Unfinished Business* (1985) examined the Japanese American experience during World War II. Okazaki later won an Academy Award for his short documentary *Days of Waiting: The Life and Art of Estelle Ishigo* (1990).

Wayne Wang's *Chan Is Missing* (1982) is notable for being the first Asian American film to receive theatrical distribution and to screen extensively outside of the Asian American community. *Chan Is Missing* premiered at the New York Film Festival and was shown theatrically in several U.S. cities. An offbeat, humorous and idiosyncratic look at San Francisco's Chinatown, *Chan Is Missing* challenged stereotypes about the homogeneity of the Asian American community and helped to bring Asian American films to a broader audience. *Chan Is Missing* has since been followed by several successful independent Asian American feature narratives, including *A Great Wall* (1984), *Mississippi Masala* (1991), *The Wedding Banquet* (1993), *Picture Bride* (1994), and *Better Luck Tomorrow* (2002), all of which were nationally distributed and screened.

The 1990s saw an increase in the diversity of the demographics of Asian American community. In addition, video production equipment became widely accessible with the introduction of lower-cost, portable video cameras and desktop media editing. Correspondingly, many Asian American film productions from that period used the new, affordable technology to address personal and cultural identity. *AKA Don Bonus* (1993) used a diaristic, first-person approach to follow a Cambodian American teenager's daily tribulations. Narrated by co-director Sokly Ny (whose pseudonym is Don Bonus) and shot with a Hi8 palmcorder, this personal documentary revealed the everyday challenges of a low-income teen immigrant's life, including struggles with crime, the lure of gangs, and an indifferent public education system.

My America, or Honk If You Love Buddha (1997) used as its framework director Renee Tajima-Pena's nationwide travels in search of Asian Americans. As she journeyed around the United States, Tajima-Pena visited a cross-section of the Asian American community, including a New York Chinatown entrepreneur with four jobs, Seattle-based Korean American rappers known as The Seoul Brothers, and white-identified Filipino sisters in New Orleans, among many others. She also profiled older Asian American activists Bill and Yuri Kochiyama and actor Victor Wong, as well as younger members of the community, including Korean American community organizer Allyssa Kang and a self-defined "queer South Asian," half-German woman nicknamed Madds. Throughout the film Tajima-Pena encompassed an inclusive rather than exclusive criterion of Asian American identity, community, and culture. As with many Asian American productions of the time, the film attempted to expand the definition of Asian American identity, reflecting the increased diversity of the Asian American community at large.

Since the turn of the twenty-first century, Asian American independent film has further reflecting the community's growth and change. Some Asian American films continue to champion political causes. *Muni to the Marriage* (2004) examined marriage equality, drawing parallels between racism and homophobia through director Stuart Gaffney's attempts to wed his longtime male partner. *Saigon USA* (2004) looked at the controversy surrounding the display of a poster of Communist leader Ho Chi Minh in the Vietnamese American enclave of Westminster, CA. Tad Nakamura's short documentary *Pilgrimage* (2006) traced the history and significance of the annual trek to the site of the Manzanar concentration camp in California's Owens Valley. Spanning nearly one hundred years, Arthur Dong's *Hollywood Chinese* (2007) examined stereotypes, discrimination, identity politics, and the mysteries of yellowface in its detailed look at the experiences of Chinese and Chinese Americans in mainstream American films.

Other recent Asian American films continue to examine and expand the definition of Asian American identity. Deann Borshay-Liem's personal documentary *First Person Plural* (2000) followed an adopted Korean American woman's painful journey of self-discovery. *The Flipside* (2000) satirically looked at a teenager's attempts to reconcile his Filipino and American cultural backgrounds. Souchata Poeuv's lyrical, poignant personal documentary *New Year Baby* (2007) traced the director's attempts to place her family's history in relation to the tyranny of the Khmer Rouge.

Ham Tran's film *Journey from the Fall* (2007) provides an interesting example of community-based film production. This feature-length narrative recounts the story of a Vietnamese family's struggles following the 1975 fall of Saigon—most the family flees to the United States as refugees, with the father remaining in a re-education camp in Vietnam. According to the film's Web site, *Journey from the Fall*'s entire $1.6 million production budget was raised from within the Vietnamese American community. The film's producers also independently distributed it, targeting cities with large Vietnamese populations, including Westminster, CA, New York City, and San Jose, CA. In the opening weekend, playing in just four theaters, the film earned $87,442, giving the film the largest per-theater average of any film that weekend ($21,861)·

A newer development in Asian American productions is films that use conventional genres with an Asian American twist. *Undoing* (2007) and *East 32nd* (2008) reworked the gangster film; *Shanghai Kiss* (2007) and *Charlotte Sometimes* (2002) are relationship films; *American Zombie* (2007) revisited the monster movie.

However, some newer Asian American films differ from earlier films in that they do not specifically examine issues of identity or culture. *Colma: The Musical* (2006) used song and dance to outline the story of three youthful residents of Colma, CA. Though not explicitly about identity formation, two of the three main characters are Filipino American and the story takes place in a city with a large Filipino population. The story, however, focuses primarily on universal rites of passage, such as relationship problems, party-crashing, and the difficulties of leaving home. *The Motel* (2005) is a coming-of-age film about a pubescent Chinese American boy working in his family's run-down motel off of an unidentified stretch of highway. Though its main characters are of Chinese descent, the story makes little overt reference to themes of culture, race relations, or other concerns common to earlier Asian American films. Gina Kim's *Never Forever* (2007), dealt with a love triangle involving a white woman and two Korean American men, yet focused not on race and identity but instead on less culturally specific themes such as desire, marriage, and loyalty. The Korean Americans in the film possess some culturally related characteristics (devout Christianity, illegal immigration) while also exhibiting some more universal qualities (success at business, sensitivity, and empathy). The most racially significant element of the film may be extraneous to the main story—both of the Korean American males are virile and desirable, in opposition to the common stereotype of the emasculated Asian male.

Another recent development in Asian American independent films has been the rise of creative distribution strategies that bypass traditional, mainstream distribution and advertising channels. Instead, these films extensively use new media such as e-mail and the Internet to identify and focus on a narrow target audience. Several of these techniques were first successfully used by *The Debut* (2000), a narrative set amid the backdrop of a Filipino American "debut" party. The film deftly paired traditional and contemporary Filipino and Filipino American arts—a kulintang orchestra and turntablism, and tinikling and break dancing—reflecting the Filipino American arts explosion of the 1990s.

The Debut was the closing night film at the 2001 San Francisco International Asian American Film Festival. Immediately following this screening the producers "four-walled," or rented out, the AMC Kabuki 8, a commercial San Francisco movie theater, to screen the film daily. They also targeted the large Filipino American community in the Bay Area, visiting Filipino and Asian American Studies programs, community groups, churches, and classes at colleges and high schools to publicize the film, distribute posters and placards, and to sell T-shirts and soundtracks. At each screening throughout the run of the film, either the producer, the director or cast members made personal appearances and answered questions before and after screenings. The filmmakers also compiled a large e-mail contact list to notify interested parties of the film's future bookings and to encourage repeat viewings of the film. Through this aggressive, viral word-of-mouth campaign the film sold out nearly all of its shows during the first weekend of its run. It went on to play for three months at eleven theaters in the San Francisco Bay Area, as well as fifteen other cities nationwide. As noted on the film's official Web site: "The movie ultimately expanded to other parts of the Bay Area with theater venues in Milpitas, Union City, Fairfield, Vallejo, Oakland, South San Francisco, Santa Clara, and Pittsburg. At one point, eight theaters were playing *The Debut* simultaneously. In Milpitas alone, *The Debut* lasted an amazing 10 weeks at the Century Great Mall Theater."

In later bookings the producers specifically picked cities with high Filipino American populations such as Seattle, New York, and Honolulu. Noting the success of this targeted, grassroots distribution campaign, director Gene Cajayon stated, "You shore up core constituency and once your core is buzzing and excited first, the other communities on the periphery hear about it and want to check it out, too." The film eventually grossed $1.8 million without the benefit of a traditional, well-funded advertising and distribution budget and was released in Manila in August 2003. Because of its surprising success among its target audience, in 2003 the film received DVD distribution from Columbia/Tristar. *The Debut's* unorthodox distribution methods, including Q & A sessions by cast and crew, targeted demographics and extensive use of e-mail and the Internet, have been emulated by several other Asian American independent films, including *The Flipside, The Motel,* and *Red Doors* (2006), to bypass more costly conventional distribution and advertising campaigns.

For decades, many of these developments in independent Asian American film production have relied on Asian American organizations for exposure and support. By contributing funding, screening, and distributions opportunities, Asian American media arts centers have provided key assistance for independent Asian American filmmakers. Visual Communications (VC), founded in 1971 in Los Angeles, helped produce several early Asian American independent films, such as *Hito Hata: Raise the Banner* and *Cruisin' J-Town*, in addition to mounting an enormously popular annual film festival. Asian Cinevision (ACV) was founded in New York 1976 to produce a Cantonese-language news program. It later expanded its operations to include the New York Asian American Festival. San Francisco's National Asian American Telecommunications Association (NAATA), later renamed the Center for Asian American Media (CAAM), was founded in 1980. CAAM identifies as "a non-profit organization dedicated to presenting stories that convey the richness and diversity of Asian American experiences to the broadest audience possible [through] funding, producing, distributing and exhibiting works in film, television and digital media."

Asian American independent films in the twenty-first century can perhaps best be characterized by the description "anything goes." Although many continue exploring similar themes and issues as earlier Asian American films, the sheer number of productions ensures a wide range of subject matter, stylistic approaches, and intended audiences. This reflects the increasingly diverse demographics of the Asian American community at large.

FURTHER READING

Asian American Film. http://www.asianamericanfilm.com/.

Center for Asian American Media. http://asianamericanmedia.org/.

Feng, Peter. *Identities in Motion: Asian American Film & Video.* Durham, NC: Duke University Press, 2002.

Garcia, Roger, ed. *Out of the Shadows: Asians in American Cinema.* Olivares Press, 2001.

Hamamoto, Darrell, and Sandra Liu, eds. *Countervisions: Asian American Film Criticism.* Philadelphia: Temple University Press, 2000.

Leong, Russell, ed. *Moving The Image: Independent Asian Pacific American Media Artists.* Los Angeles: UCLA Asian American Studies Center Press, 1992.

NOTES

1. Russell Leong, ed. *Moving the Image: Independent Asian Pacific American Media Artists.* Los Angeles: UCLA Asian American Studies Center Press, 1992.

2. Oliver Wang, "History" and "Mission," http://asianamericanmedia.org/who-we -are/history.

NEWS COVERAGE

Paul Niwa

REPRESENTATION IN MAINSTREAM NEWS

Before the 1980s, Asian Americans were a relatively small proportion of the general population, and the mainstream news media barely covered them; however, the community has grown considerably during the past two decades and has expected a greater share of the headlines. In some media markets such as San Francisco, Fremont, CA, and Honolulu, Asian Americans comprise 32.6 percent, 39.8 percent and 67.7 percent of the regional population respectively.[1] They have become a demographic group that is hard for newsrooms to ignore.

Although Asian American news coverage has improved during the past twenty years in print and broadcast news media, the community's issues are often overshadowed in the overall media landscape. Some prominent examples of "missing" Asian American coverage include the destruction of Vietnamese American neighborhoods by Hurricane Katrina, the economic hardship on New York's Chinatown following the attacks of 9/11 or the intimidation of South Asians as a part of the War on Terror.

A study of Asian American neighborhood coverage in metropolitan daily newspapers found that only .3 percent of articles published by the Boston Globe in 2006 contained the word "Chinatown." Boston's Chinatown is arguably newsworthy considering its large population, large percentage of residents living in poverty, and importance in the city's urban redevelopment plan.[2] Most other journalistic studies have found that articles broadcast or published on Asian Americans are so infrequent that it is statistically difficult to perform meaningful analyses.[3]

Hurricane Katrina News Coverage

Hurricane Katrina was one of the most important domestic news events of 2005. The images of the storm's devastation opened a discussion about poverty and race in America. But, Asian Americans were virtually invisible in the mainstream media, even though 53,000 of them were caught in the six parishes and counties most severely hit by the hurricane.

Most of the 12,000 Vietnamese Americans in the New Orleans area lived in a housing complex known as Versailles. The community was evacuated, but dozens of seniors were left stranded. More than 24,000 Vietnamese Americans, 7,000 Indian Americans, and 6,500 Chinese Americans lived in the worst hit areas. U.S. Census data indicates that about 70 percent of Asian Americans in the area were immigrants, further complicating their escape from the hurricane and their access to services to help rebuild their lives.

Journalists have largely praised each other for their coverage of the disaster. Journalistic trade publications have recounted stories of heroic reporters and their sensitive and intelligent stories about race. Columbia University awarded the *Times-Picayune* of New Orleans and the *Sun Herald* of Biloxi and Gulfport, Alabama, the 2006 Pulitzer Prize for Public Service, the most prestigious award in journalism for coverage of Hurricane Katrina.

However, out of the nearly 2,500 news articles published by the two newspapers in 2005 about the storm, only six stories (0.25%) were about Asian American Communities. The news coverage was proportionally well below the 2.8% of the population that Americans of Asian ethnicities comprise in the worst hurricane-hit areas.

Journalists rarely acknowledge this disparity of content. None of the industry's major trade journals have mentioned the lack of hurricane coverage of Asian American neighborhoods. Only one sentence in the influential journalism ethics website poynter.org mentions that reporters forgot Asian American communities during Hurricane Katrina.

Ethnic media often filled the hunger for hurricane information. A priest in Versailles gave an interview to Saigon Television Broadcasting Network from a flooded church that was a shelter for dozens of stranded seniors. The sewage-filled waters had reportedly risen four meters and were precariously close to the survivors on the second floor of a building. *KoreAm* wrote about a church in Baton Rouge that became a refuge for Korean Americans and a focal point for donations from Korean American churches around the country. India West reported about a group of Sikhs who hired a private security company to rescue a sacred book and other relics in New Orleans.

Mainstream media overlooked many dramatic stories involving Asian Americans that could have appealed to a broader audience. Lack of general media coverage can influence access to governmental services and the ability to garner charitable donations. However, mainstream newsrooms have reported that Vietnamese Americans returned to rebuild their communities at higher rates than African Americans and that Asian American business were among the first to reopen in New Orleans.

—Paul Niwa

When Asian Americans do appear in the news, they are often framed as foreigners. After Virginia Tech student Seung-Hui Cho killed thirty-two people and himself in April 2007, CNN and other news organizations went to Korean American Churches on the night of the attack to ask people for their reaction to the attack.[4] Koreans in Seoul were shown apologizing for the shooting, saying "our reputation is ruined." A CNN reporter described the country as having "collective guilt."[5] Journalists interviewed psychologists to ask whether Korean culture had some relationship to mass killings.[6]

Shrimp fisherman Dung Nguyen sits on a dock next to shrimp boats destroyed by Hurricane Katrina in D'Iberville, Mississippi, September 2005. (AP Photo/Darron Cummings)

These kinds of story angles have not been pursued in white neighborhoods when whites have perpetrated similar mass shootings. Journalists did not investigate the ethnicities of former Northern Illinois University student Steven Phillip Kazmierczak or Columbine shooters Eric Harris and Dylan Klebold. No questions were raised about whether their ethnic cultures were related to the school shootings they perpetrated.[7]

The mass media has made efforts to stop exoticizing Asian Americans and other ethnic groups. Journalism industry groups have convinced their members to stop sending reporters to ethnic restaurants to get someone to comment about events occurring in the restaurant's ethnic homeland. Today, it would be considered absurd for a newsroom to send a reporter to a Chinese restaurant to get an informed perspective on an earthquake in Sichuan.

ASIAN AMERICAN JOURNALISTS

The most common technique to improve coverage of ethnic minorities is for newsrooms to hire more journalists of color. Organizations like the Asian American Journalists Association (AAJA) have made it easier for news managers to find qualified Asian American employees. AAJA also runs programs to improve the skills of Asian American journalists. AAJA organizes dozens of workshops at its national convention on writing, editing, and multimedia skills.

Asian American reporters have been found to be more effective in reporting on their racial group. A study of metropolitan daily newspapers found that Asian American reporters are 139 percent more likely to quote an Asian Americans than a non-Asian reporter when covering Asian American neighborhoods.[8] Another study found that newsrooms with Asian Americans are more likely to report on Asian American topics.[9]

However, it is far more likely that a non-Asian journalist will be assigned to write about an Asian American neighborhood than an Asian American journalist.[10] Part of this may be caused by Asian American reporters being reluctant to be "pigeonholed" into covering their own racial group. The lack of Asian Americans covering their community could also be caused by the lack of Asian Americans in positions of influence who can change newsroom culture.[11]

It is extremely difficult to find an Asian American news manager in print, broadcast, or online newsrooms. Only 2.4 percent of newsroom supervisors were Asian American in 2008. Asian Americans are also less likely to be promoted to senior editor positions. One out of four editorial employees are supervisors in newspaper newsrooms. However, only one out of five Asian American newspaper journalists are in a supervisory position.[12]

Virtually all Asian American editors were found at large newspapers. Gaining experience at a small or midsized newspaper is an important employment track for newspaper journalists. So, this lack of representation in smaller newsrooms limits the pool of qualified Asian American news managers.[13]

Overall, 3.2 percent of newspaper journalists were Asian American in 2007, compared to 2.3 percent in 1999. Although their proportion of newsroom employment is growing, representation is still weak considering that Asian Americans comprise 4.5 percent of the U.S. population.[14]

Representation within television newsrooms has been traditionally stronger than in newspaper newsrooms because of federal employment regulations that were imposed following the Kerner Commission's recommendation to prevent a repeat of the 1967 riots. Deregulation and a history of lack of enforcement, however, have largely removed the threat of regulation. The Federal Communications Commission has never revoked a broadcast license because a station failed to comply with a requirement to employ a workforce similar to the audience it serves. Asian American representation in local television newsrooms declined to 2.7 percent from 3 percent between 2008 and 2000. Asian Americans are virtually nonexistent in radio news, comprising only .4 percent of editorial employees.[15]

Asian Americans are rarely found in positions to influence what television stories are selected and how the stories are framed for the public. Only 1.7 percent of local television news directors in 2008 were Asian Americans, compared to 2 percent in 2000.[16]

Newspaper editors and TV news managers in large media markets say that Asian Americans are underrepresented in management because of the small pool of Asian American applicants and the lack of Asian Americans in their audience. Among television managers, Asian Americans were perceived to be more interested in working on-air than on the production-management track or more interested in higher-paying jobs outside of journalism.[17]

The Asian American Journalists Association has been trying to increase the number of Asian American newsroom supervisors. It has a program called the Executive Leadership Program (ELP) to train midlevel newsroom managers.

AAJA has also been trying to raise the number of Asian American males in visual, on-air positions. A 2003 survey found that in the top twenty American broadcast markets, 81 percent of the Asian Americans in on-air positions were female. Only one Asian American male out of 104 Asian American on-air employees was an anchor, and he was assigned to a minor newscast. Research indicates that low starting salaries, lack of community support, and a lack of applicants were likely factors for the gender imbalance.[18] Asian Americans are also well placed in the fastest-growing segment of mainstream newsrooms. A survey showed that Asian Americans are well represented in newsroom Web site positions.[19] As the revenue of news Web sites grows, Asian Americans could find themselves in influential roles.

Another prominent strategy to increase news coverage of Asian American issues is to make the community more accessible to journalists. Services like New American Media, New York Voices, and New England Ethnic News gather stories from ethnic newspapers so that journalists can go to a single source to look for stories about ethnic communities. Newsrooms have become more interested in stories produced by ethnic newspapers and broadcasters because it is one of the three growth areas in journalism.[20] Mainstream journalists often troll the ethnic press for story ideas that they can rewrite for a broader audience.

Ethnic Press

The ethnic press serves an important function in Asian American communities. Newspapers and newscasts provide information to Asian Americans that is overlooked by mainstream media, and they help Asian Americans find and support businesses and services within their own community. Ethnic newspapers can also become important research documents because they chronicle the lives of Asian Americans.

The first Asian American newspapers, such as the Kim Shan Jit San Luk, Chinese Daily News and Nichibei Shimbun, started publishing in the nineteenth century. Ethnic newspapers often start as newsletters from an organization and develop as journalists gain editorial independence. They are also started by entrepreneurs or as North American expansions of newspapers based in Asia.

The more established an immigrant group becomes, the more likely the community members prefer to read, listen, and watch media in English. Because U.S. Census data shows that virtually all Asian Americans speak English competently, Asian American media is expected to eventually become primarily English-based instead of "in-language." Gidra, Bridge, and AsianWeek are several examples of influential English language Asian American newspapers that are no longer published.

Handling the transition from in-language to English publication can be financially difficult. Some "early adopters" like AZN Television, A. Magazine, and AsianWeek struggled to convince media buyers to access Asian Americans through English language ads.

Asian American media are also sensitive to economic recessions due to limited access to advertising revenue. Ethnic media are reputed to inflate their unaudited viewership and circulation numbers, making them less likely to attract high paying national advertisers and more reliant on cheaper, less sophisticated local advertisers.

Tables 1, 2, and 3 list major Asian American newspapers, radio broadcasters, and television broadcasters, respectively.

Table 1. Major Asian American Newspapers

Publication	Frequency	Circulation	Established	Ethnicity
World Journal	Daily	462,000	1975	Chinese
The Korea Daily	Daily	320,000	1972	Korean
Philippine News	Weekly	150,000	1961	Filipino
Little India	Monthly	143,322	1991	Indian
Ming Pao Daily	Daily	142,000	1997	Chinese

Note: These circulation figures are claimed by the publishers and unaudited. Compare with the Audit Bureau of Circulations' September 2008 figures for the *New York Daily News* (465,779), *Boston Globe* (319,508), and *Riverside Press-Enterprise* (149,608). *Source: Asian American Yearbook* 2008/2009.

Table 2. Major Asian American Radio Broadcasters

Call Letters	Antenna	Owner	Frequency	kW	Programming
KMRB-AM	San Gabriel, CA	Multicultural Broadcasting	1430	50	Cantonese
WNWR-AM	Philadelphia, PA	Global Radio	1540	50	Chinese
KGOL-AM	Humble, TX	Entravision Holdings	1180	50	Asian
KAZN-AM	Pasadena, CA	Multicultural Broadcasting	1300	5	Mandarin
KVNR-AM	Santa Ana, CA	LBI Radio License	1480	5	Vietnamese
KNDI-AM	Honolulu, HI	Broadcast House of the Pacific	1270	5	Multicultural
WZRC-AM	New York, NY	Multicultural Broadcasting	1480	5	Cantonese
KREH-AM	Pecan Grove, TX	Bustos Media Holdings	900	5	Vietnamese
KYND-AM	Cypress, TX	Matthew Provenzano	1520	3	Vietnamese

Source: Asian American Yearbook 2008/2009, FCC.

Table 3. Major Asian American Television Broadcasters

Call Letters	Antenna	Owner	kW
WMBC-TV	Newton, NJ	Mountain Broadcasting	5000
KSCI-TV	Long Beach, CA	KSLS	2583
KTSF-TV	San Francisco, CA	Lincoln Broadcasting	2510
KXLA-TV	Rancho Palos Verdes, CA	Rancho Palos Verdes Broadcasters	2354
KMTP-TV	San Francisco, CA	Minority Television Project	1320
KIKU-TV	Honolulu, HI	KHLS	215
KBFD-TV	Honolulu, HI	The Allen Broadcasting	145

Source: Asian American Yearbook 2008/2009, FCC.

—Paul Niwa

ETHNIC AND COMMUNITY NEWS OUTLETS

There are more than 700 Asian American media outlets compared to 200 newsrooms a decade ago.[21] Advertisers have identified Asian American English-language radio and English-language magazines as the strongest mediums for growth. Radio is considered promising because of the medium's ability to target audiences and because Asian Americans are clustered in coastal cities. Magazines are considered to have potential because of the ability to target demographics that are geographically dispersed. There are also relatively few magazines written for Asian Americans compared with the size of the population.[22]

However, the closures of AZN, MTV's Asian American Channels, and *AsianWeek* and the financial struggles of Imaginasia's iaTV and *KoreAm Magazine* indicate the difficulty of creating information content for Asian American in mass communication mediums. Many newsrooms are dependent on foreign parent companies like United Daily News, China Press, and Global China Group for both financial backing and content to fill their pages.[23] Giant Robot, a magazine on pop "otaku" culture, relies on the interest of non-Asians to supplement its Asian American readership.

Asian American media is also limited by the lack of advertising infrastructure. Asian Journal is the only community newspaper that regularly audits its circulation. The small size of the Asian American population also makes national media buying impractical for large advertising agencies. Asian American media have been unable to adapt to commoditized media buying models, so they are unable to access the larger streams of advertising money. Advertising revenues for the top five Asian American newspaper groups is estimated to be well below $100 million.[24]

Distribution on traditional mass media may be too broad and too commercially challenging for Asian America. Recently, the community has embraced the Internet to distribute information, and it uses Web sites, personal digital assistants and cell phones more frequently than other racial groups.[25] Blogs like Angry Asian Man, Asian-Nation and Jeff Yang's Instant Yang review cultural trends and events. E-mail listservs create micro-communities to share information and mobilize members.

The effective use of the Internet by Asian America can be illustrated in its response to a remark by celebrity Rosie O'Donnell in December 2006. Asian Americans instantly debated online whether the O'Donnell's remark about people in China saying "ching chong," was racist. Internet users quickly posted the video on YouTube so that other members of the community could see the remark for themselves.[26]

The lively Internet discussions caught the attention of several newspapers, and O'Donnell made an acknowledgement on ABC's *The View* within days of her remark.[27] However, Asian American discussions groups were largely unsatisfied. In February 2007, Chinese American poet Beau Sia posted a commentary on YouTube that was produced by Viacom's MTV Chi channel.[28] Within days, the video was viewed more than 250,000 times, which is more viewings than the average major market newscast in America. One viewer believed to be O'Donnell posted a lengthy apology on Beau Sia's YouTube page.[29]

Since the O'Donnell remarks, Asian Americans have used the Internet to spread information on the Virginia Tech shooting, remarks by Don Imus, and the LPGA's English rule. Asian America has filled the void in news coverage left by mainstream media, and it is creating news with its own citizen-based reporting on the Internet.

FURTHER READING

All American: How to Cover Asian America. http://www.aaja.org/resources/apa _handbook/2000aaja_handbook.pdf. Book written to help journalists cover Asian America with sensitivity.

New America Media. http://news.newamericamedia.org/news/view_category.html? category_id=521. Aggregates news from the Asian American ethnic press.

Poynter's Diversity at Work Blog. http://www.poynter.org/column.asp?id=58. Weblog gives tips to journalists on how to cover communities of color.

Society of Professional Journalists Diversity Guide. http://www.spj.org/divguidelines.asp. Contains guidelines for reporting on diverse communities.

NOTES

1. Jessica S. Barnes and Claudette E. Bennett, *The Asian Population: 2000* (Washington, DC: U.S. Census Bureau, 2002).

2. Paul Niwa, *Source Diversity Within a Reporter's In-Group: Metropolitan Daily Newspapers and Sourcing Within Asian Pacific Communities* (Washington, DC: AEJMC National Meeting, 2007).

3. Paula M. Poindexter, Laura Smith, and Don Heider, "Race and Ethnicity in Local Television News: Framing, Story Assignments and Source Selections," *Journal of Broadcasting and Electronic Media* 47 (2003): 524–536.

4. John King, Gary Tuchman, Tom Foreman, et al., "Deadliest Shooting; Massacre at Virginia Tech," *CNN*, April 17, 2007, http://www.lexisnexis.com.proxy.emerson.edu/us/ lnacademic/frame.do?tokenKey=rsh-20.34184.03813022264&target=results_listview _resultsNav&reloadEntirePage=true&rand=1232479996262&returnToKey=20_T55758 01732&parent=docview.

5. Susan Lisovicz, Allan Chernoff, John Zarrella, et al., "Virginia Tech Victims Remembered; Interview With Deepak Chopra; Warning Signs Missed in Virginia Tech Massacre?; Democrats Speak to President Bush About Iraq Funding," *CNN*, April 18, 2007, http:// www.lexisnexis.com.proxy.emerson.edu/us/lnacademic/frame.do?tokenKey =rsh-20.327362.4271932963&target=results_listview_resultsNav&reloadEntirePage =true&rand=1232480223274&returnToKey=20_T5575826563&parent=docview.

6. David Mattingly, Anderson Cooper, Randi Kaye, et al., "Massacre at Virginia Tech; Deadliest Shooting," *CNN*, April 20, 2007, http://www.lexisnexis.com.proxy .emerson.edu/us/lnacademic/frame.do?tokenKey=rsh-20.486741.0563430021& target=results_listview_resultsNav&reloadEntirePage=true&rand=1232478473897& returnToKey=20_T5575611975&parent=docview.

7. Yang, Jeff. "Killer Reflection," April 19, 2007, http://www.salon.com/opinion/ feature/2007/04/19/cho_shooting/.

8. Niwa, *Source Diversity.*

9. Denis Wu and Ralph Izzard, *Representing the Total Community: Relationships between Asian-American Staff and Asian-American Coverage in US Newspapers* (Baton Rouge, LA: Manship School of Communication, 2005).

10. Niwa, *Source Diversity.*

11. C. A. Steele, "Newspapers' Representations of Tolerance and Intolerance," *Mass Communications Review* (1994): 173–186.

12. American Society of Newspaper Editors, "ASNE—Newsroom Employment Census," *ASNE.org.* April 3, 2008. http://www.asne.org/index.cfm?id=1138 (accessed Sept. 24, 2008).

13. Larry Stuelpnagel, *Asian Americans in Newsroom Management* (Evanston: Medill School of Journalism, Northwestern University, 2004).

14. American Society of Newspaper Editors, "SNE—Newsroom Employment Census."

15. Bob Papper, "The Face of the Workforce," *RTNDA Communicator* (July/August 2008): 10–12.

16. Papper, "The Face of the Workforce."

17. Stuelpnagel, *Asian Americans in Newsroom Management.*

18. Patricia Riley and Cynthia Kennard, *Asian American Male Broadcasters on TV: Where Are They?* Survey for AAJA (Los Angeles: Annenberg School, University of Southern California, 2003).

19. American Society of Newspaper Editors, "ASNE—Newsroom Employment Census."

20. Projects for Excellence in Journalism, *The State of the News Media* (New York City: Project for Excellence in Journalism, 2005).

21. Bill Imada, *The State of Marketing to Asian Americans* (New York: IW Group, 2008).

22. Magna Global, *The Pollo or the Dan: An Overview of Multicultural Media,* (New York City: Magna Global, 2005).

23. Global, *The Pollo or the Dan.*

24. Global, *The Pollo or the Dan.*

25. Imada, *The State of Marketing to Asian Americans.*

26. ptrinh123. *Rosie O'Donnell's Racist 'Ching Chong' Chinese SLUR.* Dec. 13, 2006. http://www.youtube.com/watch?v=A0HtTReGt08 (accessed Sept. 24, 2008).

27. Vanessa Hua, "Asian American Advocates Decry Parody by TV's O'Donnell," *The San Francisco Chronicle*, Dec. 14, 2006: A5.

28. Beau Sia, *YouTube,* Feb. 27, 2007. http://www.youtube.com/watch?v=VJCkHu3trKc (accessed Sept. 24, 2008).

29. Guest Contributor, *Racilicious.* March 1, 2007. http://www.racialicious.com/2007/03/01/rosie-finally-seems-to-get-it-all-because-of-beau-sia/ (accessed Sept. 24, 2008).

POPULAR MUSIC

Allan Aquino

During the first half of the twentieth century, countless Asian American artists avidly engaged popular music by way of jazz ensembles and rock 'n' roll bands. Access to the fledgling American recording industry was limited, so Asian Americans were primarily known for their live performances. In the 1950s, Mexican American Ritchie Valens, on the strength of his hit single "La Bamba," opened the doors for people of color in rock 'n' roll music. While Valens is a pioneer in that regard, he first began as a lead guitarist and covocalist of a Los Angeles–based garage band called The Silhouettes, which featured Japanese American bandmates throughout its early years.

Since the emergence of the "Asian American" paradigm in the 1960s and 1970s, music has been an integral part of Asian American life. Bound much more by parallel social and historical experiences than culture, Asian American activists shared chants and protest songs, along with common musical tastes. Musicians who were involved with the Asian American movement of the 1970s included the Japanese American jazz-fusion group Hiroshima, and the trio of Chris Iijima, Charlie Chin, and Nobuko Miyamoto, whose seminal recording, *A Grain of Sand* (1973), set to music many themes and issues in the Asian American community. The presence and contributions of Asian American artists in popular music is deeply rooted in history and has grown tremendously in the present day.

A number of contemporary popular music groups feature prominent Asian American members. Beginning in the 1980s, Metallica, icons of the heavy metal movement, became known for the edgy compositional choices of lead guitarist Kirk Hammett, who is of Irish and Filipino descent.[1] Alternative rockers The Pixies are similarly defined by the distinctive "mellow verse/hard chorus" sensibilities of lead guitarist Joey Santiago, a Filipino American whose style has directly influenced more widely known bands like Nirvana.

By the 1990s, popular rock bands featured more and more prominent Asian American bandmates. One of the most recognized is James Iha, a Nisei native hailing from suburban Chicago, who was lead guitarist of the enormously popular Smashing Pumpkins. Iha's original songs and vocals were featured on some of Smashing Pumpkins' bestselling albums, and Iha himself, prior to forming his own independent record label, Scratchie Records, released a well-received solo album, *Let It Come Down*, in 1998.

Audiences could often and easily overlook the ethnicities of these musicians because, as guitarists, their ethnicity was secondary to their musical abilities. Even in Iha's solo effort, he wrote songs with more universal and archetypal themes, rather than dealing directly with his Japanese American roots. But by the early twenty-first century, via cyberspace-based media, a fast-growing number of independent Asian American artists have emerged in the popular American music scene.

Because growing numbers of music consumers acquire music through online downloads (rather than via CD purchases), many recording artists now choose these media tools in lieu of more conventional distribution methods. Resources like YouTube and social networking sites such as Facebook and MySpace also greatly aid the exposure and publicity of these artists.

It is also through the Internet that consumers can indulge in the diversity of styles and genres of Asian American artists. While singer-songwriters like Corrinne May, a Singapore-born Chinese American from Los Angeles, may be known for her tender, pop-friendly, and universally appealing ballads, artists such as Boston's Kevin So tackle ethnicity and social issues head-on. Early in her career May reached a large audience with her song "If You Didn't Love Me" a songwriting collaboration with the illustrious Carol Baker Sayer.[2] Kevin So, on the other hand, gained notice by the strength of his catchy "Average Asian American" a funk-inflected number that tackles anti-Asian stereotypes with wit and humor.

Vietnamese American Tila Nguyen, better known as Tila Tequila, became enormously popular through her personal MySpace Web site. An import-car model, singer, and television personality, Tequila's Internet success propelled her into her own MTV show and record deal. Though controversy surrounds the creative merit and moral appropriateness of her work, Tequila is one of the most visible and well known of popular Asian American music artists.

Likewise, Japanese American Marié Digby gained notice and popularity by way of YouTube posts. Though Digby had been signed to a label, she was fairly obscure until she posted her homemade acoustic renditions of songs by more popular artists on YouTube. Much like Tila Tequila, her cover of Rihanna's chart-topping "Umbrella" garnered for her a large and swiftly growing fan base, and on the strength of her YouTube ventures, Digby has produced successful national tours and music videos.

The most notable YouTube "recognition miracle" is the story of Arnel Pineda, a Filipino émigré who for years, had struggled as an independent rock vocalist in the Philippines. Enter Neal Schon, lead guitarist and founder of Journey, the popular U.S. rock 'n' roll band.

After the unceremonious departure of lead singer Steve Perry, Journey had struggled for years to secure a competent lead vocalist. Out of frustration, Schon turned to YouTube, browsing it for days in search of potential vocalists who might carry on Steve Perry's mantle. Upon discovering Arnel Pineda singing covers of songs by The Police, Led Zeppelin, and Journey, Schon immediately consulted his fellow bandmates, and, in late 2007, Pineda flew to the United States for a quick audition process. Pineda was immediately hired as Journey's lead vocalist. Amid a successful 2008 world tour, Journey released an album of new material entitled *Revelation*, which has sold well despite its limited Wal-Mart Exclusive release. In addition to featuring more than a dozen new songs, the album comes with a supplemental disc featuring Arnel Pineda's vocal interpretations of Journey's heyday hits.

Behind the scenes, Asian Americans have also played influential roles as producers. Chad Hugo, one half of the creative duo known as The Neptunes, has produced, cocomposed, and coarranged hit songs for an eclectic array of artists including Britney Spears, Gwen Stefani, Justin Timberlake, and Snoop Dogg. While Asian American recording artists have thus made inroads in rock and pop music, they have also had considerable influence in the roots of hip-hop culture as well.

FURTHER READING

Hess, Mickey, ed. *Icons of Hip-Hop: An Encyclopedia of the Movement, Music, and Culture.* Westport, CT: Greenwood Press, 2007.

Model Minority: A Guide to Asian American Empowerment, www.modelminority.com.

Murray, Derek Conrad. "Hip-Hop vs. High Art: Notes on Race as Spectacle." *Art Journal* 63, no. 2 (2004).

Wei, William. *The Asian American Movement.* Philadelphia: Temple University Press, 1999.

Yellow Buzz: Exploring and Documenting Asian American Music Production, www.yellowbuzz.com.

NOTES

1. Metallica Web site, http://www.metallica.com.
2. Corrinnemay Web site, http://www.corrinnemay.com.

RAPPERS AND "TURNTABLISTS"

Allan Aquino

Asian Americans, like many artists of color, often negotiate the margins of mainstream media production. "Making it" as a media artist inevitably concerns gaining access to, and popularity in, mainstream institutions. The musical element of American hip-hop culture—known worldwide primarily through rap music—is rooted in the historical experiences of socioeconomically marginalized peoples of color. Hip-hop "wears its alterity like a badge of honor," a whole and dynamic culture founded by poor and working-class black and Latino youth in the Bronx during the 1970s.[1] Unbeknownst to many, the growth and cultivation of hip-hop and its international and transnational appeal has always involved the contributions and innovations of various Asian American artists, most notably in the elements fields of rapping and turntablism.

Grand Wizard Theodore, inventor of "scratching" (the manual rhythmic and melodic manipulation of vinyl records in hip-hop music), succinctly defines hip-hop-as-culture as consisting of "four elements": rapping, deejaying, breakdancing, and graffiti art. The earliest known Asian American artist to record a hip-hop recording was Joe Bataan, a Harlem-based singer, bandleader, and "godfather" of the Salsoul movement, a melodic syncretism of soul music with Puerto Rican and Cuban salsa music from Harlem. A self-identified "mestizo" (one of his albums was aptly titled *Afrofilipino*), Bataan released "Rap-O Clap-O" in 1979, around the same time as the Sugar Hill Gang's iconic "Rapper's Delight." In keeping with the positive, original mission of hip-hop ("peace, love, unity, havin' fun"), "Rap-O Clap-O" was a pure party jam where Bataan's, through vocal rhyming, backed by disco rhythms, calls upon all peoples of the world to dance and clap their hands to the beat. Bataan prophesies the fast-growing transnational appeal of hip-hop culture.

By the mid-1980s, with the worldwide popularity of rap music by artists like Run-DMC and The Beastie Boys, the first Asian American rap star emerged as a member of the controversial 2 Live Crew of Miami. Chris Wong Won-War, known by his rapper alias Fresh Kid Ice, was one of 2 Live's lead rappers. Despite a hurricane of social and legal controversies over the apparent obscenity of their second album, 2 Live Crew maintained an undeniably strong fan base. Fresh Kid Ice, well-aware of popular media stereotypes of the emasculated, asexual Asian man, embodied the uber-confident braggadocio so expected of rappers at the time—his image, like many of his non-Asian ilk, bespoke a gangster's toughness, coupled with a boldly hypersexual party-animal sensibility. In 1992 he released a self-titled solo album as a new rapper persona known as The Chinaman.

As rap music gained exposure and popularity in mainstream media through the 1990s and early 2000s, other Asian American "emcees," as hip-hop vocalists are often known, emerged. Allan Pineda, known by the stage name apl.de.ap., made a name for himself as one of the lead vocalists of the enormously popular Black Eyed Peas (also known as BEP). In the independent hip-hop scene, groups with Asian American members such as Blue Scholars, Far East Movement, The Visionaries, and Native Guns emerged as reaction to the stereotypically violent and misogynist "gangsta" aesthetic propagated in the corporate commodification of hip-hop. Such groups, featuring well-respected emcees and DJs, also created music that called for social consciousness and activism, especially in light of the post-9/11 world. Rapper Jin Auyeung, known simply as Jin, gained an internationally known reputation as a highly skilled "freestyle" emcee. After working with highbrow hip-hop producers like Wyclef Jean, with whom he recorded his most well-known hit "Learn Chinese," Jin founded his own record label, Crafty Plugz. During his independent years, Jin has recorded songs intended to inspire awareness of anti-Asian stereotyping in popular media; in particular, his music has addressed the aftermath of Hurricane Katrina and the Virginia Tech shootings. In 2008, Jin was an avid supporter of Senator Barack Obama's presidential campaign.[2]

Asian American hip-hop artists have been most innovative through the art form of DJing, most notably "turntablism." While Asian American communities in metropolitan centers, notably in California, have had a steady presence in the mobile DJ business since the early 1980s, many modern "turntablists" credit "Rockit," Herbie Hancock and Grandmixer DST's postmodern jazz hit, as a catalyst for the rise of internationally renowned Asian American DJ "crews" such as The World Famous Beat Junkies and The Invisibl Skratch Piklz. "The Piklz," as they are known by various fans and fellow artists, swept a number of prestigious DJ "battle" competitions during the 1990s, most notably the international Disco Mix Club (DMC) competition. The Piklz's pioneering performance dynamics entailed each member scratching as if he were a member of a band. DJ QBert was the "drummer" while Mix Master Mike emulated a trumpet soloist. Their raw skills and crowd-pleasing showmanship were so cutting edge that they were requested by the DMC organizers to "step down" from competition, to give their fellow artists a more competitive chance to win. They then served the competition as honorary judges.

FURTHER READING

Hess, Mickey, ed. *Icons of Hip-Hop: An Encyclopedia of the Movement, Music, and Culture.* Westport, CT: Greenwood Press, 2007.

Model Minority: A Guide to Asian American Empowerment, www.modelminority.com.

Murray, Derek Conrad. "Hip-Hop vs. High Art: Notes on Race as Spectacle." *Art Journal* 63, no. 2 (2004).

Wei, William. *The Asian American Movement.* Philadelphia: Temple University Press, 1999.

Yellow Buzz: Exploring and Documenting Asian American Music Production, www .yellowbuzz.com

NOTES

1. Mickey Hess, ed., *Icons of Hip-Hop: An Encyclopedia of the Movement, Music, and Culture* (Westport, CT: Greenwood Press, 2007).

2. MySpace Music, "Ayojin," http://www.myspace.com/therealjin.

RESOURCE GUIDE

Suggested Reading

Chan, Jachinson. *Chinese American Masculinities: From Fu Manchu to Bruce Lee.* New York: Routledge, 2001.

Feng, Peter. *Identities in Motion: Asian American Film & Video.* Durham, NC: Duke University Press, 2002.

Hamamoto, Darrell Y. *Monitored Peril: Asian Americans and the Politics of TV Representation.* Minneapolis: University of Minnesota Press, 1994.

Hamamoto, Darrell and Sandra Liu, eds. *Countervisions: Asian American Film Criticism.* Philadelphia: Temple University Press, 2000.

Lee, Robert G. *Orientals: Asian Americans in Popular Culture.* Philadelphia: Temple University Press, 1999.

Leong, Russell, ed. *Moving the Image: Independent Asian Pacific American Media Arts.* Los Angeles: UCLA Asian American Studies Center, 1991.

Marchetti, Gina. *Romance and the "Yellow Peril": Race, Sex, and Discursive Strategies in Hollywood Films.* Berkeley: University of California Press, 1993.

Mimura, Glen M., *Ghostlife of Third Cinema: Asian American Film and Video,* Minneapolis: University of Minnesota Press, 2009.

Ono, Kent, and Vincent N. Pham. *Asian Americans and the Media.* Urbana, University of Illinois Press, 2009.

Xing, Jun. *Asian America through the Lens.* Walnut Creek, CA: AltaMira Press, 1998.

Films

Hollywood Chinese: The Chinese in American Feature Films, directed by Arthur Dong, Los Angeles: DeepFocus Productions, 2008. (60 min.). An encyclopedic documentary looking at Chinese Americans in Hollywood, including interviews with actors, directors, writers, and film scholars, and featuring rare and significant clips from many important films.

Picturing Oriental Girls: A (Re) Educational Videotape, directed by Valerie Soe, San Francisco; Center for Asian American Media Distribution, 1991. (14 min.). A brief, impressionistic examination of stereotypes of Asian women in U.S. film and television.

The Slanted Screen, directed by Jeff Adachi, San Francisco: Center for Asian American Media Distribution, 2007. (56 min.). Documentary that discusses roles and stereotypes of Asian American men in mainstream American film and television, with interviews with more than two dozen actors, directors, and producers.

Slaying The Dragon, directed by Asian Women United, San Francisco: Center for Asian American Media Distribution, 1988. Documentary critiquing roles of Asian women in Hollywood film and television.

Organizations

Asian American Justice Center. http://www.advancingequality.org/tv%5Fdiversity/. AAJC and the Asian Pacific American Media Coalition work closely with the major networks—NBC, ABC, CBS, and FOX—to ensure diversity both on and off camera. They produce a nationally recognized annual report card grading the networks on their diversity efforts.

Center for Asian American Media. http://asianamericanmedia.org/. Advocates for Asian American representation in media through exhibition, distribution, and funding of independent Asian American film, television, and digital media.

Media Action Network for Asian Americans. http://www.manaa.org/. Dedicating to monitoring the media and advocating balanced, sensitive, and positive coverage and portrayals of Asian Americans.

Web Sites

All American: How to Cover Asian America. http://www.aaja.org/resources/apa _handbook/2000aaja_handbook.pdf. Book written to help journalists cover Asian America with sensitivity.

Angry Asian Man. http://www.angryasianman.com. Clearinghouse for news and information about Asian American arts and culture, as well as activism in support of fair representations of Asians in the media.

Asian American Film. http://www.asianamericanfilm.com/. Information about Asian American films and filmmakers, with many links to film festivals, screenings, and other news and opportunities.

Asian American Justice Center. http://www.advancingequality.org/tv%5Fdiversity/. Produces a nationally recognized annual report card grading the networks on their diversity efforts, which has yielded initiatives by the networks to heighten opportunities for Asian Americans.

Asian Americans in the Television Media: Creating Incentives for Change. http://www.bc.edu/schools/law/lawreviews/meta-elements/journals/bctwj/ 24_2/05_FMS.htm. This Web site looks at race, representation, and other issues pertinent to the study of Asian Americans in mass media.

Center for Asian American Media. http://asianamericanmedia.org/. Media arts organization that provides funding, exhibition, networking, and distribution for Asian American films.

Media Action Network for Asian Americans. http://www.manaa.org/. Organization dedicated to monitoring the media and advocating balanced, sensitive, and positive coverage and portrayals of Asian Americans.

Media Representations of Asian Americans. http://sitemaker.umich.edu/psy457 _tizzle/home. Summarizes the various stereotypes and representations of Asian Americans in mainstream U.S. media and suggests further research on the topic.

Model Minority: A Guide to Asian American Empowerment. http://www.modelminority.com. Dedicated to Asian American empowerment, through a collection of research articles, commentaries, stories, poems, pictures, and other documents on the Asian American experience.

New America Media. http://news.newamericamedia.org/news/view_category.html? category_id=521. Aggregates news from the Asian American ethnic press.

Restrictive Portrayals of Asians in the Media and How to Balance Them. http://www .manaa.org/asian_stereotypes.html. Outlines various stereotypes of Asian Americans in Hollywood and suggests strategies for countering those stereotypes.

Visual Communications, http://vconline.org. Visual Communications promotes intercultural understanding through the creation, presentation, preservation, and support of media works by and about Asian Pacific Americans.

Yellow Buzz: Exploring and Documenting Asian American Music Production. http://www.yellowbuzz.org. Blog that looks at Asian American music production.

Section 9:

POLITICS

Section Editor:
Andrew L. Aoki

VOTING BEHAVIOR AND POLITICAL PARTICIPATION

James S. Lai

Asian Americans have been labeled as the "next sleeping giant" in American politics in key geopolitical states such as California, Texas, New York, New Jersey, Maryland, and Washington.[1] Much of this perception is fueled by the dramatic growth of Asian American communities in these and other states as a result of federal immigration reforms beginning in 1965. This section highlights the major areas of Asian American political participation and behavior that will likely determine whether Asian American politics will live up to this label. These include voter behavior and turnout in local, state, and federal elections as recently as the 2008 presidential election, their roles in multiracial and panethnic coalition-building, historical and contemporary social movements, and recent trajectories in local politics.

The partisanship of Asian American voters has traditionally been limited to the Democratic Party because of the predominantly working-class backgrounds of the early immigrants in the United States and the salient issues that matter to them. Recent scholarship has found an upswing of both Republican and independent voters in Asian American immigrants who have arrived since 1965 because of their higher socioeconomic statuses, immigrant experiences, and political ideologies.[2] As a result, the Asian American vote is seen as a potential racial voting bloc and subsequently a swing vote in states with large Asian American populations in a two-party system during important statewide elections, ranging from the state legislature to the U.S. presidency.

While the potential for Asian American politics is great at the state level in key geopolitical states such as California, it is even greater at the local level. For example, Asian Americans comprise nearly 14 percent of California's state population and nearly 1.1 million voters, and there are currently six Asian American–majority cities in California (where they account for more than 50 percent of the city's population).[3] In comparison, in 1980, only one Asian American majority city (the suburb of Monterey Park in Los Angeles County) existed in the continental United States. All of these Asian American–majority cities are small- to medium-size suburbs, with populations between 25,000 to 100,000. They have witnessed tremendous demographic shifts and subsequent local political incorporation efforts as Asian Americans have chosen to live in these cities because of their high-quality public schools, established ethnic networks, growing economic opportunity because of globalization patterns, and gravitational migration based on these factors. While many challenges exist both within and outside of the Asian American community in attaining political power in these suburbs, the pathways to political incorporation, beginning with elected representation of Asian Americans, are moving faster in the suburban context than in traditionally large urban metropolitan cities, such as San Francisco, Los Angeles, and New York City.

Beyond these recent Asian American–majority suburbs, even more suburbs in California exist where Asian Americans are the plurality population, the largest racial group where no racial majority is present, and those suburbs where Asian Americans are a substantial population base of greater than 20 percent of the city population. Such findings are in stark contrast to the pre-1965 era in which a majority of Asian Americans lived in self-contained ethnic enclaves, such as Chinatowns and Little Tokyos, in major metropolitan cities that served as gateways for predominantly working-class immigrants. Currently, a broader socioeconomic range of Asian American immigrants are moving directly to the suburbs at a rate of nearly 40 percent in recent years.[4]

In California state and local electoral districts that contain these Asian American–influenced suburbs, Asian American–elected representation has gradually followed. In California state level politics, after the June 2008 state primary elections, a historic eleven Asian American state representatives will serve in the state capitol, in comparison to the period of 1980–1993 when no Asian American served in the state legislature. A majority of these newly elected Asian American state representatives are emerging from electoral districts of suburban cities that include significant Asian American populations, such as California Assemblyman Michael Eng (D-49th Assembly District, which contains large portions of suburbs like Monterey Park, Rosemead, San Marino, and Alhambra), who was elected in November 2006, and California Assemblyman Paul Fong (D-22nd Assembly District, which contains large portions of suburbs like Cupertino, Sunnyvale, Milpitas, and Santa Clara), who was elected in November 2008.

Attorney Linda Nguyen, left, gestures during a debate with school board member Madison Nguyen, right, in San Jose, CA, August 2005. The city council race between two candidates named Nguyen marks the political awakening of San Jose's Vietnamese community, a fast-growing immigrant group that began arriving three decades ago as political refugees from war-ravaged Vietnam. (AP Photo/Paul Sakuma)

Even more impressive than Asian American candidates' recent successes in California state level elections has been their electoral success in small to medium suburbs, where they are not only winning city council elections, but are also sustaining and building on Asian American–elected representation in their respective local governments, an important measuring stick for group political power. One of the most important challenges that Asian Americans have faced historically has been matching their minority counterparts in replacing Asian American representatives with other coethnics at the state level. One study found that among the thirteen Asian American state-level officials who served in the California State Legislature during 1960–2004, none was replaced by a coethnic. In comparison, 81.3 percent of Latino Democrats and 85 percent of black Democrats were replaced by co-ethnics during this period.[5] Reasons for this inability to sustain Asian American–elected officials include intense competition for limited seats with other racial groups, entrenched party interests that make it extremely difficult for recent immigrants to gain their support, a low voter-turnout rate of Asian American immigrants because of low U.S. naturalization rates among the majority foreign-born population, districts that contain few heavily concentrated Asian American populations that can serve as a base, and the lack of a formal pipeline to develop experienced candidates.[6]

The inability to sustain Asian American–elected representation at the state level is not as acute of an issue in small to medium suburbs for the following reasons: local elections are typically citywide, which allows for the racial mobilization of Asian American voters and contributors to support Asian American candidates' campaigns; and the emergence of various political loci, such as panethnic community-based organizations and the ethnic media, in the Asian American community that facilitate group political mobilization. For example, in California suburbs like Cupertino (Santa Clara County), Gardena (Los Angeles County), and Westminster (Orange County), where Asian Americans account for 46 percent, 27 percent, and 31 percent of their respective city populations and many of these community loci are civically engaged around Asian American candidates' campaigns, Asian Americans have achieved a majority or near majority representation on their respective city councils. In Gardena, for two successive generations a majority of Japanese American city council members have served on the five-person council. In Cupertino, Asian Americans will likely attain a majority of the city council in the next local election cycle in 2009. Asian American majority–led local governments had occurred only in cities in Hawai'i, but they are now beginning to happen slowly in California.

While California leads the charge in the suburbanization of Asian American politics, it is certainly not alone. In suburbs throughout the United States, such as Bellevue (outside of Seattle, WA), Sugar Land (outside of Houston, TX), and Eau Claire (in Wisconsin, near the Minnesota border), Asian American immigrants and refugees are building on elected representation in their respective local governments. In the case of Eau Claire, Hmong Americans are defying the belief that low socioeconomic status determines low political participation, as this Asian American refugee community has elected four different Hmong

Americans to its city council over the past decade. Two primary reasons for Asian American electoral success in these suburbs are the socioeconomic backgrounds that Asian American candidates share with whites and other racial groups and the significant Asian American populations that serve as a base for their electoral support.

At the forefront of group political mobilization efforts in these transformed suburbs are Asian American immigrants, who are beginning to awaken politically, going beyond the well-documented campaign contributions to seeking and running for elected positions in these cities, from school boards to the mayor's office. Those Asian American immigrants who decide to run for elected office are typically educated professionals who have been in the United States for several decades, who want to give back to the larger community. It is this stage of Asian American immigrant political behavior, often reserved for later generations, that is challenging the traditional assumption that immigrants do not participate extensively in electoral politics beyond voting.

The electoral successes of Asian Americans running for local offices in such cities beget future Asian American candidates. In California, multiple Asian American candidates running for the same seat is becoming more common. For example, at the state level, during the 2008 California State Assembly, District 22 election (located in Santa Clara County), three of the four candidates running in the Democratic primary were Asian American, with one of them eventually winning. A local election example occurred recently in the city of San Jose, the third largest city in California and home to the largest Vietnamese American community in any major U.S. city. In a 2005 election for the San Jose City Council, District 7 seat, two Vietnamese Americans (Madison Nguyen and Linda Nguyen) ran against each other in an attempt to become the city's first Vietnamese American city council member. The concern, as has been historically the case, is that the Vietnamese American vote would be split with multiple candidates, but what eventually happened was that the Vietnamese American community's voter turnout was so great that it propelled both Vietnamese American candidates into the general election, ensuring that history would be made. In many ways, these recent examples illustrate that Asian American candidates are not only running for elected positions more frequently, but that they are also more politically sophisticated than previous ethnic candidates who solely relied on their Asian ethnic constituencies. One recent study of successful Asian American candidates found that they focus on both multiracial and pan-Asian American ethnic coalition strategies in the areas of voters and contributors.[7]

MULTIPLE STAGES

Asian American suburban transformations do not occur overnight but instead are shaped by historical and contemporary community settlement patterns, as well as the formation of important community political agents (e.g., community-based organizations and the ethnic media) and networks that

provide the necessary institutional infrastructure for local political incorporation efforts. Similar to Latinos, who were labeled as the previous political sleeping giant in California and the Southwest, Asian Americans face unique
challenges that are reflective of their community's demographics and experiences in the United States. As a result, the current state of Asian Americans in
American politics is the culmination of multiple stages of their experiences in
the United States, beginning with their legal challenges of racial exclusionary
laws to the contemporary suburbanization of Asian American politics. To
understand better the current and future political trajectories of Asian Americans in politics, these multiple stages of Asian American political behaviors,
which extend beyond traditional forms such as voting, must be examined
closely. In doing so, a comprehensive understanding of the major contemporary
issues can be fully ascertained and addressed as this community comes of political age in the near future.

Early Forms of Political Participation, Late 1800s to the 1950s

The history of Asian Americans in the United States is long and rich, encompassing more than 160 years and beginning with the arrival of the first wave of
Chinese gold miners to California in 1848.[8] Since this period, many political
events have affected their citizenship and political rights in the United States.
Such elderly Asian American immigrants in the mid-nineteenth century have
been perceived as "apolitical" in the traditional sense of political participation,
defined as voting, but they were unable to vote because they could not become
naturalized U.S. citizens. Although early Asians in America could not vote, they
did practice other forms of political participation in order to protect themselves
against discriminatory laws.

Because of anti-Asian sentiments in the form of discriminatory laws,
early Asian leaders used avenues that were available to them, such as the
U.S. court system.[9] Chinese immigrants during this period were outsiders to
mainstream political institutions because they could neither vote nor testify
in court. Nevertheless, early Chinese community leaders were able to use
the U.S. court system with the help of white lawyers to contest for constitutional rights, such as equal protection under the Fourteenth Amendment.
Many of the late nineteenth century Chinese leaders arose from labor associations such as the Chinese Consolidated Benevolent Association (CCBA),
also known as the Chinese Six Companies in San Francisco. Often, their
interests would have to be pursued in the courts. One important case decided
in 1886 by the U.S. Supreme Court was *Yick Wo v. Hopkins* (118 U.S. 356),
in which the majority ruled that the San Francisco Ordinance requiring
wooden laundry facilities to obtain permits unfairly discriminated against
Chinese businesses and therefore was a violation of their Fourteenth
Amendment equal protection status. This case stands as an important case
today and is often cited as a precedent. *Yick Wo* illustrates one historical

instance where early Chinese in America challenged discriminatory laws through the U.S. court system. Moreover, it illustrates that early Asians in America were indeed politically conscious despite—or perhaps because of—their lack of basic constitutional rights. This form of political activity was not only practiced among early Chinese in America, but among other Asian ethnic groups as well.

Another example of nontraditional political participation can be seen with Japanese American community leaders who also struggled for constitutional rights and protections. Perhaps the most famous historical examples are the World War II internment cases decided by the U.S. Supreme Court, where individual Japanese Americans challenged curfew and removal orders issued by government authorities. In the 1944 case, *Korematsu v. U.S.* (323 U.S. 214), the U.S. Supreme Court used the strict scrutiny standard for the first time in addressing an equal protection violation of the Fourteenth Amendment. The U.S. Supreme Court's majority decided that Executive Order 9066 did not violate equal protection status of American citizens of Japanese ancestry, and thus required them to report to relocation centers across the west. Almost fifty years later, President George Bush signed the Civil Liberties Act of 1988, which issued a formal apology to Japanese American survivors and a sum of $20,000 to all internment camp survivors. This act resulted from the efforts of Japanese American national and local leaders who lobbied to rectify this past civil rights injustice by framing the issue of Japanese American internment as a civil liberty issue, and by their building multiracial coalitions with whites and African Americans, in particular, that extended this civil rights issue beyond the Japanese American community.[10]

A final example of early Asian American political participation through the U.S. court system for greater civil protections was the Japanese American community's successful overturn of the discriminatory California Alien Land Laws of 1913 and 1920, which prevented those with alien status from owning land and limited the length of leases. These land laws were a direct threat to the burgeoning Japanese American–owned agricultural businesses and were eventually overturned in a series of California State Supreme Court cases during the 1930s.[11]

The ability for Asian Americans to sustain a viable second generation of U.S.-born offspring who could participate in U.S. civic institutions would be delayed by state and federal antimiscegenation laws that forbade interracial marriages with whites, and the National Origins Act of 1924, which prevented immigrants from national origins that were declared "ineligible for citizenship" by the U.S. Constitution. Only Japanese Americans saw a substantial second generation emerge in the early twentieth century, because the Gentlemen's Agreement had enabled Japanese immigrants to bring spouses from Japan, despite restrictions otherwise preventing immigration from Asia. Other Asian Americans, however, found marriage prospects very limited by the combination of antimiscegenation laws and immigration restrictions. For Asian Americans during this period of anti-Asian sentiment, the idea of becoming full partners in the American society was a distant dream.

Asian American Movement and Immigration Reform

The 1960s and 1970s represent a crucial period in the formation of the political identity of Asian Americans today. This is when the second generation of Asian Americans came of age politically in the era identified as the "Asian American Movement." On the continental United States, particularly along the West Coast, Asian American activists, students, community leaders began to form multiracial and panethnic coalitions to achieve greater social and economic opportunities for its largely immigrant population. This was a microcosm of the civil rights and the antiwar movements of this era. For Asian Americans, like their minority counterparts, a new group consciousness as "Asian Americans" emerged out of these struggles. As community-based organizations and its leadership emerged and developed in the subsequent decades, so did their political vision regarding the Asian American community. In particular, the pursuit for greater Asian American–elected representation at all levels of American government would be a logical extension of the Asian American movement in the subsequent decades. However, this goal would be challenged by the very root of this community's potential—the contemporary formation of the Asian American community as a result of immigration reform that would change the face and politics of this community.

Social movements involving Asian and Pacific Islander groups were not limited to the U.S. mainland. In Hawai'i, for those who identified as whole or in part as Native Hawaiian or as Hawaiian nationals, the Hawaiian Sovereignty movement would begin to take shape and coincide with the social movements of the 1960s and 1970s, such as the Red Power Movement of Native Americans on the continental United States. Its goals, similar to the Red Power Movement, emphasized self-determination, sovereignty, and self-governance primarily for Native Hawaiians who had their lands stripped from them illegally as part of the United States' annexation of Hawai'i in 1898. The issue of how to address this issue varies among activists, ranging from the idea of a "nation within a nation" status proposed by U.S. Senator Daniel Akaka (D-HI), to monetary reparations from the U.S. government for their economic grievances, to complete independence of Hawai'i from the United States.

The current national Asian American population on the continental U.S. is a young and foreign-born community with the majority arriving in the United States during the past three decades. This trend was the result of dramatic reforms to immigration laws by the U.S. Congress that would allow for inclusion rather than exclusion of Asian immigrants to the United States. Particularly key was the monumental Immigration Act of 1965, which allowed a second generation of Asian Americans to develop because families could arrive en masse after forty years of racial exclusion by the National Origins Act of 1924. Along with the opportunity to immigrate after 1965 was the opportunity for immigrants from Asia to become naturalized U.S. citizens as soon as the standard waiting period was fulfilled, an opportunity that some earlier generations of Asian immigrants did not have until 1956. These two monumental developments would usher in a second stage of Asian American political participation that would provide the foundation for the contemporary period and subsequent stages of Asian American politics. During this stage, established U.S.-born Asian American political leadership and community leaders would attempt to naturalize and bring together their growing and diverse immigrant population.

The term Asian and Pacific Islanders encompasses more than twenty-five different ethnic groups, all with unique cultures and histories of migration and settlement in the United States. In 2000, more than 2 million Asian Americans were biracial or multiracial. As multiracial and ethnic Asian Americans become more politically involved, one of the primary challenges for the general Asian American community will be to create inclusive political organizations that can represent the diverse interests of Asian Americans, as well as can reach out and build viable coalitions with other communities. Underlying this challenge is the shift from the traditional biracial, black-white paradigm that has historically defined American race relations to a multiracial one that includes Latinos and Asian Americans.[12]

If the political maturation of Asian Americans is to signal a new era in racial politics, then the group will have to overcome at least two major challenges. First, Asian Americans have comparatively low voter registration and turnout rates.[13] Second, they are the most geographically dispersed and residentially integrated minority group.[14] Both of these conditions have tended to deflate the impact that their recent population increases might suggest. On the other hand, the rapid population growth of Asian Americans during the 1990s has laid the foundation for increased representation, particularly in the formation of political districts with substantial Asian American populations. According to the Democratic National Committee, for instance, congressional districts with an Asian American population of 5 percent or more have increased from sixty-three districts in 1990 to ninety-six in 2000. While California is leading the charge, it is certainly by no means alone. This population growth is also occurring in states such as New Jersey, Minnesota, Oregon, Nevada, and Pennsylvania. In New Jersey, during the last decade, the number of congressional districts with an Asian American population of 5 percent or more increased from one to eight.[15] As a result, Asian American voters have the potential to play a greater role in future state and federal politics on the continental United States, and it is more likely that more Asian American candidates will also emerge.

EMERGENCE OF ELECTED REPRESENTATIVES

For Asian Americans, the decades after the 1960s symbolized a period of increased political activity.[16] The struggle for Asian American–elected officials is very much a continuation of the goals of the Asian American Movement, which sought self-empowerment in the electoral political arena. This was evident with the emergence of Asian American–elected officials at the federal level, particularly from Hawai'i and California. In Hawai'i, where Asian Americans represent the majority population, the first Asian American federal elected officials were U.S. Senators Spark Matsunaga (D-HI) and Daniel Inouye (D-HI), who were both elected in 1962. The late Patsy T. Mink (D-HI) would be elected to the U.S. House of Representatives in 1964.

While Asian American representation grew in Hawai'i, Asian Americans were relatively underrepresented on the continental United States. A majority of the Asian American elected federal officials on the U.S. mainland were from California. S. I. Hayakawa (R-CA) served as a U.S. Senator from 1976 to 1982. Norman Mineta (D-CA) served in U.S. House of Representatives from 1974 to 1996. The late Robert Matsui (D-CA) was first elected in the U.S. House of Representatives in 1978 and eventually served 13 full terms. One Asian American (Mike Honda from District 15) from California serves in the U.S. House of Representatives, after being elected in 2000.

Despite these pioneer Asian American–elected officials at the federal level, Asian American political representation has been extremely limited in the major metropolitan cities where many substantial Asian American communities were forming. For example, in the large gateway cities of Los Angeles and New York City, only two Asian American city council members have ever been elected in their respective histories. Michael Woo became the only Asian American to be elected to Los Angeles' fifteen-person city council in 1985, and most recently, John Liu, was elected to the New York City's fifty–one–person city council in 2001. Given the large Asian American immigrant populations and the lack of mainstream civic institutions engaging this community, Asian American community-based organizations would play an important role in providing social services and a political voice.

Differences exist in regard to the political experiences for Asian American–elected officials on the continental United States compared with those in Hawai'i, where Asian Americans have historically attained the most elected representation. The first difference is that Asian Americans in Hawai'i represent the majority, whereas this is not the case on the continental United States. Therefore, for Asian American candidates running on the continental United States, it would be an unwise political strategy to rely solely on this racial group's bloc vote. Successful Asian American candidates must pursue two-tiered campaign strategies that involve mandatory cross-racial alliances with white voters and contributors, the first tier, and strategic targeting of Asian American resources within and outside of their districts, the second tier.

A second difference is that Asian American–elected officials and candidates on the continental United States tend to rely more heavily than their Hawaiian counterparts for support by Asian American community elites (namely community-based organization leaders, community activists, and the ethnic media) for access to political resources.[17] One of the most important among these political resources is campaign contributions, an area where Asian

Americans on the continental United States have historically wielded their political muscle in local, state, and federal politics.[18] In 1996, Asian Americans were at the center of a campaign contribution scandal that involved allegations of foreign interests gaining access to the White House through illegal campaign contributions to former Vice President Al Gore and the Democratic National Committee. This prompted a bipartisan Senate investigation into the matter, and a federal civil rights investigation fueled by Asian American community leadership who declared it to be a second invocation of the "yellow peril" image.[19]

The experiences of Asian American–elected officials on the continental United States are also different from African American and Latino elected officials in one important aspect—they tend to be nonethnic representatives in state districts.[20] State level Asian American–elected officials on the continental United States emerge from non-Asian districts that are either heavily white or multiracial. African American and Latino elected officials at the local, state, and federal levels tend to emerge from political districts in which they represent the majority or a substantial portion of the total population.[21] At the federal level, twenty-three of thirty-nine African American House Representatives represented districts in 1998 where this group's voting age population was 50 percent or more of the population.[22] For Latinos, seventeen of nineteen members of Congress were in districts where the Latino population was at least 50 percent.[23] In contrast, Asian American–elected officials on the continental United States typically represent non-Asian majority districts at all three levels of government where Asian constituents are a minority or nonexistent. A vivid example is U.S. Representative David Wu (D-OR), who is one of three Asian Americans elected to the U.S. Congress from the mainland and whose district contains less than 5 percent Asian Americans. One notable exception to this trend is U.S. Representative Mike Honda (D-CA) who is elected from a congressional district in Santa Clara County that contains many suburbs with large Asian American populations.

Community Political Leaders and Mobilization

Asian American community-based organizations and other community elites undertake a variety of roles in group political mobilization such as get-out-the-vote drives to organizing candidate forums and training sessions. These roles depend on the geographic context of the cities they are located within and the type of political district. For Asian Americans in large metropolitan gateway cities on the continental United States, the lack of ethnic representation has led to a political void as seen with gateway cities such as Los Angeles and New York City, where the two largest Asian American aggregate populations reside. As a result of this electoral void in such large metropolitan cities, Asian American community leaders, organizations, and activists have played a significant role in representing and advocating Asian American interests to local and state representatives through a variety of ways.

Asian American community-based groups can act as a conduit with mainstream elected officials and institutions, particularly in large metropolitan gateway cities with large Asian American populations. For example, in Los Angeles Koreatown, the commercial and organizational focal point for the largest population of Korean Americans in the nation, Korean American community-based organizations have provided their substantial ethnic community with a political voice in expressing their concerns to mainstream elected representatives and institutions. One such organization is the Korean American Coalition (KAC), which is nonprofit and nonpartisan, representing the interests of more than 500,000 Korean Americans living in Southern California. During its existence, KAC has conducted an annual legislative luncheon in Southern California with local and statewide elected officials and legislative aides, who are invited to Koreatown to meet with Korean American community leaders/organizations. In the past, the elected officials who have been invited to their legislative luncheons included a formidable list of former local, state, and federal elected officials including California Governor Gray Davis, former Governor Pete Wilson, U.S. Senator Barbara Boxer, U.S. Congressman Xavier Bacerra, and Los Angeles Mayor Richard Riordan. Their luncheons have served as a forum to present and discuss issues affecting Korean Americans in Southern California.

Community-based organizations have helped to recruit and to train potential Asian American candidates with the hope of establishing a formal pipeline of candidates in key regions throughout the United States. At the local level, the Japanese American Citizens' League chapter in Los Angeles has held candidate training workshops led by Asian American–elected officials, who worked hand in hand toward the goal of increasing elected representation. These workshops usually feature current and past Asian American–elected officials, campaign strategists, and political researchers. At the national level, the Asian Pacific American Institute for Congressional Studies, the only national Asian American public policy institute in Washington, DC, and the University of California at Los Angeles Asian American Studies Center, a leading research center on Asian Americans, annually co-sponsor a National Leadership Academy for Asian American–elected officials in Washington, DC. Various Asian American candidates and elected official participants from across the country attend the three-day workshops. This event includes training sessions with current and former Asian American–elected officials, Congressional staffers, political and public relations consultants, fundraisers, and print and broadcast journalists. Such events are certainly not limited to California and Washington, DC, as emerging Asian American political mobilization is taking shape in other major states. Most recently, in March 2008, a one-day Asian American candidate training session sponsored by the Washington, DC, nonprofit, community-based organization Progressive Alliance took place in the emerging suburb of Bellevue, WA, where Asian Americans represent more than a quarter of the city population and where two Asian American city council members (Conrad Lee and Patsy Bonincontri) serve on the five-person council.

The success of the inaugural 1999 Leadership Academy for Asian American Elected Officials resulted in the formation of the Asian American Political Education Institute in California. The cosponsors of this political education institute are two of the most visible Asian American community and academic organizations in Los Angeles County, the Chinese Americans United for Self-Empowerment (CAUSE) and the University of California at Los Angeles' Asian American Studies Center. According to their press release, the mission of the institute was "to gather top notch political consultants, elected officials, community leaders, and media together with individuals who are interested in seeking elected offices for two days of interactive panel discussions and training. . . . Through this institute we strive to enhance the success rate of Asian American candidates by discussing issues facing these candidates . . . and provide our community with a better understanding of the mechanics of political campaigns."[24]

Another important Asian American community resource in the continental United States is the emergence of transnational Asian American ethnic media, which caters to the large bilingual and transnational Asian American immigrant communities. In Los Angeles and Orange Counties alone, it is estimated that there were nearly 200 different Asian and Pacific Islander media outlets ranging from newspapers and journals to radio and television programs.[25] Besides providing immigrants bilingual and unilingual information on United States and international news in their respective homelands, the ethnic print media can also provide Asian American candidates who chose to target them with important media exposure to a large segment of Asian foreign-born, bilingual population of potential voters and donors. Given this strong presence in the Asian and Pacific Islander foreign-born population, it was no surprise that high-profile candidates such as Republican Matt Fong, a Chinese American and son of former California State Secretary March Fong-Eu, targeted the Chinese American print media, in order to get his message out to prospective Chinese American voters and contributors during his closely contested 1998 bid in California for the U.S. Senate against incumbent Senator Barbara Boxer.

The advantage of targeting the ethnic media was that it provided Fong a cost-effective medium to advertise his campaign to potential Asian American voters and contributors, who could tip the balance of a close election in his favor. During the Republican primary election, Fong's greatest challenger Darrell Issa spent $2 million dollars in radio advertisements alone. While Fong targeted the mainstream media during his campaign, he also focused his limited resources on the Asian ethnic media. An example of the cost-effectiveness of advertising in Asian ethnic print media versus mainstream print media can be seen in the following: a full-page advertisement in the *San Francisco Chronicle* costs $55,000 compared with $1,200 for a full-page advertisement in *Sing Tao*, a Bay Area Chinese language newspaper with a national circulation of 60,000. Fong used the Chinese American print media to his advantage, and even credited them with helping him win his Republican primary election.[26]

These organizations, with the support of community leaders and activists through many grass-roots activities, attempt to educate and influence local and statewide elected officials. An example can be seen in Santa Clara County in California with the Asian Pacific American Silicon Valley Democratic Club (APASVDC), which has been successful in helping elect more than thirty Asian American candidates, the most for any continental U.S. county region, since 2002.[27] Historically focused on local elections, this political organization has begun to support Asian American candidates running for statewide positions with the most recent one being Paul Fong's 2008 California Assembly District 22 campaign. Fong is one of the founders of APASVDC and an important Asian American community player in Santa Clara County local politics.

PANETHNIC CHALLENGE

The challenges to constructing and maintaining any type of political coalition in American politics are many. One such challenge is the salience of race and ethnicity in today's political arenas. In regard to ethnic salience, one contemporary trend in California politics is for ethnic groups to "go it alone."[28] This is particularly the case among recent immigrant Asian ethnic groups (post-1965) who do not necessarily identify with issues that marked the political struggles of more established Asian American groups during the social movements of the sixties and with current movements that espouse similar group ideologies. As a result, panethnic coalitions among Asian Americans are difficult to construct and tend to be short-lived, given the contemporary characteristics of Asian Americans. Other factors that diminish the potential for a pan-Asian identity among recent Asian immigrants include differences in socioeconomic background such as education and income, generation issues, and homeland politics.[29]

One of the primary barriers to whether Asian Americans can form a racial bloc vote in key swing states stems from the very root of their potential, such as their extraordinary diversity and growth. One recent national survey of Asian American public opinions in several major metropolitan cities, it was found that a panethnic identity is gradually emerging in the first-generation Asian American community, in terms of the public opinion survey measure of "linked group fate" (what happens to another Asian ethnic group adversely affects their own ethnic group), although not when measured by other survey measures such as "shared cultured."[30] Such a measure of panethnic identity is likely to increase over time particularly among the latter generations, which bodes well for future panethnic coalitions.

For Asian Americans, their political success is not only defined by their ability to form panethnic coalitions within its ethnically diverse community and cross-racial coalitions with whites, but also to develop positive race relations with African Americans and Latinos. In many racially commingled cities such as Los Angeles, the challenges are there as exemplified by the 1991 Los Angeles uprisings that represented the nation's first multiracial riots in which Korean American–owned businesses suffered the greatest losses, estimated at $400 million during the several days of burning, looting, and rioting.[31] In a telling 1993

Los Angeles Times survey of southern Californians, 45 percent of African American respondents identified Asian Americans as the second most prejudiced group, only behind whites at 65 percent, which represented a 19 percent increase from a similar 1989 survey. Moreover, African American respondents most frequently identified Asian Americans as the one racial group that is gaining economic power that is not good for Southern California.[32] The challenges within such contexts are to find the common interests that exist but that are overshadowed by zero–sum–based racial politics.[33] Hate crimes in the post-9/11 era have seen increased targeting of Asian Indians and Pakistani Americans at local, state, and national levels that raise future concerns for race relations in multiracial cities, while at the same time serves as a salient issue that can potentially unite the diverse Asian American community.

OUTLOOK

Politics is an increasingly important issue for Asian Americans as they continue to participate in U.S. mainstream and community-based civic institutions. As new and old members of this community enter the political arena and participate through a myriad of ways, the trajectory of Asian Americans in politics remains extremely optimistic. Asian American–elected leadership has begun to emerge in the continental United States, primarily at the local and state levels, that rivals the number of those in Hawai'i; however, many contemporary political challenges exist for Asian Americans as they seek to naturalize and vote consistently, and attempt to build cross-racial and panethnic coalitions around both Asian and non-Asian American candidates. Whether this can be achieved and sustained in the near future remains to be seen.

If in fact the Asian American community is to sustain a positive trajectory of political growth and influence in future statewide and national elections, a triangulation must occur among the following three Asian American community loci: community-based and national organizations, Asian American candidates and elected officials, and the emerging and influential Asian American media. Concomitantly, the two major parties must legitimately focus on recruiting and incorporating Asian American voters, contributors, and candidates. This process is most evident in the South Bay of northern California and Orange County in southern California, where Asian Americans are emerging as legitimate coalition partners with whites and Latinos, and where Asian American candidates are receiving the necessary party support from both Democrats and Republicans in winning key political offices. Grassroots mobilization efforts involving these three community loci around a progressive ideology will allow Asian Americans to achieve greater political incorporation in small to medium cities in these important regions. The formation of this important political infrastructure within the regional Asian American communities has been gradually taking shape over the past three decades and will play an important role in determining whether Asian Americans can live up to their "sleeping giant status" in American Politics.

NOTES

1. Holly Kernan, "San Francisco's 'Sleeping Giant' Awakes." National Public Radio. 2002. Retrieved from http://www.npr.org/programs/atc/features/2002/aug/california/asian/index.html;UCLA Asian American Studies Center Press Release. "The New Sleeping Giant in California Politics." Nov. 7, 2006. Retrieved from http://www.aasc.ucla.edu/archives/sleepgiants.htm; Cindy Chang. Feb. 27, 2007. "The Sleeping Giant in California Politics." *International Herald Tribune* Online. Retrieved from http://www.iht.com/articles/2007/02/27/news/asians.php.

2. J.A. Garcia, "Asian American Party Dynamics: Partisan and Non-Partisan Identities," Paper presented at the annual meeting of the American Political Science Association, Marriott Wardman Park, Omni Shoreham, Washington Hilton, Washington, DC. Online. September 2005. Retrieved from http://www.allacademic.com/meta/p41297_index.html.

3. These six Asian American majority cities in California are the following according to the 2000 U.S. Census findings: Daly City (50.8 percent Asian American), Cerritos (58.4 percent), Milpitas (51.8 percent), Monterey Park (61.8 percent), Rowland Heights (50.3 percent), and Walnut (55.8 percent).

4. Sam Roberts, "In Shift, 40% of Immigrants Move to Suburbs," *New York Times* Online. Oct. 21, 2007. http://www.nytimes.com/2007/10/17/us/17census.html.

5. Fernando Guerra, Center for the Study of Los Angeles Handout. Presented at the 100th Annual Meeting of the American Political Science Association. September 2004.

6. James Lai, Wendy Tam-Cho, Thomas Kim, and Okiyoshi Takeda. "Asian Pacific American Campaigns, Elections, and Elected Officials," *PS: Political Science and Politics* 36 no. 3 (2001): 611–619.

7. James S. Lai and Kim Geron, "When Asian Americans Run: The Suburban and Urban Dimensions of Asian American Candidates in California Local Politics," *California Politics & Policy* 10 (June 2006): 62–68.

8. Sucheng Chan, *Asian Americans: An Interpretive History* (Philadelphia, PA: Temple University Press), 1991.

9. Charles McClain, *In Search of Equality: The Chinese Struggle against Discrimination in Nineteenth-Century America* (Berkeley: University of California Press), 1994.

10. Mitch Maki and Harry Kitano. *Achieving the Impossible Dream: How Japanese Americans Obtained Redress* (Urbana: University of Illinois Press), 1999.

11. Chan, *Asian Americans*.

12. Paul M. Ong, "The Asian Pacific American Challenge to Race Relations," in *The State of Asian Pacific America: Transforming Race Relations,* ed. Paul M. Ong (Los Angeles: LEAP and UCLA Asian American Studies Center, 2000), 13–39.

13. Don T. Nakanishi, "The Next Swing Vote? Asian Pacific Americans and California Politics," in *Racial and Ethnic Politics in California,* vol. 1, eds. Byran O. Jackson and Michael B. Preston (Berkeley, CA: Institute of Governmental Studies Press, 2001), 25–54; Don T. Nakanishi and Paul M. Ong, "Becoming Citizens, Becoming Voters: The Naturalization and Political Participation of Asian Immigrants," in *Reframing the Immigration Debate,* eds. Bill Ong Hing, et al. (Los Angeles, CA: LEAP and UCLA Asian American Studies Center, 1996), 275–305; Don T. Nakanishi, "When the Numbers Do Not Add Up: Asian Pacific Americans in California Politics," in *Racial and Ethnic Politics in California,* eds. Michael B.

Preston, Bruce E. Cain, and Sandra Bass (Berkeley, CA: Institute of Governmental Studies Press, 1998), 3–44.

14. Gregory Rodriguez, "Minority Leader: Matt Fong and the Asian American Voter," *The New Republic*, Oct. 19, 1998, 21–24; Raphael Sonenshein, "Do Asian Americans Count in L.A.?" *Los Angeles Times*, Feb. 28, 2005, B9.

15. Office of Asian American Outreach, Democratic National Committee Press Release, Oct. 13, 1999.

16. William Wei, *The Asian American Movement* (Philadelphia: Temple University Press, 1992); Steve Louie and Glenn Omatsu, eds., *The Movement and the Moment* (Los Angeles: UCLA Asian American Studies Center Press, 2001).

17. James S. Lai, "Asian Americans and the Panethnic Question," in *Minority Politics at the Millennium,* eds. Richard A. Keiser and Katherine Underwood (New York: Garland Publishing, 2000), 157–178.

18. Judy Tachibana, "California's Asians: Power from a Growing Population," *California Journal* 17 (1986): 534–543; Nakanishi, "When the Numbers Do Not Add Up."

19. Robert Lee, *Orientals: Asian Americans in Popular Culture* (Philadelphia: Temple University Press, 1999); Frank Wu, *Race in America: Beyond Black and White* (New York: Basic Books, 2002).

20. Bruce E. Cain, Roderick Kiewiet, and Carole J. Uhlaner, "The Acquisition of Partisanship by Latinos and Asian Americans," *American Journal of Political Science* 35, no. 2 (1991): 390–422.

21. Rufus P. Browning, Dale Rogers Marshall, and David H. Tabb, "Introduction: Can People of Color Achieve Power in City Government? The Setting and the Issues," in *Racial Politics in American Cities*, eds. Rufus P. Browning, Dale Rogers Marshall, and David H. Tabb (New York: Longman Press, 1990), 3–14.

22. David A. Bositis, *Redistricting and Minority Representation* (Lanham, MD: University Press of America, 1998).

23. Bositis, *Redistricting and Minority Representation.*

24. Asian American Political Education Institute, Press Release, Aug. 20, 1999.

25. *1998-99 Asian and Pacific Islander Community Directory for Los Angeles and Orange Counties* (Los Angeles, CA: Asian American Studies Center Press, 1998).

26. Sam Chu Lin and Bob Galbraith, "Fong Wins First Round: What His Victory Means for Boxer, for Asian Americans, for GOP," *AsianWeek*, June 4–10, 1998.

27. Katherine Corcoran, "Valley Political Group Sets Sights Higher: Asian American Club Turns to State Race After Local Success," *San Jose Mercury News*, Jan. 25, 2004, 4B.

28. Bruce Cain, "The Contemporary Context of Ethnic and Racial Politics in California," in *Racial and Ethnic Politics in California* (Vol. 1), eds. Byran O. Jackson and Michael B. Preston (Berkeley, CA: Institute of Governmental Studies Press, 1991), 9–24.

29. Yen Le Espiritu, *Asian American Panethnicity: Bridging Institutions and Identities* (Philadelphia: Temple University Press, 1992); Yen Le Espiritu and Paul M. Ong, "Class Constraints on Racial Solidarity among Asian Americans," in *The New Asian Immigration in Los Angeles and Global Restructuring*, eds. Paul M. Ong, Edna Bonacich and Lucie Cheng (Philadelphia: Temple University Press, 1994), 295–322; Pei-te Lien, *The Political Participation of Asian Americans: Voting Behavior in Southern California* (New York: Garland Publishing, 1997).

30. Pei-te Lien, M. Margaret Conway, and Janelle Wong, *The Politics of Asian Americans: Diversity & Community* (New York: Routledge, 2004), 41–56.

31. Edward T. Chang, "America's First Multi-Racial Riot," in *Asian American Politics: Law, Participation, and Policy*, eds. Don T. Nakanishi and James S. Lai (Lanham, MD: Rowman & Littlefield, 2003), 431–440.

32. Paula McClain and Joseph Stewart, *Can We All Get Along? Racial and Ethnic Minorities in American Politics* (Boulder, CO: Westview Press, 2005).

33. Manning Marable, "Building Coalitions among Communities of Color," in James Jennings, ed., *Blacks, Latinos, and Asians in Urban America: Status and Prospects for Politics and Activism* (Westport, CT: Praeger, 1994), 29–46.

ASIAN AMERICAN MOVEMENT

Diane C. Fujino

In 1968, activist-scholars Yuji Ichioka and Emma Gee approached Asian Americans, many strangers, to invite them to form an Asian caucus of the Peace and Freedom Party in Berkeley, CA. An independent organization, Asian American Political Alliance (AAPA), emerged. In 1969, Kazu Iijima and Minn Matsuda lamented the lack of any Asian organization for their college-aged children in New York City. They invited Asian Americans they saw at Vietnam War rallies to the first meeting of what became Asian Americans for Action (AAA, or Triple A). In the midst of antiwar protests and fists raised in Black Power, Asian Americans on both coasts were craving new identities, new formations, and new solidarities. When Ichioka introduced the term, "Asian American" in an AAPA meeting, he, perhaps only with partial consciousness, helped launch a new identity and new social movement.

Social factors help explain why the Asian American Movement (AAM) developed in the late 1960s and not earlier. Chinese and Japanese American youth, and to a lesser extent Filipinos and others, came of age influenced by American schools, media, and culture; spoke a common language; and often came together on college campuses. Beyond demographics, the AAM emerged in the midst of vibrant U.S. protest movements and worldwide anticolonial liberation struggles. While some lament the demise of the civil rights and early New Left movements, others celebrate the racial pride and radical freedom dreams that broke forth in the mid-1960s with the Black Power, Asian American, Chicana/o, and American Indian movements.

While those who initiated AAPA and AAA had long activist histories, the development of a widescale, multisited *Asian American* social movement was new. A hallmark of this AAM was its pan-Asian focus, developed to express a unity grounded in common experiences with racism and a need to unite numerically small communities. Panethnicity was a political strategy for increasing power rather than an assumption about common cultures. From its start, this new identity also produced tensions—a coming together across differences and ethnic hierarchies that were not easily resolved.

Though never a monolithic movement, the AAM was heavily influenced by the ideology of Black Power, with its focus on self-determination, third world unity, militancy, and dreams of radical transformations. AAM activists emphasized unity among U.S. third world peoples in opposing racism and in connecting racial and colonial domination nationally and internationally. AAM activists were responding, in part, to the model minority image of Asian Americans, popularized in two 1966 magazine articles, and to the assimilationist aspirations of many in their parents' generation.[1] In a widely read article in *Gidra*, a UCLA AAM publication, Amy Uyematsu criticized Asian Americans who "try to gain complete acceptance by denying their yellowness" and "form an uneasy alliance with white Americans to keep the blacks down." Yellow Power symbolized "a rejection of the passive Oriental stereotype" and "the birth of a new Asian, one who will recognize and deal with injustices."[2]

One of the clearest expressions of third world solidarity emerged in the struggle for ethnic studies. Stressing the idea of a shared oppression, Asian American, black, Chicano, and Indigenous students, through the Third World Liberation Front (TWLF) at San Francisco State College, waged the longest student strike in U.S. history and birthed the first school of ethnic studies in the nation.[3] Early on in the AAM, activists discussed the previously obscure history of Japanese American incarceration during World War II. AAPA and AAA made connections across time and race, alerting their newspaper readerships to the existence of six concentration camps, under Title II of the McCarran Internal Security Act of 1950, for the detention of black militants, radicals, and anyone who "might possibly" be engaged in subversive activity.[4] Asian Americans with activist credentials, primarily in the Black Power movement, were looked to for leadership, particularly Yuri Kochiyama, best known for working with Malcolm X, and Richard Aoki, a leader of AAPA, TWLF at UC–Berkeley, and the Black Panther Party (BPP).

AAM activists strongly opposed the Vietnam War. Beyond "bringing the boys home" (interpreted as saving white American lives), they condemned U.S. imperialism, connected anti-Asian racism abroad and at home, and supported self-determination for the Vietnamese people. Their opposition to U.S. imperialism also led to struggles to end the U.S. military occupation of Okinawa and to commemorations of Hiroshima Day each year with a call to stop nuclear proliferation.

Influenced by the BPP's survival programs and Mao's ideas, AAM activists emphasized "serve the people" programs. More than simply "helping people," which activist Mo Nishida asserts creates another dependency, they sought to create community institutions and simultaneously developed "knowledgeable, humane and enlightened individuals."[5] One of the best known among the many

AAM struggles for jobs, housing, health care, education, etc., was the decade-long struggle to save the International Hotel, home to working-class Filipino and Chinese elderly men. Many activists were already familiar with these Filipino *manongs* from their support of Filipino and Chicano farmworkers organizing with Cesar Chavez, Delores Huerta, and Philip Vera Cruz. Within the I-Hotel campaign, AAM groups with differing goals and ideologies struggled over whether human rights (affordable housing), racism, or capitalist exploitation (corporate gentrification) should be the main campaign goal.

This reflected differences between what William Wei, in a useful though problematic dichotomy, calls reformers versus revolutionaries.[6] Reformers tended to provide direct social services, particularly to working-class Asian Americans, without an explicit call for radical societal transformation. Groups like Chinese for Affirmative Action fought for fair employment and the Asian Law Caucus provided legal services. Revolutionaries also provided "serve the people" programs, but did so while critiquing racial capitalism and seeking far-reaching change. The Red Guard Party, organized in San Francisco's Chinatown in 1969, closely patterned itself after the BPP in ideology and street youth membership. That same year in New York City, I Wor Kuen (IWK) was formed. In 1971, these two groups merged to form the first national Asian American revolutionary organization, IWK. Their politics were both pan-Asian and third worldist, demanding "self-determination for all Asian Americans" and "all Asians" and the "liberation of all Third World peoples." IWK desired human rights and provided "serve the people" programs, but also opposed sexism and called for "a socialist society."[7]

Cultural productions flourished, inspired by and in turn helping to develop the AAM. The Kearney Street Workshop, a storefront in the I-Hotel, produced political posters, held community art classes, and ran an art gallery. Frank Chin, Janice Mirikitani, Al Robles, and others created powerful writings, poetry, and plays, exposing Asian American oppression and resistance. In the early 1970s, A Grain of Sand set powerful lyrics to folk music to become the symbol of AAM music, and a decade later, Fred Ho, Mark Izu, Jon Jang, and others developed an Asian American jazz scene that combined traditional Asian instrumentation with African American jazz to create a new hybrid form of politically explosive music.

Asian American activism still continues, with efforts to support educational reform, combat sweatshops, struggle for immigrant rights, and oppose the "war on terrorism," among other issues. The AAM of the 1960s and 1970s uncovered hidden histories of Asian American activism, created a political consciousness and pan-Asian identity, produced generations of activists, and continues to inspire resistance today.

FURTHER READING

Asian American Movement Ezine. www.aamovement.net. Progressive, radical, and revolutionary Asian American perspectives.

Fujino, Diane C. "Who Studies the Asian American Movement?: A Historiographical Analysis." *Journal of Asian American Studies 11* (2008): 127–169.

Ho, Fred, ed. *Legacy to Liberation: Politics and Culture of Revolutionary Asian Pacific America.* San Francisco: AK Press, 2000.

Liu, Michael, Kim Geron, and Tracy Lai. *The Snake Dance of Asian American Activism: Community, Vision, and Power* (Lanham, MD: Lexington Books, 2008).

Louie, Steve and Glenn Omatsu, eds. *Asian Americans: The Movement and the Moment.* Los Angeles: University of California–Los Angeles, Asian American Studies Center Press, 2001.

Wei, William. *The Asian American Movement.* Philadelphia: Temple University Press, 1993.

NOTES

1. William Petersen, "Success Story, Japanese-American Style." *New York Times Magazine* (January 9, 1966): 20–21, 33, 36, 38, 40–41, 43; "Success Story of One Minority Group in U.S.," *U.S. News & World Report* (December 26, 1966): 73–76.

2. Amy Uyematsu, "The Emergence of Yellow Power in America," *Gidra* 1, no. 7 (October 1969): 8–11; reprinted in Amy Tachiki, Eddie Wong, and Franklin Odo, eds., *Roots: An Asian American Reader* (Los Angeles: Continental Graphics, 1971), 9–13.

3. Social movement historiography virtually ignored Asian American participation in the San Francisco State College strike until *Amerasia Journal* published a special issue commemorating the strike. Asian Americans comprised three of the six groups of the Third World Liberation Front. Karen Umemoto, "'On Strike!' San Francisco State College Strike, 1968–69: The Role of Asian American Students," *Amerasia Journal,* 15 (1989): 3–41.

4. Yuji Ichioka, "Would You Believe Concentration Camps for Americans?" *AAPA Newspaper* (November–December 1968): 3; "Infamous Concentration Camp Bill: Title II-Emergency Detention Act," *Asian Americans for Action Newsletter* (October 1970): 8.

5. Mori Nishida, "Serve the People," in Steve Louie and Glenn Omatsu, eds., *Asian Americans: The Movement and Moment* (Los Angeles: UCLA Asian American Studies Press, 2001), 305–306.

6. Diane C. Fujino, "Who Studies the Asian American Movement?: A Historiographical Analysis," *Journal of Asian American Studies* 11 (2008): 127–169.

7. I Wor Kuen, 12-Point Platform and Program, http://www.dartmouth.edu/~hist32/Hist33/I%20Wor%20Kuen.pdf.

COALITION POLITICS

Andrew L. Aoki

Coalition building is essential for political success. Building effective alliances is challenging, however. Larger coalitions tend to be more influential but difficult to form and maintain, requiring a continual effort to balance widely varying interests. This problem is particularly acute for Asian Americans because of their tremendous diversity.

Nevertheless, Asian Americans have formed alliances around many issues, including civil rights, immigration, and economic opportunity. Many of the successful coalition-building efforts owe much to the groundwork laid by activists who created organizations and events that helped nurture connections between groups. Future coalitions will likely face substantial challenges, however, because of the economic and cultural diversity of Asian Americans.

COALITIONS BETWEEN ASIAN AMERICAN GROUPS

Although the term "Asian American" implies a single identity, Asian Americans in fact are a very diverse subpopulation that itself must be united through coalition building. Shared ethnicity may provide a common identity for new immigrants—for example, Hmong may identify with other Hmong—but ancestral roots in the same continent is not enough to create a common bond.[1] Pakistani immigrants, for instance, are unlikely to identify with Japanese Americans simply because Pakistan and Japan both happen to be in Asia.

There is very little scholarly research about the process of coalition building between Asian American groups, but some of this can be inferred by observing pan-Asian American groups.[2] While shared views can obviously fuel alliances, equally important factors appear to be key linkages between groups and opportunities for groups to interact. Panethnic organizations strive to attract members of different ethnic backgrounds, who then become key nodes linking together Asian American subgroups. Through their activities, panethnic groups can bring together more individuals of different ethnic backgrounds, building interethnic understanding and laying the groundwork for stronger panethnic coalitions.

An example of this is Asian Americans United (AAU) in Philadelphia.[3] When it began, AAU's membership was primarily well-educated Chinese and Japanese Americans; however, they did not want to limit their focus to their own ethnic communities, so they worked to help the city's Southeast Asian community with housing, education, and youth programs. As a result, the AAU increasingly attracted immigrant and working-class members, creating ties that connected the Philadelphia Asian American community. In 1991, when some Asian American youth were involved in a violent incident and racial tensions flared, Philadelphian Asian Americans saw the AAU as the group to lead a pan-Asian American effort to combat media bias and to present a more balanced depiction of the incident.

Although this type of coalition building is likely to be difficult, evidence from the Pilot National Asian American Political Survey (PNAAPS) suggests that there may be an emerging panethnic identity, which would make it easier to bring Asian American subgroups together. The PNAAPS found that approximately 75 percent of its respondents usually thought of themselves in ethnic-specific terms, such as Filipino, or Filipino American. But the PNAAPS also found that more than half thought of themselves as Asian American at least some of the time, and almost half felt that what happened to Asian Americans in general would affect them personally.[4]

Currently, however, Asian Americans appear to be more likely to ally with coethnics than with Asian Americans of other ethnic backgrounds. One study of Federal Election Campaign data found that there is relatively little cross-ethnic giving in congressional races where an Asian American is running, although Asian Americans appear to be more willing to contribute cross-ethnically in Hawaii.[5] And, other research has uncovered some willingness to contribute across ethnic lines in California state and local races, once again implying that there is some potential for panethnic coalition building among Asian Americans.[6]

COALITIONS BETWEEN ASIAN AMERICAN AND NON-ASIAN AMERICAN GROUPS

Asian American groups have been active in interracial coalitions. For example, the Asian American Justice Center (AAJC) is currently the chair of the Rights Working Group, which seeks to protect civil rights and civil liberties that have become weakened by efforts to combat terrorism. Among the Rights Working Group members are the Arab-American Anti-Discrimination Committee, the Mexican American Legal Defense & Education Fund (MALDEF), the Muslim Public Affairs Council, the National Council of La Raza, the Southeast

Asia Resource Action Center (SEARAC), the Sikh American Legal Defense and Education Fund (SALDEF), the National Korean American Service & Education Consortium (NAKASEC), and many other organizations (including the AAJC). Another coalition that includes many Asian American organizations is the Leadership Conference for Civil Rights, an alliance of more than 190 members representing a wide range of communities.

Individuals are often the critical links in networks that help form interracial coalitions. When the Alhambra school district in Southern California was troubled by violence between Latino and Asian American groups, local activists who had worked across ethnic lines helped to bring participants together into a new organization which came to be called the Multi-Cultural Community Association. The association successfully pushed for changes in the school district's policy for handling conflicts and for the creation of programs to help prevent future conflicts from erupting.[7]

In some cases, coalition building is driven by elected officials or candidates. In Houston, Lee Brown successfully appealed to Asian Pacific American activists in his 1997 mayoral campaign.[8] Brown's outreach to APA groups was so effective that he was able to maintain support in those communities even when some prominent APA elected officials threw their support to his opponent.

MASS ELECTORAL COALITIONS

Assessing Asian American participation in larger electoral coalitions requires a very different approach. While activists or elected officials build coalitions with each other through negotiation and much individual interaction, mass electoral coalitions are often created through mass media and other impersonal messages. Coalitions of activists or elected officials are generally composed of individuals who know each other and are conscious of their alliance with others. In contrast, many of those in mass electoral coalitions have little or no sense of being part of a larger alliance, and they often know little or nothing about others in that coalition. Many of the members of mass electoral coalitions are tied together only by their common support of a candidate or political party. Because of this, we evaluate these types of coalitions by examining survey data on political attitudes and preferences.

Some have hoped that people of color and liberal whites might rally around common candidates; however, evidence for this is mixed. While many Asian Americans appear to have joined African Americans and Latinos in helping to provide critical support for Democrats, especially in California, Asian American partisan preferences still may be divided.

Furthermore, surveys have found some significant areas of distrust or distaste between African Americans, Latinos, and Asian Americans. For example, a New American Media survey found a majority of African American respondents agreed that most Asian American business owners did not treat them with respect, and a narrow plurality of Asian respondents agreed that they are afraid of African Americans because African Americans were responsible for most crimes. In addition, for each group, respondents were far more likely to be comfortable doing business with whites than with the other two groups.[9]

Scholar George Yancey has drawn on survey and census data to argue that Latinos and Asian Americans are becoming more similar to and gaining greater acceptance from whites, while African Americans are once again being left on the margins of society.[10] Yancey's evidence does not demonstrate that Asian Americans and Latinos are natural allies, but his data show that many Asian Americans may be developing political perspectives that are increasingly different from those of black Americans.

These obstacles to interracial understanding should not be overemphasized, however. The New American Media poll noted above also found many areas of agreement between African Americans, Asian Americans, and Latinos. Overwhelming majorities in all three communities agreed that each group had similar problems and should work together to solve them, and substantial majorities of Asian Americans and Latinos agreed that they had all been helped by the African American leadership in the civil rights movement.[11] A "rainbow" electoral coalition can still exist, but it will require leaders skilled at managing the many sources of tension that can emerge between the different groups.

CHALLENGES

Coalitions face constant challenges. Affirmative action has the potential to create stress for interracial coalitions that include Asian Americans, although, given their diversity, it seems most likely to divide Asian Americans from each other. One important challenge to panethnic coalition building is the issue of Native Hawaiian self-determination, but economic issues can also create fissures in pan-Asian alliances.

While most Asian American groups continue to support affirmative action, some feel that it is contrary to their interests. In the late 1990s in San Francisco, a group of Chinese American parents challenged a program which sought to create some racial balance at prestigious Lowell High School, and in 2008, an Asian American student's complaint about Princeton's admissions policies triggered a U.S. Department of Education investigation that could further undermine affirmative action in higher education.[12] In education and hiring, affirmative action programs can create a zero-sum game, which may lead growing numbers of Asian Americans to oppose it, if they feel that they are no longer beneficiaries.[13]

Most pan-Asian American groups seek to include Pacific Islander Americans (including Native Hawaiians), and organization names usually reflect that—e.g., the Asian Pacific American Legal Center of Southern California; however, native Hawaiians' efforts to win greater political empowerment and sovereignty (political control over territory in Hawai'i) presents a major challenge to efforts to build an Asian and Pacific Islander American coalition in Hawai'i. There, the Asian American dominance of politics in the islands means that they make up much of the power structure that is denying native Hawaiians greater control. Cooperation still occurs, but tensions over this issue are unlikely to go away.

Although the issue of native Hawaiian sovereignty is not as likely to divide Asian Americans and Pacific Islanders residing on the mainland, economic issues might. In the Houston case described above, some Asian American–elected officials argued that their communities would benefit more from Republican pro-business policies—but this was a plea clearly aimed at more prosperous Asian Americans, not at the many still struggling with poverty and economic opportunity.

OUTLOOK

It is difficult to predict the composition of the future coalitions that Asian Americans will join, but it seems likely that they will continue to participate actively in broader alliances. As groups gain political experience, they learn that they will be more successful when they can gain the support of other groups.

It has been argued that political involvement has helped build an Asian American identity. Separate ethnic groups have found it beneficial to work together in their battles for their rights. As these coalitions form, the sense of a panethnic—an Asian American—identity has grown.[14]

Broader coalition building is likely to help Asian Americans become more deeply embedded in American society. Alliances are usually built on reciprocity, and so Asian American groups will gain support by giving it. Ample evidence of this exists already. For example, the National Association of Korean Americans warned of threats to civil liberties in the "war on terror," although Korean Americans were not among those most likely to be targeted.[15] As coalition building grows, Asian Americans will become more familiar with groups that had previously been foreign to them, and other groups will develop a greater understanding of Asian Americans. This will not always happen easily, and the benefits will not always be evenly distributed, but the long-term result will likely be a society more open to all.

FURTHER READING

Asian American Justice Center. http://www.napalc.org/.

Fuchs, Lawrence H. *The American Kaleidoscope: Race, Ethnicity, and the Civic Culture.* Hanover, NH: Wesleyan University Press, 1990.

Kim, Claire Jean. *Bitter Fruit: The Politics of Black-Korean Conflict in New York City.* New Haven, CT: Yale University Press, 2000.

Lien, Pei-te. *The Making of Asian America through Political Participation.* Philadelphia: Temple University Press, 2001.

Rights Working Group. http://www.rightsworkinggroup.org.

NOTES

1. Ethnic groups can be defined in different ways. Here they are defined as groups of people who see themselves as sharing common traditions and cultural patterns, and who usually originate in the same nation-state—for instance, Chinese Americans, Filipino Americans, or Korean Americans—however, some, such as the Hmong, do not have

geographical origins that can be easily connected to a single nation state. In addition, in other contexts, some ethnic groups could be seen as panethnic entities. China, for example, can be seen as containing many different ethnic groups, so "Chinese" would be a panethnic identity.

2. The term "panethnic group" is usually used to refer to entities that bring together people of different ethnicities. A list of panethnic groups in the United States would be very similar to a list of racial groups: for example, both would include African Americans, American Indians, and Asian Americans.

3. This section draws on Scott Kurashige, "Pan-Ethnicity and Community Organizing: Asian Americans United's Campaign Against Anti-Asian Violence," *Journal of Asian American Studies* 3, no. 2 (June 2000): 169–190.

4. Pei-te Lien, M. Margaret Conway, and Janelle Wong, *The Politics of Asian Americans: Diversity & Community* (New York: Routledge, 2004), 41–53.

5. Wendy K. Tam Cho, "Tapping Motives and Dynamics Behind Campaign Contributions: Insights from the Asian American Case," *American Politics Research* 30, no. 4 (2002): 347–383.

6. James S. Lai, "Asian Pacific Americans and the Pan-Ethnic Question," in *Minority Politics at the Millennium*, eds. Richard E. Keiser and Katherine Underwood (New York: Garland Publishing, 2000), 203–226.

7. Leland T. Saito and Edward J. W. Park, "Multiracial Collaborations and Coalitions," in *The State of Asian Pacific America: Transforming Race Relations,* vol. IV, ed. Paul M. Ong (Los Angeles: LEAP and UCLA Asian American Studies Center, 2000), 435–474.

8. Saito and Park, "Multiracial Collaborations and Coalitions," 444–448.

9. New American Media, "Deep Divisions, Shared Destiny," December 2007. PowerPoint summary available at http://media.newamericamedia.org/images/polls/race/poll_presentation.ppt.

10. George Yancey, *Who Is White? Latinos, Asians, and the New Black/Nonblack Divide* (Boulder, CO: Lynne Rienner, 2004).

11. New American Media, "Deep Divisions, Shared Destiny."

12. For the Lowell case, see Bill Ong Hing, "Asians Without Blacks and Latinos in San Francisco: Missed Lessons of the Common Good," *Amerasia Journal* 27, no. 2 (2000): 19–27. For the Princeton case, see "Education Department Investigating Allegations of Racial Discrimination Against Asian American Applicants to Princeton University," *The Journal of Blacks in Higher Education Weekly Bulletin,* June 19, 2008, http://www.jbhe.com/latest/index061908.html.

13. See Paul M. Ong, "The Affirmative Action Divide," in Paul M. Ong, ed., *The State of Asian Pacific America: Transforming Race Relations,* vol. IV (Los Angeles: LEAP and UCLA Asian American Studies Center, 2000), 313–361.

14. Pei-te Lien, *The Making of Asian America through Political Participation* (Philadelphia: Temple University Press, 2001), 42–197.

15. National Association of Korean Americans, " 'War on Terrorism': Fundamental Civil Liberties Must be Preserved," no. 2 (Feb. 2002), http://www.naka.org/news/news.asp?prmid=3.

"DONORGATE" AND WEN HO LEE

Michael Chang

In 1996, top-level Asian American Democratic National Committee (DNC) fund-raisers were indicted for violating Federal Election Commission (FEC) laws. The experience demonstrated the tenuous political status of Asian Americans, and their vulnerability to being labeled disloyal foreigners. Asian American activists argued that the "Donorgate" discourses served to "denaturalize" Asian Americans, reinforcing an already deeply seated perception of Asian Americans as aliens in the United States. Battles over campaign finance are likely to continue to involve concerns over race, rights, and citizenship.

From one perspective, the Asian Donorgate controversy was about allegations of illegal campaign finance fund-raising practices in the fall of 1996. But, if viewed from a broader context of globalization and the related concern of the growing economic and political power of China, the Donorgate discourses continued for several years, culminating in allegations of Chinese nuclear espionage in the winter of 1999.

Prior to the unfolding of "Asian Donorgate," 1996 was viewed in the Asian American communities as a watershed year in terms of mainstream national-level political attainment by Asian Americans.[1] John Huang had been named head fund-raiser for the Democratic National Committee, seen by many as a sign that the Democratic Party was serious about its Asian American constituency. But soon after the first charges of DNC fund-raising irregularities emerged, it became clear that these gains were greatly susceptible to partisan politics and sensationalist media coverage.

In September 1996 during the re-election campaign of President Bill Clinton, the *Los Angeles Times* published a story charging that DNC fund-raiser Huang had collected an illegal $250,000 donation from John K. H. Lee, a South Korean businessman. Soon after this, Republican politicians and media outlets began to scrutinize the fund-raising practices of the DNC, those of Huang in particular. Of most concern were allegations that the DNC had accepted foreign campaign contributions, a violation of the Federal Election Committee rules. The DNC tried to distance itself from the scandal, hiring the accounting firm of Ernst & Young, which called all Asian surnamed donors on the DNC's donor lists and asked them about their citizenship status, among other questions.

Huang, the vice chair of finance at the DNC, came under suspicion for his connection to his former employer, the Indonesian-based Lippo Group conglomerate. As Bob Woodward (of Watergate fame) and Brian Duffy reported in the *Washington Post*, the Lippo Group sold 50 percent of its holdings in Hong Kong Chinese Bank (where Huang worked in the mid-1980s) in 1993 to a corporation run by the Chinese government.[2] This circumstantial information suggested to reporters that the Lippo Group, owned by the Riady family, was acting in the interests of the Chinese government, and that Huang was their point man. Woodward and Duffy's reporting was highly influential and gave validity to accusations from the Republican Party of a "China connection" to the fundraising scandal.

Republican representative Gerald B. H. Solomon (R-NY), chairman of the powerful House Rules Committee, requested an FBI investigation of Huang for "potential economic espionage against the United States by a foreign corporation having direct ties to the People's Republic of China."[3] Representative Solomon claimed that he had "new information" that was the "smoking gun," proving Huang was a spy for China.[4] Solomon told reporters that he had received "reports from government sources that say there are electronic intercepts which provide evidence . . . that John Huang committed economic espionage and breached our national security by passing classified information [to Lippo Group]."[5] Solomon's charges made front-page news and helped to propel the Huang investigation in the direction of espionage.

When the FBI later questioned Solomon about the "electronic intercepts," Solomon told them that he never had actual intercepts, only information from a Senate staffer who had told him that "a Department of Commerce employee had passed classified information to a foreign government."[6] Solomon only assumed that the staffer was speaking about Huang and that the foreign government was China. During FBI interviews Solomon could not name the staffer, and he admitted that the Senate staffer did not make the very specific comments (about wire intercepts) that Solomon had claimed.

In a common cycle of news media coverage and political partisanship, the Senate's Committee on Governmental Affairs investigation (led by Fred Thompson, R-TN) used media accounts and still unreleased classified information to piece together its claim of a link between fund-raising infractions and espionage. The conclusions of the Thompson committee's final report were then used to validate the original news stories.[7] This circular reasoning continued throughout the Asian Donorgate controversy.

The Woodward article used the questionable claims of Representative Solomon, and helped to generate intensive media and political concentration on a "China connection." These allegations elevated the fund-raising controversy to a much more serious level, giving the Justice Department investigation a "foreign counterintelligence component."[8]

In March 1998, the *New York Times* and the *Washington Post* gave front-page coverage to allegations that the Clinton administration had allowed a leak to China of important military technology by giving the Loral and the Hughes Aerospace Corporations (major Democratic donors) the right to have their satellites launched from Chinese rockets. After several Loral and Hughes satellites had been destroyed in failed Chinese rocket launches, both companies gave technical advice to the Chinese to improve their launching technology.

The *New York Times* and the *Washington Post* alleged that these transferences of knowledge greatly improved China's ability to launch long-range ground-based nuclear weapons.[9] Representative Christopher Cox (R-CA), who chaired a House select committee investigation on Chinese military espionage, saw connections between these allegations and DNC fund-raisers Huang and Johnny Chung. The Cox Committee searched for evidence for this "China connection," concluding that nuclear arms miniaturization technology had been given to China by a government scientist most likely based at Los Alamos National Laboratory in New Mexico. Led by the Thompson and Cox committees and high-profile reporting by the *New York Times*, the narrative of illegal foreign campaign money morphed from campaign finance reform and DNC fund-raisers peddling influence with foreign dollars into an issue of heightened national security.

In Asian Donorgate, the interests of people and governments in Asia were seen as the same as the interests of Asian Americans. Asian Donorgate was described in ways that portrayed Asian Americans as foreigners, leaving them more vulnerable to charges of disloyalty.

Wen Ho Lee experienced the consequences of that vulnerability.

Lee was incarcerated in December 1999 after allegations that he had helped give the "crown jewels" of U.S. nuclear technology, the miniaturized W-88 nuclear warhead technology, to the Chinese government. Under political pressure, and without a trial, Lee was fired from his job at Los Alamos National Laboratory, after having been employed as a nuclear scientist there for twenty-five years. Lee was placed in solitary confinement and required to wear shackles on his hands and feet during his daily one hour of exercise.[10] He was released from federal prison on September 13, 2000, after nine months of solitary confinement. The federal judge who released him, James A. Parker, strongly criticized the prosecution for having misled him into believing that Lee was a great security risk, and he apologized to Lee.[11] Although Lee was released, and the judge recognized that the prosecution had exaggerated its case, the Donorgate scandal and the experiences of Wen Ho Lee demonstrate the political vulnerability of Asian Americans, and the ease with which they can be depicted as dangerous foreigners.

FURTHER READING

Chang, Michael. *Racial Politics in an Era of Transnational Citizenship: The 1996 "Asian Donorgate" Controversy in Perspective.* Lanham, MD: Lexington Books, 2004.

Stober, Dan, and Ian Hoffman. *A Convenient Spy: Wen Ho Lee and the Politics of Nuclear Espionage.* New York: Simon and Schuster, 2001.

NOTES

1. Until 2002, federal campaign finance laws made a distinction between "hard money" and "soft money." In 2002, the Bipartisan Campaign Reform Act was passed, essentially outlawing soft money. But during the Asian Donorgate events, the Asian American DNC fund-raisers raised large amounts of soft money, unregulated funds from corporations, unions, and wealthy individuals, which were donated to political parties. Soft money became the primary source of funding for the all important political party television ads. Brennan Center for Justice, "Unregulated Soft Money Now Pays for Most Party Electioneering Ads," Brennan Center for Justice, New York University, March 28, 2001, www.brennancenter.org/cmagpdf/cmag2000.03.28.01.pdf (8/11/01).

2. Bob Woodward and Brian Duffy, "Chinese Embassy Role in Contributions Probed; Planning of Foreign Donations to DNC Indicated," *Washington Post*, Feb. 13, 1997, A01.

3. Woodward and Duffy, "Chinese Embassy Role."

4. Al Kamen, "How a Story Changed Its Shape," *Washington Post Sunday Magazine*, Feb. 6, 2000, W04.

5. Art Pine and Alan C. Miller, "FBI Notes Dispel 'Evidence' of Security Breach by Huang; Allegation: Casual Remark, Not Intelligence Reports, Called Basis of Ex-Congressman's Widely Publicized Claim of 'Economic Espionage,' " *Los Angeles Times*, Dec. 17, 1999, A36.; Kamen, "Story Changed," 2000.

6. Kamen, "Story Changed," 2000.

7. Chapter 18 of the Senate investigation's final report, titled "The China Connection: Summary of the Committee's Findings Relating to the Efforts of the People's Republic of China to Influence U.S. Policies and Elections," describes the committee's use of early media accounts of "alleged foreign activities" in conjunction with briefings by the FBI in 1996 to members of Congress and the White House as primary sources for its claim of Chinese espionage. USSCGA, *Summary of Findings*, 2502.

8. Woodward and Duffy, "Chinese Embassy Role."

9. U.S. House of Representatives Select Committee (USHRSC), *U.S. National Security and Military/Commercial Concerns with the People's Republic of China*, vols. 1–3, Redacted/declassified version (Washington, DC: GPO, May 1999), xiv–xxiii.

10. Robert Scheer, "No Defense: How the *New York Times* Convicted Wen Ho Lee," *The Nation* (Oct. 23, 2000): 11–20.

11. James Sterngold, "A Judge's Indignation," *New York Times*, Feb. 15, 2000, A1.

NATURALIZATION AND VOTING

Don T. Nakanishi

Becoming naturalized and acquiring citizenship in the United States represents a critically important stage in the incorporation of an immigrant into American society. Naturalization is not merely a paper change in status. It requires a level of acculturation defined by a basic command of the English language, and knowledge of U.S. history and its political institutions. In becoming a citizen, in most instances, immigrants forgo allegiance to their country of origin while pledging loyalty to the United States.

In order to gain full political and social membership in the United States, acquiring citizenship is a key step. U.S. citizenship provides an important opportunity to vote and to participate in the electoral process. Naturalization and political participation also have significant implications for groups. The political strength of a largely immigrant population, such as Asian Americans, within the American electoral system hinges on three interrelated, but distinct processes: first, the group's naturalization rate, that is, the relative proportion of immigrants with citizenship; second, the rate by which naturalized and native-born citizens register to vote; and finally, the rate by which those who are registered to vote actually vote during elections. Low rates of naturalization, voter registration, and voting dilute an immigrant-dominated group's potential electoral power, thereby diminishing its influence on legislation, public policy, and the selection of leaders. At the same time, attaining citizenship and participating in society are seen by the general public as markers of a group's ability and willingness to assimilate and to be "Americanized" rather than remain as permanent aliens. While high rates of naturalization and political participation do not guarantee that all members of a group will be fully accepted as equals, low rates foster political and social isolation and may provide fodder for nativist movements.

Although becoming a citizen and becoming a voter are usually viewed as nearly simultaneous processes, they are distinct and temporally distant forms of membership and participation in American life and society. Asians and other immigrants and refugees, especially those who migrated as adults, oftentimes acquired their fundamental political values, attitudes, and behavioral orientations in countries that have sociopolitical systems, traditions, and expectations different from those of American politics. Indeed, many came from countries where voting was not permitted, limited to a privileged few, or was widely viewed as being inconsequential because of the dominance of a single political party. As such, they must undergo a process of political acculturation, which goes beyond the rudimentary exposure to the basic facts of American governmental institutions that they are required to learn in preparing for naturalization examinations through citizenship classes. Becoming a voter, and more generally becoming a participant in American electoral politics, can be a prolonged and complicated process of social learning for immigrants as much as it is for native-born citizens.

NATURALIZATION AND CITIZENSHIP

As of 2006, the nearly 15 million Asian Americans comprised approximately 5 percent of the total U.S. population, with ten states having more than 5 percent of their population Asian Americans. Many of these states, particularly California, New York, Texas, Illinois, and Florida, have the largest Congressional delegations and the most Electoral College votes, and as a result wield considerable national political influence in federal legislative decision-making and in presidential elections. For Asian Americans, what is most important in terms of their potential political impact is the percent of those who are eligible to register to vote. What is noticeable is the substantial decline in the proportion of Asian American as the analysis moves from total population to either those with citizenship or adult citizens (eighteen years and older), which can be seen in Table 1. Nationally, the declines are 1 or more percentage points. This means that one in twenty people who live in the United States may be Asian, but between one in twenty-five and one in thirty adult citizens of the country is Asian. These figures vary among the states. Asians constitute a majority of adult citizens in Hawaii. Four additional states listed in Table 1 have percentages higher than the national average (California, New York, New Jersey, and Washington).

The primary reason for the difference in the Asian American share of the total population and the Asian American share of adult citizens is the fact that this is a predominantly immigrant population. In 2006, 61 percent of all Asian Americans of all age groups were immigrants, and 76 percent of all Asian American adults were born abroad. The percent of immigrants varies greatly among the ten states listed in Table 2. They comprise a small minority of those in Hawaii, and three-quarter of those in California. The highest fraction is in New Jersey, where seven in eight are immigrants. This difference can influence the political issues that Asian Americans are most concerned about because immigrants and U.S.-born share many, but not all, issue concerns. Equally important is the naturalization rate among the immigrants. Nationally, a majority of immigrants has

Table 1. 2006 Asian American Population Estimates

Area	Total Population	Asian Population	Percent Asian	Percent Asian, Citizens	Percent Asian, 18+ Citizens
United States	299,398,485	14,656,608	4.9%	3.9%	3.6%
California	36,457,549	4,896,851	13.4%	12.2%	12.3%
New York	19,306,183	1,391,510	7.2%	5.4%	5.2%
Texas	23,507,783	859,588	3.7%	2.8%	2.7%
Hawai'i	1,285,498	725,436	56.4%	55.3%	54.0%
New Jersey	8,724,560	685,013	7.9%	5.9%	5.4%
Illinois	12,831,970	583,538	4.5%	3.5%	3.3%
Washington	6,395,798	497,782	7.8%	6.4%	6.1%
Florida	18,089,889	460,641	2.5%	2.1%	1.8%
Virginia	7,642,884	409,035	5.4%	4.0%	3.7%
Massachusetts	6,437,193	334,954	5.2%	3.8%	3.3%

Source: 2006 American Community Survey.

acquired citizenship, but there is still a substantial minority who are not citizens; the rates tend to be lower outside the West Coast states.

VOTER REGISTRATION AND VOTING PATTERNS

Even after achieving citizenship, there are two additional steps required to become fully politically engaged—registering to vote and turning out to vote. According to estimates from the Voter Supplement to the November 2006 Current Population Survey, Asian American adult citizens have a substantially lower voter

Table 2. Citizenship Status of Asian Americans

State	Adults (× 1,000)	Born Citizen	Naturalized	Not Citizen	Naturalization Rate
United States	10,951	24.1%	43.4%	32.5%	57.2%
California	3,722	25%	47%	28%	63%
New York	1,090	15%	46%	38%	55%
Texas	625	17%	46%	37%	56%
Hawai'i	551	70%	19%	11%	63%
New Jersey	515	12%	49%	39%	56%
Illinois	440	19%	46%	35%	57%
Washington	376	29%	44%	27%	62%
Florida	337	19%	48%	33%	59%
Virginia	303	18%	48%	34%	58%
Massachusetts	255	20%	39%	41%	49%

Source: 2006 American Community Survey, Public Use Microsample (PUMS).

registration rate than non-Asians, a difference of 19 percentage points (Table 3). With the exception of Hawaii, registration rates among Asian Americans by different states and regions are lower than for non-Asians. On the other hand, the voter registration rate for naturalized Asian Americans is only slightly lower than for naturalized non-Asians, which indicates that most immigrants, regardless of race, tend to register to vote at lower rates. Thus, the lower registration rate among Asian American adult citizens is partly because of the large number of naturalized immigrants. At the same time, the voter registration rate for U.S.-born Asian American citizens is lower than that of all other U.S.-born citizens, a finding that has been observed for many years. This may be because many factors, including the lingering effects of the historic disenfranchisement of early Asian immigrants who were barred from becoming naturalized citizens and therefore could not vote, as well as the lack of interest and oftentimes hostility that the major political parties exhibited toward Asian Americans in the past.

Table 3 also reports voting rates. Nationally, 15 percent fewer Asian American citizens turned out to vote in 2006 than non-Asian Americans. Only in Hawai'i did Asian American citizens vote at a higher rate than others in the population. On the other hand, the differences in voter turnout rates were substantially smaller among Asian Americans and others who were registered to vote. The differences were only 3 percentages points for Asian American registered voters, whether they were those who were born in the United States, those who were naturalized or other registered voters, reflecting a considerable narrowing of the voting gap, compared with earlier studies.

Table 3. Registration and Voting Rates, 2006

	Registered		Voted	
	Asians	**Non-Asians**	**Asians**	**Non-Asians**
U.S. Adult (18+)				
Citizens	49%	68%	33%	48%
Citizens by birth	46%	69%	31%	49%
U.S. naturalized	52%	55%	34%	38%
California	49%	64%	34%	49%
Hawaii	56%	53%	47%	39%
New York/New Jersey	51%	64%	29%	44%
All other regions	48%	69%	30%	49%
U.S. Registered				
Voters			66%	71%
Citizen by birth			68%	71%
U.S. naturalized			65%	68%
California			71%	77%
Hawai'i			83%	72%
New York/New Jersey			57%	68%
All other regions			62%	71%

Source: November 2006 Current Population Survey Voter Supplement.

2008 PRESIDENTIAL ELECTION

According to an eleven-state multilingual exit poll of 16,665 Asian American voters conducted by the Asian American Legal Defense and Education Fund (AALDEF) in collaboration with sixty national and local community groups, Asian American voters favored President Barack Obama by a 3-to-1 margin (76% to 22%) and supported other Democratic candidates in the November 2008 elections.[1] A clear majority (58%) of Asian Americans were registered Democrats, 26 percent were not enrolled in any political party, and 14 percent of Asian Americans were registered Republicans. This poll was conducted at 113 poll sites in twelve Asian languages and dialects: Chinese, Korean, Vietnamese, Japanese, Tagalog, Khmer, Arabic, Bengali, Hindi, Punjabi, Urdu, and Gujarati.

First-time voters favored Obama by greater margins. Among first-time Asian American voters, 82 percent voted for Obama, 17 percent voted for John McCain, and 1 percent for other candidates.

Although one in five (20%) identified English as their native language 35 percent of Asian Americans polled said that they were limited English proficient. A number of poll sites were mandated to provide bilingual ballots and interpreters under the federal Voting Rights Act; other jurisdictions voluntarily provided language assistance. In the 2008 elections, 18 percent of all respondents preferred to use some form of language assistance to vote.

This nonpartisan poll provides a unique snapshot of voter preferences in 30 cities with large and growing Asian American populations in New York, New Jersey, Virginia, Maryland, Michigan, Illinois, Nevada, Louisiana, Texas, and Washington, DC.

Interestingly, Asian American voters seem roughly reflective of their states. Where McCain had strong support among the general voting population, he also won over Asian American voters. The six largest Asian ethnic groups polled in 2008 were Chinese (32%), Asian Indian (16%), Korean (14%), Bangladeshi (8%), Vietnamese (7%) and Filipino (5%). Four out of five (79%) of those polled were foreign-born. More than one-third (35%) described themselves as limited English proficient, and 21 percent had no formal U.S. education. Nearly one-third (31%) were first-time voters.

Asian Americans shared common political interests across ethnic lines, with the economy/jobs cited as the most important issue in their vote for president.

Notes

1. The exit polls conducted by the National Election Pool (NEP) found that 62 percent of Asian Americans reported voting for Obama, and 35 percent for McCain. The NEP poll was a true national sample, so its sample should be more representative of the entire population. The AALDEF poll sampled areas that include most of the Asian American population, but a significant minority is not included in the sampling frame. However, the AALDEF poll was better able to interview respondents, because of its use of multilingual interviewers, so it is difficult to know which poll presents the more accurate picture of the Asian American vote for president.

—Christine Chen

FUTURE POLITICAL PARTICIPATION

It is seen that the political incorporation of Asian naturalized (and native-born citizens) into the American electoral system needs further acceleration. Some believe that the contemporary remnants of the political exclusion and isolation that Asian Americans experienced in the past must be fully confronted and eliminated not only by Asian American groups, but also by the two major political parties and others who believe that citizens should be able to fully exercise their right of franchise. Unfair redistricting of Asian American communities, lack of bilingual voter registration application forms and ballots, and opposition to the implementation of legislation such as the National Voter Registration Act of 1993 (otherwise known as the Motor Voter Act) are seen to perpetuate so-called political structural barriers, which must be challenged and replaced by fair and inclusive political practices and policies. Asian immigrants have much to contribute to all aspects of American political life—as voters, campaign workers, financial donors, policy experts, and elected officials—and advocates believe they must be allowed to and encouraged to participate fully. By doing so, Asian Americans will continue the political tradition as old as the nation itself of benefiting from the special leadership talents and contributions of individuals who came to the United States from all corners of the world, and shaped its domestic and international programs and policies.

In recent years, the incentive and necessity for Asian immigrants and their native-born counterparts to naturalize and become more involved in electoral politics have been greatly enhanced in both obvious and unexpected ways. Politicians and the major political parties, which had long neglected to address the unique public policy interests and quality-of-life concerns of Asian Americans, have become increasing responsive and attentive, especially to the growing sector of the Asian American population that contributes sizable amounts to political campaign coffers. Less interest, however, has been shown toward augmenting the long-term voting potential of Asian Americans, and few attempts have been made by the Democratic or Republican parties to finance voter registration and education campaigns in Asian American communities. The increasing number of Asian Americans, however, especially those of immigrant background, who are seeking public office appears to be stimulating greater electoral participation among Asian Americans at the grassroots level. For example, it is becoming a common practice for Asian American candidates to make special efforts in seeking monetary donations and in registering new voters among Asian Americans in the jurisdictions in which they are running for office. These activities provide Asian immigrants with important and direct vantage points from which to understand the workings of the American political system, thereby facilitating their political acculturation. At the same time, a wide array of advocacy and social services groups have formed in Asian American communities across the nation, and a number of outreach campaigns have been launched to promote citizenship and to register individuals, particularly those who have just become citizens at naturalization ceremonies. And finally, disastrous events like the civil unrest in Los

Angeles in 1992, in which more than 2,000 Korean American and Asian-owned businesses were destroyed, have underscored the need for immigrant-dominant communities to have greater organizational and leadership activities that will augment their access to and influence in local government and other policy arenas, as well as to increase their representation in voter registration rolls.

For Asian Americans, the twenty-first century is often viewed in glowing and optimistic terms because of seemingly positive demographic trends, and it will be a significant period to witness because of the extraordinary challenges and opportunities that it will undoubtedly present for Asian Americans to realize their full potential as citizens and electoral participants. The level of success that they will achieve in the future, however, will not be solely determined by the Asian American population, or its leaders and organizations. Experts see that it will require the assistance and intervention of a wide array of groups and leaders in both the private and public sectors. Whether Asian Americans become a major new political force in the American electoral system is nearly impossible to predict with any precision. But, given the history of disenfranchisement and exclusion that Asian Americans have faced, even to raise and seriously entertain such a question is quite revealing.

FURTHER READING

Asian American Justice Center. http://www.advancingequality.org/.

Asian American Legal Center of Southern California. http://www.apalc.org/.

Asian American Legal Defense and Education Fund. https://www.aaldef.org/.

Asian Law Caucus. http://www.asianlawcaucus.org/site/alc_dev/.

Chang, Gordon. *Asian Americans and Politics: Perspectives, Experiences, Prospects.* Washington, DC: Woodrow Wilson Center Press, 2001.

Lien, Pei-te, Conway, M. Margaret, and Wong, Janelle. *The Politics of Asian Americans: Diversity and Community.* New York: Routledge, 2004.

Nakanishi, Don T. and Lai, James S. *Asian American Politics: Law, Participation, and Policy.* Lanham, MD: Rowman and Littlefield, 2003.

Nakanishi, Don T. and Lai, James, eds. *National Asian Pacific American Political Almanac.* 13th ed. UCLA Asian American Studies Center Press, 2007.

RACIAL ATTITUDES IN THE TWENTY-FIRST CENTURY

Natalie Masuoka

As a central feature in American life, race represents an important social dimension that individuals use as a proxy to determine their attitudes and preferences about a variety of political issues and policies. Indeed, one's racial background generally predicts one's outlook on the trajectory of race relations in the United States, with whites being more optimistic and minorities being more pessimistic. Furthermore, how one perceives members of another racial group—whether they are based on correct or incorrect assumptions—influences how one understands the merits of socially redistributive policies, such as affirmative action, and the types of target populations that are considered deserving of such benefits. Existing scholarship has found that individual racial attitudes generally do not influence attitudes on non-racialized issues, such as abortion. However, because race is intricately entwined with so many features of American politics, the range in which racial attitudes influence an individual's politics is extensive.

While the literature on racial attitudes is well developed, the majority of that literature describes the contours of white racial prejudice and has focused on white attitudes about African Americans. As the American population grows increasingly diverse, however, the question remains whether the theories that appropriately describe white attitudes about African Americans can explain racial attitudes more generally. Many scholars acknowledge that an accurate gauge of racial attitudes today should incorporate the perspectives of white and minority respondents and that studies on racial prejudice should recognize that racial resentment may also be aimed at other minority groups besides African

Americans. The existing research on white racial attitudes may provide an important foundation to understand the role of racial attitudes on individual political attitudes, but more recent research demonstrates that the dynamics of individual racial attitudes is much more complex than what this foundational literature suggests. Most importantly, this new research demonstrates that white Americans and racial minorities have very distinctive viewpoints about race, which, in turn, influence their individual political attitudes. Thus, the application of past research on racial attitudes to a racial context that includes more than only black-white relations may be limited.

PERCEPTION OF RACE RELATIONS

The first dimension in the study of racial attitudes is how individuals perceive the state of race relations and how race influences their own individual life chances. When it comes to viewpoints about race relations, the most significant distinction exists in how whites and minority groups view American liberal democratic norms and their levels of optimism toward societal change. While white Americans embrace the ideal of the American Dream—the belief that hard work leads to individual personal success—African Americans are more likely to identify structural barriers that inhibit individual social mobility, such as racial status.[1] Thus, African American political attitudes generally reflect skepticism toward ideas of improving race relations. Early research on African American racial attitudes suggests that because African Americans witness the personal experience as being part of a marginalized minority group, African American perspectives on race relations are governed by a different set of considerations than that of whites. Because African Americans are normally perceived as the target group in any reference about race, they are more likely to understand how race influences their personal life chances, whereas for whites, race is not perceived to be a direct personal barrier. This also explains why African Americans have strong perceptions of racial group consciousness that encourages an individual to remain committed to the causes of the racial group and are supportive of policies aimed to service their racial community.[2] Thus, as a collective group, African Americans tend to be more unified on their perceptions about race relations and are much more willing to acknowledge the persistence of racial inequality in today's society as compared with whites, which as a group is much more divided on racial issues.

Research on Asian Americans' outlook about race relations is less developed. Some research suggests that when it comes to racial issues, Asian Americans are more likely to report attitudes closer to those of whites than to African Americans.[3] Scholars contend that there are two major factors that influence perceptions about race relations and racial group attachment: one's economic status and perceptions about social mobility. For some scholars, racial group attachment strengthens when individuals continue to perceive rigid barriers to economic mobility. Their findings reveal that because Asian Americans, on average, have higher levels of income and are relatively less constrained by their racial status as compared with African Americans, they are less likely to view the world in racial terms. Thus, Asian Americans are more optimistic about the state of race relations and are less likely to identify structural barriers that inhibit individual agency.

However, Asian American attitudes toward race relations should not be conflated with white attitudes. Although Asian Americans may not depict similar perspectives about race relations as African Americans, it does not mean that Asian Americans fail to recognize the role of race in society. Figure 1 presents an example of how the four major racial and ethnic groups compare with one another on race issues. As shown, on the issue of whether race is an important issue in American society, white Americans are the least likely to view race as an important issue, whereas African Americans are the most likely to want to address racial issues. Asian American and Hispanic ratings on the question fall between white and black attitudes. This pattern, which depicts whites and African Americans on two opposing poles with Asian Americans (and Hispanics) falling somewhere in between, can be found on a number of public opinion questions about race, suggesting that each of the major racial/ethnic groups view race relations through their own unique lens.[4]

Figure 1. Comparison of Racial Groups on Attitudes toward Racial Issues

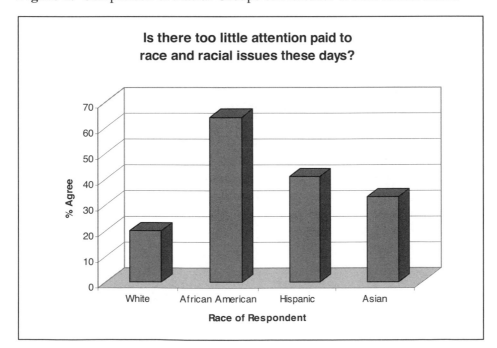

Source: Washington Post/Kaiser/Harvard, "Race and Ethnicity in 2001: Attitudes, Perceptions and Experiences."

RACIAL ATTITUDES AND INTERGROUP RELATIONS

The second dimension in the study of racial attitudes falls in the area of political psychology. This literature focuses on the formation of racial prejudice and how prejudice influences intergroup relationships. Longitudinal trends on white public opinion demonstrate that racial prejudice against African Americans has declined since the civil rights era, leading many to conclude that white racism is slowly disappearing and no longer dictates intergroup relations in the United States.[5] Others argue, however, that white racial prejudice continues to persist but rather is expressed in a form that conforms to today's norm of "color-blindness."[6] One well-documented debate in this literature is over how to explain the nature of this new racism. One position posits that ideology and other personality traits, such as authoritarianism, explain an individual's position on racial issues, while the opposing position argues that whites express their racism indirectly and through their opposition to policy issues implicitly coded as racial issues, such as school busing.[7]

Although less is known about racial prejudice among minorities, psychological studies using implicit attitude tests show that, for example, African Americans report negative affect toward other African Americans, demonstrating how strong racial tropes persist through society and how even those who are themselves marginalized develop racial animosity toward their own in-group.[8] Studies on African American public opinion also offer some information on how African Americans view other minority groups, although the majority of this work examines African American views about Latinos.[9] A significant share of this research relies on the theory of realistic group conflict, which argues that intergroup relations are best described in terms of the competitive relationship between one or more groups.[10] When members of an in-group perceive that an out-group threatens their position on the social hierarchy or that the out-group has a monopoly on the benefits that they perceive to be rightfully theirs, they begin to express resentment and hostility toward that out-group and intergroup hostility ensues. Thus, although all racial and ethnic minority groups share a marginalized status on the racial hierarchy in relation to whites, studies have found that minorities express resentment toward other minorities.

The prevailing example of intergroup relations involving Asian Americans is the black-Korean conflicts that occur in urban areas. Since the 1970s, there have been numerous documented incidents involving violence or conflicts between Korean immigrant merchants and African American customers. According to scholar Claire Kim, the conventional wisdom describes black-Korean conflict as a story of "racial scapegoating."[11] Korean immigrants are pictured as hard-working and industrious, while blacks are described to be resentful toward Koreans who African Americans perceive as monopolizing the service economy that should rightfully belong to African American entrepreneurs. This story mirrors a similar sentiment as the realistic group conflict theory described above. Kim offers a contrasting position to the realistic group conflict theory by arguing that contrary to the racial scapegoating story, intergroup relations between Koreans and African Americans is better described as a byproduct of white racial dominance and racial ordering. By using the frame of the racial scapegoat, minorities are effectively misdirected away from the heart of the problem—their social marginalization by whites—and aim their frustrations toward each other. Kim points to the structural barriers that prevent African Americans from owning their own businesses, which explains their racial antagonism. Further, the persistent framing of Koreans as foreign outsiders forces them to become merchants in poor urban areas rather than as competitive professionals in white society.

While two competing theories seek to describe intergroup relations today, one important conclusion is that racial attitudes are strongly determined by the dominant racial stereotypes and tropes (evocative images) that are used to frame minority groups.[12] Although theorists propose that Asian Americans are strongly governed by two competing racial tropes—the perpetual foreign outsider and the model minority—public opinion studies suggest that the most predominant stereotype is the model minority image today. Like the racial scapegoat frame identified by Kim, other racial groups view Asian Americans as a relatively privileged group whose race does not impair their individual life chances. As Figure 2 demonstrates, white, African Americans, and Hispanic respondents are all more likely to view Asian Americans as having similar opportunities in life as whites in contrast to the two other minority groups, African Americans and Hispanic Americans. Interestingly, Asian Americans also believe that they are less disadvantaged than African Americans or Hispanics.

Figure 2. Attitudes toward Opportunity among U.S. Racial Groups

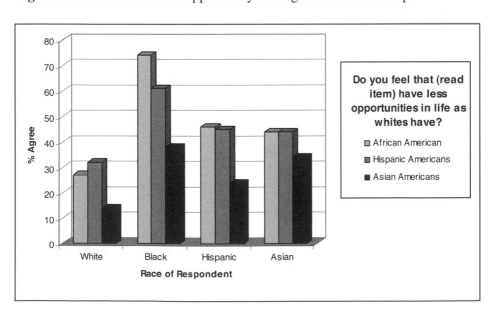

Source: Washington Post/Kaiser/Harvard, "Race and Ethnicity in 2001: Attitudes, Perceptions and Experiences."

What must be acknowledged, however, is that scholars have limited understanding about racial prejudice toward Asian Americans. The pattern demonstrated in Figure 2 can be misleading because some pundits may interpret these patterns as evidence that no prejudice against Asian Americans exists. Yet, evidence from public opinion polls only measure explicit racial attitudes, those attitudes that individuals are comfortable expressing openly because they feel these attitudes do not violate existing societal norms of racial equality. Most of the political psychology literature on racial prejudice uses experimental methods that can identify and measure hidden or implicit prejudices. However, no such studies include a manipulation using Asian Americans. Until a study is conducted, scholars cannot make relative assessments on the degree of racial prejudice aimed at Asian Americans nor how that racial prejudice influences public opinion.

FURTHER READING

APIAVote.org. http://www.apiavote.org/.

Asian American Legal Defense and Education Fund (AALDEF) Voting Rights. http://www.aaldef.org/voting.php.

Kim, Claire. *Bitter Fruit: The Politics of Black-Korean Conflict in New York City*. New Haven, CT: Yale University Press, 2000.

Lien, Pei-te, M. Margaret Conway, and Janelle Wong. *The Politics of Asian Americans: Diversity and Community*. New York: Routledge, 2004.

Sears, David, Jim Sidanius and Lawrence Bobo. *Racialized Politics: The Debate About Racism in America*. Chicago: University of Chicago Press, 2000.

NOTES

1. Jennifer Hochschild, *Facing Up to the American Dream: Race, Class and the Soul of the Nation* (Princeton, NJ: Princeton University Press, 1995).

2. Darren Davis and Ronald Brown, "The Antipathy of Black Nationalism: Behavioral and Attitudinal Implications of an African American Ideology," *American Journal of Political Science* 46 (2002): 239–252; Michael Dawson, *Behind the Mule: Race and Class in African American Politics* (Princeton, NJ: Princeton University Press, 1994); Katherine Tate, *From Protest to Politics: The New Black Voters in American Elections* (New York: Russell Sage Foundation, 1993).

3. Dennis Chong and Dukhong Kim, "The Experiences and Effects of Economic Status Among Racial and Ethnic Minorities," *American Political Science Review* 100 (2006): 335–351.

4. de la Garza, Rodolfo, Louis DeSipio, F. Chris Garcia, and Angelo Falcon, *Latino Voices Mexican, Puerto Rican and Cuban Perspectives on American Politics* (Boulder, CO: Westview Press, 1992); Lien, Pei-te, M. Margaret Conway and Janelle Wong, *The Politics of Asian Americans: Diversity and Community*. (New York: Routledge, 2004); Tate 1993.

5. Howard Schuman, Charlotte Steeh, Lawrence Bobo, and Maria Krysan, *Racial Attitudes in America: Trends and Interpretation* (Cambridge, MA: Harvard University Press, 1997); Steven Tuch, Lee Sigelman, and Jason Macdonald, "Trends: Race Relations and American Youth, 1976–1995," *Public Opinion Quarterly* 63 (1997): 109–148.

6. Lawrence Bobo and James Kluegel, "Opposition to Race-Targeting: Self-Interest, Stratification Ideology or Racial Attitudes?" *American Sociological Review* 58 (1993): 443–464; David Sears and Donald Kinder, "Racial Tensions and Voting in Los Angeles," in *Los Angeles: Viability and Prospects for Metropolitan Leadership*, ed. Werner Hirsch (New York: Praeger, 1971), 51–88; Paul Sniderman and Edward Carmines, *Reaching Beyond Race* (Cambridge, MA: Harvard University Press, 1997).

7. Sniderman and Carmines, *Reaching Beyond Race*; Donald Kinder and Lynn Sanders, *Divided by Color: Racial Politics and Democratic Ideals* (Chicago: University of Chicago, 1990); Donald Kinder and David Sears, "Prejudice and Politics: Symbolic Racism versus Racial Threats to the Good Life," *Journal of Personality & Social Psychology* 40 (1981): 414–431; John McConahay, "Modern Racism and Modern Discrimination: The Efforts of Race, Racial Attitudes, and Context on Simulated Hiring Decisions," *Personality & Social Psychology Bulletin* 9 (1986): 551–558.

8. Gordon Allport, *The Nature of Prejudice* (Cambridge, MA: Addison Wesley, 1958); Paul M. Sniderman and Thomas Piazza, *The Scar of Race* (Cambridge, MA: Harvard University Press, 1993); Margaret Spencer and Carol Markstrom-Adams, "Identity Processes among Racial and Ethnic Minority Children," *Child Development* 61 (1990): 290–310; Jim Sidanius and Felicia Pratto, *Social Dominance: An Intergroup Theory of Social Hierarchy and Oppression* (Cambridge, MA: Cambridge University Press, 1999).

9. Claudine Gay, "Seeing the Difference: The Effect of Economic Disparity on Black Attitudes Toward Latinos," *American Journal of Political Science* 50 (2006): 982–997; Kenneth Meier, Paula McClain, J. L. Polinard, and Robert Wrinkle, "Divided or Together? Conflict and Cooperation Between African Americans and Latinos," *Political Research Quarterly* 57 (2004): 399–409.

10. Herbert Blumer, "Race Prejudice as a Sense of Group Position." *Pacific Sociological Review*. 1 (1958): 3–7; Lawrence Bobo and Vincent L. Hutchings, "Perceptions of Racial Group Competition: Extending Blumer's Theory of Group Position to a Multiracial Social Context," *American Sociological Review* 61 (1996): 951–972.

11. Claire Kim, *Bitter Fruit: The Politics of Black-Korean Conflict in New York City* (New Haven, CT: Yale University Press, 2000).

12. Jane Junn and Natalie Masuoka, "Asian American Identity: Racial Status and Political Context," *Perspectives on Politics* 6 (2008), 729–740.

WOMEN'S ACTIVISM AND POLITICS

Diane C. Fujino and Chrissy Lau

While Asian American women have long participated in struggles for labor rights, homeland politics, and racial equality, it was only in the late 1960s that an Asian American women's movement developed. Women held rap sessions and wrote about sexism, gender equality, and women's issues; formed Asian American women's organizations; created Asian American women's classes; and developed women's grassroots leadership. Many Asian American women felt alienated from the mainstream women's movement and instead worked largely within the Asian American Movement (AAM). Drawing from black and Chicana feminism, the Asian American women's movement promoted a politic of intersectionality to simultaneously address sexism, racism, class inequality, and colonialism. By the 1980s and 1990s, there was greater focus on professional and leadership development, electoral politics, immigration issues, and sexuality and gay rights.

EARLY ORGANIZING

Until the 1960s, Asian American women's political participation was hampered by widespread racial and economic discrimination, political disenfranchisement, linguistic barriers, and patriarchal ideas relegating women to domesticity. Still, Asian American women—mostly Chinese and Japanese and mostly working-class—worked within their own ethnic communities for labor rights, homeland politics, and racial equality.

In Hawai'i in the early 1900s, labor strikes abounded, as Japanese women worked alongside their husbands on sugar cane plantations. Though men predominated as workers and activists, women supported the strikes and women-centered issues such as maternity leave were included in the labor demands. In 1938, Chinese immigrant and U.S.-born women engaged in their first collective struggle against labor exploitation in the garment industry, the largest employer in San Francisco's Chinatown. Their strike against the National Dollar Stores was the longest strike in Chinatown's history up to that point. After 105 days, the workers won a contract that included higher wages, a closed union shop, and a forty-hour workweek, reduced from forty-eight hours. Significantly, the women gained a sense of their own political and economic power, organizing skills, and an awareness of race, class, and gender dynamics in Chinatown and American labor unions.[1]

Asian American and immigrant women also actively supported homeland struggles. There were few Koreans in the United States and Hawai'i in the early 1900s. Men and women alike worked with fierce determination to support the Korean independence movement. In the 1930s, when Japan invaded Manchuria and North China, numerous Chinese women's organizations were formed throughout the United States to aid China's war relief. Moreover, when Japanese Americans were placed in concentration camps during World War II, women participated as journalists and editors of camp newspapers, rallied support for Japanese American soldiers, and participated in the camp's self-governance.

WOMEN'S MOVEMENT, 1960s–1970s

Still, it wasn't until the advent of the AAM in the late 1960s that large numbers of Asian American women became politically active and a widespread, sustained pan-Asian women's movement emerged. This movement developed within the overall AAM, influenced by the ideas and achievements of the Black Power, civil rights, and New Left movements. As Asian American women activists struggled for racial equality, they were confronted with other forms of inequality. They held consciousness-raising rap sessions, where Asian American women told moving stories about the ways sexism affected their lives and shared frustrations, anger, hopes, and struggles in safe and supportive spaces. They developed small and intensive study groups, where participants examined the historical roots of women's oppression. As they protested being relegated to so-called women's roles within the movement and marginalized from leadership, they pushed several AAM publications, notably *Gidra*, *Bridge*, and *East Wind*, to devote special issues to women's liberation. Articles focused on women leaders and rank-and-file activists, working-class women, labor resistance, and women's experiences historically. They offered feminist analyses of Asian American women's subordination and liberation. *Gidra*'s special issue on women's liberation included a script depicting two male activists demanding that a female activist get their coffee, type a leaflet, and book rooms, while repeatedly interrupting her and ignoring her ideas.[2] One particularly poignant moment occurred at an AAM meeting during a period of self introductions when one man introduced himself and then said, "[T]his is my wife; she has nothing to say."[3] The women exploded—a response that likely would not have occurred outside of this developing collective feminist consciousness. Some Asian American women came to identify as feminists. Others rejected the term, wanting to distance themselves from white feminism, militant politics, or what they perceived as a call for separation from men. Still, regardless of whether or not they used the term feminism, Asian American woman developed an ideology that viewed sexism as intricately linked to racism and classism and advocated a multi-issue approach to equality.

Most Asian American women chose to work alongside their Asian "brothers" within the AAM challenging racism, economic exploitation, and sexism in society, even as they protested male chauvinism within the AAM. Their analysis viewed sexism as arising from systemic structures, rather than individual men's ideas and actions per se. Their experiences growing up in a society organized by race—segregated residences, churches, organizations, communities, marriage and dating practices—created a stronger ethnic/racial than gender identity. Moreover, the women's movement of the 1960s had only a few years earlier popularized the idea of "the problem that has no name" and introduced a vocabulary to address sexism.[4] While initiating a new feminist consciousness, the women's movement simultaneously alienated women of color. In universalizing women's experiences, liberal or mainstream feminism assumed middle-class white women's issues represented the concerns of all women and thereby neglected the issue of racism, economic exploitation, and the continuing discrimination against third world men. Black feminism's focus on triple oppression, or the idea that women's inequality needed to be analyzed in relation to racism and class inequality, strongly influenced the development of Asian American feminism. The idea of examining the intersection of race, class, and gender oppression is contained in a 1971 article on "G.I.'s and Asian Women." The article began by focusing, not on women as the title implies, but on Asian American men—on how the draft consigns "our brothers" to face racism in the U.S. military and the killing other Asians. The author denounced the stereotypic images of Asian women as dolls and sex toys, not only because they objectify Asian women, but also because they dehumanize all Asians, rendering them easier to kill. The article advocates opposition to not only the Vietnam War, but also to the racism, sexism, and imperialism contained in U.S. militarism.[5]

In the early phase of the Asian American women's movement (late 1960s to mid-1970s), activists tended to focus on three interrelated types of activities: education and consciousness raising, community service, and radical politics. One major focus of the early AAM was educational transformation and the establishment of ethnic studies. Though men predominated, Asian American women were also active in the struggles for ethnic studies. At San Francisco State College, the birthplace of the first school of ethnic studies in the nation, Penny Nakatsu was a key leader of the Asian American Political Alliance and Third World strike. Participating in that strike transformed the political and racial consciousness of poet-activist Janice Mirikitani. Mirikitani went on to edit *AION*, one of the first Asian American cultural and political magazines, and today is a primary organizer of community service programs at Glide Memorial church in San Francisco. Emma Gee was already active with the Peace and Freedom Party when she cofounded the Asian American Political Alliance at UC–Berkeley. In 1970, students in her Asian women course at UC–Berkeley lamented the dearth of materials on Asian American women and decided to publish a journal. The *Asian Women* journal became a classic text in Asian American women's courses and played an influential role in shaping the Asian American women's movement. Through the process of producing this journal, the *Asian Women* staff discovered that "personal experiences are not private but common to all women" and that "out of common experiences political struggle is created."[6] They were moving away from individual expressions of sexism to structural analyses of patriarchy. Their views of women's liberation also promoted third world radicalism and internationalism, and they forged solidarities with U.S. black, Chicana, and indigenous women and with women in Asia. They charged the U.S. government with genocide based on its use of toxic chemicals in Vietnam and the sterilization of third world women. They also highlighted a conference in Montreal on Vietnamese women's liberation and profiled Pat Sumi, who developed anti-imperialist politics after traveling to North Korea, North Vietnam, and China on a delegation led by Black Panther leader Eldridge Cleaver.

As women talked and studied, they felt a need to provide direct services to ameliorate the social problems facing Asian American women. By the late 1960s, drug use had become a significant problem in the Japanese American community in Los Angeles, but it was ignored by middle-class parents and their ethnic organizations. Self-help drug abuse groups such as Asian Hardcore had recently formed to serve Asian American men. Asian Sisters was established in 1971 to deal with Asian American women's drug use and the gendered manifestations of drug addiction and recovery, including sexual abuse and suicide. The following year, Asian Sisters helped to found the Asian Women's Center in Los Angeles, with funding from the Department of Health, Education, and Welfare. The organization provided health, counseling, childcare, and education services. To the Asian Sisters, service delivery was intricately linked to political consciousness raising and collective structures. Their program explicitly promoted self-determination, self-defense, third world solidarity, and a democratic centralist organizational structure emphasizing collective decision-making.

The emergence of Black Power in the mid-1960s exerted a radicalizing influence on the AAM. I Wor Kuen (IWK), a socialist organization in New York, was known for its women's leadership. IWK's twelve-point platform and program, patterned after but extending beyond the Black Panther Party's, included the explicit goal of women's liberation: "We want an end to male chauvinism and sexual exploitation." IWK not only had women in top leadership positions, it also implemented collective child care, where men and women, parents and nonparents rotated as care providers, so that parents, particularly mothers, could attend meetings and assume leadership roles. Influenced by the Black Panther Party and Mao's essay, "On Practice," IWK promoted "serve the people" programs to directly address social needs. Working with the working-class and immigrant community in New York's Chinatown, IWK launched afterschool childcare programs and organized Chinese mothers to develop bilingual language programs, developed an extensive door-to-door tuberculosis testing campaign, and organized draft counseling services for Asian American youth. As members developed direct services, they also worked to develop a critique of capitalism, racism, sexism, and imperialism among their community base. In the late 1970s, when IWK merged into the League of Revolutionary Struggle, Carmen Chow and other IWK women continued to exert key leadership in the new multinational formation.

While students and youth predominated, the AAM also involved multiple generations of activists. The few older, more experienced Asian American women activists, notably Yuri Kochiyama, Grace Lee Boggs, and Kazu Iijima, were sought after as political leaders. Based on her interactions with Malcolm X and activist experience gained in the black movement in Harlem, Kochiyama was viewed as one of the most influential political mentors to the predominantly young activists in the AAM. Her commitments to Asian American, black, and Puerto Rican liberation influenced the focus on third world solidarity, internationalism, and radicalism emerging in the AAM. Like Ella Baker, Kochiyama embodied a "centerperson" leadership model, elevating networking and nurturance in struggle to leadership qualities.[7] Boggs helped shape political theory and social movement activity through her writings. After earning a PhD in the 1940s, Boggs turned away from academics to become a fulltime activist, working in the socialist, black labor, and black radical movements, particularly in Detroit. Iijima was among the small cadre of Japanese Americans who became leftists in the 1930s and helped found the Japanese American Committee for Democracy in postwar New York City. In the late 1960s, she cofounded one of the first AAM community organizations, Asian Americans for Action, and later was active with the Organization of Asian Women.

CONTEMPORARY ORGANIZING

Since 1980, major demographic changes, including a post-1965 surge of middle-class Asian immigrants and increased educational and professional opportunities for Asian American women, resulted in a growing middle-class within Asian America. Moreover, writings by and about U.S. third world women abounded in the 1980s, enabled by the gains of the Black Power, Asian American, women's, and gay rights movements. As a result, a sharp rise in the number of Asian American women's organizations emerged. Compared with the early years of the Asian American women's movement, these organizations focus on career goals and electoral politics, immigrant issues, and/or the intersection of gender and sexuality.

There has been a substantial rise in the number of organizations that support the career and leadership development of middle-class, professional Asian American women. These groups tend to be more formal in structure, with bylaws, elected officials, and steering committees, and they tend to have larger membership with national networks, compared with the smaller, local activist groups of the 1960s and 1970s. These professional women's groups include the Asian Pacific Women's Network, the National Network of Asian and Pacific Women, and Asian Women in Business. The gains of multiculturalism in the 1980s and 1990s have filtered into corporate America, with, for example, Price Waterhouse supporting a South Asian Women's Leadership Forum. While these professional organizations work to counter racial and gender barriers to career advancement—known as the glass ceiling—some activists charge that such professional organizations focus on individual enhancement at the expense of collective progress for the most marginalized.

Asian American women's political participation in voting has also increased over time. Decades of political disenfranchisement, along with linguistic barriers and normative constructions of gender that placed women outside of the political arena, diminished Asian American women's participation in electoral politics. But Asian American women's voting rates have risen and in 2004, for the first time, slightly exceeded the voting rates of Asian American men.

Two prominent Asian American women politicians are Patsy Takemoto Mink and March Fong Eu. As early as 1956, Mink was elected to the Hawai'i state legislature, and in 1965, became the first Asian American–elected to the U.S. Congress. Eu was elected to the California Assembly in 1966 and became Cal-

Democratic presidential hopeful, Senator Hillary Rodham Clinton (D-NY) is introduced by Rep. Doris Matsui (D-CA) at a gathering of the Asian American and Pacific Islanders in Washington, 2007. (AP Photo/Manuel Balce Ceneta)

ifornia's Secretary of State in 1974. While the Asian American women's movement spurred substantial grassroots activism and contributed to women's political participation in voting, it has had mixed success as a catalyst to electoral office. After Eu in 1966, it was not until 2000 that another Asian American woman was elected to California Assembly (Wilma Chan and Carol Liu in 2000 and Judy Chu in 2001). In 2001, Elaine Chao, as U.S. Secretary of Labor, became the first Asian American woman given a Cabinet-level appointment. Asian American women, like other minorities and women, have had more success at running for local offices, such as school boards and boards of supervisors. But barriers remain at higher levels. Of the eighty-eight women in the 110th Congress, only two are Asian American, Doris Matsui (D-CA) and Mazie Hirono (D-HI), and of the 1,749 women in state legislatures, only thirty are Asian American, mainly from Hawai'i.

Asian American women continue to participate in a variety of grassroots activism as labor union organizers, student-activists, community workers, and artists and cultural workers. With demographic and social movement changes, two areas—immigrant rights and queer rights—have taken on greater prominence. With the sharp rise in Asian immigration since the 1965 Immigration Act and with the increased attention on globalization, it is not surprising that Asian American women's groups focus on issues affecting immigration women. Since the mid-1980s, when Manavi was established in suburban New Jersey, the growth of South Asian women's organizations has been striking. While many groups formed to address general issues facing South Asian women immigrants, the urgency of domestic violence in South Asian communities demanded that this become a priority issue. As they organized to provide support and services to abused women, South Asian Women's Organizations (SAWOs), especially the more politically transformative groups like Manavi, Sakhi for South Asian Women, and South Asian Women for Action, developed an analysis of domestic violence that connects violence in the home with the violence of racism, patriarchy, capitalism, and state policies that keep women, especially immigrant women, subordinated and vulnerable to abuse.[8]

In the 1980s, the Asian Pacific Lesbian Bisexual Transgender (APLBT) movement developed out of the influences and the limits of race-based and gay organizing. The gay rights movement exploded on the scene after the 1969 Stonewell rebellion, but it often ignored issues of race. The AAM assumed heteronormativity and often ignored issues of sexual identity. The first Asian American lesbian organization, Asian American Feminists, formed in San Francisco in 1977 as a support group that also fostered discussions of politics and family issues. The late 1970s and 1980s became a period of path-breaking cultural work for Asian American lesbians, including the formation of Unbound Feet, the first Chinese American feminist performance group. Open lesbians comprise half of the group. By the 1980s and 1990s, there was a visible Asian American gay and lesbian community. Asian/Pacific Sisters in San Francisco countered the invisibility of Asian lesbians by creating a contingent in the city's annual Gay Pride Parade and fostered a sense of belonging and cohesion among

Asian American lesbians and bisexuals through rap sessions. The national Asian/Pacific Lesbian Network (APLN) for the first time brought together a community of Asian Americans from across the nation. When the Broadway musical sensation *Miss Saigon* hit the stage in the 1990s, it was Asian American lesbians and gay men who organized protests of the play's racial and sexual stereotypes of Asian women and racially problematic hiring practices. This issue, as well as the naming of groups like Asian American Feminists and Asian/Pacific Sisters, reveals the intersectional politics of the APLBT movement and ways the APLBT movement aligns itself with the AAM.

The Asian American women's movement, while remaining small, continues to the present. Perhaps the most significant gain of the various women's movements, including Asian American feminism, is the change in ideology. The idea of thinking about race, class, gender, and now sexuality as intersecting rather than separate issues is well established. There has been an explosion of scholarship on women of color feminism and Asian American gender and sexuality. University courses on Asian American women are now regularly, if sparingly, offered, mostly in Asian American Studies. In the 1990s, the successful campaign of the Asian Immigrant Women's Advocates in the Bay Area in support of Chinese American garment workers who sewed for Jessica McClintock helped to make a new generation of youth aware of labor struggles and capitalist exploitation. In part because of the 1960s and 1970s AAM, more nonprofit agencies and institutions now support Asian American women's organizing. Today's Asian American feminism draws on ideas generated in the 1970s and remains a contested and developing construct.

FURTHER READING

Asia Pacific Online Network of Women in Politics, Governance and Transformative Leadership. http://www.onlinewomeninpolitics.org/.

Asian Women. Berkeley: Asian American Studies, University of California Berkeley, 1971; reprinted by AASC, UCLA, 1975.

Asian Women United of California, ed. *Making Waves: An Anthology of Writings by and About Asian American Women.* Boston: Beacon Press, 1989.

Ling, Susie. "The Mountain Movers: Asian American Women's Movement in Los Angeles," *Amerasia Journal* 15 (1989): 51–67.

Shah, Sonia, ed. *Dragon Ladies: Asian American Feminists Breathe Fire.* Boston: South End Press, 1997.

NOTES

1. Judy Yung, *Unbound Feet: A Social History of Chinese Women in San Francisco* (Berkeley: University of California Press, 1995), 209–222.

2. Killer Fawn, "In the Movement Office," *Gidra*, (January 1971): 13.

3. Susie Ling, "The Mountain Movers: Asian American Women's Movement in Los Angeles," *Amerasia Journal* 15 (1989): 54.

4. In her immensely influential *The Feminist Mystique*, Betty Friedan discussed women's dissatisfaction the Cold War constructions of gender that confined them to

domesticity (New York: W. W. Norton, 1963). Whereas Friedan's analysis aligned with liberal feminism's focus on middle-class white women's housebound confinement, given that most poor women and women of color were forced by economic circumstances to do double duty, working outside and inside their homes. See also Rebecca E. Klatch, "The Formation of Feminist Consciousness among Left- and Right-Wing Activists of the 1960s," *Gender & Society*, 15 (2001): 791–815.

5. Evelyn Yoshimura, "G.I.'s and Asian Women," *Gidra* (January 1971) 4, 15.

6. *Asian Women* (Berkeley: Asian American Studies, University of California Berkeley, 1971); reprinted by AASC, UCLA, 1975, 6.

7. Diane C. Fujino, "Grassroots Leadership and Afro-Asian Solidarities: Yuri Kochiyama's Humanizing Radicalism," in *Want to Start a Revolution: Women in the Black Revolt*, eds. Jeanne Theoharis, Dayo Gore, and Komozi Woodard (New York: NYU Press, 2009).

8. Monisha Das Gupta, *Unruly Immigrants: Rights, Activism, and Transnational South Asian Politics in the United States* (Durham, NC: Duke University Press, 2006); Margaret Abraham, *Speaking the Unspeakable: Marital Violence among South Asian Immigrants in the United States* (New Brunswick, NJ: Rutgers University Press, 2000).

RESOURCE GUIDE

Suggested Reading

Aoki, Andrew, and Okiyoshi Takeda. *Asian American Politics*. Cambridge, UK: Polity Press, 2009.

Chang, Gordon, ed. *Asian Americans and Politics: Perspectives, Experiences, Prospects*. Palo Alto, CA: Stanford University Press, 2001.

Fujino, Diane C. "Who Studies the Asian American Movement?: A Historiographical Analysis," *Journal of Asian American Studies* 11 (2008): 127–169.

Junn, Jane, and Natalie Masuoka. "Asian American Identity: Shared Racial Status and Political Context." *Perspectives on Politics* 6, no. 4 (December 2008): 729–740.

Lien, Pei-te. *The Making of Asian America through Political Participation*. Philadelphia: Temple University Press, 2001.

Lien, Pei-te, M. Margaret Conway, and Janelle Wong. *The Politics of Asian Americans: Diversity and Community*. New York: Routledge, 2004.

Nakanishi, Don T., and James S. Lai, eds. *Asian American Politics: Law, Participation, and Policy*. Lanham, MD: Rowman and Littlefield, 2003.

Tam, Wendy. "Asians—A Monolithic Voting Bloc?" *Political Behavior* 17 (1995) 223–249.

Watanabe, Paul Y. "Global Forces, Foreign Policy, and Asian Pacific Americans." *PS: Political Science & Politics* 34, no. 3 (September 2001): 639–644.

Wong, Janelle. *Democracy's Promise: Immigrants and American Civic Institutions*. Ann Arbor: University of Michigan Press, 2006.

Films

Golden Venture. 2006. Peter Cohn. New Day Films. DVD, VHS. Documentary about unauthorized immigrants from China who became national symbols when their ship ran aground near New York City.

Vincent Who? 2008. Curtis Chin and Tony Lam. An updated look at the Vincent Chin case, and the important ways it shaped the Asian American community.

Who Killed Vincent Chin? 1987. Christine Choy and Renee Tajima-Pena. Filmakers Library. DVD, VHS. Documentary exploring the landmark events around the murder of Vincent Chin, a watershed for pan-Asian American political efforts.

Organizations

Asian Pacific American Institute for Congressional Studies. http://www.apaics.org/. One of the leading groups working to increase Asian Pacific American political participation.

Japanese American Citizens League (JACL). http://www.jacl.org/. The oldest Asian American civil rights organization, formed in 1929, now with an expanded focus that takes in concerns across all Asian Pacific American communities.

Leadership Education for Asian Pacifics (LEAP). http://www.leap.org/. One of the most prominent organizations providing leadership training and education for Asian Pacific Americans.

National Association of Korean Americans (NAKA). http://www.naka.org/index.asp. Contains considerable useful information on Korean Americans and issues of concern to them.

Organization of Chinese Americans (OCA). http://www.ocanational.org/. One of the major Asian American organizations working on greater political inclusion and other issues; like the JACL, the OCA has expanded its focus to encompass all Asian Pacific Americans.

Web Sites

APIAHF. http://www.apiahf.org/. A key source of information on health concerns facing Asian Americans, and public policy efforts to address those concerns.

APIAVote. http://www.apiavote.org/. This organization played a leading role connecting the major parties to Asian American communities during the 2008 election campaign, and its Web site provides a wealth of information on national political developments relevant to Asian Pacific Americans.

Asian American Justice Center (AAJC). http://www.advancingequality.org/. A leading Asian American civil rights organization which is also part of major civil rights coalitions, the AAJC maintains a Web site that gives information on these larger alliances, as well as on some of the key issues facing Asian Pacific Americans.

Congressional Asian Pacific American Caucus (CAPAC). http://honda.house.gov/capac/. Composed of members of Congress (House and Senate); an excellent source of information on national legislative proposals important to Asian Pacific Americans.

http://www.aamovement.net. Asian American Movement Ezine—progressive, radical, and revolutionary Asian American perspectives.

National Federation of Filipino American Associations. http://www.naffaa.org/main/. Umbrella organization for a long list of groups, its Web site offers extensive resources for information on Filipino Americans.

Office of Hawaiian Affairs. http://www.oha.org/. Contains a large volume of information that can serve as an excellent introduction to Native Hawaiian issues, which are unknown to most on the mainland.

Sikh American Legal Defense and Education Fund (SALDEF). http://www.saldef.org/. Evolved out of the Sikh Mediawatch and Resource Task Force (SMART); works to protect civil rights of Sikh Americans; contains great deal of information on religious freedom cases.

South Asian Americans Leading Together (SAALT). http://www.saalt.org/. Site with links to many South Asian American groups and wide range of information on South Asian Americans and their public policy concerns.

Southeast Asia Resource Action Center. http://www.searac.org/index.html. Probably the best collection of links to information and issues of importance to Cambodian, Laotian, and Vietnamese Americans.

UCLA Asian American Studies Center. http://www.aasc.ucla.edu/. The most important Asian American research center; Web site offers an overview of the Center's many activities, including how its scholarship serves community needs.

Section 10:

WAR

*Section Editors: Wei Ming Dariotis
and Wesley Uenten*

OVERVIEW OF WAR AND ITS EFFECTS: PAST AND PRESENT ISSUES UNRESOLVED

Wei Ming Dariotis and Wesley Ueunten

Because of the model minority myth, which is the stereotype that Asian Americans have few social problems and have high rates of success and achievement, and because of a general lack of historical knowledge about Asian Americans, the issue of war in context of contemporary Asian American communities is often invisible to most Americans and even to many Asian Americans. Even those who remember the wars personally may make no connection between those wars and current issues and circumstances that continue to affect Asian American communities. Yet these issues are in fact relevant, not only to those who directly experienced the wars themselves, but also for other Asian Americans—and on many levels, from the intimately personal to the broadly political. Asian Americans of all generations are affected by the ghosts of wars in Asia, the Pacific, and Europe in myriad ways that vary distinctly by community. For example, Asian American veterans of World War II, the Korean War, the Vietnam War, the first Gulf War, and the war in Iraq, especially those who were asked to fight other Asians, have had very particular experiences, including being racialized as "enemies." They and their spouses, children, extended families, and communities are still dealing with the aftereffects and continuing resonances of these wars. Other Asian Americans once were Asians living in countries at war with the United States. They and their families and communities have complex relationships with these and other wars.

Previous attempts to write about these wars have often been in the form of memoirs about the drama of wartimes themselves, and they have often focused on presenting these stories to dominant audiences rather than on offering a more balanced view. This section focuses on the continuing effects of these wars on various Asian American communities, and by doing so, suggests how these wars relate to important contemporary issues for Asian Americans. Some of the lingering effects of these wars include post-traumatic stress disorder (PTSD), legislation relating to such issues as reparations and redress, ongoing family issues related to silences, crises in Asian/Asian American male masculinity, and the violent and violating sexualization of Asian/Asian American women. All of these specific and concrete issues have their overarching logic in the construct of Orientalism, as described by postcolonial theorist Edward Said. Said criticized the construction of a romanticized image of an exotic, foreign, and feminized Asia and Middle East (collectivized as "the Orient") that has validated and continues to justify European and U.S. colonialism and imperialism in these regions.

The Philippine-American War (officially 1898–1902) set up the pattern for military colonization against the will of the local population, patterns of immigration following war and colonization, maintenance of subsequent continuous U.S. military presence, and a racialization of the Asian as enemy in ways that have constructed both the image of Asian women as the spoils of war and the image of Asians in America as being more than just the perpetual foreigners of the past—with U.S. imperialism, Asians in the United States become perpetual enemy spies, the fifth column. These patterns have been subsequently mirrored in the Pacific theater of World War II, the Korean War, the Vietnam War, and the two Gulf Wars. Contemporary historians have called the Philippine-American War the United States' first Vietnam, in reference to what has been seen as the U.S. military's slash and burn genocidal policies against a local population that often had to resort to guerrilla tactics to respond to the numerical and military superiority of the United States.

Asian Americans who are affected by these issues include Asian American veterans of the U.S. military, Asian ally veterans who are now in the U.S., civilian victims of war who have come to the U.S. as refugees, Asian Americans who have been viewed and treated as enemy aliens, and the children, grandchildren, and larger communities of the aforementioned groups. By this count, nearly every Asian American has been and continues to be directly or indirectly touched by these histories of war.

Asian Americans have now begun to consider the lingering presence of war in Asian American individual, familial, and community psyches. Until recently, too frequently Asian Americans have been silent on these issues, even within the privacy of Asian American families and communities. Asian Americans have only just begun to make public how individuals and communities of Asian Americans have resisted, demanded redress and recognition, and engaged in both legislative and community activism to support each other through the difficult process of recuperating suppressed histories and thus healing the wounds caused by the original traumas that have been exacerbated by continuing suppression. Asian American community leaders and members, as well as Asian American Studies scholars, have begun to articulate the importance of understanding how these histories of war continue to affect Asian Americans and how they are linked to contemporary issues, including post-traumatic stress disorder tied to U.S. military service; North Korean refugees; Iraq war resistance; redress and recognition for Japanese Latin Americans relocated and imprisoned during World War II; Filipino World War II *veteranos* who had their veterans benefits rescinded and are still struggling for their rights; the contemporary struggles of Southeast Asian veterans of the Vietnam War; Korean "comfort women" and issues of contemporary rape and sex slavery related to militarism; the politics of communities in diaspora; and contemporary legislative activism. The following entries also explore contemporary issues of community advocacy, the relationships of diasporic communities to their homelands, silences around histories of violence, and post-9/11 "anti-terrorism" racial profiling. All of these current concerns of Asian American communities are inextricably related to Asian American communities' histories with war.

It is also important to consider how the general population views Asian Americans in the context of war. For the most part, histories of wars are written by the victors—and the victims' stories are written only in a language of silence. But Asian American stories have also been silenced through misrepresentations in the mass media. Asians in war movies are largely limited to roles as screaming hordes of suicidal enemy combatants; weak, helpless peasants; or sexually available women. The heroes of these stories are inevitably European American men. For Asian Americans to recenter their own stories in relation to war thus requires a massive effort—not only to overcome the inclination to bury painful memories, but also to push back against inaccurate, Orientalist media portrayals.

The lens of Asian Americans and contemporary issues related to war provides a unique view through which to understand Asian American migration, history, and identity development, as reflected in the Asian American Movement slogan, "we are here because you were there." Most of Asian America would not exist if it had not been for the push-pull effect exerted by the destabilization of Asian homelands through U.S. military actions, pushing Asians out of Asia (beginning with the mid–nineteenth–century Opium Wars that destabilized southern China) and the related increased wealth the U.S. enjoys that pulls Asians to the United States. This overview also provides another way to review Asian Americans in the context of histories of war. It helps provide a broader context for Asian immigration to the United States, contemporary issues of violence and pain in Asian America, and struggles by Asian Americans for social justice.

Too often, writing about war focuses only on the details of the war itself, rather than on the continuing human effects of that war—what remembering or trying to forget that war does to human beings. By looking at the issues tied to multiple wars in connection with one another, it is possible to see beyond the specifics of any one war.

The entries in this section reflect contemporary issues for Asian Americans that are rooted in war. In these histories there are connections to 9/11 and the current war in Iraq, issues with racial profiling by Immigrations and Customs

Enforcement (ICE), questions around human rights related to immigration and war, and the need to provide justice to those who have not received recognition or redress. Ultimately, these issues are contemporary because as long as justice is not served, the wars are not over.

FORGOTTEN WARS/FORGETTING WARS

From the time of the Mexican-American War of 1846–1848, the U.S. has justified wars through an injunction to remember: Remember the Alamo! Remember the Maine! Remember Pearl Harbor! Remember 9/11! These declarations of collective memories situate the United States as a victim of attacks on U.S. soil, and they provide an impetus to war. Simultaneously, aggressive actions by the U.S. military are softly forgotten through a process of minimization: reducing the actual number of years involved and of people killed, and minimizing the significance of the war itself, until virtually the only legacy is people of that country dispersed into diaspora. Thus the war is forgotten and people learn, instead, the cuisine.

The Spanish-American war of 1898 resulted in the United States gaining many of Spain's former colonies, including the Philippine Islands and Guam. In 1898, Guam was captured by the United States during the Spanish-American war to be used, in part, for its access to the Philippines. By 1899, the Philippine-American War ensued between the United States and the Philippine revolutionaries. The United States proclaimed the war ended when Aguinaldo was captured by American troops in 1901, but the rebellion by Filipino independence fighters continued until 1913. This war is often called The Forgotten War, as even many Filipinos and Filipino Americans are unaware of this history.

In the Korean War, which lasted from 1950 to 1953, and later in the war in Vietnam, not all Asian soldiers were the enemy. South Koreans, like South Vietnamese, were U.S. allies. Like the U.S.-Philippine War, the Korean War is also often called, with great bitterness at the lack of recognition for the many lives lost and destroyed, The Forgotten War.

VIOLENCE AGAINST WOMEN

War, with its languages of domination, penetration, and exploitation, is always sexualized, and combatants, then, are always gendered. The sexualization of Asian women as spoils of war parallels the image of Asia itself, in Orientalist terms, as a supine, feminine figure, ripe for the taking.

Korean "Comfort Women," Filipina "Comfort Women," and the Chinese women victims of the "Rape of Nanking" have survived the literal brutalities of the Japanese military and have spoken out against the denials of the Japanese government. In doing so, they opened the dialogue about the ongoing pervasive international sex trade in Asian women's bodies. This directly or indirectly state-supported sex-work/rape continues around U.S. military bases in Korea and Okinawa, where reports of gang rapes of schoolgirls are paralleled by the institutionalization of prostitution in these areas. The phrase "Subic Bay" conjures years of U.S. military occupation in the Philippines and a parasitic thriving sex industry. The Vietnam War established the internationally known sex industry in Thailand, which is now a significant component of the Thai tourist economy. For example, the small oceanside village of Pattaya in Thailand, once a rest and recreation layover for the U.S. Navy, is now a hot spot of bars and nightlife with high levels of prostitution. Older men from Europe often retire there and find a local "wives" or girlfriends, and the streets are filled with men walking with women half their age pushing baby carriages.

Representations of Asian women in popular media have followed U.S. wars in Asia, introducing the image of the geisha during the U.S. occupation of Japan and the bargirl/whore of Vietnam War movies. The ever-popular Asian peasant girl may be less refined than her "China doll" counterpart, but she similarly exists largely to be saved by the white male hero. The concomitant portrayal of Asian men as evil and simultaneously weak reinforces the nobility of the white male savior in these media images (books, movies, video games, etc.) of Asian women. A resulting fetishization of Asian women makes them preferred as sexual partners, especially for European and African American men, as demonstrated through personal ads and the thriving "mail order bride" industry that has largely moved onto the Internet. These images may also increase sexual violence against Asian American women of any class, background, and sexuality, as they are assumed to be passively waiting for sexual attention from men of the dominant culture, but they are also seen as victimizable representatives of the enemy culture.

Whether in Internet porn, Internet "mail-order bride sites," dating and personals, massage parlors, or in both the intra- and international sex trade, images of Asian women have at their root a sexualization tied to the Orientalist construction of Asia itself as "sexually" available for the macho, virile "West."

REFUGEES AND EXILES

North Korean refugees, and Vietnamese and other Southeast Asian refugees, such as the Khmer (Cambodian), Lao, Hmong, Iu-Mien, Lahu, Kmhmu, and others, face issues different from those of other Asian ethnic groups that migrated to the United States as immigrants rather than as refugees. Immigrants, in general, are able to plan their departure from their homeland. They may be able to bring family members, material wealth, and family treasures. They are also more likely to immigrate into a more stable situation, supported by family and extended ethnic enclaves. Refugees, in contrast, are often torn apart from family members in the process of departure and may bring very little in the way of resources.

Vietnamese and other Southeast Asian refugees of the late 1970s and the 1980s did not come into long-established ethnic enclaves such as those set up by Chinese, Japanese, and Filipino Americans a century before. Because of government policies of dispersal, they were not able to bring material wealth with them, and because of other factors contributing to their ongoing economic fragility, refugees from the Vietnam War have often ended up living in impoverished areas. This has led to the irony of Vietnamese war refugees who had settled in and near New Orleans becoming refugees again in the wake of Hurricane Katrina. Many of the Southeast Asian ethnic groups also struggled with coming from cultures with no written language, little formal education, and few skills other than subsistence farming and soldiering. This has lead to an uncomfortable shift in gender roles, as the women in these communities have become the breadwinners, often taking jobs in factories and as garment factory workers, while the men have struggled to adjust culturally and deal with the psychological damage of PTSD. This may be particularly difficult for Southeast Asian refugees of the Vietnam War, who went from being seen as valued allies of U.S. forces during the "Secret War" in Southeast Asia, to being forced to rely on government assistance and Christian church group sponsors. This indignity compounds other issues related to the refugee experience.

Like Vietnamese and Southeast Asian refugees, North Korean refugees often find themselves beholden to the Christian church groups that sponsor their relocation. They also face issues relating to other Korean American groups because of resentment over their years of deprivation under North Korea's regimes, their inability to go home to see friends and family, and suspicions of their loyalties.

The history of Asian America has been told largely as an immigration story, and refugees disturb this narrative. Frictions with established Asian American communities add to the difficulties faced by refugees.

PTSD AND OTHER VETERANS' RIGHTS ISSUES

After annexing the Philippines, the U.S. government embarked upon a re-education scheme to indoctrinate Filipinos according to a U.S.-centric educational system. Filipinos were U.S. "nationals" and many therefore believed they would be treated in the United States according to the values of equality and freedom that they had been taught to associate with the United States. Thus, when Filipinos were called to serve in the U.S. military against Japan during World War II, they had every expectation that the promises made to them would be honored. The Philippines, it was thought, had a special relationship with the United States, which makes the rescission of their veterans benefits by the U.S. Congress passing of the Rescission Act of 1946 even more difficult to understand. The Filipino *veteranos*—who have still not yet received their promised benefits from their service in World War II—continue to struggle daily with this betrayal. This situation has affected subsequent generations of Filipinos and Filipino Americans. First affected have been the many families that were broken when the *veteranos* came to the United States to try to claim their benefits. And many of the *veteranos* simply could not have families because they did not receive their due. Younger generations of Filipino Americans have been affected as they have learned of the *veteranos*' more than sixty-year struggle to receive fair treatment—they have learned through these stories that their elders were not respected because of their race, and therefore that they, as Filipino

Americans, are in many ways second-class citizens. This is particularly brought home by the fact that the extremely small number of *veteranos* living today have only recently won some degree of remedy for their years of discriminatory treatment as veterans who served in the U.S. military, even at a time of war when our government's treatment of its veterans is a politically sensitive issue.

Other Asian American veterans may not face the extreme injustice of the rescission of their veterans benefits, but they do face the effects of racism while in service, compounding PTSD issues.

Civilians may also experience PTSD because of bearing witness to the horrors of war, survival of torture and extreme political repression, and the terrors inherent in the process of fleeing their homelands as refugees. The effects of these psychological traumas are often aggravated because cultural reasons may discourage both veteran and civilian Asian American sufferers of PTSD from seeking psychological services.

CONFLICTS WITHIN COMMUNITIES IN DIASPORA

War often continues in immigrant and refugee communities through contentions over political differences that arise between the immigrant/refugee generations and those generations raised in the United States. The strong emotions and political ideologies of the first generation are not necessarily shared by younger generations, and this causes the community to be fractured along age and generational lines. This generation gap has been expressed, for example, in Vietnamese American communities that struggle with political perspectives that have divided this diasporic community between hyper-U.S. nationalism and centrist or even leftist perspectives. Either of the last two might be grounds for being labcled "communist." These community discords create complicated relationships with homelands that are controlled by communist governments.

REPARATIONS

Within the United States, the issue of reparations for Japanese American internment took many years to develop. Inspired by the civil rights movement, Japanese Americans began to seek reparations for the many losses they experienced—both of property and opportunity. Starting in 1980, a congressional Commission on Wartime Relocation and Internment of Civilians began to investigate the issues, eventually holding hearings that were integral in the process of Japanese Americans breaking their silence on this issue. In 1988, President Ronald Reagan signed the Civil Liberties Act. This began the process of healing for Japanese Americans.

Japanese Latin Americans, who had been seized by the U.S. government from Latin America to be used as hostages to exchange for U.S. prisoners of war, were not U.S. citizens at the time of their relocation and incarceration, so they were left out of the 1988 Civil Liberties Act. A lawsuit against the U.S. government to include the Japanese Latin Americans in the Civil Liberties Act resulted in a controversial settlement that gave only one-fourth of the redress to Japanese Latin Americans ($5,000) as was given to Japanese Americans ($20,000). The redress struggle for Japanese Latin American internees has subsequently taken two routes: legislation in Congress and international redress through the Organization of American States. Japanese Latin Americans are also working in coalition with German and Italian Americans and other Latin Americans who were interned as "enemy aliens" during World War II to get redress.

A related contemporary issue is recognition that patterns of rendition that were established by the United States entering Latin American countries during World War II and rounding up Japanese Latin Americans in the name of military necessity are currently being used in the case of Muslims and Muslim Americans being sent to Guantanamo Bay. Japanese Latin American activism lays the ground work for coalition with other social justice struggles by holding the United States accountable for not only civil rights of U.S. citizens, but also for the human rights of people beyond the borders of the United States.

LEGISLATIVE ACTIVISM

U.S. Congressman Mike Honda (D-CA) is well known as a "legislative activist" who has supported Filipino *veteranos* seeking the reinstatement of their promised benefits, Japanese Latin Americans seeking redress equity, and comfort women demanding an apology from the Japanese government. Latino Congressman Rep. Xavier Becerra (D-CA) and Senator Daniel Inouye (D-HI) introduced the Commission Hearing Bill (HR 662, S381), which will allow for congressional commission hearings on the Japanese Latin American redress issues, while the Wartime Parity and Justice Act introduced by Congressman Becerra, would, if passed, provide comprehensive redress legislation for Japanese and Japanese Latin Americans who have not received proper reparations, as well as providing the $45 million to fulfill the original educational mandate of the Civil Liberties Act of 1988.

Significantly, the legislators who support these issues are exercising the rights for which their own parents had to struggle as immigrants of color.

IRAQ/AFGHAN WAR RESISTANCE

Lt. Ehren Watada has become a leader among military personnel refusing to serve in the war in Iraq. Such Asian American war resisters are in a difficult position; they have a fragile status as Asian Americans because they will always be seen as being somewhere between being "enemy others" and "loyal citizens." Watada's criticism of U.S. military action is seen as "un-American" by many Asian Americans and non-Asian Americans, while others see it as the ultimate expression of loyalty to America.

Similar to conflicts that have split Vietnamese American communities over communism, the question of Iraq War resistance often polarizes Asian American communities. Japanese Americans may be, on the whole, more antiwar than other Asian American ethnic groups, especially where their war resistance might be informed by their awareness of wartime racial profiling. There is no monolithic Chinese or Korean or Filipino or Indian or Pakistani or Iranian or Vietnamese American perspective on the Iraq War. There are, however, extreme feelings on either side of the question; there is little complacency in Asian American communities when it comes to the War in Iraq and the military action in Afghanistan.

POST-9/11 "ARAB/MUSLIM" RACIAL PROFILING

After the events of September 11, 2001, there were immediate assumptions played out in the media that the perpetrators had been Muslims. In the days following, Americans engaged all of their media-fed assumptions and stereotypes about Muslims and Arabs, and hate crimes began to be perpetrated on South Asian Americans, especially Sikhs, as well as Muslims of various ethnic backgrounds, and Arabs, Arab Americans, non-Arab West Asians and North Africans. Even Latinos and African Americans who appeared to fit the Arab/Muslim stereotype were threatened. A particularly gendered aspect of this profiling is because of the high visibility of women and girls wearing the hijab or abaya. Even the young had epithets hurled at them on the street in the first days and even months following 9/11. "No-fly" lists, rumors of FBI internment lists, and other abrogations of civil liberties have brought back chilling memories for Japanese Americans, for whom 12-07-41 will forever be marked in the same way that 9-11-01 is now marked for West Asian and North African Americans, Muslim Americans, and South Asian Americans.

Because of the strong parallels, many Asian American—especially Japanese American—activists have come out and organized in support of Muslim Americans and other groups affected by the racial profiling of Arab and Muslim Americans. This movement offers some hope, as it brings together coalitions between people separated by different cultures, religions, and racialized experiences. For example, the annual Japanese American community Day of Remembrance celebrations and pilgrimages to internment camps now regularly involve participation of Arab and Muslim and other West Asian Americans. More significantly, Asian American activists and community leaders have stood shoulder to shoulder with those groups affected most deeply by the current wave of "anti-terrorist" racial profiling; they have promoted anti-hate crime activities and legislation; they have devoted community resources such as newspapers and well-established community events; and they have shared strategies and techniques learned form their own struggles.

OUTLOOK

Some other war-related issues with which Asian Americans are concerned that are not covered in the following entries include the development of larger coalitions around social justice issues, the "war baby" phenomenon, ongoing conflicts between U.S. military bases and local communities in East and West Asia and the Pacific, and the ways in which continued anti-terrorist legislation leads to deportation for some Asian American immigrants.

On the Bases: U.S. Military Occupation and the Future

What happens after a war? If the United States wins a war, then it establishes bases of military occupation. Some of these bases have been in operation for more than half a century and show no signs of being dismantled. The social fabric of the communities around the bases becomes weighted by the gravitational pull of objects heavy in capital and power. Profound issues endemic to these bases include prostitution, the sexualization of Asian women, rape, illegitimate pregnancy, and mixed race children left at the bottom of the social order. U.S. military bombing ranges in all of these locations, combined with chemical waste from military activities, mean that U.S. military bases cause environmental degradation—and related health crises—to local communities. High percentages of Asian Americans from these countries are directly affected by these military bases. In many ways, Asian American diasporas follow similar contours as the global U.S. military base network, further complicating the definition of "Asian American."

Philippines

For nearly a century, Clark Air Force Base and Subic Naval Station were used by the U.S. military. Decades of protests by activists for environmental justice and for rights for Filipina women subjected to sex work finally ended the long U.S. military occupation in 1991.

Korea

The South Korean government and the U.S. military have been accused of colluding in developing the sex trade around U.S. military bases in Korea. Bombing ranges have also caused public outcry, including riots by villagers affected by the use of their land for target practice.

Okinawa, Japan

Okinawan bases are used as staging and training grounds for U.S. wars in West Asia and North Africa. Okinawans have no say in how their land is being used to stage U.S. forces in Iraq and Afghanistan. The social effects of this in Okinawa and for Okinawan Americans have been all-encompassing; for example, the Okinawan diaspora in the United States is largely composed of Okinawan women married to U.S. servicemen and their mixed-heritage children.

—Wei Ming Dariotis and Wesley Ueunten

Social justice includes the environmental justice issue of cleanup around former U.S. military bases—an issue shared with many communities of color in the United States. (For example, San Francisco's former Hunter's Point Shipyard is still years away from full environmental remediation; meanwhile generations of mostly African American children are growing up among toxic levels of military-related chemicals).

Another generation of war also means another generation of mixed-race Asian Americans confronting their image of being "war babies." This image has been so strong in the past that Asian Americans of mixed heritage have been assumed to be the products of wars that were ended years before they were born. And those who are born directly as a result of war or of subsequent military occupation have to negotiate the difficult terrain of enmity—members of their Asian country of origin may see in their faces the face of the enemy. Those born in Asian countries, with fathers of other nationalities, may not have citizenship because nationality in the country of their birth was determined by paternity. In the context of the United States, those born in Asia may have come here as children or young adults, culturally Asian, but expected, again because of their phenotypes, to be more "American" than other Asian immigrants. Those whose parentage may be related to U.S. military bases in Asia also face stigmas associated with presumptions about their mother's professions and social status.

The maintenance of U.S. military bases and occupying military forces is an ongoing and often critical issue for Asian countries and for Asian American communities. Since the Spanish American war ended in 1898, the U.S. has maintained a military base in Cuba: Guantanamo Bay. Since World War II ended in 1945, the U.S. has continued to keep military bases throughout Japan and Okinawa, and the Visiting Forces Agreement continues to allow U.S. military to dock in the Philippines. Since the Korean War, which ended in 1953, the United States has continued to maintain military bases in South Korea. Will these bases continue to be maintained? What new bases might be opened and maintained indefinitely in Iraq and Afghanistan? Asian Americans, particularly those with ancestry from these Asian countries, will continue to question the validity of this U.S. military presence, particularly when conflicts erupt with local communities.

Ironically, this presence of the United States within the territories of other nations is not comfortably balanced by the presence of Asian nationals within the body of the United States. Some Asian immigrants to the United States either chose to not attain citizenship, or they do not have the means to do so; thus, when 9/11 was followed by anti-terrorist legislation that clamped down on immigrants with criminal records, some Asian immigrants have been placed in a position of being deported to countries from which they may have left as children and which they may barely remember.

Asian America, or rather, many diverse Asian Americas, will continue to develop multiple axes through which to understand war-related issues in Asian American communities. Just as some issues have taken years to surface and have yet to be resolved even decades later, new issues will arise as new wars begin. One thing that may hold Asian Americans together in future responses to war-related issues is a refusal to remain silent for generations, as has happened in the past. Asian Americans will not forget lessons of wartime experiences; they will work to heal these open wounds. Now that war issues are collectively remembered, Asian Americans will continue *re-membering*, as in putting themselves and their communities back together, and as in claiming membership within the larger political and social community of the United States. Part of the process of Asian American re-membering is understanding that the term "Asian American" partially emerged from the anti-war movement; it was constructed in 1968 as a rejection of the term "Oriental," and as a way to recognize both Asia and America as influences in the construction of complex identities and communities.

COMFORT WOMEN

Annie Fukushima

The "Comfort Women" have multiple names: *Jūgunianfu* translates to "comfort women" in Japanese, and, in Korean, *Chŏngshindae* translates to "Women's Volunteer Labor Corps," conveying the different understandings the women had when they went abroad to "work" for the Japanese military. In the Philippines they are referred to as Lolas, signifying their respected status (the term means "grandmother"). By the 1940s, in a piece of Japanese correspondence, the women were referred to as "Special Service Personnel Group," suggesting that the women and girls were recruited in a highly systematic manner.[1]

Despite these various names, "Comfort Women" is the term most commonly used in international discussions because of the diversity of Asians that were "recruited." It is estimated that 80,000 to 200,000 women and girls were recruited as "Comfort Women."[2] Women and girls recruited as comfort women were told that they would work in factories or hospitals; they were told that they would do manufacturing or service jobs. However, they found themselves instead trapped in a system of normalized sexual violence, or, rather, institutionalized rape. Comfort women were recruited from Japanese-occupied territories, including China, Okinawa, East Timor, and Guam, to serve as comfort women or prostitutes/sex slaves at Japanese military "comfort stations."

The comfort women movement exposes the "dirty" secret of war, especially in the Asia-Pacific region: the use of rape as a weapon.[3] It also articulates the need for redress and reconciliation. While no nation's hands are clean from human rights violations, the unveiling of the role of rape as torture committed as part of systemic militarized operations has been highly documented by the comfort women movement that, for some scholars and activists, is also considered the most organized movement to raise awareness on military rape and torture.[4] Such mass mobilization in the United States is because of the numerous Asian Americans who identify with the issues directly affecting comfort women: the hypersexualization of Asian women and men; histories of colonialisms; U.S. expansion being linked to other histories of violence, racism, and sexism; and the need for redress during and after wartime crimes. The issue of the comfort women is a reminder of how wars affect civilian lives, particularly those of women and children. The comfort women movement illuminates how women and children experience war during times of a "hot war," as well as during militarized peace. The movement also documents the long-term effects of sexual violence against women. The development of the comfort women movement has occurred largely through the work of survivors who testified to their experience. This showcases the need to center testimonies in Asian American history. Testimonials by surviving comfort women have shifted the paradigm of what counts as truth in Asian American history because the movement is defined by the voices of the comfort women, who suggest that there is a need to tell stories from the "ground up" and to hear the words of those who directly experience struggle. Testimonies convey that there are no words that can easily describe what the women went through.[5] Such testimonies have proved valuable to the work of historians. Testimonies also proved critical for conveying to the Asian American movement what the comfort women experienced.

In January 1992, Japanese historian Yoshiaki Yoshimi found direct evidence of Japan's military's role in managing the "comfort stations" or brothels in spite of Japan's continued silence concerning wartime atrocities.[6] Yoshimi's work made its way through Asian American networks and fueled the ongoing global movement seeking redress for comfort women. While there remains a struggle to confront Japan's denial continuing well into the twenty-first century, the comfort women movement is one of the most visible global initiatives to break the silence surrounding wartime atrocities and sexual violence.

The reasons Asian Americans have joined this international movement are diverse. Many Asian Americans themselves are not comfort women survivors nor are they directly related to survivors, but the comfort women movement has been popularized in the United States partly because of the Japanese American redress movement, which provides a model for the seeking of redress on behalf of the remaining comfort women. The passage of the Civil Liberties Act of 1988, an apology, and economic retribution for the more than 120,000 internees have led many Asian Americans to understand the need for acts of reconciliation for wartime crimes.[7] While the U.S. Congress pushes for policies that address wartime crimes by the Japanese government and military during and before World War II, ongoing Asian

American activism through the arts, writing, scholarship, films, student organizations, and policies suggest that there is still a need for further gestures of reconciliation.

HISTORICAL CONTEXT

Innumerable news reports, personal accounts, photographs, films and physical remains have helped shape twenty-first century Asian American and global popular conceptions of the comfort women.[8] The comfort women experience is the militarized prostitution of thousands of women and girls from military-occupied zones by the Japanese government. Early recruiting by the Japanese began during the Russo and Sino Japanese Wars (1894–1895 and 1904–1905), but the comfort woman system would not become a full-scale operation until the Nanjing Massacre of December 1937. In Shanxi, China, testimonies indicate that women and girls were both randomly raped as well as systematically prostituted in Japanese comfort stations or brothels.[9] Women were recruited to prevent the Japanese soldiers from gang-raping women in the occupied territories in Manchuria. Thus, it was ostensibly in an attempt to "control" rape that the Japanese government set up "comfort stations."

Comfort women became known as a Korean issue because Korean Americans have heavily mobilized in the United States because of the sheer number of Korean women who were used as comfort women. It is estimated that Korean women and girls comprised 80 percent to 90 percent of those recruited primarily from Kyongsang and Cholla Provinces, although not exclusively these regions, to be comfort women. Stereotypes of Korean values surrounding chastity and Confucianism led the Japanese government to believe that Korean women were ideal prostitutes for the Japanese military. The Japanese government hesitated using Japanese prostitutes for military use in large numbers because of fear of spreading venereal diseases. Japanese and Korean women were not the only ethnic groups affected. Starting in 1938, Taiwanese women and girls were recruited, and soon after the outbreak of war in the Asia Pacific (1941) with Japan's invasion of the Philippines, Singapore, and Indonesia, Filipina Lolas, Dutch, and Indonesian women and girls would find themselves in systemic militarized prostitution as comfort women.[10] By 1941, Japanese government legislation was enacted requiring that the age of the women and girls recruited be between the ages of 14 years to 45 years old, also conveying that virgins were preferred.[11]

The experiences for comfort women were diverse; they varied from complete isolation to less isolation, but violence was normalized for all. Many of the women and children died as comfort women, servicing countless numbers of men; on average, they were expected to serve for two years.[12] It is estimated that 25–35 percent of the comfort women survived.[13] For those who survived, they live with the physical markers of scars and disfigurement from rape and other forms of physical torture, venereal disease including gonorrhea and syphilis, the inability to give birth, as well as post-traumatic stress disorder and other mental disorders from rape and head traumas that they accrued as military comfort women.

RESPONSES OF ASIAN AMERICANS

During the 1980s and 1990s the comfort women movement progressed with only a few hundred survivors coming forward.[14] It is a credit to Korean mobilizations that began in Korea that the comfort women movement became global. In 1990, the Korean Council supported surviving comfort women. With the support of the council, two important events would take place: a public testimonial by Kim Hak-sun on August 1991 that was soon followed by the first class-action suit against Japan by a Korean comfort woman survivor in December 1991.[15] These events suggest that at the core of the beginnings of the comfort women movement was an impetus for redress and visibility. In 1992, surviving comfort women in Korea organized by protesting every Wednesday in front of the Japanese Embassy, requesting that the Japanese government formally apologize. And in 1993, eighteen Filipina former comfort women filed lawsuits against Japan.

The public protests, testimonials by survivors, and lawsuits made visible to the United States and to the world Japan's war atrocities of sexual violence in spite of their abbreviated treatment in Japanese textbooks. This increasing visibility also led to other survivors coming forward with governmental and organizational support and the development of organizations to address these issues, including: Taipei Women's Rescue Foundation (Taiwan, 1992); Asia Center for Human Rights (Philippines, 1990s); the Task Force on Filipino Comfort Women (Philippines, 1992); the Washington Coalition for Comfort Women Issues (USA, 1992); the establishment of a home for survivors in Korea, called The House of Sharing (1992); Lila-Pilipina (Philippines, 1994); the Foundation for Japanese Honorary Debts (Netherlands, 1994); the Violence Against Women in War Network (Japan, 1998); the Shanghai Comfort Women Research Centre (China, 1999); and Forum Komunikasi Untuk Perempuan Timor Lorosa'e, or the East Timor Women's Communication Forum (East Timor, 2000).[16]

The international organizing would lead to the creation of the Asian Women's Fund (1995) in Tokyo by a private group with heavy government support, which was to make cash payments to surviving wartime sex slaves. The fund only compensated 285 women (from the Philippines, South Korea, and Taiwan), who each received 2 million yen, at the time about $17,800. A handful of Dutch and Indonesian women were also given assistance.[17] Many victims rejected aid from the Asian Women's Fund because it had not come directly from the government nor was it accompanied by an official apology. As the debates surrounding redress boiled in Asia, it was clear that by 1996, the movement was no longer confined to the Asia-Pacific region.

In 1996, the comfort women movement became visible in the United States through an international conference titled, "The 'Comfort Women' of World War II: Legacy and Lessons," which was held at Georgetown University from September 30 to October 2, 1996.[18] Not only would this conference bring together students, scholars, and survivors' testimonies, but it would also inspire creative writers, such as mixed heritage Asian American author Nora Okja Keller, to write about the comfort woman experience in fictionalized form in her novel, *Comfort Woman*. Comfort women's struggles for redress and reparations have captured widespread sympathies that have inspired a range of creative, scholarly, and activist works by Asian/Americans in the United States. These have ranged from hosting testimonies by surviving women, art exhibits such as the "Quest for Justice: The Story of 'Comfort Women' as Told through Their Art," community forums, academic conferences, and Web sites. Asian Americans are creatively writing about the comfort women, making art, and portraying this complex history through film and other visual media.[19] In 2001, in response to the lack of representation of the comfort women in Japan's high school textbooks, Gabriela Network (a Filipina/o network against sex-trafficking of Filipinas), Okinawa Peace Network of Los Angeles, and Young Koreans United of Los Angeles held a joint press conference and rally.[20] Producers of the internationally acclaimed play *The Vagina Monologues* have also joined the international comfort women movement with the launch of the Global V-Day Campaign for Justice to comfort women (February 28, 2005). While these popular mediums have proved important for spreading awareness, it would not be until 2007 that the comfort women issue received attention from Asian Americans through legislative activism.

MOBILIZING THROUGH POLICY

Former comfort women are increasingly seeking political support from the international community as their lawsuits against the Japanese government continue to fail. In the United States, the 121 Coalition worked to mobilize the Asian American community and the larger U.S. community through policy. On January 31, 2007, Michael Honda introduced House Resolution 121 that was shepherded by House Foreign Affairs Committee Chairman Tom Lantos. Titled, "Relative to the War Crimes Committed by the Japanese Military during World War II," the resolution urges the government of Japan to bring closure to the issue by formally issuing a clear and unambiguous apology for the atrocious war crimes committed by the Japanese military during World War II and immediately paying reparations to the victims of those crimes. Michael Honda's role in the HR 121 initiative illuminates the complexity in Asian American solidarities: Honda, a third-generation Japanese American who experienced Japanese internment for fourteen months in a Colorado camp, when asked in a 2007 interview about spearheading HR 121, invoked the idea of a multicultural coalition in his response.[21] Honda's identification as a Japanese American and the survivors being women and children from the Asia-Pacific region and Europe illustrates the need for solidarity within the Asian American community when calling for a redress for violence that affects Asian Americans. This would be most apparent in the mobilization of a coalition to support the passage of HR 121, the HR 121 Coalition.

Bringing Public Recognition to War and Asian Americans: Mike Honda

Born in California, Mike Honda spent his early childhood during World War II in the Granada internment camp in Colorado. His family returned to California, working as strawberry sharecroppers in San Jose. After two years of serving in the Peace Corps in El Salvador, Honda embarked on a career in education. In 1981, he joined the San José Unified School Board, and in 1990, he was elected to the Santa Clara County Board of Supervisors. He served on the California State Assembly from 1996 to 2000. Since 2001, Honda has represented the 15th Congressional District of California in the U.S. House of Representatives. As the chair of the Congressional Asian Pacific American Caucus, Honda coordinates with Congressional Black Caucus and the Congressional Hispanic Caucuses to fight for social justice, racial tolerance, and civil rights—all of which connect Asian Americans and war. In 2005, Honda was elected vice chair of the Democratic National Committee, and, in 2007, he was appointed House Democratic senior whip. Congressman Honda has been a legislative leader in the following specific issues related to Asian Americans and war:

On July 30, 2008, Honda's five-year struggle to recognize significant service by hundreds of soldiers of Asian and Pacific Islander heritage during the Civil War met success as the House passed a resolution honoring them.

Under Honda's guidance, the Appropriations Committee recently garnered a one-time payment of $198 million for Filipino veterans.

In 2007, Honda proposed House Resolution 121, requesting that the Japanese government formally acknowledge, apologize, and accept historical responsibility for the comfort women, and educate current and future generations.

Honda has supported community efforts to educate the public about government violations experienced by immigrants of Italian, German, and Japanese ancestry in the United States who were abducted from Latin America during World War II.

Honda has spoken and acted publicly to condemn the scapegoating of Muslim Americans in the aftermath of the September 11 attacks.

—Wei Ming Dariotis and
Wesley Ueunten

Asian Americans have participated in linking comfort women to the United States through the national campaign of Asian Americans titled 121 Coalition. It is creating mass visibility and participation by Asian Americans, despite beginning with just a small listserv of friends.[22] House Resolution 121 is a national U.S. campaign led by filmmaker and national coordinator for House Resolution 121, Annabel Park. In support of the coalition, Asian American film director and screenwriter Eric Byler created YouTube videos to help mobilize the international movement via the Internet. As the organizers made progress through community educational forums and campus visits across the United States, the movement took a quick turn on March 2007.

On March 1, 2007, Japanese Prime Minister Shinzo Abe stated that there was "no evidence" of the prostitution of thousands of women in Japanese military camptowns. Abe said there would be nothing to apologize for, even if the U.S. House passed the resolution. Abe's statement was accompanied by the placement of an ad in the *Washington Post* by forty-five Japanese lawmakers and a number of intellectuals saying the resolution distorted the truth, making clear the need for international support. This ad reportedly worsened American sentiment toward Japan's handling of the issue because two weeks earlier Asian and European women had offered vivid testimony before a House hearing on comfort Women. Major news outlets, including the *New York Times,* criticized Abe's comments, which in turn solidified international support for the comfort women. The nonbinding resolution was soon approved 39 to 2 by the House of Representatives' International Relations Committee and passed the full House on July 30, 2007. The passage of U.S. House Resolution 121 in December 2007 would lead to similar adoptions in the European Parliament, Canada, and the Netherlands. While redress has been important to the comfort women movement, what exactly the resolution will look like in practice continues to be in question.[23]

During March 2008, HR 121 Coalition coordinator Park and mixed heritage Asian American filmmaker Eric Byler visited Japanese activists advocating for the rights of comfort women. Park recalls in the piece "Justice for 'Comfort Women,' Our Trip to Asia, and Pulling the Rope" (published in *Asian Week: The Voice of Asian America*) that during the March 2008 conversations with Japanese advocates she thought of the image of a tug-of-war. Tugging on one side were those who struggled for reconciliation for comfort women; on the other side were those who wished to forget. For Park, it was imperative for her to join the tug-of-war for justice, peace, human rights, and dignity. In this struggle she was joined by survivors of many nationalities, activists from all around the world, scholars, teachers, and students, members of the U.S. Congress, Japanese Diet members, Japanese citizens, Dutch women, feminists, and ordinary people who belonged to none of these categories.[24] The coalition that Park heads is reflective of the larger movement in the United States; the comfort women issue has transitioned from being "just" an older-generation Korean issue to one that is multigenerational and pan-Asian in the United States and globally.[25] Redress and a formal apology by the Japanese government for the militarized prostitution of thousands of women and children during World War II became urgent at the turn of the twenty-first century, as many of the surviving comfort women are now in their seventies and eighties and in failing health. Also other similar abuses of women by military occupiers are coming to light.[26]

In part, the comfort women movement for Asian Americans during the twenty-first century has been fueled by the long history of the movement to end violence against Asian American women that took on force during the 1980s. The first Asian women's shelter to open in San Francisco in 1992 was inspired by the organizing of Becki Masaki and other Asian American activists during the 1980s to respond to the silences surrounding violence against women in the domestic sphere. Since the United States passed the Violence Against Women Act in 1992, the anti-violence against women movement has broadened understandings of violence against Asian Americans in the United States to conceptualizations that draw upon how Asians experience violence and trauma in their countries of origin. Such a shift has also impacted twenty-first-century mobilization surrounding the comfort women experience.

LINKING THE "PAST" TO THE PRESENT

Sixty-plus years after the violence was committed, the comfort women have yet to hear an official apology from the Japanese government. Some survivors believe that the Japanese government assumes that when all of the survivors die, the past will be forgotten.[27] But, because the comfort women will soon die, does this mean that so will their stories? The project of the comfort women movement in the twenty-first century will continue through the efforts of student organizations such as Babae in California, public displays such as the Asian American Women's Coalition exhibit "Comfort Women—Now and Then—From Exploration to Empowerment" (2008), public education forums, and other modes for the passing on of stories. But such mobilizations are not just about memorializing the situation. U.S. social services such as the Polaris Project, which is a federally funded comprehensive social service for trafficked people, have found that comfort woman history is also a part of the present. For example, the U.S. military presence in Korea has led to high levels of prostitution, sexual violence, and rape around U.S. military bases.[28] While Asian Americans have mobilized to call for reconciliation for the comfort women and to remember it through continued initiatives to raise awareness, they have also moved toward making other connections to enable an understanding of how the comfort women history connects to the present-day understanding of "Modern Day Slavery," or the trafficking of people into prostitution. It is most evident in cases such as the 2005 "Operation Gilded Cage," when the Federal Bureau of Investigation found more than one hundred Korean women trafficked into San Francisco brothels living in slave-like conditions. Groups such as the Asian

Women's Shelter and the *SAGE Project* (Standing Against Global Exploitation) work to ameliorate such situations.[29] This and similar cases have illustrated the need for coalitions not only within the Asian American community but also internationally.[30] What the comfort women movement means for Asian Americans in the twenty-first century is re-memory, recovery, and making deeper connections that continue to sustain coalitions that are not only local, but are also global in scope.

FURTHER READING

Babae. http://babaesf.blogspot.com/.

Comfort Women: A Cry for Justice. Directed by Celso Ad. Castillo. Philippines: Alyssa Films, 1989.

Comfort Women: A Web Reference. http://online.sfsu.edu/~soh/cw-links.htm.

Henson, Maria Rosa. *Comfort Woman: A Filipina's Story of Prostitution and Slavery under the Japanese Military.* Lanham, MD: Rowman and Littlefield, 1999.

Hicks, George. *The Comfort Women: Japan's Brutal Regime of Enforced Prostitution in the Second World War.* New York: W. W. Norton & Company, 1994.

The House of Sharing. Directed by Hein Sook. Korea: 2007.

The House of Sharing Web site. http://www.nanum.org/eng/.

Keith, Howard. *True Stories of the Korean Comfort Women: Testimonies.* New York: Continuum International Publishing Group, 1995.

Kim-Gibson, Dai Sil. *Silence Broken: Korean Comfort Women.* Iowa: Mid-Prairie Books, 1999.

San Francisco State University Web Reference. http://online.sfsu.edu/~soh/cw-links.htm.

Silence Broken: Korean Comfort Women. Directed by Dai-Sil Kim Gibson. USA: NAATA, 2000.

Stetz, Margaret, and Bonnie B. C. Oh. *Legacies of the Comfort Women of World War II.* Armonk, NY: M. E. Sharpe, 2001.

Taipei Women's Rescue Foundation. http://www.wiserearth.org/organization/view/c50bf390aa44e7485824be5f3f454fbc.

Tanaka, Yuki. *Japan's Comfort Women: Sexual Slavery and Prostitution during World War II and the U.S. Occupation.* London and New York: Routledge, 2002.

Violence Against Women in War Net-Japan. http://www1.jca.apc.org/vaww-net-japan/english/.

Washington Coalition for Comfort Women Issues. http://www.comfort-women.org/history.html.

NOTES

1. Ustinia Dolgopol, "Women's Voices, Women's Pain," *Human Rights Quarterly* 17, no. 1 (1995): 133.

2. Alice Yun Chai, "Asian-Pacific Feminist Coalitions Politics: The Chonghindae/Jugunianfu ("Comfort Women") Movement," *Korean Studies* 17 (1993): 70.

3. Anne Llewellyn Barstow, ed., *War's Dirty Little Secret: Rape, Prostitution, and Other Crimes Against Women.* Edited by The Asian Center for Women's Human Rights (ASCENT) (Cleveland, OH: Pilgrim Press, 2000).

4. Congresswoman Diane E. Watson, "Congresswoman Watson Cosponsors 'Comfort Women' Legislation—Delivers Remarks." Feb. 15, 2007, press release, http://www.house.gov/list/press/ca33_watson/070215.html; Rochelle Jones, "Gender and Reparations: An Interview with Ruth Rubio-Marin," *AWID—Association for Women's Rights in Development*, Aug. 17, 2007, http://www.awid.org/eng/Issues-and -Analysis/Library/Gender-and-reparations-An-interview-with-Ruth-Rubio-Marin -Editor-of/(language)/eng-GB.

5. Dai Sil Kim-Gibson, *Silence Broken: Korean Comfort Women* (Parkersburg, IA: Mid-Prairie Books, 1999); George Hicks, *The Comfort Women: Japan's Brutal Regime of Enforced Prostitution in the Second World War* (New York: W. W. Norton & Company, 1994); Howard Keith, *True Stories of the Korean Comfort Women: Testimonies* (New York: Continuum International Publishing Group, 1995).

6. Norimitsu Onishi, "Historian Documents Japan's Role in Sex Slavery," International Herald Tribune Asia-Pacific, March 30, 2007, http://www.iht.com/articles/2007/ 03/30/asia/japan.php.

7. Alice Yang Murray, "Military Necessity, World War II Internment, and Japanese American History," *Reviews in American History* 25, no. 2 (1997): 319.

8. Jordan Sand, "Historians and Public Memory in Japan: The 'Comfort Women' Controversy: Introduction," *History & Memory* 11, no. 2 (1999): 123.

9. Kandice Huh, "Discomforting Knowledge: Or, Korean 'Comfort Women' and Asian Americanist Critical Practice," *Journal of Asian American Studies* 6, no. 1 (2003): 33.

10. Dolgopol, "Women's Voices, Women's Pain," 127.

11. Dolgopol, "Women's Voices, Women's Pain," 129.

12. Dolgopol, "Women's Voices, Women's Pain," 137.

13. Civil Action 00-02233 (HHK). Oct. 4, 2001. U.S. District Court for the District of Columbia. Hwang Geum Joo et al., versus Japan. Decision: Ordered and Adjudged, Complaint Dismissed.

14. Kandice Huh, "Discomforting Knowledge," 5; Dolgopol, "Women's Voices, Women's Pain," 138.

15. Sarah Soh, "Japan's Responsibility Toward Comfort Women Survivors," *Japanese Policy Research Institute* JPRI Working Paper No. 77 (2001): http://www.jpri.org/ publications/workingpapers/wp77.html.

16. A tribunal was originally proposed by VAWW-NET Japan at the Asian Women's Solidarity Conference in Seoul. Kim Puja, "Global Civil Society Remakes History: "The Women's International War Crimes Tribunal 2000," *positions: east asia cultures critique* 9, no. 3 (2001): 611–620.

17. CNN, "Documents: U.S. Troops Used 'Comfort Women' after WWII." Posted April 25, 2007, http://www.cnn.com/2007/US/04/25/comfort.women.ap/index. html.

18. Margaret Stetz and Bonnie B. C. Oh, *Legacies of the Comfort Women of World War II* (Armonk, NY: M. E. Sharpe, 2001).

19. See, for example, Duk-Kyung Kang et al., "Quest for Justice: The Story of Korean 'Comfort Women,' As Told Through Their Art," September–December 2000, http://www.museology.org/final.swf; Koon Ja Kim, Former Comfort Woman, House of Sharing and NAKASEC. Feb. 15, 2007. Testimonial. U.S. House Committee on Foreign Affairs, Subcommittee on Asia, the Pacific and the Global Environment; Duk-Kyung Kang et al., "Quest for Justice"; "The 'Comfort Women' of World War II: Legacy and Lessons," Sept. 30 to Oct. 2, 1996. Georgetown University. See note 21; Jerry D. Boucher

and Chunghee Sarah Soh. June 13, 2002. "Comfort Women: A Web Reference," http://online.sfsu.edu/~soh/cw-links.htm. Also, Washington Coalition for Comfort Women Issues, 2008, http://www.comfort-women.org; Chang-rae Lee, *A Gesture Life* (New York: Riverhead, 1999); Therese Park, *A Gift of the Emperor* (Duluth, MN: Spinsters Ink, 1997); Nora Okja Keller, *Comfort Woman* (New York: Viking Penguin, 1997); Ishle Park, "House of Sharing Comfort Women," *Manoa* 13, no. 2 (2001): 51–53; Bino A. Realuyo, "Pantoum: The Comfort Woman," *In Spite of Open Eyes,* was selected for the Poetry Society of America's Lucille Medwick Memorial Award in 1998; Miran Kim's paintings, the sculpture and installation works by Yong Soon Min and Mona Higuchi, the photo-based work of Sasha Y. Lee, the issue of "Comfort Women; Celso Ad. Castillo's Comfort Women: A Cry for Justice (1989), Soo Jin Kim "Comfort Me" (1993), Dai-Sil Kim Gibson's documentary film *Silence Broken: Korean Comfort Women* (2000), Hein Sook's documentary film *The House of Sharing* (2007), and *63 Years On* (2008).

20. Young Koreans United of Los Angeles, "Los Angeles Organizations Protest Legacy of Japanese Militarism," Press Release. Contact: Haena Cho, April 17, 2001: http://www.uchinanchu.org/about/comfort_women_press_release.htm.

21. During an interview, Congressman Honda, when asked how he could support a resolution when he has a "Japanese face," responded, "I told her I could have a black face, a brown face, a white face—I could be Mexican, I could be Indian—it doesn't matter." Norimitsu Onishi, "A Congressman Faces Foes in Japan As He Seeks an Apology," *New York Times,* May 12, 2007, http://www.nytimes.com/2007/05/12/world/asia/12honda.html?pagewanted=print.

22. "USA-California: Breaking the Silence: Truth and Reconciliation for Comfort Women," conference, April 8, 2008, University of California Berkeley, guest speakers Annabel Park and Eric Byler.

23. "A Woman's Plight: Comfort Women of WWII." *Manila Town Heritage,* March 28, 2008, I-Hotel Manila Town Center, speakers Marissa Mariano and Elaine Villasper of Babae, Evelina Galang and Annie Fukushima.

24. Annabel Park, "Justice for 'Comfort Women,' Our Trip to Asia, and Pulling the Rope," *AsianWeek: Through Our Lens. Eric Byler & Annabel Park*, March 18, 2008: http://throughourlens.asianweek.com/?p=4.

25. Jean Han, "Sex Slaves Resolution Expected to Reach Floor Vote in Congress," *AsianWeek*, June 22, 2007: http://www.asianweek.com/2007/06/22/sex-slaves-resolution-expected-to-reach-floor-vote-in-congress/.

26. The Korea Society, "The Long March for Justice: Comfort Women v. Japan," 1957–2007: The Korea Society 50th Anniversary. http://www.koreasociety.org/contemporary_issues/contemporary_issues/the_long_march_for_justice_comfort_women_v._japan.html Heisoo Shin, vice-chair person, Committee on the Elimination of Discrimination Against Women, Office of the High Commissioner of Human Rights, the United Nations is quoted.

27. Amnesty International, "'Comfort Women': Waiting for Justice After 62 Years," July 5, 2008, Appeals for Action, http://www.amnesty.org/en/appeals-for-action/comfort-women-waiting-justice.

28. Katherine Chon and Derek Ellerman, "Modern-Day Comfort Women: The U.S. Military, Transnational Crime, and the Trafficking of Women," *Violence against Women* (forthcoming), http://www.uri.edu/artsci/wms/hughes/pubtrfrep.htm.

29. Jaxon Ban Derbeken and Ryan Kim, "Alleged Sex-Trade Ring Broken Up in the Bay Area: Police Say Koreans in Massage Parlors were Smuggled in," *San Francisco*

Chronicle, July 2, 2005, http://www.sfgate.com/cgi-bin/article.cgi?file=/c/a/2005/07/02/MNGDLDIDVD1.DTL.

30. Ellen-Rae Cachola, Lizelle Festejo, Annie Fukushima, Gwyn Kirk, and Sabina Perez, "Gender and U.S. Bases in Asia-Pacific," March 14, 2008 (Washington, DC: Foreign Policy in Focus).

CONTINUING IMPACT OF GENOCIDE ON CAMBODIAN AMERICANS

Cathy J. Schlund-Vials

Cambodian American activism in the twenty-first century reflects a larger Asian American movement focused on antiracism, cultural reclamation, and community formation. The first documented Cambodian American demonstration occurred in 1986 in Chicago, where more than 200 Cambodian and Lao Americans gathered to protest evictions resulting from a planned building sale.[1] The following year, in Lowell, MA, Cambodian Americans worked with Latinos to push for bilingual education in public schools. Nineteen eight-seven also witnessed a Cambodian American protest against racially motivated arson in Revere, MA.[2] Following the September 11 attacks, the planned deportation of more than one thousand Cambodian Americans fomented a series of community protests. In November 2002, Cambodian American community members, leaders, parents, and students publicly protested the deportations in Long Beach, CA, and Lowell, MA. Alongside these antiracist and communally focused efforts, Cambodian Americans have organized efforts to build temples within communities and fund efforts to retain Khmer culture in the country of settlement through sponsorships of traditional art forms. In March 2008, an international conference was held at California State University in Long Beach to facilitate through panel discussions and presentations the gathering of refugee testimony for the current United Nations/Cambodian War Crimes Tribunal. The effort to collect testimony from Cambodian Americans in the United States is manifest in oral history projects like the one launched by Mardine Mao, the current president of the Cambodian American Community of

Oregon, in the summer of 2008, in which second-generation Cambodian Americans record the experiences of first-generation Cambodian survivors of the Cambodia Civil War and Khmer Rouge "killing fields."[3]

What connects these Cambodian American activist moments and movements is a sustained, albeit at times implicit, cultural, political, and social engagement with an unreconciled genocidal past that collides with dominant U.S. racial hierarchies. It is this past that makes Cambodian American activism transnational in scope, for the events in the country of origin continue to have an impact on experiences and movements in the country of settlement. Specifically, contemporary Cambodian American identity is shaped by the three-year, eight-month, twenty-day period of Democratic Kampuchea, during which an estimated 1.7 million Cambodians (roughly 21% of the extant population) died as a result of execution, starvation, disease, and forced labor.[4] Between 1975 and 1979, the communist Khmer Rouge–run Democratic Kampuchean government enforced a series of totalitarian policies meant to eliminate Western and prerevolutionary influence from all facets of Cambodian life. Labeled by Cambodian journalist and activist Dith Pran as the time of "the Killing Fields," the reign of the Khmer Rouge ended with the 1979 Vietnamese invasion. To date, no Khmer Rouge official has been successfully tried for war crimes and crimes against humanity, although five former leaders of the regime are currently in custody and slated to stand trial as part of the UN/Cambodian War Crimes Tribunal.[5] The leader of the regime, Saloth Sar (Pol Pot), died under house arrest in 1998 without ever standing trial in an international court. Similarly, Ta Mok, the person in charge of Khmer Rouge military forces, passed away in 2006.

The brutal policies of Democratic Kampuchea and the subsequent occupation of the nation by the Vietnamese caused the migration of Cambodian refugees to the United States, and memories of genocide and the absence of international forms of justice continue to have an impact on experiences in the country of asylum. From 1975 to 1992, an estimated 145,000 Cambodian refugees came to the United States; the majority of these refugees arrived after the passage of the 1980 Refugee Act, which further expanded U.S. immigration law to accommodate individuals seeking asylum for humanitarian reasons.[6] Hence, genocidal experiences immediately circumscribed the formation of Cambodian American identity in the United States. Furthermore, relocation to the United States has not been a seamless process for the majority of Cambodians and Cambodian Americans. According to the 2000 U.S. Census, the average per capita income for Cambodian Americans was $10,215 in 1999, and 29.3 percent lived below the poverty line. Twenty-two percent of Cambodian American households relied on public assistance income, and only 6 percent of Cambodian Americans graduated with a college degree.[7] Crime among Cambodian Americans is higher than among most other Asian American groups, as is the 7.3 percent rate of incarceration for native-born Laotian and Cambodian American males.[8]

Such statistics highlight the extent to which Cambodian Americans and other Southeast Asian Americans fall outside the rubric of the "model minority stereotype," which is partially grounded in the dominant, monolithic assumption that all Asian Americans have achieved a high degree of socioeconomic success. Cambodian refugee survivors also suffer from higher rates of post-traumatic stress disorder than any other Asian American group. Within Democratic Kampuchea, silence was fundamental to survival, and as a consequence, many first-generation Cambodians and Cambodian Americans are often unwilling to talk about the past, which partially impedes contemporary attempts to collect survivor testimonials for the current war crimes tribunal. Moreover, the task of developing and maintaining Cambodian American communities becomes even more difficult given the host of economic and psychological obstacles that face first-generation and 1.5-generation Cambodian Americans. Political activism in these communities is often necessarily focused on the implementation and facilitation of social service programs. In 2005, The National Cambodian American Health Initiative (NCAHI), a wide-ranging consortium of community-based organizations and mental health activists, noted that Cambodian American mortality rates due to diabetes, heart disease, post-traumatic stress disorder, and depression were higher than any other ethnic American group, and the organization has continued to examine the connection between the genocide and contemporary Cambodian American health.[9]

Responding more generally to the influx of Southeast Asian refugees and the emergence of Southeast Asian American communities following the conclusion of both the Vietnam conflict and the dissolution of Democratic Kampuchea, the Southeast Asia Resource Action Center (SEARAC) was founded in 1979 to assist in the resettling of refugees from Indonesia in the United States.[10] Initially named the Indochina Refugee Action Center (IRAC), SEARAC has developed into a national organization that advocates on the national stage for specific economic and political needs of Southeast Asian American communities. Working closely with local and state mutual aid associations (MAAs) and faith-based organizations (FBOs), SEARAC provides leadership training, sponsors community development workshops, and facilitates program evaluation. Though admittedly more focused on pan-Southeast Asian American issues, SEARAC was nevertheless heavily involved in raising awareness about and advocating against the post–September 11th deportations of an estimated 1,200–1,500 Cambodian Americans, which represents one of the major issues facing contemporary Cambodian American communities.

The 1996 Illegal Immigration Reform and Immigrant Responsibility Act (IIRAIRA) and the Anti-Terrorism and Effective Death Penalty Act (AEDPA) expanded the definition of "aggravated felony," so minor crimes such as shoplifting were included among more major crimes such as murder and assault. Touted by proimmigrant advocacy groups as a "one–size–fits–all" approach, the punishment of deportation was retroactively applied to crimes committed before 1996.[11] Individuals could face deportation whether or not time had been served for the crime. Moreover, fairness hearings—which would enable judges to apply a case-by-case standard in the review of deportation cases—were prohibited. This particular provision was initially enabled by a bilateral agreement between the U.S. and Cambodia in March 2001 to regulate deportation and enforced by the October 2001 passage of the Uniting and Strengthening America by Providing Appropriate Tools Required to Intercept and Obstruct Terrorism Act (USA PATRIOT Act). Cambodian Americans were not the only group targeted by the Immigration and Naturalization Service (INS), but this deportation is noteworthy given the actuality of the Cambodian genocide and the continuing legacy of this past on current sociopolitical dynamics in Cambodia. The amnesia over the very conditions that brought Cambodians to the United States, coupled with the refugee political status of those slated for deportation, is inextricably tied to a narrative of asylum from the Khmer Rouge as well as a tenuous connection to contemporary Cambodia.

Culturally, the majority of Cambodian American subjects facing deportation had been born in refugee camps, had spent most of their lives in the United States, and were predominately 1.5-generation men in their twenties and thirties. Disconnected from Cambodia with no guarantee that their human rights would be protected, those slated for deportation would be forced to return to a nation they sought refuge from as a consequence of genocidal policies and practices. Economically, as former SEARAC director KaYing Yang asserted, Cambodian American families would potentially be devastated by the deportations because deportees were often primary wage-earners within households.[12] The threat of deportation and its possible repercussions promulgated the formation of the Southeast Asian Freedom Network, a conglomeration of Southeast Asian American activists and activist organizations who opposed the proposed deportations.[13] The Committee Against Anti-Asian Violence (CAAV) responded with the formation of both the Khmer Freedom Committee and the more expansive Southeast Asian Freedom Network, which, in conjunction with non-Asian American groups, organized a "Day of Action against Deportation" on November 8, 2002, to protest deportations.[14] As of 2008, more than 1,500 Cambodian Americans were still awaiting deportation, and between 2002 and 2008, a total of 169 Cambodian Americans had been deported.[15] Fundamental to antideportation efforts within various Cambodian American communities are narratives about life under the Khmer Rouge, which are more striking given that former members of the Khmer Rouge still occupy positions of power in the Cambodian government.[16]

Cambodian American community organizations reflect the demographic realities of particular locations and often engage both business and cultural interests. The majority of Cambodian Americans live in Long Beach, CA, which contains the largest concentration of Cambodians outside of Cambodia.[17] In 2001, Cambodian American community organizers pushed to rename a one-mile section of the city—Anaheim Street—"Cambodia Town," to further highlight the many Cambodian and Cambodian American–owned businesses in the district, and this request was granted on July 3, 2007.[18] Lowell, MA, is home to the second largest population of Cambodians and Cambodian Americans. These refugees initially came in the 1980s to fill positions in the then-thriving computer parts industry, though refugee sponsorships also brought individuals to other places in the United States.[19] The Cambodian American League of Lowell was formed in 1993 to promote Cambodian American entrepreneurship, community engagement, and awareness through local programs and sponsored arts events related to traditional Khmer forms and remembering the genocide.[20] The communal support of traditional Khmer musical and dance arts is especially important because such forms were almost lost because of the systematic suppression and execution of an estimated 90 percent of classically trained musicians and dancers affiliated with the Royal Cambodian Classical Ballet.[21] Thus, arts organizations dedicated to the preservation of traditional Khmer forms culturally reclaim what has been lost as a result of the genocide.

The collapsing of space between social justice initiatives and arts activism is apparent in other Cambodian American organizations in the United States. For example, the Chicago-based Cambodian Association of Illinois (CAI), founded in 1976, is a nonprofit group dedicated to working with the resettlement of Cambodian refugees who have survived the genocide, and their mission of community development in many ways echoes the efforts of SEARAC, the work of mutual aid associations in Lowell and analogous organizations in Long Beach.[22] The Cambodian Association of Illinois offers bilingual education programs, health initiatives, and social service assistance to an estimated 5,000 Cambodian Americans at the state level. The Cambodian Association of Illinois directly addresses the issue of genocidal remembrance in its fund-raising campaigns, which allow donors to contribute money toward scholarships for Cambodian American students, aid in the promotion of education about the genocide, and facilitate the preservation and ongoing production of Khmer arts in the United States as part of a national campaign, titled the "Cambodian Killing Fields Endowment."

Moreover, in 2004, the Cambodian Association of Illinois opened the Cambodian American Heritage Museum and Killing Fields Memorial, which includes traveling and permanent exhibits focused on Cambodian history, Khmer culture, images from the genocide, and experiences of Cambodian Americans. In a similar vein, Cambodian American Dara Duong, who was a child during the reign of the Khmer Rouge, founded the Cambodian American Cultural Museum and Killing Fields Memorial in Seattle, WA. This museum is dedicated to educating subsequent generations of Cambodian Americans about the genocide through the revelation of survivor accounts and the promulgation of Khmer arts and culture.[23] The reclamation of artistic forms operates in tandem with genocidal remembrance, and such exhibits are marked by the question of justice, which remains unanswered until the completion of the current war crimes tribunal. Therefore, rooted in a genocidal past and guided by a refugee present, Cambodian American arts and activism implicitly and explicitly engage with issues of memorialization, notions of cultural reclamation, calls for political justice, and questions of sociopolitical reconciliation within the country of origin and the country of settlement.

As individuals who grew up under the Khmer Rouge or who were born in refugee camps, contemporary Cambodian American activists, writers, filmmakers, and artists foreground the actuality and continuing impact of the genocide in community organizing efforts, memoirs, documentaries, musical productions, and dance. Cambodian American hip-hop artist praCh (Prach Ly) incorporates familial stories about surviving under the Khmer Rouge in his *three-part Dalama* album series. The artist juxtaposes lyrical memorials with a more contemporary consideration of how the genocide continues to impact his experiences in the United States. In this regard, praCh's work is connected to Cambodian American literary production, which characterized by a similar bifurcated sensibility. Two full-length memoirs of the killing fields have also been published in the United States—Chanrithy Him's *When Broken Glass Floats: Growing Up Under the Khmer Rouge* (2000) and Loung Ung's *First They Killed My Father: A Daughter of Cambodia Remembers* (2000). Each full-length autobiography recounts the story of life in Cambodia's killing fields from the perspective of one who had experienced the Khmer Rouge regime as a child and who had also grown up as a refugee in the United States. Imbued with the task of commemorating those who were lost under the regime, constituted by testimonial narration, and dominated by repeated calls for justice, Him and Ung engage in a form of literary activism that reminds readers of both the genocide and the degree to which those responsible have yet to be prosecuted.[24]

This form of activism is mirrored by each author's work outside of literary production. Chanrithy Him foregrounds this other role in the introduction of the memoir, in which she writes about her experiences working with Cambodian refugees suffering from post-traumatic stress disorder as part of the Khmer Adolescent Project in Eugene, Oregon.[25] Ung's work as a Cambodian genocide activist, author, and lecturer is prominently featured on her Web site. From 1997 to 2003, Ung worked for the Vietnam Veterans of America Foundation's (VVAF) Campaign for a Landmine-Free World from 1997–2003, served as a community educator for the Abused Women's Advocacy Project of the Maine Coalition Against Domestic Violence, and is currently a national spokesperson for the Campaign for a Landmine-Free World.[26] Ung's second memoir, *Lucky Child: A Daughter of Cambodia Reunites with the Sister She Left Behind* (2005) centers on Ung and her sister, Chou. The autobiography is divided equally between Ung's recollections of growing up in the United States and Chou's experiences in Cambodia after the fall of the Khmer Rouge. In this regard, Ung's *Lucky Child* represents the first Cambodian American work largely focused on life after the Khmer Rouge. Also in 2005, Cambodian American Theary C. Seng, executive director of the Center for Social Development, a human rights organization located in Phnom Penh that monitors contemporary Cambodian and global politics, published *Daughter of the Killing Fields*. Seng, who received a law degree in 2000 from the University of Michigan, serves as a tribunal representative for victims in Cambodia.[27]

Cambodian American documentary filmmaker Socheata Poeuv takes a similar trajectory in her cinematic negotiations of the Cambodian genocide. Embedded in documentary, travel narrative, and memoir, Poeuv's debut production, *New Year Baby* (2006), returns the discussion of remembrance back to

Cambodia with a narrative about what it means to return to a country that has forever been changed as a result of the Khmer Rouge. *New Year Baby* follows the filmmaker as she returns to the various labor camps and villages that marked her parents' experiences during the Democratic Kampuchean regime. Grounded firmly in the question of what it means to be Cambodian and American, Poeuv's narrative brings the issue of genocidal remembrance full circle by returning the displaced Cambodian refugees to the country of origin. In this regard, her work is emblematic of Cambodian American activism and art, which continues to remember the genocidal past while simultaneously acknowledging what it means to be a refugee in the United States. Poeuv's current archival video project, *Khmer Legacies*, includes interviews of Democratic Kampuchean survivors conducted by the children of survivors and is part of a larger nonprofit organization headed by the filmmaker.[28] Such a project continues the memory work of Cambodian American organizations, activists, and artists who continue to push for remembrance and justice.

FURTHER READING

Cambodian Association of Illinois. http://www.cambodian-association.org.

Chan, Sucheng, ed. "Introduction." *Not Just Victims: Conversations with Cambodian Community Leaders in the United States.* Interviews conducted by Audrey U. Kim. Urbana: University of Illinois Press, 2003.

Chan, Sucheng. *Survivors: Cambodian Refugees in the United States.* Urbana: University of Illinois Press, 2004.

Etcheson, Craig. *After the Killing Fields: Lessons from the Cambodian Genocide.* Westport, CT: Praeger Publishers, 2005.

Shaffer, Teri Yamada. "Cambodian American Autobiography" *Form and Transformation in Asian American Literature.* Zhou Xiaojing and Samina Najimi, eds. Seattle: University of Washington Press, 2005.

Smith-Hefner, Nancy J. *Khmer American: Identity and Moral Education in a Diasporic Community.* Berkeley: University of California Press, 1999.

Southeast Asian American Resource Center. http://www.searac.org/resourcectr.html.

Yale Cambodian Genocide Program. http://www.yale.edu/cgp/.

NOTES

1. Christine Su, "Cambodian-Americans and Political Empowerment," Cambodian Community of Hawai'i Web site, 2006, http:/Hawaii.cambodiaworldwide.com/poelm power3.html/.

2. Su, "Cambodian-Americans and Political Empowerment."

3. Erin Hoover Barnett, "Recovered Identity: Cambodian Community in Portland Moves Beyond the Horror of Khmer Rouge Killing Fields," *The Oregonian,* "Metro Portland Neighbors," Oct. 2, 2008, 8, http://www.oregonlive.com/clackamascounty/index.ssf/2008/11/recovered_identity_cambodian_c.html.

4. Yale Cambodian Genocide Program, "Introduction," 2008, http://www.yale.edu/cgp/.

5. Currently, the UN Cambodian War Crimes Tribunal has five Khmer Rouge officials in custody: Kaing Guek Eav ("Duch") (the person in charge of S-21), Khieu Samphan (Democratic Kampuchean Prime Minister), Nuon Chea (Brother No. 2, the

Khmer Rouge's chief ideologist), Ieng Sary (Deputy Prime Minister/Foreign Minister/Democratic Kampuchea), and his wife, Ieng Thirith (Minister for Social Affairs/Democratic Kampuchea). However, the tribunals have been plagued by accusations of corruption, contestations over the nature of genocide (including the assertion that claims of genocide are not substantiated), and fears of funding.

6. Sucheng Chan, ed. "Introduction," *Not Just Victims: Conversations with Cambodian Community Leaders in the United States*. Interviews conducted by Audrey U. Kim. (Urbana: University of Illinois Press, 2003), 29–31.

7. Max Niedzwiecki and T. C. Duong, "Southeast Asian American Statistical Profile" (Washington, DC: Southeast Asia Resource Action Center, 2004), http://www.searac.org/seastatprofilemay04.pdf.

8. Rubén G. Rumbaut and Walter A. Ewing, "The Myth of Immigrant Criminality," *Border Battles: The U.S. Immigration Debates, Social Science Research Council,* May 23, 2007, http://borderbattles.ssrc.org/Rumbault_Ewing/index1.html.

9. "Cambodian Refugees Gripped by Severe Depression in the U.S," Agence France-Presse, Aug. 3, 2005; and "Webcast Examines Cambodian-American Health Emergency," press release, 2006, http://www.uchc.edu/ocomm/newsreleases06/apr06/webcast.html.

10. Southeast Asian Resource Action Center, 2008, http://www.searac.org/.

11. Melissa Hung, "One Way Ticket to Cambodia," *East Bay Express*, Nov. 20, 2002, http://www.modelminority.com/article358.html.

12. Sophia Hanifah, "A New Nightmare: Cambodian American Deportations Carries History's Weight," *AsianWeek* Nov. 22–28, 2002, http://asianweek.com/2002_11_22/feature.html#TOP.

13. Southeast Asian Freedom Network, 2003, http://www.caaav.org/coalitions/seafn.

14. Quoted in Sophia Hanifah, "A New Nightmare: Cambodian American Deportations Carries History's Weight," *AsianWeek* November 22–28, 2002, http://asianweek.com/2002_11_22/feature.html#TOP.

15. Robynn Takayama, "Cambodian Refugee Faces Return Home," Day to Day: NPR, Jan. 10, 2006; Dori Chan and John Stansall, "U.S. and Vietnam Need to Rethink Deportation," *International Examiner*, Feb. 16, 2008, http://news.newamericamedia.org/news/view_article.html?article_id=d4ae7849572770c46e0f3d0fc33a7007.

16. A former Khmer Rouge soldier, current Prime Minister Hun Sen continues to hold power in Cambodia, along with many other former Khmer Rouge members and officials.

17. Anna Gorman, "Cambodia Town on the Map," *Los Angeles Times,* July 18, 2007, http://articles.latimes.com/2007/jul/18/local/me-cambodian18.

18. Nuch Sarita, "Long Beach 'Cambodia Town' Approved," *Voice of America Khmer*, July 20, 2007. http://www.voanews.com/Khmer/archive/2007-07/2007-07-20-voa4.cfm.

19. Suzanne Presto, "Cambodian Immigrants Make Impact on City in US Northeast," *Voice of America*, May 4, 2005, http://www.voanews.com/english/archive/2005-05/2005-05-04-voa72.cfm.

20. Cambodian American League of Lowell, Inc., 2008, http://www.cambodianamerican.net/.

21. Deborah Jowitt, "True Love Triumphs, Gently in Cambodian Classical Dance," *The Village Voice*, Jan. 22, 2008. http://www.villagevoice.com/2007-10-09/dance/true-love-triumphs-gently-in-cambodian-classical-dance/.

22. Cambodian Association of Illinois, 2008, http://www.cambodian-association.org/.

23. Cambodian Cultural Museum and Killing Fields Memorial, 2008, http://www.killingfieldsmuseum.com/.

24. Soon after the publication of the memoir by W. W. Norton, Eugene, OR, reporter Kimber Williams claimed that she and Him worked together on the manuscript and that Williams was responsible for crafting the majority of the text. Williams was not named as a contributor, nor was she acknowledged within the text. Sydney Schanberg, the well-known journalist whose experiences in Cambodia provided a partial foundation for the film, *The Killing Fields*, sided with Williams. Initially Schanberg had written a blurb that praised *When Broken Glass Floats* but later asked to be disassociated with Him's memoir. The controversy over authorship was resolved through an out-of-court settlement in 2001, and Him later acknowledged Williams as a contributor in subsequent printings of the book. Nonetheless, no clear verdict has been rendered with regard to authorship, although the shifts in acknowledgement support Williams's allegation; The recently defunct online Cambodian American site, the Khmer Institute, put forth the following proclamation against Loung Ung: "We are not engaged in a crusade against the author; our crusade, if it can be described as such, is to expose the truth so that people may know what the Killing Fields really meant for Cambodians who lived through it. Although Ung's book is sub-entitled 'A Daughter of Cambodia Remembers,' it is apparent that she neither truly considers herself a "daughter of Cambodia" (except for the purpose of publicity) nor does she with any kind of accuracy "remember." Unlike the acclaim and support given to the movie "The Killing Fields," many survivors of the Democratic Kampuchea regime find this book inaccurate, distasteful, and insulting. We believe in this case that misinformation is more dangerous than no information. It is sad that a person would distort and sensationalize such a tragic experience for personal gain. It dishonors the memory of the 1.7 million people who died and the legitimate stories of countless others who have and still suffer because of the Khmer Rouge." The Khmer Institute, "First They Killed My Father reviews," 2001, http://www.khmerinstitute.org.

25. Chanrithy Him, 2008, http://www.chanrithyhim.com/.

26. Loung Ung, 2008, http://www.luongung.com/.

27. Theary Seng, 2008, http://www.thearyseng.com/.

28. Khmer Legacies, 2008, http://www.khmerlegacies.org/.

CONTINUING IMPACT OF THE KOREAN WAR ON KOREAN AMERICANS

Raina Han

The Korean War took place from June 25, 1950, when the North attacked the South, until July 27, 1953, when an official armistice was signed by the United Nations, the North, and China. To this date, the South has not signed the armistice, and because a peace treaty has not been signed, the communist North and democratic South are still at war, at least in principle.

After the armistice was signed, the Korean peninsula's official demilitarized zone (DMZ) came into place and this 2-mile-wide zone has separated families and communities ever since. Many of those that either escaped to one side or the other during the war would never see their families again. During the Korean War, the 1.2 million people who fled the North came to comprise at least 15 percent of the South Korean population.[1] As of 2008, the war's impact in the region still resounds, with 28,500 U.S. troops continuing to reside in South Korea as the South is still technically considered a combat zone.[2]

Of the more than 1.2 million Korean Americans (per the 2000 U.S. Census), anywhere from 200,000 to 500,000 have direct ties to family in North Korea, but as of 2006, only 80 Korean Americans have been reunited with family members in the North under government-sanctioned arrangements versus the approximately 1,000 family reunifications between South Koreans and North Koreans.[3] As North Korea is careful in its interactions with the United States, Korean Americans are less likely to be chosen for reunification meetings, while South Koreans are chosen by their government's lottery to reunite with North Korean family members.[4]

The Korean War has a continuing presence in the lives of Korean Americans due to the struggle over reuniting with family members, the plight of North Korean refugees, and how ongoing tensions between the United States and North Korea shape the daily lives of Korean Americans. This war is a contemporary issue for Korean Americans because so many are affected by these ongoing legacies.

The impact of a civil war on its people can have drastic long-term consequences, especially when the war has never officially ended. More than fifty years after the Korean War, the Korean American reaction to issues related to the war include mixed feelings between generations, specifically between the older Koreans who lived through the Korean War and immigrated to the United States, and the younger generations, those who are ethnically Korean but either U.S.-born or immigrated as children. Older generations recall and continue to comprehend the long-time U.S. military presence in South Korea. On the opposite end, younger generations have expressed concern that the Bush administration, especially when initially applying the "axis of evil" term to North Korea in 2002, did not attempt meaningful discourse to prevent the possibilities of war. There was widespread sentiment throughout the Korean American community that such a negative designation would only hurt relations between the two countries. Also at this time, younger generations felt that until verbal communication occurred between the United States and North Korea about the situation on hand, there would continue to be a likelihood that North Korea would engage in more nuclear activities, thus causing a likely arms marathon and making the DMZ separating the two Koreas an even more complicated and fragile area.[5]

Beginning in 2003, dialogue in the form of "Six Party Talks" (both Koreas, the United States, China, Russia, and Japan) began, and there have been signals that North Korea has begun cooperating in slowly retiring its nuclear activities. Overall, while the nuclear weapons issue still plays a more visible role in the media, the other major international issues—reunification, North Korean refugees and human rights, and family separation—continue to be significant, multifaceted concerns that directly affect the Korean American population, regardless of generation or nationality. Current events on the peninsula affect all Korean Americans as this community's roots—and many family members—still reside in both Koreas. The first decade of the twenty-first century has highlighted these issues—increasingly attracting U.S. congressional attention—and they will only become more prominent in the next decade, as the divisions of families and a country continue to exist.

IMPACT ON FIRST-GENERATION KOREAN AMERICANS

The Korean War is considered "forgotten" for several reasons. In the American psyche, it is often overlooked and not easily recognized as the start of the Cold War. Additionally, few Koreans in America have publicly addressed the war and its continuing impact on Koreans who have survived the war and moved to the United States. The lingering impact on Korean families and the effect on second and third generations of these Korean American families also are not extensively covered by the popular media or even in much scholarly research.

In recent years, scholars have begun to address the issues facing the Korean American community. A professor at Boston College, Ramsay Liem, has conducted significant research into the impact of the Korean War on Korean Americans through interviews and oral surveys. Additionally, his research was included in the only art and multimedia exhibition of its kind known to date, called "Still Present Pasts: Korean Americans and the 'Forgotten War'" (2006–2008), which chronicles first-person oral-testimony accounts of Korean Americans who have survived the war. Liem's research has uncovered the war as a reverberating theme among Korean Americans. Primarily, especially for first-generation Korean Americans, there is still the pain from either having lost a family member during the war or being permanently split from family in the North. Another consistent theme is that many immigrants to the United States left directly because of the war and continue to feel the war's devastating impact on the peninsula. Many were seeking better opportunities and livelihoods in emigrating to the United States during the postwar period when the South was slowly developing as a struggling economy during the 1960s and 1970s.[6] The population who survived the war had also just lived through Japan's colonization of Korea (1910–1945). These Korean American war survivors' existence in and memory of Korea have constantly been filled with domestic turmoil and political strife.

IMPACT ON SECOND-GENERATION KOREAN AMERICANS

Older relatives' feelings of insecurity about the future and a constant search for stability for themselves and the younger generations in their families can be traced to first-generation Korean Americans' experiences during and after the war, yet these feelings are often not well understood by younger generations. For second-generation Korean Americans, being able to hear their parents' and grandparents' experiences during the war and later reflections may address a lot of questions concerning behavior, reactions, and thought processes of their elders. There is a notable misunderstanding and a silence of the unspoken between generations that continues. Some younger generations may think that their elders' particular behaviors and mindsets are because of a cultural frame of mind without realizing that these might be side effects of war. Sometimes they may misinterpret their elders as being or acting "Korean" when in actuality, the demonstrated behavior might be of someone scarred with the emotional remains of surviving a civil war. Often, many younger generations simply are not informed of their family's history or trauma during the war, aside from what they may have briefly learned in a formal school setting. Some younger generations may simply not be interested, or some may have parents or relatives who are not comfortable sharing their stories. There is a need to discuss these experiences more openly within families, and to understand the impact on the generations, given that the older generations are aging and time is limited.[7]

INTERGENERATIONAL DIFFERENCES

There is a significant difference between how first-generation Korean Americans and second-generation Korean Americans view the impact of the war on the Korean American population and collective experience. Even among second-generation Korean Americans, opinions differ, as some younger generations feel that the United States should take a tougher stance on the North's nuclear activities and reneged promise to halt such activities. Other second-generation Korean Americans feel that the United States must be careful not to pursue a military approach in dealing with the North.[8]

From Washington to Southern California, from Wisconsin to New Jersey, from Minnesota to Georgia, throughout the large clusters of Korean American populations, there are sharply conflicting feelings among Korean Americans: some feel that the Bush Administration should have engaged in more dialogue instead of increasing sanctions on the "axis of evil" member state, North Korea. At the same time, many Korean Americans of all generations were disappointed with the North for retracting from a previous commitment to stop nuclear involvement and for continuing to take and expect international aid despite such actions. Across the country, Korean Americans reacted sharply when the North carried out its nuclear weapons test in 2006. On the international scale, North Korea's nuclear weapons testing is a threat to global security and peace; however, to Korean Americans, it is personal. Some Korean Americans were dismissive of the threat, but many were concerned. Some Korean Americans believe that there is much more concern among the Korean American population than among South Koreans. Most of the Korean American population has family on the peninsula. Not only are Korean Americans concerned about family members in North Korea, they are also deeply concerned about family in South Korea and especially in Seoul, where 25 percent of the South Korean population lives and which is close to the DMZ.

At the same time, many Korean Americans were distressed with the anti-American sentiment in South Korea during Roh Moo-Hyun's presidency. During President Roh's administration, his Sunshine Policy (which included more interactions and dialogue with the North) led some South Koreans to develop anti-American feelings, which were further fueled by the death of two young Korean girls who had been run over by a U.S. military tank around this time. In the United States, many first-generation Korean Americans were not supportive of President Roh's policies, which they viewed as liberal and left-leaning. Younger generations were less critical of his Sunshine Policy.

THE 2002 STATE OF THE UNION ADDRESS
AND THE "AXIS OF EVIL"

In his 2002 State of the Union address, President George W. Bush came up with the encompassing term "axis of evil" for Iran, Iraq, and North Korea, based on these countries' presumed nuclear weapons ownership or production. At the time, this designation became a prominent issue for the Koreans in America and for the larger Asian American population, which constituted 4.2 percent of the overall U.S. population in 2000.[9] The "axis of evil" label raised concerns for Korean and Asian Americans about the potential for discrimination, racial profiling, and terrorist association. In the immediate post-9/11 world, this designation raised specters of racial profiling cases of Muslim Americans, as well as of the xenophobic suspicion of Japanese Americans and other Asian Americans right after the Pearl Harbor bombing. And when North Korea's leader, Kim Jong Il, announced in December 2002 that he was going to reactivate the country's nuclear reactor to produce weapons-grade plutonium, and when he then actually carried out tests, this caused far-reaching concern for not just South Koreans but also for immigrant Koreans and Korean Americans in the United States. These moves toward nuclear armament raised concerns about other issues that hit closer to home—about the future potential for the peninsula's reunification, about the health and well-being of North Korean refugees (starvation was still an issue even after the more widespread famine of the 1990s), and about family separation.

September 11th and the "axis of evil" designation have only made anti-immigrant and antiforeigner laws and sentiments increase. Since the establishment of the Antiterrorism and Effective Death Penalty Act (AEDPA) and the Illegal Immigration Reform and Immigrant Responsibility Act, which were both passed by President Clinton in 1996, more than 1 million people have been deported by the United States. The Bush administration's USA PATRIOT Act of 2001, which permits law enforcement officials to execute surveillance techniques and hold suspicious persons in custody, is a descendant of the AEDPA. These laws affected the law of habeas corpus, and many immigrants and foreigners have seen their rights threatened by this law. Noncitizens who commit or are convicted of a minor crime, including petty theft, could face deportation retroactively, even after serving their sentences. These laws have, in effect, made it easier for law officials to process deportations.

According to Families for Freedom, a New York–based defense network for immigrants, since 1996, 1,148 Korean Americans have been deported. In comparison, 2,621 Filipino Americans have been deported; 1,975 Indian Americans have been deported; 1,841 Pakistani Americans have been deported.[10] One notable cause Korean American permanent resident Hyung Joon Kim, who immigrated to the United States at age six, was arrested without due process of law and faced deportation under the Illegal Immigration Reform and Responsibility Act, which constrained his rights as a noncitizen. His ruling was protested by the executive director of the National Korean American Service and Education Consortium (NAKASEC), a civil and immigrant rights support group based in New York.[11]

IMPACT OF NORTH KOREA'S ACTIONS ON THE KOREAN AMERICAN COMMUNITY

For many Korean Americans, the initial prospect of and then eventual war with Iraq made war with North Korea a real possibility. In 2002 and 2003, prior to the invasion of Iraq, many Korean Americans became concerned when North Korea test-fired missiles and the tensions between the United States and the North escalated. In areas where a large Korean American population conducts business with South Korea, such as southern California, Korean Americans grew worried about the impact on businesses and also an increase in racial discrimination. During this time, Koreans in America were concerned that they would be treated similarly to how Arab Americans were shortly after 9/11.[12]

It is an ongoing fear that a war with North Korea will follow the war with Iraq, especially with North Korea's nuclear activities, both suspected and actual. With such a possibility, the Korean American community faces multiple fears, including the threat of North Korea attacking South Korea with weapons. Koreans in America are concerned that their families in both Koreas will be hurt if any belligerence were to occur on the peninsula, and they are also concerned about the growing tensions between the United States and North Korea. Throughout the United States in various Korean American enclaves, there are generational clashes in viewpoints as some first-generation Korean Americans expect the United States to take a hard stance with the North, while younger second-generation Korean Americans want more dialogue.[13]

When the nuclear threats and active nuclear program in North Korea became clear in late 2002, despite North Korea's previous agreement to disband its nuclear activities, many Korean Americans grew concerned that their chances for family reunification were even more diminished. Hundreds of thousands of Korean Americans continue to wait for the day when reunification will be feasible, and many families continue to be dispirited by the uncertainty of the peninsula's future.[14] Despite Korean Americans' mixed feelings toward the Sunshine Policy, there was some hope with such efforts; however, when North Korea openly announced its once-covert nuclear programs, Korean Americans' hopes were again diminished.

OTHER CHALLENGES IN THE KOREAN AMERICAN COMMUNITY

A common ongoing concern is that Korean Americans feel that many non-Koreans do not comprehend the difference between South and North Koreans; hence, they do not realize that a majority of Korean Americans did not recently come from the North nor are they communists. Additionally, Korean Americans do not want to be associated with any Korean American spy cases. There have been cases of Korean Americans suspected of being spies for North Korea. In early 2003, a Santa Monica Korean American shop owner named John Yai was indicted by a grand jury for not registering as a foreign government agent. He was arrested on charges of espionage for the North Korean government. His wife, Susan Yai, a bank employee, was also indicted. Those who knew Yai were suspicious of the timing of his arrest, which occurred when tensions were elevated between the United States and North Korea, as he had already been under surveillance by the FBI for seven years.[15]

FAMILY SEPARATION

After the U.S. Immigration Act was signed in 1965 and as postwar South Korea slowly recovered economically, many Koreans emigrated from the 1960s to the 1980s. Thirty-five thousand emigrated per year from 1985–1987, the height of Korean immigration to the United States.[16] Perhaps up to 40 percent of the Koreans who arrived after 1965 were from the northern region of Korea.[17]

As it has been more than fifty years since the war, for those who have family members in the North, with the population aging for those who have survived through the war, it is becoming a frantic concern to find out whether a family member is alive or dead. The first cross-border reunion occurred in 1985, but more significantly, since 2000, there have been more than thirteen reunions for divided family members; at least 13,600 Koreans from both Koreas have been reunited.[18] However, few of these were Korean Americans, as these arrangements occurred between the two Koreas and not North Korea and the United States. In May 2007, the first family reunion for Koreans living in the United States occurred, as a group of fifteen went to Pyongyang, the capital of North Korea. The group went with the help of the Los Angeles branch of South Korea's National Unification Advisory Council.[19]

Structured organizations to assist with reunification are necessary for these efforts. A number of Korean Americans have been able to reunify with relatives in the North through an organization called the Overseas Compatriot Protection Committee; however, such rare arrangements generally were possible for those with money or connections. A majority of older first-generation Korean Americans do not have such access.[20]

Another organization, Saemsori, which is based in Washington, DC, and Seoul, has been playing a pivotal role in family reunification efforts for Korean Americans. As of March 2006, 1,300 people from the United States (including Hawai'i) have signed up with Saemsori, seeking the organization's help in reuniting divided families. Therefore, organizations such as Saemsori, one of the few of its kind, help Korean Americans seek reunification with the help of a U.S. congressperson.[21]

Notably, one prominent Korean American author, Helie Lee, brought much U.S. media attention to the war's impact on her immediate family and by extension, the Korean American community. Her nationally best-selling book, *In the Absence of Sun* (2002), garnered her much attention in the media for illustrating the story of reuniting her family with her long-lost uncle in North Korea. The book also shares how her family rescued her uncle and the rest of his family from North Korea in a dangerous attempt. The footage and story have been shared in the media, including on CNN, *Nightline*, and *Oprah*. Lee has since been a vocal advocate for North Korean refugees and human rights.[22]

In 2001, the Korean American community garnered 20,000 signatures for a petition to send to the U.S. State Department so that North Korea could address the family reunification issue.

KOREAN AMERICAN REACTION TO THE NORTH
KOREAN FAMINE AND FLOODS OF THE 1990s

While the "Great Famine" of the mid-1990s in which more than 2 million North Koreans died from starvation and crop-destroying floods has passed, but most North Koreans continue to endure hardships from lack of food and agricultural resources. Previously, North Korea had received significant support, especially during the 1960s, from the Soviet Union, a fellow communist ally. The Soviet Union's collapse drastically affected the North, as the region no longer received the aid that had helped them thrive so rapidly after the war. With less financial support from North Korea's communist ally and in need of assistance, the United Nations World Food Program entered the North. This support was not sufficient for all, however, especially those in the more rustic regions of the northern part of the peninsula. Therefore, many North Koreans, including hundreds of thousands of political prisoners, seek refuge in China, and of these refugees, many attempt the trek to South Korea. The U.S. State Department estimates that between 30,000 and 50,000 North Korean refugees live in China, while some nongovernmental organizations approximate the number at 300,000.

The Korean American community provides significant financial support to North Koreans in need. As of 2001, it was reported that Korean Americans had provided the North with $46 million in assistance.[23] When news and photographs of the famine in North Korea reached Korea Americans, the Korean American community collectively reacted by gathering funds to help support those facing starvation. The community is also supportive of survivors of other tragedies. For instance, when a train crash killed 161 people and thousands became homeless in 2004 in a North Korean city bordering China, called Ryongchon, Korean Americans also collected funds to help the victims.[24]

Korean American activists continue to believe that more of the Korean American community needs to raise a voice in shaping the U.S. foreign policy regarding the Korean peninsula; however, in recent years, although the Korean American community as a whole provided community and financial support during the famine in the 1990s, after the North's nuclear activities were discovered, some Korean Americans became reluctant to provide food and humanitarian aid to the North, presuming that such support might be sent to the military instead.

NORTH KOREAN REFUGEE MIGRATION
TO THE UNITED STATES

In 2004, the U.S. Congress passed and President Bush signed the North Korean Human Rights Act of 2004 (NKHRA). Among other items, the act authorized up to $20 million per fiscal year from 2005 to 2008 to be used to aid North Korean refugees. The act also permitted North Koreans to be considered eligible for refugee status in the United States, allowing the State Department to accept applications by North Korean refugees seeking asylum. As a result of the act, in 2006 the first six North Korean refugees received asylum in the United States. From 2006 to 2008, forty-three refugees have arrived in the United States.[25] Overall, there are few documented North Korean refugees, and the history of their acceptance into the United States is brief. When refugees do give interviews, it is usually under a pseudonym in order to protect their family members in North Korea. Those that have emigrated to the United States may not realize that their experience may be similar to North Korean refugees in South Korea. That is, these refugees find it difficult to assimilate because of the cultural and language barriers and their poor educational background. The Korean dialect that North Koreans speak varies greatly from the dialect of the South Koreans; hence, even in the United States, North Koreans would find it difficult to communicate with the Korean American population. In addition, their limited education backgrounds make it difficult to move beyond menial occupations.

KOREAN AMERICAN GROUPS RAISING AWARENESS

Many Korean American North Korean refugee or reunification advocacy groups are Christian in nature. These groups include the aforementioned Saemsori, founded by the Eugene Bell Foundation, a Christian organization. One of the more prominent organizations with a nationwide network in the United States, the Irvine, CA–based Korean Church Coalition for North Korea Freedom (KCC), includes three thousand Korean American pastors and millions of congregation members. The organization works to liberate North Korean refugees in China and also actively raises awareness throughout the United States. This group regularly holds candlelight vigils across the nation. Leaders and members also effectively assisted the integration process when the first six North Korean refugees were accepted by the United States in 2006. The KCC's "Let My People Go" campaign, launched in 2007 prior to the 2008 Summer Olympics in Beijing, was intended to raise awareness in providing refugee protection and status to the North Korean refugees currently residing in China.

Another prominent organization, the Washington, DC–based U.S. Committee for Human Rights in North Korea, is a group of foreign policy and human rights experts that aim to promote human rights in North Korea. Prominent Korean Americans on this board include Helie Lee, the aforementioned Korean American author, who also lectures about human rights for North Korean refugees.

Some Korean Americans are concerned with ensuring that they do not come across as anti-American and do not want their U.S. loyalties to be doubted, especially when there was a period of strong anti-American and anti-Bush sentiment in South Korea. For instance, when a New York–based fifty-member North Korea advocacy group that provides social services to immigrants, called Nodutdol for Korean Community Development, organized an antiwar gathering in 2003 in reaction to the war in Iraq, some other Korean Americans felt that the action seemed anti-American. Some Korean Americans feel that the group is pro–North Korean, and they do not want to be associated with the "enemy." This kind of reaction is common among immigrant groups in the United States. [26]

Alliance of Scholars Concerned About Korea (ASCK) was started by a group of scholars in the United States and a group of Korea Studies experts, including Korean American scholars, to raise awareness about North Korea and its surrounding issues. This group feared that the Bush administration would take bellicose actions toward the North. This group has started efforts such as "Peace Day," which is meant to explore peaceful solutions.[27]

REUNIFICATION EFFORTS BY KOREAN AMERICANS

There are several active Korean American–run or –supported North Korean refugee support and advocacy organizations in the United States. Many of these organizations, including nongovernmental organizations, are Christian groups or missionary organizations and may operate under secretive methods to avoid detection from both the Chinese and North Korean governments. The Korean American Sharing Movement is a NGO that gives humanitarian aid to North Koreans and is managed by a Korean American reverend. Exodus 21, also led by a Korean American reverend, is a group that helps North Koreans escape.

Chun Ki Won, a well-known Seoul-based pastor helped the first group of North Korean refugees into the United States. He received help from Korean American churches and has become well known for his work helping refugees. These refugees have an opportunity to receive shelter and work from one of the 2,300 churches of the Korean American Church Coalition. These refugees have sought occupations in nail salons and construction sites.[28]

In April 2004, "North Korea Freedom Day" took place on Capitol Hill, drawing younger generation Korean Americans, including the founder of an organization called Liberty in North Korea (LiNK), and twenty North Korean refugees to the Hill's steps. And on the same day, across the country in Los Angeles, a group of young Korean Americans organized a concert to bring more attention to the issue of North Korean refugees.[29]

KOREAN AMERICANS VISITING NORTH KOREA

In July 2008, five Korean American university students (as part of a group of nine American university students) from International Strategy and Reconciliation (ISR), a group that has given medical supplies valued at $32 million to North Korea, visited North Korea for twelve days to teach English to middle- and high-school students. Supposedly, it was the first such visit to teach American English in Pyongyang, North Korea. This project, called a "Global Research Internship," was meant to provide U.S. college students with an opportunity to go to North Korea.[30]

LiNK is one of the few non-Christian nonprofit groups to address human rights issues for North Koreans. Based in Washington, DC, the group has attempted to unify the efforts of young Korean Americans nationally. In 2008, LiNK went to Seoul, South Korea, to meet with North Korean refugees, defectors, and officials from North Korean resettlement agencies, and to learn more about awareness of North Korean rights and issues in South Korea.

Tongjin Samuel Lee, 90, holds an old photograph of his sister, Hwasil, and her husband, in 2006 in Honolulu. Lee, a retired Christian minister, is originally from North Korea. He emigrated from what was then Japanese-occupied Korea in the 1940s to the United States to continue his theological studies. Lee lost contact with his family when the Korean Conflict began. He has no knowledge of his younger sister since he immigrated to the U.S. and wishes to make contact with her. (AP Photo/Marco Garcia)

OUTLOOK FOR KOREAN AMERICANS

The status of North Korea and the U.S. foreign policy regarding the peninsula will continue to affect the Korean American community. While the media and the government approach the situation solely from a political standpoint, for Korean Americans, the division is also significantly about the split of families. The intergenerational differences and perspectives will continue to challenge the community, while views on issues concerning the peninsula can even differ between members of the same generation. Within the Korean American community, various internal dialogues are taking place, often through local roundtables. These kinds of events help encourage younger generations to vote and share their opinions with the public and their congressional representatives.

For many Korean Americans, a chief concern is the possible future threat of war on the peninsula, especially with the past Bush administration's preemptive war doctrine. Another major concern is that reunification will be delayed, and that the aging first-generation Korean American population will not have an opportunity to be reconnected with lost family members. Future concerns and mutual desires include a peaceful reunification. More than anything, it is the not knowing—whether family members survived or died—that is of much torment to Korean American families. If there is a reunification, however, the challenges that come with how the two regions would be integrated will be unique and complex. Other fears include an implosion of North Korea. In the interim, an ongoing hope for the Korean American community will be that bilateral talks sustain between the United States and the North. The year 2003 marked the fiftieth anniversary of the war. Overall, moving forward, to effect change, it will continue to be important for Korean Americans to make their voices heard on the political stage. One recurring issue in studies and interviews of Korean Americans is that Korean Americans do not have a major impact in effecting change on Korea-related issues in Congress, other than, most prominently, the North Korean Human Rights Act of 2004.[31] Korean Americans are still a minority in the United States, but their population and economic pull is increasing, while the time left to reunite families is only diminishing.

FURTHER READING

Liem, Ramsey. "History, Trauma, and Identity: The Legacy of the Korean War for Korean Americans," *Amerasia Journal*, 29, no. 3 (2003): 111–129.

Save North Korean Refugees. http://www.snkr.org/.

Still Present Pasts: Korean Americans and "the Forgotten War." http://www.stillpresent pasts.org/spp/home/home.html.

Stories Untold: Memories of Korean War Survivors. http://userwww.sfsu.edu/~gracey/films.htm.

Yoo, Grace. "The Not So Forgotten War," *Peace Review* 16, no. 2 (2004): 169–179.

NOTES

1. Bay Fang, "Talk of Kith and Kims," *U.S. News & World Report* 128, no. 25 (June 26, 2000): 9.

2. Eric Schmitt, "Gates Approves of 3-Year Tours for U.S. Troops in South Korea," *New York Times*, June 4, 2008, http://www.nytimes.com/2008/06/04/washington/04gates.html?_r=1&fta=y&oref=slogin.

3. Audrey McAvoy, "Korean-Americans Seeking to Reunite with Family in North Korea," *The America's Intelligence Wire*, March 28 2006, http://www.saemsori.org/press/2006-03/20060328-Hawaii-AP.htm.

4. Sang Lee, "Brother, Where Art Thou?" *San Gabriel Valley Tribune*, July 19, 2006.

5. Calvin Sims, "A Nation at War: An Immigrant Community; for Korean-Americans, Concerns for a New War," *New York Times*, April 16, 2003, http://www.nytimes.com/2003/04/16/us/nation-war-immigrant-community-for-korean-americans-concerns-for-new-war.html?pagewanted=2.

6. Ramsay Liem, "History, Trauma, and Identity: The Legacy of the Korean War for Korean Americans," *Amerasia Journal* 29, no. 3 (2003–2004), 111–129.

7. Ramsay Liem, "History, Trauma, and Identity: The Legacy of the Korean War for Korean Americans," *Amerasia Journal* 29, no. 3 (2003–2004), 111–129.

8. Sun Hung Lee, "Uniting Hearts and Minds over Korea," *AsianWeek*, Oct. 21–27, 2004, http://www.asianweek.com/2004/10/22/uniting-hearts-and-minds-over-korea/.

9. Jessica S. Barnes and Claudette E. Bennett, "The Asian Population: 2000," U.S. Census 2000 Brief, U.S. Census Bureau, U.S. Department of Commerce, 2002.

10. Neela Banerjee, Shirley Lin, "Tearing Us Apart," *AsianWeek*, May 21, 2003, 21.

11. Julie Ha, "Court Says Yes to Detention: A KA Who Challenged a Controversial 1996 Immigration Law Loses in the U.S. Supreme Court," *KoreAm Journal*, June 2003.

12. Kate Berry, "Korean Businesses Brace for Losses as Diplomacy Falters," *Los Angeles Business Journal*, 25, no. 11, March 17, 2003.

13. Louise Roug, "A House Divided by War's Specter: With Trouble Brewing in the Koreas, Immigrants Here—Even Families—Are Split over a Solution," *Los Angeles Times*, April 9, 2003.

14. Catherine Holahan, "New Jersey's Koreans not Surprised; Many Saddened by North's Nuclear Revelation," *The Record*, Oct. 20, 2002.

15. Julie Ha, "The United States Vs. John Yai," *KoreAm Journal*, March 2003.

16. Bruce Cumings, *Korea's Place in the Sun* (New York: W. W. Norton & Company, 2005).

17. Bong-Youn Choy, *Koreans in America* (Chicago: Nelson-Hall, 1979).

18. Yonhap News Agency of Korea, "First Group of Korean-Americans Heads to North Korea for Family Reunion," *Yonhap News Agency of Korea*, May 17, 2007.

19. Audrey McAvoy, "Korean-Americans Seeking to Reunite with Family in North Korea," *The America's Intelligence Wire*, March 26, 2006, http://www.saemsori.org/press/2006-03/20060328-Hawaii-AP.htm.

20. Barbara Demick, "Korean Reunion Project Aimed at Americans: Many Don't Know Whether Relatives in the North Survived the War," *Los Angeles Times*, Feb. 9, 2006, http://articles.latimes.com/2006/feb/09/world/fg-families9.

21. Audrey McAvoy, "Korean-Americans Seeking to Reunite with Family in North Korea," *The America's Intelligence Wire*, March 28 2006, http://www.saemsori.org/press/2006-03/20060328-Hawaii-AP.htm.

22. Kate McLaughlin, "Journey to Freedom: Author Recounts North Korean Ancestors' Struggles in Hopes of Raising Awareness," *Daily Breeze*, Feb. 6, 2003.

23. "Korean Americans' Assistance to North Korea Tops $46 Million," *Korea Herald*, Feb. 7, 2001.

24. "Korean Americans in New York Aid North Korea Train Blast Victims," *Yonhap News Agency of Korea*, April 28, 2004.

25. "Seven N. Korean Asylum Seekers Arrive in U.S.," *Yonhap News Agency of Korea*, March 23, 2008.

26. Denny Lee, "In Search of a Delicate Balance, Koreans Clash Over an Antiwar Protest," *New York Times*, March 23, 2003, http://www.nytimes.com/2003/03/23/nyregion/neighborhood-report-chelsea-search-delicate-balance-koreans-clash-over-antiwar.html.

27. Jimmy Lee, Ki-Min Sung, Charse Yun, "All They are saying . . .," *KoreAm Journal*, January 2004.

28. Valerie Reitman, "Defecting from Despair: A Perilous Odyssey Aided by the Internet Gives N. Korean Refugees a Chance to Settle in the U.S." *Los Angeles Times*, Oct. 16, 2006, http://fairuse.100webcustomers.com/fuj/latimes96.htm.

29. K. Connie Kang, "Southlanders Join Capitol Hill Rally for Rights in North Korea," *Los Angeles Times*, April 28, 2004, http://articles.latimes.com/2004/apr/28/local/me-gulag28.

30. "US College Students Visited N. Korea to Teach English," *Yonhap News Agency of Korea*, July 24, 2008.

31. Bo Kyung Choi, Daniel Lim, and Jeffrey Mitchell, "The K Factor: Korean-American Attitudes Towards and Impact on U.S.-Korea Policy," Center for Strategic and International Studies, March 25, 2008.

FILIPINO WORLD WAR II VETERANS

Ben de Guzman

One of the recurring themes of any discussion concerning the Philippines and the United States is the "special relationship" between the two nations. As the first subject of the U.S. colonial imperial project, the Philippines has been inextricably intertwined with the United States since Admiral Dewey first sailed into Manila Harbor in 1898. The unequal power dynamic between the colonial "master" and "subject" has affected many aspects of Philippine culture and society; Filipino migration to the United States has re-enacted this dynamic in their new land. One of the longstanding examples of how this power imbalance has played itself out through the "special relationship" between the United States and the Philippines has been the unequal treatment of Filipino World War II veterans and their quest for treatment equitable to that of the other soldiers with whom they fought side by side. During the sixty-three years of this longstanding inequity, it has evolved from a specific issue for a relatively small group of aggrieved individuals and their advocates into the largest legislative campaign ever undertaken by the Filipino American community. This issue has also leveraged support from broader range of allies and supporters. With a recent victory that provides official recognition of the service of Filipino World War II veterans by the U.S. military as well as a monetary benefit, the campaign now takes a new turn.

During World War II, the proximity of Japan to the Philippines made it a strategically important location. At that time, the Philippines was in the process of transitioning from being a U.S. territory to being an independent nation, as set forth in the Tydings-McDuffie Act (PL 73-127), which governed procedures around military bases and personnel in the Philippines. Based on his authority through that act, on July 26, 1941, President Franklin D. Roosevelt called the

Philippine Commonwealth Army into service under the command of the newly formed United States Armed Forces of the Far East. In total, approximately 300,000 Filipinos fought in the Pacific theater during the war.[1]

Some of the most enduring images of the war anywhere come from the Philippines and the battles waged there. General Douglas MacArthur's iconic, "I Shall Return!" was uttered as he left the Philippines for a strategic retreat. The Bataan Death March, in which more than 75,000 American and Filipino soldiers were forcibly marched 90 miles in the tropical heat, continues to live in infamy. The Raid at Cabanatuan, in which five hundred soldiers were liberated from a Japanese prison camp, is called the most successful of its kind in U.S. military history.[2] These events are indelibly inked in the American psyche and are evidence of the key role played by the Philippines and the Filipinos who fought there in World War II.

After the war, the U.S. Congress took proactive steps against these very soldiers. On February 18, 1946, the First Supplemental Appropriations Rescission Act of 1946 (PL 79-301) struck the first blow, stating that these soldiers' service "shall not be deemed . . . active military, naval, or air service for the purposes of conferring rights, privileges, or benefits" (PL 79-301, sec. 107). A Second Supplementary Rescission Act (PL-79-391) further restricted access to U.S. veterans benefits for these soldiers. These acts were opposed by President Harry S. Truman. In a signing statement to the First Rescission Act, he wrote that despite this legislation, the U.S. government has a "moral obligation to provide for the heroic Philippine veterans who sacrificed so much for the common cause during the war."[3]

The U.S. Congress' passing of the 1946 Rescission Acts denied U.S. veteran status for these soldiers. In the years since, the U.S. Department of Veterans Affairs has reported disbursement of payments to veterans in sixty-six countries, both U.S. citizens and noncitizens, as well as dependents and spouses.[4] In essence, it is by virtue of the passage of the Rescission Acts that veterans from the Philippines were proactively singled out for unequal treatment and inequitable access to benefits based on service in the U.S. Armed Forces. The U.S. government took advantage of the changing status of the Philippines from U.S. territory to independent nation as an opportunity to remove them from the rosters of U.S. veterans. Ironically, the "special relationship" between the U.S. and the Philippines becomes the basis of and justification for the discriminatory treatment.

UNDERLYING FRAMEWORK FOR VETERANS CAMPAIGN

In the years since, Filipino World War II veterans and their advocates have fought for redress of what they perceive to be discriminatory treatment. For them, the quest for "full equity" means equal treatment for their service on par with other veterans who served under U.S. command during World War II.

Following the war, the struggle for equitable treatment of Filipino World War II veterans focused on eligibility for naturalization by virtue of military service. Despite passage of the wartime legislation that allowed for naturalization of noncitizens during wartime, efforts were made to discourage Filipino veterans from achieving U.S. citizen status. Court cases throughout the 1960s and 1970s went back and forth on the issue of naturalization for Filipino World War II veterans until the Supreme Court held in favor of the INS that the courts had no power to circumvent congressional limitations on citizenship.[5] This case, in effect, placed the equity struggle out of the purview of the judicial branch and into the legislative branch, where it has remained since.

Generally speaking, there are four groupings of Filipino World War II veterans, classifications on which benefits are based. These groupings refer to specific military units in which Filipinos served and are also determined in part by the time they joined.

1. Regular Philippine Scouts (also referred to as "Old Philippine Scouts"): Soldiers who enlisted as Philippine Scouts before October 6, 1945. These scouts were part of a regular component of the U.S. Army considered to be regular active service. Generally, they are entitled to all benefits administered by the Department of Veterans Affairs.
2. Commonwealth Army of the Philippines: Soldiers enlisted in the organized military forces of the Government of the Philippines per the Philippine Independence Act of 1934. They were called into service per the order of President Roosevelt on July 26, 1941.
3. Recognized Guerrilla Forces: Individuals who served in units recognized by the U.S. Armed forces during the Japanese occupation. After the war, they became part of the Commonwealth Army of the Philippines.
4. New Philippine Scouts: These Philippine citizens served with the U.S. Armed Forces between October 6, 1945, and June 30, 1947. They served through the Armed Forces Voluntary Recruitment Act of 1945 (PL 79-190) and were primarily involved in "mop-up" work in Japan and the Pacific theater.[6]

These categories and the Filipinos' pursuit of full equity have evolved over the years. The categories have achieved a number of adjustments to eligibility for benefits and access to services for Filipino World War II veterans, and in general, these adjustments have increased access to benefits and services for Filipino World War II veterans.

EVOLVING EQUITY STRUGGLE

If the basis of the quest for full equity lies in the power imbalance of the "special relationship" between the United States and the Philippines, it is perhaps no mistake that the Filipino American community's emerging political clout has coincided with progress of the Filipino World War II Equity campaign. The signing of the 1990 Immigration and Naturalization Act (PL 101-649) and subsequent influx of immigration by Filipino veterans to the United States was originally perceived to be a legislative victory. By 1998, about 20,000 Filipino veterans had naturalized and 17,000 came to the United States.[7] Upon their arrival, however, it quickly became evident that in some ways their problems had only increased. As citizens, they were eligible for certain benefits such as Medicare and Social Security; however, they continued to be denied status as U.S. veterans and remained largely ineligible for programs administered by the U.S. Department of Veterans Affairs. The unsuccessful efforts to achieve equity through the judicial system moved veterans and advocates to more fully pursue redress through the legislative process.

The equity campaign hit full stride in the mid- to late 1990s, when it became a signature issue for emerging national networks of Filipino Americans. The movement for Veterans' Equity became national in scope through efforts of groups such as the National Network for Veterans Equity (NNVE) and the American Coalition of Filipino Veterans (ACFV). These organizations and networks emerged from the work of the veterans themselves and of the locally based organizations and agencies that served them.

Perhaps the main impetus for the exponential growth the movement experienced in this time is the evolution of the issue beyond the immediate scope of the veterans and their direct advocates. At this stage of the campaign, the Filipino American community as a whole began to embrace the Filipino World War II Veterans Equity struggle and positioned it as a key priority issue. This coincided with the emergence of national Filipino American networks that took on broader sets of issues, including that of the veterans. Filipino Civil Rights Advocates (FilCRA) was formed in 1994 and at national conventions in 1994 and 1997, the Veterans Equity Campaign was discussed. In 1997, the National Federation of Filipino American Associations (NaFFAA) was formed and positioned itself as an "umbrella group" for Filipino American organizations of all types around the country. At its Founding Convention, the Filipino World War II veterans campaign emerged as its top legislative priority and has been a key area of concern for the organization since.

By moving the issue beyond the scope of the veterans themselves and positioning it as a self-consciously unifying issue that all Filipino Americans could ostensibly support, the campaign was better able to leverage the resources of the entire community to the effort. This move toward unanimity has experienced its own ups and downs, and in many ways has served as the Filipino American community's version of the internal dialogues that all advocacy campaigns have around strategies and tactics. For the Filipino veterans, this dialogue generally revolved around the notions of "piecemeal" versus "full equity" approaches during this time. Advocates of a more piecemeal approach argued that it was more realistic to pursue incremental advances in the struggle for equitable treatment of Filipino World War II veterans and that other strategies were unrealistic "all or nothing" gambits. Supporters of full equity, on the other hand, maintained that it was necessary to articulate their perceived goals of full and equitable treatment of Filipino World War II veterans and eschewed strategies that favored watering down these goals.

These at times conflicting strategies have played a role in the introduction of a multiplicity of pieces of legislation in the U.S. Congress since the late 1990s. While bills providing for full equity for Filipino World War II veterans have been introduced in every Congress since 1990, bills containing smaller, more limited provisions for Filipino veterans have also moved. With different bills covering varying ranges of benefits, it muddied the waters and made a more coherent legislative strategy more difficult. Thus, for almost twenty years, these bills languished in Congress, with only limited fixes able to pass. The progress until this point only served to create a web of eligibilities and benefits structures for Filipino WII veterans based on a variety of variables, including military unit of service, citizenship and health status or nature of war-related injuries.[8]

POLITICS AND PROGRESS

This issue has come to a head in recent years. After almost twenty years of piecemeal achievements for the veterans and little to no progress in the underlying question of full and equitable status for Filipino World War II veterans, legislation restoring U.S. veteran status to these veterans experienced exponential progress starting with the 110th Congress. The Democratic takeover of the Congress in 2006 laid the groundwork for this progress, when many of the key champions for this legislation rose from minority status to leadership positions in key committees. The House Veterans Affairs Committee became chaired by Bob Filner (D-CA) who had been involved with this issue since his arrival to Congress in 1993, and Senator Daniel Akaka (D-HI), whose home state of Hawai'i is home to a large Filipino American population, became chairman of the Senate Veterans Affairs Committee. These champions were aided by members of the House and Senate on both sides of the aisle.

With a coordinated, national campaign from the community and unprecedented levels of support from the Congress, Filipino World War II veterans legislation moved quickly and was voted out of the House and Senate Veterans Affairs Committees. Despite opposition from Senate Veterans Affairs Ranking Member Larry Craig (R-ID), until scandal removed him from his leadership post, and then Senator Richard Burr (R-NC), the Senate voted down an unfriendly amendment 56 to 41 and took an historic and resounding 96-1 vote in favor of Filipino World War II veterans equity legislation. Unfortunately, opposition in the House led by Veterans Affairs Ranking Member Steve Buyer (R-IN) was able to block a floor vote and wait out the clock until Congress convened in the fall of 2008. In the closing days of the 110th Congress, Senator Inouye worked with Congressman Bob Filner to lay the groundwork for the 111th Congress by appropriating a $198 million Filipino World War II Veterans Compensation Fund.

Increased majorities in the House and Senate after the 2008 elections, along with the election of President Barack Obama (who had cosponsored the Senate bill when he was a member of the Veterans Affairs Committee) brought momentum into the 111th Congress. Senator Inouye moved forcefully to include Filipino World War II veterans legislation in the economic stimulus package, which was the first moving bill in the new Congress. The bill authorized spending the Filipino World War II Veterans Compensation Fund they had created in the previous Congress in the amount of $15,000 for U.S. citizen veterans and $9,000 for noncitizens. On February 13, 2008, the Congress finally passed Filipino World War II veterans legislation that provides a payment to Filipino World War II veterans and recognizes their service by the U.S. military. In a moment ripe with symbolic meaning for the Filipino American community, President Barack Obama signed this bill into law on February 17, 2008, one day shy of the sixty-third anniversary of the 1946 Rescission Act that took away their status in the first place.

FILIPINO AMERICANS FINDING THEIR PLACE

One of the notable advancements of the Filipino Veterans Equity movement starting in the 110th Congress has been the more direct engagement of allied, non-Filipino communities and organizations in coalition-building efforts. While such groups have always shown support, strategies in the 110th Congress intentionally included efforts to garner direct support and partnership of other communities. In December of 2006, the Philippine Embassy convened all the currently existing organizations leading the efforts on the Filipino veterans' campaign to plot strategy for the 110th Congress, resulting in the establishment of the National Alliance for Filipino Veterans Equity (NAFVE). NAFVE's leadership structure leveraged its relationships with Asian Pacific American and civil rights organizations to bring them on board. Organizations such as the National Council of Asian Pacific Americans—the leading coalition of national Asian Pacific American organizations—and its members issued letters of support and actively participated in the campaign. Several leading national civil rights and Latino organizations issued a letter of support calling for Filipino World War II veterans legislation as well.

Veterans Service Organization (VSOs) also played a key role in the campaign. Initially, several key VSOs actively supported passage of this legislation. The American Legion, one of the nation's largest veterans' groups, testified in support of the bill and included it in its list of legislative priorities for 2007. Other VSOs also lined up in support. Unfortunately, the budget offset to pay for the bill proved to be a challenge for VSOs. The offset was presented by the opposition in the House as a wedge that would take money away from old, disabled veterans in the United States and send it abroad. Despite efforts by the bill's champions, including a public statement by Senator Daniel Akaka to clarify the offset, some VSOs backed off.[9] The American Legion stated that while they support Filipino World War II veterans legislation, they were opposed to the budget offset. Other VSOs, most notably Vietnam Veterans of America (VVA), Jewish War Veterans, and Catholic War Veterans, continued to support the bill and raised concerns that the opposition to the offset was not based on substantive issues related to the bill, but on procedural matters.

Jose V. Juachon wears his favorite military cap, adorned with medals from the U.S. and Philippine governments, at his home in Chicago, 2005. The eighty-six-year-old veteran was inducted into the U.S. Armed Forces in 1941, when his country was under American control and the United Stated promised Filipino fighters the same benefits as American soldiers in return for their service. (AP Photo/Nam Y. Huh)

During the 2008 election year, Filipino Americans and Asian Pacific Americans made this issue a key component in its political and civic engagement work. Along with broader issues such as immigration and education, the Filipino World War II veterans issue was the highest profile ethnic specific issue discussed in Asian Pacific American political discussions.[10] With the passage of Filipino World War II veterans legislation, the journey of these veterans takes a new turn. While by and large, the Filipino American community recognizes the magnitude of the victory this bill represents, many recognize the limitations of the legislation. Since the bill's passage, advocates in the short term are focused on implementation and making sure that every eligible veteran is able to take advantage of the benefit they have secured. In the long run, advocates will face larger questions of how they can turn the political capital won by this battle into more legislative victories not just for veterans specifically, but on the broader set of issues of concern for all Filipino Americans.

FURTHER READING

American Coalition for Filipino Veterans. http://usfilvets.tripod.com/.
APIA Vote YouTube Video Clips from Presidential Town Hall. http://www.apiavote.org/newsroom/press-releases/2008/historic-presidential-town-hall-availabl.

Filipinos for Affirmative Action (FAA). http://www.filipinos4action.org.

House Veterans Affairs Committee (HCVA) 1998. Hearings on Benefits for Filipino Veterans. Serial No. 105-44.

National Alliance for Filipino Veterans Equity (NAFVE). http://www.nafve.org.

Panangala, Sidath Viranga, Christine Scott, and Carol D. Davis. "Overview of Filipino Veterans' Benefits." Congressional Research Service (CRS). Updated Oct. 10, 2008.

San Francisco Veterans Equity Center (VEC). http://home.att.net/~smpch/index.html.

Sides, Hampton. *Ghost Soldiers: The Forgotten Epic Story of World War II's Most Dramatic Mission*. New York: Doubleday, 2001.

Vergara, Vanessa. "Broken Promises and Aging Patriots: An Assessment of US Veteran Benefits Policy for Filipino World War II Veterans." *Asian American Policy Review* VII (1997): 163–182.

NOTES

1. Vanessa Vergara, "Broken Promises and Aging Patriots: An Assessment of US Veteran Benefits Policy for Filipino World War II Veterans," *Asian American Policy Review* VII (1997): 163.

2. Hampton Sides, *Ghost Soldiers: The Forgotten Epic Story of World War II's Most Dramatic Mission* (New York: Doubleday, 2001).

3. Harry Truman, *Public Papers of the Presidents of the United States, Harry S. Truman, Containing the Public Messages, Speeches, and Statements of the President*, vol. 2 (Washington, DC, Government Printing Office, 1962).

4. U.S. Department of Veterans Affairs, *1967 Annual Report of the Administrator of Veterans Affairs,* (Washington, DC: Government Printing Office, 1968), 122. cited in Vergara, p. 171.

5. *INS v. Pangilinan,* 486 U.S. 875 (1988).

6. Sidath Viranga Panangala et al., *Overview of Filipino Veterans' Benefits* (Congressional Research Service: Updated October 10, 2008), 1–2.

7. House Veterans Affairs Committee (HCVA) 1998, *Hearings on Benefits for Filipino Veterans,* Serial No. 105-44.

8. Panangala et al., *Overview of Filipino Veterans' Benefits,* 12.

9. U.S. Senate Committee on Veterans' Affairs Press Release, http://veterans.senate.gov/public/index.cfm?pageid=12&release_id=11734.

10. APIA Vote YouTube Video Clips from Presidential Town Hall, http://www.apiavote.org/newsroom/press-releases/2008/historic-presidential-town-hall-available.

HMONG AND LAO AMERICAN VIETNAM VETERANS

Davorn Sisavath

The United States entered the war in Vietnam as part of the Cold War containment strategy and to prevent a communist takeover of South Vietnam. The Vietnam War was highly publicized, but the "Secret War" in Laos (1961–1973) was a clandestine operation. The U.S. government feared that if Laos fell to communism, it would create a domino effect on other Southeast Asian countries.[1] Without direct military involvement, the U.S. Central Intelligence Agency hired local Hmong and Lao to support U.S. interests in the war. Despite these aids, the United States' failure to achieve its objective in Vietnam and Laos had a major impact on U.S. politics and foreign relations. After several decades and only in the late 1990s, the U.S. government finally acknowledged its involvement in Laos. In 1997, national recognition was bestowed upon the Lao Veterans of America by members of Congress, and by representatives of the U.S. intelligence, military and diplomat communities. On October 10, 2002, under the House Concurrent Resolution 406, the House of Representatives honored and commended the Lao Veterans of America, Lao and Hmong veterans of the Vietnam War, and the families of the Lao and Hmong veterans.[2] This was an important signal for Lao and Hmong veterans because they have fought for a long time to be recognized and honored. The end of the Vietnam War changed and diversified the demographics of the Asian American population because it brought an influx of refugees to the United States from Vietnam, Laos, and Cambodia. With this influx, it has also reshaped the concept of a monolithic Asian American community and raised awareness of contemporary issues surrounding immigration laws, welfare policy reforms, mental health, and the myth of the model minority.

LAOTIAN CIVIL WAR

After Laos gained independence in 1953 through the Franco-Lao Treaty, the United States feared the spread of communism and, therefore, conducted a covert operation in the country during the Vietnam War. From 1960 through 1975, the Central Intelligence Agency and the U.S. Armed Forces recruited, organized, trained, and assisted more than 30,000 Hmong and Lao guerrilla units known collectively as the Special Guerrilla Unit. The unit was also composed of Khmu, Mien, Lahu, and other diverse ethnic groups. Under the command of Royal Lao Army General Vang Pao, a Hmong military leader, the guerrilla units were used to block the Ho Chi Minh Trail, which was the main military supply route for the North Vietnamese army. Lao and Hmong veterans risked their lives to block the supply line and to rescue American pilots and aircrews who were shot down over Laos and North Vietnam. They also blocked and helped to destroy enemy units. By 1969, Lao and Hmong veterans had already fought for more than twelve years in the Secret War. It was in 1970 that the war in Laos became public to the Americans; however, the United States continued to deny any involvement because it would have meant admitting it had broken the signed agreement at the Geneva Conference in 1962, which called for the neutrality of Laos. In 1973, the Paris Peace Accord was signed that stipulated the United States was to pull out of Laos; however, under the treaty, North Vietnam was not required to remove its forces.[3] This forced Laos' national government to accept the communist Pathet Lao regime into the government because Vietnamese and Pathet Lao forces attacked the government. An agreement was then signed that gave power to the Pathet Lao in order to save the government from destruction. Once in power, the Pathet Lao cut all economic ties with its neighbors. Many members of the Lao and Hmong guerrilla units and their families who were trapped in Laos were persecuted, imprisoned, or killed because of their roles during the Secret War. It is estimated that more than 40,000 Hmong and Lao were killed and many more are missing in action, injured, or disabled.[4] Although many Hmongs and Laotians have found new homes in the United States, some of their family members remain stranded in their home country and in refugee camps. Consequently, a multinational tie has been strengthened within the Southeast Asian and Asian American communities in Asia. This connection has led to strong political and cultural ties to Asia and creating a bridge between Asian Americans and Asians.

IMMIGRATION TO THE UNITED STATES

After the communist Pathet Lao regime took over the country in 1975, more than 300,000 Hmongs and Laotians fled the country to refugee camps in Thailand in fear of retaliation and persecution. Their immigration to and resettlement in the United States were facilitated by the following acts: Indochina Migration and Refugee Assistance Act (1975), Refugee Act (1980), Immigrant Reform and Control Act (1986), and Immigration Act (1990). In 1976, the first wave of immigrants was primarily made up of individuals directly associated with Vang Pao's guerilla units. The second-wave of Hmong and Lao immigration to the United States began in 1980 with the passage of the Refugee Act. For humanitarian reasons, family members of members of the Special Guerrilla Unit were permitted to immigrate into the United States, as were other refugees from Southeast Asia. Specifically, Hmongs and Laotians were unable to return to Laos because of fear of persecution from the communist Pathet Lao government. Despite the federal government's plan to widely disperse Southeast Asian refugees throughout the fifty states, many refugees have resettled in California (137,000), Minnesota (57,000), and Wisconsin (42,000).[5] In California, the presence of a Southeast Asian community, sponsoring relatives, and tropical climate made the transition less difficult. The United States is home to significant communities of Lao and Hmong veterans and their families.

Southeast Asians have played a significant role in refocusing attention on Asian American issues, especially across racial and class lines. Their impact is not limited to demographic statistics; Southeast Asian Americans have reshaped how Asian Americans are perceived by others and themselves. Many Southeast Asian refugees are undereducated and live below the poverty line, which counters the model minority myth and how most Asian Americans perceive themselves. This has led Asian American leaders and Asian American communities to work with each other to address issues of poverty, mental illness, crime, and education. For example, the impact on this community of the Welfare Reform Act in 1996, also known as the Personal Responsibility and Work Opportunity Reconciliation Act, brought Asian Americans together to work and act as a cohesive group.

LAO VETERANS OF AMERICA

After a decade of resettling in the United States, the Lao Veterans of America, a nonprofit veteran organization headquartered in Fresno, CA, was established in 1990 to honor and assist Lao and Hmong veterans who served or assisted the U.S. Armed Forces during the Vietnam War. The organization has chapters throughout the United States such as in California, Hawai'i, Minnesota, North Carolina, Washington, Wisconsin, and many other states. Its objectives are to serve the Lao and Hmong communities and to educate the public about the historic contribution made by Lao and Hmong veterans during the Vietnam War. According to the organization, it is estimated that there are about 12,000 Lao and Hmong veterans in the United States. The organization also led national efforts to lobby Congress to provide citizenship for elderly Lao and Hmong veterans, their spouses or widows.

LAOS MEMORIAL

On May 15, 1997, the Laos Memorial was dedicated in the Arlington National Cemetery in Arlington, VA. The memorial was approved by the U.S. Department of Defense but fully paid for by Lao and Hmong veterans. The commemoration of the memorial represented the first time the U.S. government officially and publicly recognized the contributions of Hmong and Lao veterans who fought alongside the United States during the Vietnam War. The following words appear on the Laos Memorial:[6]

> Dedicated To The U.S. Secret Army In The Kingdom Of Laos (1961–1973)
> In Memory Of the Hmong And Lao Combat Veterans And Their American Advisors Who Served Freedom's Cause In Southeast Asia. Their Patriotic Valor And Loyalty In The Defense Of Liberty And Democracy Will Never Be Forgotten
> YOV TSHU TXOG NEJ MUS IB TXHIS
> LAOS VETERANS OF AMERICA
> May 15, 1997

The Laos Memorial is located on the grounds of the Arlington Cemetery between the John F. Kennedy Eternal Flame and the Tomb of the Unknown Soldier.

Other memorials include the Lao Hmong American War Memorial in Fresno, CA, which was unveiled in December 2005. The memorial stands 16 feet tall and weighs 14 tons. It depicts heroic Hmong and Lao veterans coming to the aid of a downed American military pilot in Laos. In Wisconsin, where more than 42,000 Hmong and Lao reside, the Lao, Hmong and American Veterans Memorial is commemorated in Sheboygan. The circular memorial is 44 feet in diameter and made of black granite, and it tells the story of Hmong and Lao veterans who fought in the Secret War. In addition, the granite panels bear the names of the hundreds of soldiers who fought in the war.

BILLS PASSED

On May 26, 2000, the Hmong Veterans' Naturalization Act of 2000 became law. The law provides an exemption from the English language requirement and special consideration for civics testing for certain refugees from Laos applying for naturalization. It does, however, place a cap: the benefit is limited to no more than 45,000 eligible refugees from Laos applying for naturalization.[7] Furthermore, in 2001, Congress passed a resolution honoring and commending the Lao Veterans of America, Laotian and Hmong veterans of the Vietnam War, and their families, for their contributions to the United States during the Vietnam War. In California, Assembly Bill AB 78 was approved. The Bill's purpose is to introduce the "Secret War" (1961–1973) in Laos as a part of the curriculum in social sciences or in history at California public schools.

OUTLOOK

The outlook is bright for Lao and Hmong veterans as they are being increasingly recognized and honored. Organizations in local communities have formed to assist the veterans, and the public has taken interest to learn about their contribution to the U.S. government during the Vietnam War. For Lao and Hmong veterans who have recently immigrated to the United States, their transition to American culture is assisted by the abundance of social services provided throughout various communities. These services were created by Lao and Hmong who had immigrated as refugees in the late 1970s and early 1980s, by religious organizations, and by local and national governments. Many continue to suffer, however, from mental health issues related to the war. Studies have shown many refugees living in the United States have symptoms of post-traumatic stress disorder and depression after their exposure to war trauma. The trauma they live with affects their health mentally and physically; elders are at the highest risk. As human assistance and social services have become increasingly accessible, many Southeast Asian refugees have become more willing to seek and receive medical help. Lastly, for the younger generation, the legacy of the Secret War is their continued struggle for recognition. Their adaptation to United States' society means their social roles and values are evolving. Their contributions as productive citizens have brought awareness to a diversity of Asian American communities in transition.

FURTHER READING

Hamilton-Merritt, Jane. *Tragic Mountains: The Hmong, the Americans, and the Secret Wars for Laos, 1942–1992.* Bloomington: Indiana University Press, 1993.

Hmong National Development. http://www.hndinc.org.

Lao Veterans of America. http://www.laoveterans.com.

Minnesota Lao Veterans of America. (MLVA). http://minnesotalaoveteransofamerica.org.

Morrison, Gayle. *Sky is falling: An oral history of the CIA's evacuation of the Hmong from Laos.* Jefferson, NC: McFarland & Company, 1999.

Quincy, Keith. *Harvesting Pa Chay's Wheat: The Hmong and America's Secret War in Laos.* Spokane: Eastern Washington University Press, 2000.

NOTES

1. Arthur J. Dommen, *Conflict in Laos: The Policy of Neutralization* (New York: Praeger, 1065).

2. *U.S. Government Printing Office, 107th Congress, 2D Session,* http://frwebgate .access.gpo.gov/cgi-bin/getdoc.cgi?dbname=107_cong_bills&docid=f:hc406ih.txt .pdf, accessed 02 December 2008.

3. Joshua Castellino, "The Hmong Struggle in Laos: Freedom Fighters or Terrorists?" American Chronicle, posted June 8, 2007, http://www.americanchronicle.com/articles/ 29164.

4. Paris Peace Accords, http://www.aiipowmia.com/sea/ppa1973.html, accessed Dec. 3, 2008.

5. Southeast Asia Resource Action Center, "Southeast Asian American Statistical Profile 2004," http://www.searac.org/seastatprofilemay04.pdf.

6. Laos Memorial Arlington National Cemetery, http://www.arlingtoncemetery.net/ laosmem.htm (accessed Dec. 2, 2008).

7. U.S. Department of Justice, "'Hmong Veterans' Naturalization Act of 2000," Immigration and Naturalization Service, http://www.uscis.gov/propub/ProPubVAP.jsp ?dockey=2aae2d001699aac96aa3f0f5c5c732a1 (accessed Dec. 3, 2008).

THE IRAQ WAR

Wei Ming Dariotis, Wesley Ueunten, and Kathy Masaoka

The U.S.-Iraq War started on March 20, 2003, when the U.S. military invaded Iraq under the pretext of searching for weapons of mass destruction and under the assumption that Iraqi President Saddam Hussein was harboring members of al-Qaeda, the terrorist group responsible for the attacks on the World Trade Center of September 11, 2001. Eventually, no weapons of mass destruction were found.

However, thousands of Americans have been serving in this war. Many Asian Americans serve in the U.S. military at every rank, as well as those who are veterans and casualties of the Iraq War. About sixty-four Asian Americans have died during service in the Iraq War, comprising about 1.55 percent of those killed as of February 2009.[1] This number is difficult to calculate, however, particularly given the fifty-nine deaths attributed as "multiple races, pending, or unknown" and the large percentage of mixed race Asian Americans in this age range. Many more Asian Americans are still serving in the military and many others have returned as veterans and are reintegrating into U.S. society. There are also some individual Asian American members of the U.S. military who have dedicated themselves to protesting against the war, as well as Asian American groups that have organized antiwar activities.

ISSUES FOR ASIAN AMERICAN VETERANS OF THE IRAQ WAR

The public account of issues faced by Asian American veterans returning from Iraq remains limited. This may reflect the positive image of Asian American military service that overshadows those issues, yet there is the ongoing invisibility of Asian American veterans.

Joining the ranks of those who served valiantly before them, many Asian American Iraq War veterans generally receive heroes' welcomes and recognition for their military service. Many Asian American veterans point out the positive aspects of military service. For example, Matthew Inchun Briaiotta, despite being badly wounded in Iraq, credits his military experience with giving his life direction and purpose.[2]

Even when reporting difficulties that Asian American Iraq War veterans face in transitioning back to civilian life, the issue of being Asian American is downplayed. For some, the issues are similar to those experienced by veterans—of any race—of the Vietnam War: the war in Iraq has become very unpopular, and there is a great deal of public censure about the war. Others are just struggling because veterans' benefits have dwindled in the face of inflation and a poor economy. For example, Thomas Sim, a twenty-four-year-old Korean American senior at the University of California–Irvine, has been facing the difficult task of transitioning back into civilian life after serving in the Iraq war. One difficulty has been the limited provisions of the GI Bill, which pays at most $9,600 per year for college, even though the average cost of a public university runs more than $16,000 per year.[3]

Thai American Iraq War veteran Tammy Duckworth, director of the Illinois Department of Veterans Affairs and former Democratic candidate for Congress, lost both her legs in November 2004, when the Blackhawk helicopter she was copiloting was struck by a rocket-propelled grenade. Duckworth, who identifies as an Asian American, as well as being both a daughter of the American Revolution and the daughter of an immigrant, spoke before the 2008 Democratic National Convention to argue against the Bush Administration's decision to fight the war in Iraq. She argued that the U.S. military should focus on Afghanistan rather than Iraq. She has also been a strong advocate for veterans' care through the Veterans' Administration, of which she notes returning wounded veterans are faced with many obstacles in attaining service and benefits. Duckworth is one of many Asian American veterans who has been disillusioned by the war in Iraq.[4]

While Asian Americans serving in the military have had experiences particular to being Asian American in the post-9/11 period, particularly racism, a hopeful attitude regarding the acceptance of Asian American veterans as "American" is evident. An article about a meeting of Chinatown's American Legion Post 1291 in New York describes the anti-Asian racism that Chinese veterans faced in the military in earlier wars, but quotes Kingston Lam, a twenty-eight-year-old veteran of the Iraq War, as saying that his Chinese American identity was not a factor in his military experience. Lam says that being an American soldier is primary during his service in Iraq—he feels his uniform overrides his ethnicity.[5]

ASIAN AMERICAN ORGANIZATIONS RESPONDING TO WAR

Across the country, Asian American community organizations have responded to the war by organizing events, programs, marches, and educational forums. Asian and Pacific Islanders for Community Empowerment (APIFORCE), an

Oakland, CA–based organization, was part of the larger coalition called Southeast Asian Freedom Network (SEAFN), which is a national campaign to stop the deportation of Southeast Asians in the post-9/11 period. An intergenerational alliance of people of Taiwanese, Chinese and Hong Kong heritage, Moving Forward for Peace (CJWP, *Chin Jurn Wor Ping/Chien Jin He Ping*) works in the San Francisco Bay Area for peace and social justice, which they interpret as ranging from local issues like housing rights to global issues such as the Iraq War, engaged from a specifically Chinese American perspective. The Alliance of South Asians Taking Action (ASATA) educates, organizes, and empowers Bay Area South Asian American communities to end violence, oppression, racism, and exploitation. ASATA is a member of the United Response Collaborative, which formed to address the backlash of anti-Asian hate, violence, and discrimination that surfaced after 9/11, specifically targeting South Asian Americans. Also in the Bay Area, Filipino Coalition for Global Justice, Not War (FilsGLOBE) facilitates educational discussions on issues related to U.S. militarism, especially related to the continuing presence of the U.S. military in the Philippines, but also related to the Iraq War. Filipinos for Global Justice, Not War is a coalition of organizations and individuals that brings the Filipino community together to call for an end to the cycle of violence brought on by retaliatory war, racism, and state repression. Member organizations include: Committee for Human Rights in the Philippines, Filipinos for Affirmative Action, Filipino Left Network, Gabriela Network/SF Bay Area, Lakas Diwa Kapatid, League of Filipino Students, Philip Vera Cruz Justice Project, PEACE/City College, Solid Thoughts, 8th Wonder, and Kappa Psi Epsilon.

The organization Korean Americans Against War and Neoliberalism (KAAWAN) is a coalition group working with approximately 280 national groups in Korea that was organized in opposition to free trade talks between South Korea and the United States and against war.

In New York City, Organizing Asian Communities, also known as Committee Against Anti-Asian Violence (CAAAV), was founded in 1986 to mobilize Asian American communities to counter anti-Asian violence. CAAAV organizes diverse poor Asian communities in New York City to develop self-determination, and this has involved antiwar activism. Desis Rising Up and Moving (DRUM) is an organization of South Asian immigrants in New York City, including people of South Asian descent, to identify as people from Afghanistan, Bangladesh, Bhutan, India, Nepal, Pakistan, Sri Lanka, and parts of the diaspora, including Africa, England, Fiji, Guyana, and Trinidad. Founded in 2000, DRUM organizes for immigrant rights, racial, economic, and social justice, including legalization for immigrants and ending deportation policies. DRUM views justice for immigrants in the United States as it relates to foreign policy issues, such as the Iraq War. Boston's Asian American Resource Workshop (AARW) promotes community, identity, and social justice through education, advocacy, and arts and culture. In addition to cultural activities, the Asian American Resource Workshop advocates for an end to the Iraq War.

Like these other organizations, Nikkei for Civil Rights and Redress (NCRR) has developed a strong antiwar stance, which is, in this case, especially

connected to the history of Japanese Americans and that community's memories of World War II. As during that war, the war in Iraq has been a locus for
debates within Asian American communities about what it means to be truly
"American." One side argues that to be "American" means to be loyal to the
U.S. government and especially to show that loyalty through military service.
Another side argues that the ultimate demonstration of "Americanness" is to
question the government through the processes of free speech and to protest
against military actions that are deemed to be unjustified. NCRR was formed in
1980 during the struggle for redress for Japanese Americans interned during
World War II. NCRR was a major force in pushing for the passage of the Civil
Liberties Act of 1988, which gave redress and an apology to former Japanese
American interns. NCRR organized a contingent in the early marches against
the war and joined with other Asian Pacific Islander organizations to build
opposition to the war.

As concern for Asian American civil liberties increased, so too did concern
regarding the continued abuses of military prisoners and the innocent people of
Iraq. In October 2005, the NCCR September 11 Committee organized a week-
long speaking tour for Chaplain James Yee, the Chinese American Muslim who
had been charged with spying and possession of pornography after serving at
Guantanamo Bay, Cuba. His duties were not only to minister to the religious
needs of the detainees but also to recommend changes that would help the
prison run more smoothly. He worked with the high command, including Major
General Geoffrey Miller of Abu Ghraib fame, and was given high evaluations,
yet he was charged with espionage and thrown into prison for seventy-six days.
Eventually all the charges were dropped but his military career was destroyed.
Chaplain Yee spoke on college campuses and to an overflow crowd in Little
Tokyo, which learned about the abuses at Guantanamo and the fact that many
of these prisoners had committed no crimes yet were being held without the
right to an attorney or a trial.

Lt. Ehren Watada, a commissioned officer and a mixed Japanese and Chinese
American, had refused to go to Iraq because he believed that the war was illegal
and immoral. Charged with missing a movement and conduct unbecoming an
officer, Watada faces up to eight years in prison and a dishonorable discharge.
A Southern California speaking tour for Lt. Watada's father and stepmother,
Bob Watada and Rosa Sakanishi, was organized by NCRR and the Asian
American Vietnam Veterans Organization, which, composed of former Vietnam
veterans and their families, opposes the U.S. government's policies in Iraq but
supports unconditionally the fighting men and women stationed in Iraq.
Japanese American and Asian American activists and organizations, including
Nikkei for Civil Rights and Redress, continued to build support for Watada by
circulating petitions, setting up tables for letter writing in Little Tokyo, and
organizing an educational program about the effect of the war on Iraqi veterans.
At this program, Helga Aguayo eloquently explained how her husband, a
Filipino American medic, had served in Iraq but could no longer participate in
the war in good conscience. In preparation for the court martial of Watada in

February 2007, NCRR and AAVV organized the largest march of youth, Nisei, Latino, and Asian Americans in Little Tokyo since the 1970s. With Helga Aguayo and Carolyn Ho, Ehren Watada's mother, in the lead, the marchers chanted "Drop the Charges Now" and "Free Aguayo" all the way to Higashi Hongwanji Temple.

As of February 2008, Lt. Ehren Watada was awaiting a second court martial under the objection of his attorneys who argue that this constitutes "double jeopardy" or trying a person twice for the same offense. NCRR and the Asian American Vietnam Veterans Organization continue to support Watada with weekly vigils in Little Tokyo and a petition calling for the military to drop the charges against him and for the district courts to uphold his Fifth Amendment protections against "double jeopardy." This coalition and many of Watada's other supporters also oppose any retrial for Watada and any persecution of other military war resisters. After news of renditions and torture, and with almost 4,000 U.S. soldiers killed and more than 1 million Iraqis dead, the majority of the United States population, including a significant portion of the Asian American population, now agrees that this war is immoral and illegal, or at the very least ill-advised.

CONTRIBUTIONS OF ASIAN AMERICANS AND THE IRAQ WAR

Exemplary Asian American military service in the Iraq War follows a tradition of Asian American contributions to earlier wars. For example, Lt. Gen. Eric Shinseki, a Japanese American from Hawai'i, is the highest-ranking Asian American in the active military, and Major Gen. Edward Soriano, a Filipino American is the second-highest-ranking Asian American on active duty. Soriano is director of operations, readiness, and mobilization at the Office of the Deputy Chief of Staff for Operations and Plans, and he is responsible for the mobilization of U.S. forces in Haiti, Bosnia, Somalia, Europe, and the United States. Soriano is a veteran of the Gulf War, and his work demonstrates the drive and loyalty of Asian Americans serving in the U.S. military during the era of the Iraq War.[6] These contributions are an important part of the Asian American story—then and now. Asian American responses to the Iraq War also highlight the diversity of Asian American communities. Service to the United States through the military continues to be an important part of the Asian American experience, as does grassroots, antiwar activism. Consequently, not only have Asian Americans defined themselves as American through acts of perceived loyalty to the U.S. government, but also by being willing to challenge the United States' record on domestic and international human rights. As the Iraq War continues, Asian Americans will continue to have complex, diverse reactions, including serving in the military and protesting against the war.

FURTHER READING

Leong, Russell C. *World, War, Watada* (Los Angeles: *Amerasia Journal,* UCLA Asian American Studies Center, 2007).

Nikkei for Civil Rights and Redress (NCRR).http://www.ncrr-la.org/.

Thank You Lt. Ehren Watada Web site. http://www.thankyoult.org/.

Yee, James. *For God and Country: Faith and Patriotism Under Fire*. New York: Public Affairs, 2005.

NOTES

1. iCasulaties.org, "Iraq Coalition Casualty Report," http://icasualties.org/oif/Ethnicity.aspx.

2. The Library of Congress, "Matthew Inchun Braiotta: Veterans History Project," http://lcweb2.loc.gov/diglib/vhp-stories/loc.natlib.afc2001001.43113/.

3. Thomas Sim and Alex Cohen, "Making the Transition from Serviceman to Student," Day to Day: NPR, http://www.npr.org/templates/story/story.php?storyId=88402838.

4. Hokubei.com, "Asian American Veteran of Iraq War Addresses DNC," http://www.hokubei.com/en/news/2008/08/Asian-American-Veteran-Iraq-War-Addresses-DNC.

5. Victoria Moy, "Chinese Vets Reflect on Iraq, Racism and Serving 2 Cultures," *Downtown Express*, http://www.downtownexpress.com/de_251/chinesevets.html.

6. Bert Eljera, "Joining the Highest-Ranking APAs in Active-Duty Military Service," *AsianWeek*, http://www.asianweek.com/082297/newsmaker.html.

JAPANESE LATIN AMERICAN REDRESS FOR WORLD WAR II INTERNMENT

Grace Shimizu and Wesley Ueunten

The passage of the Civil Liberties Act of 1988 by the U.S. Congress was a historic achievement in the struggle of Japanese Americans for redress of government violations during World War II. This hard-fought legislation established a ten-year redress program whereby the majority of former internees of Japanese ancestry, both U.S. citizens and legal permanent residents, received an apology letter and symbolic compensation, and a public education fund was created. The U.S. Office of Redress Administration denied redress to internees of Japanese ancestry abducted from Latin America. The struggle for government accountability for constitutional and human rights violations in the name of "national security" during World War II continues today and has gained additional relevance in the aftermath of the 9/11 tragedies.

It is not well known that the World War II incarceration of "nonaliens" (a euphemism for U.S. citizens) and "enemy aliens" of Japanese ancestry in the ten War Relocation Authority camps was part of a larger plan of how the U.S. government dealt with "the enemy." The World War II Enemy Alien Program affected nearly 1 million noncitizen immigrants and their families from the Italian, German, and Japanese communities in the United States. The U.S. government also went outside its borders to Latin America and apprehended more than 8,000 men, women, and children of Italian, German, and Japanese ancestry under the Latin American rendition scheme. More than 31,000 of these "enemy aliens" in the United States and from Latin America were interned in U.S. Department of Justice camps and Army facilities on the basis of being "potentially dangerous." More than 4,800 (including U.S.–born children) were traded for U.S. citizens held in the war zones of Europe and the Far East.[1]

Discussions and planning for the treatment of "enemies" began before the attack on Pearl Harbor. By the mid-1930s as war spread in Europe, the United States had become concerned with Axis influence in Latin America. By the end of the 1930s, U.S. officials suspected that the Japanese, German, and Italian communities in Latin America would engage in subversive activities (i.e. espionage, sabotage, and pro-Axis propaganda). In 1940, U.S. diplomats and intelligence agents began preparing lists of "dangerous enemy aliens" residing in Latin America. In October 1941, the U.S. ambassador and Panamanian foreign minister secretly agreed on plans for the wartime detention of persons of Japanese, German, and Italian ancestry in Panama, with the United States assuming all expenses and responsibility.[2]

With the Japanese military attack on Pearl Harbor on December 7, 1941, President Franklin D. Roosevelt authorized the FBI to arrest without warrant any Japanese citizen fourteen years or older in the United States. The next day this was applied against German and Italian aliens as well. Overnight 1 million law-abiding immigrants were transformed into "enemy aliens." No distinction was made between resident immigrants and aliens in the United States on a temporary basis.[3] Local police in Latin America began arresting "potential subversives," which included businessmen, teachers, priests, journalists, and leaders of community and cultural organizations. No search warrants were issued, no charges of crimes were filed, and no hearings were given.[4]

The rendition of Japanese Latin Americans occurred from December 1941 to 1945. The U.S. government orchestrated the forcible deportation of 2,264 men, women, and children of Japanese ancestry—both citizens and immigrant residents—from thirteen Latin American countries, in the name of national security and to be used as hostages in exchange for U.S. citizens held by Japan.[5] Of these, about 1,800 (80%) were abducted from Peru.[6] The U.S. government financed their transportation over international borders and their internment in U.S. Department of Justice camps and Army facilities, separate from the ten War Relocation Authority camps that held Japanese Americans.[7] The government justified its control over the Japanese Latin Americans by confiscating their passports upon entry to the United States and then labeling them as "illegal aliens."[8]

More than 800 Japanese Latin Americans were included in the two prisoner exchanges that took place in 1942 and 1943 between the U.S. and Japan.[9] This left about fourteen hundred Japanese Latin Americans who continued to be interned in the United States. Their ordeal did not end with the close of World War II in 1945. Classified as "illegal aliens," the remaining Japanese Latin Americans were told that they would be deported from the U.S. to Japan.[10] At first, the Peruvian government refused to readmit any Japanese Peruvians, even those who were Peruvian citizens or married to Peruvian citizens.[11] As a result, between November 1945 and June 1946, more than nine hundred Japanese

Peruvians and more than one hundred other Japanese Latin Americans were deported to war-devastated Japan.[12] More than three hundred Japanese Peruvians remained in the United States and fought deportation through the courts.[13] More than two-thirds were paroled by the U.S. government, placed under the sponsorship of Seabrook Farms in New Jersey, and used as cheap labor.[14] Eventually fewer than one hundred Japanese Peruvians were able to return to Peru.[15] In 1954, the Refugee Relief Act of 1953 was amended so that the former internees from Latin America who resided in the United States could begin the process of becoming permanent residents. Many became U.S. citizens.[16]

The experiences of Japanese Americans and Japanese Latin Americans have been integrally related through internment in the Department of Justice camps, the wartime prisoner exchanges, and later through the process of resettlement and the redress struggle for acknowledgment, empowerment, and justice. Japanese Latin Americans gave testimony at the Congressional Commission Hearings in 1981 and shared in celebration when the Civil Liberties Act of 1988 was passed. Japanese Latin Americans were informed that they were ineligible for redress, however, because the U.S. government considered them "illegal aliens" at the time of their internment, despite the fact that the U.S. government forcibly brought them to the United States. In 1991, the Japanese Peruvian Oral History Project was founded by former Japanese Peruvian internees and their families. During the 1990s, Japanese Latin American internees joined with Japanese Americans in several community delegations to Washington, DC, to seek redress for hundreds of Japanese Americans and Japanese Latin Americans who were being denied redress. In 1996, the Campaign For Justice: Redress NOW For Japanese Latin Americans! was founded. Also that year, the *Mochizuki* lawsuit was filed on behalf of the Japanese Latin American internees. The lawsuit ended in 1999 with a controversial settlement agreement whereby eligible Japanese Latin American internees received apology letters and compensation payments (one-quarter of that granted to Japanese American internees) and pursuit of legislative relief from the U.S. Congress was not prohibited. Seventeen Japanese Latin American internees rejected the *Mochizuki* settlement. Four additional lawsuits were filed, all dismissed at the lower courts; one reached the U.S. Supreme Court but was denied a hearing.[17]

Feeling that justice could not be attained through U.S. courts, three former Japanese Peruvian internees and the Japanese Peruvian Oral History Project filed a petition in 2003 at the Inter-American Commission on Human Rights (IACHR), a body of the Organization of American States. This *Shibayama* petition seeks to hold the U.S. government accountable for the ongoing failure to provide redress for war crimes and crimes against humanity perpetrated against the Japanese Latin Americans during World War II. The merit of the Japanese Latin American cause was affirmed when the IACHR accepted the Japanese Latin American petition and rejected efforts by the U.S. government to prevent review of the human rights violations on technical grounds.[18] A decision on the *Shibayama* petition is pending.

Legislation has also been introduced on the behalf of Japanese Latin Americans. In 2000 and three subsequent sessions of Congress, the Wartime Parity and Justice Act was introduced by Rep. Xavier Becerra, a Latino congressman from California. This act sought comprehensive redress legislation for hundreds of Japanese Americans and Japanese Latin Americans who had been denied proper redress as well as reestablishment of $45 million to fulfill the original education mandate of the Civil Liberties Act.

In 2006, Rep. Becerra and Sen. Daniel Inouye (D-HI) introduced legislation, the "Commission on Wartime Relocation and Internment of Latin Americans of Japanese Descent Act," to investigate the treatment of Japanese Latin Americans during World War II and make appropriate recommendations (HR662, S381).[19] This commission would build on a similar fact-finding study authorized by Congress in 1980, which examined the treatment of Japanese Americans during World War II. The recommendations from that study led to the passage of the Civil Liberties Act of 1988. During the course of that study, information began to be uncovered about the treatment of the Japanese Latin Americans. It was found significant enough to be included in the published study and noted to warrant deeper investigation. The Japanese Latin American commission bill would extend the study of the 1980 Commission.[20]

In addition to legislative and litigation efforts, former Japanese Latin American internees, their families, and supporters have engaged in efforts to educate the public, in the United States and internationally, about their little-known wartime history and the ongoing struggle for government accountability and redress. Since 2000, Japanese Latin American internees have worked with Japanese, Italian, German American, and Latin American internees and scholars, as well as with Muslim, Arab, and South Asian community members, to promote dialogue and draw lessons from the World War II and post-9/11 experiences. In 2001, ten days after the 9/11 tragedies, a ground-breaking traveling exhibit, "The Enemy Alien Files: Hidden Stories of WWII," opened. In 2005, a two-day public event, "Here, In America? The Assembly of Wartime Relocation and Internment of Civilians (AWRIC)," was organized to take testimony from former World War II internees of Japanese, Italian, German, and Latin American ancestry, along with Middle Eastern/South Asians and Muslims in the post-9/11 period. There were also a variety of panel discussions on topics related to relocation and internment. In 2006, a community delegation delivered the AWRIC Report and DVD to members of the U.S. Congress and Inter-American Commission on Human Rights. In 2008, a ground-breaking, cross-cultural educational event, "Inalienable Immigrant Rights—Youth Voices from WWII and Post 9/11," was organized as a step toward understanding the immediate and long-term human impact of policies such as restrictions, special registration, detention, incarceration, deportation, and rendition on diverse youth, families, and communities during World War II and today.

FURTHER READING

Campaign for Justice Web site. http://www.campaignforjusticejla.org/.

Donald, Heidi Gurcke. *We Were Not the Enemy: Remembering the United States' Latin-American Civilian Internment Program of World War II.* iUniverse.com, 2006.

Gardiner, C. Harvey. "The Latin American Japanese and WWII." In *Japanese Americans: From Relocation to Redress*, eds. Roger Daniels et al. Salt Lake City: University of Utah Press, 1983.

Gardiner, C. Harvey. *Pawns in a Triangle of Hate: The Peruvian Japanese and the United States.* Seattle: University of Washington Press, 1981.

Hidden Internment: the Art Shibayama Story. Directed by Casey Peek and Irum Shiekh. Peek Media in association with the Japanese Peruvian Oral History Project, 2004. (English, Japanese, available soon in Spanish).

Higashide, Seiichi. *Adios to Tears: The Memoirs of a Japanese-Peruvian Internee in U.S. Concentration Camps.* Seattle: University of Washington Press, 2000.

Masterson, Daniel M., and Sayaka Funada-Classen. *The Japanese in Latin America.* Urbana: University of Illinois Press, 2004.

Ueunten, Wesley. "Japanese Latin American Internment from an Okinawan Perspective." *Okinawan Diaspora*, Ronald Y. Nakasone, ed. (Honolulu: University of Hawai'i Press, 2002).

NOTES

1. Enemy Alien Files Consortium, *Here, In America? Immigrants as 'The Enemy' During WWII and Today. Report of the Assembly on Wartime Relocation and Internment of Civilians, April 8–9, 2005* (San Francisco: National Japanese American Historical Society, 2006).

2. P. Scott Corbett, *Quiet Passages: The Exchange Of Civilians Between the United States and Japan* (Kent, OH: Kent State University Press, 1987).

3. Michi Weglyn, *Years of Infamy: The Untold Story of America's Concentration Camps* (Seattle: University of Washington Press, 1976, 1996).

4. Enemy Alien Files Consortium, *Here In America?* 19.

5. C. Harvey Gardiner, "The Latin American Japanese and WWII," in *Japanese Americans: From Relocation to Redress*, edited by Roger Daniels et al. (Salt Lake City: University of Utah Press, 1983), 142. The 13 nations are Bolivia, Colombia, Costa Rica, Dominican Republic, Ecuador, Panama, Peru, El Salvador, Guatemala, Haiti, Honduras, Mexico, and Nicaragua.

6. C. Harvey Gardiner, *Pawns in a Triangle of Hate: The Peruvian Japanese and the United States* (Seattle: University of Washington Press, 1981) 7; Joan Z. Bernstein (chair), *Personal Justice Denied—Report of Commission on Wartime Relocation & Internment of Civilians* (Seattle: Civil Liberties Public Education Fund and University of Washington Press, 1997), 305.

7. Gardiner, "The Latin American Japanese and WWII," 143; Weglyn, *Years of Infamy,* 58–59.

8. Gardiner, *Pawns in a Triangle of Hate*, 290.

9. Gardiner, *Pawns in a Triangle of Hate*, 48, 84–85.

10. Gardiner, *Pawns in a Triangle of Hate*, 115; Personal Justice Denied, 311.

11. Weglyn, *Years of Infamy,* 64.

12. Gardiner, *Pawns in a Triangle of Hate*, 124–125, 127, 130.

13. Bernstein, *Personal Justice Denied*, 313.

14. Gardiner, *Pawns in a Triangle of Hate*, 155.

15. Bernstein, *Personal Justice Denied,* 313.

16. Gardiner, *Pawns in a Triangle of Hate*, 170–171.

17. Campaign for Justice, "What We Do," http://www.campaignforjusticejla .org/whatwedo/index.html.

18. Campaign for Justice, "What We Do."

19. Campaign for Justice, "What We Do."

20. Bernstein, *Personal Justice Denied*, 493.

POST-TRAUMATIC STRESS DISORDER IN REFUGEES AND WAR VETERANS

Meekyung Han and Julian Chun-Chung Chow

The study of war trauma and its important role in mental health problems among Southeast Asian refugee populations and Asian American Vietnam War veterans has received considerable attention in the past three decades to the point that there is now substantial knowledge about rates of trauma and associated problems. More specifically, extensive empirical studies have found high rates of both trauma and post-traumatic stress disorder (PTSD) in community samples, as would be expected given the brutal circumstances faced by many of the Vietnamese, Cambodians, Hmong, and Laos who migrated to the United States during and after the Vietnam War era.[1] Studies also find high rates of PTSD among Asian American Vietnam veterans.[2] In both cases, it is increasingly recognized that adaptation to war trauma is a complex process and should be viewed within a broader context, i.e., not only of the direct effect of trauma itself but also of the situational factors surrounding the event, including the race and ethnicity of the person experiencing the trauma.[3] Indeed, studies of PTSD in general show that race and ethnicity are critical factors in furthering the understanding of PTSD in relation to the diagnosis and to treatment.[4] In order to better understand how "being Asian American," including not only racialization but also issues of culture, gender roles, and class, affects war-related psychiatric distress such as PTSD, this discussion presents a brief overview of the PTSD diagnosis, a contextual framework for perspectives on PTSD, a survey of the prevalence of PTSD among Southeast Asian refugee populations and Asian American Vietnam veterans, and suggestions related to mental health service delivery for Asian Americans with PTSD.

DIAGNOSIS

Post-traumatic stress disorder is related to war trauma in the American Psychiatric Association's Diagnostic and Statistical Manual of Mental Disorders (DSM-III).[5] A unique psychiatric diagnostic category, PTSD is kind of "survivor syndrome." The significance of the PTSD diagnosis in DSM-III is that it is the first mental illness recognized as requiring an initiating external event—in this case, war.[6] By specifying that such events would evoke "significant symptoms of distress in almost everyone," the American Psychiatric Association's DSM-III implicitly includes subjective perception as well as environmental objectivity within the PTSD construct. The diagnosis listed in DSM-III was modified in DSM-IV to suggest that the event needed to be "outside the range of usual human experience." Additionally, in order to clarify the difference between the subjective (i.e., perception) and objective (i.e., event) components, DSM-IV broke the stressor criterion into two parts, where the first criterion offers the objective description of the event and the second criterion describes the subjective reactions, such as intense fear, terror, and helplessness.[7] Thus, PTSD is defined as encompassing the historical syndromes known as "shell shock," "war neurosis," and "combat fatigue."

REFUGEES

Following traumatic exposure during war, escape, re-education camps, refugee camps, and resettlement in the United States, many Southeast Asian refugees still experience mental health problems. In a psychiatric clinic population, PTSD represents the most common psychiatric disorder, affecting perhaps 50–70 percent of the Southeast Asian refugees.[8] Indeed, despite almost three decades having passed since the end of the Cambodian war, a randomly selected group of Cambodians in Long Beach, CA, still suffered a high rate of PTSD (62%) and major depression (51%).[9] Also, there appears to be a gender difference with mental health problems among Southeast Asian refugees. Researchers have found that Southeast Asian refugee women reported significantly higher levels of distress than their male counterparts.[10]

While relatively few empirical studies have examined the psychological adjustment of refugee children, those that have been conducted found that the enduring nature of PTSD was also evident with children and youths. For example, a twelve-year longitudinal study (beginning at the time of arrival, and returning three years later, six years later, and twelve years later) was conducted using interviews with Cambodian refugee children. This study found that 35 percent of the sample suffered PTSD for twelve years, and about 18 percent of subjects developed PTSD at least five years after resettlement. Despite the persistence of PTSD over time, however, the study also found that these children appeared to make the transition into American culture quite well, for instance, by pursuing either occupational or educational goals.[11]

For Southeast Asian refugees, their subjective perception of trauma should be viewed within a cultural context because, as refugees, their decision to leave was often a forced option for survival purposes rather than being a personal choice to make a new home in a foreign land. Southeast Asians began arriving in the United States in large numbers at the conclusion of the Southeast Asian wars in 1975, and according to the U.S. Census (2002), an estimated 2 million are living in the country, with the largest proportion from Vietnam.[12]

Of the estimated 2 million who fled Vietnam, more than 500,000 died attempting to flee, mostly by small boats. Their mass exodus was filled with horrors, including brutal attacks by pirates, rape, torture, and cannibalism because of the lack of food. Cambodians suffered the worst ordeal of all refugees, even before their exodus. Almost all educated people were killed during the Cambodian genocide. Those who escaped successfully were mostly illiterate, making the adjustment to a new life extremely difficult. Similarly, at the fall of Laos, like other Southeast Asians, many Laotians fled their country, crossed the Mekong River, and entered Thailand. Also, the Laotian Hmong fought the "secret war" for the U.S. government in Laos and suffered severe casualties.[13]

Southeast Asian refugees have to face many challenges due to cultural differences after resettlement in the United States. As a result, they experience additional perceived traumas associated with their acculturation and have thus developed ongoing PTSD long after their settlement in the host country. Family is the primary social unit in many Asian cultures and the most important source of identity for its members. Roles and positions of hierarchy are apparent in many traditional Asian families so that adults are placed in roles of authority over children. However, these traditional values of Southeast Asian refugee families have been affected by war trauma. Parents whose daily functioning has been negatively impacted by the trauma endured at home and during the migration may cede more power and authority to their children. In addition, because of difficulties of acculturation such as language barriers and cultural differences, adults often lose their status within the family. Children, who usually acculturate faster than their parents, become communication facilitators between their parents and the mainstream society, thereby reversing the traditional parent-child relationship and disrupting cultural roles within the family structure.[14]

Men are considered to be higher in the hierarchy than women in some traditional Asian cultures. Southeast Asian refugee women's status has also been altered, as their male counterparts became unemployed or underemployed, which results in women needing to find work to support their families. Indeed, while Southeast Asian men faced downward mobility in employment, women have generally experienced increased occupational opportunities following migration to the United States.[15] These challenges in gender roles have created conflicts between familial values and have placed severe pressure on traditional marriage and family relationships. This shift in gender roles often compounds trauma experienced during war and migration.

Research shows that financial difficulties and economic disadvantages are strongly associated with acculturative stress among Southeast Asian refugees.[16]

Southeast Asian refugees have lower social and economic status than the average American. Because of language and cultural barriers, they also face difficulties in the areas of bilingual education, job training, business development, representation in government, as well as access to technology and social services.[17] In addition, more than 21 percent of Southeast Asian families were living below the poverty line compared to 13 percent of the U.S. population. A higher proportion of Southeast Asians held minimum-wage occupations (21% among Vietnamese, 31% among Cambodians, 44% among Laotians, and 33% among Hmong, compared with 15% for the general population) and a disproportionate segment of Southeast Asians has to rely on public assistance for survival (25% of Vietnamese, 51% of Cambodian, 35% of Laotian, and 32% of Hmong, compared with 8% of the general population).[18]

Southeast Asian refugees have suffered from manifold losses: material losses, physical losses, spiritual losses, loss of community support and cultural milieu, and loss of family members. These losses exacerbate their vulnerability and prolong the impact of the traumatic event. Similarly, factors such as poverty and cultural conflicts in the host country may additionally influence their daily functioning as they experience persistent intrusions of memories related to the trauma, which in turn prevent them from healing psychological and emotional wounds, such that they continue to be subjected to repeated post-traumatic syndrome.[19]

VIETNAM VETERANS

In comparison with the Southeast Asian refugee population, very few empirical studies have been conducted with veterans of Asian ancestry. This may be due to the small number of Asian American veterans (1.2%) in the 2002 U.S. veteran population compared with European Americans (85.5%), African Americans (9.75%), and Latinos/Hispanics (4.3%).[20] The existing studies, however, clearly show that race-related stressors are important predictors of PTSD symptoms among Asian American veterans. Asian Americans fighting a war in Asia or the Pacific might be at greater risk for developing PTSD symptoms and other psychiatric sufferings because of experience with negative race-related events associated with appearing racially similar to the Asian "enemy." The level of reported PTSD among Asian American Vietnam veterans in a national study was comparable to or higher than that of the European American population. In other words, 13 percent of Chinese American veterans, 29 percent of the Native Hawaiian veterans, and 40 percent of "other" Asian American veteran groups met PTSD criteria, compared with 24 percent of European American veterans. Another study found that 37 percent of Asian American veterans suffered from PTSD.[21] While it is too early to know whether Asian American veterans disproportionately suffer PTSD from the war in Iraq, they are vulnerable because of the persistence of racial and religious stereotypes, particularly for Asian American Muslim populations.

Asian American veterans experience unique issues because of race-related stress in addition to all the other stressors experienced by veterans in general. In particular, Asian American soldiers serving in the Vietnam War—during the time of the development of the Asian American Movement—were exposed to violence, suffered terror and horror because of the war itself, and also experienced psychological conflicts that arose because of their ethnic and racialized identities.

In a survey of Asian American Vietnam veterans conducted by the U.S. Department of Veterans Affairs, the majority of Asian American soldiers felt they were similar or very similar to the Vietnamese in terms of physical characteristics, which increased perceived terror about being shot at by fellow U.S. soldiers when mistaken for the enemy, being harassed and physically injured because of being perceived as resembling or symbolizing the enemy, and being captured and abandoned because they would not be recognized as American.[22] They also felt their ethnicity affected how the Vietnamese people treated them; their increased connection with local Vietnamese populations may have made it more difficult to carry out orders that they knew would cause harm to people with whom they identified racially or ethnically (for example, in the case of Chinese American soldiers meeting ethnic Chinese in Vietnam). The combination of the combat experience and psychological distress related to ethnicity and racialization appear to magnify the trauma among Asian American veterans.

Research has revealed that failure to assess race-related stressor experiences of Asian American and Pacific Islander veterans could result in missing as much as 20 percent of veterans' PTSD symptoms.[23] This means that 20 percent of Asian American veterans who need to be treated might not receive the appropriate disability assessment, compensation, and/or mental health services. Simply put, it is the professional's responsibility to accurately assess and treat the full range of problems faced by Asian Americans experiencing PTSD.

Empirical studies that have investigated readjustment problems of ethnic minority Vietnam veterans have mostly focused on African Americans or Latinos/Hispanics. Not unlike African Americans and Latinos/Hispanics whose rate of PTSD tends to be higher than European Americans, as shown above, a few existing empirical studies with Asian American and Pacific Islander veterans also show the high rate of PTSD, but the record remains relatively silent on Asian American and Pacific Islander Vietnam veterans. Even the National Vietnam Veterans Readjustment Survey limits their definition of "ethnic minority" to African Americans and Latinos/Hispanics.[24] Larger scale studies with full inclusion of Asian American and Pacific Islander veterans are needed.

OUTLOOK

Since the phenomenon of transgenerational traumatization was first noted in 1966 among Nazi Holocaust survivor families, there has been significant evidence showing a strong association between parental trauma and children's psychological dysfunction.[25] However, very little research has been conducted on this issue in Asian American communities. Indeed, Southeast Asian refugees and their children are a potentially high-risk population for the intergenerational transmission of trauma because many Southeast Asian refugees were highly traumatized in their homeland, and parents' trauma was related to psychological distress in their children. To address the needs, there have been efforts of healing and recovery from war trauma in Asian American communities. As suggested by researchers, clinical interventions with Southeast Asian populations have focused on parents' mental health (with emphasis on PTSD), resolution of trauma and mourning, and parenting effectiveness, with cultural and contextual issues included in treatment plans.[26]

For example, many community-based social service agencies have been working diligently to create an innovative, culturally sensitive, and culturally specific model for intervention with Southeast Asian refugee populations. Some agencies provide group intervention, which has combined cultural traditions, spirituality (e.g., meditation), and religious (Buddhist) philosophy with standard Western mental health techniques for treatment of Southeast Asian people with PTSD. No studies have yet been conducted on the children of Asian American Vietnam veterans, but this work would help develop a fuller picture of the mental health of Asian American populations. In sum, mental health practitioners working with Asian Americans suffering with PTSD are trying to help bring about a change in the meaning that has been assigned by patients to these traumatizing war events, and are working to change that way PTSD is viewed in order to encompass the significance of race and ethnicity in diagnosing and treating patients.

FURTHER READING

Danieli, Yael. *International Handbook of Multigenerational Legacies of Trauma*. New York: Plenum Press, 1998.

National Center for Posttraumatic Stress Disorder. http://www.ncptsd.va.gov/ncmain/index.jsp.

Southeast Asian Resource Center. http://www.searac.org/.

NOTES

1. Richard F. Mollica, "Invisible Wounds: Waging a New Kind of War," *Scientific American* 282, no. 6 (2000): 54–57; Richard F. Mollica, *Healing Invisible Wounds: Paths to Hope and Recovery in a Violent World* (New York: Harcourt Press, 2007); Ruben Rumbaut, "Vietnamese, Laotian, and Cambodian Americans" in *Asian Americans*, ed. Pyung Gap (Thousand Oaks, CA: SAGE Publications, 1995), 232–270; Yu-Wen Ying, "Psychotherapy with Traumatized Southeast Asian Refugees," *Clinical Social Work Journal* 29, no. 1 (2001): 65–78.

2. Chalsa Loo et al., "Measuring Exposure to Racism: Developing and Validation of a Race-Related Stressor Scale (RRSS) for Asian American Vietnam Veterans," *Psychological Assessment* 13, no. 4 (2001): 503–520.

3. Yu-Wen Ying, "Psychotherapy with Traumatized Southeast Asian Refugees," 65–78.

4. Eugenia Hsu, Corrie Davies, and David Hansen, "Understanding Mental Health Needs of Southeast Asian Refugees: Historical, Cultural, and Contextual Challenges," *Clinical Psychology Review* 24, no. 2 (2004): 193–213; Grant Marshall, et al., "Mental Health of Cambodian Refugees 2 Decades after Resettlement in the United States," *Journal of American Medical Association* 294, no. 5 (2005): 571–579; Barbara Nicholson, "The Influence of Pre-Emigration and Postemigration Stressors on Mental Health: A Study of Southeast Asian Refugees," *Social Work Research* 21, no.1 (1997): 19–31; Barbara Nicholson and Tali K. Walters, "The Effects of Trauma on Acculturative Stress: A Study of Cambodian Refugees," *Journal of Multicultural Social Work* 6, no. 3/4 (1997): 27–46.

5. Loo et al., "Measuring Exposure to Racism," 503–520; Chalsa Loo and Peter Nien-chu Kiang, "Race-Related Stressors and Psychological Trauma: Contributions of Asian American Vietnam Veterans," in *Asian Americans: Vulnerable Populations, Model Interventions and Clarifying Agendas*, ed. Lin. Zhan (Sudbury, MA: Jones and Barlette Publishers Inc., 2003), 19–42.

6. John Marsh, "What Constitutes a Stressor? The Criterion A Issue," in *Posttraumatic Stress Disorder: DSM-IV and Beyond,* ed. Jonathan Davidson and Edna Foa (Washington, DC: American Psychiatric Press, 1993).

7. American Psychiatric Association, *Diagnostic and Statistical Manual of Mental Disorders* 4th ed. (Washington, DC: American Psychiatric Association, 2000).

8. Grant Marshall et al., "Mental health of Cambodian Refugees," 571–579; Richard F. Mollica et al., "Dose-Effect Relationships of Trauma to Symptoms of Depression and Post-Traumatic Stress Disorder among Cambodian Survivors of Mass Violence," *The British Journal of Psychiatry* 173 (1998): 482–488; J. D. Kinzie, P. K. Leung, and J. Boehnlein, "Treatment of Depressive Disorders in Refugees," in *Working with Asian Americans: A guide for Clinicians*, ed. Evelyn Lee (New York: Guilford Press, 1997).

9. Marshall et al., "Mental Health of Cambodian Refugees," 571–579.

10. Rita Chi-Ying Chung, Fred Bemak, and Marjorie Kagawa-Singer, "Gender Difference in Psychological Distress among Southeast Refugees," *Journal of Nervous and Mental Disease* 186, no. 2 (1998): 112–119.

11. William H. Sack, Chanrithy Him, and Dan Dickason, "Twelve-Year Follow-Up Study of Khmer Youths Who Suffered Massive War Trauma as Children," *Journal of American Academy of Child and Adolescent Psychiatry* 38, no. 9 (1999): 1173–1179.

12. Sucheng Chan, *Survivors: Cambodian Refugees in the United States* (Champaign: University of Illinois Press, 2004); Southeast Asian Reaction Center, *Southeast Asian American Statistical Profile*, 2000, Retrieved from http://www.searac.org/seastat profilemay04.pdf; U.S. Census Bureau, *The Foreign-Born Population in the United States* (Washington, DC: U.S. Department of Commerce, March 2002), P20-539, http://www.eric.ed.gov/ERICWebPortal/contentdelivery/servlet/ERICServlet?accno =ED478282.

13. Chan, *Survivors: Cambodian Refugees in the United States*; Southeast Asian Reaction Center, "Southeast Asian American Statistical Profile"; Pho, Gerson, and Cowan, *Southeast Asian Refugees and Immigrants in the Mill City.*

14. Hsu, Davies, and Hansen, "Understanding Mental Health Needs of Southeast Asian refugees," 193–213; Chung, Bemak, and Kagawa-Singer, "Gender Difference in Psychological Distress," 112–119.

15. Chung, Bemak, and Kagawa-Singer, "Gender Difference in Psychological Distress," 112–119.

16. Hsu, Davies, and Hansen, "Understanding Mental Health Needs of Southeast Asian Refugees," 193–213.

17. Chan, *Survivors: Cambodian Refugees in the United States*; Southeast Asian Reaction Center, "Southeast Asian American Statistical Profile," 1-30; Pho, Gerson, and Cowan, *Southeast Asian Refugees and Immigrants in the Mill City;* Theresa Liu and Chieh Li, "Psychological Interventions with Southeast Asian Students: An Ecological Approach," *Special Services in the Schools* 13, no. 1/2 (1998): 129–148; Leng Mouanoutoua Vang, "Depression and Posttraumatic Stress Disorder: Prevailing Causes and Therapeutic Strategies with Hmong Clients," in *Healing by Heart: Clinical and Ethical Case Studies of Hmong Families and Western Providers*, ed. Culhane-Pera, Kathleen Vawter, Dorothy. E and Xiong, Phua (Vanderbilt University Press. 2003), 216–221.

18. Southeast Asian Reaction Center, "Southeast Asian American Statistical Profile," 1–30.

19. Devon Hinton et al., "Panic Disorder among Cambodian Refugees Attending a Psychiatric Clinic: Prevalence and Subtypes," *General Hospital Psychiatry* 22 (2000): 437–444; R. Jay Turner and Donald Lloyd, "The Stress Process and the Social Distribution of Depression," *Journal of Health and Social Behavior* 40, no. 4 (1999): 374–404.

20. U.S. Department of Veterans Affair, *Veterans of Culturally Diverse Populations*, 2002, http://www1.va.gov/centerforminorityveterans/.

21. Chalsa Loo et al., "Race-Related Stress among Asian American Veterans: A Model to Enhance Diagnosis and Treatment," *Cultural Diversity and Mental Health* 4 (1998): 75–90.

22. U.S. Department of Veterans Affair, *Veterans of Culturally Diverse Populations*.

23. Turner and Lloyd, "The Stress Process and the Social Distribution of Depression," 374–404.

24. Loo et al., "Measuring Exposure to Racism," 503–520; Loo and Kiang, "Race-Related Stressors and Psychological Trauma," 19–42; Chalsa et al., "Race-Related Stress Among Asian American Veterans," 75–90.

25. Rachel Yehuda et al., "Vulnerability to Posttraumatic Stress Disorder in Adult Offspring of Holocaust Survivors," *American Journal of Psychiatry* 155 (1998): 1163–1171.

26. Hsu, Davies, and Hansen, "Understanding Mental Health Needs of Southeast Asian Refugees," 193–213; Meekyung Han, "Relationship among Perceived Parental Trauma, Attachment, and Sense of Coherence in Southeast Asian Late Adolescents," *Journal of Family Social Work* 9 (2006): 25–45.

POST–VIETNAM WAR TENSIONS IN THE VIETNAMESE AMERICAN COMMUNITY

C. N. Le

The Vietnamese American community contains a complex mix of many seemingly contradictory elements. On the one hand, Vietnamese Americans tend to be one of the youngest Asian ethnic groups on average, with a fast-growing second generation. On the other hand, many are still firmly focused on what happened more than thirty years ago and the ongoing legacy of the Vietnam War. These two elements form the basis for much of the tension among Vietnamese Americans today, which is the topic of this entry.

Based on their hatred of the communist regime in Vietnam and the communists' status as "the enemy" who drove them from their homeland and brutalized their family members, relatives, and friends, many Vietnamese Americans continue to have very strong emotions regarding the communist government. Since Vietnamese Americans' departure after the fall of Saigon in 1975, their goal has been to overthrow the regime and restore democracy and individual freedoms for all Vietnamese. To achieve such goals, Vietnamese Americans have been willing to do basically anything—overt and covert, legal and illegal. Within this historical and social environment, any suggestion that the overseas Vietnamese population (popularly referred to as the *Viet Kieu*) should learn to accept the current situation as permanent, or to consider the communist government in their homeland as legitimate by advocating normalized relations between the United States and Vietnam has provoked much outcry, anger, and resentment.[1]

Since their resettlement into the United States, and particularly once a critical mass of Vietnamese converged on Westminster, CA, to form their own enclave that became known as Little Saigon, any Vietnamese American who dared to make such a statement or engage in any activity that was perceived to be legitimizing or strengthening the communist regime back in Vietnam was immediately, loudly, and publicly denounced as a traitor or a *Viet Cong* (the term for a South Vietnamese communist). Starting in the early 1980s, individuals perceived to be sympathetic to the communists—many of whom were journalists—were harassed, physically assaulted, had their property vandalized, and in some extreme instances, were kidnapped, murdered, or just disappeared. Between 1980 and 1992, at least a dozen such disappearances occurred, mostly in California.[2] One of the most highly publicized deaths was that of Tap Van Pham, who, at the time, was editor of *Mai*, a Vietnamese-language entertainment magazine. In the early hours of August 9, 1987, Pham died of smoke inhalation when his office in Little Saigon was firebombed, apparently for running advertisements for companies that did business with the communist government. (To this day, and despite FBI involvement, the case remains unsolved.) It has been documented that "Liberal Vietnamese community leaders" were so threatened they had to take extreme measures to protect themselves, including wearing bulletproof vests. Some also used ads in Vietnamese-language newspapers to deny rumors that they sympathized with the communist regime.[3]

However, in 1994, President Bill Clinton lifted the trade embargo against Vietnam that had existed since the communists unified the country in 1975. A 1994 *Los Angeles Times* survey of Vietnamese in southern California showed that 54 percent of respondents approved of the action, with a similar proportion favoring full normalized relations between the United States and Vietnam, which occurred the following year.[4] Nonetheless, while Vietnamese Americans may be moderating their strategies on how to best deal with the communist government in their homeland, many remain very sensitive to perceived expressions of communist sympathy within their own community. No other incident illustrates this continuing sentiment and the still-fresh wounds of war more than the Ho Chi Minh portrait incident in Little Saigon in 1999.

OPENING FRESH WOUNDS

In January 1999, after returning from a tourist trip to northern Vietnam, Truong Van Tran, a video store owner in Southern California's Little Saigon, put up a poster of Ho Chi Minh, along with the flag of the current Vietnamese communist government, inside his store. In subsequent interviews, Tran claimed that he felt Ho Chi Minh had some beneficial impact on Vietnam, that the portrait was meant to provoke discussion among the Vietnamese American community, and that ultimately, as a resident of the United States, he had the right to freely express himself. The community reaction was swift and massive. Almost immediately, Tran's store was beset with daily protests, with many enraged protesters coming from San Jose and other locations outside of Southern California to participate. At the height of the protests, approximately

15,000 demonstrators gathered outside his store, shouting insults such as "Viet Cong!" and carrying signs that read, "Our Wounds Will Never Heal!" and "Be Aware! Communists are Invading America!" At times, the crowd became so large and agitated that police in riot gear had to be called in; hundreds of demonstrators were ultimately arrested throughout the course of the protests.

After two months of continuous protests outside Tran's store, his business was eventually evicted by its corporate landlord for unpaid rent and insurance violations. With his store gone, the offending display was removed and soon afterward, thousands of Vietnamese Americans gathered in and around the location of the former store for a candlelight "healing" ceremony and gathering. For many Vietnamese, especially the older and first generation who had a direct connection to the events that led to their exile, Tran had a right to personally believe whatever he wanted to believe. Nonetheless, many felt that he had crossed the line by publicizing his beliefs, and, by praising Ho Chi Minh, being blatantly disrespectful of the painful memories that so many members of his own community have of the legacy of the Vietnam War. Many likened Tran's act of provocation to displaying a portrait of Hitler in a Jewish community or Fidel Castro in a U.S. Cuban community. As a *Time* magazine article from March 8, 1999, described, Vietnamese American protesters argued that they respected his freedom of speech but felt he abused that freedom by causing dissension in his community.[5]

Many protesters said that they were exercising their own freedom of expression to denounce Tran as a communist traitor. Others said that, at best, Tran was rather naïve and perhaps even crazy in thinking that he could put up a picture of Ho Chi Minh in public view without provoking anger in Little Saigon and as such, he deserved the scorn leveled at him. On the other side, other Vietnamese Americans, more likely to be younger and/or 1.5 generation or later, felt that Tran had a right to express his opinion and that protesters overreacted to a simple picture. Many noted in their efforts to squelch dissent, anticommunist Vietnamese Americans were replicating the same form of oppression that they consistently condemn the communists for and that further, living in the United States means that they need to be more tolerant of dissenting views.

CONTINUING TENSIONS AND PROTESTS

More than 30 years after the end of the Vietnam War, many Vietnamese Americans are still very sensitive to any public display that is perceived to legitimize the communist regime back in Vietnam. In recent years, many local and state government offices and educational institutions around the country have displayed flags from countries all around the world. However, in displaying the current flag of Vietnam, many have encountered fierce protests from Vietnamese American community members and students. In a recent incident, officials at Irvine Valley Community College in California, located only a few miles from Little Saigon, chose to take down an entire display of 144 international flags in their student center after receiving numerous calls and threats of a large-scale demonstration from leaders of the Vietnamese American community.[6]

Even more interpretive displays such as works of art have not escaped scrutiny and protests. In early 2008, a Vietnamese American graduate student displayed an art installation that included a yellow-and-red foot-spa tub, meant as a tribute to Vietnamese refugees like her mother-in-law who toiled in a nail salon after the family came to America. But once word spread of the exhibit, many Vietnamese Americans criticized the imagery as disrespectful of the old flag of South Vietnam and therefore implicitly supportive of the communist regime. In further escalation of this incident, after one of the longest-running the Vietnamese language newspapers in Little Saigon, *Nguoi Viet*, published a story and picture of the art display, its offices were besieged by protesters. In one incident, protesters stormed and blocked the newspaper's office lobby, and one protester urinated on a mural dedicated to freedom of speech and the Bill of Rights. After numerous other acts of vandalism, threats of physical violence and of bombing its office, the newspaper ultimately fired two of its editors, hoping to alleviate the tensions.[7]

While many tensions within the Vietnamese American community center around public images and symbols related to the communist government, other controversies involve perceived loyalty among its leaders. Specifically, in 2005, with the enthusiastic and overwhelming support of the Vietnamese American community, Madison Nguyen became the first Vietnamese American elected to the city council of San Jose, CA, home to the second largest Vietnamese community in the U.S. But in late 2007, a deep split developed within San Jose's Vietnamese American community over whether to name its distinctive enclave "Little Saigon" or "Saigon Business District." Amid accusations that she secretly worked on behalf of businesses sympathetic to the Vietnamese government in support of the "Saigon Business District" name, protests eventually denounced Nguyen as a traitor. Even after the initial decision in favor of "Saigon Business District" was reversed and private "Little Saigon" banners were allowed to be hung, protesters launched an unsuccessful recall campaign against her, garnering only 44 percent of voters.[8]

ASSIMILATION VERSUS ETHNIC SOLIDARITY

Until the ultimate goal of overthrowing the communist government is achieved, it is unlikely that anticommunist fervor within the Vietnamese American community will subside significantly. Two other developments, however, are likely to complicate the nature of tensions among Vietnamese Americans. The first is Vietnam's economic emergence in the global economy. In the last twenty years or so and following the lead of China, Vietnam has developed its own mix of capitalist development with communist oversight, and also like China, the economic results have been remarkable. Vietnam's economy has averaged around 10 percent gross domestic product (GDP) growth each year and is the second-fastest growing economy in the world (after China).

Along with joining the World Trade Organization in 2006, Vietnam currently has an unemployment rate of only 2 percent, one of the lowest in the world, and its GDP per capita has increased almost sixfold since the late 1980s. Perhaps its most notable accomplishment is that its level of "deep poverty" (percent of the population living under $1 per day) has declined significantly (down to 8% in 2006, from 51% in 1990) and is now smaller than that of China, India, and the Philippines.

Such economic advancements have led to a growing number of Vietnamese Americans who have returned to their homeland to start their own businesses to try to cash in on the economic prosperity inside Vietnam. While Vietnamese American–owned businesses have had financial ties to their homeland for decades (i.e., money transfer services, typically in small local shops located in Little Saigon, to send remittances to family, relatives, and friends who stayed back in Vietnam), recent years have seen much larger and more frequent business ventures into Vietnam led by *Viet Kieu*, whether they involve Vietnamese Americans being the owners and direct proprietors of their ventures, or as leaders and managers of large-scale corporate expansion ventures into the country involving corporations from all virtually industries of the Fortune 500.[9] In this context of Vietnam's rising economic power, the gradually improving quality of life for its citizens, and the trend of Vietnamese Americans returning to their homeland to do business, the question that emerges is: will these developments improve or worsen ideological tensions within the Vietnamese American community?

To complicate this question further, the second emerging trend is the growing numbers of U.S.-raised Vietnamese Americans—those who were either born in the United States or the 1.5 generation who immigrated when they were young children. These U.S.-raised Vietnamese Americans tend to be much more assimilated and integrated into mainstream America, and just as important, are more likely to have moderate, liberal, or even apathetic views toward the Vietnamese government and communism in general. Among younger Vietnamese Americans, "opposing communism" is not the "top priority" it is to those in the older generation. Only one in five of those aged 25–34 consider "opposing communism" to be a critical issue; this group feels similarly to the issue of "encouraging Vietnam to improve its policy on human rights"—while both of these issues are significant to those over the age of 45.[10]

The general consensus among observers and scholars is that, all other things being equal, as the U.S.-raised Vietnamese American generation becomes more prominent, the community's anticommunist stance is likely to gradually moderate or at the least become less confrontational. Nonetheless, scholars argue that based largely on their wartime and refugee experiences, Vietnamese Americans tend to exhibit the highest levels of ethnic solidarity among all Asian American ethnic groups.[11] Further, Vietnamese American political participation has always been more about quality and intensity, rather than quantity, as exemplified by studies that show that while Vietnamese Americans have lower voter registration rates than most other Asian American ethnic groups, among those who are registered, Vietnamese Americans are near the top in terms of actual voting rates.[12] Therefore, even though U.S.-raised Vietnamese Americans may not have the same level of attachment to the events and trauma surrounding the Vietnam War, nonetheless they are likely to still feel the influence and sentiments of anticommunism in their community.

Anticommunist activism can easily be reignited and re-energized if the communist government continues to crackdown on prodemocracy dissidents or if its human rights abuses become even more egregious. The memories of the Vietnam War, the re-education camps, and their refugee experiences are still powerful influences for many Vietnamese Americans, and their high levels of ethnic solidarity likely mean that parents will continue to exert influence over their children and grandchildren for the foreseeable future. With that in mind, younger Vietnamese Americans are not likely to completely reject or ignore their history, as may have been more common among Asian immigrant groups in the past. Rather, as Vietnam continues to emerge as an economic power, as U.S. companies increasingly look to countries such as Vietnam as partners in capitalism, as global "quality of life" issues such as human rights continue to grow in prominence, as Vietnamese Americans continue on their path of political activism and influence, and as the communist regime in Vietnam continues to squelch dissent, anticommunism among Vietnamese Americans may not necessarily die out so quickly after all.

While the social forces of assimilation are undeniable, so too are the human rights abuses that Vietnam's government commits. Even while the communists modernize their economy and strive to elevate their status on the international stage, they continue to deny many basic human rights, individual liberties, and social freedoms to large numbers of their citizens. As long as these abuses exist, Vietnamese Americans will continue to criticize, condemn, and try to undermine the legitimacy of Vietnam's government by using their own personal experiences as inspiration and their developing political power at the state and national levels as ammunition. While the tactics of anticommunist resistance might change and become focused more on humanitarian efforts to improve the lives of ordinary Vietnamese citizens, the wish to restore democracy in their homeland is likely to continue to unite Vietnamese Americans for years to come.

FURTHER READING

Lam, Andrew. "U.S.-Vietnam Thaw Hazardous to Dissidents." *New America Media.* 2007.

Le, C. N. "'Better Dead Than Red': Anti-Communist Politics Among Vietnamese Americans" in *Anti-Communist Minorities in the US: The Political Activism of Ethnic Refugees*, ed. Ieva Zake. New York: Palgrave-MacMillan, 2009.

Nguoi Viet 2 (English language version). http://www.nguoi-viet.com/nv2_default.asp.

Texeira, Erin. "The Vietnamese American Community." *Asian-Nation: The Landscape of Asian America.* 2005. http://www.asian-nation.org/vietnamese-community.shtml.

"U.S.-Vietnam Thaw Hazardous to Dissidents." http://news.newamericamedia .org/news/view_article.html?article_id=e4468651bad0af6f2eddd02e5fbddb96.

Zhou, Min, and Carl L. Bankston. *Growing Up American: How Vietnamese Children Adapt to Life in the United States*. New York: Russell Sage Foundation, 1998.

NOTES

1. Min Zhou and Carl L. Bankston, *Growing Up American: How Vietnamese Children Adapt to Life in the United States* (New York: Russell Sage Foundation, 1998).
2. Zhou and Bankston, *Growing Up American.*
3. Zhou and Bankston, *Growing Up American*, 86.
4. Zhou and Bankston, *Growing Up American.*
5. Jeffery Ressner, "The Man Who Brought Back Ho Chi Minh," *Time*, March, 8, 1999, http://www.time.com/time/magazine/article/0,9171,990385,00.html (accessed August 2008).
6. Marla Jo. Fisher, "Vietnamese Flag Removed at Irvine Valley College," *Orange County Register*, Feb. 25, 2008, http://www.ocregister.com/news/flag-college-flags-1987450-vietnamese-student (accessed August 2008).
7. Kenneth Kim, "Fired Vietnamese Editor Launches Blog," *New America Media*, May 27, 2008, http://news.ncmonline.com/news/view_article.html?article_id=a92925856d7d969bb895f3ab851311e8 (accessed August 2008).
8. John Vu, "Vietnamese Americans Thirst for Blood Over A Name," *New America Media* Web site, Online August 2008, http://news.newamericamedia.org/news/view_article.html?article_id=97b3bcdd0aaa74a5a4bc148d0674c8c4.
9. James Flanagan, "Little Saigon Exports Its Prosperity," New York Times Website, Online August 2008, http://www.nytimes.com/2006/01/19/business/19sbiz.html; "Nguyen Beats Back Recall Effort," NBC Bay Area Web site, March 4, 2008, http://www.nbcbayarea.com/news/local/A-Win-for-Nguyen-Councilmember-Beating-Recall-Effort.html.
10. Christian Collet and Nadine Selden, "Separate Ways. Worlds Apart? The 'Generation Gap' in Vietnamese America as Seen Through The San Jose Mercury News Poll," *Amerasia Journal* 29 (2003): 199–217.
11. C. N. Le, *Asian American Assimilation: Ethnicity, Immigration, and Socioeconomic Attainment* (New York: LFB Scholarly Publishing, 2007).
12. Pei-Te Lien, M. Margaret Conway, and Janelle S. Wong, *The Politics of Asian Americans: Diversity & Community* (New York: Routledge, 2004).

RESOURCE GUIDE

Suggested Readings

Chan, Sucheng. *Survivors: Cambodian Refugees in the United States*. Urbana: University of Illinois Press, 2004.
Enloe, Cynthia. *Bananas, Beaches and Bases: Making Feminist Sense of International Politics*. New York: HarperCollins, 1989.
Enloe, Cynthia. *Maneuvers: The International Politics of Militarizing Women's Lives*. Berkeley: University of California Press, 2000.
del Rosario, Carina A., Ken Mochizuki, and Dean Wong, eds. *A Different Battle: Stories of Asian Pacific American Veterans*. Seattle: University of Washington Press, 2000.
Etcheson, Craig. *After the Killing Fields: Lessons from the Cambodian Genocide*. Greenwood, CT: Praeger Publishers, 2005.

Gardiner, C. Harvey. *Pawns in a Triangle of Hate: The Peruvian Japanese and the United States*. Seattle: University of Washington Press, 1981.

Henson, Maria Rosa. *Comfort Woman: A Filipina's Story of Prostitution and Slavery under the Japanese Military.* (Lanham, MD: Rowman and Littlefield, 1999).

Ignacio, Abraham, Enrique de la Cruz, Jorge Emmanuel, and Helen Toribio. *The Forbidden Book: The Philippine-American War in Political Cartoons*. San Francisco: T'Boli Publishing, 2004.

Kiang, Peter. "About Face: Recognizing Asian and Pacific American Vietnam Veterans in Asian American Studies." *Amerasia Journal* 17, no. 3 (1991).

Kim-Gibson, Dai Sil. *Silence Broken: Korean Comfort Women*. Iowa: Mid-Prairie Books, 1999.

Masterson, Daniel M., and Sayaka Funada-Classen. *The Japanese in Latin America*. Urbana: University of Illinois Press, 2003.

United States Commission on Wartime Relocation and Internment of Civilians. *Personal Justice Denied: Report of the Commission on Wartime Relocation and Internment of Civilians:* Report for the Committee on Interior and Insular Affairs by George Miller, chairman. Washington: U.S. Government Printing Office, 1992.

Films/Videos

Air America: The CIA's Secret Airline, DVD, directed by Jason Markham and Arthur Kent. A&E Home Video. 2000. (50 min.). Examines the history of this airline, how it began and its key role throughout the Vietnam War and Southeast Asian conflicts. Pilots of Air America and military historians recount their operations in Laos, from transporting personnel to delivering humanitarian aid.

New Year Baby, DVD, directed by Socheata Poeuv. Film-Baby. 2006. (80 min.). Embedded in documentary, travel narrative, and memoir, Socheata Poeuv, a Cambodian American, goes back to visit the genocide, including visiting labor camps and revisiting lost family members.

Regret to Inform, DVD, directed by Barbara Sonneborn. New York Films. 1998. (72 min.) The widow of a U.S. soldier in the Vietnam War, Sonneborn's very personal documentary traces her journey to Vietnam, where she talks with widows of Vietnamese soldiers who died during the conflict.

Second Class Veterans, DVD, directed by Donald Young. Asian American Media. 2002 (27 min.). Documentary that reveals the little-known story of Filipino World War II veterans who have been struggling to receive the military benefits promised by the U.S. government but never delivered.

Sentenced Home, DVD, directed by David Grabias and Nicole Newnham. Independent Lens. 2005 (76 min.). Documentary featuring three Cambodian men who face deportation to Cambodia. The three escaped the violence of the Khmer Rouge in the 1980s and came to the United States, where they joined street gangs as part of their response to a new and unfamiliar environment. As teenagers, they were found guilty of serious crimes and served sentences in the United States; however, under a new agreement between Cambodia and the United States, all three men face deportation to Cambodia, which would in effect punish them for crimes for which they have already served.

Silence Broken: Korean Comfort Women, DVD, directed by Dai-Sil Kim Gibson. Asian American Media. 2000 (88 min.). A combination of historical footage, interviews, and dramatic reenactments that portrays the story of Korean women who were forced into sexual labor during World War II by the Japanese Army. The first part of the film features interviews with several survivors of this experience, while the second part is a dramatic reenactment of three of the survivors.

Stories Untold: Memories of Korean War Survivors, Video, directed by Sulgi Kim. San Francisco State University, Asian American Studies, 2001. (53 min.). A documentary exploring the memories of older Korean immigrants who have lived through the Korean War.

The House of Sharing, directed by Hein Seok. Two Fish Pictures. 2007 (84 min.). A documentary that features eight elderly Korean women living at the House of Sharing in Korea. While the women are lively and humorous, the pain and anguish from their experiences as comfort women forced into sexual slavery by the Japanese Army during World War II are expressed in their words, paintings, and songs.

The Last Ghost of War, directed by Janet Gardner. PBS 2006 (54 min.). A look at the lasting effects of Agent Orange on the Vietnamese decades after the Vietnam War. It asks whether Agent Orange herbicides were chemical weapons. And if so, who should be held accountable for what could be the largest chemical warfare operation in history?

The Story of Vinh, DVD, directed by Keiko Tsuno. Asian American Media. 1990 (60 min.).This documentary follows Vinh, a Vietnamese Amerasian, during his failed struggle to find his identity after coming to America.

Voices of Challenge: Hmong Women in Transition, DVD, directed by Candace Lee Egan. Asian American Media. 1996 (39 min.) A documentary that features candid discussions by several women who share their experiences of fleeing Laos in the wake of Vietnam War and the challenging resettlement process in the United States.

Whose Children Are These? DVD, directed by Theresa Thanjan. Asian American Media. 2004 (27 min.). A documentary that raises the issues surrounding America's treatment of immigrants, particularly South Asian, Muslim and Arab immigrants, since the September 11 attacks. The three teenagers featured in the film talk about the impact of immigration policies that have separated their families through detentions and deportations.

Organizations

Hmong National Development. http://www.hndinc.org. National nonprofit organization that works to promote educational opportunities, increase community capacity, and develop resources for Hmong in U.S. society.

Lao Veterans of America. http://www.laoveterans.com. Nonprofit organized headquartered in Fresno, CA, that serves the general needs of former soldiers who served with the CIA during the "Secret War" in Laos during the Southeast Asian Conflict.

Minnesota Lao Veterans of America (MLVA). http://minnesotalaoveteransofamerica.org. Community-based nonprofit organization founded in 1991. The organization's mission is "to facilitate and promote the success of Hmong and Laotian Veterans and their families in Minnesota, while also recognizing and supporting other immigrant and refugee populations."

National Alliance for Filipino Veterans Equity (NAFVE). http://www.nafve.org. Coalition of local, national and international organizations and individuals that are working toward securing justice for Filipino World War II Veterans through restoration of U.S. veterans status for purposes of benefits.

Save North Korean Refugees. http://www.snkr.org/. Devoted to bringing to attention the continuing issues facing North Korean refugees.

South East Asian Resource Action Center. http://www.searac.org. Founded in 1979 as the Indochina Refugee Action Center to assist the relocation of Southeast Asian refugees into American society. The center serves as a coalition builder and leader to advance the interests of Southeast Asian Americans.

Violence Against Women in War—Network Japan. http://www1.jca.apc.org/vaww-net -japan/english/. Committed to eliminate violence against women in war and armed conflicts.

Washington Coalition for Comfort Women Issues. http://www.comfort-women.org/ history.html.

Yale Cambodian Genocide Program. http://www.yale.edu/cgp/. Tribunal news, photographs, maps of Cambodia, databases.

Web Sites

Asian-Nation. http://www.asian-nation.org/index.shtml. Founded by Vietnamese American Asian American Studies professor C. N. Le, the Vietnam section of this site covers the history of Vietnam, the war and the subsequent refugee exodus, as well as other related topics, in useful detail.

Asian/Pacific Americans in the U.S. Army. http://www.army.mil/asianpacificsoldiers/.

Covering the U.S. Civil War, World War I, World War II, the Korean War, the Vietnam War, the Gulf War and the Iraq War, this site provides basic information about Asian and Pacific Islander American service in these wars through short articles and video clips.

Babae Blog (Filipina Women). http://babaesf.blogspot.com/. Women's organization that serves to address the rights and welfare of Filipinas in the San Francisco Bay Area. It includes frequently updated blogs and YouTube videos.

Conscience and the Constitution. http://www.pbs.org/itvs/conscience/index.html. PBS site for the film *Conscience and the Constitution* that provides links to organizations, a list of texts for further reading, and a viewers guide.

JARDA: Japanese American Relocation Digital Archives. http://www.calisphere.universityofcalifornia.edu/jarda/. Provides primary sources and historical context for the Japanese American Relocation and Internment including photographs, letters and diaries, oral histories (transcribed), and art.

Still present pasts: Korean Americans and "the forgotten war." http://www.stillpresentpasts .org/spp/home/home.htm. Chronicling a multimedia exhibit on Korean Americans and their memories of the Korean War, this site includes a brief history of the Korean War and a study guide to accompany the exhibit.

The House of Sharing (Comfort Women). http://www.nanum.org/eng/. Focuses on the women who live in The House of Sharing, a home for living survivors of the Korean Comfort Women experience. It includes the history and profiles of comfort women, information about The Museum of Sexual Slavery by Japanese Military, and a bulletin board.

The Vietnam Center and Archive. http://www.vietnam.ttu.edu/. Vietnam Archive at Texas Tech University provides information on the "American Vietnam experience" through, among other supports, a virtual resource archive, teaching guides, an oral history project, the Vietnam Graffiti Project, news, and updates.

Section 11:

YOUTH, FAMILY, AND THE AGED

Section Editors: Alan Y. Oda and Grace J. Yoo

OVERVIEW: UNDERSTANDING GENERATIONS

Alan Y. Oda and Grace J. Yoo

Unlike the model minority myth, Asian Americans throughout their lives have had critical issues affect their sense of selves, their families and their communities. Generation, region, ethnicity, culture, and class all have an impact on the life course for Asian Americans. This diversity encompasses ethnic Japanese, many who are now four or more generations removed from the early immigrants. Stories of *Baachan* and *Jiichan* (Grandma and Grandpa) and other *Issei* (first immigrant generation) being forced into World War II Relocation Centers are still being told to children born to one Japanese parent and one non-Japanese or even non-Asian parent. It includes ethnic Cambodians, who found refuge in the United States from the murder and the forced labor of the Khmer Rouge. Ethnic Koreans made their presence known on the West Coast during the 1980s, becoming small business owners throughout Los Angeles, then found themselves later targeted during Sa-I-Gu (4/29), the start date of the 1992 L.A. riots. Within the diversity there are shared stories of struggle, racism, successes, and achievements, as well as shortcomings and frustrations. The entries through this section focus on the critical issues facing Asian Americans throughout the life course. This overview elaborates and identifies trends affecting the young, old, and families in Asian America today.

YOUTH AND FAMILY

An individual's understanding of cultural traditions, practices, behaviors, expectations, and history is introduced through family. In other words, a child initially learns about of what it means to be Chinese, Japanese, Korean,

Filipino, Vietnamese, or a member of any other group based on their interaction with parents, and further supported by other family members. In the past, the successful Asian American family has been defined as one able to adapt and accept Westernized cultural standards, including preferring to communicate in English, read and view less foreign media, veer away from traditional diet, and appear less ethnic in dress and appearance. Current research questions these standards, sometimes emphatically.

Part of this is because of the shift and general acceptance toward multiculturalism and away from a dominant—and often exclusive—Euro-American perspective about children and families. Much of the literature has been from Euro-American researchers who view development from their own cultural perspective. Put simply, whether intended or not, a primary developmental goal has been the acquisition of American culture.[1] More recent theories about child development are beginning to reflect greater diversity in childrearing practices and families from a cross-cultural viewpoint.

Another notable shift involves viewing minority American children as doing more than adapting to discrimination. Much of the scholarship on Asian Americans and other minorities has been focused on how families respond to racism, poverty, and/or other stresses that impede progress toward assimilation into the mainstream culture. Lost in the discussion until recently were the positive characteristics associated with becoming Asian American.[2] Rather than viewing development simply as progress in acculturating to mainstream culture, a more constructive view of development can be viewed from criteria determined by standards and values important—and perhaps distinctive—to Asian Americans.

One corollary to consider is that Asian Americans may experience stressors unique to their culture, irrelevant to acculturation and other processes. The same cultural values that encourage educational achievement can also cause tensions and conflict between parents and children. The strong support resulting from the extended family can also grate against a desire for greater independence and freedom for Asian American youth. And sometimes, the younger generation more strongly identifies with cultural roots compared with their parents who made acculturation and acceptance into mainstream society their priority. The third generation often addresses the issues forgotten in the second generation.[3]

Much of the current literature on the effects of family on the developing child addresses issues of mainstream individuals, with an inadequate breadth of studies on the uniqueness of minority American populations and in particular, Asian Americans.[4] Theories of youth development are either extrapolated from Western developmental models or from the problematic "deficit" models of Asian Americans described earlier.[5] One common characteristic observed in many Asian American populations is filial piety, which defines the relationship between the young and elderly. Children are expected to have a life-long respect of the authority of one's parents and the family name. Filial piety also emphasizes an interdependence and loyalty between children and parents, as the actions of a child can bring either honor or shame to the entire family, not just the individual. The concept of filial piety is linked with the Confucian origins of many Asian philosophies and cultures. This contrasts with the Western emphasis on parents fostering independence and individualism in their children.

Another commonality is the extended family. This family structure offers one of the more conspicuous differences of Asian American families. Specifically, Westernized cultures largely emphasize the nuclear family, stressing the importance of independence, individual achievement and individuation. By contrast, the extended family fosters interdependence, group identity, and shared achievement. To illustrate, the success of a child reflects well on the parents and other family members. Beyond the nuclear family, the extended family can incorporate grandparents, aunts, uncles, and even close family friends.

The prominence of the extended family assists in facilitating the maintenance of certain values and traditions. For example, it is widely accepted among Asian cultures that education and respect for ones' parents are valued principles. These values are often shared by parents and reinforced by other family members within the extended family structure. Accordingly, there is evidence that high standards of children's educational achievement and respect for authority are indeed values commonly retained by Asian American families. One other possibility as to why Asian cultural beliefs are retained is because of the reticence of Asian Americans to seek assistance from nonfamily members and instead rely upon family members.

Besides the processes of acculturation, enculturation is another process affecting the cultural development of youth. It is common to confuse acculturation and enculturation in the study of Asian Americans and other minority Americans.[6] However, enculturation is defined separately as learning without specific teaching.[7] Certain values and beliefs are not deliberately taught but instead are "absorbed" in a sometimes unintentional and nonevaluative manner. Arguably such beliefs become embedded into youth and are not easily changed or challenged. From a developmental perspective, enculturation is a powerful conduit for familiarizing children with traditions and culture-based behaviors.

There are also more deliberate behaviors observed between parents and children which help convey traditional family practices and values. Infants commonly sleep with their mothers, and later may prefer to share the bedroom with their parents versus their own individual bedroom, a physical demonstration of the bonds and interdependence between parent and child. When children begin school in middle childhood, parents teach their children to respect and obey their teachers, again highlighting the significance of youth submitting to their elders, be it teachers or parents. Older siblings are expected to take on the responsibility of caring for their younger brothers and sisters, encouraging the belief of family before individuality. The adolescent is expected to continue to assist in caring for siblings, plus make other contributions to the well-being of the family, underpinning the prioritization of family and collectivistic community.[8] By middle childhood, children are reminded about respecting parents as authority. Another prominent trait of Asian American families is parent-centered (authoritarian) childrearing, differing from child-centered parenting practices observed in Westernized families.[9] Parental authority is largely unqualified and dominant.[10] Authoritarian practices helps reinforce the respect that children are expected to have toward their parents.

At the same time, the parental role in filial piety is also demanding. Compared to other ethnicities, American families of Asian origin are more aggressive in providing financial, human, and within-family social capital for their children.[11] Because there is a shared concern for the success of the group, there is mutual support offered between family members.[12] Both parents and children are expected to make personal sacrifices to benefit each other and the group as a whole.

Yet the description of Asian American parenting as "authoritarian" has its own hazards, a lucid example of the shortcomings of the scholarship on Asian Americans. Ruth Chao, a developmental psychologist, has stated that the concept of authoritarian parenting is based on an ethnocentric perspective that is inadequate to capture distinctive features of Asian American parenting. The Western labels used to describe parenting practices miss the unique nuances and idiosyncrasies of non-mainstream cultures. For example, the Chinese term *chiao shun* help describes a mother's "training" of children, involving more strict and deliberate teaching and educating of their daughters and sons. This may sound militaristic and rigid compared with Western parenting practices emphasizing the "nurturance" of children. Another unique term is *guan*, which is literally translated as "to govern" but can also mean "to care for." Chinese American mothers believe they must be strict to protect and enhance—and not inhibit—their children's successful growth.[13]

A related cultural distinction is observed in Japanese culture. *Amae* is at least partly defined as indulgent dependence between mother and child.[14] Like the Chinese terms of *chiao shun* and *guan*, the Japanese term *amae* lacks a precise or even adequate English translation, and may be disdained by Western standards, particularly in its perceived pampering and coddling. An example of *amae* is given where a six-year-old child climbs on the knees of her mother and expects to be read a storybook while the mother is busy with another task.[15] The authority of the parent is respected, yet the child also expects that his mother will fulfill and even indulge her needs. Again, describing such a relationship as "authoritarian" would be severely limiting.

The complex inimitability of Asian parenting traits may help explain how such practices persist throughout generations even within the mainstream culture. First, Asian childrearing practices can reinforce the traditional collectivistic, extended family system. Second, the strength of the parent-child relationship may lie in the variety of ways parents demonstrate their commitment to their children, while in return, children are expected to meet their parents' numerous expectations. Such intricate and subtle relationships, while potentially beneficial to both sides, can also be the source of stressors and challenges on both sides of childrearing. Contrasted with Westernized expectations of children's individuation and independence, the possibility of conflict between parents and children may be further aggravated.

Consequently, the parent-child relationship has evolved over many years. Changes have been noted as early as the 1930s, with the Americanization of traditions raising the concerns of early immigrant families. First-generation Japanese parents (*Issei*) lamented the dissolution of filial piety and respect for patriarchal authority in the behaviors of their American-born, second-generation (*Nisei*) children.[16]

Among Chinese families, it is expected—by both recent immigrant Chinese (from Taiwan) and Chinese American mothers—that their children will revere their parents; however, it is noted that Chinese American mothers, as a likely influence of mainstream culture, tended to be a bit less restrictive than more recent Chinese immigrant mothers. Similar observations have been observed for Japanese American mothers and other Chinese American mothers.[17]

Likewise, traditional beliefs among Korean immigrant families include their children's expected obedience to their parents and an emphasis on high educational achievement. One mediating factor observed among Korean families is language assimilation, whether or not Korean-speaking parents and their English-speaking children can communicate effectively in spite of language barriers.[18]

The experience of Vietnamese and Cambodian immigrant families has been further exacerbated by their migratory status. One observation is that as parents make the difficult transition into mainstream society with varying degrees of success, parental authority may be compromised.[19] Of particular interest is the effect of cultural discrepancy between the more tradition-bound parents and the more rapidly acculturating children, specifically a decline in the affective relationship between generations which can predict future problem behaviors in youth.[20]

One illustration of this discrepancy—and a largely unexplored question—is whether the eventual loss of native language reflects differing educational levels between parents and children; in other words, advice offered in the "mother tongue" of the parents may be dismissed by children as being naive or irrelevant. Nonetheless, this may instead reflect a consequence of language barriers, as children lose their family's native language, more complex thoughts and emotions become harder to express. Further, some research links language loss as being detrimental to parent-child bonding. Psychological barriers and language barriers in Chinese American families may be enmeshed.[21]

INTERGENERATIONAL TENSIONS

The common assumption in American families—particularly during the adolescent years—is that concerns, conflicts, and even clashes are normal. For Asian American families, the standard of "normal" is much more variable. The mainstream society stresses the importance of forming an independent identity, emphasizing individualism. Yet the collectivistic Asian traditions not only accentuate group identity, an important value is harmonious dependence.[22] Therein exists a further complication, that any desire to establish individualism is stifled by both the traditional value of group identity but also group harmony.

Thus, there is a competition of values within an Asian American family. This is likely most pronounced for children who are either U.S.-born or who arrived in the States at a young age. Besides the growing pains associated with the childhood-to-teen transition, an Asian American youth must somehow resolve the obvious conflict between traditional family, group interdependence and mainstream individualism, all within the context of a culture that stresses harmony within the family.

It prompts another review of the childrearing practices of Asian Americans. It was stated previously that many Asian Americans, across all ethnic groups, exercise strong parental control, expect respect for the elderly and other adults, and emphasize the importance of family. Although these ideals are prevalent, these same ideals can be inappropriately used to negate the tensions, stresses, and differences that Asian Americans experience throughout the life course. The same ties that promote family cohesion can also be the ties that bind.

Complicating this dilemma even further is the reticence of Asian Americans to seek counseling or other help resources. Once again, traditional Asian values can strongly influence such behaviors. Discussing family issues with outsiders is considered to be disloyal and can adversely affect the family's reputation ("family shame"). Additionally, one's own resources and inner strength should suffice in resolving personal distress; psychological help is a sign of weakness.[23]

One illustration of this phenomenon is observed among Vietnamese immigrant families and their America-born children. More than half of children of Vietnamese immigrants find it difficult to discuss their problems with their parents, as the latter are often non-English speaking laborers engaged in low-wage arduous work.[24] However, discussing either personal or family issues with an outsider may be viewed as disloyalty to the family ties. Help is sought only when the family is in some sort of psychosocial crisis.[25]

There are other sources of stressors for Asian American youth. What could be characterized as "violation of personal boundaries" in Western psychology instead may be considered normal behaviors in Asian American families. Chinese American mothers, whether recent immigrants to the United States or mothers more established in mainstream culture, agree that children should not challenge their parents, that parents can and should have the power to approve (and disapprove) children's activities, and that active intrusion by parents into their children's lives is not just acceptable, but desirable.[26] Higher expectations and participation from parents with their children's education are associated with better educational achievement in Chinese and Korean immigrant families, again noting that parents are often actively involved in their children's lives. Interestingly, one study of Korean American adolescents viewed parental control as being associated with parental warmth and caring, a sharp contrast to data obtained from North American youth.[27] Asian immigrant parents are also more demanding, expecting high achievement in many areas of academic activity, while white parents were satisfied if children excelled in at least one area (school, athletics, music, among others).[28]

So in addition to high parental involvement based on fostering interdependence—conflicting with the individualistic emphasis of main-stream culture—Asian American youth also must answer to high demands for academic excellence. Adolescents in particular may resist such demands derived from cultural values, traditions, and lifestyles imposed by parents, particularly when such expectations diverge with the Western-oriented values that the Asian American adolescent is exposed to on a daily basis. Compared with other ethnic groups, Asian Americans reported the highest likelihood of family conflict.[29] Although it was difficult to distinguish whether minor and severe psychopathology was related to cultural conflicts or acculturation stress, studies have documented that Asian Americans have at least the same incidence of personal and emotional issues when compared to white and other ethnic students, challenging the assumptions of the "model minority" stereo-type. Another complication is the observation—for numerous reasons—that Asian Americans are least likely to seek counseling and psychological help compared with any other American ethnic group, although differences between different ethnic subgroups has been noted.[30] Interestingly, there appears to be no significant relationship between values acculturation and professional help-seeking attitudes.[31]

Several topics having an impact on Asian American youth and families require more discussion and scholarship. Not all Asian Americans are success-ful in education. It is true that a large percentage of Asian Americans are suc-cessful academically, yet many students are not at the top of their class. Economic class of an Asian American family can make a difference between a mother who can devote much of her time supporting her children's education versus a mother who must engage in long hours of low-wage labor to support her family. The educational background of the parents can also make a signifi-cant impact, as many recent Asian immigrants, such as Cambodian, Hmong, Laotian, and Vietnamese parents, have less than a high school education, a stark contrast to more acculturated Filipino, Japanese, Asian Indian, and Korean immigrant parents.[32] A comparable study assessed the difference between academically successful Korean Americans students versus dropouts. Class differences, educational resources, and social networks were all implicated in predicting student achievement.[33]

Another topic of interest is Asian American at-risk youth. Already there is scholarship discussing gang activity, yet there is little consensus as to the etiology or the nature of such gangs.[34] Still, there is little doubt that economic and social divides will continue to exacerbate delinquency and other antisocial behaviors among Asian American youth. Conflict within and between genera-tions is probable.[35]

In general, one wonders whether or not the future of Asian America will be viewed in a bimodal manner, a bifurcated population. There continue to be examples of Asian American youth who appear to fulfill the stereotype of the "model minority." In 2006, Asian Americans surpassed whites as the largest ethnic group admitted to the University of California.[36] Yet the number of Asian American youth who are neither academically nor economically successful is likely to continue to grow. In both situations, the reticence of Asian Americans to engage in support services and assistance can only aggravate the divide.

CARING ACROSS GENERATIONS

Many of the different entries in this section focus on caring within families. Asian American families are unique in that they wrestle between the values of filial piety and family interdependence. Yet the concept of family interdependence is worth review as a separate characteristic as it further elucidates the collectivistic nature of Asian cultures. Such interdependence emphasizes in-group goals and prioritizing of the group over personal agendas, versus Western cultures, which emphasize independence and the importance of personal achievement over group achievement and success. Generally, Asian American families assume members can rely on, assist, and provide resources for one another, yet as stated earlier, such family ties can also be the ties that bind.

There is a widespread assumption within and outside the Asian American community that Asian American families take care of their own—more specifically that they take care of their aging and sick family members. The literature on Asian American ethnic families furthermore promotes this common assumption that there is a willingness of adult children to care for their aging parent and an expectation of the old to be cared by them. Although the traditional Asian family is seen as strong with filial ties, there is lack of critical discussion of how adult children in a new country who are overworked, lack resources, and lack time and money can provide the emotional, social, and financial needs of their aging parents.[37] Despite this common assumption that Asian Americans can "take care of their own," not all Asian Americans have the capacity and ability to care for aging relatives. Not all Asian Americans are considered to be financially successful—there is a greater percentage of Asian Americans below the poverty line compared to whites, plus the median income is lower for Asian Americans compared to whites with similar academic degrees and experience. At the same time, Asian Americans who are caring for their parents are often "sandwiched" between caring for aging parents and young children. Asian Americans who are sandwiched experience more guilt compared with other racial/ethnic groups about not doing enough for their aging parent.[38] In fact, two out of five Asian Americans caring for an aging parent have taken time off work to help care for an aging parent and one in two regularly accompany their parents on doctor's visits.[39] Caring for the older generation comes at a cost, including caregiver stress. One in three Asian Americans providing care to an aging parent experiences caregiver-related stress, such as exhaustion, lacking concentration, and feeling of being overwhelmed.

Despite the difficulties of caring for an aging family member, many younger, American-born Asians still cling to the ideal that they plan to take care of their parents.[40] Asian Americans, especially those with immigrant parents, are socialized to think about caring for their parents because they have a better English ability and understanding of cultural American norms. Even though Asian Americans may cling to the ideals that they will care for their parents in old age, many adult Asian Americans have not discussed issues such as wills, advance directives, and other important legal and health matters with their aging parents, and they are often unprepared when an aging family member needs care.[41] At the same time, there are changes in the beliefs and expectations among Asian Americans and their aging parents about caregiving and living independently. Researchers have found that for many Asian immigrant elderly living independently is often more preferred that residing with adult children. Beliefs about who is supposed to care for an aging family member and how to provide that care are changing with time and with generation. For example, older Korean immigrants are caught between two different traditions: one that is strongly collective-oriented, where the interests of the family are primary, and an American tradition of independence and individuality. Migrating to the United States many older Koreans immigrants strive to continue to maintain their independence and do not want to depend on their children for financial or tangible support.[42] Rather they would rather rely on more formal support for assistant. At the same time, with increasing acculturation and subsequent generations of Asian Americans, ideals of filial piety are changing.

Social service providers may not have the knowledge and the wherewithal to provide culturally appropriate and helpful services, which are often lacking for Asian American populations. Children can provide a valuable bridge in navigating through complicated and convoluted processes in order to secure needed aid and programs, though the adequate fulfillment of such responsibilities has been historically variable at best. Aging, frail family members may face burn out and exhaustion.[43] Previous research has shown that Asian Americans have avoided use of long-term care facilities, such as skilled nursing facilities, because of costs, stigma of family abandonment, fear of social isolation, and low quality of care.[44] For Asian immigrant elderly, three significant losses occur for those entering into a nursing home: loss of family, loss of culture, and loss of community.[45] Throughout the United States, there are innovative programs that service Asian immigrant families around long-term care. Unique programs include the Keiro Services in the Los Angeles area and the Asian community nursing home in Sacramento. Started in 1961, Keiro Services is the largest eldercare provider for the Japanese American community in the nation. Started by community members, the Asian community nursing home in Sacramento provides a 24-hour skilled nursing facility as well as drop-in respite care for care providers. Both of these eldercare services provide care in a culturally sensitive environment with close attention food, language and values.

EVER-CHANGING FAMILIES

What will be of interest to both scholars and families alike will be the persistence of distinctive behaviors singular to Asian American families. More and more common are mixed marriages, defined as an individual marrying someone of a different ethnicity or race. The trend was first documented in the 1980s, when it was noted that almost two-thirds of Japanese Americans and half of Chinese Americans in Los Angeles County were marrying someone of differ-

Increases in the Divorce Rate

Like other populations, Asian Americans are seeing an increase in the divorce rate. Yet unlike other communities, the impact of divorce may be more convoluted for Asian Americans. The number of divorces, though increasing, is still less than other American ethnic groups. Consequently, there are few available resources for divorcees for support and recovery within the Asian American community. Making it more difficult is the perception of failure and shame associated with the dissolved marriage, which can affect the response and encouragement offered by the extended family.

In addition, the extended family can become the "ties that bind," making a tenuous situation more exigent. Many are largely unfamiliar with divorce, and are often confused at best. What happens to the relationship between uncles, aunties, cousins, grandparents, and other family members with the divorced couple and their children is potentially perplexing. It is not just about whom to visit during the holidays, it is also about sorting out loyalties and penchants for all parties involved throughout the entire year.

The patriarchical nature of Asian American families can also become a stressor, particularly in shared custody arrangements. Traditionally, the mother is responsible for the day-to-day care of children, making sure homework is completed, chores are fulfilled, and other tasks are accomplished. Time spent with Dad often ranges from unfulfilling and boring to being totally entertained and pampered because the maternal parent is responsible for the "business" of childrearing.

With successive generations of Asian Americans, differences with the mainstream population may become attenuated, yet the question is whether or not the multigenerational structure of extended Asian American families will maintain and perhaps continue to complicate the already unfortunate conditions surrounding divorce.

—Alan Y. Oda

ent ethnic or racial heritage.[46] Whereas some theorists view this as a sign of successful assimilation by Asian Americans into the mainstream culture, at least one author has challenged this assumption, stating that racial inequality is a more appropriate explanatory construct.[47] As far as the children of mixed-raced marriages, one study stated that more than 40 percent these children identify with their Asian heritage.[48]

Asian Americans are also experiencing higher divorce rates than a decade ago. These changes are attributed to acculturation to more American norms regarding marriage and divorce.[49] Divorce tends to be less culturally acceptable in Asian countries, but with the increasing numbers of Asians born in this country, divorces have increased. Nonetheless, U.S. Census figures state that the divorce rate among Asian Americans is roughly half of whites. There is very little scholarship addressing any unique facets of Asian Americans and divorce.

Another trend of note is the continued entry of Asians into the United States via adoptions. While overall adoption rates tripled between 1990 and 2005, more than four out of every ten children adopted was from an Asian country. This is another topic not widely discussed in the literature, although there appears to be far less controversy about transnational Asian adoptions compared with children from Africa and Native American populations, considered by some to be a form of "cultural genocide."[50] Anecdotally, it has been observed that many of the adoptees from China, Korea, and other Asian countries are being placed in Asian American families.

The configuration of Asian American families is also changing as well as the support for such families. In California, 57 percent of Asian Americans opposed Proposition 8, which would recognize marriage between men and women and not same-sex couples. Also in California, one in ten same-sex couples is an Asian American.[51] At the same time, more than 50 percent of these couples are raising children. Asian American same-sex couples with children have a lower average household income and rate of home ownership than non–same-sex Asian American households with children.[52] Researchers and practitioners have stated that Asian American same-sex families face "triple minority" status because of racial and sexual orientation discrimination, as well as inadequate support from community, institutions, and their own families.[53]

Researchers have indicated that different ethnic groups under the umbrella of Asian American cannot and should not be viewed as part of one homogeneous group. Aside from different characteristics of each ethnic community, diverse emigration histories factor into any discussion of whether distinguishing practices will be passed down from generation to generation. Still, Asian Americans continue to stand out as a distinct population demonstrating at least some similar characteristics. Many of these distinctions have been, and continue to be, idealized, as in the model minority stereotype, which despite challenges by scholars and other authors, continues to persist. Such stereotypes affect public policy, where Asian American communities are deprived of resources and needed funding to assist both recent immigrants and later generations, who require at least the same level of services as other ethnic communities.

Much of the past scholarship on Asian America has been focused on Chinese, Japanese, Korean, and Filipino populations. Studies of Southeast Asian communities have largely focused on the immigrant experience. Just recently, findings about second-generation Southeast Asian Americans have become available, stating that Vietnamese have appeared to find success in mainstream culture, yet Cambodians, Hmong, and Laotians have not yet attained similar measures of achievement.[54]

Another question not explored here is whether the persistence of culturally based behaviors among Asian American families is a testimony to the strength and the advantageous nature offered by certain traditions and practices, or whether such behaviors are a reaction to continued racism and stereotyping. Such far-reaching questions will require a multidisciplinary view to better understand the current and future of Asian America.

NOTES

1. P. M. Greenfield and R. R. Cocking, *Cross-Cultural Roots of Minority Child Development* (Mahwah, NJ: Lawrence Erlbaum Associates, 1994).

2. Greenfield and Cocking, *Cross-Cultural Roots*, 11.

3. D. Montrero, *Japanese Americans: Changing Patterns of Ethnic Affiliation over Three Generations* (Boulder, CO: Westview, 1980).

4. D. B. Qin, N. Way, and P. Mukherjee, "The Other Side of the Model Minority Story: The Familial and Peer Challenges Faced by Chinese American Adolescents," *Youth and Society* 39 (2008): 480–506.

5. Greenfield and Cocking, *Cross-Cultural Roots*.

6. B. S. K. Kim, "Adherence to Asian and European American Cultural Values and Attitudes Toward Seeking Professional Psychological Help among Asian American College Students," *Journal of Counseling Psychology* 54 (2007): 474–480.

7. U. Kim and S. Choi, "Individualism, Collectivism, and Child Development: A Korean Perspective," in *Cross Cultural Roots of Minority Child Development*, ed. P. Greenfield and R. Cocking (Hillsdale, NJ: Lawrence Erlbaum, 1994), 259–274.

8. A. Lau, "Family Therapy and Ethnic Minorities," in *Meeting the Needs of Ethnic Minority Children*, 2nd ed., ed. K. N. Dwivedi (London: Jessica Kingsley, 2002), 91–107.

9. J. Steinberg, S. M. Dornbusch, and B. B. Brown, "Ethnic Differences in Adolescent Achievement. An Ecological Perspective," *American Psychologist* 47 (1992): 723–729.

10. D. Baumrind, "The Influence of Parenting Style on Adolescent Competence and Substance Use," *The Journal of Early Adolescence* 11 (1991): 56–95.

11. Y. Su, "The Academic Success of East-Asian-American Students—An Investment Model," *Social Science Research* 27 (1998): 432–456.

12. A. J. Fuligni, V. Tseng, and M. Lam, "Attitudes toward Family Obligations among American Adolescents with Asian, Latin American, and European Background," *Child Development* 70 (1999): 1030–1044.

13. R. Chao, "Beyond Parental Control and Authoritarian Parenting Style: Understanding Chinese Parenting through the Cultural Notion of Training," *Child Development* 65 (1994): 1111–1119.

14. T. Matsudaira, T. Fukuhara, and T. Kitamura, "Factor Structure of the Japanese Interpersonal Competence Scale," *Psychiatry and Clinical Neurosciences* 62 (2008): 142–151. Retrieved Nov. 29, 2008, from MEDLINE.

15. Y. Niiya, P. C. Ellsworth, and S. Yamaguchi, "Amae in Japan and the United States: An Exploration of a 'Culturally Unique' Phenomenon," *Emotion* 6 (2006): 279–205.

16. E. H. Tamura, *Americanization, Acculturation, and Ethnic Identity: The Nisei Generation in Hawaii* (Urbana: University of Illinois Press, 1994).

17. H. L. Chiu, "Child-Rearing Attitudes of Chinese, Chinese-American, and Anglo-American Mothers," *International Journal of Psychology* 22 (1987): 409–419.

18. E. Kim and S. W. Wolpin, "The Korean American Family: Adolescents versus Parents Acculturation to American Culture," *Journal of Cultural Diversity* 15 (2008): 108–116.

19. N. Foner and P. Kasinitz, "The Second Generation," in *The New Americans: A Guide to Immigration since 1965*, eds. M. C. Waters, R. Ueba, and H. B. Marrow (Cambridge, MA: Harvard University Press, 2007), 270–282.

20. Qin, et al., "The Other Side," 483.

21. Qin, et al., "The Other Side," 480–506.

22. R. Fan, "Self-Determination vs. Family-Determination: Two Incommensurable Principles of Autonomy: A Report from East Asia," *Bioethics* 11 (1997): 309–322.

23. S. K. Kim, D. R. Atkinson, and D. Umemoto, "Asian Cultural Values and the Counseling Process: Current Knowledge and Directions for Future Research," *The Counseling Psychologist* 29 (2001): 570–603.

24. Maria Cramer, "Disconnected: The City's Vietnamese Population is Turning to Harvard for Help in Understanding the Problems Its Youth Are Facing—Problems that Are Often Manifested through Violence," *The Boston Globe,* May 27, 2008. Retrieved on Dec. 15, 2008 http://www.boston.com/news/local/articles/2008/05/27/disconnected/.

25. S. C. Kim, "Family Therapy for Asian Americans: A Strategic-Structural Framework," *Psychotherapy* 22 (1985): 342–348.

26. L. Hao and M. Bonstead-Burns, "Parent-Child Differences in Educational Expectations and the Academic Achievement of Immigrant and Native Students," *Sociology of Education* 71 (1998): 175–198; R. P. Rohner and S. M. Pettengill, "Perceived Parental Acceptance-Rejection and Parental Control among Korean Adolescents," *Child Development* 56 (1985): 524–528.

27. Rohner and Pettengill, "Perceived Parental Acceptance," 524–528.

28. B. Schneider and Y. Lee, "A Model for Academic Success: The School and Home Environment of East Asian Students," *Anthropology and Education Quarterly* 21 (1990): 358–377; G. Kao, "Asian Americans as Model Minorities? A Look at Their Academic Performance," *American Journal of Education* (1995): 121–159.

29. University of California–Davis, "Suicide In Asian Americans: Family Conflict Increases Risk Of Suicide Attempts," Science Daily, Aug. 20, 2008, http://www.sciencedaily.com/releases/2008/08/080817223446.htm (accessed Nov. 11, 2008).

30. S. Sue et al., "Mental Health Research on Asian Americans," *Journal of Community Psychology* 22 (1994): 61–67; F. T. L. Leong, "Asian Americans' Differential Patterns of Utilization of Inpatient and Outpatient Public Mental Health Services in Hawaii," *Journal of Community Psychology* 22 (1994): 82–96.

31. Kim, "Adherence to Asian and European American Cultural Values," 474–480.

32. W. Au and Benji Chang, "You're Asian, How Could You Fail Math?" *Rethinking Schools* 22 (2007), http://www.rethinkingschools.org/archive/22_02/math222.shtml

(accessed Dec. 6, 2008); J. Lew, *Asian Americans in Class: Charting the Achievement Gap among Korean American Youth* (New York: Teachers College Press, 2006).

33. Lew, *Asian Americans in Class.*

34. G. T. Tsunokai and A. J. Kposowa, "Asian Gangs in the United States: The Current State of the Research Literature," *Crime, Law, and Social Change* 37 (2002): 37–50.

35. E. T. Trueba et al., *Myth or Reality: Adaptive Strategies of Asian American* (New York: Routledge, 1992).

36. L. M. Krieger and L. Fernandez, "Asians Surpass Mark at UC: White Admissions Fall to Second Place for the First Time," *San Jose Mercury News* 4 (2006), http://www.accessmylibrary.com/coms2/summary_0286-14943001_ITM (accessed on July 24, 2009).

37. Grace Yoo and Barbara Kim, "Remembering Sacrifices, Negotiating Cultures and Institutions: Second-Generation Korean Americans and Their Caregiving Expectations and Responsibilities to Aging Immigrant Parents," unpublished paper (2008), 1–25.

38. Belden, Russolleno, and Stewart Research, Strategy, and Management, AARP Report: "In the Middle: A Report on Multicultural Boomers Coping with Family and Aging Issues," July 2001, http://assets.aarp.org/rgcenter/il/in_the_middle.pdf (accessed on Dec. 15, 2008).

39. Belden, Russolleno, and Stewart, "In the Middle: A Report on Multicultural Boomers."

40. Yoo and Kim, "Remembering Sacrifices.

41. Yoo and Kim, "Remembering Sacrifices.

42. Sabrina Wong, Grace Yoo & Anita Stewart, "An Empirical Evaluation of Social Support and Psychological Well-Being in Older Chinese and Korean Immigrants," *Ethnicity and Health* 12, no.1 (2007): 43–67.

43. Belden, Russolleno, and Stewart "In the Middle: A Report on Multicultural Boomers,"

44. Nancy Hikoyeda and Steven Wallace, "Do Ethnic-Specific Long Term Care Facilities Improve Resident Quality of Life? Findings from the Japanese American Community," in *Social Work Practice with the Asian American Elderly*, ed. Namkee Choi (New York: Haworth Press, 2002).

45. Michael Maclean and Rita Bonar, "Ethnic Elderly People in Long Term Care Facilities of the Dominant Culture: Implications for Social Work Practice and Education," *International Social Work* 2 (1986): 227–236.

46. H. Kitano et al., "Asian-American Interracial Marriage," *Journal of Marriage and the Family* 46 (1984): 179–190.

47. S. Chow, "The Significance of Race in the Private Sphere: Asian Americans and Spousal Preferences," *Sociological Inquiry* 70 (2000): 1–29.

48. R. Saenz et al., "Persistence and Change in Asian Identity among Children of Intermarried Couples. Identity among Children of Intermarried Couples," *Sociological Perspectives* 38 (1995): 175–194.

49. The Associated Press, "Census: Divorce Rate Up among Asians," *USA Today*, posted May 28, 2003, http://www.usatoday.com/news/nation/census/2003-05-28-asians-census_x.htm (accessed Dec. 15, 2008).

50. K. Condit, "Familial Legacies: Rethinking Transnational Asian Adoption in the 21st Century," Paper presented at the annual meeting of the American Studies Association, Oct 12, 2006, http://www.allacademic.com/meta/p113665_index.html (accessed Dec. 7, 2008).

51. UCLA Williams Institute, "Asian and Pacific Islanders in Same Sex Couples in California: Data from the 2000 Census," http://www.law.ucla.edu/williamsinstitute/publications/API_Report.pdf (accessed Dec. 15, 2008).

52. UCLA Williams Institute, "Asian and Pacific Islanders."

53. Diane Hayashino and Sapna Batra Chopra, "Parenting and Raising Families," in *Asian American Psychology,* ed. Nita Tewari and Alvin Alvarez (New York: Taylor and Francisco, 2008), 317–336.

54. A. Sakamoto and H. Woo, "The Socioeconomic Attainments of Second-Generation Cambodian, Hmong, Laotian, and Vietnamese Americans," *Sociological Inquiry 77* (2007): 44–75.

AT-RISK YOUTH

Roderick Daus-Magbual and Jonell Molina

In January 2008, a Vietnamese gang in the south Boston neighborhood of Dorchester was caught on video beating a 14-year-old girl and 15-year-old boy into bloodied oblivion.[1] A report on teen pregnancy showed a higher percentage of teenage pregnancy among Cambodian and Laotian teenagers than any other Asian American subgroup.[2] These stories represent the issues and challenges that at-risk Asian American youth face in the United States. Historically, Asian American youth have often been depicted as "whiz kids," but these stories demonstrate that Asian Americans also face issues that put them at risk.[3] Although the definition of the term "at-risk" varies and stigmatizes particular groups, the term is nonetheless widely used in schools and among service providers, funders, policy makers, scholars, and media.[4] Being at-risk means events, relationships, circumstances, or conditions that influences and/or limits an individual's access to succeed.[5] At-risk youth often face more issues, such as a higher high school dropout rate, gangs, suicide, teenage pregnancy, drugs, and substance abuse.

Being Asian American brings into focus the delicate balance of traditional values, customs, and the pressure to assimilate to American norms.[6] Asian American youth face the challenge to "fit in" within educational institutions, among peers, and social networks.[7] A common stereotype of Asian American youth as the whiz kid continues a pattern that is harmful and threatens the relationships between youths and their families, as well as how youths understand their identity.[8] An example of this phenomenon is the depiction of Asian American youth as academic achievers who rarely get in trouble, which keeps many immigrant parents complacent about the dangers their children face.[9]

One of the many challenges Asian American families face is the disappearing family unit in America.[10] This disruption of the Asian American family is creating a generation of Asian American youth who are lacking a social support unit. Like many Latino immigrant families, Asian American families are finding it tough to connect to their children.[11] Many Asian American youth find direction and their sense of identity from peers and messages in popular culture. With no place to turn but the environment and influences in their neighborhood, youth may feel the anxiety and pressure of being misunderstood. To make up for the absence of family and parental guidance, Asian American youth begin to model behavior from their peers or completely withdraw.[12]

For Asian American youth who struggle, at-risk indicators can include: declining academic performance, such as poor grades, truancy, and expulsion; the lack of friends; mental health issues; and experimentation and use of substances such alcohol, tobacco, and other drugs.[13] Vietnamese, Cambodia, Laotian, Hmong, and Mien are more at risk than other Asian American subgroups because of academic performance issues that include language backgrounds and abilities, history of schooling, reasons of migrating to America, trauma, issues of identity, and sense of self-efficacy.[14]

Commonly overlooked in Asian American youth experiences is the wide array of societal and local community problems that they face in their communities. Issues of poverty, immigration, the pressure to assimilate, the failure of urban schools, and the lack of a cultural identity are various factors that can contribute to Asian American youth in becoming at risk.[15] For example, at-risk Southeast Asian youth face cultural differences and hardships often attributed to their relocation and settlement in America.[16] Similar to these experiences, many Asian immigrant groups share experiences of overcrowded households and immigrant parents working longer hours.[17] In order to survive, families are left to assimilate and acculturate themselves into new environments and surroundings. These factors contribute to Asian American youth feeling isolated, depressed, and helpless, and lead to generational conflicts between parents and children.

GANGS

Racial tension and violence are concerns for many Asian American youth.[18] Connie Vang, a Hmong American high school sophomore, described in 2005 the tension between African Americans and Asian Americans at her Central Valley high school in California. A simple food fight at the high school between Asian and African American students escalated into a near riot, and almost 600 students did not attend school because of fears of continued violence.[19] Many Asian American youth reported staying home from school because they were afraid for their safety.[20] Racial conflict and tensions remain present in many school sites that instill a sense of fear to attend school.

Like many youth of color growing up in communities of failing schools and high rates of violence and murder, Asian American youth choose to align and involve themselves with gangs for safety, community, and camaraderie.[21] For many Asian American youth who feel disenfranchised not only from their parents but also from school, street gangs serve as familial unit that offer youth a sense of ethnic pride.[22] As a response to being neglected in school, threats from other racial groups and street gangs, and the deterioration of the immigrant family, street gangs provide security, confidence, and social networks for these at-risk youth. [23] Asian American street gangs also instill a sense of cultural pride that is rooted within maintaining language and history, and producing youth culture through party culture.[24] Gangs provide safety, protection, recognition, and a sense of power that Asian American youth find themselves unable to acquire individually.

Many parents of at-risk Asian American youth are unaware that their child might be involved in gang activities because of the generational conflicts and language barriers.[25] Asian American youth involved in gangs may keep their "gang lifestyle" a secret from their home life.[26] Many Asian Americans who join street gangs start as early as eleven years old, when they are impressionable and older teenage gang members can offer a sense of belonging.[27] Asian American adolescents that were in California Youth Authority (CYA) wards were often identified as having the highest percentages of gang membership.[28] The leaders of the Asian American street gangs are generally older youth ranging from eighteen and twenty-four years of age who can serve as an older brother/sister or father/mother figure and can use the insecurity, the little parental supervision, and the allure of drugs in their recruitment practices.

As Asian American youth become more involved in gangs, their association, allegiance, and responsibility to the gang become more dangerous by engaging and/or witnessing violence, robbery, drugs, sex, and gambling.[29] These actions are seen as acceptable ways of behavior and success in their new "family." Youth copy and embody these lifestyles to make up for what has been missing at home and at school, a development of confidence in their identity. Their involvement in gang activity leads to more aggressive and daring acts of crime.

Asian American street gangs have captured the attention of local and national media through their highly documented rap sheet of violence, theft, drug trafficking, and murder. Shows such as "Gangland," featured on the History Channel, have highlighted such gangs as the Joe Boys, Wah Ching, Wo Hop To, Tiny Rascal Gang, and Asian Boyz.[30] Other Asian American street gangs that have gained notoriety are the Filipino gangs Bahala Na Gang and Satanas.[31] Such gangs have had roots that started in the mother country, street gangs that have started locally and expanded their gangs internationally.[32]

TEENAGE PREGNANCY

The perception of teenage pregnancy is that it solely lies within African American or Latino communities, but Asian American youth also face this issue.[33] When the teenage birthrate numbers are examined, sorted by different Asian American subgroups, certain communities bear much of the cost and burden of teen pregnancy.[34] Asian American teen birthrates in certain sub-groups rank among the highest compared with any other major racial/ethnic groups in the United States.[35] In California, Cambodians represent one-tenth and Laotians one-fifth of all teen births.[36] In Minnesota, Asian American represent one-third of all births to teens.[37] As the number of Asian American teenagers continue to grow, teen pregnancy is expected to be a long-term problem.[38]

Although Cambodian and Laotians comprise some of the highest birthrates, other Asian ethnic groups such as Chinese, Korean, and Asian Indian groups represent some of the lowest.[39] Exploring beyond the numbers of Asian American teenage pregnancy, issues of cultural traditions versus American norms present challenges. Some of these challenges include: lack of communication between immigrant parents and bi-cultural teenagers about sex and sexuality, generally a culturally taboo topic; diminished communication between parent and child because of both parents working long hours; and in some cases, teens becoming pregnant as an act of rebellion.[40] Teenage pregnancy among the Cambodian and Laotian communities is also related to issues of poverty, lack of educational access, and strict traditional family values.[41] There are also specific cultural issues unique to different Asian American subgroups, where Hmong teenage girls are bound by cultural tradition. Cultural and gender expectations of teenage Hmong girls are that they are expected to be married and pregnant before their twenties.[42]

The rate of acculturation of second-generation teenage Asian Americans compared to their immigrant parents also presents challenges. Within the Filipino American community, some Filipina Americans perceive pregnancy as a form of rebellion to the strong Roman Catholic beliefs and strict parental upbringing common in their families.[43] Teenage issues such as dating, sex, and abortion are difficult subjects to talk about with their parents. Many young Filipina Americans keep these issues to themselves out fear of rejection, shame, or anger from their parents.[44] These are issues that keep Asian American teens at risk become contributing factors to the high numbers of dropouts in high school and suicides.[45]

OUTLOOK

Although considerable research has focused on factors associated with becoming an at-risk Asian American youth, little has been written on programs that offer effective intervention strategies. Nationally, there are many Asian American community-based organizations that provide services to ethnic-specific Asian communities as well as panethnic Asian American youth. In Los Angeles there are ethnic specific agencies such as Search to Involve Pilipino Americans (SIPA), which has served the historic Filipino-town neighborhood for the past thirty-six years.[46] SIPA continues to work with at-risk youth, engaging them in programs that deal with teen pregnancy, tobacco prevention, and gang prevention.[47] In San Francisco, the Asian Youth

Prevention Services (AYPS) is represented by a consortium of Asian and Pacific Islander community-based organizations that assist both the larger panethnic population of Asian Americans as well as ethnic-specific groups.[48] The consortium is composed of Asian American Recovery Services (AARS), Community Youth Center (formerly the Chinatown Community Center), Filipino Community Center (FCC), Japanese Community Youth Council (JCYC), Korean Center (KCI), Samoan Community Development Center (SCDC), and the Vietnamese Youth Development Center (VYDC). The goal of AYPS is to reduce or delay the use and abuse of alcohol, tobacco, and other drugs among Asian and Pacific Islander youth. These agencies provide mental health and drug education services to middle and high school youth. Youth participants identified as "at-risk" are provided with in-depth case management or referred to professional social workers.

Addressing the need for ethnic specific services, the Pin@y Educational Partnerships (PEP), a program of San Francisco State University's Asian American Studies Department in the College of Ethnic Studies, partners with San Francisco public schools and the Filipino Community Center located in the Excelsior neighborhood of San Francisco to address the issues of Filipina/o immigrant and Filipina/o American youth.[49] Filipina/o American urban youth face issues of poverty, immigration issues, gangs, drugs, racial confusion, and the alarming rates of Filipina suicide.[50] Using education as a tool for social justice, PEP integrates the experiences of Filipina/o and Filipina/o American youth within the classroom to address their social and personal issues. PEP addresses the issues of colonization, immigration, and contemporary social issues and helps students understand the historical and cultural impact of their identities and behaviors. PEP also addresses the lack of Filipina/o teachers by recruiting undergraduate and graduate students, who serve as mentors and role models. Through a critical, cultural, and creative curriculum, PEP engages students to learn about the root causes of racism, sexism, and poverty through a yearlong class that allow students to voice their issues and take action in their own lives, as well as in their communities. Involvement in programs such as these serves as an alternative to gangs, drugs, and violence by providing students the academic, personal, and transformative space needed to change their lives, as well as their communities.

FURTHER READING

Alsaybar, B. D. "Filipino American Youth Gangs, 'Party Culture,' and Ethnic identity in Los Angeles." In *Second Generation: Ethnic Identity among Asian Americans,* ed. P.G. Min. Lanham, MD: Altamira Press, 2002, 129–152.

Le, T. N., and J. L. Wallen. "Youth Delinquency: Self-Reported Rates and Risk Factors of Cambodian, Chinese, Lao/Mien, and Vietnamese Youth." *aapi nexus* 4, no. 2 (2006): 15–44.

Services and Advocacy for Asian Youth Consortium. *Moving Beyond Exclusion: Focusing on the Needs of Asian/Pacific Islander Youth in San Francisco.* http://www .yvpcenter.org/media/docs/4608_moving_beyond_exclusion.pdf.

Siu, S. F. *Asian American Students At-Risk: A Literature Review.* (Center for Research on the Education of Students Paced at Risk, 1996), 8.

Umemoto, K., and P. Ong. "Asian American Pacific Islander Youth: Risks, Challenges, and Opportunities." *aapi nexus* 4, no.2 (2006): v–ix.

NOTES

1. Maria Cramer, "Viet-American Gangs Stir Worry in Dorchester," *Boston Globe*, Jan. 31, 2008, http://www.boston.com/news/local/articles/2008/01/31/viet_american_gangs_stir_worry_in_dorchester/.

2. Tracy A. Weitz, "Asian Pacific Islander Subpopulations: A True Look at Teen Pregnancy," *SIECUS US Report* 30, no. 3 (2002): 16–20.

3. Kim Doan, "A Sociocultural Perspective on At-Risk Asian American Students," *Teacher Education and Special Education* 29, no. 3 (2005): 157–167; Sau-Fon Siu, "Asian American Students At Risk: A Literature Review," *Center for Research on the Education of Students Placed at Risk* 8 (CRESPAR, 1996); Bob Suzuki, "Education and the Socialization of Asian Americans: A Revisionist Analysis of the 'Model Minority' Thesis," *Amerasia Journal* 4, no. 2 (1977): 23–51.

4. Karen Umemoto and Paul Ong, "Asian American Pacific Islander Youth: Risks, Challenges, and Opportunities," *aapi nexus* 4, no. 2 (2006): v–ix; Richard R. Valencia and Daniel G. Solorzano, "Contemporary Deficit Thinking" in *The Evolution of Deficit Thinking: Educational Thought and Practice,* ed. Richard R. Valencia (New York: Routledge, 1997), 160–210.

5. Nicole Robinson, "Redefining 'At-Risk' to Meet the Needs of the Contemporary Classroom," *Action, Criticism, & Theory for Music Education* 3, no.3 (2004): 2–12; Robert C. Pianta and Daniel J. Walsh, *High Risk Children in Schools* (New York: Routledge, 1996); Valencia and Solorzano, "Contemporary Deficit Thinking."

6. Stacey J. Lee, *Up against Whiteness: Race, School, and Immigrant Youth* (New York: Teachers College Columbia University, 2005).

7. Sara Exposito and Alejandra Favela, "Reflective Voices: Valuing Immigrant Students and Teaching with Ideological Clarity," *The Urban Review* 35, no. 1 (2003): 73–91.

8. Doan, "A Sociocultural Perspective on At-Risk Asian American Students."

9. Miriam Camar, "Viet-American Gangs Stir Worry in Dorchester." *The Boston Globe*, 31 January 2008, http://www.boston.com/news/local/articles/2008/01/31/viet_american_gangs_stir_ (accessed Oct. 30, 2008).

10. Lee, *Up against Whiteness.*

11. Carola Suárez-Orozco and Irina L. G. Todorova, "The Social Worlds of Immigrant Youth," *New Directions for Youth Development* 100 (2003): 15–24.

12. Suárez-Orozco and Todorova, "The Social Worlds of Immigrant Youth."

13. *Moving beyond Exclusion: Focusing on the Needs of Asian/Pacific Islander Youth in San Francisco* (Services and Advocacy for Asian Youth (SAAY) Consortium, 2004).

14. Siu, "Asian American Students At Risk."

15. Stacey J. Lee, *Up against Whiteness*; Thao N. Le and Judy L. Wallen, "Youth Delinquency: Self-Reported Rates and Risk Factors of Cambodian, Chinese, Lao/Mien, and Vietnamese Youth," *aapi nexus* 4, no. 2 (2006): 15–44; Kevin L. Nadal, "A Culturally Competent Classroom for Filipino Americans," *Multicultural Perspectives* 10, no. 3 (2008): 155–161.

16. Stacey J. Lee, *Up against Whiteness*; Thao N. Le and Judy L. Wallen, "Youth Delinquency; Kevin L. Nadal, "A Culturally Competent Classroom for Filipino Americans."

17. Lee, *Up against Whiteness.*

18. "Statewide Dialogue on Asian & Pacific Islander Youth Violence," Aug. 17, 2005, Sacramento Convention Center, Cycle of Violence. Asian and Pacific Islander (API) Youth Victimization, General Workshop, Session 1.

19. "Statewide Dialogue on Asian & Pacific Islander Youth Violence."

20. *Moving Beyond Exclusion.*

21. Suárez-Orozco and Todorova, "The Social Worlds of Immigrant Youth."

22. Bangele D. Alsaybar, "Filipino American Youth Gangs, 'Party Culture,' and Ethnic Identity in Los Angeles" in *Second Generation: Ethnic Identity Among Asian Americans,* ed. Pyong Gap Min (Lanham, MD: AltaMira Press, 2002), 129–152.

23. Alsaybar, "Filipino American Youth Gangs," 134–140.

24. Alsaybar, "Filipino American Youth Gangs," 143–146.

25. David Castellion, "Asian Gangs amongst the Bloodiest," *Visalia Times-Delta,* July 14, 2008, http://www.visaliatimesdelta.com/apps/pbcs.dll/article?AID=/20070714/NEWS01/707140329 (accessed Oct. 30, 2008).

26. Jason B. Johnson, "From Southeast Asia to a Violent East Bay: Gang Rivalries Turn Immigrants' Hopes into Urban Miseries," *San Francisco Chronicle*, June 13, 2004; accessed Oct. 30 2008. http://www.sfgate.com/cgi-bin/article.cgi?file=/c/a/2004/06/13/MNGBH75IGB1.DTL 27; Alsaybar, "Filipino American Youth Gangs."

28. National Council on Crime & Delinquency, "Juvenile Justice Fast Facts," http://www.nccd-crc.org. Several API ethnicities have the highest levels of gang membership, Cambodian youth (91%), Laotian (88%), and Thai (87%) had the highest levels of gang membership in 2002.

29. Douglas R. Kent and George T. Felkenes, *Cultural Explanations for Vietnamese Youth Involvement in Street Gangs* (Westminster, CA: Westminster Police Department, Office of Research and Planning, 1998), 1–92.

30. A&E Television Networks, History.com, "Gangland," http://www.history.com/minisites/gangland, accessed Nov. 18, 2008; "State Department Release on Chile Shows Suspicions of CIA Involvement in Charles Horman 'Missing' Case," http://www.gwu.edu/~nsarchiv/news/19991008/, Dec. 12, 2003.

31. Shannon Sims, "Va. Beach Teen's Arm Nearly Cut Off in Sword Attack," WVEC.Com, http://www.wvec.com/news/vabeach/stories/wvec_local_072407_sword_.a921429f.html, accessed Nov. 18, 2008; Pasckie Pascua, "FilAms In Crossfire as L.A. Gang Violence Rages," *Philippine News*, April 11, 2008, http://www.philippinenews.com/article.php?id=2204&catId=1 (accessed Nov. 18, 2008).

32. Alsaybar, "Filipino American Youth Gangs."

33. Ray Kim, "Asian Teen Mothers a Quiet State Crisis: Problem Will Be Addressed in Oakland Tonight," *SFGate,* June 7, 2001, A17, http://www.sfgate.com/cgi-bin/article.cgi?f=/c/a/2001/06/07/MNL198711.DTL.

34. Weitz, "Asian Pacific Islander Subpopulations."

35. U.S. Department of Health and Human Services, Centers for Disease Control and Prevention (CDC), National Vital Statistics Reports (55) 1, *Births: Final Data for 2004,* data from CDC, National Center for Health Statistics.

36. Weitz, "Asian Pacific Islander Subpopulations."

37. Laurie Meschke, "Hmong Pregnancy Planning Grant" (unpublished document). St. Paul, MN: Lao Family Community of Minnesota, 2003.

38. Tom Lee, "Some Groups See Rise in Teen Pregnancy," *AsianWeek*, June 8, 2000. http://asianweek.com/2000_06_08/news_teenpregnancy.html; Tracy A. Weitz, "Asian Pacific Islander Subpopulations."

39. Weitz, "Asian Pacific Islander Subpopulations."

40. Margaret Magat, "Teenage and Pregnant: Despite the Statistics and Stereotypes, Teen Pregnancy Among Asian Americans is a Very Real Problem" *a Magazine*, March 31, 2001, 55.

41. Kim, "Asian Teen Mothers a Quiet State Crisis."

42. Ji Hyun Lim, "Teen Pregnancy a Tradition," AsianWeek.com, March 2–8, 2001, http://asianweek.com/2001_03_02/bay2_hmongteenpregnancy.html.

43. Magat, "Teenage and Pregnant."

44. Barbara Posadas, *The New Americans: The Filipino Americans* (Westport, CT: Greenwood Press, 1999).

45. A. Barretto Ogilvie, ed., *Filipino American K-12 Pubic School Students: A National Survey* (Washington, DC: National Federation of Filipino American Federations, January 2008).

46. Pascua, "FilAms In Crossfire as L.A. Gang Violence Rages."

47. Search to Involve Pilipino Americans Web site, SIPA, "Search to Involve Pilipino Americans," October 2008, http://www.esipa.org.

48. Japanese Community Youth Council (JCYC), "Asian Youth Prevention Services," http://www.jcyc.org/programs/ayps.htm, accessed Nov. 18, 2008.

49. Gender-neutral term representing Filipino and Filipina American experiences that was popularized by Filipina/o American college students at UC–Berkeley in the 1990s; Allyson Tintiangco-Cubales, *Pin@y Educational Partnerships, A Filipina/o American Studies Sourcebook Series, Volume 1: Philippine History and Filipina/o American History.* (Santa Clara, CA: Phoenix Publishing House International, 2007).

50. Allyson Tintiangco-Cubales and Jeffrey C. Ponferrada, "Filipina/o Students in San Francisco Student Survey Project," *Filipino American K-12 Public Schools: A National Survey*, A national report from the National Federation of Filipino American Associations (Washington, DC, 2008); Kevin L. Nadal, "A Culturally Competent Classroom for Filipino Americans." 155–161; A. Barretto Ogilvie, ed., *Filipino American K-12 Pubic School Students.*

CHILDREN AS LANGUAGE AND CULTURAL BROKERS

Nina H. Wu and Su Yeong Kim

For many Asian immigrants, their arrival in the United States gives them hopes for a new beginning and a brighter future. However, as much as some Asian immigrants want to thrive quickly in the host country, they can face many challenges. For those with limited English proficiency, simply communicating in and understanding the new language and culture may be one of the greatest of these challenges. Encounters in the educational, administrative, economic, social, and many other aspects of life in the United States may require Asian immigrants to have interactions with others who do not speak or write their heritage languages. These situations can occur in places where Asian immigrants go to apply for legal documentations (e.g., Social Security), register children to attend school, obtain health insurance and receive health care, apply for government assistance, look for employment, or shop. Asian immigrants can also face language and cultural challenges at home when letters, notices, and documents are sent to them written in English. With more than 10 million Asians living in the United States, and about 40 percent of them aged five and older who speak English less than "very well," the survival and success of this group depends on having someone trustworthy to help them with translation and interpretation.

Research on Asian immigrant families shows that many adults in these families (usually the parents) involve the children to assist with translation and interpretation. Children of Asian immigrants who take on the role in their families as designated translators and interpreters are known as language or cultural brokers.[1] Here, the term "language broker" is used to represent both terms. Some children of Asian immigrants find themselves performing language and cultural brokering tasks for their families even as they themselves are learning the new language and culture.[2] They are usually the first in their families to gain exposure to the English language. This often happens in school, where children of Asian immigrants are also immersed in U.S. culture.

In addition to helping their family members and relatives accomplish simple everyday tasks, many children of Asian immigrants become an important bridge between their families' heritage cultural identity and the U.S. culture and institutions. These children use their newly acquired bilingual and bicultural knowledge to help their families gain access to opportunities, resources and information. They negotiate between two cultural environments: one within their families where their heritage languages are spoken and the world outside the family, where the dominant language is English.

As the percentage of foreign-born Asians arriving in the United States continues to increase, child language brokers are becoming even more important in the Asian communities, as they use their bilingual and bicultural knowledge to help others in their communities to adapt to and succeed in the host country. According to the Census 2000, about 24.1 percent of Asians living in the United States were foreign-born before 1980; nearly 32.4 percent were foreign-born in the years 1980 and 1990; and 43.5 percent were foreign-born in the years 1990 to year 2000. Inevitably, many children in Asian immigrant families find themselves translating and interpreting not only for their parents, but also for other family members, friends, and community members who are not familiar with the English language.

The literature on language brokering suggests that perceptions of the language broker by children of immigrants vary greatly: from feeling a sense of efficacy (e.g., feeling proud, helpful, and useful) to feeling a sense of burden (e.g., feeling embarrassed, burdened, and uncomfortable). For example, some children who language broker demonstrate more symptoms of depression, withdrawal, and sadness.[3] Other children are also likely to perceive more conflicts with their parents.[4] Collectively, studies have shown that some children of immigrants are negatively affected by the language brokering experience, while others benefit. As such, research on language brokering and its potential consequences on children of Asian immigrants might help those whose work is related to these children to better understand this special group of population, not only for their current circumstances and future prospects but also for the important role that they will take part in determining the fate of the United States economy in the future.

CHARACTERISTICS

Child language brokers share some similar characteristics. First, they have acquired some knowledge of the English language and the U.S. culture. Second, they have familiarity with their heritage language and culture.

Prevalence

Child language brokering is very common in many Asian immigrant families. Adult Chinese, Vietnamese, Cambodian, and Korean immigrant study participants recalled performing language brokering tasks when they were younger. Many children of Asian immigrants begin performing brokering tasks within three years of arrival in the United States. Some begin performing language brokering tasks in the early grade school years, the youngest being five years old. Two studies of high school participants from Vietnamese and Chinese backgrounds found that at least 90 percent took on the role as language brokers.[5] In one study, 52 percent of the participants began brokering within a year of arrival in the United States and 62 percent began brokering within two years of arrival. [6] Similarly, another study reported that almost 70 percent of the 1,000 Chinese and Korean high school students studied performed language brokering tasks.[7]

Where Language Brokering Occurs

Language brokering frequently occurs in the home and school. A study reported that 80 percent of their participants brokered at home and 65 percent brokered at school.[8] Study participants frequently filled out school forms, wrote notes, and translated school letters and notices for their parents. Many participants also recalled having to perform language brokering tasks among parents, teachers, and school staff. Language brokering is not limited to the home and school contexts. It can also occur at government offices, hospitals/clinics, banks, grocery stores, restaurants, on the street, and in post offices.

Child language brokers primarily broker for their parents, siblings, relatives, and friends. Other people involved in language brokering, both oral and written, could be neighbors, teachers, school officials, peers in school, clerks, and parents' acquaintances. One study found that the most frequent language brokering tasks performed by children were translating for their parents (86%) and answering the phone (85%), followed by answering the door (78%) and scheduling or accompanying parents on appointments (73%). In addition, participants reported frequently interacting with institutional and government officials (46%).[9]

Process

Language brokering is a complex phenomenon that entails more than simply the act of translation and interpretation on the part of the broker. In a typical child language brokering event, the child has to actively engage one or more people (often adults) to convey messages between two different languages. While doing so, the child language broker assumes the role of a mediator to facilitate communication and linguistic translation for other participants in the language brokering event. The child usually has to interact with adults in many different settings.[10] Therefore, it is common for the child to find himself or herself in situations where complex social relationships are involved. The child language broker often has to acquire sophisticated vocabulary and knowledge to perform language brokering tasks.[11] The child must also understand complex aspects of the adult world in order to competently and accurately convey messages between the parties involved.

To become more competent performing language brokering tasks, many children are motivated to seek knowledge and information to help provide assistance for their families. Many Asian children use dictionaries, search for information, involve their parents and siblings, and develop wide personal networks when performing language and cultural brokering tasks.[12] Far from being passive translators, these children are active in acquiring the skills, information and connections they needed to accomplish brokering tasks.

Benefits and Challenges

The existing research on Asian American children's language brokering has reported inconsistent findings on how these children are being affected by language brokering. For example, children believe that brokering helps them learn more about their heritage languages and culture and increases their English proficiency.[13] Some also feel pride in being language brokers.[14] In a 1995 study, most participants enjoyed and benefited from language brokering.[15] Those participants recounted that language brokering gave them opportunities to learn, to become more independent, and to broaden their knowledge of both their heritage and host cultures. By taking advantage of the learning opportunities that brokering tasks provided, many participants reported that language brokering enhanced their cognitive skills, increased their comprehension of adult-level texts, helped them gain the trust of their parents, and helped them become more bicultural. As a result of performing language brokering tasks for their parents, many child language brokers also reported that language brokering provided them the opportunities to learn about and become more aware of their parents' life experiences in the host country.[16] Language brokering also helped many to increase their sense of maturity and self-esteem.

However, some participants in the same study disliked performing language brokering tasks. Those participants felt a sense of stress, burden, frustration, and embarrassment when performing brokering tasks. In addition, participants believed that assuming the role of language broker required them to take on too many responsibilities, and that taking on such responsibilities interfered with their schoolwork and left them little time to socialize with peers. Other studies also reported detrimental consequences for immigrant children who performed language brokering. For example, a 2007 study found that the Vietnamese language brokers in their studies reported high levels of emotional distresses and disagreements with parents.[17] In another study, the Chinese and Korean language brokers reported symptoms of depression, anxiety, and withdrawal.[18] The Korean participants in this study also exhibited more aggressive and delinquency behavior as the number of language brokering tasks they perform for parents increased. For some children of Asian immigrants, the negative psychological experiences associated with language brokering can put them in a vulnerable position for a host of risky health and social problems.

A 2007 study provides some insights into why language brokering poses an immense burden on some children.[19] Many of the children often had to assume responsibilities on behalf of their parents that affected the welfare and safety of the whole family. For example, participants reported that they had to translate and interpret legal letters (e.g., contracts), fill out business and administrative forms, write legal letters and notes, accompany their parents to doctors' offices to interpret medical information, and interact with government officials and others (e.g., lawyers, doctors) who were in authority and power. Taking on such a responsibility may put child language brokers in states of fear and uncertainty.[20] In circumstances where child language brokers have limited knowledge to deal with complex adult matters, they can find themselves experiencing high levels of stress. Additionally, some children might feel discomfort when their parents have to depend on them to language broker and where children must make decisions on behalf of their parents. In traditional Asian families, parents wield great authority and power, and children are expected to defer to their parents. However, role reversal may occur when children language broker for their parents. Thus, children's language brokering may undermine the traditional power relationship between parents and children in Asian families. Consequently, such discomfort between parents and children can put strains on the family relationship.

Role of Cultural Orientation

As there are both positive and negative consequences for children of Asian immigrants who are language brokers, what remains unanswered in the literature is why the psychological meaning of language brokering differs so greatly for these children. In addition, the potential mechanisms and processes that may be responsible for the variations in their perceptions of the language brokering experience, such as perceiving a sense or burden or efficacy, are relatively unknown. In order to understand how and why some children of Asian immigrants become negatively affected as language brokers while others benefit, researchers tested potential mechanisms that lead to a sense of efficacy and a sense of burden in children's psychological experiences as language brokers.[21] Using data from two waves of a prospective longitudinal study of Chinese American adolescents, researchers examined the role of the adolescents' orientation toward the Chinese culture and family mediators (sense of family obligation and the quality of perceived relationships with parents) both in middle school and high school as potential mechanisms that might help in understanding the variations in the adolescents' perceptions of the language brokering experience while in high school.

Data from more than 200 Chinese American adolescents demonstrated that adolescents were more likely to feel a sense of efficacy in their experiences as language brokers when language brokering for their parents if they were more Chinese oriented, and that these relations were partially explained by the importance they placed on family obligation and the perceptions that they mattered to their parents. On the other hand, adolescents were more likely to feel a sense of burden as language brokers if they had a weak sense of family obligation and felt alienated from their parents. It appears that the adolescents' Chinese orientation sets in motion a family process that helps to understand the variations in the perceptions of their language brokering experience.

The results of this study provided supporting evidence that categorizing Chinese American adolescents' perceptions of the language brokering experience into two types (one to capture the positive feelings, and the other the negative) is a useful way to capture the psychological meaning of language brokering in this sample of adolescents and to use it as a future tool for understanding their language brokering experiences. Such a finding is important for school psychologists and clinical practitioners who work directly with children language brokers of Asian immigrants. Language brokering for such children is an experience that can have psychological consequences for these children, which in turn can affect their general well-being and daily functioning, both at home and in school.

OUTLOOK

As the influx of Asian immigrants continues, many more children of Asian immigrants will inevitably have to become their families' designated language brokers. As language brokers, these children will be put in positions and situations where they may have to perform tasks and take on responsibilities that are beyond their cognitive and language abilities. These children, however, may not have the skills, knowledge, or sense of maturity to carry out their responsibilities. A number of these children might take the initiatives to seek out and acquire the resources, knowledge, and skills to help themselves become more competent as language brokers in order to contribute to the success of their families in the host country. In the process, these children will likely acquire valuable skills and knowledge that can be beneficial and useful to them in other areas (e.g., school achievement and competence in social and cognitive areas of development). At the same time, the demanding and challenging aspects of language brokering might also put some children at risk for a host of health, personal, and psychological problems. Perhaps focusing on the role of heritage cultural orientation and family-related variables as modifiable mediators for intervention may be particularly useful for school psychologists and practitioners who work with children of Asian immigrants.[22]

FURTHER READING

Chao, Ruth. "The Prevalence and Consequences of Adolescents' Language Brokering for Their Immigrant Parents." In *Acculturation and Parent-Child Relationships: Measurement and Development,* ed. Marc Bornstein and Linda Cote. Mahwah, NJ: Lawrence Erlbaum, 2006, 271–296.

Trickett, Edison, and Curtis Jones. "Adolescent Culture Brokering and Family Functioning: A Study of Families from Vietnam." *Cultural Diversity and Ethnic Minority Psychology* 13 (2007): 143–150

Tse, Lucy. "Language Brokering in Linguistic Minority Communities: The Case of Chinese- and Vietnamese-American Students." *The Bilingual Research Journal* 20 (1996): 485–498.

YouTube. "Childhood in Translation." http://www.youtube.com/watch?v=HfLH -Z71diA&feature=related. Provides a clip of Asian child language brokers; explores how the child felt during the brokering event.

NOTES

1. Jeffrey McQuillan and Lucy Tse, "Child Language Brokering in Linguistic Minority Communities: Effects on Cultural Interaction, Cognition, and Literacy," *Language and Education* 9 (1995): 195–215.

2. Nigel Hall, and Sylvia Sham, "Language Brokering as Young People's Work: Evidence from Chinese Adolescents in England," *Language and Education* 21 (2007): 16–30.

3. Ruth Chao, "The Prevalence and Consequences of Adolescents' Language Brokering for Their Immigrant Parents," in *Acculturation and Parent-Child Relationships: Measurement and Development,* eds. Marc Bornstein and Linda Cote (Mahwah, NJ: Lawrence Erlbaum, 2006), 271–296.

4. Edison Trickett and Curtis Jones, "Adolescent Culture Brokering and Family Functioning: A Study of Families from Vietnam," *Cultural Diversity and Ethnic Minority Psychology* 13 (2007): 143–150; Curtis Jones and Edison Trickett, "Immigrant Adolescents Behaving as Culture Brokers: A Study of Families from Former Soviet Union," *The Journal of Social Psychology* 4 (2005): 405–427.

5. Lucy Tse, "Language Brokering in Linguistic Minority Communities: The Case of Chinese- and Vietnamese-American Students," *The Bilingual Research Journal* 20 (1996): 485–498; Trickett and Jones, "Adolescent Culture Brokering and Family Functioning," 143–150.

6. Tse, "Language Brokering in Linguistic Minority Communities," 485–498.

7. Chao, "The Prevalence and Consequences of Adolescents' Language," 271–296.

8. Jeffrey McQuillan and Lucy Tse, "Child Language Brokering in Linguistic Minority Communities: Effects on Cultural Interaction, Cognition, and Literacy," *Language and Education* 9 (1995): 195–215.

9. Trickett and Jones, "Adolescent Culture Brokering and Family Functioning," 143–150.

10. Hall and Sham, "Language Brokering as Young People's Work," 16–30

11. McQuillan and Tse, "Child Language Brokering in Linguistic Minority Communities," 195–215.

12. Hall and Sham, "Language Brokering as Young People's Work," 16–30; McQuillan and Tse, "Child Language Brokering in Linguistic Minority Communities," 195–215.

13. Tse, "Language Brokering in Linguistic Minority Communities," 485–498.

14. Tse, "Language Brokering in Linguistic Minority Communities," 485–498.

15. McQuillan and Tse, "Child Language Brokering in Linguistic Minority Communities," 195–215.

16. McQuillan and Tse, "Child Language Brokering in Linguistic Minority Communities," 195–215.

17. Trickett and Jones, "Adolescent Culture Brokering and Family Functioning," 143–150.

18. Chao, "The Prevalence and Consequences of Adolescents' Language Brokering," 271–296.

19. Hall and Sham, "Language Brokering as Young People's Work," 16–30.

20. Hall and Sham, "Language Brokering as Young People's Work," 16–30.

21. Nina Wu and Su Yeong Kim, "Chinese American Adolescents' Perception of the Lanugage Brokering Experience as a Sense of Burden and Sense of Efficacy," *Journal of Youth and Adolescence* 38(2009): 703–718.

22. Wu and Kim, "Chinese American adolescents' perception of the lanugage brokering experience as a sense of burden and sense of efficacy," 703–718.

DISABILITIES WITHIN FAMILIES

Rooshey Hasnain

Asian Americans have historically been overlooked in discussions pertaining to individuals with disabilities. Today, approximately 54 million Americans, one in six, have some form of disability—sensory, physical, cognitive, developmental, emotional/ behavioral, or mental illness.[1]

Despite their increasing visibility in the United States, Asian Americans with disabilities, along with their families, have remained the most poorly understood and underserviced racial group. These individuals are largely overlooked, both in their communities and in mainstream American social and educational systems, including mental health systems, vocational rehabilitation, and special education. In fact, because of the traditional stigma of disability as well as various cultural factors, Asian Americans with disabilities often find limited or no opportunities in society, and thus maintain an invisible presence. In addition, because of inadequate data and research, state and federal disability programs in special education and rehabilitation have traditionally underexamined the needs and challenges of Asian Americans and their families.

INCIDENCE, PREVALENCE, AND CENSUS DATA

In the past few decades, the number of native and foreign-born Asian Americans in the United States has increased significantly, with many families living with disabilities. Asian Americans, the fastest growing racial group in the United States, report 26.5 percent of families have at least one member with a disability. This compares with 38.5 percent of American Indian/Alaska Native, 35.7 percent of blacks, 33.2 percent of Latinos, 31.6 percent of Native Hawaiian/Pacific Islanders, and 27.5 percent of whites.[2] Based on this percentage,

Asians have the lowest disability rate of any other racial and ethnic groups in the country. It is questioned whether these statistics—along with related findings—provide an accurate report of disabilities among Asian Americans.

Asian Americans with disabilities encounter social, attitudinal and environmental barriers both in their own ethnic communities as well as the mainstream culture-at-large.[3] For example, stigma, racism, and injustice toward Asian Americans in general make it harder for Asian Americans with disabilities to access opportunities. In many cases, such factors can lead to injustices in all aspects of life: employment, education, recreation, housing, travel, and religion.[4] For example, like other ethnic groups, Asian Americans with disabilities who receive Social Security benefits may find it difficult to decide to seek work. However, fear of losing their Social Security checks or their medical benefits may cause many Asian Americans with disabilities to not pursue well-paying and meaningful work, a phenomenon seen in many different populations. But an additional consideration is few working-age Asian Americans with disabilities know about various government work incentive programs that give them the option of gradually working their way off Social Security benefits into a full-time or part-time job.[5]

Another issue for Asian American families is they can be denied their rights and entitlements by school districts regarding their child's education. Some educators have told Asian American families not to bother showing up for their children's educational plan meeting because the school system lacks the linguistic capacity to translate. After these families were denied the opportunity to meet with their child's teacher, these parents were nonetheless instructed to sign and mail in the educational plan, thereby restricting or denying parental participation in the process.[6] Despite various laws and rights, some Asian American parents are discouraged from offering their input in their child's future educational planning process and placements, adversely affecting their children's opportunity to receive a free and appropriate education.

IMPACT

Asian Americans with a disability may rely on family supports or other resources in their Asian American community before seeking "outside" professional help.[7] In fact, members of large Asian American families may use fewer resources or may not seek any assistance from disability programs, such as independent living centers or vocational rehabilitation agencies, because they mistrust the social service system and government bureaucracy.[8] In addition, the complex bureaucratic structure (e.g., federal, state, county, and local) of disability services and the fragmented organization of U.S. disability service programs and supports, as well as the seemingly endless paperwork—often offered only in English or Spanish—adds to the confusion and frustration experienced by Asian American families, reinforcing their tendency to seek support within their native communities.[9]

Furthermore, like many other ethnic minority and mainstream families, many Asian Americans dealing with disability issues for the first time simply do not know where to go for services or support. Lack of knowledge and little trust in available resources, as well as access issues, can adversely affect how Asian Americans use social services available for individuals with disabilities.[10] This distrust may also be related to a family's fear of compromising their immigration status and/or the concern that the system could even remove their child from the family. It also suggests that the U.S. disability and rehabilitation systems provide inadequate outreach to Asian American communities.

Other characteristics associated with the insular nature of Asian American communities can make access to disability services difficult. In some situations, Asian American families choose to bring their family member to their family physician instead of a neurologist, psychologist, psychiatrist, or mental health counselor who could provide professional insight and information. This is likely because of the perceived stigma associated with seeking mental health counseling from such professionals.[11]

The aforementioned lack of information about services and supports can lead to poorer social, economic, and quality-of-life outcomes for Asian Americans with disabilities. Given this reality, it helps clarify why Asian Americans have been underserved for decades in the disability system. Additionally, little research has been conducted on various Asian American subgroups with disabilities that depict their overall status, needs and strengths.

Difficulties related to language and communication are other significant matters. More than one out of three Asian Americans are classified as living in households that primarily speak their culture's native language. Moreover, more than 80 percent of Cambodian, Hmong, Laotian, and Vietnamese Americans, ages 65 and older are limited English proficient (LEP) and live in linguistically isolated households.[12] Since English language proficiency is critical to accessing disability and rehabilitation services, one probable reason Asian Americans access available disability services is such language barriers. This is further exacerbated because of the dearth of translation and interpretation services for Asian American clients in disability and rehabilitation service agencies.

With the large variety of Asian languages and cultures comes an array of cultural perspectives of the various disabilities and attributions that Asian Americans use to describe and depict Western-constructed definitions of disabilities and related terminology. Specifically, labels such as developmental disability, mental retardation, autism, and mental illness are subject to culturally based nuances in translation and understanding. A disability may be attributed to specific metaphysical, cultural, or spiritual factors in some Asian American cultures. To illustrate, a Korean mother of a child with autism reported that "she attributed her child's inconsolable crying to having attended a funeral when she was pregnant; she also indicated that her son's condition was compounded by her frequent mood swings and temper outbursts during her pregnancy and that she had failed in her duty to counsel her unborn in physical, intellectual, and moral ways and to act as a positive role model during her pregnancy."[13]

In general, how Asian American families recognize disability is largely based on cultural, personal, and societal beliefs. Asian American families customarily tend to associate greater stigma with visible physical and developmental disabilities, especially cognitive impairments, rather than less apparent or invisible conditions such as dyslexia or various forms of learning disabilities.

It is important to reiterate that Asian Americans' cultural perception of "disability" may differ greatly from the mainstream American (i.e., white middle-class) notion of disability. Similarly, within the community, Asian Americans hold varying definitions and views of disability. The degree to which Asian Americans are acculturated to American culture is positively correlated with the degree to which they seek help for a disability. For example, some families attribute disabilities as a punishment for their disobedience to a higher power (God) or to the work of evil spirits. Similarly, among various ethnic/racial groups worldwide, disability may be looked upon as bad luck or misfortune.[14] In one study (2002), many Asian Americans viewed traumatic brain injury as bringing shame to the entire family, reflecting the emphasis on family over individuals in their cultures. Such differing perceptions and cultural beliefs may strongly influence a family's decision to seek services for their family member with a disability.[15]

Another dynamic influencing the use of public disability services is that Asian American families tend to be more involved in direct care for their relatives with disabilities compared with other cultural groups. Specifically, Asian Americans are more likely to accompany a family member with a disability to medical clinic visits and to actively participate in decisions associated with the individual's use of disability services. For example, a study of forty Korean-American patients with schizophrenia in the Los Angeles area found that 65 percent lived with their parents, other relatives, or both.[16] Yet the advantages of a family-centered approach may also deprive the person with a disability from seeking beneficial support services and accommodations from outside resources. Such resources could provide access to assistive technology or adaptive equipment such as personal digital gadgets, electronic book player, or Braille printers, for example, to support a person who is blind to pursue work or go to school.

CONTEXTUAL BARRIERS TO RECEIVING APPROPRIATE CARE

Asian Americans with disabilities and their families often experience more discrimination and social disadvantages than mainstream groups, resulting in decreased access to disability services and supports programs. Many factors contribute to this underrepresentation, including discrimination because of race/ethnicity, low income, and educational levels, and refugee/immigrant status.[17] Certain Asian American groups are more likely to be poor, undereducated, and underemployed, and have fewer opportunities to succeed in mainstream American life. This further restricts the ability of the family to seek and provide services to disabled family members. Other considerations making an Asian American less likely to seek mainstream disability services include geographic isolation or—for children with disabilities—having parents unfamiliar with the U.S. social service system, a by-product of their limited education, immigration status (especially illegal immigrants), and limited English language skills. Both institutional bias (because of race/ethnicity, gender, and/or social class) and the aforementioned inadequate number of trained bilingual, bicultural professionals can result in decreased access to resources or support for members of these cultural groups.

Socioenvironmental factors also contribute to underuse of disability services by Asian Americans. Like many other ethnic groups and mainstream families, disabilities are disproportionately concentrated in vulnerable Asian American populations, including those living in poor housing conditions, those who lack access to resources, and those who experience and observe difficult lifestyles because of financial problems. Many lack health insurance and its related benefits, such as medicine and adaptive equipment. [18] Higher exposure to crime and lack of transportation may also place Asian American consumers at a disadvantage, restricting either their desire or ability to consider appropriate resources. Furthermore, many Asian Americans with disabilities, because of a variety of mitigating reasons, are judged ineligible for services, and those who are accepted into the system are often not adequately served.[19] Again, as a consequence, Asian Americans with disabilities, especially those who are minority and low-income, are often denied complete access to helpful services.

Complex acculturation factors, such as time spent in the United States, proximity to traditional and native culture, degree of adherence to ethnic customs, and social class, can also influence access to or help-seeking behaviors for disability services by Asian Americans. There is also the issue of preserving family pride. Seeking assistance outside of the family and Asian American community may be seen by both as a signal of the family's inability to care for its own and supposed inadequacy to function well. Studies have also shown that the combined effects of poverty and high rates of disability in some ethnic groups, compounded by language and communication barriers, are associated with lower levels of disability service use.[20]

Given the limited resources and linguistic capacity of a significant number of Asian Americans, those with disabilities and their families continue to underutilize critical programs in education, rehabilitation, and training. Currently, community-based disability groups are forming partnerships with grassroots organizations to improve policies and service delivery practices for Asian American families. These agencies, such as the Boston Chinatown Neighborhood Center in Boston and Great Wall Center in Malden, MA, have started Asian American–specific parent support groups for parents and family members who are caring for a child or other family member with a disability. Such groups have served a number of Chinese American and Vietnamese American families who have children with developmental disabilities and special needs, providing parents with a forum for networking, socializing and support.

FURTHER READING

Fanlight.com. "The Eyes of Raymond Hu." http://www.fanlight.com/eyesofray mondhu.php.

National Disability Council on Disability. "Lift Every Voice: Modernizing Disability Policies and Programs to Serve a Diverse Nation," http://www.ncd.gov/newsroom/ publications/ 1999/lift_report.htm.

National Technical Assistance Center (NTAC)-AAPI Information Brief Series. "Outreach Brief: Effective Community Outreach Strategies for Service Providers to Increase Delivery to Services to Asian Americans and Asian Pacific Islanders" 3(1). http://www.ntac.hawaii.edu/downloads/products/briefs/outreach/pdf/OB-Vol3-Iss01 -Providers.pdf.

NOTES

1. "Barack Obama and Joe Biden's Plan to Empower Americans with Disabilities," BarackObama.com, July 1, 2008. http://www.barackobama.com/pdf/DisabilityPlan FactSheet.pdf.

2. Keh-Ming Lin, and Freda Cheung, "Mental Health Issues for Asian Americans," *Psychiatric Services* 50, no. 6 (1999): 774–780.

3. U. S. Census Bureau. Disability and American Families: 2000, July 2005, http://www.census.gov/prod/2005pubs/censr-23.pdf.

4. President's Advisory Commission on Asian Americans and Pacific Islanders. Asian Americans and Pacific Islanders: A people Looking Forward—Action for Access and Partnerships in the 21st Century. Interim Report to the President and the Nation, Jan. 30, 2001.

5. Jean Chin, Jeffery Mio, and Gayle Iwamasa, "Ethical Conduct of Research in with Asian and Pacific Islander American Populations," in *The Handbook of Ethical Research with Ethnocultural Populations and Communities,* eds. Joseph Trimble and Celia Fisher (Thousand Oaks, CA: SAGE Publications, 2006), 117–137.

6. Nan Hampton, "Access to Education, Health Care, and Rehabilitation Services," in *Asian Americans: Vulnerable Populations, Model Interventions, and Clarifying Agendas*, ed. Lin Zhan (Sudbury, MA: Jones and Bartlett Publishers, 2003), 69–77.

7. Willie Bryan, *Multicultural Aspects of Disabilities: A Guide to Understanding and Assisting Minorities in the Rehabilitation Process (*Springfield, IL: Charles C. Thomas Publisher, 2007).

8. Research Exchange, "Disability, Diversity, and Dissemination: A Review of the Literature on Topics Related to Increasing the Utilization of Rehabilitation Research Outcomes among Diverse Consumer Groups," *National Center for the Dissemination of Disability Research* 4, no. 2 (1999): 2–15.

9. Hampton, "Access to Education, Health Care, and Rehabilitation Services," 69–77.

10. Lin and Cheung, "Mental Health Issues for Asian Americans," 774–780.

11. Sam Chan and Evelyn Lee, "Families with Asian Roots," in *Developing Cross-Cultural Competence*: 3rd ed.*,* eds. Eleanor Lynch and Marci Hanson (Paul H. Brookes Publishing Company, 2004), 219–299.

12. National Council for Asian Pacific Americans, "Call to Action: National Council of Asian American and Pacific Islander National Policy Priorities," http://www .apiahf.org /downloads/NCAPA2008Platform.pdf.

13. Chan and Lee, "Families with Asian Roots," 219–299.

14. Lin Zhan, *Asian Americans: Vulnerable Populations, Model Interventions, and Clarifying Agendas* (Sudbury, MA: Jones and Bartlett Publishers, 2003).

15. Grahame Simpson, Richard Mohr, and Anne Redman, "Cultural Variations in the Understanding of Traumatic Brain Injury and Brain Injury Rehabilitation," *Brain Injury* 14, no. 2 (2002): 125–140.

16. S. Bae and W. W. Kung, "Family Interventions for Asian Americans with a Schizophrenic Patient in the Family," *American Journal of Orthopsychiatry* 70, no. 4 (2000): 532–541.

17. Thomas LaVeist, *Minority Populations and Health: An Introduction to Health Disparities in the United States* (Hoboken, NJ: Jossey-Bass, 2006).

18. LaVeist, *Minority Populations and Health.*

19. Hampton, "Access to Education, Health Care, and Rehabilitation Services," 69–77; Research Exchange, "Disability, Diversity, and Dissemination," 2–15

20. Research Exchange, "Disability, Diversity, and Dissemination," 2–15; Zhan, *Asian Americans*; LaVeist, *Minority Populations and Health.*

ELDERLY POOR

Barbara W. Kim

In 2006, more than 35 million or 12 percent of the U.S. population was sixty-five and older; this population is projected to grow as the first of the cohort known as the "baby boomers"—about 78 million people born between 1946 and 1964— reach retirement age (65) in 2011.[1] Older people are also living longer into retirement. While many in their sixties are healthy, financially sound, and enjoying a leisurely period of their lives, the "oldest old" population—those eighty-five and older—are divided into those who are healthy and living independently and those who have serious and often multiple chronic health problems and need extensive health services and benefits.[2] The population in the United States and other nations is aging, accompanied by a diverse and complex array of social and economic needs of the elderly. These profound demographic shifts are affecting cultural values, informal and formal institutions, and social and economic policies.

The Asian American population is one of the fastest growing and socioeconomically heterogeneous racial groups in the United States. Further, the number and proportion of its elders (age 65 and older) are projected to increase at faster rates than the general Asian American population. Older Asian Americans, who comprised 1.8 percent of the total elderly U.S. population in 1995, is projected to make up 6.3 percent of the total of older Americans by 2050, which will also be 9.3 percent African American and 17.5 percent Latino.[3]

Older people exhibit the most diversity within the Asian American population with respect to ethnicity, immigration history, language, religion, and other cultural and socioeconomic characteristics. They are also likely to be foreign-born individuals who immigrated as parents of U.S. citizens, resident aliens, or refugees. Generally, they emigrated later in their lives because of a series of exclusionary and discriminatory legal acts, laws, and policies that limited Asian immigration and civil rights for much of U.S. history.[4]

While there are older Asian Americans who were born in the United States or arrived in the first half of the twentieth century, most did not arrive in the United States until after post-1960s immigration law reforms and refugee resettlement acts. The majority of Asian immigrant elders came to accompany or reunite with their children and to provide intergenerational support as a part of immigration and adaptation to American life. Many Asian elders, especially those who live in urban ethnic enclaves, are living independently but are, in general, less likely to speak and comprehend English or have years of formal education. They are often not culturally and structurally integrated into the dominant American society.[5] Combined with a lack of formal work history in the United States, it is not surprising that compared with their U.S.-born counterparts, Asian immigrant elders are more likely to be poorer because they are not eligible for Social Security and pension benefits.[6] The higher rates of poverty among Asian American elders are significant because they are less likely to use formal support systems such as services, programs, and facilities because of language barriers and cultural differences.[7]

The aging population is affecting all aspects of American society. All elderly groups face economic disadvantages compared with the general population as they exit the labor market, but black, Latino, and Asian American elderly exhibit higher poverty rates compared to their non-Latino white counterparts.[8] Combined with their diverse immigration history and demographic and cultural diversity, the rapid growth of Asian American elderly poses a number of challenges for families, researchers, practitioners, and policy makers.

DEMOGRAPHICS

In 2006, Asian Americans as a group had a larger percentage of older people than blacks and Latinos. Asian American elders exhibit bifurcated patterns of education, occupation, and income distributions.[9] A 2000 study of 407 Chinese, Filipino, Indian, Japanese, Korean, and Vietnamese immigrant elders age sixty-five and older in New York City, one of the few studies to use a representative sample of the six largest Asian ethnic groups for elders, found significant demographic variations among ethnic groups in gender, marital status, education levels, religiosity, and English fluency.[10] Chinese and Japanese elders had, on average, lived in the United States longest but Chinese elders, followed by Vietnamese, had the highest percentage of people who could not read or write in English. Filipino, Japanese, and Indian elders reported the highest percentage of people who could speak and read English very well or at least somewhat well.

Overall, 13 percent of Asian elders reported that "could not get by" economically, with variations in income amount and sources by ethnicity, with Vietnamese elders reporting the highest percentage (24%). More than one-third of the respondents reported receiving Supplemental Security Income (SSI) or food stamps. Vietnamese (79%) and Korean (64%) elders reported the highest usage of SSI compared with Chinese (36%), Filipino (27%), Japanese (13%) and Asian Indian (8%) elders. Vietnamese elders reported receiving food stamps (84%) and Medicaid (91%) at much higher rates than other groups (34% and 37% for all groups, respectively).

Less than half (48%) of the sample received Social Security, but the percentages also varied greatly by ethnicity. While Japanese (78%), Koreans (67%), Filipino (53%) and Asian Indians received Social Security, none of the Vietnamese and 29 percent of the Chinese elders received such payments. Similarly, just more than half (51%) of respondents received Medicare Part A, and two-thirds (66%) had Medicare Part B insurance coverage. More than a quarter of Filipino (27%) and Indian (25%) elders did not have any health insurance.[11]

The 2006 Current Population Survey showed that elderly Asians have lower poverty rates than band a Latino elderly, but slightly higher rates than non-Latino whites. It is also interesting that by race/ethnicity, poverty rates were higher for all age groups compared to the elderly population only, with the exception noted for Asian Americans; specifically, Asian American elders were more likely to be poorer than those under sixty-five years of age. Foreign-born noncitizens, 7.7 percent of the U.S. population, had the highest poverty rates when compared with native-born and naturalized citizens (comprising 87.4% and 4.9% of the population, respectively).[12] Asian American elderly, especially those who came to the United States later in their lives, tend to be designated as foreign-born noncitizens for a variety of reasons, such as choosing to remain a citizen of their home country or failing citizenship tests administered in English. Their lack of U.S. citizenship had a significant effect on their economic condition during the welfare reform of the late 1990s.

WELFARE REFORM

In 1996, President Bill Clinton signed the Personal Responsibility and Work Obligations Reconciliation Act (PRWORA), a welfare reform act, into law.[13] The new law cut off public funds from all immigrants including legal permanent residents and refugees, such as elderly immigrants from East Asia and Southeast Asian families (who had been largely admitted as refugees in the aftermath of the Vietnam War) who collected SSI. In this backlash against immigrants, stereotypes of wealthy Asian Americans and cultural values of filial piety portrayed all elderly Asian immigrants as those supported "in reality" by their wealthy children while receiving assistance that they did not need.[14]

Welfare reform denied noncitizens and new immigrants access to SSI—for many, their only source of income—for the first five years of U.S. residency. Distressed older and disabled immigrants and refugees contacted community-based organizations, which met with representatives and coordinated demonstrations at state and national capitals with Asian and Latina/o immigrants and refugees. Elderly, disabled, and war/genocide survivors overcame their language barriers and fear of public attention and repercussions to give testimonies and speak out about their plight.[15]

As a result of these collective efforts, Congress reinstated SSI eligibility to noncitizens who were receiving benefits as of August 22, 1996, under the 1997 Balanced Budget Act. Without it, many Asian and Latino elders would have lost their sole source of income. Such public assistance is crucial to the livelihood of elderly poor, such as Southeast Asian survivors of war and trauma. The 2000 Census revealed that in California, high percentages of Cambodian (24.8%), Hmong (33.5%), and Laotian (21.6%) elders live in poverty, compared with Vietnamese (11.7%). Cambodian, Hmong, and Laotian elders, who also have higher rates of disability compared with other elders, received SSI and other public assistance at higher rates than Vietnamese, Asians, and Californians.[16]

Elderly, disabled refugees and other humanitarian immigrants who arrived after August 22, 1996, remained SSI-eligible for seven years but lost their benefits if they did not become U.S. citizens during that period. The collective efforts of national advocacy organizations, local community organizations, and congressional offices resulted in the Supplemental Security Income Extension for Elderly and Disabled Refugees Act, which extends SSI eligibility to nine years for elderly and disabled refugees, asylees, and other humanitarian immigrants. The law, effective October 1, 2008, also provided an additional two years of retroactive provisions for those who lost their SSI benefits because of their inability to become citizens within the time limit and an additional third year for those who have applied for U.S. citizenship. Still, the two-year extension is set to expire in 2011. While this amendment of the 1996 welfare reform will restore the only source of income for many elderly and disabled refugees, community members and advocates are concerned about those who will not be able to become naturalized citizens because of factors such as increased fees, increased length of application processing, and the difficulty of learning English.

ACCESS TO SUPPORT, SERVICES, AND PROGRAMS

As a group, Asian American elders have longer life expectancy and better health than their racial counterparts but exhibit significant differences by nativity, ethnicity, and gender.[17] However, a study of Asian American seniors in New York City found that 40 percent reported symptoms of depression and Asian Americans had the highest suicide rate of all elderly women. Another study of Asian Indian elders found that higher body mass index, longer residence in the United States, being older, and being female were associated with poorer health.[18] Asian American elders experience stressful life events associated with aging (e.g., widowhood, death of friends and relatives, physical illnesses and declining health, loss of income and livelihood) and immigration (e.g., adjusting to a new country, culture, and/or language). Immigrant elders in particular may have been cut off from the familiarity, networks, resources, and knowledge that formed their identity, influence, and activities in their home country. Social, economic, and emotional support from family and friends, religion and faith communities, and ethnic communities helped alleviate stress, anxiety, and depression.

Older Asian Americans, especially those who do not have or live near close family members and coethnics, also need access to formal health and social services. Factors such as language barriers, cultural incompatibility, lack of service providers with cultural sensitivity and competence, lack of recognition of Asian American elders' unique and diverse needs, and public assistance eligibility based on citizenship contribute to their underutilization of existing services and programs for the aging population. These programs include recreational activities, home-delivered meal programs, adult day care and assisted-living facilities, and assistance with activities of daily living (ADL).[19]

OUTLOOK

The Asian American elderly population is projected to grow dramatically, as those who arrived after 1965 through immigration reforms and refugee acts enter this age group. There is a lack of research and data that could provide an overview, as well ethnically and geographically disaggregated socioeconomic and demographic profiles. Compared with data sets for other racial groups, existing data sets for Asian American elders are not large enough to provide accurate portraits of this heterogeneous group. Most research has focused on one or two ethnic groups residing in specific geographic locations, so that while they provide rich details and needed discussions of elder issues, needs, and care, findings may not be generalizable to other ethnic groups and/or elders residing in different geographic locations in the United States.[20] Such research and findings will be useful for elders, family members, service providers, and policy makers to address the needs of a national population growing older and more diverse.

Asian American families and communities are often viewed to practice filial piety, thus adult children are expected—by themselves and the dominant community—to financially, physically, and emotionally take care of aging family members. While research has shown that filial piety—values such as respecting the elderly and obeying the wishes of one's parents—remains a core value especially for first-generation immigrants and their children, this family value is not a culturally unique one; research on the general U.S. population demonstrates that the elderly obtain as much as 80 percent of their care from private, informal sources such as family, friends, and neighbors.[21] More significantly, Asian American elderly face significant linguistic and cultural barriers to accessing social services, programs, and facilities. National organizations, local community-based and faith-based organizations, and other advocates are working to ease or remove such barriers. In one example that sought to increase access to health care and social services, the National Asian Pacific Center on

Aging (NAPCA), a national advocacy group based in Seattle, WA, partnered with twenty-five local organizations in targeted communities across the United States to provide information about Medicare prescription drug coverage to low-income and limited–English-fluent Asian American and Pacific Islander seniors in 2005–2006. Their outreach strategies included developing simplified, senior-friendly, bilingual materials and establishing national language-specific toll-free numbers that provided direct assistance and information in Chinese, Korean, and Vietnamese, the three Asian ethnic communities with the highest percentages of seniors who do not speak English fluently.

Many Asian American elders are economically and politically vulnerable. Their lack of access to traditional retirement savings, such as Social Security and pension benefits, means that older Asian immigrants rely on SSI for their primary source of income. As the 1996 PRWORA example has shown, Asian American elderly, majority first-generation immigrants are subject to changing policies that threaten to withhold services and programs from noncitizens, even legal permanent residents. The 2008 annual report estimates that U.S. Social Security trust funds will run out of money by 2041, and the Medicare trust fund by 2019, because of rising health costs. Many scholars agree that a shift in policy is necessary to address socioeconomic, psychological, and health needs of the aging population.

FURTHER READING

Choi, Namkee G. "Diversity within Diversity: Research and Social Work Practice Issues with Asian American Elders." *Journal of Human Behavior in the Social Environment* 3 (2001): 301–319.

Choi, Namkee G., ed. *Social Work Practice with the Asian American Elderly*. Binghamton, NY: Haworth Press, 2001.

Mui, Ada C., Duy D. Nguyen, Dooyeon Kang, and Margaret Dietz Domanski. "Demographic Profiles of Asian Immigrant Elderly Residing in Metropolitan Ethnic Enclave Communities." *Journal of Ethnic & Cultural Diversity in Social Work* 15 (2006): 193–214.

National Asian Pacific Center on Aging (NAPCA). www.napca.org.

National Indo-American Association for Senior Citizens (NIAASC). www.niaasc.org.

Niedzwiecki, Max, KaYing Yang, and Saroeun Earm. *Southeast Asian American Elders in California: Demographics and Service Priorities Revealed by the 2000 Census and a Survey of Mutual Assistance Associations (MAAs) and Faith-Based Organizations (FBOs)*. Washington, DC: Southeast Asia Resource Action Center, 2003. http://www.searac.org/sea-eldersrpt-fin.pdf.

NOTES

1. Carmen DeNavas-Walt et al., "Income, Poverty, and Health Insurance Coverage in the United States: 2006," U.S. Census Bureau, Current Population Reports, P60-233 (U.S. Government Printing Office, Washington, DC, 2007), http://www.census.gov/prod/2007pubs/p60-233.pdf.

2. Tonya M. Parrott et al., "The United States: Population Demographics, Changes in the Family, and Social Policy Challenges," in *Aging in East and West: Families,*

States, and the Elderly, ed. Vern L. Bengtson, Kyong-Dong Kim, George. C. Myers, and Ki-Soo Eun (New York: Springer, 2000), 193.

3. Namkee G. Choi, "Diversity within Diversity: Research and Social Work Practices Issues with Asian American Elders," *Journal of Human Behavior in the Social Environment* 3 (2001): 302.

4. Choi, "Diversity within Diversity," 305–306.

5. Ada C. Mui et al., "Demographic Profiles of Asian Immigrant Elderly Residing in Metropolitan Ethnic Enclave Communities," *Journal of Ethnic & Cultural Diversity in Social Work* 15 (2006): 193.

6. Choi, "Diversity within Diversity," 306.

7. Angela Shen Ryan, Ada C. Mui, and Peter Cross, *Asian American Elders in New York City: A Study to Assess Health, Social Needs, Quality of Life and Quality of Care* (New York: The Asian American Federation of New York, 2003).

8. DeNavas-Walt et al., "Income, Poverty, and Health Insurance Coverage in the United States," 11.

9. Namkee G. Choi, "Diversity within Diversity," 302.

10. Choi, "Diversity within Diversity," 306.

11. Mui et al., "Demographic Profiles of Asian Immigrant Elderly," 193.

12. Mui et al., "Demographic Profiles of Asian Immigrant Elderly," 211.

13. DeNavas-Walt et al., "Income, Poverty, and Health Insurance Coverage in the United States," 11–13.

14. Lynn Fujiwara, *Mothers without Citizenship: Asian Immigrant Families and the Consequences of Welfare Reform* (Minneapolis: University of Minnesota Press, 2008), 9.

15. Choi, "Diversity within Diversity," 311.

16. Fujiwara, *Mothers without Citizenship*, 75–80.

17. Max Niedzwiecki, KaYing Yang, and Saroeun Earm, *Southeast Asian American Elders in California: Demographics and Service Priorities Revealed by the 2000 Census and a Survey of Mutual Assistance Associations (MAAs) and Faith-Based Organizations (FBOs).* (Washington, DC: Southeast Asia Resource Action Center, 2003). http://www.searac.org/sea-eldersrpt-fin.pdf.

18. Choi, "Diversity within Diversity," 307.

19. Ryan, Mui, and Cross, *Asian American Elders in New York City: A Study to Assess Health, Social Needs, Quality of Life and Quality of Care*, 28; Choi, "Diversity within Diversity," 309; Sadhna Diwan and Satya S. Jonnalagadda, "Social Integration and Health among Asian Indian Immigrants in the United States," in *Social Work Practice with the Asian American Elderly*, ed. Namhee G. Choi (Binghamton, NY: Haworth Press, 2001), 45–62.

20. Choi, "Diversity within Diversity," 313.

21. Parrott et al., "The United States," 191.

FAMILY VIOLENCE

Hee Yun Lee

Family violence is generally considered to encompass child abuse, intimate partner violence (IPV), and elder mistreatment. Family violence is a universal experience crossing all racial/ethnic communities, so that no group is immune to this type of violence here in the United States. It is often reported that cultural beliefs and social contexts in which an individual lives permeate relationships regardless of the individual's ethnic or racial group, but they are especially evident in an individual's interactions with his/her family, whether these interactions are healthy or abusive. As a result, to some extent, culture and social contexts inform family structure, roles, child-rearing practices, and violence among family members.

Among Asian Americans, accounts of family violence are occurring with disturbing frequency, yet such incidents appear to be underreported. Consequently, the response of the Asian American community has been limited at best. There is also a paucity of empirical evidence available that examines the phenomenon of family violence among Asian Americans; however, available studies suggest the risk factors associated with this experience may differ from those typically attributed to the majority culture.[1] The findings suggest that socially and culturally determined relationships with parents, children, or a spouse are significant variables in understanding this phenomenon. Therefore, it may be useful to examine family violence in Asian Americans in terms of traditions and immigration experience, along with other factors.

There are several dynamics that merit consideration. Confucian ethics are an example of a cultural belief that can shape the definition, perception, and help-seeking behavior in cases of family violence for Asian Americans. Confucianism has been frequently revisited as a conceptual framework in comprehending the dynamics of family violence. Specifically, these ethics can contribute as a risk factor in preventing, detecting, and intervening in family violence among Asian Americans. One feature is the consideration of family well-being as a priority over individual welfare. Asian American women experiencing abuse may delay or avoid seeking help for the sake of keeping the family unit intact. The experience of immigration can compound the circumstances because of language issues and unfamiliarity with social service resources or other aid. In general, the characteristics of immigrants often present barriers in seeking access to appropriate services, further impeding immigrants' understanding of the family violence laws in their new country. Similarly, acculturative stress has also been identified as a risk factor for family violence in Asian Americans.[2]

While the Asian American community shares many cultural values, traditions, and beliefs, as well as many commonalities in their immigration experiences, it is important to recognize that the Asian American community is a diverse group. The 2000 Census data counted twenty-four racial/ethnic groups in the Asian American communities, with each Asian American group having its own cultural belief, language, immigration background, length of time since arrival to the United States, and socioeconomic status.[3] These differing characteristics that are unique and distinct to each Asian American subgroup, as well as shared traditions and cultural values of Asian Americans, can contribute to each population's unique experience with family violence.

CHILD ABUSE

The Federal Child Abuse Prevention and Treatment Act defines child abuse and neglect as "at a minimum, any recent act or failure to act on the part of a parent or caretaker which results in death, serious physical or emotional harm, sexual abuse or exploitation; or an act or failure to act which presents an imminent risk of serious harm." This definition represents a minimum national standard, leaving each state in the United States to set its own definition.[4] Consequently, in many states, child abuse is not merely physical abuse but also includes psychological abuse, and neglect.

While there are no reliable population-based estimates of prevalence of child abuse in Asian Americans or other racial/ethnic groups, every year 3 million children in the United States are estimated to be victims of child abuse and neglect.[5] Most of these child victims were white (67%) and African American children (30%), while Hispanic and Asian American and Pacific Islander children represented 13 percent and 1 percent of victims respectively.[6] These statistics may help explain why Asian Americans are not typically identified as a community at risk of such abuse; however, it is hard to say that the low percentage of child abuse victims among Asian Americans equates to a low number of actual incidents of child abuse and neglect. A recent investigation examining family violence among Cambodian, Chinese, Korean, South Asian, and Vietnamese reported that 69 percent of these children experienced being hit by their parents.[7] Another study reported that known child abuse cases were not reported to child protective services (CPS) by Korean immigrant ministers.[8] These findings suggest that Asian Americans have a low reporting pattern to authorities of known child abuse incidents.

Other factors that may contribute to low reporting rates include a victim's sense of shame about the mistreatment or a concern about involving CPS.[9] In addition, the child may be more reticent to report abuse out of fear that the report will not seem credible or a belief that the child is responsible for or deserving of parental abuse.[10] Many Asian Americans perceive child maltreatment to be extreme physical torture exerted on a child.[11] Consequently, more modest cases are less likely to be recognized than blatantly abusive ones. For many Asian American families, the general assumption is that physical punishment or discipline by striking a child does not qualify as abuse.

Cultural Views on Child Rearing and Risk for Child Abuse

Certain traditional values in Asian cultures have been implicated in assessing the risk of parent-to-child aggression and abuse.[12] For example, the emphasis on filial piety in Confucian ethics—which stress children's absolute obedience to parents' rules—has led children to heed and follow the authority of the parents, whether abusive or not.[13] Consequently, corporal punishment is not regarded as abuse, but necessary for discipline. For example, in Korean culture, physical punishment is interpreted as the "whip of love" and frequently viewed as a tool used to educate children.[14] Chinese parents promote filial piety both by enhancing physical and emotional closeness and by establishing parental authority and child obedience through harsh discipline.[15] It is not unusual for Asian parents— for whom Confucian tradition is a central part of their culture—to experience and accept ambiguity as they strive to find the right harmony in their roles as strong disciplinarian and primary nurturer of their children.[16] Indeed, parental use of force may be seen as reflecting parental dedication.

Impact of Immigration Experience

There are numerous stressors related to the experience of immigration, including downward social mobility, differing rates of acculturation between parents and children, and unfamiliarity with Western cultural norms. Such stressors can contribute to the occurrence of child abuse. In general, when parents are experiencing extreme and difficult challenges, the role of parenting can be particularly taxing. Parents may be more susceptible to behaviors associated with child abuse or neglect. One study found that factors associated with immigrant status, such as perceived discrimination and a reduced social standing, were more reliable predictors of parent-child aggression in Asian American families than level of education and income, the latter risk factors often attributed to the majority culture in the United States.[17] Moreover, in Asian Americans as with other minority American populations, intergenerational conflict resulting from different rates of acculturation has also been identified as a risk factor for physical aggression toward children and in turn elevated risk of child abuse.[18]

The circumstances surrounding immigration are possible contributors to the level and type of abuse perpetrated on children. For example, Cambodian parents, who arrive in the United States having experienced war trauma, can later encounter post-traumatic stress disorder or depression. Because of inappropriate coping behaviors such as alcohol or drug abuse, there is a greater risk for the parent to compromise childrearing responsibilities. There are reports that the majority of child abuse incidents reported to CPS agencies were child neglect cases in Cambodian refugee families. In these instances, a frequently cited circumstance under which the child neglect occurred was parental substance abuse and mental health problems.[19]

Children's Experience of Witnessing Domestic Violence

Aside from direct child abuse, children's witnessing domestic violence is another important issue in Asian American families. According to the Children's Defense Fund, millions of children witness domestic violence annually, and exposure to such violence elevates a child's risk of being victimized themselves.[20] A recent investigation found that 27 percent of Vietnamese children and 30 percent of Korean children had witnessed their mothers being struck by their fathers on a regular basis.[21] This abuse can also take the form of emotional abuse. For example, emotional abuse to children among Korean families occurs mainly under circumstances in which children witness domestic violence.[22] This phenomenon reflects the prevalence of domestic violence incidents in Asian American families and its negative ramifications on children in the form of emotional trauma.[23]

INTIMATE PARTNER VIOLENCE

The Centers for Disease Control defines intimate partner violence (IPV) as "abuse that occurs between two people in a close relationship."[24] Like child abuse, IPV can include psychological or emotional abuse (intimidation, isolating from other relationships, or name-calling), sexual abuse, and physical abuse between spouses (current or former) or a dating partner. Until the late 1990s, there was a general lack of understanding of the prevalence of IPV. Most recently, the CDC estimates nearly 5.3 million incidents occur annually among women age eighteen and older in the United States.[25]

To date, while there are no population-based estimates of IPV in Asian Americans, there have been some small-scale studies estimating the IPV prevalence rate in Asian Americans that have emerged in the past decade. In one study, 80 percent of Chinese Americans in Los Angeles County disclosed an experience of a sustained form of verbal aggression by a spouse or partner in the last twelve months and 85 percent during their lifetime.[26] An Asian Task Force study found between 44–47 percent of Cambodians reported knowing a woman who had been the victim of domestic violence.[27] Japanese American women have reported experiencing physical violence during their lifetime at rates as high as 52 percent, while South Asian American women have reported rates as high as 40.8 percent.[28] Another study reported that about 19 percent of Korean couples experienced at least one incident of physical violence during the year.[29] After categorizing types of marriages, the same study reported that male-dominant marriages had higher levels of violence, with 33 percent experiencing at least one type of physical violence during the year compared with more egalitarian marriages (12%).[30] Such reports of IPV in the Asian American community are deemed alarming to both researchers and service providers.

Cultural Gender Role and Perception of IPV

Although there is an increased awareness that IPV exists among Asian American families, there is a lack of understanding about how IPV is manifested within the unique cultural values of Asian women. Recent studies indicate cultural differences that affect the perception of IPV and employment of help-seeking behaviors, potentially increasing the vulnerability of Asian American women.[31] For example, one of the core ethics of Confucianism is patriarchal values. Such values can pervade the attitudes and awareness of IPV.[32] Traditional gender roles, where men have power and control over women, are related to high levels of violence against women. Accordingly, an Asian American may regard an IPV incident as a normal aspect of marital relations.[33] The prevalence of IPV in one's country of origin also may play a role in viewing these behaviors as a marital norm.[34]

Similarly, the inability to recognize an IPV incident as abuse can, in turn, decrease the likelihood that these women would seek help for themselves.[35] If Asian American women live in a community where marital violence is accepted and not challenged by the community members, it would follow that women may believe that IPV is part of their everyday life. The belief that these issues should not be discussed outside the family also reduces the likelihood that an Asian American woman would seek help or report an incident to the authorities.[36] Because these women often experience pressure by their immigrant community to keep the family together, keeping shameful family incidents within the family is highly valued, hence seeking outside help is considered breaking close family ties and losing family face in the Asian American community.

The results of the Project AWARE study revealed that 35 percent of the women who reported IPV felt ashamed. Furthermore, these women were more likely to seek informal sources of help from a family member or friend rather than seek help from an agency or the police.[37] Interestingly, another study found heterogeneity in the rate that Asian American women sought help from a friend as the result of experiencing IPV. Specifically, 82 percent of South Asian women indicated a belief that a woman should seek such help compared with 44 percent of Cambodian women, 37 percent of Chinese women, 41 percent of Korean women, and 29 percent of Vietnamese women.[38]

One population-based study of Japanese American women in Los Angeles revealed that 71 percent of the respondents linked their experiences with IPV to their Japanese heritage. Moreover, culturally related beliefs contributed to their reaction to IPV, including highly valuing the ability to endure such treatment, prioritizing family welfare over individual welfare, and believing in male dominance.[39] The belief that women play a subservient role in a marital relationship is not unique to the Japanese community. Research has also found that 71 percent of Vietnamese American women state that their husbands believe that men have the dominant role in the relationship.[40]

Immigration Experience and Help-Seeking

In addition to the cultural barriers, the immigration status of an Asian American woman can affect her reaction to IPV. Fear of deportation was identified as a common theme for deciding not to seek help, particularly among Asian women immigrants who are in the United States on temporary papers.[41] Another recurrent theme is a sense of isolation likely associated with their lack of English speaking ability.[42] The language challenges likely affect Chinese, Vietnamese, Laotian, and many other ethnic subgroups in accessing related resources and domestic violence services, including shelter and legal services.[43] Combined with the aforementioned lack of awareness of resources and other protective services, immigrant woman who seek help for abuse are more likely to seek informal sources of support.[44]

Whether an Asian American couple came to the United States as immigrants or refugees contributes to their risk of IPV. In a study proposing an explanatory model of domestic violence among the refugee community, several characteristics are regarded as unique to refugee domestic violence cases.[45] Key among such characteristics are the individual's sense of powerlessness to control his or her own destiny, stemming from the involuntary nature of the journey to the United States.[46] This loss of intellectual and social competence as refugees can exacerbate marital conflict, a potential source of marital violence.

ELDER ABUSE

Similar to definitions of child abuse and IPV, elder mistreatment is characterized by physical abuse, psychological abuse, or neglect that results in the bodily harm, emotional suffering, or financial exploitation of a person over the age of sixty, regardless of whether that harm is intentional or unintentional.[47] Like child abuse, a specific definition of elder mistreatment is defined by each individual state. Elder mistreatment is a rapidly growing and pervasive social problem in the United States, as well as in the Asian American community. It is estimated that anywhere from 1 to 10 percent of the elderly population becomes a victim of elder mistreatment annually.[48] Along with the rapid aging of the population, there is a potential for elder mistreatment to increase simultaneously. One estimate states there will be more than 2.2 million mistreated and abused older adults in 2030 based on the current, widely reported prevalence rate of 3.2 percent.[49] The potential for "an epidemic" has been posited by scholars in the field.[50]

Among most of the prevalent studies, it is likely that Asian elders have been underrepresented because of their tendency to underreport elder mistreatment incidents to authorities.[51] For example, the 1998 NCEA report indicated that the proportion of Asian American elders as victims of all types of mistreatment was only 2.1 percent of all substantiated elder abuse and neglect cases in 1996, while white and African American elders accounted for more than 92 percent.[52] Such reports could lead to the conclusion that elder mistreatment is not an important social issue in the Asian American community.

Research on elder mistreatment among Asian American elders, however, revealed elder mistreatment as a growing social problem. About 34 percent of one hundred Korean elderly respondents in one study indicated knowledge of at least one incident of elder abuse and neglect that had occurred in their community.[53] A review of active cases of elder mistreatment by the San Francisco Protective Services found that Asian Americans were involved in 10.6 percent of those cases.[54] Disaggregation of those cases revealed that 6.81 percent were Chinese Americans, 2.7 percent were Southeast Asian Americans, .57 percent were Korean Americans, and .09% were Japanese Americans.[55]

Despite the fact that a considerable number of minority elderly may experience various forms of elder abuse and neglect, research on this topic among Asian American elders, as is the case with other family violence issues, is extremely limited, and most studies have focused on Korean elderly immigrants. Studies that do exist have asserted that culture plays a critical role in an Asian American elder's perception and response to elder mistreatment. In cross-cultural comparisons, elderly Korean immigrants were identified to be significantly less sensitive and more tolerant of potential elder mistreatment scenarios, and more likely to blame the victims for the occurrence of abuse, compared to African American and white elderly.[56] A recent investigation found that elderly Chinese participants were more likely to not only tolerate but also justify a husband's abusive behavior toward his wife.[57]

Likewise, as with other forms of family violence, Confucian values undergird elder mistreatment in the Asian American community. Confucian ethics, such as saving a family's face, are well ingrained in elderly Asian Americans' response, or lack thereof, to the problem of elder mistreatment. One study found that help-seeking intentions among Korean elderly were less likely than among Caucasian and African American elders, citing cultural expectations, including reluctance to reveal family shame.[58] They further explain Korean elderly concerns for keeping problems to oneself, maintaining family harmony, and assigning virtue to a certain amount of human suffering.[59]

While little attention has been given to the immigration experience in the research about elder mistreatment, a review of elder mistreatment research asserts that level of acculturation among Asian elderly immigrants affects how elder mistreatment is manifested, perceived, and reported.[60] Differing perceptions of elder mistreatment associated with acculturation have been captured in previous studies. Filipino and Korean respondents in Honolulu, who were mostly born in Hawai'i, provided answers that were more similar to the responses of Caucasians residing in Minnesota, more so than Korean elderly immigrants also living in Minnesota.[61] Such findings indicate that cultural norms or values may be diluted as Asian American elderly immigrants acculturate into American culture and lifestyles.

Elderly Asian immigrants are also reported to have very limited knowledge of formal services related to elder mistreatment. In one study, only a small portion of Korean elderly immigrants knew about Adult Protective Services (21%) and the Elder Abuse Hotline (12%).[62] In the same study, only 28 percent of Korean respondents, compared with 62 percent of the Caucasian sample, knew of an organization or a professional person to assist them in a case of elder mistreatment.[63]

Furthermore, elderly Asian immigrants who recently immigrated to the United States are more liable to hold negative attitudes toward the involvement of people outside of the family in elder mistreatment incidents. In a study focused on four Asian American elderly groups, it was found that the American-born Chinese, Japanese, and Taiwanese groups were more likely to favor reporting elder abuse to the authorities, while Korean elderly immigrants were less likely to favor such reporting.[64]

OUTLOOK

Researchers and practitioners refer to the model minority myth as a possible reason why abuse within Asian American families has been inadequately identified and researched. Researchers and practitioners have generally believed the myth that Asian American families are more successful and well adjusted than other minority groups, and this belies the reality that family violence does occur in this community. Additionally, scholars and service providers appear to concur on the premise that increasing understanding of family violence in all of its forms among Asian Americans is critical to promoting a more a realistic portrayal of Asian American family life.

Accordingly, cultural competency is an important issue for social service providers in the detection, prevention, and intervention of family violence in Asian Americans. The sensitive nature of family violence and its occurrence in private situations necessitates a culturally sophisticated approach by service providers when working with the Asian American community. Research or documentation of a standardized culturally sensitive method for assessing and detecting family violence and developing service intervention programs for culturally diverse Asian Americans is sparse.

In addition, little is known about how the social and cultural background of Asian Americans influences their definition, perception, and help-seeking with respect to child abuse, IPV, and elder mistreatment. Early research indicates that while there are many shared family violence characteristics among this population, there are marked differences as well. Some of these differences may be embedded in cultural beliefs or traditions that are unique to a specific Asian American subgroup. Certain immigration factors, such as a family's migration experience, may also affect the level or type of violence in a family.

Experts agree that more investigation in this arena is needed, particularly research that disaggregates the Asian American population into more culturally relevant subgroups. Gaining a more complete understanding of how different Asian American subgroups experience family violence will encourage the development of more culture- and ethnic-specific family violence prevention and intervention programs and policies.

FURTHER READING

Asian and Pacific Islander Institute on Domestic Violence. http://www.apiahf.org.
Asian Task Force on Domestic Violence. http://www.atask.org.
Bui, Hoan, and Merry Morash. *In the Adopted Land: Abused Immigrant Women and the Criminal Justice System.* Westport, CT: Greenwood Press, 2004.
Child Welfare Information Gateway. http://www.childwelfare.gov.
DasGupta, Shamita, ed. *Body of Evidence: Intimate Violence Against South Asian Women in America.* New Brunswick, NJ: Rutgers University Press, 2007.
Nguyen, Tuyen. *Domestic Violence in Asian American Communities.* Lanham, MD: Rowman & Littlefield, 2005.

NOTES

1. A. Lau, D. Takeuchi, and M. Alegria, "Parent-to-Child Aggression among Asian American Parents: Culture, Context, and Vulnerability," *Journal of Marriage and Family* 86 (2006): 1261–1278.

2. Lau, Takeuchi, and Alegria, "Parent-to-Child Aggression among Asian American Parents."

3. U.S. Census Bureau, 2002, "The Asian Population: Census 2000 Brief," http://www.census.gov/prod/2002pubs/c2kbr01-16.pdf (accessed Dec. 7, 2007).

4. Child Welfare Information Gateway, "Definitions in Federal Law," http//www.childwelfare.gov/can/defining/federal.cfm (accessed Oct. 27, 2008).

5. Children's Defense Fund, "The State of America's Children 2005," http://www .childrensdefense.org/child-research-data-publications/data/state-of-americas-children -2005-report.pdf (accessed Sept. 8, 2008).

6. R. E. Clark, J. F. Clark, and C. Adamec, *The Encyclopedia of Child Abuse, Second Edition* (New York: Facts on File, 2001).

7. M. R. Yoshioka and Q. Dang, *Asian Family Violence Report: A Study of the Cambodian, Chinese, Korean, South Asian, and Vietnamese Communities in Massachusetts* (Boston: Asian Task Force Against Domestic Violence, 2000). Available at www.atask.org (accessed Oct. 24, 2008).

8. S. Rhee, J. Chang, and S. Youn, "Korean American Ministers' Perceptions and Attitudes toward Child Abuse," *Journal of Ethnic & Cultural Diversity in Social Work* 12, no. 3 (2003): 27–46.

9. Yoshioka and Dang, *Asian Family Violence Report.*

10. Yoshioka and Dang, *Asian Family Violence Report.*

11. S. WuDunn, "Japan Admitting, and Fighting, Child Abuse," *New York Times,* 1999, http://www.nytimes.com/1999/08/15/world/japan-admitting-and-fighting-child -abuse.html?pagewanted=3 (accessed July 2, 2003).

12. J. Chang, S. Rhee, and D. Weaver, "Characteristics of Child Abuse in Immigrant Korean Families and Correlates of Placement Decisions," *Child Abuse & Neglect* 30, no. 8 (2006): 881–891.

13. Chang, "Characteristics of Child Abuse," 881–891.

14. Chang, "Characteristics of Child Abuse," 881–891.

15. C. K. Ho, "An Analysis of Domestic Violence in Asian American Communities: A Multicultural Approach to Counseling," *Women & Therapy* 9, no. 1–2 (1987): 129–150.

16. S. Chan, "Families with Asian Roots," *Developing Cross-Cultural Competence: A Guide for Working with Young Children and Their Families,* eds. E. Lynch and M. Hanson (Baltimore, MD: Paul H. Brookes Publishing, 1992), 181–250.

17. Lau, Takeuchi, and Alegria, "Parent-to-Child Aggression," 1261–1278.

18. M. S. Park, "The Factors of Child Physical Abuse in Korean Immigrant Families," *Child Abuse and Neglect* 25, no. 7 (2001): 945–953.

19. J. Chang, S. Rhee, and M. Berthold, "Child Abuse and Neglect in Cambodian Refugee Families: Characteristics and Implications for Practice," *Child Welfare* (2008): 141–160.

20. Children's Defense Fund, "The State of America's Children."

21. Yoshioka and Dang, "Asian Family Violence Report."

22. S. Rhee, J. Chang, and S. Youn, "Korean American Ministers' Perceptions" 27–46.

23. A. Mullender and R. Morley, *Children Living with Domestic Violence: Putting Men's Abuse of Women on the Child Care Agenda* (London: Whiting & Birch, 1994).

24. Centers for Disease Control and Prevention and National Center for Injury Prevention and Control, "Understanding Intimate Partner Violence, Fact Sheet," http://www.cdc.gov/ncipc/dvp/ipv_factsheet.pdf (accessed Oct. 29, 2008).

25. Centers for Disease Control, "Morbidity & Mortality Weekly Reports," 55, no. 19: 532–535, http://www.cdc.gov/mmwr/preview/mmwrhtml/mm5519a3.htm (accessed Aug. 27 2008).

26. A. G. Yick, T. Shibusawa, and P. Agbayani-Siewert, "Partner Violence, Depression, and Practice Implications with Families of Chinese Descent," *Journal of Cultural Diversity* 10, no. 3 (2003): 96–104.

27. Yoshioka and Dang, *Asian Family Violence Report.*

28. M. Yoshihama and B. Gillespiel, "Age Adjustment and Recall Bias in the Analysis of Domestic Violence Data: Methodological Improvement through the Application of Survival Analysis Methods," *Journal of Family Violence* 17, no. 3 (2002): 199–221; A. Raj and J. G. Silverman, "South-Asian Women in Greater Boston," *Journal of American Medical Women's Association* 57, no. 2 (2002): 111–114.

29. J. Y. Kim and K. T. Sung, "Conjugal Violence in Korean American Families: A Residue of the Cultural Tradition," *Journal of Family Violence* 15, no. 4 (2000): 331–347.

30. Kim and Sung, "Conjugal Violence in Korean American Families."

31. A. Raj and J. G. Silverman, "Intimate Partner Violence against Immigrant Women: The Roles of Immigrant Culture, Context, and Legal Status," *Violence Against Women* 8, no. 3 (2002): 367–398; Ahmad et al., "Patriarchal Beliefs and Perceptions of Abuse among South Asian Immigrant Women," *Violence Against Women* 10, no. 3 (2004): 262–282; Fugate et al., "Barriers to Domestic Violence Help Seeking: Implications for Intervention," *Violence Against Women* 11 (2005): 290–310; R. E. Latta and L. A. Goodman, "Gaining Access: An Assessment of Community Responsiveness to the Needs of Haitian Immigrant Women Who Are Survivors of Intimate Partner Violence," *Violence Against Women* 11 (2005): 1441–1464; Sullivan et al., "Participatory Action Research in Practice: A Case Study in Addressing Domestic Violence in Nine Cultural Communities," *Journal of Interpersonal Violence* 20 (2005): 977–995.

32. Kim and Sung, "Conjugal Violence in Korean American Families," 331–347; A. G. Yick, "Domestic Violence Beliefs and Attitudes in the Chinese American Community," *Journal of Social Service Research* 27, no. 1 (2000): 29–51.

33. S. Bhanot and C. Y. Senn, "Attitudes towards Violence against Women in Men of South Asian Ancestry: Are Acculturation and Gender Role Attitudes Important Factors?" *Journal of Family Violence* 22, no. 1 (2007): 25–31; S. K. Murnen, C. Wright, and G. Kaluzny, "If 'Boys Will Be Boys,' Then Girls Will Be Victims? A Meta-Analytic Review of the Research that Relates Masculine Ideology to Sexual Aggression," *Sex Roles* 46 (2006): 359–375; Bhuyan et al., "Women Must Endure According to Their Karma: Cambodian Immigrant Women Talk About Domestic Violence," *Journal of Interpersonal Violence* 20 (2005): 902–921.

34. T. D. Nguyen, "Prevalence of Male Intimate Partner Abuse in Vietnam," *Violence Against Women* 12, no. 8 (2006): 732–739.

35. S. K. Shiu-Thornton and M. S. Senturia, "'Like a Bird in a Cage': Vietnamese Women Survivors Talk about Domestic Violence," *Journal of Interpersonal Violence* 20 (2005): 959–976.

36. Bhuyan et al., "Women Must Endure According to Their Karma," 902–921.

37. K. McDonnell and S. Abdulla, *Project AWARE*. Washington, DC: Asian/Pacific Islander Domestic Violence Resource Project, 2001, www.DVRP.org accessed Oct. 24, 2008.

38. Yoshioka and Dang, *Asian Family Violence Report*.

39. Yick and Agbayani-Siewert, "Perceptions of Domestic," 832–846.

40. H. Bui and M. Morash, "Domestic Violence in the Vietnamese Immigrant Community: An Exploratory Study," *Violence Against Women* 5, no. 7 (1999): 769–795.

41. Sullivan et al., "Participatory Action Research in Practice," 977–995; Fugate et al., "Barriers to Domestic Violence Help Seeking: Implications for Intervention," *Violence Against Women* 11 (2005): 290–310.

42. Crandall et al., "No Way Out": Russian-Speaking Women's Experiences with Domestic Violence," *Journal of Interpersonal Violence* 20 (2005): 941–958; Bhuyan et al., "Women Must Endure According to Their Karma," 902–921; Fugate et al., "Barriers to Domestic Violence," 290–310; Sullivan et al., "Participatory Action Research in Practice," 977–995; E. M. Ingram, "A Comparison of Help Seeking Between Latino and Non-Latino Victims of Intimate Partner Violence," *Violence Against Women* 13 (2007): 159–171.

43. A. Raj and J. G. Silverman, "Immigrant South Asian Women at Greater Risk for Injury from Intimate Partner Violence," *American Journal of Public Health* 93, no. 3 (2003): 435–437; Bhuyan et al., "Women Must Endure According to Their Karma," 902–921.

44. McDonnell and Abdulla, *Project AWARE*.

45. W. Judith, "Refugees and Domestic Violence: Model-Building as a Prelude to Services Research," *Journal of Social Work Research* 2, no. 2 (2001): 237–245.

46. Judith, "Refugees and Domestic Violence," 237–245.

47. Lawyers.com, "Elder Abuse," http://elder-law.lawyers.com/Elder-Abuse.html. Accessed Oct. 29, 2008; Violence Affecting Asian-American and Pacific Islander Communities, "Definitions," http://www.sph.umich.edu/apihealth/2006/childelder.htm (accessed Oct. 24, 2008).

48. P. Brownell and I. Abelman, "Elder Abuse: Protective and Empowerment Strategies for Crisis Intervention," in *Battered Women and their Families,* ed. A. R. Roberts (New York: Springer, 1998); K. A. Pillmer and D. Finkelhor, "The Prevalence of Elder

Abuse: A Random Sample Survey. *The Gerontologist* 28 (1988): 51–57; M. Young, "Recognizing the Signs of Elder Abuse," *Patient Care* 34 no. 20 (2000): 56–62.

49. Pillmer and Finkelhor, "The Prevalence of Elder Abuse," 51–57.

50. Mouton, C. P., et al., "Multiethnic Perspectives on Elder Mistreatment," *Journal of Elder Abuse and Neglect* 17, no. 2 (2005): 21–44.

51. T. Tatara, *Understanding Elder Abuse in Minority Populations* (Philadelphia: Brunner/Mazel, 1999).

52. National Center on Elder Abuse, 1998, *Final Report*. Prepared for the Administration for Children and Families, and the Administration on Aging in the U.S., Department of Health and Human Services. Washington, DC: National Center on Elder Abuse.

53. J. Chang and A. Moon, "Korean American Elderly's Knowledge and Perceptions of Elder Abuse: A Qualitative Analysis of Cultural Factors," *Journal of Multicultural Social Work* 6, no. 1/2 (1997): 139–154.

54. Violence Affecting Asian-American and Pacific Islander Communities, "Definitions."

55. Violence Affecting Asian-American and Pacific Islander Communities, "Definitions."

56. Perceptions of Elder Abuse and Help-Seeking Patterns among African-American, Caucasian American, and Korean American Elderly Women, *The Gerontologist* 33, no. 4: 386–395; A. Moon and D. Benton, "Tolerance of Elder Abuse and Attitudes toward Third-Party Intervention among African American, Korean American, and White Elderly," *Journal of Multicultural Social Work* 8, no. 3/4 (2000): 283–303.

57. Yoshioka and Dang, *"Asian Family Violence Report."*

58. A. Moon and O. J. Williams, "Perceptions of Elder Abuse and Help Seeking Patterns among African American, Caucasian American and Korean American Elderly Women," *The Gerontologist* 33, no. 3 (1993): 386–395.

59. Moon and Williams, "Perceptions of Elder Abuse," 386–395.

60. Moon and Benton, "Tolerance of Elder Abuse," 283–303; A. Moon and T. Evans-Campbell, "Awareness of Formal and Informal Sources of Help for Victims of Elder Abuse Among Korean American and Non-Hispanic White Elders in Los Angeles," *Journal of Elder Abuse and Neglect* 11, no. 3 (1999): 1–23.

61. S. Pablo and K. L. Braun, "Perceptions of Elder Abuse and Neglect and Help-Seeking Patterns among Filipino and Korean Elderly Women in Honolulu," *Journal of Elder Abuse & Neglect* 9, no. 2 (1997): 63–76.

62. Moon and Evans-Campbell, "Awareness of Formal and Informal Sources of Help," 1–23.

63. Moon and Evans-Campbell, "Awareness of Formal and Informal Sources of Help," 1–23.

64. A. Moon, S. K. Tomita and S. Jung Kamei, "Elder Mistreatment among Four Asian American Groups: An Exploratory Study on Tolerance, Victim Blaming and Attitudes toward Third Party Intervention," *Journal of Gerontological Social Work 36* (2001): 153–169.

FILIAL PIETY AND CAREGIVING

Grace J. Yoo and Barbara W. Kim

Filial piety remains an important value that defines and regulates appropriate attitudes and behaviors toward parents and elderly in Asian societies; however, rapid industrialization, urbanization, internal migration, and demographic changes in marriage and childbearing in nations such as China, Korea, and Japan have redefined the meanings, duties, and arrangements of respecting and supporting aging parents.[1] As earlier generations of Asian Americans age, Asian American families are also negotiating ways to modify yet uphold the meanings and intergenerational expectations and practices around filial piety and caregiving. Physical, emotional, and social work of caregiving significantly affect women who make up the majority of informal (unpaid) and formal (paid) caregivers. The impact of cultural values, resources, and social policies around caregiving within and beyond Asian American families will be discussed in this entry.

FILIAL PIETY

The value of filial piety in the context of Confucianism has guided traditions, intergenerational relations and the treatment of elderly for centuries in many Asian societies—in particular, China, Japan, the Philippines, and Korea. While other societies also value filial obligation, they may attribute its basis to other religions and philosophies such as Christianity and Buddhism. By contrast, as an ideal virtue of moral behavior, filial piety stresses that children obey and care for their parents as they age. It is often demonstrated through responsibility, respect, sacrifice, and family harmony.[2] Adult children are to be attentive to their parents' desires and are expected to set aside their own interests for the well-being of their elderly parents. According to the practice of primogeniture that has accompanied the value of filial piety in traditional China, Japan, and Korea, the oldest son and his wife would live with and take care of his parents, inherit family properties, and continue to honor family ancestors as the rightful heir. Younger generations of Asians, however, define relationships with parents using concepts of affection and reciprocity in addition to duty and obligation.

Filial piety remains a core social value for Asian Americans of different ethnic groups and generations. As U.S.-born and/or raised children of Asian ethnicity continue to adapt and participate in mainstream American culture, conflicts with their immigrant parents, who cling to the values and cultures of the home country, are often inevitable. Yet the younger generation of Asian Americans still report feelings of duty and emphasize caring for their parents and other family members into old age.[3] The concept of filial piety has been especially important to first-generation Asian immigrants—especially those who are aging themselves and taking care of elderly parents—but the concepts of filial piety are modified even within these later intergenerational relationships, influencing expectations, practices, and types of caregiving.[4]

CAREGIVING

The definition of caregiver is anyone who provides assistance to an older adult or someone with a disability. Caregiving is the help provided to someone—generally a senior—who is unable to live independently and who needs assistance with eating, bathing, or dressing. It is estimated that informal caregivers, unpaid individuals who care for a family member, friend, or a neighbor provide up to 80 percent of care for frail elders in the United States, and caregivers tend to be middle-aged women across all ethnicities who are already juggling a combination of occupational, marital, childcare, and/or social obligations. Worldwide, spouses, adult daughters, and daughters-in-law are among the women who serve as the primary caregivers to the aged and those in frail health.

As the global economy changes and as more women enter the labor markets, informal caregiving for the growing aging population becomes more of a challenge in nations around the world. For example, in the United States, the economic burden and costs have fallen harder on the shoulders of women who provide the majority of the care to older family members. Those who decide to cut back hours, take time off without pay, or retire early in order to take care of an elderly or sick family member lose their earnings and benefits in the present and the future because Social Security benefits are based on years in the labor force multiplied by annual wages.[5] Caregivers may also experience chronic fatigue, anger, depression, frustration, stress, and worsening of their own health as a consequence of their duties especially as demands of the tasks grow.[6] Caregivers undergo many different encounters in caring for an ailing family member, including identifying a diagnosis, finding support, decision-making about treatment, and determining long-term care done at home or in a formal care setting.

Support that meets the multiple demands of caregiving plays an imperative role in community education, prevention, and treatment of senior health issues. For Asian immigrant families, barriers to support are compounded by significant language barriers. Elderly immigrants often encounter language and cultural barriers and often do not receive the services and support they need, placing additional burdens on the caregivers as well as their English-speaking children.

Moreover, concerns regarding shame and concerns about encumbering the family may prevent seeking out and accepting support both within and outside their families. Examining caregiving cross-culturally has shown that the meaning and process of caregiving is heavily influenced by cultural norms; however, cultural norms, such as filial piety and family expectations, can also produce barriers for support for both the caregiver and the frail relative. A recent study of Asian American caregivers found that personal issues of the caregivers, such as feeling too proud or unwilling to accept outsiders coming in to help, created barriers to accessing services as much as the lack of services that met diverse linguistic and cultural needs.[7] In another example, foreign-born Vietnamese caregivers did not access formal services for family members experiencing dementia because of concerns about shame and "loss of face." Understanding cultural conceptualizations of certain medical and health conditions could assist burdened caregivers to find appropriate help and for agencies to outreach sensitively and effectively to first-generation ethnic communities.[8]

FILIAL PIETY ACROSS GENERATIONS

Certain Asian American groups retain filial piety as a cultural tradition, demonstrated through intergenerational coresidence. An analysis of 1980 U.S. Census data found that despite differences in personal reasons for immigration and ethnic immigration history, elderly Chinese and Japanese were more likely to live in extended family households than non-Hispanic white elders, regardless of the elderly person's marital status, the state of residence, and gender.[9] In a 2001 survey of 2,300 baby boomers between ages forty-five and fifty-five, Asian American respondents (Japanese, Korean, Chinese, Filipino, Vietnamese, and Asian Indian) were most likely to care for their parents and older relatives (whether they lived in or outside the United States) and also were the most likely to say they had adjusted their lives and plans around their family responsibilities compared to other racial/ethnic groups. Almost half of Asian Americans reported providing care for an aging parent or relative, which was higher than other racial/ethnic groups. Foreign-born individuals were also more likely to provide care than native-born individuals, and those with lower incomes reported feeling more overwhelmed by caregiving responsibilities. Despite providing the most care to their aging relatives, Asian Americans also expressed the most guilt that they were not providing enough care. Almost three-fourths of Asian American adults said they should do more for their parents, compared with two-thirds of Latinos, slightly more than half of the African Americans, and fewer than half of the whites. Foreign-born Asian Americans were much more likely to feel guilt than U.S.-born Asians.[10]

There were racial/ethnic differences in caregiving as well as with attitudes about and perception of caregiving. For example, the majority (73%) of Asian Americans believed that the children in their families should care for elderly parents, compared with less than half (49%) of all respondents, and they were more likely to agree that their children should plan to care of them (38% compared to 22% of total respondents). However, factors such as income and foreign birth also determined personal caregiving and financial support behaviors.

At the same time, notions regarding the expectations of support from adult children are also changing and evolving among Asian immigrants who arrived later in their lives. Given the norm of dual-income families and increased mobility for educational and occupational reasons, traditional beliefs about filial piety are often challenged and altered upon immigrating to the United States. Studies of Korean American families have found that a major shift in filial piety expectations stems from the fact that many older immigrants find that their adult children fall short of their expectations.[11] They find that soliciting support from adult children often creates friction between themselves and their adult children's spouses.[12] As a result of these unexpected alterations (often downward) in their roles and status within the family, older Korean immigrants prefer to live independently from their adult children, valuing their independence and freedom. Many elders also do not wish to burden their children.[13]

Many studies that emphasize strength of cultural values without a social context ignore how the cultural concept of filial obligation interacts with financial and structural factors—such as proximity in residence, financial resources, parent need variables, and availability of other sibling or other kin/friend support—in influencing an adult child's support for his/her elderly parents. In a comparison of Chinese, Japanese, and Korean Americans, Korean American respondents were most likely to provide various types of support, such as financial assistance. Factors associated with this finding may include shorter years of residency in the United States, younger mean age, and the fact that Korean Americans are most likely to have younger children, which may result in more frequent reciprocal exchanges between parents and children. Proximity in residence, adult children's financial resources, and parental needs for assistance resulted in different fulfillment of filial obligations, dispelling the idea that all Asian Americans are rooted in traditional Asian culture.[14] Adult children may not always feel the affection or duty to care for their aging parents, or they may be geographically or financially unable to do so because of other multiple obligations.

Taking Care of Elders

The decision for a family to place a frail loved one in a nursing home can often be one of the most difficult decisions. Many Asian Americans are socialized to care for family members, but often they are saddled with work and care of young children. Over the last four decades, various Asian American communities in different part of the United States have organized to create nonprofit, community-based long-term care facilities that are linguistically and culturally familiar. These long-term care facilities include assisted living facilities, which are homes to assist elderly with activities of daily living, such as eating, bathing and taking medication. Others include nursing homes for frail elderly who need 24-hour nursing care and assistance with activities of daily living.

These nonprofit long-term care facilities often have been developed, in part, by an intergenerational coalition of concerned community members, advocates, and health and social service providers. In 1998, the Legacy House in Seattle's Chinatown opened its doors for assisted living to low-income Asian immigrant elderly. Developed in the 1980s in Sacramento, CA, the Asian Community Center of Sacramento nursing home has served as a model for culturally and linguistically competent care for Asian American elders. In the Japanese American community, throughout the United States in cities such as Los Angeles, San Francisco, and Seattle, there are assisted-living facilities and nursing homes like Keiro Homes and Nikkei Manor, long-term care facilities often started by third-generation Japanese Americans, who saw language and cultural barriers their immigrant grandparents were facing.

—Grace J. Yoo

CULTURAL VALUES, FAMILY SUPPORT, AND SOCIAL POLICIES

As in many industrialized nations around the world, the U.S. population is aging and living longer. The growth and diversity of the aging population have implications for social structures, relationships, and policies that can meet the rising needs of the elderly. The establishment and expansion in the 1950s through the 1970s of federal programs to address economic, health, and housing needs of the elderly slowed in the 1980s. In this new "renegotiation of the contract across generations" in the twenty-first century, politicians and researchers are reevaluating Medicare, Social Security, and other programs for the elderly so that caregiving responsibilities for older persons may shift from the public (government) to the private (family). The current U.S. long-term care system is built on the premise that the elderly will be cared for by their younger family members—most likely a daughter or a daughter-in-law—with other jobs. As more older people are living longer, current caregiving policies do not meet the available realities and resources of the elderly and their families.[15]

Asian American families may express respect for parents and desire to take care of aging adults, but they may not always be able to provide it. In time, the burdens of caregiving negatively affect the physical, mental, and emotional well-being of the caregiver (and family), who often need additional help. Although many Asian Americans see the traditional concept of filial piety as a core value of their ethnic group, the ideal that Asian Americans will take care of their own have been used by U.S. policy makers to assume that families could do even more to meet the needs of their aging family members. Various bills in past sessions in the U.S. Congress have proposed that Asian American family members, especially adult children, should be held fiscally responsible for the financial obligations of their aging immigrant parents.[16]

The first of the 78 million baby boomers will turn sixty-five in 2011, and some have already become eligible for Social Security benefits. The Medicare and Social Security trust funds are estimated to run out of money by 2019 and 2041, respectively, especially because of rising health costs. While the federal government seeks to find solutions to the rising needs of an aging population, shifting even more responsibility to the family alone will not address the dramatic population aging and its implications.

According to social scientists, expressions and practices of filial piety are changing in Asian societies as family members adapt to rapid industrialization, urbanization, rising female labor participation, family structures, and changing intergenerational relations. At the same time, social service providers are noting that Asian American adult children of different ethnic backgrounds, nativity, income, occupations, and English fluency need outside services to take care of their elderly parents. Despite a general view that Asian Americans are strongly influenced by and abide by traditional Asian values and practices, such as filial piety, economic and social factors are significantly interrelated with cultural factors in determining what types of financial, social, and emotional support adult children provide for their elderly parents.

Seniors who live in or near ethnic communities have been fortunate to have access to health care, ethnic senior centers, meal programs, religious services, leisure and recreational activities, assisted living centers, respite care, adult day care, and nursing homes that cater to characteristics and needs of particular ethnic backgrounds. Independent and home-bound older individuals have also been able to receive assistance with activities of daily living (ADL) from bilingual caregivers who can communicate with and interpret for them. To meet the diverse needs of the rapidly growing, Asian American older population, family members, mainstream and ethnic community providers, agencies, and institutions are continually working and advocating for linguistically and culturally appropriate programs and services. As the need for caregiving often comes unexpectedly, health and social service providers have noted that older and younger family members should discuss the process and economic feasibility of formal long-term care that families and friends are unable to provide.

FURTHER READING

Li, Hong. "Barriers to and Unmet Needs for Supportive Services: Experiences of Asian-American Caregivers." *Journal of Cross-Cultural Gerontology* 19, no. 3 (2004): 241–260.

Navaie-Waliser, Maryam, et al. "When the Caregiver Needs Care: The Plight of Vulnerable Caregivers." *American Journal of Public Health* 92 (2002): 409–413.

Wong, Sabrina T., Grace Yoo, and Anita Stewart. "The Changing Meaning of Family Support among Older Chinese and Korean Immigrants." *Journals of Gerontology Series B: Psychological Sciences and Social Sciences* 61 (2006): S4–S9.

NOTES

1. Kyu-taik Sung, "An Asian Perspective on Aging East and West: Filial Piety and Changing Families," in *Aging in East and West: Families, States, and the Elderly*, ed. Vern L. Bengtson, Kyong-Dong Kim, George. C. Myers and Ki-Soo Eun (New York: Springer Publishing Company, 2000), 41–56.

2. Sung, "An Asian Perspective on Aging East and West," 45.

3. Masako Ishii-Kuntz, "Intergenerational Relationships among Chinese, Japanese, and Korean Americans," *Family Relations 46* (1997): 24.

4. Sabrina T. Wong, Grace J. Yoo, and Anita L. Stewart, "The Changing Meaning of Family Support among Older Chinese and Korean Immigrants," *Journals of Gerontology Series B: Psychological Sciences and Social Sciences* 61 (2006): S4–S9.

5. Tonya M. Parrott et al., "The United States: Population Demographics, Changes in the Family, and Social Policy Challenges," in *Aging in East and West: Families, States, and the Elderly*, ed. Vern L. Bengtson, Kyong-Dong Kim, George C. Myers, and Ki-Soo Eun (New York: Springer Publishing Company, 2000), 193.

6. Ada C. Mui, Namkee G. Choi, and Abraham Monk, *Long-Term Care and Ethnicity* (Westport, CT: Auburn House, 1998), 171; Maryam Navaie-Waliser, et al., "When the Caregiver Needs Care: The Plight of Vulnerable Caregivers," *American Journal of Public Health* 92 (2002): 409–413.

7. Hong Li, "Barriers to and Unmet Needs for Supportive Services: Experiences of Asian-American Caregivers," *Journal of Cross-Cultural Gerontology* 19 (2004): 241–260.

8. Gwen Yeo et al., "Conceptions of Dementia among Vietnamese American Caregivers," in *Social Work Practice with the Asian American Elderly*, ed. Namhee G. Choi (Binghamton, NY: Haworth Press, 2001), 131–152.

9. Yoshinori Kamo and Min Zhou, "Living Arrangements of Elderly Chinese and Japanese in the United States," *Journal of Marriage and the Family* 56 (1994): 544–558.

10. AARP, *In the Middle: A Report on Multicultural Boomers Coping with Family and Aging Issues* (Washington DC: AARP, 2001), http://assets.aarp.org/rgcenter/il/in_the_middle.pdf.

11. Kwang Chung Kim, Shin Kim, and Won Moo Hurh, "Filial Piety and Intergenerational Relationships in Korean Immigrant Families," *International Journal of Aging and Human Development* 33 (1991): 233–245; Judith Treas and Shampa Mazumdar,

"Older People in America's Immigrant Families: Dilemmas of Dependence, Integration and Isolation," *Journal of Aging Studies* 16 (2002): 243–258.

12. Kwang Chung Kim, Won Moo Hurh, and Shin Kim, "Generational Differences in Korean Immigrants' Life Conditions in the United States," *Sociological Perspectives* 36 (1993): 257–270.

13. Tae-Ock Kauh, "Changing Status and Roles of Older Korean Immigrants in the United States," *International Journal of Aging and Human Development* 49 (1999): 213–229.

14. Ishii-Kuntz, "Intergenerational Relationships among Chinese, Japanese, and Korean Americans," 30.

15. Tonya M. Parrott et al., "The United States: Population Demographics, Changes in the Family, and Social Policy Challenges," 208.

16. Grace Yoo and Barbara Kim, "Remembering Sacrifices, Negotiating Cultures and Institutions: Second-Generation Korean Americans and Their Caregiving Expectations and Responsibilities to Aging Immigrant Parents," Unpublished paper, 2008.

INTERGENERATIONAL RELATIONS

Linda P. Juang

Asian American immigrant parents and their children face challenges, losses, opportunities, and complex relationships. On the one hand, many children deeply appreciate their parents' sacrifices for a better life. Yet on the other hand, many children experience an immense and sometimes distressing pressure to live up to those high hopes and expectations. Prior to 1965, there were very few psychological studies that involved ethnic minority Americans, including Asians.[1] In 1965, a major amendment to the Immigration and Nationality Act was approved. This amendment stimulated a new wave of immigrants—including many from Asian countries—to the United States. Notably, this new wave of immigrants was much more culturally, linguistically, educationally, and economically diverse than previous waves.[2] Concurrent with this increase in immigrants of Asian origin was the increasing appreciation and use of the term "Asian American" as a label and as an identity. These two factors stimulated a growing interest in understanding the dynamics of Asian American families. Thus, the focus here is on studies conducted with post-1965 Asian Americans.

Scholars of various disciplines—psychologists, sociologists, and anthropologists—have long emphasized the important role of the family, and especially parents, to child and adolescent development. For families of many different ethnicities and backgrounds, children who experience more positive relationships with their parents generally experience better mental health and greater well-being. The growing body of research on Asian American families supports this robust finding. Specifically, Asian American parent-child relationships that are cohesive and supportive are associated with better child and adolescent adjustment in numerous ways: better academic achievement, less depression, higher self-esteem, less loneliness, and more positive social adjustment. In contrast, negative parent-child relationships, such as those characterized by high parent-child conflict, have been associated with poorer adjustment in terms of greater depression, feelings of alienation, and poorer academic achievement. Indeed, family conflict and disagreement may be detrimental to Asian American families in particular, as there is a cultural emphasis on family interdependence, obligation, and cohesion.[3]

PARENTING STYLES

There is a long-standing history of exploring the style of parenting that encourages positive parent-child relationships and child outcomes. Four broad styles of parenting have been identified: authoritative, authoritarian, permissive, and uninvolved.[4] *Authoritative* parents are sensitive to the child's maturity level and are firm, fair, and warm. *Authoritarian* parents expect unquestioned obedience and view the child as needing to be controlled. *Permissive* parents are warm and nurturing to their children; however, they allow their children to regulate their own lives and provide few firm guidelines. *Uninvolved* parents are often too absorbed in their own lives to respond appropriately to their children and may seem indifferent to them. In general, research indicates that children benefit the most from the authoritative parenting style. Compared with children of other parenting styles, children of authoritative parents tend to have high self-esteem, do well in school, and get along well with their peers and family.[5] The benefits of authoritative parenting, however, differ depending on the particular ethnic group. For example, in a study comparing several thousand U.S. adolescents from four ethnic groups (European American, African American, Asian American, and Latino American), results show that authoritative parenting significantly predicted higher school achievement for European American, African American, and Latino American adolescents, but not for Asian Americans.[6] Further, European American adolescents were the most likely, and Asian American adolescents the least likely, to report that their parents were authoritative.

These findings (that Asian American adolescents seemed to benefit the least from authoritative parenting and were the least likely to report their parents as being authoritative) led some scholars, such as Ruth Chao of the University of California–Riverside, to challenge the notion that these particular styles adequately describe parenting across various ethnic groups. For example, Asian American parents have been thought to be more authoritarian than European American parents. However, the significance and meaning attached to this parenting style originates from a set of cultural beliefs that differ from the European American cultural belief system.[7] For example, for many Asian American families, there is a heavy emphasis on family interdependence and obligation to parents. As such, parental control (an aspect of authoritarian parenting) may be seen as a very positive and caring aspect of parenting. In contrast, for many European American families there is less emphasis on family interdependence and obligation to parents, thus, parental control may be seen as a negative, or even hostile, aspect of parenting. Consequently, the meaning and outcomes associated with the original four parenting styles may differ depending on the ethnic group. Chao has identified a type of parenting characteristic of Chinese parents, called *training*, that emphasizes close supervision in order to promote children to become disciplined and adherent to family obligation. Chao's work with Asian American parents underscores the need to understand parenting, parent-child relationships, and child adjustment within the particular cultural context.

FAMILY ISSUES

Several issues salient to Asian American families have consequences for the parent-child relationship: a high emphasis on achievement, less emphasis on independence, and high emphasis on family obligations. Many Asian American families are characterized by a strong parental emphasis on academic achievement. Ethnographies of Punjabi Sikh and Vietnamese families show that many parents believe that poor school performance reflects negatively on the entire family. Research has shown both positive and negative consequences to this strong emphasis on achievement. Positively, many parents are eager to support and provide numerous resources for education and learning (e.g., after-school programs, tutoring, music lessons) even in the face of economic hardship. Negatively, there can be immense pressure for children to succeed academically. This can be problematic in several ways. For example, studies have found that Asian American children often interpret high parental expectations for academic achievement negatively, believing their parents expect impossibly much or that their parents are never satisfied with their academic performance.[8] These pressures may result in excessive anxiety, self-doubt, and resentment, leaving some children with an overwhelming sense of alienation from their achievement-oriented parent, and vice versa.

Nonetheless, research has also shown that many Asian American children share the belief that doing well in school is an important way of repaying their parents' efforts and sacrifices. In one large-scale study of second-generation adolescents (including Asian American participants), one resounding theme appeared frequently in the interviews: the indebtedness the adolescents felt to their parents. Many adolescents understood the many hardships and sacrifices their parents endured to ensure they (the children) would have a better life.[9] One way Asian American youth cope with demanding expectations is by turning to their siblings and same-ethnic peers who may share the same pressures to succeed. Same-ethnic youth gatherings, facilitated by community or religious organizations, are important contexts for this type of support to emerge.[10]

Another issue salient for Asian American families is the cultural de-emphasis on independence (e.g., making independent decisions, focusing on individual needs over the needs of the family) in a culture where independence is promoted and encouraged. For European American (and other Western/mainstream culture) families, this independence is demonstrated in the fact that as children get older, much less time is spent with the family and greater time is spent with peers. As a result, parent-child relationships become more distant, at least for this period of time. This gradual separation from parents may signify the adolescent's developing sense of self and identity in preparation for adulthood, a process described by Erik Erikson as *identity formation.* Because of a cultural emphasis on family *interdependence,* however, research shows that Asian American parents tend to allow less independence and supervise their children more than other parents. For example, European and African American parents tend to allow their children to date, go to mixed-gender parties at night, spend time with friends rather than family, and choose their own friends, at earlier ages than Asian American parents.[11] Also important to note, however, are differences between different generational statuses. For example, Asian American adolescents born in the United States tend to look more similar to their European American counterparts in expectations for behavioral independence compared with Asian American adolescents born outside the United States. One study found that the age at which Hong Kong adolescents expected to go to boy-girl parties at night was 16–17 years, similar to Chinese American foreign-born adolescents. In contrast, Chinese American U.S.-born adolescents expected to go to boy-girl parties around 15 years and European American adolescents even earlier, around 14–15 years. These findings show that one important variation within Asian American families is generational status of the parent and child (foreign-born vs. U.S.-born).

Another salient issue for Asian American families is the strong role of family obligation. Family obligation refers to a set of behaviors and attitudes involving the support, assistance, and respect that children provide to their family. It is a key cultural value of many Asian cultures. Family obligation assigns great importance to the roles and duties of the child to the parents and family. There is a strong emphasis on respect for elders, obedience to parents, and putting the needs of the family before individual needs. Importantly, conciliation rather than disagreement in the home is encouraged, and different views within the family, particularly between children and parents, are discouraged. Studies have shown that Chinese and Filipino American adolescents report the highest levels of family obligation attitudes compared with their European American and Mexican American peers. For example, they report greater assistance to the family (e.g., help out around the house, run errands for the family), greater respect (e.g., treating parents with great respect, doing well for the sake of the family) and greater sense of future obligation (e.g., having parents live with you when older, helping out parents financially in the future) compared to European American and Mexican American adolescents. European American adolescents reported the lowest levels of family obligation on the three dimensions, reflecting the cultural emphasis on independence and less orientation to the family.[12]

Asian American adolescents who strongly endorse family obligation benefit in multiple ways; they derive a sense of pride by contributing to the family and enjoy more positive family relationships. Importantly, studies have found that many Asian American adolescents fulfill their obligations to the family without experiencing psychological distress.[13] Indeed, studies have found that Asian

American adolescents with a greater sense of family obligation report closer family relationships, greater academic motivation and achievement, and lower levels of behavioral misconduct.[14] Prevention programs that reinforce youths' collective identity, that strengthen their ties to their family and culture, and that remind youth of their family obligation may be particularly effective for Asian Americans.

IMMIGRATION

A majority of Asian Americans (88%) are immigrants or have at least one immigrant parent. As such, issues related to immigration are important considerations for understanding parent-child relations. Parents and children of immigrant families have unique difficulties not shared by nonimmigrant families, in part because family relationships are undergoing the process of acculturation. Acculturation refers to the changes in values, attitudes, and behaviors when individuals come into prolonged contact with one or more cultures.[15] Some important issues include adapting to a new language and culture while maintaining one's heritage culture, dealing with the loss of leaving family and friends behind, experiencing discrimination as an ethnic minority in the new culture, and struggling to navigate through unfamiliar job markets and education systems.

With respect to families, one of the greatest acculturation challenges is the growing differences between parents and children in values and behaviors. Because Asian American children from immigrant families tend to acquire the values and behaviors of the new culture at a faster rate than their parents, a large difference in values and behaviors (i.e., "acculturation gap") may result.[16] Researchers have hypothesized that the greater the acculturation gap, the greater potential for parent-child conflict. The acculturation gap has been highlighted in the popular and news media as the classic cultural clash between the Americanized, rebellious teen and the traditional, strict parent. For example, a story in *The New York Times* in 2002 focused on the cultural clash that arose with high school prom night. In one New York high school, teens of immigrant families expressed a strong desire to participate in this American rite of passage, but were forbidden by their immigrant parents to do so.[17]

The acculturation gap may be expressed in various family issues sensitive to the acculturation process, such as family obligation and autonomy expectations. For example, differences concerning family obligation grow larger with time in the United States among Asian American families. More specifically, Asian American parents endorse higher levels of family obligation than their adolescents, and this difference widens over time. Furthermore, and perhaps more importantly, parent-child differences in family obligation are associated with lower levels of life satisfaction for Asian American adolescents. Greater parent-child differences concerning autonomy expectations are also associated with more depressive symptoms, lower self-esteem, and greater conflicts with parents among Asian American youth.[18] For example, adolescents who desire independence at an earlier age in areas such as dating, choosing their own friends, or being able to attend parties, but whose parents do not allow their adolescents to engage in these behaviors, report engaging in greater conflict with parents. And greater conflict with parents has been found to be one of the strongest predictors of poor adolescent mental health in terms of depression and self-esteem.

Having different views from parents concerning values and attitudes is normal for almost all adolescents, not just those from Asian American families; however, because many Asian cultures greatly emphasize respect for parents and family harmony, these differences may be less acceptable and more disturbing to Asian American adolescents, especially if these differences erupt into family conflict. Indeed, parent-adolescent conflicts are more highly correlated with problem behavior (e.g., antisocial behavior, cigarette smoking, alcohol use, school misconduct) among Chinese American adolescents compared to European American adolescents.[19]

Another challenge for Asian American immigrant families is language differences. Often, parents and children speak different languages in the home. The majority of Asian American children (with the exception of Filipino and Japanese children) speak a language other than English in the home. English monolinguals (those who speak English only) are most common among Filipinos and Japanese and least common among Vietnamese and other Southeast Asians. Language is important for understanding the quality of parent-child relationships. In families where parents have difficulty speaking English and children lose their heritage language, effective communication is compromised and may only occur on a superficial level. More meaningful communication may be lost.[20] Over time, parent-child relationships may become impaired, as the language to convey complex thoughts and emotions is limited. In contrast, for parents and children who manage to maintain a common language (either both fluent in English, or both fluent in the heritage language), communication and quality of parent-child relationships become more positive over time.

In addition to differences in language spoken, there may be differences in expectations for ways of communicating. Asian parents may expect children to obey their words without talking back. Parents may also focus more on issues such as school and studying, and less on other areas such as social relationships and emotional well-being. Children, on the other hand, may desire more open communication (e.g., being able to share their thoughts honestly and freely) and to discuss not only school performance, but also their feelings and ideas. These differences in ways of communicating set the stage for parent-child conflict that may intensify.

However, although it is assumed that Asian American parents are acculturating at a slower rate than their children, and therefore embody more traditional cultural ideals, this is not always the case. Some parents are less traditional than their children, and some children are more traditional than their parents. As such, there may be much greater variation in rates of acculturation within Asian

American families than commonly assumed. Asian American children who are more traditional than their parents may experience different challenges compared with children who are just as or less traditional than their parents. Among Chinese Americans, the first generation immigrants are more likely to identify themselves with Chinese cultural values while the second and third generation are more likely to identify themselves with both American and Chinese values. On the other hand, fourth-generation Chinese Americans often identify with Chinese values rather than American values.[21] Members of the later generation often realize they have lost a great deal of their cultural heritage, and begin to reach back to their cultural roots to regain what was lost. It could be, then, that children who are more culturally traditional than their parents feel the need to accentuate and maintain their culture in the context of a family that did not emphasize their cultural heritage. Attention to such variations provides a richer, more accurate picture of how Asian American family members are adapting to the new culture in relation to one another.

Although there are many challenges for Asian American families, it is also important to highlight that parents are an essential source of comfort and identity for children and adolescents. Parents provide the link between the child and broader society. Parents can help their children and adolescents adjust to and navigate the new culture while providing a connection to the heritage culture. Parents who instill a sense of cultural pride in their children contribute to their children's resilience in situations such as facing racial or ethnic discrimination.[22] Asian American children and adolescents who maintain strong heritage cultural ties (e.g., through language, adopting heritage culture values and beliefs, identifying with and being proud of their culture) experience better adjustment in terms of greater self-esteem, lower depression, and higher academic achievement.[23]

To understand Asian American parent-child relations one must also go beyond the individual relationships to consider the broader contexts in which they live.[24] Some Asian American families live in a strong, cohesive, and robust ethnic community, while others live in a community that is ethnically isolated. Community-based ethnic institutions that provide opportunities for parents, children, and families to connect with one another, reinforce cultural traditions and in turn, promote positive youth development.[25]

To address the challenges faced by Asian American families, community advocates and scholars have created programs geared toward supporting Asian American families. One such program, developed specifically for Chinese American immigrant parents but intended for expansion to immigrant parents in general, was developed by community psychologist Yu-Wen Ying of the University of California–Berkeley. The goal of Ying's parenting program is to prevent and reduce parent-child conflict that may arise because of acculturation challenges and, further, to strengthen parent-child relationships. In this eight-week program, parents gather to discuss issues such as understanding cultural differences in notions of ideal parent-child relationships (between mainstream vs. heritage culture), and the challenges Asian American children face (e.g., balancing two cultures, experiencing racial discrimination in school, developing a strong ethnic identity). Three months after the intervention, the parents reported greater confidence in their parenting skills and, importantly, also reported an improvement in their relationships with their children. These preliminary findings are a promising start. Another community advocate and scholar, clinical psychologist Anna Lau of UCLA, is also designing a prevention program aimed at Asian American parents. Based on a national data set of Asian American adults, Lau reports that almost one-third of Asian American parents reported minor parent-to-child assault, and 2 percent reported major assault. She argues these numbers may be an underrepresentation because of cultural pressures against disclosing family problems. Lau seeks to uncover and address culturally salient factors (such as acculturative stress, acculturation gaps, culturally based child-rearing values) that would place Asian American families at risk for abuse. The goal of her program is to prevent parent-child conflict from evolving into abusive violence.

An understanding of intergenerational relations between Asian American parents and children is still far from complete. Future work should focus on including more various Asian groups. To date, most of the research on Asian American families has focused on Chinese, Japanese, and Filipino parents and children. Less is known about family processes among Southeast Asian and Asian Indian parents and children. It is believed that future research on intergenerational relations should also focus on subgroups that have been, until recently, invisible in discussions of Asian American families. Some examples are low-achieving Asian American students, Asian American families in poverty, and families with sexual minority adolescents.

FURTHER READING

Garrod, Andrew and Robert Kilkenny. *Balancing Two Worlds: Asian American College Students Tell Their Life Stories.* Ithaca, NY: Cornell University Press, 2005.
Portes, Alejandro and Ruben Rumbaut. *Legacies: The Story of the Second Generation.* Berkeley: University of California Press, 2001.
Tewari, Nita and Alvin Alvarez. *Asian American Psychology: Current Perspectives.* Mahwah, NJ: Lawrence Erlbaum, 2008.

NOTES

1. Laura Uba, *Asian Americans: Personality Patterns, Identity, and Mental Health* (New York: Guilford Press, 1994).

2. Alejandro Portes and Ruben Rumbaut, *Legacies: The Story of the Immigrant Second Generation* (Berkeley: University of California Press, 2001).

3. Andrew Fuligni, "Authority, Autonomy, and Parent-Adolescent Conflict and Cohesion: A Study of Adolescents from Mexican, Chinese, Filipino, and European Backgrounds," *Developmental Psychology* 34, no. 4 (July 1998): 782–792; Uba, *Asian Americans.*

4. Diana Baumrind, "Current Patterns of Parental Authority," *Developmental Psychology Monographs* 4, no. 1 (1971): 1–103; Eleanor Maccoby and John Martin,

"Socialization in the Context of the Family: Parent-Child Interaction," in *Handbook of Child Psychology: Vol. 4. Socialization, Personality, and Social Development,* 4th ed., ed. E. M. Hetherington (New York: Wiley, 1983), 1–101.

5. Andrew Collins and Lawrence Steinberg, "Adolescent Development in Interpersonal Context," in *Handbook of Child Psychology,* 6th ed., ed. W. Damon and R. Lerner (New York: Wiley, 2006).

6. Lawrence Steinberg, et al., "Impact of Parenting Practices on Adolescent Achievement: Authoritative Parenting, School Involvement, and Encouragement to Succeed," *Child Development* 63, no. 5 (Oct. 1992): 1266–1281.

7. Ruth K. Chao, "Beyond Parental Control and Authoritarian Parenting Style: Understanding Chinese Parenting through the Cultural Notion of Training," *Child Development* 65, no. 4 (Aug. 1994): 1111–1120; Ruth K. Chao, "Cultural Explanations for the Role of Parenting in the School Success of Asian-American Children," in *Resilience across Contexts: Family, Work, Culture, and Community*, ed. M. C. Wang and R. D. Taylor (New York: Routledge, 2000), 333–363.

8. Desiree Qin, "'Our Child Doesn't Talk to Us Anymore': Alienation in Immigrant Chinese Families," *Anthropology & Education Quarterly* 37, no. 2 (June 2006): 162–179.

9. Alejandro Portes and Ruben Rumbaut, *Legacies: The Story of the Second Generation* (Berkeley: University of California Press, 2001).

10. Min Zhou and Carl Bankston, *Growing up American: How Vietnamese Children Adapt to Life in the United States* (New York: Russell Sage Foundation, 1998).

11. Christopher Daddis and Judith Smetana, "Middle-Class African American Families' Expectations For Adolescents' Behavioural Autonomy," *International Journal of Behavioral Development* 29, no. 5 (2005): 371–381; Shirley S. Feldman and Doreen A. Rosenthal, "Age Expectations of Behavioral Autonomy in Hong Kong, Australian, and American Youths: The Influence of Family Variables and Adolescent Values," *International Journal of Psychology* 26, no. 1 (1991): 1–23.

12. Andrew Fuligni, Vivian Tseng, and May Lam, "Attitudes toward Family Obligations among American Adolescents with Asian, Latin American, and European Backgrounds," *Child Development* 70, no. 4 (July–Aug. 1999): 1030–1044.

13. Andrew J. Fuligni, Tiffany Yip, and Vivian Tseng, "The Impact of Family Obligation on the Daily Activities and Psychological Well-Being of Chinese American Adolescents," *Child Development* 73, no. 1 (Jan.–Feb. 2002): 302–314.

14. Fuligni, Tseng, and Lam, "Attitudes toward Family Obligations," 1030–1044; Linda Juang and Huong Nguyen, "Misconduct among Chinese American Adolescents: The Role of Acculturation, Family Obligation and Autonomy Expectations," *Journal of Cross-Cultural Psychology* 40, no. 4 (July 2009): 649–666.

15. John Berry, "Conceptual Approaches to Acculturation," in *Acculturation: Advances in Theory, Measurement, and Applied Research,* ed. K. Chun, P. Balls-Organista, and G. Martin (Washington, DC: American Psychological Association Press, 2003), 17–37.

16. Kyunghwa Kwak, "Adolescents and their Parents: A Review of Intergenerational Family Relations for Immigrant and Non-Immigrant Families," *Human Development* 46, nos. 2–3 (2003): 115–136.

17. Susan Sachs, "Prom Night, Lost in Translation: Teenagers Want to Go but Immigrant Parents Frown," *New York Times,* B1, June 13, 2002, http://www.nytimes.com/2002/06/13/nyregion/prom-night-lost-in-translation-teenagers-want-to-go-but-immigrant-parents-frown.html?pagewanted=1.

18. Jean S. Phinney, Anthony Ong, and Tanya Madden, "Cultural Values and Inter-generational Value Discrepancies in Immigrant and Non-Immigrant Families," *Child Development* 71, no. 2 (April–May 2000): 528–539; Linda Juang et al., "The Goodness of Fit of Autonomy Expectations between Asian American Late Adolescents and their Parents," *International Journal of Behavioral Development* 23, no. 4 (Dec. 1999): 1023–1048.

19. Chuansheng Chen et al., "A Cross-Cultural Study of Family and Peer Correlates of Adolescent Misconduct," *Developmental Psychology* 34, no. 4 (July 1998): 770–781.

20. Qin, "Our Child Doesn't Talk to Us Anymore," 162–179.

21. Stella Ting-Toomey, "Ethnic Identity and Close Friendships in Chinese American College Students," *International Journal of Intercultural Relations* 5 (1981): 383–406.

22. Richard Lee, "Resilience Against Discrimination: Ethnic Identity and Other-Group Orientation as Protective Factors for Korean Americans," *Journal of Counseling Psychology* 52, no. 1 (Jan. 2005): 36–44.

23. Lisa Kiang et al., "Ethnic Identity and the Daily Psychological Well-Being of Adolescents from Mexican and Chinese Backgrounds," *Child Development* 77, no. 5 (Sept.–Oct. 2006): 1338–1350; Richard Lee and Hyung Chol Yoo, "Structure and Measurement of Ethnic Identity for Asian American College Students," *Journal of Counseling Psychology* 51, no. 2 (Apr. 2004): 263–269; Jeanne L. Tsai, Yu-Wen Ying, and Peter A. Lee, "Cultural Predictors of Self-Esteem: A Study of Chinese American Female and Male Young Adults," *Cultural Diversity and Ethnic Minority Psychology* 7, no. 3 (Aug. 2001): 284–297.

24. Kwak, "Adolescents and Their Parents," 115–136.

25. Min Zhou and Carl Bankston, *Growing Up American: How Vietnamese Children Adapt to Life in the United States* (New York: Russell Sage Foundation, 1998).

INTERRACIAL AND INTERETHNIC DATING AND MARRIAGE

Sachiko K. Wood

Interracial or interethnic marriages occur between individuals who marry someone of a different ethnicity or race. The phenomenon is so common that the late Japanese American scholar Harry Kitano stated that well more than 50 percent of Japanese Americans married someone of a different ethnicity.[1] According to a study, 43 percent of second-generation Asian women and 35 percent of second-generation Asian men marry outside their respective Asian ancestry.[2] This is important to Asian America as identity and family structure (e.g. traditions, values and cultures) are constantly evolving. Growing numbers of interracial and interethnic couples in Asian communities means the merging of not only the couple but of their respective families and friends. This in turn, creates more alliances and bridges among different racial and ethnic groups that might not otherwise be formed. In the twenty-first century, one begins to see a new generation of Asian Americans and a constant blurring of ethnic and racial boundaries. Interracial relationships include two people who have different racial origins from each other (e.g., one partner might be Asian and the other might be white), whereas interethnic relationships might include a couple of the same race (e.g., Asian) and of different ethnic background (e.g., Korean and Vietnamese). The U.S. Census in 2000 estimated that 1.5 million marriages were interracial, which is an increase since 1970.[1] In 2005, more than 7 percent of the United States' 59 million married couples were interracial.[2]

ANTIMISCEGENATION LAWS

In the 1700s and 1800s, Asian immigrant workers at the time—mainly Chinese and Filipino men—arrived onto the U.S. mainland. Over time, more and more Asian men courted—and eventually married—white American women. White Americans viewed Asians as a threat to society, so consequently, antimiscegenation laws were passed to illegalize marriages between Asians and whites. However, these laws were not new to the United States; the first anti-miscegenation laws were passed in the 1600s to prevent black slaves from marrying whites. These laws were only part of the anti-Asian movement; later, the Page Law of 1875 prevented Chinese women from immigrating to the United States. Shortly afterward, the Chinese Exclusion Act in 1882 prevented naturalization of any Chinese people in the United States and banned the immigration of all Chinese to America, including the wives and children of those already residing within the country. The trend however, of Asian men marrying non-Asian women turned around after World War I and World War II. Servicemen, mainly but not exclusively whites, began marrying Asian women from countries overseas, such as Japan, Korea, and Vietnam. These women were often referred to as *war brides.*

Antimiscegenation laws did not illegalize all interracial marriages, only marriages of people of color to white people (i.e., Asians could marry blacks, Latinos could marry American Indians, etc.). The 1924 legislation defined a white person as one "who has no trace whatsoever of any blood other than Caucasian."[3] These laws were designed to protect and maintain white supremacy (e.g., protecting voting rights, property rights), establishing people of color as inferior to whites. Nonwhites marrying whites meant the possibility of producing mixed race children and losing one's power and position in the family and/or society. This racial caste system meant that white women served as producers of white children thereby securing those rights. It took forty-three years before *Loving v. Virginia*, a landmark civil rights case, to end all race-based legal restrictions on marriage in the United States.

Since the Supreme Court decision in *Loving v. Virginia* set the federal precedent, interracial dating and marriages have increased each year. The U.S. Census Bureau stated that interracial marriages doubled between 1970 to 1980 and again doubled in the 1990s.[4] In 2003, according to the Pew Research Survey, more than 77 percent of randomly polled Americans (compared to 48 percent in 1987) thought interracial relationships were socially acceptable.[5] There is more dialogue and attention paid to racial mixture in America than ever before.[6]

Asian Americans have one of the highest out-marriage rates to whites (second only to Hispanic and white couples). Some argue that Asians marrying whites can be seen as moving up the social or economic ladder, and they are integrating into white neighborhoods faster than any other group.[7] Research shows that it is more common for Asian women to marry white men than Asian men to marry white women. In the majority of Asian-white marriages, the husband is white.[8]

This phenomenon is more complex than it reads. White men might date or marry Asian and Asian American women for various reasons, including having grown up in or with an Asian community, or having interest or curiosity in a different culture. Some argue that misguided media images and stereotypes of Asian women being more domesticated, submissive, and erotic make Asian women more desirable. On the other hand, possible reasons for Asian women marrying whites (rather than Asians) might be their perception white men tend to be more culturally liberated while often (mis)perceiving Asian and Asian American men to be more traditional and patriarchal about gender roles.[9] There are stereotypes of Asian men not being "Americanized" enough, not being masculine enough, or being too sexist which can contribute to Asian women marrying out.

INTERETHNIC RELATIONSHIPS

Interethnic relationships refers to couples that share a common racial group (i.e. Asian American) but who also belong to different ethnic groups (e.g., Japanese, Korean, Vietnamese, etc.) For example, a Japanese American dating a Korean American would be considered an interethnic relationship.

The odds of having an interethnic relationship increase if the individual has a ethnically diverse friendship network and supports interethnic dating.[10] Asians who are born or raised in the United States are more likely to date or marry outside their ethnic group.[11] This may be attributed to the fact that those who are raised in the United States are more likely to interact with members of different racial and ethnic groups than Asian immigrants who come to the United States already married or who have not interacted with different racial and ethnic groups prior to immigrating.

Cultural assimilation through marriage is historically an important part of Asian American communities adapting and acculturating to U.S. society.[12] Assimilation refers to the multitude of social processes that bring ethnic minorities into mainstream U.S. society, including economic, political, and family life.[13] To individuals belonging to an ethnic minority group, marrying a white American signifies cultural assimilation and the attainment of higher socioeconomic status.[14]

The 2000 Census reported that among the largest Asian American groups (i.e., Asian Indian, Chinese, Filipino, Japanese, Korean, and Vietnamese Americans), Japanese Americans had the highest out-marriage rates, with another Asian ethnic group (e.g., Japanese-Chinese) or another race (e.g., Japanese-white) at 31 percent.[15] Conversely, Vietnamese Americans had the lowest rates (8.3 percent), which might be because of their more recent immigration patterns and being less assimilated to U.S. culture.[16]

CRITICAL ISSUES

There has been a long history of debates regarding the idea of miscegenation, as some biologists, anthropologists, historians and sociologists viewed racial mixing as "social pathology."[17] One of the reasons this taboo of interracial dating subsists is that there is still a racial caste system in the United States. Whites have historically been on the top of this racial hierarchy, followed by Asians and Hispanics, and with American Indians and blacks on the bottom. This caste system can cause tension in interracial and interethnic relations.

One of the most common challenges for interethnic or interracial couples is dealing with opposition from family, friends, and/or society. Past taboos of interracial dating and marriages, as well as stereotypes of racial groups, are still prevalent in society and experienced by those involved in interracial relationships. Maria Root, a clinical psychologist, interviewed some two hundred people from different ethnic and racial backgrounds to discuss their experiences. While some respondents in the study shared that they felt barriers and discriminatory attitudes toward interracial couples were declining, others felt that there remains opposition from family and society.[18] For example, some interracial couples were upset or hurt when strangers in their community might look at them disapprovingly.[19] Some report that family would be insulted by dating someone outside of their ethnicity and that the union would not be respected by immediate or extended family.[20] A Korean college student explained in one study, that being a firstborn son of a Korean family, there is pressure to marry a Korean, or at least another Asian.[21]

Interracial and interethnic couples who do not live in urban areas or who do live in areas where racial and ethnic diversity are lacking might deal with this community's resistance toward interracial and even interethnic dating and marriages. These couples, then, might face some issues dealing with the social images and stereotypes that society still holds and perpetuates in mainstream media.

Language barriers, communication style, and/or conflicting childrearing perspectives are some other factors that can complicate interracial and interethnic relationships.[22] Different upbringings and cultural backgrounds might make it difficult for a couple to understand where one is coming from. These factors are not limited, however, to just interracial/interethnic relationships and can actually serve to strengthen and build strong relationships.

BENEFITS

An empirical study, comparing thirty-two interracially dating couples with eighty-six intraracially dating couples, disproved the notion that interracial relationships are aberrant or dysfunctional compared with intraracial relationships.[23] There is no research that proves interracial and/or interethnic couples have higher divorce rates; in fact, divorce rates and divorce factors are comparable for both interracial and same race couples.[24] Furthermore, interracial couples appear to have similar levels of satisfaction as same-race couples.[25]

Learning about and being exposed to another culture than one's own can be an enriching experience that can benefit the relationship as well as enrich family and friends of the couple. Learning a new language, eating new foods, celebrating different traditions, learning about new religions and observing different holidays can be positive and eye-opening for both partners and their families. Successful interethnic couples see past ethnicity and race and appreciate one another as loving partners who they mutually respect and benefit from sharing with one another.

OUTLOOK

Growing numbers of interethnic marriages have blurred traditional Asian ethnic boundaries and have created an emerging pan-Asian American identity.[26] Like white ethnics during the twentieth century, this process of intermarriage among diverse Asian ethnic groups resembles this similar phenomenon. Current demographics illustrate that there will be a continual increase in interracial and interethnic dating and marriages as the U.S. population continues to grow more diverse. In the 2000 Census, more than 6 million individuals reported that they have more than one race. By the year 2020, one in five Asian Americans will be multiracial.[27]

In the twenty-first century, it is not only legal to interracially and interethnically marry, but it is also somewhat probable—especially among younger generations.[28] One in five Americans have a family member married to someone of another race, and almost all of Generation Y-ers say, "Interracial dating is perfectly normal."[29] The movement of interracial and interethnic marriages and dating also reflects the growing social acceptance of interethnic and interracial relations.[30] The increase in interethnic and interracial dating and marriages will lead to a more diverse society and culturally rich country.

FURTHER READING

iPride: Interracial, Intercultural Pride Web site. http://www.ipride.org/.

Kennedy, Randall. *Interracial Intimacies: Sex, Marriage, Identity, and Adoption.* New York: Pantheon Books. 2003.

Koshy, Susan. *Sexual Naturalization: Asian Americans and Miscegenation.* Stanford, CA: Stanford University Press, 2004.

New Demographic—Better than Diversity Training Web site. http://www.newdemographic .com/.

Root, Maria P., and M. Kelley, eds. *The Multiracial Child Resource Book.* Seattle, WA: Mavin Foundation, 2003.

Root, Maria. *Love's Revolution: Racial Intermarriage.* Philadelphia: Temple University Press, 2001.

NOTES

1. David R. Harris and Hiromi Ono, "How Many Interracial Marriages Would There Be If All Groups Were of Equal Size in All Places? A New Look at National Estimates of Interracial Marriage," *Social Science Research* 34 (2005) 236–251.

2. The Associated Press, "Interracial Marriage Flourished in U.S.: Since Landmark 1967 Ruling, Unions Have Moved from Radical to Everyday," *MSNBC,* http://www.msnbc.msn.com/id/18090277/.

3. Walter Wadlington, "The Loving Case: Virginia's Anti-Miscegenation Statute in Historical Perspective," in *Mixed Race American and the Law*, ed. Ken Johnson (New York: New York University Press. 2003).

4. Zhenchao Qian, "Who Intermarries? Education, Nativity, Region, and Interracial Marriage, 1980 and 1990," *Journal of Comparative Family Studies* 34 (1999): 263–276.

5. Paul Taylor, Cary Funk, and Peyton Craighill, "Guess Who's Coming to Dinner," Pew Research Center Publications, posted March 14, 2006, http://pewresearch.org/pubs/304/guess-whos-coming-to-dinner.

6. Kim Williams, *Mark One or More: Civil Rights in Multiracial America* (Michigan: The University of Michigan Press, 2006).

7. Zhenchao Qian, "Breaking the Last Taboo: Interracial Marriage in America," *The American Sociological Association* 4, no. 4 (2005): 33–37.

8. Paulette Chu Miniter, "New Generation Navigates Interracial Marriage," *New American Media*, May 23, 2007, http://news.newamericamedia.org/news/view_article.html?article_id=ea125ffa1a0aadaec58bd953b2e0585e.

9. Qian, "Breaking the Last Taboo: Interracial Marriage in America," 33–37.

10. Clark-Ianez and Diane Felmlee, "Interethnic Relationships: The Role of Social Network Diversity," *Journal of Marriage and Family* 66 (2004): 293–305.

11. C. N. Le, "Interracial Dating & Marriage," *Asian-Nation: The Landscape of Asian America*, http://www.asian-nation.org/interracial.shtml.

12. Zhenchao Qian and Daniel T. Lichter, "Measuring Marital Assimilation: Intermarriage among Natives and Immigrants" *Social Science Research* 30 (2001): 289–312.

13. Qian and Lichter, "Measuring Marital Assimilation," 289–312.

14. S. Hwang, R. Saenz, and B. E. Aguirre, "Structural and Assimilationist Explanations of Asian-American Intermarriage," *Journal of Marriage and the Family* 59 (1997): 758–772.

15. Le, "Interracial Dating & Marriage."

16. Le, "Interracial Dating & Marriage."

17. Jayne Ifekwunigwe, "Rethinking 'Mixed Race' Studies," in *'Mixed Race' Studies: A Reader*, ed. Jayne Ifekwunigwe (2003), 53–55.

18. Maria Root, *Love's Revolution: Interracial Marriage* (Philadelphia: Temple University Press, 2001).

19. Root, *Love's Revolution: Interracial Marriage.*

20. Rahwa Ghebre, "Interracial Dating Has Benefits for Students," *The Michigan Daily*, Feb. 13, 2003, http://www.michigandaily.com/content/interracial-dating-has-benefits-students.

21. Keramet Reiter, "AAA Hosts Panel On Interracial Dating," *The Harvard Crimson,* March 9, 2000, http://www.thecrimson.com/article.aspx?ref=99835.

22. P. M. Usita and S. Poulsen, "Interracial Relationships in Hawaii: Issues, Benefits, and Therapeutic Interventions," *Journal of Couple and Relationship Therapy* 2 (2003): 73–83.

23. Adam B. Troy, Lewis-Smith, Jamie and Jean-Philippe Laurenceau, "Interracial and Intraracial Romantic Relationships: The Search for Differences in Satisfaction, Conflict, and Attachment Style," *Journal of Social and Personal Relationships* 23, no. 1 (2006): 65–80.

24. Maria Root, *Love's Revolution: Interracial Marriage.*

25. Marina Lanstman, "Relationship Satisfaction as Function of Congruence of Acculturation Levels and Ethnic Identification in Interracial Couples," PhD dissertation, Hofstra University, 2003.

26. Qian and Lichter, "Measuring Marital Assimilation," 289–312.

27. Le, "Interracial Dating & Marriage."

28. Taylor, Funk and Craighill, "Guess Who's Coming to Dinner."

29. Taylor, Funk and Craighill, "Guess Who's Coming to Dinner."

30. Martin Fiebert et al., "Dating and Commitment Choices as a Function of Ethnicity Among American College Students in California," presented at Western Psychological Association convention in Phoenix, Arizona (April 23, 2004).

LGBTIQ PEOPLE COMING OUT

Anneliese A. Singh

"Coming out" is an important issue for Asian Americans who are lesbian, gay, bisexual, transgender, intersex, and/or queer (LGBTIQ). The term refers to a process where LGBTIQ people share their sexual orientation or gender identity with others in their lives—from friends and family to coworkers and employers.[1] Although there are no specific numbers of how many LGBTIQ people of Asian/Pacific Islander heritage there are in the United States, general statistics estimate that between 6–16 percent of the general population claim an LGBTIQ identity.[2]

Regardless of the actual number of LGBTIQ Asian Americans, there is ample evidence of their presence in the organizations around the United States, such as Trikone and GAPA, that have focused on Asian Americans LGBTIQ, providing opportunities for support, networking, and friendship in a safe environment that respects the racial/ethnic, sexual orientation, and gender identity of this group. In fact, a National Queer Asian American/Pacific Islander Association (NQAAPA) has been proposed by national and community Asian American LGBTIQ leaders to organize these social organizations nationally into a coalition of groups that advocates for the rights of LGBTIQ Asian Americans.[3] As LGBTIQ issues in general become more visible in the United States through the media and other institutions, the visibility of Asian American LGBTIQ issues will continue to grow.[4]

There are some specific terms that help individuals familiarize themselves with the LGBTIQ community. *Sexual orientation* refers to one's affectional attractions to either same-sex or opposite sex partners.[5] *Lesbians* are women who are attracted to female-identified partners, while *gay* is a term acknowledging men's attractions to male-identified partners. *Bisexual* refers to people who have attractions to both women and men. *Queer* is a term acknowledging the broad array of sexual and gender identities that are nonheteronormative.[6]

Sexual orientation is often confused with gender identity, the latter term defined as an individual's internal understanding of personal gender and/or gender expression.[7] Some lesbian, gay, bisexual, or queer Asian Americans may also identify their gender identity as *transgender* or *intersex*. Transgender Asian Americans have been assigned "male" or "female" at birth, yet this sex assignment may not be congruent with their internal understanding of their own self. Further, intersex Asian Americans are those people born with reproductive and/or sexual anatomy atypical of what society generally defines as "male" or "female."[8] Having a strong grasp of appropriate terms that are affirmative is a critically important aspect of working with LGBTIQ Asian Americans and their issues.

INTERSECTION OF MULTIPLE IDENTITIES

There are many barriers, challenges, and benefits associated with LGBTIQ Asian Americans. The National Gay and Lesbian Task Force conducted the largest national survey on LGBTIQ Asian Americans in 2007.[9] The results of this survey illustrated the complexity of LGBTIQ Asian Americans' lives, including the impact of both racism and homophobia. Almost all participants reported one or more experiences of discrimination based on race/ethnicity or sexual orientation; 75 percent of participants shared they experienced discrimination based on their sexual orientation. Eighty-nine percent of the participants reported that homophobia was a significant challenge in their Asian American/Pacific Islander community, while 78 percent of participants reported they experienced racism from the larger white LGBTIQ community.

These statistics portray the stark challenges that exist for Asian American LGBTIQ people. These individuals experience marginalization from their own ethnic community because of their sexual orientation and/or gender identity, yet they experience further prejudice attributed to their ethnic identity within white LGBTIQ communities.

There are additional barriers and challenges to coming out and embracing both their racial/ethnic and LGBTIQ identities. There are very few empirical studies examining the lives of LGBTIQ Asian Americans. One of the first studies to examine the intersection of Asian American and LGBTIQ identities suggested that LGBTIQ Asian Americans want affirmation and validation of both their racial/ethnic identity and their sexual orientation; however, the participants reported they were often perceived and/or treated *as either* LGBTIQ or an Asian American.[10] The result of this "splitting" of identities can produce mental health stressors for this group resulting in depression, anxiety, and even suicide.

Coming out is a process that has been traditionally defined as occurring in stages across the lifespan of LGBTIQ people. There are six stages of coming out: confusion, comparison, tolerance, acceptance, pride, and synthesis.[11] The first stage of confusion refers to the recognition of one's same-sex attractions, searching for information on LGBTIQ issues, and experiences of shame as a result of such attractions. In the second stage of comparison, a person begins to accept the possibility of being LGBTIQ —rejecting typical LGBTIQ labels, but acknowledging LGBTIQ behaviors. The third stage of tolerance refers to the acknowledgement of emotional needs for sexual intimacy and social networks in the LGBTIQ community, including both positive and negative experiences involved in establishing community. In the fourth stage of acceptance, the person begins to accept—not just tolerate—the LGBTIQ identity, spending more time in LGBTIQ community and less time in heterosexual spaces. The fifth stage of pride involves being immersed in LGBTIQ community and making distinctions between LGBTIQ or heterosexual culture—with greater acceptance of being LGBTIQ and more rejection of the heterosexual paradigm. In the sixth stage of synthesis, one's LGBTIQ identity becomes merely one aspect of identity along with other salient components of identity, and there is increased acceptance of both LGBTIQ and heterosexual people.

Because the research is so nascent with LGBTIQ Asian Americans, it is challenging to make broad generalizations about how relevant the traditional coming out model applies to LGBTIQ Asian Americans. Interestingly, there have been some areas of contradiction in the literature. In a national study examining the relationship between lesbian and bisexual women and psychological health, the study found three predictors of being out as LGBTIQ, which also predicted fewer levels of mental health stress and were consistent with the subsample of Asian American participants.[12] The three factors were lesbian or bisexual sexual orientation, number of years identifying as a lesbian or bisexual, and participation in LGBTIQ communities. The authors also found lower rates of suicidal ideation were predicted as well.

Other findings indicate resilience in managing multiple identities of race/ethnicity and sexual orientation. The present research proposes that the coming out process is a predominantly white construct that may not be one that is best suited to discussing and evaluating LGBTIQ Asian Americans racial/ethnic and sexual orientation identities. Rather, this research has suggested, LGBTIQ people have parallel and interactive identity process development of their sexual orientation and race/ethnicity.[13] The parallel processes include identifying with either whites in the United States or heterosexual people in the United States; discovering feelings of conflict resulting to an enhanced awareness of one's cultural identification as Asian American or as LGBTIQ; immersing in one's Asian American or LGBTIQ group; and then integrating both one's racial/ethnic and sexual orientation and/or gender identity.

There are other considerations applicable to the conceptual model of dual identity development of Asian American LGBTIQ people. A recent study with Asian American lesbian and bisexual women suggests that Asian-identified participants had lower levels of internalized homophobia than their Western-identified counterparts.[14] These findings are interesting on several levels. It is hypothesized that Asian American LGBTIQ people may be able to dissociate their racial/ethnic and sexual orientation identities from one another when necessary. It could also be that as Asian American LGBTIQ people become more acculturated to Western values, they are exposed to increased LGBTIQ resources that may, in turn, increase their discomfort with both their racial/ethnic and sexual orientation identities. Although the research is limited, it nonetheless suggests that the concept of coming out may be too Western a construct to fully capture the complexities of Asian Americans LGBTIQ people's multiple identities.

FAMILY

For many Asian American LGBTIQ people, coming out about one's sexual and/or gender identity includes negotiating some complex family issues. Because many Asian American families might equate being LGBTIQ with adopting Western values, many family members may feel that their LGBTIQ family members are rejecting their Asian culture. Depending on acculturation status and primary language spoken, there even may be difficulty communicating with family members what being LGBTIQ means because many Asian languages have few words describing LGBTIQ identity.

Another major issue for families is the lack of support in Asian American communities for families with LGBTIQ members. Family support organizations that do exist in the United States—such as PFLAG (Parents, Friends, Families, and Loved Ones of Lesbians and Gays) and Colage (support network for children of LGBTIQ parents)—may not feel like culturally responsive spaces for Asian American family members.

Asian American LGBTIQ groups such as Trikone and Asians and Friends are offered as a potential place for establishing support for family members. Commonly, a family member of an Asian American LGBTIQ person may be willing to talk individually with the family of a person who has more recently come out. In these instances, supportive family members can address typical concerns such as potential loss of face, confusion about what being LGBTIQ means, denial of family member's LGBTIQ identity, and provision of resources for family members. Because younger generations appear to be more accepting of LGBTIQ people, there may also be very different types of support in both their family of origin and their extended family, who may potentially be supportive or offer assistance to resource providers and other sources of support.

IMAGES IN THE MEDIA

Typically when Asian Americans are portrayed in the media, there has been a demasculinization of Asian American men, while Asian American women are exoticized.[15] A similar situation exists in the portrayal of LGBTIQ Asian Americans. Recently there have been more positive portrayals of LGBTIQ Asian Americans in mainstream media. In particular, *Saving Face*, a film by Alice Wu, highlighted not only the romance of a Asian American lesbian couple but also the cultural intricacies involved with coming out in both Asian and white communities. The main character, a Chinese American surgeon, negotiates both fear and excitement in her coming out process, so the title referencing "loss of face" is an appropriate one. There have also been many independent Asian American LGBTIQ film festivals around the country. *A Jihad for Love* is a documentary film that is commonly featured. In this film by Parvez Sharma, the documentary follows the lives of LGBTIQ Muslim South Asians in eleven different countries who share their stories as LGBTIQ Asian Americans managing the extensive homophobia of their culture, while also negotiating Islamophobia as well.

Media portrayals highlighting the strength and resilience of LGBTIQ Asian Americans do not appear solely limited to cinema. There are several books and magazines that also seek to depict the lives of LGBTIQ Asian Americans in all their complexity. *Trikone* magazine is a bimonthly publication focused on the lives of LGBTIQ South Asian Americans. In the book, *Asian American X*, there is a poignant chapter written by gay Korean American Christian Michael Kim entitled "Out and About: Coming of Age in a Straight White World."[16] In this chapter, Kim discusses the joys and hardships of his intersecting identities of race/ethnicity, religion, and sexual orientation, identifying the salient forces (e.g., family, church, political environment, immigration) shaping his multiple identities as he came out and embraced all of these identities.

RELIGION AND COMMUNITY

Although little research exists on the importance of religion and community for LGBTIQ Asian Americans, these constructs merit consideration.[17] There is an immense diversity of religious and spiritual beliefs, practices, and worldviews within the Asian American community. For LGBTIQ Asian Americans this is also true. Buddhism, Confucianism, Islam, Sikhism, Christianity, Judaism, and Hinduism are only a few of the major strains of religions that may have special importance to LGBTIQ Asian Americans. In fact, many of these religions—especially the Eastern practices—have worldviews that portray a belief in the balance of the masculine and feminine in all people, or these religions may be silent on issues of LGBTIQ people. In addition, the non-Western religions may be an alternative to the heterosexism embedded in Judeo-Christian religious views as well as Asian cultural worldviews. Regardless, religious and spiritual worldviews of LGBTIQ Asian Americans can be an avenue to affirm salient aspects of their identity that do not solely relate to their racial/ethnic, sexual orientation, and/or gender identities, particularly because religion can also be the source of condemnation for one's sexual identity.

OUTLOOK

With the turbulent state legislation on national LGBTIQ issues such as gay marriage and the absence of federal employment discrimination for LGBTIQ people, there remain considerable challenges for LGBTIQ Asian Americans in the United States. When coming out, the negotiation of multiple identities will continue to be a salient issue for this group. Coming out as LGBTIQ in general U.S. society still has consequences, including be fired solely for being LGB-TIQ. This is a difficult challenge especially for LGBTIQ Asian Americans, who may be involved with supporting extended family members both in the United States and in their country of origin. Coming out in white LGBTIQ communities may entail managing racism, exotification, and other experiences that minimize the value of LGBTIQ Asian Americans.

Most importantly for some, just coming out within Asian communities may be the most challenging for this group. There remains a lack of understanding of LGBTIQ identities in Asian groups, despite the numerous references in the history of LGBTIQ (e.g., Hijra of India, Mahu of Hawai'i, Kathooey of Thailand) experiences in countries of Asian origin.[18] The future of LGBTIQ Asian Americans likely rests on a continuum. There will be activists and community organizers who will continue to work on creating safe, positive spaces and images of LGBTIQ Asian Americans, while demanding respect and rights for their communities. Simultaneously, there will be LGBTIQ Asian Americans who quietly live in the "in-between" spaces between their race/ethnicity and sexual orientation and/or gender identity. Regardless, for service providers and supporters of LGBTIQ Asian Americans, the future issues will likely be the consideration and evaluation of ways to respect and affirm the choices, decisions, and experiences of this group as they create lives meaningful to them.

FURTHER READING

Asian and Friends Chicago. http://www.afchicago.org/.

Asian and Pacific Islander Family Pride. http://www.apifamilypride.org.

Gay Asian Pacific Alliance. http://www.gapa.org.

Gay Asian Pacific Support Network. http://www.gapsn.org/.

Kim, Michael. "Out and About: Coming of Age in a Straight, White World." In *Asian American X: An Intersection of Twenty-First Century Asian American Voices.* Eds. Arar Han and John Hsu. Ann Arbor, MI: University of Michigan Press, 2004.

Kumashiro, Kevin. *Restoried Selves. Autobiographies of Queer Asian American activists.* Binghamton, NY: Harrington Park Press, 2004.

Leng, David M., and Alice Hom. *Q & A: Queer in Asian America.* Philadelphia: Temple University Press, 1998.

Leong, Russell. *Asian American Sexualities: Dimensions of the Gay and Lesbian Experience.* New York: Routledge, 1996.

Nishioka, Joyce, and AsianWeek Magazine. "Young, Gay, and APA." *Asian-Nation: The Landscape of Asian America.* 1999. http://www.asian-nation.org/gay.shtml, Dec. 21, 2008.

San Francisco Bay Area Lesbian, Gay and Transgender South Asians. http://trikone.org.

NOTES

1. Vivian C. Cass, "Homosexual Identity Formation: A Theoretical Model," *Journal of Homosexuality* 4 (1979): 219–235.

2. National Gay and Lesbian Task Force. http://ngltf.org.

3. Personal correspondence with Deepali Gokhali of Trikone-Atlanta, Oct. 25, 2008.

4. Yiu-man B. Chung and Anneliese A. Singh, "Lesbian, Gay, Bisexual, and Transgender Asian Americans," in *Asian American Psychology: Current Perspectives*, eds. N. Tewari and A. Alvarez (New York: Taylor & Francis, 2009), 223–246.

5. Yiu-man B. Chung and Motoni Katayama, "Ethnic and Sexual Identity Development of Asian-American Lesbian and Gay Adolescents," *Professional School Counseling* 1 (1998): 21–25.

6. Asian Pacific Islander Health Forum. http://www.apiahf.org.

7. Lynn Carroll and Paula J. Gilroy, "Transgender issues in counselor preparation," *Counselor Education and Supervision* 41 (2002): 233–242.

8. Intersex Society of North America. http://www.isna.org.

9. National Gay and Lesbian Task Force, "Living in the Margins: A National Survey of Lesbian, Gay, Bisexual, and Transgender Asian and Pacific Islander American. http://www.ngltf.org.

10. Connie S. Chan, "Issues of Identity Development among Asian-American Lesbians and Gay Men," *Journal of Counseling and Development* 68 (1997): 16–20.

11. Vivian C. Cass, "Homosexual Identity Formation: A Theoretical Model," *Journal of Homosexuality* 4 (1979): 219–235.

12. Jessica F. Morris, Craig R. Waldo, and Esther D. Rothblum, "A Model of Predictors of Outness among Lesbian and Bisexual Women," *American Journal of Orthopsychiatry* 71 (2001): 61–71.

13. Yiu-man Chung and Dawn M. Szymanski, "Racial and Sexual Identities of Asian American Gay Men," *Journal of LGBT Issues in Counseling* 1 (2006): 67–93.

14. Anneliese A. Singh and Yiu-man B. Chung, "Acculturation Level and Internalized Homophobia of Asian American Lesbian and Bisexual Women: An Exploratory Analysis," *Journal of LGBT Issues in Counseling* 1 (2006): 3–19.

15. Anneliese A. Singh and Arpana Inman, "Beyond Geishas and the Kama Sutra: AAPI Women and Sexuality," Paper presented to the Asian American Psychological Association, Boston, MA, August 2008.

16. Michael Kim, "Out and About: Coming of Age in a Straight, White World," in *Asian American X: An Intersection of Twenty-First Century Asian American Voices.* Eds. Arar Han and John Hsu. (Ann Arbor, MI: University of Michigan Press, 2004), 139–148.

17. Yiu-man B. Chung and Anneliese A. Singh, "Lesbian, Gay, Bisexual, and Transgender Asian Americans," in *Asian American Psychology: Current Perspectives*, ed. N. Tewari and A. Alvarez (New York: Taylor & Francis, 2009), 223–246.

18. Michael G. Peletz, "Transgenderism and Gender Pluralism in Southeast Asian since Early Modern Times," *Current Anthropology*, 47 (2006): 309–325.

SAME-SEX MARRIAGES

Raymond San Diego and Margaret Rhee

While rarely studied within the context of the Asian American community, same-sex marriage remains critical for various reasons. In particular, the issue of marriage equality is pressing for Asian Americans in same-sex partnerships. Although relatively invisible within mainstream media, a 2005 UCLA Williams Institute study reported that there were more than 38,000 Asian American and Pacific Islanders living with a same-sex partner, which is 3 percent of all individuals in same-sex couples in the United States.[1] Moreover, nearly one in ten same-sex couples in California (8,854 couples) includes an Asian Pacific Islander partner.[2] Federal recognition of same-sex marriage would grant full rights as citizens for Asian American and Pacific Islanders around immigration, health, and parenting issues. In particular, debates for and against same-sex marriage within the Asian American community remain pressing and contested. As the issue of marriage equality retains political currency within our public sphere, understanding same-sex marriage and the Asian American community is vital, as governmental restrictions on marriage have historically affected and been contested by the Asian American community.[3] The various debates and legal stakes for civil rights remain a crucial issue for Asian Americans, who have been historically subjugated and silenced. As Russell C. Leong notes, by speaking out on same-sex marriage Asian Americans provide insights to the important struggle of the first decade of the twenty-first century.[4]

LEGAL PROTECTIONS, SECURITY, AND MARRIAGE

Recognition of same-sex marriage may provide legal protections, civil security, and financial support for Asian American same-sex partnerships. Home ownership, cohabitation for a period of time, or parenting may indicate partners are pooling resources and making long-term decisions together. As reported in the UCLA Williams Institute Report on Asian American and Pacific Islander same-sex partnerships, there is a relatively small difference between homeownership rates of Asian American and Pacific Islander same-sex couples and heterosexual counterparts. Asian American and Pacific Islander same-sex couples are actually more likely to have lived together for at least five years (59%) than both Asian American and Pacific Islander (52%) and non-Asian American and Pacific Islander (55%) different-sex couples.[5] However, Asian American and Pacific Islander same-sex couples may face considerable economic disparities. Same-sex couples have substantially lower incomes than non-Asian Americans and Pacific Islanders in same-sex couples ($34,869 vs. $42,532) and individuals in Asian American and Pacific Islander heterosexual couples ($36,283).[6] Despite these income and employment disparities, Asian American same-sex couples often make decisions without the protections that marriage provides.

Issues of marriage, health, and parenting are vital for Asian American same-sex couples to be recognized fully as partners. Most same-sex couples cannot subscribe to health care plans, as domestic partnerships are not recognized for benefits.[7] While most employers provide health care coverage to heterosexual couples, same-sex couples in domestic partnerships and/or non-legally recognized same-sex marriage are not recognized.[8] As many Asian American same-sex individuals struggle with the cost of living and make less than their heterosexual counterparts, partners have to go without health insurance at times because of the lack of legal recognition.[9] Additionally, taking time to take care of a sick spouse and other benefits of marriage that heterosexual partners enjoy are rights that same-sex partners do not have access to.[10]

In particular, Asian American same-sex partners also have higher rates of parenting than white same-sex partners.[11] For Asian American same-sex couples, rights such as legally filing taxes together, legal rights as parents, issues of inheritances and wills, and the subtle discrimination of recognition as dual parents of a child at school remain vital issues. Many Asian American same-sex parents have created various organizations, media publications, and books to shed light on same-sex parenting and families. The organization Asian and Pacific Islander Family Pride serve API families with lesbian, gay, bisexual, and transgender members, while Angeline Acain, a Filipino American, started "Gay Parent" magazine in September 1998 to dispel the stereotypes and empower LGBT families.[12] Asian American public figures also are involved. Actor B. D. Wong, for example, published a book, *Following Foo: The Electronic Adventures of the Chestnut Man,* which chronicles his family's journey of same-sex parenting.[13] Asian Americans have continued to create resources and networks of support around same-sex parenting and families.

IMMIGRATION

In 1996, Congress enacted the Defense of Marriage Act (DOMA), which denies federal recognition of same-sex marriages and allows individual states to do the same.[14] Same-sex couples do not have federal recognition for their marriages and are unable to sponsor a same-sex partner for immigration benefits. Moreover Asian Americans who are members of the transgender community face considerable challenges. While legal documents such as a driver's license and passport can be changed to reflect proper gender, immigration authorities can reject validity of marriage between transgender partnerships.[15] The rights of the transgender community are compromised within same-sex marriage issues, and some would argue the right to determine one's identity takes precedent over the right to marry. Moreover, for Asian immigrants living with HIV/AIDS, the opportunity to become a citizen and the benefits of a legalized same-sex marriage is not an option. Under the Immigration and Nationality Act, HIV-positive diagnosed immigrants could be denied permanent residence or green card status and are subjected to mandatory HIV testing.[16] A barrier to receiving permanent residency status, government officials deny HIV-positive immigrants with a place to live, and thus are choosing who is eligible for marriage.[17] Moreover, the right of hospital visitation is a marriage protection that does not extend to same-sex partners. For Asian American sexual health advocates, removing the stigma of HIV and AIDS from the immigration process may be a more pressing issue than marriage equality.

POLITICAL OPPOSITION FROM ASIAN AMERICANS

In 2004, Korean American churches organized rallies in Southern California, while 7,000 Chinese American Christians marched against same-sex marriages in San Francisco.[18] The Asian American religious community largely voices sentiments against same-sex marriage, mainly those of Christian denominations, as the dominant Religious Right remain the largest opponent of same-sex marriage.[19] Much of Asian American opposition may stem from religious and cultural values. The notion of a normative heterosexual family also extends to various ethnic groups in the Asian American community. For many Asian Americans, maintaining marriage as a heterosexual practice may maintain their culture and normative values. However, while Asian Americans are depicted in mainstream media as opponents to same sex marriage, there is evidence of complicated negotiations being made in respective ethnic communities.[20]

RADICAL LEFT CRITIQUES

Radical left responses from LGBTQ Asian Americans are critical of the same-sex marriage debate. Many LGBTQ Asian Americans do not want to participate in this issue because they do not believe in the heterosexist institution of marriage.[21] It has been noted that many critics of same-sex marriage argue that marriage ideologically goes against the very core of gay and lesbian identity and lifestyle: its acceptance and validation of multiple forms of relationships.[22]

Marginalized sectors of the LGBTQ community, such as homeless LGBTQ youth of color, may have pressing issues of survival rather than same-sex marriage as a necessary issue. For radical LGBTQ Asian Americans, political campaign funding toward same-sex marriage may take away from issues that LGBTQ of color may face, which is illustrated in day-to-day survival.[23] For LGBTQ radical left Asian American critics, same-sex marriage may be a movement that privileges a particular group: white middle class LGBTQ .[24]

SUPPORT FROM ASIAN AMERICANS

On February 12, 2005, Assessor-Recorder Mabel Teng officiated the wedding of Phyllis Lyon and Del Martin, the first same-sex people to get married.[25] Asian Americans served as plaintiffs, lawyers, organizers, and allies in efforts to secure marriage equality. Despite the variety of neutral to negative messages circulating around Asian Americans and marriage equality, there is a large and powerful contingent dedicated to ensuring the right to marry freely for all. For many Asian Americans, the fight for full-fledged marriage equality is grounded in social justice grassroots effort for human rights. The Japanese American Citizens League became one of the first civil rights organizations to support same-sex marriage in 1994, when then Congressman Norman Mineta (D-CA) spoke out for the need for all citizens in the country to have equal rights.[26] The case for marriage equality takes steps beyond tolerance and moves toward the validation and acceptance of same sex sexuality and marriage.

The Asian American community has been pivotal in galvanizing the marriage equality movement. With two headquarters located in San Francisco and Los Angeles, the nonprofit organization API Equality has spearheaded numerous efforts to gain support for the legalization of same-sex marriage in California. Formed in 2004 following the demonstrations by Asian American Christian churches against same-sex marriage, API Equality has since dedicated itself to providing advocacy and education in both English and API languages. API Equality has worked collaboratively with many organizations and institutions, including National Council of Asian Pacific Americans, Gay Asian Pacific Alliance (GAPA), and the Family Acceptance Project at San Francisco State University. One of their greatest hurdles overcome in mobilizing the community to support same-sex marriage was the formation of a coalition of API faith leaders who supported LGBT families and equality.[27] Their perseverance in raising support and awareness around this issue has been key in the struggle to legalize marriage.

In September of 2007, led by the Asian Pacific American Legal Center in Los Angeles, more than sixty Asian American organizations signed on to file an amicus brief with the California Supreme Court in support of same-sex marriage.[28] This was one of many briefs in support of same-sex marriage, which ultimately led to marriage equality in the state of California. On May 15, 2008, the California Supreme Court in a 4–3 ruling declared that denying same-sex couples the right to marry was unconstitutional, and that equality for all will be granted.[29] Organizations such as API Equality, Let California Ring, and Lambda Legal plan on continuing the fight for the legalization of same-sex marriages federally. Many countries around the world such as the Netherlands, Belgium, Canada, Spain, and South Africa have already legalized same-sex marriage.[30] With the momentum in California and other states growing stronger every day, it may not be too unrealistic to believe that marriage for all will become a reality not only in the United States, but internationally as well.

PROPOSITION 8

A hot ticket issue during the 2008 election season concerned Proposition 8 in California, which proposed amending the constitution of California to state that marriage is to be defined as only between a man and woman.[31] Social justice organizations such as API Equality were a huge part of the campaign against this discriminatory proposition. Before the election, a poll was conducted about Asian American perceptions of this initiative and found that 57 percent of the population had planned on voting against the passage of Proposition 8.[32]

Despite the strong opposition from multiple communities that strive to provide and protect civil rights, Proposition 8 passed 52 to 48 percent.[33] As people began to search for explanations as to how it was passed, the Latino and African American communities were held responsible, even though they only make up 26 percent of California's voting population.[34] Asian Americans, who make up 6 percent of the voting bloc, maintained their same view before the election and voted against the passage of Prop 8 at 51 to 49 percent.[35]

The fight was not yet over. Although Proposition 8 was based in California, its effects reached far and wide. Communities throughout the nation and all over the world continued their resistance against Proposition 8 with massive protests and demonstrations.[36] Legally, the Asian Pacific Legal Center, Mexican American Legal Defense and Education Fund, Equal Justice Society, California NAACP and the NAACP Legal Defense and Education Fund Inc. filed a petition to the California Supreme Court to prevent the enactment of Proposition 8.[37] In May 2009, the California Supreme Court upheld Prop 8; efforts are now underway to get another California ballot initiative to overturn Proposition 8 in the 2010 election.[38]

FURTHER READING

API Equality. http://www.apiequality.org/getinformed/articles.php.
Asian Pacific Family Pride. http://www.apifamilypride.org/resources.html.
Eng, David, and Alice Hom. *Q & A: Queer in Asian America*. Philadelphia: Temple University Press, 1998.
Leong, Russell, ed. *Asian American Sexualities: Dimensions of the Gay and Lesbian Experience*. New York: Routledge, 1996.

Sueyoshi, Amy, and Russell Leong, eds. "Asian Americans on the Marriage Equality Debate," *Amerasia Journal*. University of California Press, 2006.

NOTES

1. Gary Gates, Holing Lau, and R. Bradley Sears, "Asian and Pacific Islanders in Same Sex Couples in the United States: Data from Census 2000," *Amerasia Journal* 32, no. 1 (2006): 16.

2. Gates, Lau, and Sears, "Asian and Pacific Islanders," 16.

3. Bryant Yang, "Seeing *Loving* in Gay Marriages: Parallels of Asian American History and the Same-Sex Marriage Debates," *Amerasia Journal* 32, no. 1 (2006): 33.

4. Russell Leong, "Sister Subject: In the Marriage Equality Debate," *Amerasia Journal* 32, no. 1 (2006): 3–9.

5. Gary Gates and R. Bradley Sears, "Asian and Pacific Islanders in Same-Sex Couples in California: Data from Census 2000" (Los Angeles: The Williams Project on Sexual Orientation Law and Public Policy, 2005), http://www.law.ucla.edu/williamsinstitute/publications/API_Report.pdf.

6. Gates and Sears, "Asian and Pacific Islanders," 8.

7. Than Ngo, "Why We Got Married," *Amerasia Journal* 32, no. 1 (2006): 119–122.

8. "Our Stories," API Equality, http://www.apiequality.org.

9. Ela Dutt, "Thousands of Same-Sex Couples Struggling to Get Marriage Licenses around Country," *New India Times.com*, 2004, http://www.newsindia-times.com/nit/2004/04/16/tow-top23.html.

10. Margot and Koko, "7 Months Pregnant . . . We Were Spouses for Life! At Last . . . ," Let California Ring, http://www.letcaliforniaring.org/site/apps/nl/content2.asp?c=ltJTJ6MQIuE&b=3389649&ct=4477713 (accessed Dec. 10, 2008).

11. "Asian Pacific American Same-Sex Households: A Census Report on New York, San Francisco, and Los Angeles," Asian American Federation of New York, March 22, 2004, http://www.aafny.org/cic/report/GLReport.pdf.

12. Lynda Lin, "LGBT APA Family Portraits," *IMDiversity.com*, Oct. 15, 2004, http://www.imdiversity.com/villages/asian/family_lifestyle_traditions/paccit_lgbt_families_1004.asp; Asian Pacific Islander Family Pride home page, 2008, http://www.apifamilypride.org/ (accessed Dec. 29, 2008).

13. Christopher Stone, "B. D. Wong: Out Author, Actor and Parent," *AfterElton.com*, Nov. 16, 2005, http://www.afterelton.com/archive/elton/people/2005/11/bdwong.html.

14. "Same Sex Marriage, Civil Unions and Domestic Partnerships," National Conference of State Legislatures, http://www.ncsl.org/programs/cyf/samesex.htm (accessed November 2008).

15. Pauline Park, Willy Wilkinson, and Jessi Gan, "Pauline Park and Willy Wilkinson: A Conversation about Same-Sex Marriage," *Amerasia Journal* 32, no. 1 (2006): 89.

16. Jih-Fei Cheng, "HIV, Immigrant Rights, and Same-Sex Marriage," *Amerasia Journal* 32, no. 1 (2006): 99–107

17. Cheng, "HIV, Immigrants," 99–107.

18. Elena Shore, "Ethnic Communities Speak Out against Same Sex Marriage," June 8, 2004, http://news.newamericamedia.org/news/view_article.html?article_id=c76120f9bd844ba78ddab4e4f327992a.

19. Corina Knoll, "The Right to Say, 'I Do'," *KoreAm Journal* 19, no. 5 (2008): 46–50.

20. Margaret Rhee, "Towards Community: KoreAm Journal and Korean American Cultural Attitudes on Same-Sex Marriage," *Amerasia Journal* 32, no.1 (2006): 75–86.

21. Amy Sueyoshi, "Friday the Thirteenth—Love, Commitment, and then Catastrophe: Personal Reflections on the Marriage Equality Movement," *Amerasia Journal* 32, no. 1 (2006): xi–xvii.

22. Glenn D. Magpantay, "The Ambivalence of Queer Asian Pacific Americans Towards Same-Sex Marriage," *Amerasia Journal* 32, no. 1 (2006): 109–117.

23. Mala Nagarajan and Vega Subramaniam, "Plaintiff's Plight: Joining the Washington State Lawsuit for Marriage Equality," *Amerasia Journal* 32, no.1 (2006): 67–73; Magpantay, "The Ambivalence of Queer Asian Pacific Americans," 109–118.

24. Sueyoshi, "Friday the Thirteenth."

25. Mabel Teng, "The Right Place at the Right Time: Cultural and Political Controversy of San Francisco's Gay Marriage," *Amerasia Journal* 32, no. 1 (2006): 63–66; Wyatt Buchanan, "S. F. Same-Sex Couple Ready To Be First Again," *San Francisco Chronicle*, June 10, 2008, http://www.sfgate.com/cgi-bin/article.cgi?f=/c/a/2008/06/09/MN51116A6H.DTL.

26. Helen Zia, *Asian American Dreams: The Emergence of an American People* (New York: Farrar, Straus, and Giroux, 2000).

27. "API Equality What We Do," AP Equality, http://www.apiequality.org (accessed Dec. 10, 2008).

28. "The Power of Allies," National Center for Lesbian Rights Newsletter (Fall 2007): 5, http://www.nclrights.org/site/DocServer/Newsletter_Fall_Web.pdf?docID =2421.

29. "Let California Ring Facts," National Center for Lesbian Rights Newsletter, http://www.letcaliforniaring.org/site/c.ltJTJ6MQIuE/b.3348081/k.B080/Facts.htm (accessed Dec. 10, 2008).

30. Ivan Natividad, "Survey Indicates Asian American Opposition to Gay Marriage Ban," *AsianWeek*, Oct. 18, 2008, http://www.asianweek.com/2008/10/18/survey -indicates-asian-american-opposition-to-gay-marriage-ban/#more-8913.

31. John Wildermuth, "Many Obama Supporters also Backed Prop. 8," *San Francisco Chronicle*, Nov. 6, 2008, http://www.sfgate.com/cgi-bin/article.cgi?f=/c/a/2008/11/06/MNH413UTUS.DTL&hw=prop&sn=019&sc=408.

32. "Civil Rights Groups Petition California Supreme Court to Stop Enactment of Proposition 8," API Equality Press Release issued on Nov. 14, 2008, 1–2, http://apiequality.org/about/PressRelease-CivilRightsGp20081114.pdf (accessed Dec. 10, 2008).

33. Bob Egelko, "State Supreme Court Rejoins Prop. 8 battle" *San Francisco Chronicle,* Nov. 20, 2008, http://www.sfgate.com/cgi-bin/article.cgi?f=/c/a/2008/11/20/MNJC147QAJ.DTL&type=.

34. "Exit Polls," *CNN Politics.com*, http://www.cnn.com/ELECTION/2008/results/polls/#val=CAI01p1 (accessed Dec. 10, 2008).

35. "Exit Polls," *CNN Politics.com*.

36. "Ban on Gay Marriage Protests Go Global," *The California Chronicle* Nov. 17, 2008, http://www.californiachronicle.com/articles/81841.

37. API Equality Press Release.

38. Egelko, "State Supreme Court rejoins Prop. 8 battle."

TRANSNATIONAL FAMILIES

Yeon-Shim Lee and Melissa-Ann Nievera

A dramatic increase in globalization and migration in recent years has created a growing number of transnational families. Transnational families are families in which one or more core members live their lives across two or more nation states, yet continue to maintain a sense of collective welfare and unity.[1] According to a 2000 United Nations report, an estimated 90 million women live outside their countries of origin, constituting 49 percent of international migration.[2] Transnational families are in stark contrast to conventional family households. While the latter is shaped by the idea of coresidency and physical unity of family members, "in transnational households, one parent, both parents, or adult children may produce income abroad while other family members carry out the functions of reproduction, socialization, and consumption in the country of origin.[3] Despite different cultural, social, economic, and political contexts, many countries worldwide observe the basic pattern of transnational families—frequent movement from Asia and Latin America (e.g., China, Korea, the Philippines, or Mexico) to more advanced industrialized countries (e.g., United States, United Kingdom, or Australia).

Current research on transnational families focuses on the economic structural context, accounting for an increase in private domestic employment in many advanced industrialized countries.[4] Like many immigrants of color, Asian immigrants are often employed for cheap domestic labor, including child care, caregiving for elderly persons, or house cleaning.[5] A considerable amount of research uncovers the multifaceted nature of global transfer of care work, citing a global shift from poor countries to rich ones, and its impact on care arrangements in geographically distant families.[6] Still, more research is needed to help develop policies and service programs that can adequately address the specific needs of Asian transnational families.

CAUSES

Transnational family forms can be better understood in the context of shifting patterns of immigration and economic integration across a fluid global market.[7] With the rise of communication and transportation technologies, transnational families are becoming more common. Additionally, those who provide sustenance for the family find work in a wide range of occupational fields, from day laborers to overseas contract workers, as well as professional elites.

Asians frequently migrate particularly to the United States to pursue better opportunities in education and employment; however, Asian families often cannot afford to leave their home country as an entire unit. Thus many Asian families opt to split so that some family members leave, while others stay behind. Sacrificing the traditional home in one geographical location, these families acquire and secure education, economic resources, and status in the United States, in hopes of enhancing the overall well-being of the family.[8] As a result, the transnational Asian family recognizes multiple locations they can call home, acknowledging identities and relationships linked between their country of origin and the new country to which some members relocate for work.[9] The majority of Asian migrants sustain ties to their home country through financial remittances (sending money home), correspondence via telephone and the Internet, and travel to their homeland. In fact, financial remittance serves as the key source of income for many poor and working class families, providing a substantial share of family earnings.[10] Financial remittance also plays a significant role in strengthening notions of shared responsibility and strong bonds with family members in the home country, hence developing and maintaining transnational family ties and networks.[11]

New developing scholarship examines multiple dimensions of transnationality, focusing not only on the migration, but also the familial, psychological, cultural, political, economic, and social dimensions of living transnationally.[12] Prior studies also emphasize the substantial differences in the motives for migration. Some migrants are pressured to leave the poverty of their homelands, whereas others migrate for educational or professional growth.[13] These differences are likely to be related to their socioeconomic and demographic conditions, and ethnic identity, as well as adaptive strategies to maintain transnational family relations (e.g., frequency and duration of visiting home countries). This description may be appropriate for many Asian transnational migrants.

STRUGGLES AND CHALLENGES

"Parachute Kids" and Education

A growing phenomenon that has emerged with the existence of split-household transnational families is the migration of Asian children with or without parents to the United States, largely to obtain education: so-called "parachute kids" (e.g., high school or college students staying with an alternate caregiver/guardian). During the early 1990s, some nonworking Asian families with economic means sent children to the United States to attend school and advance to U.S. colleges or universities.[14] The influx of children, particularly from South Korea, Hong Kong, and Taiwan, is driven by this desire to provide children educational opportunities. They are frequently accompanied by their mothers, while their fathers remain working in the home country to finance the families' living and educational expenses in the United States.[15] Some mothers even attend school with a student visa and later seek employment in order to ease the financial burdens for the family.[16]

In 1990, there were 40,000 Taiwanese parachute children ages eight to eighteen residing in the United States without their parents; smaller numbers came from Hong Kong and South Korea.[17] About a billion dollars was sent from fathers in Korea to their separated families every year. Korean officials estimated that approximately 10,000 school-age children left to study overseas in 2002, an increase from 4,400 in 2000.[18] In Korean culture, these families are referred to as *"kirogi kajok"* (wild geese families). *Kirogis,* well known for their dedication to their offspring, travel long distances to bring back food for their young. The *kirogi kajok* phenomenon demonstrates how South Koreans are becoming global consumers of educational services, immersing their children in a foreign language, thereby obtaining educational achievement as a dominant source of upward mobility.[19] Such a trend is located at the nexus of rapid globalization, English as the hegemonic language in the global economy, and everchanging local and global relationships.[20] The migration of parachute kids is part of a family's long-term survival including increasing social networks and options in the United States.[21]

Despite a paucity of scientific inquiry, the work on *kirogi kajok* and parachute children stresses the hardships and adverse affects some of these families experience, such as intergenerational clashes, suicide, and divorce. Newspapers report that some fathers living apart from their wives and children for years on end are struggling with emotional and financial difficulties.[22] Family separation is intensely challenging to children. They have to cope with the stress of learning the language and adapting to the environment of the new country. These children often suffer from feeling caught between two nations and marginalized in both.[23] Behavioral and psychological problems are frequently found among parachute children, more than among their immigrant counterparts. These include depression, cigarette and alcohol use, gang involvement, and sexual behavior.[24] Adolescent boys are particularly at high risk for these problems, not only because of the absence of adult supervision, but more so to the lack of father figures in their lives.[25] While some parachute children successfully adjust to mainstream American culture, some may begin failing school, and a few give up entirely and return to their home country. Cases in which the youth become targets of racism and anti-immigration sentiments also occur.[26]

Transnational Parenthood

Recent studies examine how transnational families negotiate with networks of care—performing responsibilities of childcare in local and transnational contexts.[27] Since the early migration years of the mid-1800s and 1900s, numerous Asian populations made their way to the United States in pursuit of better-paying jobs or better education, leaving their families behind. Many Asian migrant women used their extended family and kinship networks to look after their children in their countries of origin, while employed in the United States as childcare providers for white, middle-class families. This practice is still common today.

Research on women and caregiving continues to examine social norms and cultural values pertaining to gender.[28] One of the key issues on transnational motherhood is the traditional gender role attitude toward mothers as primary providers of the family in terms of child rearing and nourishment.[29] The challenges and struggles related to shifting family structures are particularly pronounced for Asian migrant mothers, in which gender roles and divisions of labor are clearly predefined.[30] In a study of Sri Lankan migrants, the painful process of negotiations in relation to changing gender norms and family dynamics is a result of female migration.[31] When transfers of care occur from a mother to other family members, the mother becomes subject to "social disapproval and stigmatization."[32] A study of Philippine transnational mothers highlights the significant cultural and ideological components to the representation of "good mothering"—that is, "the gender-based expectations of children for mothers to nurture them."[33] The culturally and ideologically inscribed duties and self-imposed expectations of mothers aggravate the difficult experiences of separation and feelings of pain in transnational families.[34] Similar to other migrant women of color, Asian transnational mothers in their new economic role face the dual demands of breadwinning for their distant families, as well as parenting for children in other families.

Particular attention is paid to the impacts of separation on children left behind in the home country.[35] In a study of recently arrived children of immigrants (including newcomers from China, Central America, the Dominican Republican, Mexico, and Haiti) in the areas of Boston and San Francisco, most children in this study were separated from one or both parents for a few months to a few years, including children who stayed in their country of origin with one parent (33%); children who stayed in their country of origin with relatives (29%); family who came to the United States together (20%); children who came to United States with one parent (15%); and children who came to the United States and stayed with relatives (3%). Based on their cultural socialization, children respond to such separations based on their family socialization.[36] For example, separation may not be detrimental if the arrangement is considered normal in the child's native culture and if healthy relationships thrive among children, parents, and other family members providing care. On the other hand, there is documentation covering the adverse effects of separation on children.[37] During the separation-reunification process, children suffer a sense of anger and abandonment by their mothers. When reunification takes place, children often become distant from their mothers, particularly after lengthy separations. The negative effects on transnational mothers who live apart from their children include guilt, anger, depression, and hopelessness. Although such studies concern primarily non-Asian transnational families, the findings are still indicative for Asian transnational families.

Kin relationships have been pivotal to family care, provision, and maintenance of transnational families.[38] Particularly, grandparents are a crucial resource of financial, emotional, and social support for children while parents work.[39] Intergenerational interaction is critical in sustaining kinship ties and family networks. In many Asian transnational families where parents migrate to the U.S. without their children, grandparents often serve as primary childcare providers. The "flyer grandmothers" phenomenon is present in some transnational families, in which grandparents living in the home country frequently travel to care for their grandchildren in the United States.[40]

Another prominent factor of care in Asian transnational families is informal care provision within the community, wherein churches or a variety of associations look after children. The research on Asian migrants emphasizes the influential role of religion and spiritual leaders, a salient element in social support. A strong sense of responsibility for caring for members of the community has been a critical component of religious practice in most Asian immigrant communities. As a result, many Asian migrants are involved in a range of religious activities not only to seek faith, but also to establish social networks in a new country through which they can receive formal and informal services.[41] Catholic churches, Buddhist temples, or Islamic mosques are powerful religious and social institutions, playing the alternative role of extended families for many Asian ethnic immigrant groups.[42]

ELDER CARE: MAINTAINING FAMILY TIES

There is little scholarship or any other information about the impact transnational families has on either the family itself or its individual members. Arguably, such arrangements should have profound effects on youth and elderly left behind in the home country, but the lack of research allows only speculation. Although caring relationships lie at the heart of all families and communities, the ability for members to support one another in Asian American transnational families would likely be challenging, yet this phenomenon is rarely studied.

The traditional notion of intergenerational caregiving practices (given by adult children to aging parents) is based on a significantly close connection between caring relations requiring geographic proximity.[43] Yet despite changes because of migration that affect social networks, resources, and support, families find ways to stay in touch and care and often find that "adaptive strategy enables emotional and financial support for members."[44]

Sustaining family connections and participating in caregiving involves a multitude of emotional and practical tasks. This includes regular return visits to the home country to care for aging parents; remittances in money and gifts; letters, phone calls, and e-mails of support; and engagement in decisions about matters of health, finance, and housing. Research frequently points to "a strong sense of family obligation" and particularly "a sense of guilt toward the parents" for not being in close proximity.[45] Consequently, the obligations and responsibilities for care appear to be mixed with a sense of burden and conflict involving the time and expenses spent on each visit. Additionally, the existence of transnational families commonly relies on siblings, cousins, extended relatives, or well-established networks of neighbors who are able to care for aging parents.[46] Research on the transnational family means looking at the wider definition of care and kin networks including "non-blood, fictive kin."[47]

Transnational families test the strengths and limitations of the loyalty of family members to each other, as well as the support of the extended family. The continuance of the phenomenon of transnational families will be defined by a complex dynamic of changing economic realities and changes in the structure of these Asian American families.

FURTHER READING

Chee, Maria W. L. *Taiwanese American Transnational Families: Women and Kin Work.* New York: Routledge, 2005.
Ong, Aihwa. *Flexible Citizenship: The Cultural Logics of Transnationality.* Durham, NC: Duke University Press, 1999.
Orellana, Marjorie F., Barrie Thorne, Wan S. E. Lam, and Anna Chee. "Transnational Childhoods: The Participation of Children in Processes of Family Migration." *Social Problems* 48 (2001): 572–591.
Parreñas, Rhacel S. *Children of Global Migration: Transnational Families and Gendered Woes.* Stanford, CA: Stanford University, 2005.
Tsong, Yuying, and Yuli Liu. "Parachute Kids and Astronaut Families." In *Asian American Psychology: Current Perspectives*, eds. Nita Tewari and Alvin N Alvarez. Boca Raton, FL: CRC Press, 2008. 365–381.

NOTES

1. Linda G. Basch, Nina G. Schiller, and Cristina S. Blanc, eds., *Nations Unbound: Transnational Projects, Postcolonial Predicaments, and Deterritorialized Nation-States* (Langhorne, PA: Gordon and Breach, 1994); Shirlena Huang and Brenda Yeoh, "Transnational Families and their Children's Education: China's "Study Mothers" in Singapore," *Global Networks* 5, no. 4 (2005): 379–400; Elisabetta Zontini, *Encyclopedia: Transnational Families*, http://wfnetwork.bc.edu/encyclopedia_entry.php?id=6361andarea=All (accessed Sept. 14, 2008); Deborah Bryceson and Ulla Vuorela, *The Transnational Family: New European Frontiers and Global Networks*, ed. (Oxford: Berg, 2002).

2. Department of Economic and Social Affairs: Division for the Advancement of Women, *2004 World Survey on the Role of Women in Development: Women and International Migration.* (New York: United Nations, 2006).

3. Zontini, *Encyclopedia: Transnational Families*, 1.

4. Grace Chang, *Disposable Domestics: Immigrant Women Workers in the Global Economy.* (London: South End Press, 2000); Maria de la Luz Ibarra, "Transnational Identity Formation and. Mexican Immigrant Women's Ethics of Elder Care." *Anthropology of Work Review* 23, no. 3–4, (2002): 16–20.

5. The most commonly used definition of "Asians" is derived from the U.S. Census Bureau's (2003) definition of Asian, "a person having origins in any of the original peoples of the Far East, Southeast Asia, or the Indian subcontinent including, for example, Cambodia, China, India, Japan, Korea, Malaysia, Pakistan, the Philippine Islands, Thailand, and Vietnam." However, the U.S. Census Bureau acknowledged that the Asian and/or Pacific Islanders are not a homogeneous group. Instead, it constitutes many groups who differ in language, culture, and length of residence in the United States. For example, some of the Asian groups (e.g., the Japanese and Chinese) have been in the United States for several generations whereas others (e.g., the Hmong, Vietnamese, Laotians, and Cambodians) are relatively recent immigrants (U.S. Census Bureau, 2003).

6. Barbara Ehrenreich and Arlie R. Hochschild, eds., *Global Woman: Nannies, Maids, and Sex Workers in the New Economy.* (London: Granta Books, 2003); Rhacel S. Parreñas, *Children of Global Migration: Transnational Families and Gendered Woes.* (Stanford, CA: Stanford University, 2005); Rhacel S. Parreñas, *Servants of Globalization: Women, Migration and Domestic Work.* (Stanford, CA: Stanford University Press, 2001).

7. Brenda Yeoh, "Report on International Workshop on Asian Transnational Families" (paper presented at the Asian MetaCentre for Population and Sustainable Development Analysis, Singapore, February 2–4, 2005).

8. Brenda Yeoh, Elspeth Graham and Paul J. Boyle, "Migration and Family Relations in the Asia Pacific Region," *Journal of Asian and Pacific Migration* 11, no. 1 (2002): 1–12; Bryceson and Vuorela, *The Transnational Family.*

9. Diane L. Wolf, "Family Secrets: Transnational Struggles Among Children of Filipino Immigrants," *Sociological Perspectives* 40, no. 3, (1997): 457–482.

10. Holger Henke, *The West Indian Americans.* (Westport, CT: Greenwood Press, 2001); Tracey Reynolds and Elisabetta Zontini, "A Comparative Study of Care and Provision Across Caribbean and Italian Transnational Families," *Families and Social Capital ESRC Research Group Working Paper* 16 (London: London South Bank University, 2006).

11. Reynolds and Zontini, "A Comparative Study of Care and Provision."

12. Yeoh, "Report on International Workshop on Asian Transnational Families."

13. Loretta Baldassar and Cora Vellekoop Baldock, "Linking Migration and Family Studies: Transnational Migrants and the Care of Ageing Parents," in *Theoretical and Methodological Issues in Migration Research: Interdisciplinary and International Perspectives,* ed. Biko Agozino (Aldershot, UK: Ashgate, 2000), 61–89.

14. Marjorie F. Orellana et al., "Transnational Childhoods: The Participation of Children in Processes of Family Migration," *Social Problems* 48 (2001): 572–591.

15. Michael Ha, "'Kirogi' Families Weigh Risks and Rewards," *Korea Times*, Oct. 31, 2007, http://www.koreatimes.co.kr/www/news/special/2008/06/229_12942.html.

16. Ha, "'Kirogi' Families Weigh Risks and Rewards."

17. H. T. Hwang and T. Watanabe, "Little Overseas Students from Taiwan: A Look at the Psychological Adjustment Issues" (Master's thesis, University of California–Los Angeles, 1990), quoted in Yuying Tsong and Yuli Liu, "Parachute Kids and Astronaut

Families," in *Asian American Psychology: Current Perspectives, ed.* Nita Tewari and Alvin N. Alvarez (Boca Raton, FL: CRC Press, 2008), 365–381.

18. Phuong Ly, "A Wrenching Choice," *Washington Post*, Jan. 9, 2005, A01, http://www.washingtonpost.com/wp-dyn/articles/A59355-2005Jan8.html.

19. Anna Fifield, "S. Koreans Make Big Sacrifices to Study Overseas," *Los Angeles Times,* Jan. 16, 2006, C-4, http://articles.latimes.com/2006/jan/16/business/ft-korea16; Aihwa Ong, *Flexible Citizenship: The Cultural Logics of Transnationality* (Durham, NC: Duke University Press, 1999).

20. Seung-Kyung Kim, "Globalization and Transnational Korean Families: '*Kirogi Kajok*'" (paper presented at the annual meeting for the Association for Asian Studies, San Francisco, CA, April 6–9, 2006).

21. Orellana et al., "Transnational Childhoods," 576.

22. Ha, " 'Kirogi' Families Weigh Risks and Rewards."

23. Orellana et al., "Transnational Childhoods."

24. Chien-hung Cheng, "Assessment of Depression among Young Students from Taiwan and Hong Kong: A Comparative Study of Accompanied and Unaccompanied Minors," in *In Pursuit of Education: Young Asian Students in the United States,* ed. Josh C. H. Lin (El Monte, CA: Pacific Asian Press, 1998), 95–112; Christy Chiang-Hom, "Transnational Cultural Practices of Chinese Immigrant Youth and Parachute," in *Asian American Youth: Culture, Identity and Ethnicity*, eds. Jennifer Lee and Min Zhou (New York: Routledge, 2004), 143–339.

25. Ha, "'Kirogi' Families Weigh Risks and Rewards."

26. Ha, "'Kirogi' Families Weigh Risks and Rewards"; S. C. Kim, "Young Korean Students in the United States," *In Pursuit of Education: Young Asian Students in the United States,* ed. Josh C. H. Lin (El Monte, CA: Pacific Asian Press, 1998), 44–54.

27. Reynolds and Zontini, "A Comparative Study of Care and Provision."

28. Maria W. L. Chee, *Taiwanese American Transnational Families: Women and Kin Work* (New York: Routledge, 2005); Sheba M. George, *When Women Come First: Gender and Class in Transnational Migration* (Berkeley: University of California Press, 2005).

29. Judith Bernhard, Patricia Landolt, and Luin Goldring, "Transnational, Multi-Local Motherhood: Experiences of Separation and Reunification among Latin American Families in Canada" (Toronto: Joint Centre of Excellence for Research on Immigration and Settlement, 2005), http://www.yorku.ca/cohesion/LARG/PDF/Transantional_Families_LARG_May_05.pdf.

30. Evelyn Lee, "Asian American Families: An Overview," in *Ethnicity and Family Therapy,* eds. Monica McGoldrick, Joseph Giordano, and John K. Pearce, (New York: Guilford, 1996); Chang-sik Shin and Ian Shaw, "Social Policy in South Korea: Cultural and Structural Factors in the Emergence of Welfare." *Social Policy and Administration* 4, no. 37, (2003): 328–341; R. Story and E. Park, *Korea* (Melbourne, Australia: Lonely Planet Publications, 2001).

31. Michele R. Gambaurd, *The Kitchen Spoon's Handle: Transnationalism and Sri Lanka's Migrant Housemaids* (Ithaca, NY: Cornell University Press, 2000).

32. Bernhard, Landolt, and Goldring, *Transnational, Multi-Local Motherhood, 5.*

33. Parreñas, *Servants of Globalization.*

34. Parreñas, *Servants of Globalization,* 387; Bernhard, Landolt, and Goldring, *Transnational, Multi-Local Motherhood.*

35. Parreñas, *Children of Global Migration.*

36. Carola Suárez-Orozco and Marcelo M. Suárez-Orozco, *Children of Immigration.* (Cambridge, MA: Harvard University Press, 2001).

37. Bernhard, Landolt, and Goldring, "Transnational, Multilocal Motherhood."

38. Bryceson and Vourela (2002) have advanced two useful concepts in understanding transnational family in relation to kin ties being sustained: frontiering and relativizing. "Frontiering" is defined as "the ways and means transnational family members use to create familial space and network ties in a terrain where affinal connections are relatively sparse" (p. 11). "Relativizing" is referred to the ways "individuals establish, maintain, or curtail relational ties with specific family members" (p. 42).

39. Anne Gray, "The Changing Availability of Grandparents as Carers and its Implications for Childcare policy in the UK," *Journal of Social Policy* 34, no. 4 (2005): 557–577; Diane L. Wolf, "Valuing Informal Elder Care," in *Family Time: The Social Organization of Care*, eds. Nancy Folbre and Michael Bittman (London: Routledge, 2004); Reynolds and Zontini, "A Comparative Study of Care and Provision."

40. Wai H. M. Leung, *"Who Cares? Managing the Family in Transnational/ Transborder Space: Stories from Migrants in Hong Kong"* (paper presented at the International Workshop on Asian Transnational Families, Singapore, Feb. 2, 2005); Reynolds and Zontini, "A Comparative Study of Care and Provision."

41. Eunju Lee, "Domestic Violence and Risk Factors among Korean Immigrant Women in the United States," *Journal of Family Violence* 22, no. 3 (2007): 141–149.

42. Jung Ha Kim, *Bridge-makers and Cross-bearers: Korean-American Women and the Church.* (Atlanta, GA: Scholars Press, 1997).

43. Baldassar and Baldock, "Linking Migration and Family Studies"; Vern L. Bengtson and Robert A. Harootyan, *Intergenerational Linkages: Hidden Connections in American Society* (New York: Springer Publishing Company and AARP, 1994); Ge Lin and Peter A. Rogerson, "Elderly Parents and the Geographic Availability of their Adult Children," *Research on Ageing* 17, no. 3 (1995): 303–331.

44. James Coleman, *Foundations of Social Theory* (London: Harvard University Press, 1990); Robert D. Putnam, "The Decline of Civil Society: How Come? So What?" (John L. Manion Lecture presented at the Canadian Centre for Management Development, Ottawa, Ontario, Feb. 22, 1996); Zontini, "Italian Families and Social Capital," 2.

45. Baldassar and Baldock, "Linking Migration and Family Studies," 79.

46. Mand, "Social Capital and Transnational South Asian Families."

47. Rogers, "Transnational Families: Bridging into Family Support"; Mand, "Social Capital and Transnational South Asian Families"; Zontini, "Italian Families and Social Capital."

TRANSRACIAL ADOPTION

Mia H. Tuan, Elizabeth S. Rienzi, and Jiannbin Lee Shiao

Adoptions have occurred throughout history and among all cultures, but transracial adoptions involving the permanent and legal union of racially different children and parents are a relatively recent phenomenon in the United States. Strict legal and social prohibitions such as Jim Crow laws restricted intimate relations across racial lines. The first significant effort to encourage transracial placements did not take place until the aftermath of World War II when white American families adopted orphaned children from Japan and China.[1] Since then, transracial adoption has increasingly become a socially accepted means for individuals and couples seeking to create families, although some racial combinations remain much more controversial than others. In recent decades, researchers and some adoption agencies such as Holt International Children's Services have uncovered the significant yet often unrecognized role of Asian adoptees, specifically international transracial adoptees from Asia and the Pacific, within the history of transracial adoption.

In addition, the growing numbers of Asian transracial adoptees in the United States have increased their unique influence in the constantly changing history and character of Asian America. As first-generation immigrants, Asian transracial adoptees represent a slice of a long history of Asian American immigration influenced by global political relations and exchange. There has been an increased interest in the flow of people and ideas across and between national boundaries: how people's understanding of themselves and the group they identify with is influenced from both within and outside of an imagined "homeland." This is evident in both new research and resources available on the Internet, such as international chat rooms and media outlets. In this way, Asian adoptees represent "particular cases of Asian American identity formation in a transnational context."[2]

With their integration into American families, Chinese transracial adoptees have been poised as cultural and national ambassadors for China and Chinese culture and representations of racial harmony in the United States.[3] However, Asian-white transracial adoptees' acceptance is often formed in relation to black adoptees' undesirability rather than a "true" colorblindness.[4] Asian American cultures are often presented as admirable and savable, the model minority, in contrast to a deficient, irredeemable African American culture. Representations of China-U.S. transracial adoptees in pop culture have often relied on images of "exotic" female Asianness. Some adoption agencies use pictures of beautiful little girls dressed up to attract adoptive families.[5]

Scholarship on Chinese adoption is an example of emerging cultural social-ization studies that explore how racial and cultural differences are addressed within families.[6] A new trend in international adoption, an emerging belief in bicultural socialization among adoptive parents, has been noted.[7] Compared with earlier waves of white families raising Asian adoptees, current families adopting Chinese babies embrace a bicultural identity as American and Chinese. That is, the identity of the family, as a whole, shifts as a result of adopting across racial and cultural lines. This shift stands in marked contrast to parents of earlier cohorts of adoptees, who were more inclined to focus on the assimilation of their children to their American family. As such, Chinese adop-tive families have been more likely to seek, employ, and even create resources for their children to develop their racial and ethnic identities and to celebrate their birth cultures. These resources, however, often represent Chinese culture, along with other ethnic groups' cultures, as monolithic, abstracted from every-day life, and grounded in some ancient past.[8] As a result, these resources have become a concern for nonadopted ethnic communities as well.

Data on transracial adoptions are woefully inadequate because of inconsistent and incomplete data collection.[9] Adoption experts still rely on a foundational 1993 publication that used data collected in 1987 to estimate that 8 percent of all adoptions are interracial, with 1 percent involving the adoption of black children by white parents, 2 percent involving parents of color adopting white children, and approximately 5 percent involving the adoption of other children of color by white parents, the majority of whom are Asian children.[10] With the rapid expan-sion of international adoptions especially from Asia (most notably China, Korea, India, and Vietnam) and Latin America (Guatemala and Columbia) starting in the 1990s, 8 percent is likely too low a figure to capture the reality of transracial placements today. Nearly one out of every six children adopted annually in the United States, roughly 20,000 out of 125,000, is an international adoptee.[11] For children under the age of two, that figure doubles to nearly two out of every five adoptions. As the availability of healthy white babies has declined in response to rising infertility, growing birth control options, and greater acceptance of single parenthood, more prospective parents have looked abroad and across racial and cultural lines to adopt healthy children.[12]

While an African American child adopted by an Asian American family (or any other combination) is a transracial adoption, commonly associated images and notions almost always presumes a more restricted cast of characters. The term "transracial adoption" is typically reserved for those adoptions involving the domestic placement of African American children with white American parents while "international adoption" or "intercountry adoption" refers to foreign-born Asian or Latin American children adopted by white American parents. Scholars suggest that the typicality of the above usual suspects in discussions and representations arises from their association with commonly held notions of transracial adoption and international adoption: racial difference and national difference, respectively.[13] Blacks and whites dominate U.S. discourse about racial differences and therefore dominate transracial adoption discussions as well. The reality, however, is that international transracial adoptions outnumber domestic transracial adoptions by a significant margin, with Asian-white adoptions comprising the largest proportion of all transracial placements, domestic or international.

SCOPE

Figures vary from year to year in response to modifications each country makes to its policies, but in the last ten years, the majority of international adoptees coming to the United States have originated from three countries: China, Guatemala, and South Korea.[14] China, a relatively recent addition to the international adoption world, has dominated since 1995, and was responsible for sending approximately 58,000 children between 1995 and 2006, the vast majority of whom were girls. In contrast, Guatemala and South Korea sent approximately 23,000 and 21,000 children, respectively, during the same period.

Scholars have noted China's rapid rise in the international adoption scene and have speculated on the reasons behind the phenomenon. Some argue that China's "one child policy," changes in the country's adoption law that took place in 1991, and a general cultural preference for sons have combined to make international adoption an attractive solution for dealing with China's increasing numbers of abandoned children.[15] Others have pointed to the role of interest groups in China and abroad who are invested in international adoption as playing a key role in institutionalizing the practice.[16]

South Korea currently ranks third among countries with adoptions to the United States, but for decades it dominated the international adoption picture; today, the country still accounts for the largest cumulative number of international adoptees living in the United States. Placements stretch back to 1955 when Henry and Bertha Holt, an evangelical couple from Oregon, first adopted eight children whose lives were devastated by the Korean War. The Holts went on to found the first and largest international adoption agency in the United States.[17] Since that time approximately 103,000 Korean children have been adopted by American families.[18]

Given how long Korean adoption has been taking place, there are now several waves or cohorts of adoptees living in the United States ranging in age from infancy to their fifties. These cohorts differ by their parents' orientations to "difference" (adoptive, racial, and ethnic), the social climate and historic period in which the adoptees came of age, the resources and social networks available to them, and the adoptees' orientations in adulthood to the "differences" they embody.[19] Older cohorts were encouraged to deny differences and assimilate into their white families and communities. Younger cohorts, in contrast, have come of age in a very different social climate characterized by the availability of social and material resources such as parent support groups, adoptee play groups, Asian adoptee Web sites, heritage camps, motherland tours, and consumer items (e.g. "culturally appropriate" books and dolls).

CHALLENGES

Most transracial adoptive families overtly recognize their racial and ethnic differences because of their inability to "pass" as racially homogeneous nonadoptive families. As a result, adoptive parents have the dual responsibilities of incorporating adoptees into their new family while simultaneously addressing their different racial statuses. Controversy arose in the 1970s when the National Association of Black Social Workers (NABSW) vehemently opposed transracial adoption. They questioned whether white parents could prepare children of color for "survival in a racist society." Transracial placements, the NABSW argued, left children in a racial and cultural "no man's land," neither fully accepted by white majority society nor the cultural/racial community from which they originated.[20] In response to such concerns, some parents may alter the ways they deal with family differences in order to better meet their children's needs at particular moments in their lives as they mature.

Typical issues that adoptive families have to address include having to tell the child they are adopted, helping adoptees deal with the loss of biological ties, and supporting adoptees' desires to search for their biological families, to name a few. Additionally, adoptees and adoptive parents must face cultural challenges to their statuses as legitimate or "real" families, even though adoption has entered the mainstream to a higher degree. Additionally, adoptees may experience various forms of discrimination and racism. Adoptive parents will have to address such events even though they may lack personal knowledge of such experiences. How families deal with others' evaluations and expectations provides the social environment in which adoptees develop their sense of family belonging. Parents usually use a combination of strategies rather than relying on just one method to accomplish all these tasks.

Transracial adoptees, like other people of color in general, have to face cultural expectations from the society that are based on their racial and ethnic identities. For example, Asian Americans are often perceived as "forever foreigners" and are expected to have strong and ongoing ties to ethnic communities based outside the United States regardless of generational status.[21] In this way, both nonadopted and adopted Asian Americans often occupy an "in between" position concerning citizenship and foreigner/immigrant.[22] Because many adolescents desire acceptance, want to conform to mainstream white culture, and minimize a "foreigner" label, they often withdraw from participating in adoptee programs, groups, networks, and so on, in an attempt to distance themselves from such images.[23] Yet, Asian Americans also receive messages from both within and outside Asian American communities that they are expected to have an in-depth knowledge on all Asian cultural practices and to act a certain way, like speaking Korean or Chinese fluently. And while many later-generation Asian Americans cannot fulfill these expectations, Asian transracial adoptees are seen to represent a more "authentic" culture because they were born in China, Korea, and so on.[24] Thus, they, along with other people of color in general, often experience a resurgence of ethnic identity and cultural interest as adults. College experiences often introduce both adoptees and nonadopted Asian Americans to larger populations of acculturated Asian Americans like themselves for the first time.

OUTLOOK

While most parents who adopt transracially are white, middle-class heterosexual couples, Chinese transracial adoptions allowed other groups to participate in family building: gay and lesbian couples and single parents. For many gay and lesbian couples and singles, Chinese adoptions were the only viable option; however, China has recently enacted new restrictive legislation against placements with gay and lesbian couples and single parents.[25]

In contrast to such restricted options, Asian Americans have increasingly become China-U.S. adoptive parents in part because of an ethnic or racial connection to adoptees. One researcher found that in the San Francisco Bay area one-fourth to one-third of the families who adopted from China in her study included one Asian American parent, usually Chinese American.[26] This picture contrasts to earlier Korean transracial adoptive families who lacked such demographic variation.

As Asian transracial adoptees mature and increasingly participate in adoption research, practice, and policy formation as adults, they have stressed the need to shift the focus of pre- and postadoption services to race, discrimination, and racism in the United States. Some international adoption agencies such as Holt International require prospective transracial adoptive parents to attend a minimum number of preadoption course hours. Rather than postadoption services focusing on adoptee birth culture and "cultural activities," adult adoptees have called for services that directly relate to the experiences in their everyday lives at different developmental stages. Future research will show how newly enacted restrictive legislation and increased preadoption requirements affect the nature of international transracial adoption, in particular China-U.S. adoptions. The extent of Asian transracial adoptees' abilities to cross borders, both physical and ideological, will become evident as these younger adoptee populations, such Chinese adoptees, mature into adulthood.

Jenn Suomi and her five-year-old daughter Olivia share a laugh in their New York apartment, 2008. Suomi and her husband applied to adopt a second child to become a sister for Olivia. China remains the country of choice for thousands of Americans seeking to adopt a child, but the time frame for new applications is now often triple what it was a few years ago and many families are enduring uncertain, emotionally draining waits. (AP Photo/Richard Drew)

FURTHER READING

Bergquist, Kathleen, M. Elizabeth Vonk, Dong Soo Kim, and Marvin Feit, eds. *International Korean Adoption: A Fifty-Year History and Policy and Practice.* New York: Haworth Press, 2007.

Herman, Ellen. 2008. *Adoption History Project*, http://www.uoregon.edu/~adoption/.

Holt International Children's Services. Families with Children from China. http://www.fwcc.org/.

Korean American Adoptee Adoptive Family Network. http://www.kaanet.com/http://www.uoregon.edu/~adoption/

Ngabonziza, Damien. "Intercountry Adoption: In Whose Best Interest?" *Adoption and Fostering* 12, no. 1 (1988): 35–40.

NOTES

1. Richard H. Weil, "International Adoptions: The Quiet Migration," *International Migration Review* 18 (1994): 276–293.

2. Sara K. Dorow, *Transnational Adoption: A Cultural Economy of Race, Gender, and Kinship* (New York: New York University, 2006), 25.

3. Dorow, *Transnational Adoption*, 25.

4. Jiannbin Lee Shiao et. al, "Shifting the Spotlight: Exploring Race and Culture in Korean-White Adoptive Families," *Race and Society* 7, no. 1 (2004): 1–16.

5. Dorow, *Transnational Adoption,* 25.

6. Richard Lee et al., "Cultural Socialization in Families with Internationally Adopted Children." *Journal of Family Psychology* 20 (2006): 571–580.

7. Richard Tessler et al., *West Meets East: Americans Adopt Chinese Children* (Westport, CT: Bergin & Garvey, 1999).

8. Dorow, *Transnational Adoption,* 25.

9. Peter Selman, "Trends in Intercountry Adoption: Analysis of Data from 20 Receiving Countries, 1998-2004." *Journal of Population Research,* http://findarticles.com/p/articles/mi_m0PCG/is_2_23/ai_n21053961/pg_1 (accessed Jan. 9, 2008).

10. Kathy Stolley, "Statistics on Adoption in the United States," *Future of Children: Adoption* 3 (1993): 26–42.

11. Paul Placek, "National Adoption Data" in *Adoption Factbook III,* eds. Connaught Marshner and William Pierce (Washington, DC: National Council for Adoption, 1993), 24–69.

12. Wun Jung Kim, "International Adoption: A Case Review of Korean Children," *Child Psychiatry and Human Development* 25 (1995): 141–154.

13. Jiannbin Shiao and Mia Tuan, "A Sociological Approach to Race, Identity and Asian Adoption," 155–170 in K. Berquist, B. Vonk, D.S. Kim, and M. Feit, eds. *International Korean Adoption: A Fifty-Year History and Policy and Practice* (New York: Haworth Press, 2007), 155–170.

14. Ellen Herman, "Hague Convention on Intercountry Adoption, 1993," *Adoption History Project,* http://www.uoregon.edu/~adoption/topics/AfricanAmerican.htm (accessed Jan. 4, 2008); U.S. State Department, "Hague Convention on Intercountry Adoption and the Intercountry Adoption Act of 2000: Background," U.S. State Department, http://travel.state.gov/orphan_numbers.html (retrieved Jan. 10, 2008); U.S. State Department 2008. "Immigrant Visas Issued to Orphans Coming to the U.S.:

Top Countries of Origin." http://travel.state.gov/orphan_numbers.html (accessed Jan. 1, 2008).

15. Eliza Poncz, "China's Proposed International Adoption Law: The Likely Impact on Single U.S. Citizens Seeking to Adopt from China and the Available Alternatives," *Harvard International Law Journal Online*, April 27, 2007, http://www.harvardilj.org/online/112 (accessed Jan. 14, 2008).

16. Kay A. Johnson, *Wanting a Daughter, Needing a Son: Abandonment, Adoption, and Orphanage Care in China*, (St. Paul, MN: Yeong and Yeong Book Company, 2004).

17. Shiao and Tuan, *A Sociological Approach to Race, Identity and Asian Adoption*, 155–170.

18. U.S. State Department, "Immigrant Visas."

19. Shiao and Tuan, *A Sociological Approach to Race, Identity and Asian Adoption*, 155–170.

20. Mark Courtney, "The Politics and Realities of Transracial Adoption," *Child Welfare* 126, no. 6 (Nov.–Dec. 1997): 749–779.

21. Mia Tuan, *Forever Foreigners or Honorary Whites?: The Asian Ethnic Experience Today* (New Brunswick, NJ: Rutgers University Press, 1998); Miri Song, *Choosing Ethnic Identity* (Malden, MA: Blackwell, 2003).

22. Dorow, *Transnational Adoption*, 25.

23. Jiannbin Lee Shiao et al., "Shifting the Spotlight: Exploring Race and Culture in Korean-White Adoptive Families," *Race and Society* 7 (2004): 1–16.

24. Mia Tuan, *Forever Foreigners or Honorary Whites*.

25. Dorow, *Transnational Adoption*, 25.

26. Dorow, *Transnational Adoption*, 25.

RESOURCE GUIDE

Suggested Reading

Espiritu, Yen Le. *Homebound: Filipino American Lives across Cultures, Communities and Countries*. Berkeley: University of California Press, 2003.

Gates, Gary, and R. Bradley Sear. *Asian and Pacific Islanders in Same Sex Couples in California: Data from Census 2000*. http://www.law.ucla.edu/williamsinstitute/publications/API_Report.pdf.

Lee, William Poy. *The Eighth Promise: An American Son's Tribute to His Toisanese Mother*. New York: Rodale, 2007.

Leong, Fredrick T. L., Arapana G. Inman; Angela Ebreo, Lawrence Hsin Yang, Lisa Marie Kinoshita, Michi Fu, eds. *Handbook of Asian American Psychology*, 2nd ed. Thousand Oaks, CA: SAGE Publications, 2006.

Nguyen, Tuyen. *Domestic Violence in Asian American Communities*. Lanham, MD: Rowman & Littlefield, 2005.

Niedzwiecki, Max, KaYing Yang, and Saroeun Earm. *Southeast Asian American Elders in California: Demographics and Service Priorities Revealed by the 2000 Census and a Survey of Mutual Assistance Associations (MAAs) and Faith-Based Organizations (FBOs)*. http://www.searac.org/sea-eldersrpt-fin.pdf.

Park, Lisa Sun-Hee. *Consuming Citizenship: Children of Asian Immigrant Entrepreneurs*. Palo Alto, CA: Stanford University Press, 2005.

Services and Advocacy for Asian Youth Consortium. *Moving beyond Exclusion: Focusing on the Needs of Asian/Pacific Islander Youth in San Francisco*. http://www.yvpcenter.org/media/docs/4608_moving_beyond_exclusion.pdf, 2008.

Sueyoshi, Amy, and Russell Leong, eds. *Asian Americans on the Marriage Equality Debate, Amerasia Journal*. University of California Press, 2006.

Tewari, Nita, and Alvin N. Alvarez. *Asian American Psychology: Current Perspectives.* New York: Psychology Press. 2008.

Trickett, Edison, and Curtis Jones. "Adolescent Culture Brokering and Family Functioning: A Study of Families from Vietnam." *Cultural Diversity and Ethnic Minority Psychology* 13 (2007): 143–50.

Uba, Laura. *A Postmodern Psychology of Asian Americans: Creating Knowledge of a Racial Minority.* Albany: State University of New York Press. 2002.

Umemoto, K., and P. Ong. "Asian American Pacific Islander Youth: Risks, Challenges, and Opportunities." *aapi nexus* 4, no. 2 (2006): v–ix.

Films

Coming Out, Coming Home, Asian and Pacific Islander Family Stories. VHS. Directed by Hima B. A/PI-PFLAG Family Project, 1996 (44 minutes). Documentary focuses on the coming out process for Asian Americans and Pacific Islanders. It also is a discussion of how families communicate with each other and come to accept a son or daughter who is lesbian or gay.

First Person Plural. DVD. Directed by Deann Borshay Liem. Distributed by PBS and Center for Asian American Media, 2000 (59 minutes). Documentary chronicles journey in locating her birth mother and family in Korea. It also documents her adoptive family's journey in adoption, but also race and identity. Liem brings these two families together to help her reconcile her Korean and American identities.

Silent Sacrifices: Voices of the Filipino American Family. Directed by Patricia Heras, Dist. Center for Asian American Media, 2001 (25 minutes). Documentary explores the intergenerational tensions within Filipino American families. It focuses on relationships between Filipino immigrants and their American-born children and the misunderstandings and conflicts that often accompany these relationships.

Organizations

API Equality. http://www.apiequality.org/getinformed/articles.php. Working on Asian American same sex marriage issues nationally.

Asian American Pacific Islander Youth Development and Violence Prevention Programs. http://gucchd.georgetown.edu/programs/aapi/object_view.html?objectID=2554. Directory of Asian American/Pacific Islander programs throughout the United States that focus on Asian American youth development and at-risk youth.

Families with Children from China. http://www.fwcc.org/. Devoted to families that have adopted a child from China.

Korean American Adoptees Adoptive Family Network. http://www.kaanet.com/. An online community of Korean American adoptees and their families.

Mavin. http://www.mavin.net/. Online community for support focused on mixed heritage and transracial adoptees.

National Asian Pacific Center on Aging (NAPCA). http://www.napca.org. Working nationally and locally on aging.

South Asian Youth Action. http://www.saya.org/index.html. Founded in 1996 and focused on working with South Asian youth in New York City.

Web Sites

Adoptive Families. http://www.adoptivefamilies.com/. Comprehensive site on adoption with information on adoption and the experiences of those adopted from Asian countries such as China, Korea, and Philippines.

API Family Acceptance Pride Project. http://www.lyric.org/apifamilyproject/lyc_pgs/s01/01_index.html. Sharing stories of Asian American families coming to acceptance of a gay son or lesbian daughter. It includes audio of young adults sharing their stories.

Center for Pacific Asian Families. http://www.cpaf.info/index.html. Particularly useful for individuals and families experiencing crisis. Provides information to a crisis hotline and other resources.

Maria P. P. Root, http://www.drmariaroot.com/. Features the publications and references of Maria Root, a clinical psychologist, who has done extensive research and therapy with mixed raced Asian American families. Features downloadable articles.

Model Minority.Com. http://www.modelminority.com. Variety of different topics are offered, including family issues and other contemporary topics related to Asian ethnic identity.

National Asian American Pacific Islander Mental Health Association. http://www.naapimha.org/. Has a variety of different resources in English and other Asian languages.

National Asian Pacific Families Against Substance Abuse. http://www.napafasa.org/. Los Angeles-based nonprofit organization providing resources for both the public as well as for professionals, discussing issues related to all age levels.

Online Relationship Assistance for Asian Pacific Islander Youth. http://www.thatsnotlove.org/index.html. Interactive site for Asian American and Pacific Islander youth focused on dating, relationships with family, and violence. Includes weekly chatroom discussions and bulletin boards.

Violence Impacting the Asian American and Pacific Islander Communities. http://www.sph.umich.edu/apihealth/2006/index.htm. Informational site focusing on the issues of family violence facing Asian Americans and Pacific Islanders, including suicide, domestic violence, and elder abuse.

INDEX

Note: Page numbers followed by *f* indicate figures, by *s* indicate sidebars, and by *t* indicate tables.

About the Editors and Contributors

EDITORS

EDITH WEN-CHU CHEN is an associate professor at the Asian American Studies Department at California State University–Northridge. Her research and teaching interests include Chinese in the Americas, Asian American women, food and culture, and applied research. She was the co-editor of *Teaching about Asian Pacific Americans: Effective Activities, Strategies, and Assignments for Classrooms and Workshops* (2006).

GRACE J. YOO is Professor of Asian American Studies at San Francisco State University. She is an applied sociologist who has done extensive research in the Asian American community on issues related to aging, health, social support, and public policy. Her research has been published in a variety of interdisciplinary scholarly journals.

SECTION EDITORS

ANGELO ANCHETA (Law) is an assistant professor of law at Santa Clara University School of Law.

ANDREW L. AOKI (Politics) is a professor of political science at Augsburg College (Minneapolis) and is the coauthor (with Okiyoshi Takeda) of *Asian American Politics* (2009).

ALLAN AQUINO (Media) is a lecturer in the Asian American Studies Department at California State University–Northridge.

EDITH WEN-CHU CHEN (Diversity and Demographics; Identity; and Media) is an associate professor in the Asian American Studies Department at California State University–Northridge.

WEI MING DARIOTIS (War) is an assistant professor of Asian American studies at San Francisco State University.

BILL ONG HING (Immigrants, Refugees, and Citizenship) is a professor of law at the University of California–Davis.

SHIRLEY HUNE (Education) is professor of educational leadership and policy studies at the University of Washington–Seattle.

KIMIKO KELLY (Diversity and Demographics) is a lecturer in the Asian American Studies Department at California State University–Northridge and research manager at the Orange County Asian and Pacific American Community Alliance.

BARBARA W. KIM (Identity) is an associate professor of Asian and Asian American studies at California State University–Long Beach.

SIMONA C. KWON (Health) is a research scientist at the Center for the Study of Asian American Health, Institute of Community Health and Research of the New York University School of Medicine.

DON MAR (Economy and Work) is a professor in the economics department at San Francisco State University.

RANJITA MISRA (Health) is an associate professor in the School of Allied Medical Professions in the College of Medicine at the Ohio State University.

ALAN Y. ODA (Youth, Family and Aged) is a professor of undergraduate psychology and assistant director of the honors program at the Azusa Pacific University.

JULIE J. PARK (Education) is an assistant professor of educational leadership at Miami University.

VALERIE SOE (Media) is an assistant professor of Asian American studies at San Francisco State University.

WESLEY UEUNTEN (War) is an assistant professor of Asian American studies at San Francisco State University.

GRACE J. YOO (Health; Youth, Family, and Aged) is a professor of Asian American studies at San Francisco State University.

CONTRIBUTORS

JENNIFER S. ABE is an associate professor in the Department of Psychology and associate dean in the Bellarmine College of Liberal Arts at Loyola Marymount University.

GRACE MICHELE V. ALBA is a biological sciences laboratory faculty member at the University of Pittsburgh.

ALVIN ALVAREZ is a professor of Counseling at San Francisco State University.

ANGELO ANCHETA is an assistant professor of law and director of the Katharine and George Alexander Community Law Center at Santa Clara University School of Law.

ALLAN AQUINO is a lecturer in the Asian American Studies Department at California State University–Northridge.

ANDREW L. AOKI is a professor of political science at Augsburg College.

WAYNE AU is an assistant professor in the Department of Secondary Education at California State University–Fullerton.

ROXANNA BAUTISTA is a chronic diseases program manager at the Asian and Pacific Islander American Health Forum.

JONATHAN BLAZER is a public benefits policy attorney at the National Immigration Law Center.

TANYA BRODER is a public benefits policy attorney at the National Immigration Law Center.

TRACY LACHICA BUENAVISTA is an assistant professor of Asian American studies at California State University–Northridge.

MIKE CHAN is an independent scholar in San Francisco.

EDWARD TAEHAN CHANG is a professor of ethnic studies at the University of California–Riverside.

MICHAEL CHANG is a civil rights attorney at the U.S. Department of Education's Office for Civil Rights.

CHRISTINE CHEN is an independent scholar in Washington, DC.

JYU-LIN CHEN is an assistant professor in the Department of Family Health Care Nursing at University of California–San Francisco.

CHWEE-LYE CHNG is Regents Professor of Health Promotion at the University of North Texas, Denton, TX.

JULIAN CHUN-CHUNG CHOW is an associate professor in the School of Social Welfare at the University of California–Berkeley.

PETER CHUA is an associate professor of sociology at San Jose State University.

ARISTEL DE LA CRUZ is an independent scholar in San Francisco.

WEI MING DARIOTIS is an assistant professor in Asian American Studies at San Francisco State University.

RODERICK DAUS-MAGBUAL is a doctoral candidate at the School of Education at the University of San Francisco.

R. BENEDITO FERRAO is a lecturer in the Asian American Studies Department at UCLA.

TIMOTHY FONG is an assistant professor at the David Geffen School of Medicine at University of California–Los Angeles, and codirector of the University of California–Los Angeles Gambling Studies Program.

TIMOTHY P. FONG is the director and a professor of the Asian American Studies Program at Sacramento State University.

DIANE C. FUJINO is an associate professor and chair of the Department of Asian American Studies at the University of California–Santa Barbara.

ANNIE FUKUSHIMA is a doctoral candidate in ethnic studies at the University of California–Berkeley.

JENNIFER GARCIA is a doctoral student at the University of California, Los Angeles School of Public Health.

KIM GERON is an associate professor of political science at California State University–East Bay.

DANIEL PHIL GONZALES is an associate professor of Asian American studies at San Francisco State University.

SHARON G. GOTO is an associate professor of psychology and Asian American Studies at Pomona College.

BEN DE GUZMAN is a national campaign coordinator at the National Alliance for Filipino Veterans Equity in Washington, DC.

MEEKYUNG HAN is an assistant professor at the School of Social Work, College of Applied Sciences and Arts, San Jose State University.

RAINA HAN is an independent scholar in Seoul, Korea.

ROOSHEY HASNAIN is a visiting research assistant professor in the Department of Disability and Human Development at the Center for Capacity Building on Minorities with Disabilities Research at the University of Illinois–Chicago.

BILL ONG HING is a professor of law at the University of California–Davis.

ANDREW HOM is an independent scholar in San Francisco.

LAUREEN D. HOM is project coordinator at the Center for the Study of Asian American Health Institute of Community Health and Research of the New York University School of Medicine.

SHIRLEY HUNE is professor of educational leadership and policy studies at the University of Washington–Seattle.

ANH-LUU T. HUYNH-HOHNBAUM is an associate professor in the School of Social Work at California State University–Los Angeles.

NADIA ISLAM is deputy director for the Center for the Study of Asian American Health at the New York University School of Medicine.

DEEPA IYER is executive director of South Asian American Leading Together, Takoma Park, MD.

DIMPAL JAIN is a doctoral student in the Graduate School of Education and Information Studies at the University of California–Los Angeles.

JOAN JEUNG is a pediatrician in Oakland, CA.

RUSSELL JEUNG is associate professor in Asian American studies at San Francisco State University.

LINDA P. JUANG is an associate professor of psychology at San Francisco State University.

ANGIE JUNCK is a staff attorney at the Immigrant Legal Resource Center in San Francisco.

KIMIKO KELLY is a lecturer in the Asian American Studies Department at California State University–Northridge, and research manager at the Orange County Asian and Pacific American Community Alliance.

BARBARA W. KIM is an associate professor of Asian and Asian American studies at California State University–Long Beach.

MARLENE KIM is an associate professor of economics at the University of Massachusetts–Boston.

SU YEONG KIM is Assistant Professor in the Department of Human Development and Family Sciences at the University of Texas–Austin.

REBECCA CHIYOKO KING-O'RIAIN is senior lecturer in the Department of Sociology at the National University of Ireland, Maynooth.

HYEYOUNG KWON is a lecturer in the Department of Asian American Studies at California State University–Northridge.

SIMONA C. KWON is a research scientist at the Center for the Study of Asian American Health, Institute of Community Health and Research of the New York University School of Medicine.

KAM MAN KENNY KWONG is an assistant professor at the Hunter College School of Social Work of the City University of New York.

PETER KWONG is a professor in the Department of Sociology at the Graduate Center of the City University of New York.

JAMES S. LAI is an associate professor of political science and ethnic studies at Santa Clara University.

SOPHIA LAI is a JD candidate at Harvard Law School.

MABEL LAM is an independent scholar in San Jose, CA.

CHRISSY LAU is a doctoral student in history at the University of California–Santa Barbara.

C. N. LE is a visiting assistant professor of sociology and director of the Asian and Asian American Studies Certificate Program at University of Massachusetts–Amherst.

MAI-NHUNG LE is an associate professor of Asian American studies at San Francisco State University.

AMBROSE H. LEE is an independent scholar in San Francisco.

EUN SOOK LEE is executive director of the National Korean American Service and Education Consortium (NAKASEC) in Los Angeles.

HEE YUN LEE is an assistant professor at the Hartford Geriatric Scholar School of Social Work University of Minnesota, St. Paul, MN.

HELLY LEE is Director of Policy at the Southeast Asian Resource Action Center (SEARAC) in Washington, DC.

KYUNG JIN LEE is an immigration and citizenship program coordinator at the Korean Community Center of the East Bay in Oakland, CA.

MARY S. LEE is a proposal development manager at the Asian American Recovery Services in Daly City, CA.

YEON-SHIM LEE is an assistant professor of social work at San Francisco State University.

JONATHAN W. LEW is a doctoral student in the School of Educational Studies at Claremont Graduate University.

SIN YEN LING is a staff attorney at the Asian Law Caucus in San Francisco.

JOREN LYONS is a staff attorney at the nonprofit Asian Law Caucus in San Francisco.

JAYANTI MALLICK is an independent scholar in San Jose, CA.

DON MAR is professor in the Economics Department at San Francisco State University.

NATALIE MASUOKA is an assistant professor in the Department of Political Science at Tufts University.

KATHY MATSAOKA is co-chair for Nikkei for Civil Rights and Redress in Los Angeles.

DAVID K. MINETA is deputy director at Asian American Recovery Services in Daly City, CA.

RANJITA MISRA is an associate professor in the School of Allied Medical Professions in the College of Medicine at the Ohio State University.

JONELL MOLINA is an independent scholar in San Francisco.

DON T. NAKANISHI is director and professor of the Asian American Studies Center at the University of California–Los Angeles.

JENNIFER NAZARENO is a medical sociology doctoral student at the University of California–San Francisco.

MELISSA-ANN NIEVERA is a doctoral student in education at the University of California–Santa Cruz.

BRIAN NIIYA is a Resource Center Director at the Japanese Cultural Center of Hawai'i.

MAVIS NITTA is a chronic diseases program coordinator at the Asian and Pacific Islander American Health Forum.

PAUL NIWA is an assistant professor of Journalism at Emerson College.

ELIZA NOH is an assistant professor in the Asian American Studies Program at California State University–Fullerton.

CATHERINA NOU is a California Policy Advocate at the Southeast Asia Resource Action Center in Washington, DC.

ANGELA E. OH is executive director of the Western Justice Center Foundation in Los Angeles.

JONATHAN Y. OKAMURA is an associate professor in the Department of Ethnic Studies at the University of Hawai'i–Manoa in Honolulu.

GLENN OMATSU is a senior lecturer in the Asian American Studies Department at California State University–Northridge.

JULIE J. PARK is an assistant professor of educational leadership at Miami University.

R. VARISA PATRAPORN is a program officer at First 5 LA in Los Angeles.

HENRY POLLACK is an associate professor of the Saul Krugman Division of Pediatric Infectious Diseases and the Center for the Study of Asian American Health at the New York University School of Medicine, New York.

BANDANA PURKAYASTHA is an associate professor of sociology and Asian American Studies at the University of Connecticut.

RODOLFO-JOSE BLANCO QUIAMBAO is an MA candidate in Asian American studies at San Francisco State University.

RANITA RAY is a doctoral student in the Department of Sociology at the University of Connecticut.

MARGARET RHEE is a doctoral student in ethnic studies at the University of California–Berkeley.

ELIZABETH S. RIENZI is a doctoral candidate in the department of sociology at the University of Oregon.

JOANNE L. RONDILLA is a doctoral candidate of ethnic studies at the University of California–Berkeley.

JOCYL SACRAMENTO is an independent scholar in San Francisco.

RAYMOND SAN DIEGO is an MA candidate in Asian American studies at San Francisco State University.

CATHY J. SCHLUND-VIALS is an assistant professor in the Department of English and Asian American Studies Institutes at the University of Connecticut.

JIANNBIN LEE SHIAO is an associate professor of sociology at Dartmouth College and the University of Oregon and associate director of ethnic studies at the University of Oregon.

GRACE SHIMIZU is director of the Japanese Peruvian Oral History Project and coordinator for the Campaign For Justice: Redress Now for Japanese Latin Americans.

EUNAI SHRAKE is an associate professor in the Department of Asian American Studies at California State University–Northridge.

ANNELIESE A. SINGH is an assistant professor in the Department of Counseling and Human Development Services at the University of Georgia.

DAVORN SISAVATH is a doctoral student in ethnic studies at the University of California–San Diego.

VALERIE SOE is an assistant professor of Asian American studies at San Francisco State University.

PAHOLE YOTIN SOOKKASIKON is an MA candidate in Asian American studies at San Francisco State University.

NAOMI STEINBERG is deputy director at Southeast Asia Resource Action Center (SEARAC) in Washington, DC.

DOUA THOR is executive director of the Southeast Asia Resource Action Center (SEARAC) in Washington, DC.

ALLYSON TINTIANGCO-CUBALES is an associate professor of Asian American Studies at San Francisco State University.

TAM TRAN is a doctoral student in American Civilization at Brown University.

MIA H. TUAN is an associate professor of Teacher Education and Director of the Center on Diversity and Community at the University of Oregon.

WESLEY UEUNTEN is an assistant professor of Asian American studies at San Francisco State University.

KHATHARYA UM is an assistant professor of ethnic studies at the University of California–Berkeley.

KAREN UMEMOTO is a professor in the Department of Urban and Regional Planning at the University of Hawai'i–Manoa.

KEJIA WAN is project coordinator of the Saul Krugman Division of Pediatric Infectious Diseases and the Center for the Study of Asian American Health at the New York University School of Medicine, New York.

YU WAN is a master's candidate of public health at the New York University.

WINNIE W. WANG is director of sponsored research at Claremont McKenna College.

CANDICE CHIN WONG is associate adjunct professor in the Institute for Health and Aging at the University of California–San Francisco.

IVY WONG is an independent scholar in San Francisco.

SACHIKO WOOD is a doctoral student in sociology at the University of California–Santa Cruz.

MITCHEL WU is a lecturer in Asian American Studies at Hunter College, City University of New York.

NINA H. WU is a doctoral student in the Department of Human Development and Family Sciences at the University of Texas–Austin.

BO HAN YANG is a law student at the University of California–Davis School of Law.